Sport Psychology
An Introduction

Arnold LeUnes
Texas A&M University
Jack R. Nation
Texas A&M University

WADSWORTH

THOMSON LEARNING ™

Australia • Canada • Mexico • Singapore • Spain • United Kingdom • United States

WADSWORTH

★

™

THOMSON LEARNING

Publisher: *Vicki Knight*
Sponsoring Editor: *Marianne Taflinger*
Marketing Team: *Joanne Terhaar, Justine Ferguson,*
    Samantha Cabaluna
Editorial Assistant: *Stacy Green*
Production Coordinator: *Mary Vezilich*
Production Service: *Matrix Productions*
Manuscript Editors: *Pat Herbst, Vicki Nelson*
Permissions Editor: *Karyn Morrison*

Interior Design: *Carolyn Deacy Design*
Cover Design: *Laurie Albrecht*
Cover Photo: *Kevin Dodge/Masterfile*
Interior Illustration: *Mackresart*
Photo Researcher: *Sue C. Howard*
Print Buyer: *Vena Dyer*
Typesetting: *Parkwood Composition Service, Inc.*
Printing and Binding: *R. R. Donnelley—Crawfordsville*

Printed in the United States of America

10 9 8 7 6 5 4 3 2

Library of Congress Cataloging-in-Publication Data
LeUnes, Arnold D.
    Sport psychology: an introduction/Arnold LeUnes,
    Jack R. Nation.—3rd ed.
        p. cm.
    Includes bibliographical references (p.) and index.
    ISBN 0-830-41548-3
    1. Sports—Psychological aspects. I. Nation, Jack R.
II. Title.

GV706.4. L48 2002

796'.01—dc21   2001043604

Brief Contents

PART ONE

Introducing Sport Psychology and Sport History

1. An Introduction to Sport Psychology 1
2. Professional Issues 13
3. Sport History From Antiquity Through the Enlightenment 25
4. History of Sport and Sport Psychology in the United States 39

PART TWO

Behavioral Principles and Applications

5. Behavioral Principles 53
6. Anxiety and Arousal 71
7. Anxiety Reduction: Classical Conditioning and Operant Learning 87
8. Anxiety Reduction: Cognitive Learning Techniques 97

PART THREE

Social Psychological Dimensions

9. Motivation: Attribution Theory and Need Achievement 113
10. Motivation: Locus of Control and Self Theory 133
11. Social Psychology of Sport: Leadership and Group Cohesion 149
12. Social Psychology of Sport: Audience Effects 171
13. Aggression: Dimensions and Theories 185
14. Aggression: Violence in Selected Sport Populations 207

PART FOUR

Personality, Assessment, and Special Athletic Populations

15. Personality and Psychological Assessment 223
16. Psychological Assessment in Sport Psychology 241
17. Special Populations: Minority and High-Risk-Sport Athletes 263
18. Special Populations: Elite, Disabled, Injured, or Drug-Abusing Athletes 291
19. The Female Sport Experience: Historical Roots and Physiological Concerns 309
20. The Female Sport Experience: Sport Socialization, Psychological Variables, and Other Issues 321
21. Youth Sport: Motives for Participating and Withdrawing 341
22. Youth Sport: Stress and Other Issues 353

PART FIVE

Coaching and Exercise

23. The Coach: Roles, Communication, and Psychological Variables 369
24. Youth, Female, and Black Coaches; Coaching Burnout 385
25. Exercise Psychology: Physical Fitness, Adherence, and Cognitive and Affective Benefits 403
26. Exercise Psychology: Running Addictions and Exercise for Senior Citizens 421

References 437
Author Index 481
Subject Index 489

Contents

PART ONE

Introducing Sport Psychology and Sport History

CHAPTER 1

An Introduction to Sport Psychology 1

Organization of this Book 2
What Is Sport Psychology? 4
What Do Sport Psychologists Do? 5
Sport Psychology Professional Organizations 8
  The International Organization 8
  North American Organizations 8
  Australian, British, and Canadian Organizations 9
  Related Professional Organizations 9
Summary 11
Key Terms 11
Suggested Readings 12

CHAPTER 2

Professional Issues 13

Training for the Profession 14
Credentialing 14
Ethical Principles 17
Image of the Profession 18
Employment Opportunities 20
Summary 21

Key Terms 22
Suggested Readings 22

CHAPTER 3

Sport History From Antiquity Through the Enlightenment 25

The Ancient Near East and Asia 26
The Greeks 27
  Homeric Greece 27
  The Early Athenian Period 27
  The Spartan Period 28
  The Later Athenian Period 30
The Romans 31
The Middle Ages 34
  The Byzantine Empire 34
  Christianity 35
  The Age of Chivalry 35
Renaissance and Enlightenment 36
Summary 37
Key Terms 38
Suggested Readings 38

CHAPTER 4

History of Sport and Sport Psychology in the United States 39

Colonial America 40

From the Revolutionary War Through the Civil War 41

Technological Revolution, 1850–1900 42

Eight Milestones in Recent U.S. Sport History 42

A Brief History of Physical Education 45

A Brief History of Psychology 46

A Brief History of Sport Psychology 47

Summary 50

Key Terms 51

Suggested Readings 51

PART TWO

Behavioral Principles and Applications

CHAPTER 5

Behavioral Principles 53

Classical Conditioning 54

Operant Learning 55

Basic Principles 55
Behavioral Coaching Techniques 56
Public Recording 61
Changing Coaching Behaviors 62
Conditioned Reinforcement 62
Premack Principle 65
Response Cost 65
Training Variables 65
Learned Helplessness 66

Cognitive Learning 67

Summary 67

Key Terms 68

Suggested Readings 69

CHAPTER 6

Anxiety and Arousal 71

Determinants of Anxiety and Arousal 72

Neurophysiological Mechanisms 72
Psychological Mechanisms 74
Effects of Anxiety on Competitive Performance 75
Effects of Arousal on Competitive Performance: The Inverted-U Hypothesis 77

The Measurement of Anxiety and Arousal 79

Physiological Measures 80
Psychological Measures 82
Advantages and Disadvantages of Psychological and Physiological Measures 84

Summary 85

Key Terms 85

Suggested Readings 86

CHAPTER 7

Anxiety Reduction: Classical Conditioning and Operant Learning Applications 87

Classical Conditioning Techniques 88

Extinction 88
Counterconditioning 90

Operant Learning Techniques 92

Reinforced Practice 92
Biofeedback Training 92

Summary 94

Key Terms 95

Suggested Readings 95

CHAPTER 8

Anxiety Reduction: Cognitive Learning Techniques 97

Imagery 98
Visuomotor Behavioral Rehearsal 102
Stress Inoculation Training 103

Cognitive Control 104
Hypnosis 106
Yoga, Zen, and Transcendental Meditation 107
Psych-Up Strategies 108
Summary 109
Key Terms 109
Suggested Readings 110

PART THREE

Social Psychological Dimensions

CHAPTER 9

Motivation: Attribution Theory and Need Achievement 113

What Is Motivation? 114
Attribution Theory 115
  The Cognitive Model 115
  Social Cognitive Models 120
  The Functional Model 125
  Future Directions in Attribution Research 126
Need for Achievement 127
  Murray's Contribution 127
  The McClelland–Atkinson Model 127
Summary 130
Key Terms 131
Suggested Readings 131

CHAPTER 10

Motivation: Locus of Control and Self Theory 133

Locus of Control 134
  Rotter's I–E Scale 134
  Levenson's Multidimensional Approach 135
  Locus-of-Control Measurement With Youth 136
  Current Status of the Locus-of-Control Construct 137
Self Theory 137
  The Self 138
  The Self-Concept 139

  Self-Actualization 139
  Status of Research on Self Theory 141
Some Final Thoughts on Motivation 141
  Sport Self-Confidence 141
  Sport Motivation 142
  Setting Performance Goals in Sport 142
  Explanatory Style 143
Summary 147
Key Terms 147
Suggested Readings 148

CHAPTER 11

Social Psychology of Sport: Leadership and Group Cohesion 149

Leadership 150
  Theories of Leadership 151
  Chelladurai's Multidimensional Model
    of Sport Leadership 155
  Player Leadership 158
  Evaluation of Leadership Research 158
Group Cohesion 158
  Models of Team Cohesion 160
  Factors Affecting Team Cohesion 160
  Measures of Team Cohesion 164
  Two Final Notes 167
Summary 167
Key Terms 168
Suggested Readings 169

CHAPTER 12

Social Psychology of Sport: Audience Effects 171

Social Facilitation 172

Other Drive Theories 173

An Evaluation of Drive Theory 174

Alternative Nondrive Models 174

Interactive Audience Effects on Sport
Performance 174

The Home Advantage 175
Basking in Reflected Glory 179
Choking Under Pressure 180

Summary 181

Key Terms 182

Suggested Readings 182

CHAPTER 13

Aggression: Dimensions and Theories 185

Aggression Defined 186

Dimensions of Aggression 188

Provoked and Unprovoked Aggression 188
Direct and Indirect Aggression 188
Physical and Verbal Aggression 188
Adaptive and Maladaptive Aggression 188
Hostile Aggression, Instrumental Aggression,
    and Sport Assertiveness 188
Aggression and Violence: One and the Same? 190

Biological Theories of Aggression 191

Psychosocial Theories of Aggression 191

Cathartic Approaches 192
Social Learning Approach 192
Catharsis or Social Learning? 193

Sociological Explanations of Aggression
in Sport 193

Contagion Theory 193
Convergence Theory 193
Emergent Norm Theory 194
Value-Added Theory 194

The Measurement of Aggression 194

Factors Promoting Aggression 195

Physical Factors 195
Psychological Factors 198
Sociological Considerations 199

Critical Sport-Related Variables Affecting
Aggression 203

Point Spread 203
Home/Away Factor 203
Outcome 203
League Standing 203
Period of Play 203

Summary 204

Key Terms 205

Suggested Readings 205

CHAPTER 14

Aggression: Violence in Selected Sport Populations 207

Boxing 208

Football 208

Hockey 210

Smith's Violence Typology 210

Violence Among Female Athletes 214

Violence Against Females by Male
Athletes 214

Violence Against Sports Officials 216

Recommendations for Curbing Violence
in Sport 217

Management 217
The Media 218
Game Officials 220
Coaches 220
Players 221

Summary 221

Key Terms 222

Suggested Readings 222

PART FOUR

Personality, Assessment, and Special Athletic Populations

CHAPTER 15

Personality and Psychological Assessment 223

Personality Defined 224

Theories of Personality 224
- Biological Models 224
- The Psychodynamic Model 226
- The Humanistic Model 226
- The Behavioral Model 226
- Trait Theory 228
- The Interactional Model 228

Problems In Sport Personality Research 228
- Conceptual Problems 228
- Methodological Problems 230
- Interpretive Problems 231

Psychological Assessment 231

What Is a Test? 232

Validity, Reliability, and Norms 233
- Validity 233
- Reliability 234
- Norms 234

Sources of Error in Testing 236
- Faking Good 236
- Faking Bad 236

Test Ethics and Sport Psychology 236

Summary 237

Key Terms 238

Suggested Readings 238

CHAPTER 16

Psychological Assessment in Sport Psychology 241

Tests of Enduring Personality Traits 242
- Minnesota Multiphasic Personality Inventory 242
- Sixteen Personality Factor Questionnaire 244
- Eysenck Personality Inventory (EPI)/Eysenck Personality Questionnaire 245

State Measures Used in Sport Psychology 246
- Profile of Mood States (POMS) 246
- State-Trait Anxiety Inventory 248

Sport-Specific Tests 251
- Athletic Motivation Inventory 251
- Sport Competition Anxiety Test (SCAT) 252
- Competitive State Anxiety Inventory (CSAI) 253
- Competitive State Anxiety Inventory-2 (CSAI-2) 253
- Test of Attentional and Interpersonal Style (TAIS) 254
- Other Sport-Specific Measures 256
- A Final Note 257

Attitude Measurement in Sport 257
- Likert Scales 257
- Semantic Differential Scales 258
- Thurstone Scaling 258

Summary 259

Key Terms 260

Suggested Readings 260

CHAPTER 17

Special Populations: Minority and High-Risk-Sport Athletes 263

The Minority Athlete 264
- The African-American Athlete 264
- The Success of African-American Athletes 266
- The Hispanic Athlete 273
- The Asian-American Athlete 276
- The Native American Athlete 276

The High-Risk-Sport Participant 277
- Sport Parachuting/Skydiving 278
- Hang Gliding 280
- Rock Climbing 281
- Scuba Diving 284
- Correlates of High-Risk-Sport Participation 285

Summary 287

Key Terms 288

Suggested Readings 288

CHAPTER 18

Special Populations: Elite, Disabled, Injured, or Drug-Abusing Athletes 291

The Elite Athlete 292
Kroll's Personality Performance Pyramid 292
Research on Exceptional Performance 292
The Athlete With Disabilities 294
The Injured Athlete 296
The Athlete Who Uses or Abuses Drugs 298
Prohibited Classes of Substances 299
Prohibited Methods of Administering Drugs 302
Classes of Drugs Subject to Restrictions 303
Summary 305
Key Terms 306
Suggested Readings 306

CHAPTER 19

The Female Sport Experience: Historical Roots and Physiological Concerns 309

A Brief History 310
Ancient Greece 310
The Modern Olympics 310
Title IX Legislation 311
Contemporary Forces in Women's Athletics 315
The Physiological Dimension in Women's Athletics 315
Menstrual Functioning 315
Other Problems 318
Summary 319
Key Terms 319
Suggested Readings 319

CHAPTER 20

The Female Sport Experience: Sport Socialization, Psychological Variables, and Other Issues 321

Socialization Into Sport 323
Role Conflict 324
The Family 325
Acceptability of Various Sports 326
Why Women Compete 327
Psychological Variables 327
Attribution Theory 327
Fear of Success 329
Psychological Androgyny 330
Other Issues Involving Women in Sport 332
The Media 333
Homophobia 334
Eating Disorders 335
Summary 338
Key Terms 339
Suggested Readings 339

CHAPTER 21

Youth Sport: Motives for Participating and Withdrawing 341

A Brief History 342
Little League Baseball 343
Concerns About Youth Fitness 344
Motives for Participating in Sport 344
Having Fun 346
Skill Improvement 346
Fitness Benefits 347
Team Atmosphere 347
Other Reasons 347
A Final Note 347
Motives for Withdrawing from Participation 347
Primary Concerns 348
Secondary Concerns 349
AFA Recommendations for Making Youth Sport More Enjoyable 350

Summary 351

Key Terms 351

Suggested Readings 352

CHAPTER 22

Youth Sport: Stress and Other Issues 353

Stress and Youth Sport 354
Competition: Product or Process? 354
Competitive Stress 355

Measures of Stress 356

Cognitive Aspects of Competitive Stress 357
Perceived Ability 357
Success Expectancy 357

Expectancy of Negative Evaluation 357
Expectancy of Negative Affect 357

Antecedents of Competitive Stress 358
Parent–Child Interactions 358
Interactions With Other Adults and Peers 358
History of Success and Failure 358

Elite Performance in Youth Athletes 358

Violence in Youth Sports 360

Health Risks Associated With Youth Sport 362

Recommendations for Improving Youth Sport 365

Summary 366

Key Terms 367

Suggested Readings 367

PART FIVE

Coaching and Exercise

CHAPTER 23

The Coach: Roles, Communication, and Psychological Variables 369

Roles of the Coach 371

What Makes a Good Coach? 373

Advantages and Disadvantages of Coaching 375

Communication and Coaching 379

The Coach and the Sport Psychologist 379

The Coach's Personality 381
The Authoritarian Personality 381
The Machiavellian Personality 382

Summary 382

Key Terms 383

Suggested Readings 383

CHAPTER 24

Youth, Female, and Black Coaches; Coaching Burnout 385

Coaching and Youth Sport 386
The Coaching Behavior Assessment System (CBAS) 386
Other Approaches to Improving Youth Coaching 388

The Female Coach 390
The Female Interscholastic/Intercollegiate Coach 390
Reasons for the Decline in the Number of Female Coaches 391
A Final Note 392

The African-American Coach 392

Coaching Burnout 393
Smith's Cognitive-Affective Model of Athletic Burnout 393
Causes of Burnout 393
Effects of Burnout 397
Preventing Burnout 398

Summary 399

Key Terms 400

Suggested Readings 400

CHAPTER 25

*Exercise Psychology:
Physical Fitness, Adherence,
and the Cognitive and Affective
Benefits of Exercise* 403

Physical Fitness 404
Physical Fitness Defined 405
Physical Benefits 405
Psychological Benefits 406

Exercise Adherence 407
Predictors of Exercise Adherence 408
Why People Drop Out of Exercise Programs 408
Improving Exercise Adherence 410

**Cognitive and Affective Consequences
of Exercise 412**
Cognitive Effects 412
Effects on Mood 414

Summary 417

Key Terms 418

Suggested Readings 419

CHAPTER 26

*Exercise Psychology:
Running Addictions and
Exercise for Senior Citizens* 421

The Runner's Addictions 422
Positive Addiction 422
Negative Addiction 423
Mood and Running 424
Runner's High 424
Marathon Runners 425
Ultramarathoners/Ultrarunners 426

**Exercise and Competition for Senior
Citizens 430**
Fitness Issues for Seniors 430
The Competitive Senior 431
A Final Note 434

Summary 434

Key Terms 435

Suggested Readings 435

References 437
Author Index 481
Subject Index 489

Preface

In writing the first two editions of this text as well as the present one, we have been guided by a shared belief that sport and exercise psychology has been and continues to remain an emerging and important discipline. At the same time, there has been an ongoing need for a comprehensive and binding document that captures the essence of the discipline. We think we have accomplished this goal with the third edition. Many of the successful features from the previous editions have been retained. These include:

COMPREHENSIVE COVERAGE. We have covered the vast majority of important issues of concern to sport and exercise psychologists and students. In addition, we have added a number of topics that have emerged as important in the past several years.

HEALTHY BALANCE BETWEEN THEORY AND APPLICATION. The first half of the book contains abundant research applications tied to the chapters on arousal and anxiety, principles of learning, anxiety reduction and performance enhancement, motivation theories, social psychology, and aggression. Concurrent with the emphasis on research, we have attempted to show pertinent applications where possible. The latter portion of the book (Chapters 15–26) deals with topics that are less research-based and more applied, such as psychological assessment, women's issues, youth sport, coaching, and exercise psychology.

TOPIC COVERAGE. In textbook writing, there always seems to be some argument about certain topical inclusions and the order of presentation of chapters. There are three topics covered in this book that perhaps fall in this argumentative category. The first such topic is the his-

torical background material. While it is true that kinesiology majors receive training in this area, students enrolled in sport psychology courses from other disciplines do not usually receive that exposure, hence the two history chapters. A second controversial inclusion of separate topic coverage is that of women's issues. It could be argued that in today's prevailing climate women's issues should be embedded throughout the various chapters as opposed to receiving separate coverage. We feel that the recency of female sport and exercise participation merits a separate consideration. The same could be said for the coverage of minority athletes. Finally, the third topic we cover which some would argue should be deleted relates to the chapters on exercise. Again, kinesiology students may find the coverage a bit redundant, but those students from other disciplines who are taking an introductory sport psychology course would find our information about exercise to be new. We feel that some repetition actually facilitates learning.

PEDAGOGICAL AIDS. We include the following in each chapter to assist the students to further their understanding of the text:

- Chapter outlines
- Bolded key terms and glossary items located at the foot of the page
- Thorough chapter summaries
- Student-oriented suggested readings
- "Highlights" which are separate from the flow of main text but contain timelines and other material related to the text
- Carefully chosen figures and tables to aid in visual interpretation of important concepts

We have tried not to overwhelm the readership with such inclusions and have hopefully struck a proper balance with each of them.

TEST BANK. Approximately 1,000 multiple choice questions in both hard copy and electronic format will accompany the text. All have been written by your senior author, and have undergone statistical scrutiny with his students. The instructor will find them to be a valuable inclusion in instances where multiple choice items are desired.

In addition to the above-mentioned successful features that have worked well with updating, we have added the following new features for this third edition of our text:

NEW, MORE READER-FRIENDLY CHAPTER BREAKDOWN. By far the single biggest change we have implemented in this edition is to the chapter breakdown. We had originally submitted a 13-chapter manuscript through the final draft. However, we became convinced that our original structure containing chapters of 40 or 50 pages each was bulky, cumbersome, and a bit intimidating to students. To get around this liability, we have created a 26-chapter format, averaging around 20 pages each. Essentially, we divided each of the original 13 chapters at conceptually defensible breaking points, added or deleted coverage where needed, and created what we think is a much more reader-friendly format. Some chapters lent themselves to division more readily than did others. We think the reader will find that the new chapters cling together in a coherent and readable fashion. In another attempt to make things more reader friendly, when we found topic discussions that were overly technical or pedantic, we toned these down.

EXPANDED TOPIC COVERAGE. At the end of Chapter 1, we present a listing of a number of popular web sites of relevance to sport and exercise psychology professionals and students alike. Chapters 7 and 8 represent perhaps the most notable of the new additions to the book; these chapters are devoted to anxiety reduction procedures and performance enhancement techniques, respectively. Emphasis here is spread across classical conditioning, instrumental learning, and cognitive learning approaches. In Chapter 16 we give expanded coverage of the sport-specific assessment devices that have become so numerous and popular over the past decade or two. Chapter 17 presents coverage of minority athletes to include Latino, Asian American, and Native American performers. New coverage in Chapter 18 is devoted to injured athletes and athletes with disabilities. Also in the same chapter we expand the coverage of steroid abuse in sports, as well as introduce a discussion of controversial agents such as creatine, erythropoetin (EPO), human growth hormone (HGH), and beta-blockers.

NEW FEATURES. Key terms and related page references are included at the end of each of the chapters. Glossary words are found at the foot of each page. InfoTrac® search terms are presented for each chapter in cases where students may want to go beyond the bounds of the book in researching topics of interest. A free four-month subscription to the online database is packaged with the book. InfoTrac® is updated daily and includes hundreds of academic journals as well as numerous popular sources such as:

American Journal of Sports Medicine

Harvard Women's Health Watch

Journal of Physical Education, Recreation & Dance (JOPERD)

Journal of Sport Behavior

Men's Fitness

Research Quarterly for Exercise and Sport

Rodale's Fitness Swimmer

Runner's World

Sporting News

Women's Sports and Fitness

As was the case with previous editions of the text, there has been a clear division of labor between the two authors. Arnold LeUnes is responsible for all chapters except for 5, 6, 7, and 8 which, of course, were written by Jack Nation. At the same time, there have been innumerable interactions between the two authors over the past several years to ensure that the product is the best we can generate for the readership.

ACKNOWLEDGMENTS

Texts such as this could not be written without the valuable contributions of a huge array of theorists, researchers, practitioners, and others who are out constantly confronting the abundant and knotty problems within the field of sport and exercise psychology. To these dedicated professionals, we offer a heartfelt thanks.

The contributions made by the various staff members from Wadsworth—Thomson Learning have not gone unnoticed either. The guidance from Marianne Taflinger, Psychology Editor, Stacy Green, Mary Vezilich, Karyn Morrison, our reviewers—Andy Gillentine, Mississippi State University; Pamela Highlen, Ohio State University; David Kemler, Southern Connecticut State University; Patti Laguna, California State University, Fullerton; Jean Reeve, Southern Utah University; and Richard Stratton, Virginia Tech—has been invaluable.

As anyone who has undertaken a project of this magnitude will readily admit, there is a certain amount of sacrifice in terms of family and leisure time that is inherent in the process. Amassing information, writing copy, responding to reviews, editing, getting permissions, selecting a cover, choosing pictures, and proofreading are all quite demanding, and the time and energy required to do these things comes at the expense of family and other activities. In this regard, the patience, forbearance, and support given us by our families have been invaluable. Our heartfelt thanks go out to our respective families for their support. We could not have completed this project without the LeUnes group (wife, Judy and children, Leslie, Natalie, Chay, Amy, Katie, and Lyndon), and those in the Nation family (children, Derek and Shannon, Shannon's husband Brian and their children, Hunter and Strider).

A very special thanks in particular goes out to Katie LeUnes, Lyndon LeUnes, and Derek Nation, all of whom have excelled in sports and served as constant reminders of the significance of youth sport as well as the immensely important female sport experience.

Arnold LeUnes
Jack Nation

An Introduction to Sport Psychology

CHAPTER 1

Organization o
What Is Sport P
What Do Sport P
Sport Psychology
Organizations
Summary
Key Terms
Suggested Readings

Tiger Woods celebrates on the 18th green after winning the 1997 Masters Tournament at Augusta National Golf Club in Georgia. He has since emerged as perhaps the greatest golfer of all time.
©AFP/CORBIS

> *Sport is adventure, personal and vicarious.*
> *It is challenge, endeavor, and relaxation.*
> *It is, too, universal, and very few people*
> *have not succumbed to its lure, either*
> *as participant or spectator.*
>
> (BRASCH, 1970)

...scination with sports has reached epidemic proportions. On any Saturday in November, hundreds of college football teams tee up the football in front of legions of adoring fans. On Sunday, the professionals put their brand of football on display for millions of spectators and television viewers. At a point geographically removed from the pandemonium of football, professional golfers are capping off the tour. Players such as Eldrick "Tiger" Woods, David Duval, and Vijay Singh win millions of dollars. At the same time, the senior golf tour produces its own millionaires, players such as Larry Nelson, Bruce Fleisher, and Hale Irwin. At least a dozen female golf and tennis professionals take home over a million dollars in winnings. Concurrently, labor and management negotiators try to forge agreements that will allow team owners in high-profile sports to turn a profit while paying players salaries averaging around a million dollars annually.

Another area of athletic expression involves the world community. The Olympic Games represent the ultimate in athletic expression among the nations of the world. The World Games and the Pan American Games serve as tune-ups for the Olympics. International competition ranging from track and field to luge to Nordic skiing is an everyday part of our fare on sports television. Track-and-field stars such as Maurice Greene command six-figure appearance contracts from promoters of European track-and-field events. Many dollars and much energy are expended on behalf of sports as expressions of both individual pride and national prowess, and this situation is not likely to change soon.

At yet another level, children and adolescents display their skills and competitiveness in an array of youth programs—soccer leagues, peewee football, Little League baseball, and interscholastic athletics, to name only a few. Millions of youngsters play soccer, and many of these same young athletes also are members of baseball teams in one of the 8,500 leagues sponsored by Little League. Another 6 million youngsters participate in interscholastic sports such as baseball, basketball, football, track and field, and soccer.

None of this elaboration takes into account the daily games and recreational activities that captivate so many millions, things like triathlons, racquetball, jogging, and aerobic exercise. Clearly, many of us are involved in some manner with sports and exercise, so it is incumbent on the various sport sciences to do everything possible to expand our understanding and enjoyment of sports of all types and at all levels of complexity.

Our intention in this book is to capture the essence of this fascination with sports and fitness from the perspective of sport psychology and, where appropriate, other allied sport and fitness disciplines.

ORGANIZATION OF THIS BOOK

Part One is entitled "Introducing Sport Psychology and Sport History." In Chapters 1 and 2 we introduce you to the field of sport psychology and to what it is that sport psychologists try to accomplish. We identify professional organizations in sport psychology and related sport sciences. We also examine issues of concern to sport psychologists as well as to those who aspire to enter the field. Among them are training, credentialing, professional ethics, and employment opportunities.

Chapters 3 and 4 survey the history of sport and sport psychology. Sport has a long and fascinating history beginning for all practical purposes with the early Greeks. Chapter 3 traces sport history from ancient Greece to the reawakening of interest in physical activity and sport following the so-called Dark Ages, from the Renaissance into the Age of Enlightenment. Chapter 4 picks up with the colonial period of American history and extends through landmark events in the United States such as the Civil Rights Act of 1964 and the Title IX legislation of 1972. In addition to our historical survey, we provide a brief look at the history of sport psychology itself.

Money Spent on Sports and Fitness

Major League Baseball

In 1996, the most valuable franchise in professional sports was the New York Yankees, with an estimated worth of $225 million. The Yankees' estimated value in 2000 was $548 million, highest in baseball.

From 1994 through 1998 if you look at wins versus payroll costs, you will see that the Baltimore Orioles (winning percentage .538) spent $705,000 per win, followed by the New York Yankees (.607) at $697,000 per win and the Atlanta Braves (.620) at $563,000 per win. The Cleveland Indians (.594) at $534,000 per win and the Houston Astros (.550) at $438,000 per win were relative bargains for management.

The correlation between winning and payroll size in major league baseball is high. All of the 14 clubs with payrolls under $44 million in 1998 had losing records for the year.

In 2000, 404 major league baseball players, or 48% of all players, were making over $1 million. At the other end of the pay scale, 41 players were drawing the minimum salary, $200,000.

In 2001, 18 major league baseball players had contracts worth over $40 million. At the top of the list was Alex Rodriguez of the Texas Rangers, at $250 million.

National Football League

The Dallas Cowboys were valued at $663 million in 2000, making them the most valuable franchise in professional sports.

In 1999 Ricky Williams was offered a contract to play for the New Orleans Saints worth as much as $68 million over eight years. He received $8.84 million just to put his name on the contract.

During the 2001 Super Bowl, television advertisers paid $2.4 million for every 30 seconds of air time.

National Hockey League

The average player salary rose from $271,000 in 1990–91 to nearly $1.4 million in the 1999–2000 season, when Jaromir Jagr was the highest-paid NHL player at $10.4 million.

National Basketball Association

Rick Pitino ($7 million), Larry Brown ($5 million), and Larry Bird ($4.5 million) were paid handsomely for coaching teams in the NBA in the late 1990s.

Miscellany

Each college football team playing in the Rose, Sugar, Orange, or Fiesta Bowl in 2000 was guaranteed between $11 million and $13 million just to participate.

Members of the U.S. figure skating team make between $100,000 and $1.2 million annually.

Race driver Jeff Gordon won $3 million in the first five months of the 2001 NASCAR season; he has won $37 million during his 10-year career.

Professional tennis star Venus Williams has a $12 million endorsement deal with Reebok.

Over 400 new golf courses are opened in the United States each year.

British triple jumper Jonathan Edwards commands up to $1 million per appearance in track and field.

Four of the most popular spectator sports in terms of millions of paying customers are major league baseball (63), NBA basketball (21), NFL football (15), and NHL hockey (12). But, collectively, automobile and horse racing draw more spectators than all of the four so-called major professional sports combined.

Karch Kiraly, an Olympian in 1984 and 1988, has made over $3 million playing beach volleyball since turning professional.

Part Two, "Behavioral Principles and Applications," consists of chapters on learning, anxiety and anxiety management, and performance enhancement. Among the topics we discuss are classical and operant conditioning, cognitive learning, reinforcement and punishment, arousal and anxiety, the inverted-U relationship, and intervention techniques used to enhance performance.

In Part Three, "Social Psychological Dimensions," attribution theory, need achievement, locus of control, self-concept, leadership, group cohesion, audience effects, and aggression and violence in sport are discussed.

Part Four, "Personality, Assessment, and Special Athletic Populations," focuses on three areas. First we discuss psychological assessment in sport psychology, as well as various athletic groups including minority athletes, high-risk sport participants, athletes who use steroids and other alleged performance-enhancing drugs, and elite performers. Then we focus on the sport experience of women. Some might argue that separate chapters on women's issues are not warranted, but we think that the evolutionary state of women's sports justifies separate treatment. Finally, we focus on another emerging area of interest: youth sports. There has been a veritable explosion of theory, research, and practice aimed at youth sport participants and their parents and coaches.

In Part Five, "Coaching and Exercise," we look at what little is known about the psychology of coaching in terms of role demands, personality makeup, communication, and burnout. Then we conclude with a look at exercise and related topics. Millions of recreational joggers, aerobic exercisers, energetic senior citizens, softball players, golfers, swimmers, and others take part in recreation and health-related activities each day, and there are psychological reasons and consequences worthy of attention.

Critical to an understanding of each of these areas of inquiry is well-conducted research. Typically, research is published in sport psychology/sport science journals for consumption by other professionals so that they may conduct their own research, speak knowledgeably about these issues in their classes, or apply the research when working with athletes, teams, and exercise buffs. For a list of the major journals and their publishers see Table 1.1.

In the remainder of Chapter 1 we take a look at the field of sport and exercise psychology as well as what it is that sport psychologists actually do. Also, we discuss reasons for the increasing visibility of sport psychology in sport and exercise settings, and we examine an assortment of professional development issues. Chapter 1 concludes with an overview of professional organizations representing sport psychology and related sport sciences.

WHAT IS SPORT PSYCHOLOGY?

Arriving at consensus on a definition of **sport psychology** has not been easy. One of the first such efforts was that of Morgan (1972), who suggested that sport psychology is the study of psychological foundations of physical activity. An alternate definition was offered up by Martens (1980), who believed that sport psychology was too developmentally immature to overly concern itself with definitional problems and thus proposed that sport psychology be defined simply as what sport psychologists do. Three years later, Dishman (1983) challenged Martens by suggesting that defining sport psychology as what sport psychologists do shortchanged the profession and would hinder the development of useful theoretical, research, and application models.

Thanks to the efforts of the Association for the Advancement of Applied Sport Psychology (AAASP), one of the professional societies representing sport psychologists, a comprehensive and generally accepted definition of the field has been forged. According to the AAASP: "Sport psychology is (a) the study of the psychological and mental factors that influence and are influenced by participation and performance in sport, exercise, and physical activity, and (b) the application of the knowledge gained through this study to everyday settings. Sport psychology professionals are interested in how participation in sport, exercise, and physical activity may enhance personal development and

---

Sport psychology the study of psychological and mental factors affecting participation in sport, exercise, and physical activities, and the application of the knowledge thus gained to everyday settings.

TABLE 1.1

Major Sport Journals and Publishers

Journal	Publisher
Sport Psychology	
Journal of Sport & Exercise Psychology	Human Kinetics
The Sport Psychologist	Human Kinetics
Journal of Applied Sport Psychology	Taylor & Francis, Inc.
International Journal of Sport Psychology	International Society for Sport Psychology
Journal of Sports Sciences	Routledge
Journal of Sport and Exercise	Elsevier
Sports Medicine	
Sports Medicine	ADIS Press International
British Journal of Sports Medicine	British Association of Sport and Medicine
Medicine and Science in Sports and Exercise	American College of Sports Medicine
Physician and Sportsmedicine	American College of Sports Medicine
Journal of Athletic Training	National Athletic Trainers' Association
Kinesiology/Exercise Science	
Research Quarterly for Exercise and Sport	McGraw-Hill
Physical Educator	Phi Epsilon Kappa
Journal of Physical Education, Recreation and Dance	American Alliance for Health, Physical Education, Recreation and Dance
Quest	Human Kinetics
Canadian Journal of Sport Science	Canadian Association of Sport Sciences
Sport Sociology	
Sociology of Sport Journal	Human Kinetics
Journal of Sport and Social Issues	Center for the Study of Sport in Society, Northeastern University
Sport History	
Journal of Sport History	North American Society for Sport History
Sport Management	
Journal of Sport Management	North American Society for Sport Management

well-being throughout the life span" (http://www.aaasponline.org, May 2001). AAASP and organizations with similar goals promote the welfare of their respective members as well as the legions of athletes and fitness seekers everywhere.

WHAT DO SPORT PSYCHOLOGISTS DO?

Sport psychologists engage in three interrelated tasks: research, education, and application (see Figure 1.1).

Definitions of Play, Recreation, Games, and Sport

Nixon (1984) provides a useful way to differentiate among *play, recreation, games,* and *sport* (see the accompanying figure). Nixon makes the following distinctions: **Play** is exemplified by children kicking a ball back and forth or engaging in a snowball fight. **Recreation** is exemplified by jogging or skiing during the holidays. **Games,** more formalized than either play or recreation, are exemplified by a pickup game of basketball or an impromptu soccer game between neighborhood groups. **Sport,** Nixon says, is "an institutionalized competitive activity involving two or more opponents and stressing physical exertion by serious competitors who represent or are part of formally organized associations" (p. 13). An activity is a sport when "(a) it is characterized by relatively persistent patterns of social organization; (b) it is serious competition (whose outcome is not pre-arranged between two or more opponents; (c) it stresses the physical skill factor, and (d) it occurs within a formal organizational framework of teams, leagues, divisions, coaches, commissioners, sponsorship, formalized recruitment, and placement of personnel, rule books, and regulatory bodies."

Play an informal activity such as kicking a ball around by oneself or engaging in a snowball fight.
Recreation an activity engaged in for diversion or fitness, and exemplified by jogging or skiing.
Games more formal or organized activities such as a "pickup" game of basketball or a soccer match involving neighborhood groups.
Sport a competitive activity involving at least two competitors, requiring physical skill, following formal rules, and occurring within a formal organizational framework.

Low autonomy, expressiveness, spontaneity, separation from daily life

Institutionalization, bureaucratization, rationalization	Sport
Formalization of rules, external regulation	Games
Development of internal rules	Recreation
Relatively unorganized and unstructured activity	Play

Increasing organization, external regulation and constraint, seriousness, institutionalization, rationalization, bureaucratization, instrumental-task orientation

High autonomy, expressiveness, spontaneity, separation from daily life

SOURCE: Nixon (1984).

With regard to the **research function,** sport psychologists, particularly those working in universities, attempt to find answers to an infinite variety of questions through theoretical or empirical, basic or applied, and laboratory or field research. Each type of research makes an important contribution to the body of knowledge known as sport psychology.

As for the **education function,** sport psychologists teach students about the field in traditional university classroom settings, inform coaches, officials, and administrators about various sport-related issues, and

Research function conducting various kinds of research in order to find answers to questions related to sport, exercise, and physical activity.
Education function teaching students and informing coaches, athletes, exercise participants, and others about the discipline of sport psychology.

Reasons for Sport Psychology

Why sport psychology? The answers to this question are numerous and reflect long-time and worldwide fascination with sports and fitness. From the days of the ancient Greeks, with their emphasis on sport as an expression of beauty, to modern times, sport has occupied a prominent place in nearly every society. At least six factors have contributed to the evolution of the field of sport psychology over the past several decades.

1. **The pursuit of excellence by athletes.** Athletes are often open to virtually anything that will afford them the opportunity to perform at higher levels. Performance enhancement techniques drawn from psychology have been applied widely. Unfortunately, this pursuit of excellence has a downside in the form of questionable practices such as steroid use, blood doping, and abuse of stimulant drugs.

2. **Sport as a political tool.** Since the first Olympiad in 776 B.C., athletic achievement has been used to promote political ends. Sport psychologists are increasingly being asked by national sport governing bodies to assist in identifying and developing elite athletes who will serve as international spokespersons for their respective countries.

3. **High salaries in sport.** Sports is big business (see Highlight 1.1). This has led to an increase in the demand for sport psychology services among these highly paid performers.

4. **Recognition gained from sport.** Sport can be viewed as a vehicle for enhancing recognition and feelings of self-worth. There is every reason to believe that sport psychology has something to offer in this pursuit of recognition.

5. **Spectator interest.** Millions of people are regular viewers of sport-related activities. A sport psychologist can enhance their enjoyment through, for example, suggestions for reducing fan misbehavior and violence at sporting events. Also, anything that sport psychologists can do to make more of us doers rather than watchers is worthwhile.

6. **The fitness movement.** Our fascination with athletics tends to obscure another important activity, physical fitness. Sport psychologists are instrumental in assessing fitness, suggesting procedures to enhance exercise adherence, doing research and application in health psychology, and treating depression and anxiety through exercise—to name only a few of their many contributions.

enlighten top-level athletes and exercise participants about what sport psychology has to offer them.

Finally, with regard to the **application function,** sport psychologists may use psychometric instruments for purposes such as talent identification or assessment of the relationship between personality and performance. Another aspect of applied sport psychology is intervention to improve performance by means of techniques such as biofeedback, meditation, cognitive behavior modification, attentional control training, mental rehearsal, progressive relaxation, and visual imagery.

An alternate way of conceptualizing what sport psychologists do was suggested by a panel of AAASP members who identified the interests of these professionals as either academic or applied. An **academic sport psychologist** educates interested parties about

---

Application function administering psychometric evaluations to assess performance–personality relationships; using techniques such as biofeedback and visual imagery to improve performance.
Academic sport psychologist a sport psychologist interested primarily in the research and education functions of the profession.

FIGURE 1.1

Tasks of the Sport Psychologist

```
        Sport Psychologists' Tasks
        ┌──────────┬──────────┐
    Education    Research   Application
```

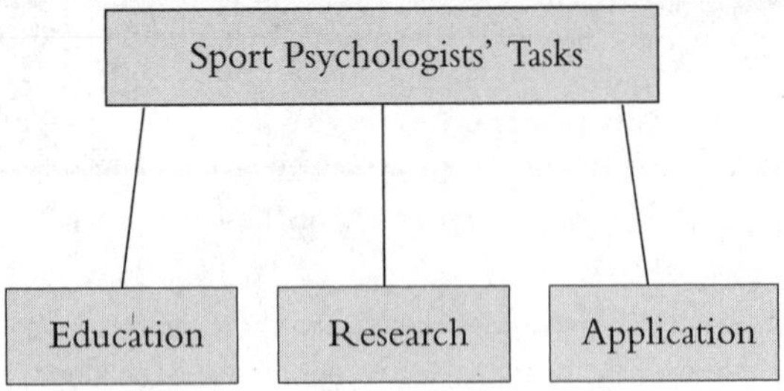

the field and conducts research on sport, exercise, and physical activity. An **applied sport psychologist** focuses on the application of sport psychology in sport and exercise settings. He or she typically devises performance enhancement strategies for athletes, conducts workshops for coaches and athletic administrators, and consults with athletic teams ranging from the youth-sport through the professional level.

SPORT PSYCHOLOGY PROFESSIONAL ORGANIZATIONS

Several professional organizations or societies aim to advance the field of sport psychology by establishing and monitoring training, credentialing, and ethical standards, as well as promoting the overall welfare of their respective members. In addition to their other responsibilities, most of the organizations and societies mentioned below also publish one or more journals dedicated to furthering communication and increasing the knowledge base. Some book publishers, too, publish journals. For a list of major sports journals and their publishers see Table 1.1.

Applied sport psychologist a sport psychologist interested primarily in the application function of the profession.

There is one international sport psychology organization. Several other organizations are primarily made up of North American sport psychologists. In addition, there are societies in Australia, Canada, and England, as well as organizations in related fields such as sport history, sports management, and sport sociology.

The International Organization

Many sport psychologists worldwide belong to the International Society for Sport Psychology (ISSP). Founded in 1965 by Feruccio Antonelli, of Italy, ISSP serves as a forum for sport psychologists from all over the world to engage in scholarly discourse while at the same time attempting to break down some of the barriers separating people with differing political and philosophical views. Quadrennial ISSP conferences have taken place in Rome (1965), Washington, D.C. (1969), Madrid (1973), Prague (1977), Ottawa (1981), Copenhagen (1985), Singapore (1989), Lisbon (1993), Wingate Institute, Israel (1997), and Skiathos Island, Greece (2001). ISSP also promotes its goals in its scholarly publications: *The International Journal of Sport Psychology* and *The Sport Psychologist*.

North American Organizations

The North American Society for the Psychology of Sport and Physical Activity (NASPSPA) has played an influential role in the evolution of sport psychology. NASPSPA was a major force in the 1970s and early 1980s when sport psychology was developing substantially as a discipline. In some ways a strange organization in terms of its composition, NASPSPA consisted of three sections: two focusing on motor learning (control and development) and one on sport psychology. The annual NASPSPA convention was really two conventions in one. The motor-learning people engaged in one mini-convention and the sport psychology people in another.

A major force propelling sport psychology to its place of relative eminence among the sport sciences is the Association for the Advancement of Applied Sport Psychology (AAASP). AAASP arose in 1986 in large part because some of the sport psychology members of NASPSPA felt that the organization was not meeting their professional interests and needs. After the creation of AAASP, NASPSPA became less of a force in sport psychology than it had been in the past.

The idea for AAASP emerged from a splinter group, spearheaded by John Silva, meeting at the 1985 NASPSPA convention. AAASP held its first annual meeting at Jekyll Island, Georgia, in 1986; since then the organization has grown in size and importance. Its approximately 1,000 members are almost evenly split between the disciplines of psychology and kinesiology. AAASP has achieved a position of leadership within sport psychology in a very short time, primarily because of its efforts to set training standards, its implementation of a credentialing process, and its stance on ethics in teaching, research, and practice.

Another prominent organization is Division 47 of the American Psychological Association (APA). Division 47, the exercise and sport psychology division, was also created in 1986 and has more than 1,000 members. In view of APA's considerable financial and political clout, Division 47 is likely to be a major player in sport psychology for the foreseeable future.

Another organization with sport psychology ties is the American Alliance for Health, Physical Education, Recreation, and Dance (AAHPERD), which has around 2,000 members with sport psychology interests. The remainder of the AAHPERD membership is devoted to traditional concerns listed in the organization's name.

An important professional society with strong ties to sport psychology is the American College of Sports Medicine (ACSM), an organization of some 17,000 members, many of whom have an interest in sport psychology. ACSM's American Board of Medical Specialties defines sports medicine as including (1) exercise as a critical component of health care throughout the life span, (2) medical management and supervision of recreational and competitive athletes, and (3) exercise as a mechanism for preventing and treating disease and injury.

Though not a professional society in the strictest sense of the term, another sport-related enterprise of importance is the Center for the Study of Sport in Society. Started by Richard Lapchick at Northeastern University in Boston, the Center has become a major force in the ongoing dialogue about racism and gender issues in sport. The Center is also active in calling attention to the interface between academics and big-time college athletics. The primary function of the Center's publication, the *Journal of Sport and Social Issues,* is to articulate serious societal concerns about sport and to promote social change.

Australian, British, and Canadian Associations

Sport psychology associations and societies are springing up all over the world as the field becomes increasingly popular. Three well-developed and active societies are found in Australia, Britain, and Canada.

AUSTRALIA. Sport psychologists in Australia are affiliated with the Australian Psychological Society (APS). There are nine colleges in APS, one of which is the College of Sport Psychologists. In order to join the College, one must meet the requirements for licensure as a psychologist as well as a number of sport-related training standards. Also, a premium is placed in the organization on continuing education designed to insure that the skill level of all APS members remains at a high level. The membership of the College is often called upon to provide sport psychology services to athletes training at the Australian Institute of Sport (AIS), the Olympic training center located in Canberra. The main sport-related journal under Australian sponsorship is the *Australian Journal of Science and Sports Medicine.*

BRITAIN. The British are represented by the British Association for Sport and Exercise Sciences (BASES). Some British sport psychologists are members of the Sport and Exercise Section of the British Psychological Society (BPS).

CANADA. Sport psychology in Canada is promoted primarily through the efforts of the Canadian Society for Psychomotor Learning and Sport Psychology (CSPLSP), which was founded in 1969 as part of the Canadian Association for Health, Physical Education, Recreation and Dance (CAHPERD). CSPLSP, which remained part of CAHPERD until 1977, represents some 200 sport psychologists in Canada.

Related Professional Organizations

In addition to the sport psychology organizations, there are three allied ones worthy of mention. The

Websites of Interest to Sport Psychologists

With the tremendous growth of the Internet, access to information about sport science and sport psychology is escalating at a rapid rate. Some important Websites are available for interested students and professionals. Information that would have taken days or weeks to gather prior to the advent of the Internet is readily available.

Sport and Exercise Psychology—American

American Alliance for Health, Physical Education, Recreation and Dance
http://www.aahperd.org/

Association for the Advancement of Applied Sport Psychology
http://www.aaasponline.org

Division 47 of the American Psychological Association
http://www.psyc.unt.edu/apadiv47/

North American Society for the Psychology of Sport and Physical Activity
http://www.naspspa.org

Sport Psychology—International

Australian Psychological Society
http://www.psychsociety.com.au

British Association for Sport and Exercise Sciences
http://www.bases.org.uk

Canadian Association for Health, Physical Education, Recreation and Dance
http://www.cahperd.ca/e/

Canadian Society for Psychomotor Learning and Sport Psychology
http://www.scapps.org/

International Olympic Committee
http://www.olympic.org/

International Society for Sport Psychology
http://nimbus.ocis.temple.edu/~msachs.issp.html

Other Sport-Related Websites

American College of Sports Medicine
http://www.acsm.org/sportsmed/

Center for the Study of Sport in Society
http://sportinsociety.org/

Institute for International Sport (University of Rhode Island)
http://www.internationalsport.com/

International Society for Comparative Physical Education and Sport
http://www.usc.edu.au/iscpes/

North American Society for the Sociology of Sport
http://playlab.uconn.edu/

North American Society for Sport History
http://www.nassh.org/

North American Society for Sport Management
http://www.nassm.com

SPORTDiscus (Sport and Fitness Information Database)
http://www.sportdiscus.com

Sport Psychology Information
http://spot.colorado.edu/~collinsj

Sportscience
http://www.sportsci.org/

United States Olympic Committee
http://www.olympic-usa.org

Women's Sports Foundation
http://www.lifetimetv.com/WoSport?

North American Society for Sport History (NASSH) boasts a membership of over 700 and serves as the main disseminator of sport history. The primary publication sponsored by NASSH is the *Journal of Sport History*. The North American Society for Sport Management (NASSM), another major player in sport science, held its first convention in Kent, Ohio, in 1986, and has over 300 members. In 1987, NASSM started its own publication, the *Journal of Sport Management,* in conjunction with the publisher Human Kinetics. The North American Society for the Sociology of Sport (NASSS) is made up of approximately 200 sport sociologists with interests in sport in the broader societal realm.

SUMMARY

1. Sport is big business in most countries, and sport psychology has much to offer in terms of understanding and enhancing the sport and exercise experience at all levels of sophistication.

2. The Association for the Advancement of Applied Sport Psychology (AAASP) defines sport psychology as "(a) the study of psychological and mental factors that influence and are influenced by participation and performance in sport, exercise, and physical activity, and (b) the application of the knowledge gained through this study to everyday settings. Sport psychologists are interested in how participation in sport, exercise, and physical activity may enhance personal development and well-being throughout the life span."

3. Sport psychologists typically engage in one or more of three interrelated tasks: research, education, and application. The research function focuses on using a variety of research techniques to ask and answer important questions. The education function, which sometimes occurs within a university setting, involves enlightening others about what the field has to offer. Sport psychologists interested in the application function are out in the field applying skills aimed at intervention or performance enhancement.

4. The International Society for Sport Psychology (ISSP) is the leading forum for communication among members of the world sport psychology community. The *International Journal of Sport Psychology* and a quadrennial world conference are ISSP's two major means of communication.

5. The North American Society for the Psychology of Sport and Physical Activity (NASPSPA) has made a substantial historical contribution to the development of sport psychology. The Association for the Advancement of Applied Sport Psychology (AAASP) and Division 47, Sport and Exercise Psychology, of the American Psychological Association (APA) are major players today in shaping the future of sport psychology. The American Alliance for Health, Physical Education, Recreation and Dance (AAHPERD) and the American College of Sports Medicine (ACSM) also have members interested in sport psychology. The Center for the Study of Sport in Society plays an important role as a watchdog on racial and gender issues.

6. Other professional societies include the North American Society for the Sociology of Sport (NASSS), the North American Society for Sport History (NASSH), and the North American Society for Sport Management (NASSM).

7. There are also professional societies in Australia, Britain, and Canada with strong ties to their respective memberships.

KEY TERMS

academic sport psychologist (7)
application function (7)
applied sport psychologist (8)
education function (6)
games (6)
play (6)
recreation (6)
research function (6)
sport (6)
sport psychology (4)

Sport Psychology Professional Organizations

American Alliance for Health, Physical Education, Recreation and Dance (AAHPERD)
American College of Sports Medicine (ACSM)

Association for the Advancement of Applied Sport Psychology (AAASP)

Australian Institute of Sport (AIS)

Australian Psychological Society (APS)

British Association for Sport and Exercise Sciences (BASES)

British Psychological Society (BPS)

Canadian Association for Health, Physical Education, Recreation and Dance (CAHPERD)

Canadian Society for Psychomotor Learning and Sport Psychology (CSPLSP)

Center for the Study of Sport in Society

Division 47 of the American Psychological Association (APA)

International Society for Sport Psychology (ISSP)

North American Society for the Sociology of Sport (NASSS)

North American Society for Sport History (NASSH)

North American Society for Sport Management (NASSM)

North American Society for the Psychology of Sport and Physical Activity (NASPSPA)

Sport Psychology Professional Journals

Australian Journal of Science and Sports Medicine
The International Journal of Sport Psychology
Journal of Sport History
Journal of Sport Management
Journal of Sport and Social Issues
The Sport Psychologist

SUGGESTED READINGS

Lidor, R., Morris, T., Bardaxoglu, N., & Becker, B. (2001). *The world sport psychology sourcebook* (3rd ed). Morgantown, WV: Fitness Information Technology, Inc.

This book serves as a starting point for exploring the world scene in sport psychology. Of particular value is the discussion of sport psychology programs, prominent sport psychologists, and related material from nearly every country.

Roberts, G. C., Spink, K. S., & Pemberton, C. L. (1999). *Learning experiences in sport psychology.* Champaign, IL: Human Kinetics.

The authors provide 20 learning experiences for use in the sport psychology classroom. The book is divided into three parts. Part 1 focuses on research design and analyzing and presenting research data. Parts 2 and 3 focus on 15 topics, including aggression, anxiety, motivation, cohesion, mental preparation, and exercise adherence.

INFOTRAC COLLEGE EDITION

For additional readings, explore Infotrac College Edition, your online library. Go to:
http://www.infotrac-college.com/wadsworth
Hint: Enter these search terms: athletic ability, sports journals, sports medicine, sport psychology, sports sciences.

Professional Issues

CHAPTER 2

Training for the Profession
Credentialing
Ethical Principles
Image of the Profession
Employment Opportunities
Summary
Key Terms
Suggested Readings

American Dan O'Brien, gold medalist in the 1996 Olympics decathlon, is an example of a prominent athlete who sought the services of a sport psychologist.
© Wally McNamee/CORBIS

Sport psychologists engage in research, education, and application tasks in a wide variety of sport and exercise settings. To fulfill these functions successfully, sport psychologists need to be alert to problematic professional issues. Five areas of concern are training, credentialing, ethics, professional image, and employment opportunities (see Figure 2.1). We will examine each one.

TRAINING FOR THE PROFESSION

Effective training in research, educational methods, and application is crucial. But who is to do the training and how it is best accomplished remain unclear. Departments of psychology, for the most part, have demonstrated little willingness to take up the challenge, typically citing other, more pressing training priorities. As a result, sport psychologists receive much of their training from professionals in departments of kinesiology, sport studies, human movement studies, and sport sciences.

Related to the training issue is a study reported by Straub and Hinman (1992), who interviewed 10 of the leading sport psychologists in North America about various professional issues. One of the interviewees, Dr. Robert Nideffer, took the position that students aspiring to be sport psychologists should seek training through clinical or counseling psychology programs, taking additional course work within the sport sciences. A 1999 recommendation from the United States Olympic Committee (USOC) added support to Nideffer's position. USOC suggested (Inside the USOC, 1999) that the movement of sport psychology into the applied area underscores the importance of sound applied psychology training. In addition to training in the traditional specialties of clinical and counseling psychology, the USOC mentioned training in industrial/organizational (I/O) psychology. With such training, students who receive a doctoral degree in psychology will qualify for licensure and be able to call themselves "psychologist."

Implicit in any discussion of training is the issue of territoriality, or what Burke (1999, p. 232) calls the

"**Who can do what debate**" the debate about whether sport psychology is a subspecialty of physical education or a subspecialty of psychology.

FIGURE 2.1

Professional Issues in Sport Psychology

"who can do what debate." Historically, sport psychology has been a subspecialty within physical education. Only in the past 15 to 20 years has psychology demonstrated anything more than passing interest in sport psychology. For at least two decades a running dialogue has been going on between the two disciplines. It goes something like this:

Psychologist: You phys-ed folks have the sport and coaching background, but your training in psychology is pretty weak.

Physical Educator: Granted, you have us beat on the psychology front, but what do you know about sports? You never played or coached anything, and you have no training in the sport sciences.

Denying that territorial disputes occasionally occur would be naive, although such verbal exchanges are conducted with cordiality and respect. Silva (1989) suggested an end to the territorial wars and the creation of a spirit of cooperation that would maximize what psychology and kinesiology have to offer each other. Sport psychologists interested in applied work could take advantage of what psychology departments have to offer, and those interested mainly in the academic side of sport psychology could seek Ph.D. training in the area that most closely corresponds with their interests. Clearly, academia has room for sport psychologists who operate from a base either in psychology or in physical education, depending on their backgrounds, interests, and training.

There are a number of complex political and monetary components related to bidding on and hosting the Olympic Games. As a result, much media attention is focused on all aspects of the Games. These highly placed men in the Olympic movement are taking part in a news conference related to the 2002 Winter Games, which were awarded to Salt Lake City, Utah.

Above and beyond the territorial issue, there is much to do to further refine the training requirements for sport psychologists. Currently, programs vary considerably, and there is much discussion but little agreement about whether this diversity is good or bad. Panels of experts from AAASP and Division 47 of the American Psychological Association are at work on the training issue, and eventually there will be a broad consensus about what constitutes good training in sport psychology.

CREDENTIALING

Credentialing is a general term for the process of ensuring that members of a profession meet certain set standards. Subsumed under the broad umbrella of credentialing are licensure, certification, and registry. Zaichkowsky and Perna (1992) suggest that the terminology surrounding the credentialing process within sport psychology is ambiguous and needs clarification.

Licensure is a restrictive, *statutory* process designed to regulate member conduct. Both physicians and psychologists are subject to licensure. **Certification** is generally a nonstatutory procedure carried out by an

organization (as opposed to a statutory body). AAASP certification, discussed below, is a sport-related example. **Registry,** another nonstatutory procedure, also indicates professional recognition. To qualify for the United States Olympic Committee (USOC) Sport Psychology Registry, for example, a professional must be both a Certified Consultant–AAASP and a member of the American Psychological Association.

All 50 states in the United States and the eight provinces of Canada have licensing laws that restrict psychological practice to individuals who have specific academic training in psychology and who have passed required state or province licensing examinations. Because of how these laws are written, most physical educators lack the educational background they would need to pass a licensing exam and become licensed psychologists specializing in sport. Thus some of these professionals are opting to return to school in psychology to do the necessary course work and acquire the practical experience they need to become licensed.

The licensure issue has generated considerable discussion in the literature and at professional meetings. It is now abundantly clear, however, that placing "sport" in front of "psychologist" does absolutely nothing to change the fact that a person must be licensed as a psychologist in order to engage in the practice of sport psychology. The word *psychologist* carries a legal definition, and no modifier changes that fact. Consequently, only licensed psychologists can *legally* call themselves sport psychologists. Actually, this restriction applies only when the person in question is offering his or her services to the public for remuneration. University professors in psychology or kinesiology who call themselves sport psychologists but do not offer their

Credentialing the process of ensuring that members of a profession meet certain set standards.
Licensure a credentialing procedure defined by statute and intended to regulate professional conduct. This is a professional and legal issue as opposed to an ethical one, and is at variance with APA and AAASP ethics codes.
Certification a nonstatutory credentialing procedure.
Registry a nonstatutory credentialing procedure.

FIGURE 2.2

Criteria for AAASP Certification

1. Membership in AAASP with attendance at two or more AAASP annual conferences.

2. Completion of a doctoral degree from an accredited university.

3. Knowledge of AAASP ethical standards.

4. Knowledge of the sport psychology subdisciplines of intervention/performance enhancement, health/exercise psychology, and social psychology.

5. Knowledge of biomechanical or physiological bases of behavior.

6. Knowledge of the historical, philosophical, social, or motor behavior bases of sport.

7. Knowledge of psychopathology and its assessment.

8. Supervised graduate-level practica training in counseling, clinical, or industrial/organizational psychology.

9. Knowledge of skills and techniques within sport or exercise gained through skills and techniques courses, formal coaching experiences, or organized sport or exercise participation.

10. Knowledge of research design, statistics, and psychological assessment.

11. Knowledge of biological bases of behavior.

12. Knowledge of the cognitive-affective bases of behavior (e.g., memory, learning, motor development, cognition).

13. Knowledge of social bases of behavior (e.g., sociology of sport, social psychology, gender roles in sport, group processes).

14. Knowledge of individual behavior (e.g., individual differences, personality theory, developmental psychology, health psychology, exercise behavior).

15. Supervised and unsupervised practica and consultation experience.

16. Three professional references.

Certified Consultant—AAASP a credential that identifies the recipient as having met AAASP's rigorous educational and training standards.

services to the public are operating within the spirit of the laws regulating the practice of psychology.

Closure has been brought to the issue of what credentials a sport psychologist must have. What is less clear is what to do about the sizable number of people in the field who do not qualify for licensure. The potential disenfranchisement of talented professionals from kinesiology backgrounds is an important concern. To deal with this problem, the Association for the Advancement of Applied Sport Psychology (AAASP) created a credentialing process that confers on qualified professionals the title **Certified Consultant— AAASP.** This credential serves several useful purposes. First, it conveys to coaches, athletes, and others that the recipient has met AAASP's rigorous educational and training standards. Second, the recipients—all well-trained professionals—achieve visibility and gain recognition through their listing in the AAASP Registry. Third, the certification process enhances the credibility of the profession of sport psychology. Finally, the certification process is a step forward in educating the public about sport psychology. As of late 1998, there were 133 Certified Consultants—AAASP: 117 from the United States, 7 from Canada, 6 from Australia, 2 from South America, and 1 from the United Kingdom.

The training requirements for AAASP certification are listed in Figure 2.2. Meeting the comprehensive interdisciplinary requirements for AAASP certification is not easy. But the standards are realistic indicators of the expertise needed to perform the myriad tasks of the sport psychologist. Zaichkowsky and Perna (1992) indicate that training in either psychology or medicine is not sufficient to call oneself a sport psychologist or an AAASP consultant. The related training in sport and exercise science must also be in place. Zaichkowsky and Perna offer some pertinent certification statistics to substantiate their argument. A review of 72 applications for certification in 1991 revealed that 32 applicants had doctorates in psychology or medicine but only 11 of them received certification. The remaining 40 applicants had training in kinesiology and related areas, and 31 of them were granted AAASP certification.

Arriving at the exacting standards listed in Figure 2.2 and getting the approval of the AAASP membership took approximately five years; this task was accomplished only after much discussion. Even after the enactment of the AAASP certification process, counterviews continued to emerge. Chief among the dissenters was Anshel (1992; 1993) who argued that the certification process was both exclusionary and based on the faulty clinical model for training that had dominated past thinking on the issue. Anshel also issued a call for sport psychologists to stop the infighting over certification and get on with the business of making their psychological skills available to teams, coaches, and athletes.

As might be expected, Zaichkowsky and Perna have taken Anshel to task for his views. Several past presidents of AAASP (e.g., Gould, 1990; Silva, 1989) are also highly supportive of the certification process, seeing it as a major step forward in establishing the validity of the discipline of sport psychology.

ETHICAL PRINCIPLES

The creation of ethical principles to guide sport psychology research and practice has been a major focus of AAASP since its creation in 1986. AAASP reviewed more than 50 codes of professional conduct before settling on standards most closely resembling the ethical principles advocated by the American Psychological Association (APA).

We addressed one important ethical issue—**who can be called a psychologist**—in the previous section, on credentialing. Other issues of professional concern include competence, integrity, professional and scientific responsibility, respect for people's rights and dignity, concern for the welfare of others, and social responsibility (see Figure 2.3).

- **Competence.** It is important that sport psychologists practice within their competencies and remain cognizant of the limitations of their expertise.

- **Integrity.** Fairness and honesty about qualifications, services, products, and fees are of paramount importance. Imbedded within this ethical principle is a prohibition against **dual relationships,** which create or might seem to create a conflict of interest. Examples of dual relationships include working with a team or individual simultaneously as coach and as sport psychologist, providing psychological services to a student–athlete in one's class, having a friendly beer at a campus

FIGURE 2.3

Ethical Issues in Sport Psychology

hangout with an athlete, or having athletes stay in one's home overnight during a local competition.

- **Professional and scientific responsibility.** It is incumbent on the sport psychologist to act professionally at all times and to cooperate with others to see that they also do so. Moral standards and conduct are expected to be of the highest quality, and nothing should be done to undermine public trust in the profession of sport psychology.

- **Respect for people's rights and dignity.** Client confidentiality, privacy, self-determination, and autonomy are of paramount concern. AAASP members are aware of individual, cultural, and role differences, including those related to age, gender, race, ethnicity, national origin, disability, language,

---

Who can be called a psychologist an ethical and a credentialing issue in sport psychology.
Competence an ethical issue in sport psychology.
Integrity an ethical issue in sport psychology.
Dual relationship a double relationship, such as being both a coach and a pal, that calls into question a person's integrity by creating or seeming to create a conflict of interest.
Professional and scientific responsibility an ethical issue in sport psychology.
Respect for people's rights and dignity an ethical issue in sport psychology.

and socioeconomic status. They are expected to work at all times to eliminate biases based on these factors, and most certainly they are expected not to engage in any form of discrimination.

- **Concern for the welfare of others.** Sport psychologists must be sensitive to real and ascribed differences in power between themselves and others and must not exploit or mislead their clients during or after professional relationships.

- **Social responsibility.** Sport psychologists must be aware of their responsibilities to the community and to society. They are expected to make public their knowledge, observe the highest principles when conducting research, and generally advance human welfare while always protecting the rights of individuals.

Petitpas, Brewer, Rivera, and Van Raalte (1994) shed light on various points of concern about ethics in sport psychology. They received responses to a questionnaire from 165 AAASP members and found, among other things, that there was reasonable congruence between the ethical beliefs and actual ethical practices of their respondents. Some issues, however, were widely regarded as difficult judgment calls. In this category were reporting gambling by an athlete, reporting college recruiting violations, consulting with athletes known to use steroids, socializing with athletes, consulting with athletes in objectionable sports such as boxing, and working with athletes known to be engaged in illegal activities. Alarmingly, only 40% of their respondents had actually completed a course in ethical behavior at some point in their professional training.

Wann (1997, p. 11), in response to those findings, suggests that "sport psychologists should feel obligated to seek out education on ethical issues, and sport psychology programs should routinely offer courses in ethical conduct." It goes without saying that AAASP and other professional sport organizations are acutely aware of the importance of ethical behavior and are devoting a lot of time and energy to the implementation and monitoring of appropriate standards of professional conduct.

Concern for the welfare of others an ethical issue in sport psychology.

Social responsibility an ethical issue in sport psychology

IMAGE OF THE PROFESSION

Any time a psychologist has more to do with who you pick in the NFL draft than the head coach, you've got to wonder about the organization.

Dan Reeves, professional football coach

What kills me is all this sport psychology crap. I've never seen so many people into sports science in my life. The USTA has these monthly seminars and all they do is this sports science. You're 15, 16 and they've got you on the couch. At 15, what the hell do you want to know more about yourself for? Hey, when I was 16, if they put me on a couch, I'd have said, "What're you crazy?" Hey man, get on the court, get working and start playing events. That's what it's all about. What all this sports psychology is about is appeasing a lot of egos, and it just kills me.

Brad Gilbert, a top professional player at one time and coach of Andre Agassi

You lie on a couch, they take your money, and you walk out more bananas than when you walk in.

Goran Ivanesevic, Croatian tennis professional

The field of sport psychology strives to present a positive and professional image to athletes, coaches, administrators, other professions, and the general public. But, as the preceding comments show, not all coaches and athletes are positive in their evaluations of sport psychology services. In the past, indiscretions by out-and-out charlatans or by do-gooders who could not deliver what they promised sent the wrong message to coaches, athletes, and sport administrators. Fortunately, today there is less charlatanism and incompetence, because of the increasing professionalization of sport psychology over the last two decades.

The media are replete with references to athletes who are making use of sport psychology services to enhance performance. At various times over the past few years, several professional golfers have spoken publicly and positively about their interactions with sport psychologists. Sport psychologists such as Dr. Richard Coop (among his clients are Greg Norman, Corey Pavin, Payne Stewart), Alan Fine (David Feherty), Dr. Jim Loehr (John Daly, Nick Faldo), and Dr. Robert

Rotella (David Duval, Davis Love, Dickie Pride, Patty Rizzo) have been cited in the media for their work with professional golfers. Professional tennis players Jim Courier, Mary Joe Fernandez, and Gabriela Sabatini have sung the praises of Jim Loehr (Loehr has also worked with NHL hockey star Eric Lindros and professional basketball player Jason Williams). Major league baseball player John Smoltz has spoken positively about his interactions with Dr. Jack Llewellyn. In professional basketball, Dr. Bruce Ogilvie was well received by the Miami Heat. Dr. Richard Suinn has been the recipient of considerable recognition on national television for his work with elite downhill skiers. Olympic ice skater Nancy Kerrigan was involved in a regular mental training program with Dr. Cindy Adams. Dr. Andrew Jacobs worked with former Kansas City field goal kicker Nick Lowery for the last twelve years of his career with the Chiefs. Jim Reardon was the sport psychologist for Olympic decathlete and world record holder Dan O'Brien. Olympic champion downhill skier Picabo Street has sung the praises of her sport psychologist, Dr. Sean McCann.

As might be expected, there are dissenters in addition to the ones quoted at the start of this section. Rick Fehr and Scott Hoch in professional golf and Marv Levy, ex-coach of the NFL Buffalo Bills, have not been impressed with what sport psychology has to offer. In general, however, anecdotal evidence casts a positive light on the field.

As an aside, anecdotal accounts from the media may seem to imply to aspiring young sport psychology students and to the general public that jobs are plentiful in sport psychology. Don't be deceived. The notion of numerous jobs offering an opportunity to work with high-profile and seemingly glamorous athletes is misleading. Many of the sport psychologists mentioned above have been or currently are professors who make their living in university settings. Their sport psychology consultation with famous athletes is done on a part-time basis. The security of a dependable salary from the university allows them to engage in this sort of consultation, which otherwise might not be possible.

Speaking of newspapers and the media in general, Brewer, Van Raalte, Petitpas, Bachman, and Weinhold (1998) conducted a 9-year study of 3 national newspapers to ascertain how sport psychology was portrayed. Using several keywords, Brewer et al. scrutinized the

Chicago Tribune, Los Angeles Times, and *Washington Post* from 1985 through 1993 and found 574 articles that focused on sport psychology. Robert Rotella (31 instances), Thomas Tutko (24), Bruce Ogilvie (21), James Loehr (20), Richard Lister (16), Jack Llewellyn (12), and Ken Ravizza (10) were the sport psychologists most often mentioned in the newspapers. The researchers drew these conclusions from their analyses: The press was objective and fair in its treatment of the discipline. Sport psychology consultation, particularly involving performance enhancement, was the most common focus. Golf and baseball were the most common sport targets. Overall, the mass media accurately portrayed sport psychology to the public.

Olympians constitute another athletic group with both experience and opinions about sport psychology. Orlick and Partington (1987) conducted interviews with 75 Canadian athletes from 19 different sports after the 1984 Olympic games. From these interviews, Orlick and Partington were able to draw up composites of good sport psychology consultants and bad sport psychology consultants.

Good consultants were seen as (1) likeable and able to offer their clients something concrete and applied; (2) flexible and knowledgeable about how to meet individual needs; (3) accessible, caring, and able to establish rapport with athletes; and (4) facilitative of mental training prior to and during competition. Bad consultants were seen as (1) lacking interpersonal skills to such a degree that they were described as "wimpy," "domineering," and "demanding" (in one case insisting that athletes carry their bags); (2) unable to apply psychological skills; (3) inflexible and unable to meet individual needs; (4) preferring group work to the exclusion of one-on-one consultation; (5) providing consulting at the competition site that interfered with mental preparation; and (6) providing little or no feedback. The best and worst behaviors that Orlick and Partington described offer strong support for the notion that elite athletes have no difficulty in assessing their sport psychology consultants.

How are athletes who seek assistance from a sport psychologist perceived? What image is projected by an athlete seeking such assistance, and what are the ramifications of this image for sport psychology? Linder, Pillow, and Reno (1989) asked introductory psychology students to respond to a hypothetical situation in which they were asked to evaluate two quarterbacks preparing to enter the professional football draft. One of the hypothetical players went to his coach, and the other went to a sport psychologist to seek help with mental skills training issues. The player seeking help from his coach was viewed as significantly more emotionally stable than his counterpart who sought out the sport psychologist. In addition, the first player was seen as more likely to fit in with management when he was eventually drafted. Overall, in this research, the field of sport psychology was viewed in a not-so-favorable light.

Following up on that line of research, Linder, Brewer, Van Raalte, and DeLange (1991) used hypothetical drafts in professional baseball, basketball, and football for evaluative purposes. In this study, psychotherapists were added to the mix for comparison purposes, and subjects once again were psychology students. However, in an effort to broaden the evaluative base, Lions Club members attending a regional convention also served as subjects. Psychology students and Lions Club members viewed in a negative light hypothetical athletes in all three sports seeking sport psychology consultation and, for the most part, did not distinguish between sport psychologists and psychotherapists. This outcome may not be all bad—being viewed in the same light as mental health professionals may actually add credibility to the work that sport psychologists do.

Speaking of mental health professionals, two surveys of attitudes about sport psychology among clinical and counseling psychologists generally cast a favorable light on the field. The first study was conducted by LeUnes and Hayward (1990), who surveyed chairpersons of APA-approved programs in clinical psychology. They mailed out 147 sets of questionnaires and received back 102 (69.4% return rate). The results indicated a generally favorable perception of sport psychology among these professionals, though few planned to expand their departmental offerings to include sport psychology. The use of the term *sport psychologist* was seen as contentious, but few respondents expected turf wars over the field.

The second study was reported by Petrie and Watkins (1994) and involved APA-approved counseling psychology departments in universities that also had physical education or kinesiology departments. Once again, sport psychology was viewed favorably. As might

be expected, the physical education departments offered more courses in sport psychology and had more students and faculty with interests in the area. However, over 70% of the counseling psychology departments had students with these same interests. Two-thirds of the counseling psychology respondents viewed the statutory restriction of the term *sport psychologist* favorably; only 30% of the physical educators agreed with such a stance. Both LeUnes and Hayward and Petrie and Watkins stressed the need for continuing cooperation between the psychology and physical education professions in dealing with issues of mutual concern.

What is evident is a generally positive image of sport psychology among professional and elite Olympic athletes, in the press, and within the clinical and counseling areas within psychology. At the same time, however, there appear to be image problems among some professional sports figures and segments of the general public, and these need to be addressed. With improvements in training, greater awareness of and adherence to good ethical practices, and general enlightening of the public, it is realistic to expect an upswing in the respect that sport psychology receives from athletes, coaches, athletic administrators, allied professions, and the general public.

EMPLOYMENT OPPORTUNITIES

Despite advances in training and increasing acceptance, the employment picture in sport psychology is not overly reassuring. Opportunities are limited, and getting a job depends on a loose combination of ability, training, creativity, entrepreneurship, luck, and the presence of persuasive advocates in one's corner. Essentially, there are two ways to become a sport psychologist. One way is to earn a Ph.D. in clinical, counseling, or industrial/organizational psychology, set up a private practice, and devote some or all of that practice to athletes and teams. The marketplace being what it is at present, few people are likely to be able to devote an entire practice to sport psychology and make a respectable living. The other way to become a sport psychologist is to be a university professor in a department of kinesiology or psychology and teach, conduct research, and work with athletes and teams in an academic setting. To be sure, a few people get their start in academia and actually become successful enough as consultants to vacate their academic appointments.

Sport psychology is indeed an exciting field, but prospective students with career goals in this area need to enter their training with both eyes open. The job market is relatively small. A somewhat dated study, reported in 1993 by Waite and Pettit, provides almost the only data-based information available concerning nuances of the job market. These investigators surveyed graduates of sport psychology programs for the period 1984 to 1989, and some interesting though tentative conclusions emerged from their efforts. Among their conclusions were the following:

1. Of their 34 respondents, all but 2 received doctoral degrees from a department of kinesiology.

2. About half were working in some capacity with athletes, although the work was unstable and the pay relatively low.

3. Two-thirds of the work was in teaching or research at a university.

4. Women made 74% of the money that men did. Men averaged slightly over $41,000, women nearly $31,000.

5. There was a marked absence of formalized practica in the respondents' doctoral training. For example, 18 reported an emphasis on intervention or performance enhancement, but 8 of them did not receive any supervised practical experience.

6. Seventy-six percent saw no advantage to having licensure, and 47% did not perceive a need for AAASP certification.

7. On a more positive note, most expressed satisfaction with their diverse work lives.

The Waite and Pettit findings suggest that jobs in sport psychology do exist (mostly in academia), salary inequities by gender are common, there are serious shortcomings in the applied aspects of doctoral training, and there is a lack of concern for licensure or certification. The last conclusion was probably an artifact of Waite and Pettit's sample, which was composed primarily of academics, and the time at which the study was reported. In all likelihood, most of the concerns expressed by Waite and Pettit are less relevant today,

what with the continuing efforts among professional societies in sport psychology to upgrade all aspects of training. The fact that AAASP certification is dependent on broad training to include supervised experience should go a long way toward remediating shortcomings alluded to by Waite and Pettit.

Clearly, some problematic issues must be addressed. It is essential to the life of the profession that efforts continue to be made to train future sport professionals. Credentialing issues will continue to need addressing in order to promote the profession in the eyes of the scientific and the athletic communities. Everyone must observe the highest ethical standards in teaching, research, and practice. Work must continue to create a favorable image. Positive outcomes in these areas will help expand the job market for sport psychologists.

SUMMARY

1. Five important professional issues in sport psychology are training, credentialing, ethics, professional image, and employment opportunities.

2. In the past, the training of sport psychologists occurred in a somewhat haphazard fashion without clear guidelines from any source. Then interested parties from AAASP and from Division 47 of the American Psychological Association established guidelines to ensure better training standards in the future.

3. Credentialing is a general term for the process of ensuring that members of a profession meet certain set standards. Subsumed under the umbrella of credentialing are certification, registry, and licensure. Certification and registry are nonstatutory processes. Licensure is restrictive and statutory. People working in the field of sport psychology may receive certification as "Certified Consultant—AAASP" if they meet AAASP requirements. They cannot, however, be licensed as sport psychologists in the United States and Canada unless they have the appropriate academic training and meet other legally mandated licensure requirements. Because the term *psychologist* is protected by law, it is illegal to sell sport-related psychological services to the public if one is not licensed first as a psychologist.

4. The ethical standards adopted within sport psychology are essentially those of the American Psychological Association. They emphasize competence, integrity, professional and scientific responsibility, respect for people's rights and dignity, concern for the welfare of others, and social responsibility. Another ethical issue is who is entitled to use the title "psychologist." There is concern that formal ethics training is not a high-priority part of the overall education of sport psychologists.

5. The image of sport psychology among professional and elite athletes appears to be good, although there is skepticism in some quarters about athletes who seek sport psychological services. Among clinical and counseling psychologists, the field of sport psychology seems to be well respected, but there is little movement among university psychology departments to institute courses or training programs.

6. The employment picture is far from rosy. Sport psychologists are likely to be found in academic jobs within universities or as private practitioners with a Ph.D. in clinical, counseling, or industrial/organizational psychology who devote part or all of their practice to athletes and teams.

KEY TERMS

certification (15)
Certified Consultant—AAASP (16)
credentialing (15)
dual relationship (17)
licensure (15)
registry (15)
"who can do what" debate (14)

Ethical Issues

competence (17)
concern for the welfare of others (18)
integrity (17)
professional and scientific responsibility (17)
respect for people's rights and dignity (17)

social responsibility (18)
who can be called a psychologist (17)

SUGGESTED READINGS

Lesyk, J. L. (1998). *Developing sport psychology within your clinical practice.* San Francisco: Jossey-Bass.

Much interest has been expressed in the past several years about how to integrate sport psychology into a private practice in either clinical or counseling psychology. Lesyk shows how to apply cognitive–behavioral and social learning theories to work with serious athletes and recreational participants. He also examines credentialing issues in sport psychology and offers some marketing tips for the clinician wanting to expand his or her practice into sport and exercise.

Meyers, A. W., Coleman, J. K., Whelan, J. P., & Mehlenback, R. S. (2001). Examining careers in sport psychology: Who is working and who is making money? *Professional Psychology: Research and Practice, 32,* 5–11.

This is one of five papers on sport psychology to appear in a special section of *Professional Psychology* early in 2001. The authors received responses from over 400 sport psychologists and concluded, among other things, that part-time supplemental involvement in sport psychology is more practical than attempting to make a living through full-time employment. They also talk about employment within academia, as well as in applied settings, and provide data related to both enterprises. This article will be helpful to students thinking about a career in sport psychology.

Parry, S. J. & McNamee, M. J. (Eds.). (1998). *Ethics and sport.* New York: Spon Press.

Contributors provide coverage of topics such as violence and aggression, cheating and self-deception, ethical conduct of sport coaches, moral development, fair play, and respect for opponents.

Poczwardowski, A., Sherman, C. P., & Henschen, K. P. (1998). A sport psychology service delivery heuristic: Building on theory and practice. *The Sport Psychologist, 12,* 191–207.

The authors focus on factors a sport psychologist should consider when planning, implementing, and evaluating psychological services. Included are professional boundaries, professional philosophy, making contact with clients, assessment, evaluating client concerns, types of service to be provided, program implementation, being aware of one's own strengths and limitations, program evaluation, and leaving the setting once the psychologist–client relationship is concluded. All of these are important considerations to be taken into account in providing sport psychology consultation.

Sachs, M. L., Burke, K. L., & Schrader, D. (Eds.). (2001). *Directory of graduate programs in applied sport psychology* (6th ed.). Morgantown, WV: Fitness Information Technology, Inc.

This book is invaluable as a resource for students planning on going to graduate school in sport psychology. One hundred three universities in the United States, Australia, Canada, and Great Britain are reviewed in terms of degree programs, admission requirements, faculty, and other relevant information. Also included are important information about the field of sport psychology, AAASP certification, ethics, and training videos, as well as suggested readings.

 INFOTRAC COLLEGE EDITION

For additional readings, explore Infotrac College Edition, your online library. Go to: http://www.infotrac-college.com/wadsworth
Hint: Enter these search terms: International Olympic Committee, professional ethics, research ethics, United States Olympic Committee.

Sport History From Antiquity Through the Enlightenment

CHAPTER 3

The Ancient Near East and Asia
The Greeks
The Romans
The Middle Ages
Renaissance and Enlightenment
Summary
Key Terms
Suggested Readings

The Parthenon serves as a reminder of the early Greeks and the Olympic tradition that began there in 776 B.C. The Olympic Games will return to Athens in the summer of 2004.
© 1993 PhotoDisc, Inc.

Sport has a long history. There is very early evidence for the existence of sports that are similar in many respects to sports that we recognize today. However, much of what we know about them is suppositional and has been amassed from a variety of fragmentary sources dating back to antiquity. From cave art, archaeological artifacts, paintings, textiles, seal stones, sculptures, and other sources we are able to get a glimpse of the sports that people long ago enjoyed.

Between the demise of the Roman Empire and the Renaissance, little useful information is available to chronicle the development of sport. During the Middle Ages, an informational blackout of major proportions occurred—and continued for over a thousand years. With the Renaissance came an awakening of interest in all facets of life, including sport. Before the 18th-century Enlightenment, however, much of what is generally accepted as accurate is somewhat speculative.

THE ANCIENT NEAR EAST AND ASIA

The first archaeological evidence of sports and games comes from the Sumerian civilization of 3000 to 1500 B.C., a society that arose between the Tigris and Euphrates Rivers. Artifacts seem to suggest participation in boxing and wrestling. Board games have also been linked to this time period (Palmer & Howell, 1973).

In reviewing a number of studies of Egyptian civilization (3000–1100 B.C.), Palmer and Howell cite evidence for the existence of acrobatics, tumbling, resistance exercises, yoga, tug-of-war, a kicking game, crawling games, and ball games. Simri (1973) also mentions evidence for the existence of ball games as early as 1500 B.C. He cites a relief showing what appears to be a pharaoh holding a bat and ball while two priests await a catch. Simri also mentions knife throwing, wrestling, the swinging of weights, swimming, board games, and a host of other activities suggestive of an interest in sports and games on the part of the early Egyptians. It has been inferred from findings in an assortment of tombs that these activities were viewed as most suitable for the nobility—kings, pharaohs, and aristocrats. Keep in mind, however, that poor people of the time were not buried in tombs and left few artifacts for analysis. They may have been as active in sports and games as the nobility but left little evidence one way or the other.

Evidence from China is also supportive of the existence of sports and games. According to Sasijima (1973), the Zhou dynasty (1100 B.C. to 256 B.C.) is of particular relevance. During the Zhou, properly raised young people were expected to be familiar with "six virtues" (wisdom, benevolence, goodness, righteousness, loyalty, and harmony) and "six arts" (rituals, music, archery, charioteering, writing, and mathematics) (Zeigler, 1973a). However, Chinese enthusiasm for physical activity appears to have been tempered somewhat by the serene, cerebral, and studious nature of the dominant religions—Taoism, Buddhism, and Confucianism. Interestingly, the founder of Buddhism, Prince Siddhartha (later known as Buddha) was "a sportsman of no mean order" (Rajagopalan, 1973, p. 51). The prince was said to have excelled in games and sports.

Rajagopalan cites evidence for hunting, fishing, archery, wrestling, boxing, the javelin throw, running, swimming, jumping, digging, and dancing as early as 1500 B.C. in India. Rajagopalan also mentions that marbles dating back to Neolithic times have been unearthed, although it is possible that they were used for weapons or valued for their aesthetic properties as much as they were used for recreational purposes.

A significant contribution to our understanding of sports in antiquity was the unearthing of the Palace of Minos in 1871. The Minoans (3000–1200 B.C.) lived on the island of Crete and seem to have been involved in acrobatics, archery, boxing, dancing, hunting, sailing, swimming, table games, wrestling, and so-called taureador sports. The **taureador sports** included bull grappling, bull vaulting, and other acrobatic activities centering on a bull. Bull grappling is probably the earliest form of the steer wrestling that we see in modern rodeos. Of the taureador sports, Palmer and Howell (1973, p. 69) state: "The representations of the bull games far outnumber any other games in the Minoan period. The bull is a common subject of Minoan artists, and is shown on seal stones, frescoes, rhytons, plaster reliefs, bronze, rings, pendants, and vases."

Taureador sports   bull wrestling, bull vaulting, and other acrobatic activities centered on bulls, on Crete, in the Minoan period.

Particularly interesting sources of information about sport during the Minoan period are seal stones carved or engraved in clay. In the Ashmolean collection at Oxford University Howell (1969) found 25 seal stones related to sports (many others in the collection were not sport-related).

THE GREEKS

Much of what we know about early Greek civilization is chronicled in the *Iliad* and *Odyssey,* attributed to Homer, a blind Ionian poet. Homer's epics are widely regarded as brilliant works that make significant contributions to our understanding of ancient Greek civilization and ancient sport. The ancient Greeks valued sports and physical activity, and their love for them influenced generations of Greeks, Romans, Macedonians, and others in the ancient world. Also, prominent archaeological discoveries have proved to be treasure troves of information.

Van Dalen, Mitchell, and Bennett (1953) divided Greek history into four periods:

1. Homeric Greece (1200–700 B.C.)
2. early Athenian (776 B.C. to c. 480 B.C.)
3. Spartan (8th century B.C. to the Macedonian conquest in 338 B.C.)
4. later Athenian (480 B.C. to the conquest of the Greek city-states by the Macedonians in 338 B.C.)

We will follow their lead and examine each in turn.

Homeric Greece

Homer is credited with creating the *Iliad* and the *Odyssey* around 850 B.C. They bring together various tales and legends transmitted by word of mouth and constitute masterpieces of world literature. Much of what we know about Greek life at the time of the Trojan War (1194–1184 B.C.) between Greece and Troy is attributable to Homer. The **Iliad** has been called a "classic epic of war" (Stull, 1973, p. 121) and the "basic source of the Greek concept of manhood" (Stull and Lewis, 1968). These authorities further suggest that the *Iliad* is a rich source of sport history. One of its unique features is its description of **funeral games,** so named because they were started by the Greek warrior

Achilles in honor of his slain companion and friend, Patroclus. The games were initiated to give soldiers respite from war and ease their mourning through physical competition. Archery, boxing, chariot racing, discus and javelin throwing, foot racing, sword fighting, and wrestling were immensely popular in the funeral games. The descriptions of athletic contests in the *Iliad* indicate an early tradition of Olympic-style competition in Greece.

As for the **Odyssey,** it recounts the trials and tribulations of Odysseus, king of Ithaca and leader of the Greeks in the Battle of Troy, who returns to his island kingdom ten years after the war. The final pages are rich in information about an amalgamation of boxing and wrestling known as the **pankration.** The *pankration* has been likened to judo (Harris, 1972) and jujitsu (Hackensmith, 1966) and described as more of a "gutter brawl than an athletic event" (Henry, 1976, p. 13). Also mentioned in the *Odyssey* are the discus, the javelin, ball games, footraces, and archery.

The Early Athenian Period

Nowhere is the early Greek reverence for sport more evident than in the Olympic Games. The **Olympic Games** were formal athletic contests held at Olympia at four-year intervals to honor the Greek god Zeus. The games were Panhellenic—that is, open to all Greeks (Hellenes); foreigners were not able to compete. Tradition says that the first competition at Olympia took place in 776 B.C.

Originally, the Olympics consisted solely of footraces. In the first 13 Olympics the only competition

---

Iliad Homer's epic about the Trojan War and an important source of information on ancient Greek sport.

Funeral games archery, boxing, racing, and other sports intended to distract Greek soldiers from the brutality of warfare through physical competition; the Greek warrior Achilles organized the first such games in honor of a slain friend.

Odyssey Homer's epic about the travels and adventures of Odysseus after the Trojan War and, in its final pages, an important source of information on Greek wrestling and other sports.

Pankration an athletic contest requiring skill in both boxing and wrestling.

Olympic Games formal athletic contests held at Olympia at four-year intervals, from 776 B.C. to A.D. 394, to honor the Greek god Zeus; forerunner of the modern Olympics.

TABLE 3.1

Typical Olympic Competitors from 520 B.C. to A.D. 394

Three Combat Events	Four Running Events	Pentathlon
Boxing	200-yard race	Javelin
Wrestling	400-yard race	Discus
Pankration	Distance	Long jump
	Race in armor	200-yard race
		Wrestling

was the **stadion,** a single-course race. In 724 B.C., at the 14th Olympic Games, a double-course race, the **diaulos,** was added. Later, in 720 B.C., a long-course race, the **dolichos,** was added. Over the next 200 years, wrestling, the pentathlon, boxing, chariot racing, horse racing, the *pankration,* and races in armor were added, and those events constituted the ancient Olympic Games until their dissolution in A.D. 394. The typical Olympic events from 520 B.C. to A.D. 394 are listed in Table 3.1.

A number of unique features characterized the earliest Olympic Games. First, the only material reward for winning an event was a crown of olive leaves. However, the athletes, like many athletes today, were very highly regarded for their skills and for the fame they brought to their respective city-states. As a result, back home they received financial and other considerations above and beyond the crown of olive leaves.

Second, after the 15th Olympic Games, in 720 B.C., all athletes competed in the nude. Harris (1972) offers two possible reasons. One is that nude competition became the norm when a highly respected runner lost his loin cloth during a race, sped away from the other runners, and won handily. The other explanation also has the loin cloth giving way, but in this version the runner trips and dies when his head strikes the ground, and the presiding magistrate promptly issues an edict banning loin

cloths from subsequent competitions. A more believable explanation is suggested by Swaddling (1980), who thinks the nudity indicates the desire of the early Greeks to show off their sleek, powerful, muscular physiques.

A third interesting feature of the early Olympics was the stadium itself. Archaeological evidence indicates that the typical Greek stadium was rectangular, perhaps 200 yards long and from 25 to 40 yards wide, with a turning post at each end. The longer races—*diaulos* and *dolichos*—added to the games in 724 and 720 B.C. required the contestants to make a series of abrupt turns at each end of the stadium.

A final noteworthy feature of the early games was the exclusion of women as competitors or spectators. The penalty for violating these prohibitions was death, and there are reports of women being thrown from a nearby mountaintop as punishment for watching the games (Yalouris, 1979). Women could be awarded an Olympic prize in the equestrian events, but as owners of horses rather than riders.

The Spartan Period

According to Yalouris (1979), the Spartans probably never numbered more than 5,000, yet the city-state of Sparta was a dominant military force for several centuries. The desire to produce the "perfect warrior" was a driving force in the success of the Spartans, who lived among 250,000 slaves known as helots. Unlike the Athenians, who saw physical activity and competition as a beautiful and harmonious expression of the self, the Spartans subjugated personal goals and individual expression to the survival of their city-state.

In order for the Spartan citizen to meet the perfect-warrior ideal, training began early. Shortly after birth,

---

Stadion a single-course footrace; the only competition in the first 13 Olympic competitions.
Diaulos a double-course footrace down one side of the stadium, around a turning post, and back; it was added to the Olympic competition in 724 B.C.
Dolichos a long-course race added to the Olympic competition in 720 B.C.

Views of Sport and Exercise from Prominent Men of Ancient Greece

Aristotle: "The education of the body must precede that of the intellect."

Euripides: "Of all the countless evils throughout Hellas [Greece], there is none worse than the race of Athletes."

Galen: "He is the best physician who is the best teacher of gymnastics."

Plato: "Gymnastics as well as music should receive careful attention in the childhood and continue through life."

Plutarch: "The exercise of the body must not be neglected; but children must be sent to schools of gymnastics. This will conduce partly to a more handsome carriage and partly to an improvement in their strength."

Socrates: "No citizen has a right to be an amateur in the matter of physical training; it is a part of his profession as a citizen to keep himself in good condition, ready to serve his state at a moment's notice."

SOURCE: Rice, Hutchinson, & Lee (1969).

---

sickly babies were left to die (or perhaps be rescued by slaves) on Mount Taygetus (Hackensmith, 1966). Spartan boys were educated at home until age 17, at which time they became wards of the city-state for training in the arts of manhood and good citizenship. Military training intensified each year, and engagement in actual combat was not unusual by age 20. The citizen–soldier was expected to engage daily in a regimen of exercise until age 30. At age 50, retirement was a possibility if military conditions were favorable. In addition to military training, an exacting regimen of diet and clothing was imposed. Spartan youth went barefoot, wore the same tunic all year regardless of weather, and were fed meager rations. Stealing to supplement the diet was encouraged, for craftiness and stealth had military value. Bathing was frowned on, though swimming in nearby rivers or streams was condoned. Beatings and floggings were commonplace as a means of building character.

Though less regimented than men, women were expected to take part in physical activity until age 20 and, at all times, to be fit and mindful of their physical appearance. Their exercise program, similar in many ways to that of the men, included dancing, discus throwing, jumping, running, swimming, and wrestling.

The Spartans were extremely successful in Olympic competition. Yalouris (1979) indicates that the first Spartan medal winner was probably Akanthos, who won the *dolichos* in the 15th Olympics. Eighty-one of the winners in the games between 720 and 576 B.C. were Spartans, as were 21 of the 36 winners of the *stadion*. It was the Spartans who introduced nudity among the Olympic athletes and also the practice of anointing themselves with oil, which became commonplace in subsequent games.

The Spartan fascination with fitness, competition, and militarism was not without cost, and perhaps Forbes (1973, p. 138) says it best:

The Spartan system of physical education achieved its limited aim and in that sense was a resounding success. Nearly every Spartan could glory in a splendid physique and in health unequaled elsewhere in Greece. Spartan courage, tenacity, and obedience were proverbial. If the battle of Waterloo was won on the playing fields of Eton, surely Sparta's many battles were won on the playing fields by the river Eurotas. Speaking of New Hampshire, Daniel Webster once said, "The

Milo of Croton

The athletic world tends to view its heroes as larger than life, and the ancient Greeks were no exception. **Milo of Croton,** a legendary wrestler, represents a case in point. Milo lived in Croton, a Greek colony in southern Italy, during the 6th century B.C. He won six consecutive Olympic wrestling championships from 536 to 512 B.C. In addition, victories in 26 competitions at the Isthmian, Nemean, and Pythian Games gave him a total of 32 national titles in his career.

As might be suspected, much folklore surrounded this athlete. Amazing feats of strength and equally amazing gastronomic excesses were attributed to Milo. Legend has it that he carried a bull on his shoulders around the stadium at

Olympia, killed it with his fists, and completely devoured it before the day was over. Milo also was said to have consumed 20 loaves of bread at one meal and quaffed 9 liters of wine in a short time to win a bet.

But there was more to Milo than strength and appetite. He was a student of Pythagoras and wrote a number of scholarly treatises. He also took up arms to defend Croton and was said to have been heroic in battle.

Milo's great strength ultimately was his downfall. According to legend, while walking through a forest, he noticed a partially split tree into which someone had driven wedges. Milo tried to tear the tree apart. His hands got caught, he was unable to free himself, and he was attacked and killed by wolves.

Milo of Croton winner of numerous wrestling championships at the Olympics and other competitions in the 6th century B.C.; also known for his great strength and huge appetite.

SOURCES: Brasch (1970); Harris (1972); Whorton (1981); Yalouris (1979).

Granite State makes men." Sparta made men. But the cost was high. Sparta deliberately neglected the education of the mind. In a country astonishingly rich in philosophers, Sparta had none. Poets were few—none of note after the seventh and sixth centuries. Books that deal in generalizing terms with the cultural contributions of Greece have little to say about Sparta. Such were the results of a one-sided educational system in the world's first totalitarian state.

The Later Athenian Period

The later Athenian period is known as the Golden Age of Greece. The defeat of a seemingly superior Persian army in 480 B.C. ushered in 50 years of peace and unprecedented prosperity among the city-states making up the Greek Empire. The city-state concept was fully developed and effective. Sparta had achieved status as a military power, and Athens had become a mecca for artists, poets, writers, and intellectuals. After the war

with the Persians, good times and a spirit of unity prevailed throughout Greece. In Athens, an expansion of the concept of democratic government gave citizens a greater voice in matters related to their own welfare. Tremendous emphasis was placed on the enhancement of individual freedoms.

Physical education became a means of self-enhancement and self-expression, and the utilitarian aspects of physical and military preparedness were neglected. The needs and wishes of individuals took precedence over the welfare of the city-state. Professionalism began to change the nature of athletic events, thus encouraging spectatorship rather than participation. The masses looked to athletic events for amusement.

Plato (427?–347? B.C.), a philosopher and outspoken social critic, was particularly dismayed by the decline of Greek values. He believed the moral values learned through participation in sports and exercise far outweighed the physical values, and he strongly opposed the professionalization of sports. Despite such subtle changes in values, life during the later Athenian period was good,

Panhellenic Games

The Olympic Games, first held in 776 B.C., became the premier athletic competition in Greek life, but Greeks also participated in other important athletic competitions. In 582 B.C. the Pythian Games emerged and eventually were held in Delphi during the year before the Olympics. In 581 B.C., the Isthmian Games began in Corinth. They were then held every two years. Eight years later, the Nemean Games began in Nemea. They also were held every two years. The Olympic, Pythian, Isthmian, and Nemean competitions were **Panhellenic games**—games open to all Greeks.

Additional evidence of the importance of athletics in ancient Greece is provided by the fact that at least 19 lesser competitions were held in places such as Alexandria, Athens, Pergamon, Sardis, Thespiai, and the island of Kos. The Leukophrynia, held in the city of Magnesia on the Menderer River (in present-day western Turkey), was probably of the stature of the Pythian Games.

SOURCE: Yalouris (1979).

Panhellenic games games open to all Greeks and forming an athletics circuit that provided venues in which athletes could compete on a regular basis; among the best known are the Olympic, Pythian, Isthmian, and Nemean Games.

and most Athenians were unaware of the gradual unraveling of the fabric of the city-state until it was too late.

Prosperity did not last long. Athens waged wars of aggression against other city-states and eventually fell under Sparta's domination. Then, a costly conflict between the various city-states under Spartan rule and Sparta itself led to a rebellion in which Sparta fell to a coalition army of city-states led by Thebes. Sparta was finally subdued in 371 B.C., ending almost a century of internal conflict. The costly warfare rekindled the spirits of the aggressive Persians. To deal with this threat, Philip II (382–336 B.C.), king of Macedonia in northern Greece, brought Sparta and Athens under Macedonian rule. The Greek Empire, for all intents and purposes, came to an end in 338 B.C. The legacy it provided, however, would influence politics, economics, and sport and physical activity throughout history.

While preparing to deal with the Persians, Philip was assassinated and his 23-year-old son, Alexander III (356–323 B.C.), known as Alexander the Great, took charge of the Macedonians. Alexander was able to marshal forces that not only dealt effectively with the Persians but also conquered Asia Minor, Egypt, and India. Alexander was consolidating his empire when he was stricken with a disease that took his life at age 33. Significantly, during his 11-year odyssey, sports competition and the Greek tradition were spread far and wide by his troops. It was said that Alexander himself was a good athlete, although he seldom competed because of his belief that kings should compete only against other royalty. Because of Alexander the Great's conquests, Greek influence spread to the east. Sports arenas were built, and athletic festivals became popular.

THE ROMANS

By 500 B.C., two civilizations were thriving in Italy, the Etruscan and the Greek. The Greeks occupied the southern part of Italy. The Etruscans occupied the region generally north of the Tiber River. Not much is known of the origins of the Etruscans; none of their literature has survived. What little is known comes from Greek and Roman writers and from the elaborate tombs in which the Etruscans buried their dead.

Wall paintings and sculptured reliefs indicate that the Etruscans held the Greeks in high esteem and developed a love of sport. Harris (1972) indicates that the Etruscans did not slavishly follow the Greek sporting traditions and instead were fascinated by gladiatorial fights and by what

Harris calls "wild beast shows." The Etruscans ceased to be a major power by the end of the fourth century B.C., but their influence on the Romans was considerable.

In 500 B.C., few could have envisioned that the Romans would dominate the Mediterranean world. In a long series of acts of aggression against their neighbors (including the Etruscans), the Romans expanded and consolidated their base of power. By 275 B.C., they had dominated their neighbors and set up a city-state rule that would be the envy of the less unified Greeks. Corsica, Italy, Sardinia, and Spain all came under Roman rule in the Punic Wars. The Greeks fell to the Romans in 146 B.C.

By the time the Greeks toppled, much of their creative genius had dissipated. The energetic, industrious Romans, at the peak of their power and prosperity, revived Greek vitality. Van Dalen et al. (1953, p. 76) draw a nice comparison of the Roman and Greek cultures:

> The Latin possessed a serious, industrious personality and a natural executive ability. On the other hand, he lacked the sparkling, aesthetic genius and the capacity for philosophical contemplation of the Greek. The empire builders were not proficient in pure art forms, did not fashion new lights of philosophical thought, or evolve new concepts of scientific truths. Nevertheless, the Western world is deeply indebted to the Romans for their practical contributions to mankind. Although the Greeks were the more profound and versatile thinkers, the Romans were the more energetic and efficient "doers."

The early Romans used physical training to produce effective soldiers. They viewed the Greeks' preoccupation with aesthetics, grace, beauty, and harmony as signs of softness and frivolousness and not conducive to developing toughness and strength of character. Unlike young Spartans educated in military barracks or young Athenians educated in the gymnasium, Roman children remained under the tutelage of their parents. Around age 17, boys were expected to enlist for military service for a period of 30 years. At all times, physical fitness was expected, but early training was largely the parents' responsibility.

Popular activities of the period included ball games, chariot racing, dancing, fencing, horse races, javelin throwing, jumping, and table games. Of special interest were the ball games. Roman youth appear to have engaged in what they called **harpastum,** an early version of handball (Van Dalen et al., 1953; Young, 1944). Evidence indicates that the players hit the ball with an open hand against a wall, hoping that the opponent would not be able to return the shot.

As the Roman Empire flourished and expanded, people had more money and free time than ever before, and the demand for leisure activities grew. Self-serving individualism, unrest among the masses, governmental corruption, outright despotism, and a decay in morality and religious values became the norm, thus creating the atmosphere of decadence that was to eventually destroy the proud Roman civilization.

Sports and physical fitness took on a new look. Professionalization of both the military and athletics led to a fragmentation of the guiding philosophy concerning the role of fitness within the culture. Fitness made sense for soldiers and athletes, but the average Roman citizen saw little need for it; like the earlier Greeks, the Romans became spectators rather than participants.

The decay of cultural values and decreasing emphasis on participation led to spectator events that appealed to many Romans. Running, jumping, and throwing generally bored them, but they found boxing, wrestling, and the *pankration* exciting. Gambling was a big part of the scene, also. To make boxing especially thrilling, pieces of lead or iron were added to the gloves, and sometimes two or three potentially lethal spikes were attached.

Another dramatic event was chariot racing. Though originally conceived in a high spirit, this form of racing degenerated in Rome. Cheating, pushing, cutting in front of opponents, and hitting opponents were all acceptable. There were many injuries and deaths.

Chariot drivers were heroes in Rome. Rice et al. (1969) noted that a slave who somehow managed to become a highly successful driver was given his freedom. Successful drivers who were free men received monetary rewards. **Diocles,** a Spaniard, is an example of what a successful driver might expect. Diocles won

---

Harpastum early version of handball, played by Roman youth.
Diocles Roman chariot driver who won a lot of races and a lot of money during a career lasting 24 years.

The gladiatorial events played a large role in the Roman Empire. The events took many forms, with men against men and men against animals featured predominantly.
© Bettman/CORBIS

the equivalent of almost $2 million during a 24-year career in which he won 1,462 of 4,257 chariot races.

A step down in its appeal to people's primitive instincts and a step down in terms of sportsmanship was **gladiatorial combat,** popular among the Etruscans and revived by the Romans in the middle of the second century B.C. Gladiators were professionally trained fighters who were paired off in an arena to engage in mortal combat for public entertainment. At first, the gladiatorial competition was conducted for the entertainment of wealthy Romans, and most of the participants were prisoners of war who preferred risking death to slavery. However, the demand for gladiatorial events became so great that schools for gladiators were instituted. Eventually, Roman spectators grew tired of watching two combatants fight to the death, so new forms of brutality were added. Scores of men were pitted against each other. Arenas were flooded, and mock naval battles were staged. The result was many deaths.

In arena events called ***venationes,*** wild animals were killed by their natural predators, or men and animals were pitted against each other in a fight for survival. Buchanan (1975) puts actual numbers to the animals killed in the Roman amphitheaters. The emperor Augustus is said to have boasted of killing 3,500 animals in his shows. Not to be outdone, Emperor Titus had 5,000 animals killed in combat in one day. To mark the 1000th year of the Roman Empire, in A.D. 249 the emperor Philip had 32 elephants, 10 elks, 10 tigers, 60 tame lions, 30 tame leopards, 10 hyenas, 6 hippos, 1 rhinoceros, 10 zebras, 10 giraffes, 20 wild asses, and 40 wild horses put to death in a one-day hunt.

Gladiatorial combat event in which professionally trained fighters were paired off in an arena to engage in mortal combat for the entertainment of the Roman public.
Venationes arena entertainment in which wild animals fought and killed each other or men and animals fought each other for survival.

Nero as Athlete

The stereotypical view of the character of the Roman emperor **Nero** (A.D. 37–68) is one of profligacy and evil. His propensity for cruelty, particularly to Christians, is legendary. Mouratidis (1985) contends, however, that historical accounts of Nero's cruelty were usually written by his enemies, hardly an impartial group. His negative image may also result from his embrace of things Greek and his admiration for athletic glory, which alienated both Christian and non-Christian Romans. According to Mouratidis, this combination of offenses against the sensibilities of Christians and the Roman power structure has given rise to less-than-objective accounts of Nero's behavior.

Nero became emperor at age 17 and committed suicide at age 30. During his brief reign, he tried to bring Roman sport (and Roman life in general) in line with earlier Greek ideas and practice. He instituted schools for athletes and masterminded the construction of a magnificent gymnasium for athletic expression. Nero attempted to lessen the brutality of gladiatorial combat by ruling that it should not cause the death of any participant. A competitor himself, Nero was fascinated with chariot racing and wrestling. He made periodic public appearances to compete in these events, much to the chagrin of the ruling class and the glee of the proletariat. His catering to the masses and his efforts to Hellenize Rome offended the upper classes and played a part in his downfall.

SOURCE: Mouratidis (1985).

Nero Roman emperor whose interest in Greek athletics prompted him to found schools for athletes, open a gymnasium, and try to lessen the brutality of gladiatorial combat.

The Roman Empire began in 753 B.C. with the founding of Rome by the wolf-suckled twins Romulus and Remus, and ended in 476 A.D.

According to Rice et al. (1969), the decline of the empire is attributable to interrelated factors such as instability in the institution of marriage, falling birth rates, economic chaos, civil war, gladiatorial combat deaths, and high suicide and homicide rates. The rise of Christianity also hastened the Roman demise. However, it was Germanic people moving in from northern Europe who provided the final and decisive blow to Roman civilization.

THE MIDDLE AGES

With the fall of the Roman Empire, a period of historical darkness began, and not until Europeans discovered the New World a thousand years later did the darkness lift.

The Byzantine Empire

One beacon of light in the period between the fall of Rome and the Renaissance was the Byzantine Empire to the east. Much of the Greek culture, language, and love of physical activity and sport had been preserved in Constantinople. Concurrently, the Byzantines followed the Romans' lead in law and governance. Christianity was their dominant religion. The Byzantine Empire endured for a thousand years: Constantinople fell to invading forces in 1453.

Among the favorite activities of the Byzantines was chariot racing. Schrodt (1981, p. 44) provides an index of this passion: "Chariot races were the most important events in the life of the ordinary Byzantine citizen, and race days were occasions for excessive gambling, roistering, eating, and shouting—providing a particular kind of excitement and entertainment not available to him in any other facet of his life." The arena in which the chariot races were held was also used for public executions.

It was during the Byzantine period that the demise of the Olympic Games took place. It is generally agreed that the emperor Theodosius I (346?–395) decreed that the games be ended in 394. Theodosius, a Christian, felt that the games glorified the paganism of body worship associated with the ancient Greeks and thus should be abolished. Of this decision, Brasch (1970, p. 414) wrote: "While one religion had given birth to the Olympic Games, in the name of another they were destroyed." The Olympic Games lay dormant for over fifteen hundred years; then in 1896 they were reinstituted by Baron de Coubertin of France.

Christianity

While Germanic peoples were dominating the West and the Byzantines the East, the influence of Christians was also growing. Christians' willingness to suffer and die for their religion, their belief in life after death, and their valuing of the spiritual over the physical had profound repercussions on sport and physical activity for many years.

Because their beliefs ran counter to the licentiousness of the Romans, early Christians suffered indignities and cruelty at the hands of the Romans. This persecution, however, reinforced rather than dissipated their piety. During the early Middle Ages (from roughly the 6th to 10th centuries), some Christians became increasingly disenchanted with worldly affairs and withdrew from the distractions of everyday life. Known as ascetics, they chose to live as hermits in caves, in the desert, or amid other primitive surroundings where they could fast, pray, and meditate undisturbed. To test their faith, they slept on beds of thorns or nails or beat themselves with sticks and branches. Physical exercise had no place in their lives.

Christian monks living in monasteries organized in Europe beginning in the early 6th century also sought to separate themselves from worldly distractions and focus on their faith through a strict discipline centered on manual labor to meet their needs, reading, study, and prayer. Physical fitness per se was of no interest to them. Historians owe a debt of gratitude to these monks because much of what we know about significant periods of early history is a result of their record keeping and preservation.

The Age of Chivalry

The Age of Chivalry in the late Middle Ages (approximately the 11th to 13th centuries) ushered in a revival of interest in physical activity. Noble landlords who emphasized fitness for military and competitive purposes presided over the feudal estates of the period. The core of this training was physical education. Intellectual growth was largely neglected; as a result, many knights were poorly educated or illiterate. Early education took place at home, but at age 7 a son of the nobility was taken from his home to serve as a page for a baron or king. At 14, he became a squire and served an apprenticeship to a knight, caring for the knight's horse and acting as a shield bearer in combat. At age 21, he became a full-fledged knight. In preparation for knighthood, some attention was paid to the arts and social graces, but most of the time after age 7 was devoted to horsemanship, swordsmanship, and hunting. A good summary of what the training for knighthood was supposed to accomplish is given in this prose passage from the 15th century (Neumann, 1936):

> The arts all seven which certainly at all times a perfect man will love are: He must ride well, be fast in and out of the saddle, trot well and canter and turn around and know how to pick something up from the ground.
>
> The other, that he knows how to swim and dive into the water, knows how to turn and twist on his back and his belly.
>
> The third, that he shoots well with crossbows, arm, and handbows; these he may well use against princes and dukes.
>
> The fourth, that he can climb fast on ladders when necessary, and that he be of use in war, in poles and ropes it is also good.
>
> The fifth art I shall speak of is that he is good in the tournament, that he fights and tilts well and is honest and good in the joust.
>
> The sixth art is wrestling also both fencing and fighting, beat others in the long jump from the left as well as the right.
>
> The seventh art: he serves well at the table, knows how to dance, has courtly manners, does not shy away from board games or other things that are proper for him.

Obviously, a knight was expected to be proficient in horsemanship, swimming and diving, archery, climbing, fencing, wrestling, jumping, dancing, and table games.

One outgrowth of this interest in readiness for combat and fitness for competition was the **joust,**

Joust combat between two mounted knights wielding lances; the goal was to unseat a competitor from his horse.

combat between two mounted knights wielding lances. The purpose of the joust was to dislodge a competitor from his horse. In its original form, both the horse and the rider were protected by armor. Eventually, however, this type of joust ceased being exciting. Blunt lances were replaced with sharp, lethal lances, and the use of protective armor was discontinued. Touring professionals, called "jousting bums" by Moolenijzer (1968), began to dominate the event, thus contributing to its demise in the sixteenth century.

RENAISSANCE AND ENLIGHTENMENT

A reawakening of interest in all facets of life was under way by the fourteenth century, and over the next 500 years incredible progress was made in philosophy, science, the arts, and education. A major reason for the rebirth of intellectual curiosity—the Renaissance—was the establishment of universities in Bologna, Paris, Salerno, and elsewhere. Loosely structured, these schools placed a lot of emphasis on grammar, logic, mathematics, and scholarly debate. The course of study did not include formal physical education or training. As a result, much youthful energy was dissipated in pranks, fights, and other shenanigans.

The intellectual reawakening fostered free trade and mercantilism, undermined the influence of the feudal aristocracy, and promoted an increasingly secular world view. Gunpowder was developed in Europe. Gutenberg devised a printing press able to print from movable type. Columbus sailed from Spain to the Western Hemisphere, and sailors from Spain and Portugal made discoveries all over the globe.

Intellectual breakthroughs of various kinds were made throughout Europe by individuals such as Copernicus (1473–1543) in Poland, Martin Luther (1483–1540) in Germany, Paracelsus (1493–1541) in Switzerland, and Rabelais (1490–1553) in France. Leonardo da Vinci (1452–1519) studied anatomy and made drawings showing the intricacies of human anatomy. Artists portrayed worldly subjects with increasing realism. Though not proponents of physical activity in the old Greek or Roman tradition, these individuals saw a place for fitness in the greater scheme of things.

Important scientific and intellectual contributions also were made by Galileo (1564–1642), Isaac Newton (1642–1727), Francis Bacon (1561–1626), and John Locke (1632–1704), among many others.

Recognition of the dignity and rights of each person and a rational and scientific approach to religious, economic, political, and social issues were the hallmarks of the eighteenth-century Age of Enlightenment. England was a constitutional monarchy, unique at the time. The French and colonists in British North America asserted that education was neither the responsibility of the church nor the right of only the wealthy or the nobility. Flames of educational reform were fanned by **Jean-Jacques Rousseau** (1712–1778), a French philosopher and author, by Johann Heinrich Pestalozzi (1746–1827), a Swiss educational reformer who, in trying to implement Rousseau's ideas, laid the foundation of modern elementary education, and by Pestalozzi's student F. W. A. Froebel (1782–1852), a German educator who designed the kindergarten system.

Rousseau's ideas about education, expressed in *Émile* (1762), represented a break with tradition. Rousseau opposed the formal curriculum, with its emphasis on Latin, Greek, and mathematics, and learning methods—principally memorization—used in schools of the time. He insisted that play, games, manual arts, and nature studies would be of equal or greater value to children. Unlike Locke and Rabelais, who were proponents of physical education in the schools for military or health reasons, Rousseau viewed physical training as contributing to the total development of the child. Rousseau also was an advocate of sports as a means of promoting national unity (Gerber, 1968).

Even more heretical than his opposition to formal learning was Rousseau's insistence that human nature is basically good, not evil or sinful as some religious thinkers were preaching. Rousseau's impact on education and philosophy extended far beyond anything he could have imagined.

Thanks in part to Rousseau, there was a veritable explosion of interest in physical activity all over Europe in the eighteenth and nineteenth centuries. The Germans developed programs in gymnastics that were

Jean-Jacques Rousseau French philosopher and author who advocated the inclusion of play, games, and physical education in educational programs for children.

broadly based physical fitness programs. In the latter part of the eighteenth century, the playground movement emerged in Germany. The Scandinavians and the British also promoted play, games, and sports.

SUMMARY

1. Artifacts dating from the period 3000–1500 B.C. seem to indicate that the Sumerians enjoyed boxing, wrestling, and board games. An even broader range of sports and games is suggested by analysis of Egyptian artifacts from that period. People in ancient China and India, too, apparently were avid sports participants.

2. The unearthing of the Palace of Minos in 1871 on Crete showed that the Minoans (3000–1200 B.C.) engaged in many activities. The so-called taureador sports seemed especially popular.

3. Much of what we know about early Greek activities comes from Homer's *Iliad* and *Odyssey*. These works reveal the Greek fascination with sport.

4. The first Olympic Games took place in 776 B.C. Not until the fourteenth Olympics, in 724 B.C., was there more than one event. By 520 B.C., the games had been expanded to include wrestling, boxing, the *pankration,* four running events, and the pentathlon. That format lasted until the demise of the early games in A.D. 394.

5. The early Olympic Games had several unique features: Winners received a crown of olive leaves. Athletes competed in the nude after 720 B.C. Women were not allowed to compete in or to view the games, and the penalty for violating either of these prohibitions was death.

6. The Spartans, unlike their contemporaries in Athens who saw physical education as a way of glorifying the body and the spirit, viewed physical activity solely as a means of creating the "perfect warrior." However, many Spartans were outstanding Olympic competitors.

7. The defeat of the Persians in 480 B.C. ushered in the Golden Age of Greece, a period of harmony among the city-states of the Greek Empire. However, over time, internecine conflict broke out,

and energy and resources were strained. The Greeks eventually were subdued by the Macedonians, and the Greek Empire ceased to exist in 338 B.C. The legacy left by those Greeks was to remain influential.

8. The Romans had ascended to power all over the Mediterranean area by 146 B.C. Much like the Spartans, they valued physical fitness because of its positive effect on military preparedness. The Romans played many sports and games. One of them, *harpastum,* appears to be the Roman version of handball. Eventually, Romans became lax in their ways and came to see fitness as a concern primarily of the military and professional athletes. Deterioration in values, a crumbling economy, and other factors eventually led to the fall of the Roman Empire.

9. Gladiatorial combat and *venationes* (fights between animals or between animals and men) became popular in the late Roman Empire. Germanic peoples from the north captured Rome in A.D. 476.

10. Europe's Middle Ages, a period of about a thousand years, were characterized by the continuing development of Christianity, warfare, devastating disease, and little intellectual development. One exception was the Byzantine culture in the East. The Byzantines carried on many of the early Greek aesthetic and athletic traditions. Chariot racing, gladiatorial combat, and *venationes* were popular. The Olympic Games died at the decree of the Byzantine ruler Theodosius I in A.D. 394, in part because of their supposed paganism.

11. The influence of Christianity led to a rejection of Greek and Roman worship of sport and physical fitness. Christians judged the needs of the body to be secondary to the needs of the soul. The ultimate expression of this point of view is evident in the self-inflicted pain and privation endured by the ascetics, and in the quiet, worshipful, reflective lives of monks sequestered in monasteries.

12. Physical competition was important in the Age of Chivalry. Knights-in-training had to acquire skills in swordsmanship and horsemanship and had to be physically prepared for competition and combat.

13. During the Renaissance, interest in worldly matters, including human anatomy and human capability,

revived; and some attention was paid to the connection between fitness and a healthy, well-rounded life.

14. During the Age of Enlightenment, new ideas emerged about education. Rousseau's criticism of the traditional curriculum and traditional approach to learning influenced education reformers such as Pestalozzi and Froebel. All of them believed in the importance of physical activity for children. Their influence is inestimable.

KEY TERMS

diaulos (28)
Diocles (32)
dolichos (28)
funeral games (27)
gladiatorial combat (33)
harpastum (32)
Iliad (27)
joust (35)
Milo of Croton (30)
Nero (34)
Odyssey (27)
Olympic Games (27)
Panhellenic games (31)
pankration (27)
Jean-Jacques Rousseau (36)
stadion (28)
taureador sports (26)
venationes (33)

SUGGESTED READINGS

Brasch, R. (1970). *How did sports begin?* New York: David McKay.
Brasch details the development of 43 sports and the Olympic Games.

Yalouris, N. (1979). *The eternal Olympics: The art and history of sport.* New Rochelle, NY: Caratzas Brothers, Publishers.
The text of this book is informative, and the pictures—primarily from the early Greek period and secondarily from the Roman era—are captivating. The author provides a list of all known Olympic winners from 776 B.C. to A.D. 369.

 ## INFOTRAC COLLEGE EDITION

For additional readings, explore Infotrac College Edition, your online library. Go to http://www.infotrac-college.com/wadsworth
Hint: Enter these search terms: ancient Rome, ascetics, Byzantium, Greek athletics, Greek civilization, Jean-Jacques Rousseau, Sparta.

CHAPTER 4

Colonial America

From the Revolutionary War Through the Civil War

Technological Revolution, 1850–1900

Eight Milestones in Recent U.S. Sport History

A Brief History of Physical Education

A Brief History of Psychology

A Brief History of Sport Psychology

Summary

Key Terms

Suggested Readings

These well-dressed tennis players in Victorian garb serve as reminders that female participation in sport was viewed with skepticism in some quarters in the early part of the 1900s.

© Gianni Dagli Orti/CORBIS

Boating was the first intercollegiate sport to gain widespread popularity. By the time members of Harvard's crew posed for this photo in 1875, Harvard and Yale had been competing in regattas for almost twenty-five years.
© CORBIS

In this chapter we take a quick look at the history of sport in the United States from colonial times to the present. Along the way, we take side trips into the histories of physical education, psychology, and sport psychology and see how these disciplines interacted with sport to create the field of sport and exercise psychology.

In the United States, there is an abundant history of sport beginning with the Revolutionary War and continuing through the 1800s with the settlement of the country by immigrants from Europe with a history of their own regarding sport and fitness. Technological developments of the last half of the nineteenth century greatly altered American life and the sports people played. In the 1900s, the advent of television, the integration of sports, and the women's movement all played major roles in shaping sport as we know it today.

COLONIAL AMERICA

The settling of Jamestown, Virginia, in 1607 and Plymouth, Massachusetts, in 1620 opened the colonial period of United States history. Early settlers faced innumerable life-threatening trials and tribulations. Houses had to be constructed, soil had to be tilled, and territory had to be defended. Strong prohibitions were placed on play and sport, because of persistent threats to survival and religious admonitions to avoid idleness and impiety.

Among the early settlers were the Puritans, who were opposed to sport because of its interference with what they viewed as proper piety and worship. In some ways, the Puritans were throwbacks to the ascetics of the Middle Ages in their rejection of the "worldliness" of sport. Prior to their departure for the New World, King James I had issued a proclamation known as the *Book of Sports,* which stated that some parts of divine services should be devoted to games, play, feasts, and physical activity. Puritans in both England and the American colonies tenaciously fought the *Book of Sports,* continually trying to prevent levity and impiety on the Sabbath.

Though influential, the Puritans were not the only people observing the Sabbath. Evangelical groups that were neither Anglican nor Puritan sprang up all over the colonies. One of the most notable was the Society of Friends (Quakers), which had been founded in England by George Fox (1624–1691). Like the Puritans, the Quakers and other evangelicals were outspoken in their opposition to sports and games.

Nevertheless, sports and games flourished. Influential historical figures of the period, such as George Washington (1732–1799) and Benjamin Franklin (1706–1790), were forceful and eloquent in their belief in physical activity as a character builder and health promoter. Much to the chagrin of the evangelicals, taverns evolved into a focal point for social life in the colonies and sponsored card games, billiards, **skittles** (bowling), and pistol and rifle competitions. Cockfighting and horse racing were also commonplace sporting events. Other popular activities were cricket, **fives** (handball), football (probably more similar to soccer than to American football), golf (called "goff"), **shinny** (hockey), **rounders** (a ball game similar to baseball), swimming, and tennis (Rice et al., 1969; Struna, 1981).

In Maryland, colonials enjoyed fox hunts, yachting, and "ball and long bullets"—a game involving the throwing of cannonballs for distance (Kennard, 1970, p. 393). Gambling on these sporting events, especially on horse races, was common. Rader (1983) tells of a southern gentleman, William Byrd III, who was an inveterate gambler, depleted his inherited fortune, and committed suicide at an early age.

FROM THE REVOLUTIONARY WAR THROUGH THE CIVIL WAR

The Revolutionary War began in 1775 and lasted until 1783. Ledbetter (1979) studied sports and games in this period. Most of what we know about the games, play, and sports of Revolutionary War soldiers is gleaned from the diaries and records of the officers; few enlisted men kept records of their activities. No specific athletic and recreation program was provided, so the soldiers had to improvise. Most of the war efforts were curtailed during the coldest weather, so in winter considerable spare time was available for recreational activities. Seldom did winning or losing in games and sports seem important to the participants, nor was competition between units utilized as a morale builder. Popular games of the Revolutionary War included those mentioned earlier plus boxing, snowball fighting, skating, and wrestling.

Between the Revolutionary War and the Civil War, sports clubs proliferated. Harvard and other universities instituted wrestling and football. Boxing clubs emerged, and various forms of racing gained in popularity. The fervor associated with horse racing inspired Stephen Collins Foster (1826–1864) to write **"Camptown Races,"** generally considered to be the first popular song with a sporting theme (Leonard, 1984).

In 1843, Yale University initiated a collegiate rowing club; a year later its friendly rival Harvard did so too. Interest in rowing produced America's first intercollegiate sport, boating, in 1852 (Lewis, 1967; Spears & Swanson, 1983). The first **rowing regatta** (race between boats powered by oars) was held on Lake Winnipesaukee in New Hampshire. Harvard won. Rowing regattas continued to grow in popularity, and other

---

Skittles ninepin bowling.

Fives a form of handball in which only the receiving side can score points.

Shinny ice, street, or field hockey; "shinny" is the name of the stick used in this game.

Rounders a game played with a ball and bat; baseball developed from it.

"Camptown Races" probably the first popular song with a sporting theme.

Rowing regatta a race between boats powered by oars.

universities created teams. The unlikely sport of rowing set a precedent for intercollegiate competition that has now reached amazing proportions.

At the outbreak of the Civil War, sport was enjoying unprecedented popularity. Many evangelical proscriptions against sport had been diluted or ignored.

Fielding (1977) studied the Civil War at length and divided the experiences of the typical Union soldier into four phases. In the first phase, initial proscription into the army—boot camp—life was arduous but monotonous when training was light. Competitive activities—shooting, horseback riding, and drilling—often had a military theme or purpose. Later, boxing, wrestling, footraces, fencing, and football were introduced. All of these sporting activities served the dual purposes of relieving boredom and boosting group morale and solidarity.

The second phase described by Fielding (1977) consisted of holidays on or near the battlefield. Recreation was quite similar to that of the boot camp period. One sport that was popular at this time was baseball. According to Crockett (1961, p. 341), it was a most welcome addition: "Baseball appears to have been the most popular of all the action sports engaged in by 'Billy Yank' and 'Johnny Reb.'" Betts (1971) indicates that prisoners of war also passed time by playing baseball. He cites an instance in which a $100 challenge game was played in Virginia between Army of the Potomac factions from New York and New Jersey. He also mentions an incident in Texas in which Confederate soldiers scattered a group of Union soldiers playing baseball and wounded and captured the center fielder.

The third dimension of soldiering was the winter camp experience. In cold weather, military activity diminished considerably, and soldiers had more free time. Cockfights were popular, but there is some evidence that the most exciting activity during cold-weather lulls was snowball fighting (Crockett, 1961; Fielding, 1977). Snowball battles became so sophisticated that weapons were stockpiled and complex plans of attack were developed.

The fourth phase of military life was marked by lulls in the fighting. During these periods, cockfights, football, and baseball were popular activities. Crockett (1961) says the opposing forces engaged in 34 different sports and recreational activities during the course of the war.

The typical Civil War battle took place at close quarters because of limitations in the range and accuracy of cannon, pistols, and rifles. Much of the fighting also involved combat with swords and knives. As might be expected, taunts, challenges, and insults accompanied this close combat and tempers flared. Fielding (1977) cites several instances in which combat was actually stopped so that combatants angered by verbal exchanges could settle their differences in a boxing match held on neutral ground. After the issue was resolved in the ring, the battle resumed.

TECHNOLOGICAL REVOLUTION, 1850–1900

Just prior to and immediately after the Civil War, great changes took place in the American way of life. From 1840 to 1880, the population tripled, increasing from 17 million to 50 million (Spears & Swanson, 1983). Immigrants arrived in great numbers, first from northwestern Europe, later from southern and eastern Europe. At the same time, African Americans in both North and South were in the early stages of assimilation into the dominant culture. Along with the effects of immigration and of the end of slavery, the effects of a technological revolution were being felt throughout the United States. Postwar surges in wealth, technology, urbanization, and industrialization were altering society in unimaginable ways. As might be expected, sport, too, was affected by these forces and events.

Betts (1953) provides an informative discussion relating technological change and sport between 1850 and 1900. Betts identifies several factors that changed the direction in sport in America from 1850 to 1900: the decline of Puritan orthodoxy, the influence of the new immigrants, the frontier spirit with its emphasis on manliness and strength, the English athletic movement, and contributions of energetic sports-minded citizens. Figure 4.1 summarizes the effect on sport of a number of technological advances of the period.

EIGHT MILESTONES IN RECENT U.S. SPORT HISTORY

Many important milestones mark the history of sport in the United States. In this section we concentrate on

FIGURE 4.1

Impact of Technology on Sport Between 1850 and 1900

1. *Railroads.* Railroads sponsored travel to athletic events in order to spur train ticket sales in the New England area. The Harvard–Yale regattas were created by a railroad company that promised to transport the participants and cover their expenses (Lewis, 1967). Railroad companies also helped to popularize baseball, boxing, and horse racing.

2. *Telegraphy.* Long-distance telegraphy greatly increased the transmission of sport information between cities. By 1870, many metropolitan newspapers were reporting sports news. The first sport section in any newspaper was created by William Randolph Hearst in New York City just before 1900.

3. *Innovations in printing.* Advances in printing technology made possible better newspapers, journals, and books with (and without) sports themes.

4. *Sewing machine.* The sewing machine made possible the creation of a greater variety and a higher quality of athletic goods.

5. *Incandescent lighting.* Incandescent lighting made possible the lengthening of the sport day by improving the lighting at nighttime events. Electrification especially helped to boost the popularity of basketball and volleyball.

6. *Vulcanization of rubber.* Vulcanized rubber had far-reaching consequences for the development of the balls used in so many sports. Pneumatic tires quickly revolutionized cycling and harness racing.

7. *Miscellany.* Stopwatches, percussion caps, ball bearings, cameras, movies, telephones, typewriters, and phonographs are just a few of the many products of the industrial revolution that enlarged the role of sport.

Source: Betts (1953).

eight. Others are listed in the time line in Highlight 4.3 at the end of this chapter.

One milestone (actually a series of events) was the formation of the **Amateur Athletic Union (AAU)** and the institution of high-profile sports. The New York Athletic Club, founded in 1868, was the first organization to attempt to bring amateur sports under one governing umbrella. This led to the creation of the AAU in 1888, and that organization remains a powerful force in the world of athletics.

Another noteworthy event was the reinstitution of the Olympic Games in 1896 in Athens, Greece. The so-called modern Olympics are the outcome of the leadership of **Pierre de Fredy, Baron de Coubertin** (1863–1937). As Spears and Swanson (1983) point out, Baron de Coubertin was not the first person to try to revive the games, but he was the one who was successful. Except during the Second World War, 1940 and 1944, the games have taken place at four-year intervals and, despite many political problems, grown in popularity.

By the early 1900s, the sport of football had become a major force in college athletics—but not without experiencing growing pains. Things were so out of hand by 1905 that President Theodore Roosevelt (1858–1919) stepped in. Critics considered collegiate football so dangerous and fraught with cheating and scandal that it needed to be altered or abolished. Roosevelt, however, believed there were lessons to be learned from football. He called it "the most valuable of all team sports because it provided each individual with an opportunity to test his courage" (Lewis, 1969, p. 719).

Roosevelt met with the presidents of Harvard, New York University, Princeton, and Yale and members of the Intercollegiate Athletic Association to see whether an agreement could be reached about the future of the game. Lewis (1969, p. 724) calls this meeting "probably the single most important event in the history of intercollegiate sport." Lewis goes on to point out that Roosevelt's role in the deliberations was significant but not crucial and that the president did not, as some have claimed, save the game, because it was really never threatened. The participants did not want to do away

Amateur Athletic Union (AAU) the sports governing body founded in 1887 that is charged with responsibility for the governance and promotion of amateur sports in the United States.
Pierre de Fredy, Baron de Coubertin French educator and sportsman whose efforts led to the revival of the Olympic Games in 1896.

with the game; they met in a spirit of reform, not abolition. Coincidentally, while the discussions were proceeding, Theodore Roosevelt Jr. suffered a broken nose and facial cuts and bruises while playing for the Harvard football team in a game against Yale. Despite the injuries to his son, President Roosevelt remained steadfast in his support of the game. Four years after the tempest, the **National Collegiate Athletic Association (NCAA)** was formed; it remains the primary governing force in collegiate athletics in the United States.

Another significant issue was prohibitions against participation in sports and games on Sundays, spelled out in so-called **blue laws,** a holdover from the colonial period. In colonial New England, laws, printed on blue paper (hence the name "blue laws"), prohibited certain forms of entertainment and recreation on Sundays. Many states had blue laws, and in some areas they were enforced. People who strongly favored keeping the Sabbath "holy" were known as Sabbatarians.

After the First World War, sports nearly became an American obsession, and inroads were made on viewing and participating in sports and games on Sundays. As early as 1919, the Philadelphia Park Commission allowed baseball, golf, and tennis to be played on Sundays in city facilities under its jurisdiction. The Philadelphia Sabbath Association took the issue to court, and the battle over Philadelphia's blue laws commenced (Jable, 1976).

A major challenge to the blue laws arose when the management of the Philadelphia Athletics, a major league baseball team, scheduled a Sunday afternoon game in August 1926. The game was played and was considered a success by team management, but the eternally vigilant Sabbatarians took the organization to court for violating the Sabbath. The presiding court issued an injunction against the team, forbidding any further such indiscretions.

After the stock market crash of 1929 state and local officials in Pennsylvania turned to sport as a source of diversion from the economic and social problems making life difficult for so many people. Again, Sabbatarians, such as the Friends of the Proper Observance of the Sabbath, took umbrage at this move to encroach on Sunday religious observance. Nevertheless, laws allowing for local option voting on Sunday sports were passed, and voters in Philadelphia and Pittsburgh approved the sports-on-Sunday option by a 7-to-1 margin. On Sunday, November 12, 1933, the Pittsburgh Steelers (known then as the Pirates) played and lost to a team from Brooklyn, 32–0, before 20,000 fans. Pennsylvania's blue laws, dating from 1794, were defeated because, as Jable (1976, p. 363) observed, "Eighteenth-century customs were not compatible with twentieth-century behavior."

Another important milestone involves President Dwight Eisenhower (1890–1969) and the youth fitness crisis of the 1950s. An athlete at West Point during his college days (he played football and baseball), Eisenhower retained a love of sport and fitness. In the early 1950s fitness testing conducted by physical educators revealed that 58% of young people in the United States (but only 9% of their European counterparts) were deficient in one or more of 6 aspects of strength and flexibility. Dismayed by these statistics, Eisenhower convened a panel of fitness experts under the leadership of Vice President Richard Nixon. The **President's Council on Youth Fitness** issued far-reaching recommendations for solving the fitness deficits. This exercise of presidential clout into the fitness realm was most noteworthy.

Two more noteworthy events are mentioned in passing here but discussed at length in later chapters. The Civil Rights Act of 1964 facilitated the integration of African Americans and other minorities into the fabric of both everyday life and the sports world. The impact of this legislation on minority involvement in sport is an important topic in Chapter 17. Eight years later, Title IX of the Educational Amendments Act of 1972 mandated that women could not be discriminated against in the workplace or elsewhere. It has had considerable impact on women's involvement in sport. We return to this important piece of legislation in Chapter 19.

Finally, Twombly (1976) calls the years since the 1950s the "Electronic Age of Sport." The growth of interest and involvement in sport and fitness in the past three decades has been spectacular. On the downside, many people are more interested in being spectators than in being participants, and this preference remains a

---

National Collegiate Athletic Association (NCAA) the primary governing force in collegiate athletics in the United States, formed in 1909.

Blue laws laws, originally printed on blue paper, that prohibited certain forms of entertainment and recreation on Sundays.

President's Council on Youth Fitness a panel of fitness experts convened during the Eisenhower administration to suggest ways to improve the physical fitness of young Americans.

The Emergence of Organizations Promoting Sports, Fitness, and Physical Education

In the late 1800s and early 1900s, a number of organizations that would exert a profound influence on the face of play, games, sports, and fitness in America sprang up. In 1885, the American Association for the Advancement of Physical Education was created. After several name changes, that organization's official name is now the American Alliance for Health, Physical Education, Recreation, and Dance (AAHPERD). The College Physical Education Association (CPEA) was formed in 1897. The Playground Association of America came into being in 1906. Amy Homans (1848–1933), a significant figure in the history of physical education, was instrumental in the creation of the National Association for Physical Education of College Women in 1910, the year in which Boy Scouts was organized. Two years later, Girl Scouts and Campfire Girls were founded to involve girls in play, games, fitness, and athletic competition. Phi Epsilon Kappa, the professional physical education fraternity, was formed in 1913.

source of concern for critics of the American lifestyle. Some of these critics attempt to draw parallels between modern society and the decadence of the Romans in the latter stages of their empire. Whether these comparisons have any validity is a subject of considerable debate.

A BRIEF HISTORY OF PHYSICAL EDUCATION

Paralleling this evolution of sports in America was the physical education movement. The early German and Swedish immigrants brought with them an enthusiasm for physical activity and in many ways were America's first physical educators. Another early advocate of physical education was Catharine Beecher (1800–1878). Her father was Lyman Beecher, a well-known preacher. Harriett Beecher Stowe, the author of *Uncle Tom's Cabin,* was her sister. She wrote two books promoting fitness in women, *Course of Calisthenics for Young Ladies* (1832) and *A Manual of Physiology and Calisthenics for Schools and Families* (1856). Her work was instrumental in the creation of the first physical education program for women at Vassar College in 1865.

The first men's collegiate physical education program was established at Amherst College in 1861. It was called the Department of Physical Education, although not until the 1920s did *physical education* generally supplant *physical culture* as the preferred name.

California, in 1866, became the first state to pass a law requiring physical education in the public schools. The law was passed primarily because of the efforts of John Swett of the Rincon School (Hoepner, 1970). By 1930, 36 states had enacted such laws. In 1916, New York became the first to have a state supervisor of physical education. Not coincidentally, New York University in collaboration with Columbia University conferred the first doctor of philosophy degree in the discipline in 1924.

The list of leaders in the physical education movement is almost endless. Several merit consideration at this point. Dr. Dudley Sargent (1849–1924) was appointed director of the Hemenway Gymnasium at Harvard in 1880. Many of the early leaders in physical education were physicians, and Sargent was no exception. He was quite interested in strength testing. It has been said that Sargent administered 50,000 anthropometric tests in his professional lifetime (Hackensmith, 1966).

In 1904, Dr. R. Tait McKenzie (1867–1938) became head of the Department of Physical Education at the University of Pennsylvania, where he distinguished himself as both a national leader and a sports sculptor for nearly three decades. In addition to his scholarly achievements, McKenzie was a most accomplished sculptor. His *Shield of Athletes* was awarded a bronze medal in the artwork competition at the 1932 Olympic Games in Los Angeles (Kozar, 1984).

Two other leaders of note, Dr. Clark Hetherington (1870–1942) and Dr. Jesse Feiring Williams (1886–1966), published books in 1922 that called for a movement away from the militaristic and moralistic influence of the Germans and Swedes. At the same time, they called for the establishment of a physical education by and for the United States, one that emphasized educating the whole person. The issuance of this challenge ushered in a new era in physical education in America.

The physical education movement was greatly served by the events of World Wars I and II. Fitness deficiencies among American youth, coupled with the importance of fitness for men inducted into military life, added impetus to the cause. The youth fitness crisis of the 1950s, mentioned earlier, also helped to advance the movement.

A BRIEF HISTORY OF PSYCHOLOGY

In 1870, Sir Francis Galton (1822–1911), an English scientist, published *Hereditary Genius,* a book that was to spur interest in psychological assessment. Historians generally agree that psychology emerged as a science in 1879 in the laboratory of Wilhelm Wundt (1832–1920) in Leipzig, Germany. The focus of the research in Wundt's laboratory was psychophysical phenomena.

In 1880, G. Stanley Hall (1844–1924), an American psychologist and educator, was appointed president of Clark University, in Worcester, Massachusetts. Hall was the leader of the child study movement, which had considerable impact on educational practices in the United States. He also started the first psychology journal, the *American Journal of Psychology;* it is still published today.

Five schools of thought have dominated psychology, and several remain influential. Structuralism is most closely associated with E. B. Titchener (1867–1927). Structural research focused on the structure of consciousness. In contrast, functionalism, associated with the work of William James (1842–1910) and John Dewey (1859–1952), focused on the functions of consciousness. Functionalism was a more applied approach and contributed to advances in education, business, and other aspects of everyday life (Benjamin, Hopkins, & Nation, 1994).

In 1913 John B. Watson (1878–1958) proposed another way of looking at behavior. Watson outlined his revolutionary behaviorism in a paper entitled "Psychology as a Behaviorist Views It." He advocated the study of *observable* behavior rather than the murky mystical mentalisms that interested the structuralists and functionalists. Also in 1913, E. L. Thorndike (1874–1949) outlined his views on behavior in a treatise entitled *Educational Psychology.* Subsequently, Clark Hull (1884–1952), Edward Tolman (1886–1961), Edwin Guthrie (1886–1959) and other behaviorists added their own subtleties and nuances to behaviorist thought. The eminent Harvard psychologist, B. F. Skinner (1904–1990), presented his ideas in such works as *Behavior of Organisms* (1938), the fictional *Walden Two* (1948), and *Beyond Freedom and Dignity* (1971). All of these American behaviorists were indebted to Ivan Pavlov (1849–1936), a Russian physiologist, who in the late 1800s demonstrated the nature of classical conditioning.

Another powerful force in psychology has been psychoanalysis, originally proposed by Sigmund Freud (1856–1938). Much has been said—both pro and con—about the psychoanalytic model, but the theory has spurred research into personality theory, psychopathology, and techniques of psychotherapy.

As a protest against the pessimism of the psychoanalysts, American psychologists such as Abraham Maslow (1908–1970) and Carl Rogers (1902–1987) championed a humanistic approach with emphasis on optimism and individual initiative. Humanistic psychology was greatly influenced by the writings of Jean-Jacques Rousseau.

Another aspect of psychology is testing and assessment. In 1902, two French physicians, Alfred Binet (1857–1911) and Theodore Simon (1873–1962), created the first paper-and-pencil test of intelligence. This attempt at objectifying intelligence assessment sparked a revolution that was to have repercussions in the assessment of personality, aptitudes, interests, and other characteristics. Some of the tests that are pertinent to sport psychology are discussed in Chapter 16.

By way of summary, structuralism and functionalism are essentially defunct; psychoanalysts are suspect scientifically and few in number; humanism, though a bit fuzzy scientifically in the view of its critics, still has

Norman Triplett

Philippe Tissie (1852–1935), a Frenchman, wrote two articles in 1894 that dealt with the physiological and psychological aspects of bicycle racing (Baumler, 1997). Tissie's articles were more naturalistic than laboratory-based, but they are important because they are among the first publications with sport psychology as the subject matter. However, Norman Triplett, a 37-year-old graduate student, is generally given credit for conducting the first sport psychology experiment, at the University of Indiana in 1898.

Vaughan and Guerin (1997) indicate that Triplett's research focused on two things. One was pacemaking. Triplett had noticed that paced bicycle racing produced faster times than unpaced. Triplett's other research interest was "dynamogenic" factors that might underlie his observation—factors such as competition, desire to win, rivalry, and audience effects on performance. He published his results in the *American Journal of Psychology* in 1898.

After receiving a master's degree that same year, Triplett moved on to Clark University, where he received a doctor of philosophy degree in 1900. After teaching for a year at Mount Holyoke College, he took a position as head of the Department of Child Study at Kansas State Normal School (later Kansas State Teachers College) in Emporia, Kansas. He signed on in 1901 for the then princely sum of $200 per month. Nineteen years later he received a raise that boosted his monthly salary to $325, where it stayed through 1929 (Davis, Huss, & Becker, 1995). He served as department head until his retirement in 1931.

Intensely interested in athletics, Triplett was a highly visible figure at sports events on campus. An ardent track fan, he temporarily took over the job of head coach at Kansas State while the search for a new coach was taking place. He and a colleague designed the new athletic stadium for the college after a fire destroyed the old facility. Triplett attended many practices in all sports, always encouraging the student athletes. According to Davis et al., Triplett's daughter described him as the "patron saint of college athletics."

Triplett was more than a sport spectator. As a young man, he ran the 100-yard dash in 10 seconds, then a very respectable time. He also played baseball for the faculty team at Kansas State for many years. His crowning achievements, however, were in the academic domain. He was passionate about his subject area, devoted to the teaching process, and active in persuading top psychologists to come to the campus to teach his students. At Triplett's retirement party, former students talked of his impact on their lives. One of them, Professor A. B. Carlisle of Butler University, told Triplett: "As I recall, you were not merely a professor of psychology, but you were an institution" (Davis et al., 1995, p. 374).

SOURCES: Baumler, 1997; Davis, Huss, & Becker, 1995; Vaughan & Guerin, 1997.

---

its proponents. In contrast, behaviorism is thriving but has undergone modification to place more emphasis on the role of cognition in shaping human behavior.

A BRIEF HISTORY OF SPORT PSYCHOLOGY

Although many believe that sport psychology is the new kid on the block, it actually is almost as old as scientific psychology itself. As early as 1898, **Norman Triplett** (1861–1934), a psychologist at Indiana University, published what many regard as the first sport psychology experiment. Triplett focused his study on the effects of an audience on cycling. He noted that cyclists performed better when competing against each other than when riding alone, and even better when riding in tandem. It was Triplett's view that an audience facilitates performance through the release of energy and incentive to increase effort (Anshel, 1997).

Norman Triplett a psychologist, who, while a graduate student, conducted the first sport psychology experiment; it focused on factors that affect the pace of cyclists.

Sports Time Line

B.C.

850	Homer creates the *Iliad* and *Odyssey*.
776	First Olympic Games are held in Greece.
520	Sixty-fifth Olympic Games establishes format for Olympics until A.D. 394.
146	Greek Empire falls to the Romans.

A.D.

394	Theodosius I ends the Olympic Games because of their glorification of the human body.
476	Rome falls to Germanic peoples from the north.
1000–1200	Age of Chivalry in Europe.
1300–1500	Reawakening of interest in physical activity during the Renaissance.
1618	King James I issues the *Book of Sports*.
1732	Schuylkill Fishing Club, the oldest sporting organization in the United States, is established in Philadelphia.
1762	In *Émile,* Rousseau espouses virtues of physical activity as part of a person's total development. The roots of the German playground movement are established.
1810	Tom Molineaux, an African American, engages Tom Cribb in the first interracial boxing match.
1832	Catharine Beecher's *Course of Calisthenics for Young Ladies* is published.
1846	First recorded baseball game is played in Hoboken, New Jersey.
1852	First intercollegiate sporting event takes place between rowing crews from Harvard and Yale.
1861	First collegiate physical education program for men is started at Amherst College.
1865	First collegiate physical education program for women is started at Vassar College.
1866	California becomes the first state to require physical education in the public schools.
1868	New York City Athletic Club is formed.
1869	Rutgers and Princeton Universities play the first collegiate football game.
1871	Palace of Minos is unearthed, yielding artifacts interesting to sport historians.

James Naismith (right) is generally given credit for inventing and popularizing the game of basketball. The original goals were made from old peach baskets. Naismith is seen here discussing the game he invented.
© Bettman/CORBIS

1872	Bud Fowler is the first African-American professional baseball player.
1874	Tennis is introduced in the United States.
1876	First collegiate track meet is held in Saratoga, New York.
1876	A. G. Spalding becomes the first major sporting goods manufacturer.
1882	Handball is introduced in the United States.
1883	Moses Fleetwood Walker becomes the first African-American major league baseball player.
1886	*Sporting News* begins publication.
1887	Legal betting takes place at a racetrack in New York.
1888	Amateur Athletic Union (AAU) is formed.
1889	Walter Camp selects the first college football All-American team.

1891	Basketball is invented by Dr. James Naismith in Springfield, Massachusetts.
1891	The world high-jump record is set by W. B. Page at 6 feet 4 inches.
1895	A newspaper owned by William Randolph Hearst publishes the first sports page.
1896	The Olympic Games are reinstituted in Athens.
1897	First marathon run in America is held in Boston.
1900	Women compete in the Olympic Games for the first time.
1901	First bowling tournament is held in Chicago.
1903	First major league baseball World Series.
1904	The Olympic Games are held on American soil for the first time, in St. Louis, Missouri.
1905	Intercollegiate Athletic Association is formed.
1911	First Indianapolis 500 automobile race is held.
1913	Jim Thorpe is stripped of his Olympic medals because he played professional baseball in 1909 and 1910.
1913	The forward pass is introduced in football.
1916	Professional Golfer's Association (PGA) is formed.
1917	National Hockey League (NHL) is formed.
1919	First coaching journal, *Athletic Journal,* is published.
1920	First radio play-by-play account of a football game—WTAW in College Station, Texas, broadcasts a game between Texas A&M and the University of Texas.
1926	Gertrude Ederle is the first woman to swim the English Channel.
1928	Women take part in Olympic track events for the first time.
1928	United States Volleyball Association is formed.
1932	Mildred (Babe) Didrikson dominates women's track at the Olympic Games.
1935	First night game in major league baseball is played, in Cincinnati.
1935	Hialeah (Florida) Race Track uses an electric eye to identify winning horses in close races.
1936	Rodeo Cowboy Association (RCA) is formed under the name Cowboy's Turtle Association.

1939	Little League baseball begins in Williamsport, Pennsylvania.
1940	The Olympic Games are canceled until 1948 because of World War II.
1947	Jackie Robinson of the Brooklyn Dodgers breaks the color barrier in the modern era of major league baseball.
1948	Fred Morrison invents the Frisbee.
1949	National Basketball Association (NBA) is formed from two other leagues.
1949	Ladies Professional Golfer's Association (LPGA) is formed.
1950	African-American players are integrated into professional basketball.
1954	*Sports Illustrated* begins publication.
1954	Roger Bannister posts the first sub-4-minute mile in Oxford, England; his time is 3:59.4.
1961	Mickey Mantle becomes the highest-paid player ($75,000) in baseball's American League.
1962	Wilt Chamberlain scores 100 points in an NBA game.
1965	Astrodome opens in Houston.
1966	First NFL Super Bowl is played.
1971	Association for Intercollegiate Athletics for Women (AIAW) is formed.
1972	The Boston marathon has its first female participant.
1972	Title IX of the Educational Amendments Act opens up athletics for women.
1973	A New Jersey court allows girls to play Little League baseball.
1975	Frank Robinson becomes the first African American to manage a major league baseball team.
1976	Janet Guthrie is the first woman to compete in the Indianapolis 500.
1980	The Olympic Games are held in the Soviet Union; the United States boycotts the games. Entertainment and Sports Programming Network (ESPN) begins broadcasting.
1982	U.S. Postal Service issues commemorative stamps honoring Bobby Jones and Babe Didrikson Zaharias.

(continued)

Sports Time Line *continued*

1984	The Olympic Games are held in Los Angeles; the Soviet Union boycotts the games.
1987	Ben Johnson of Canada runs 100 meters in world record time of 9.84 seconds; he is later stripped of his medal for testing positive for anabolic steroids.
1989	Pete Rose of the Cincinnati Reds is banned from baseball for life for wagering on baseball games.
1991	Carl Lewis sets the world record (9.86 seconds) for the 100-meter dash; 11 world records in track are broken in the next 12 months.
1991	Hall of Fame basketball player Earvin "Magic" Johnson announces that he has tested positive for HIV.
1992	The so-called USA Dream Team runs roughshod over the basketball competition at the Olympic Games.
1992	The Raybestos Brakettes of Stratford, Connecticut, win the women's national championship in fast-pitch softball for the 25th time since 1958.
1993	Tennis great Arthur Ashe dies at age 49 of AIDS contracted from a blood transfusion.
1993	Michael Jordan retires from the NBA and takes up professional baseball; he comes out of retirement in 1995 and retires again in 1998.
1994	Major league baseball goes on strike in August; World Series is canceled for the first time.
1999	Tiger Woods top the $9 million mark for the year on the PGA tour.
2000	Alex Rodriquez signs a contract worth $250 million with the Texas Rangers.

Another pioneering paper related to sport psychology, written by E. W. Scripture, a Yale psychologist, was published in *Popular Science* in 1899. It was Scripture's contention that participation in sport could exert a positive effect on personality or character. The adage "Sport builds character" has its roots in Scripture's paper.

In the early 1900s, a University of Illinois psychologist, **Coleman Roberts Griffith** (1893–1960) taught the introductory course in his discipline and became interested in what motivated the athletes in his classes. This question led him to develop the first sport psychology course in 1923 and the first laboratory devoted to sport psychology research in 1925. Griffith also wrote two pivotal books on sport psychology, *Psychology of Coaching* (1926) and *Psychology of Athletics* (1928). Because of these achievements Griffith is known as the "father of sport psychology." Unfortunately for sport psychology, Griffith left the field in the 1930s to become an administrator at the university, where he served until his retirement.

Little transpired in sport psychology from the 1930s to the mid–1960s. Then, in 1967, the field got a jump start with the creation of the North American Society for the Psychology of Sport and Physical Activity (NASPSPA). NASPSPA dominated sport psychology for two decades, at which point the Association for the Advancement of Applied Psychology (AAASP) and Division 47 of the American Psychological Association (APA) emerged and took over most of the responsibility for shaping the development of sport psychology (see Chapter 1).

SUMMARY

1. The first colonists were focused on survival and piety; sports and recreational activity were secondary concerns. By 1700, games and sports were flourishing. Taverns served as focal points for social life. Such profligacy offended Sabbatarians and was a source of conflict.

Coleman Roberts Griffith a psychologist at the University of Illinois who in 1923 developed the first sport psychology course and two years later opened the first sport psychology research laboratory.

2. The Revolutionary War was a time of considerable interest in recreational diversions and fitness for military preparedness and to relieve boredom during lulls in the fighting.

3. During the Civil War, soldiers on both sides enjoyed baseball and boxing.

4. From 1850 to 1900, there was a technological revolution with ramifications for every aspect of American life, including sports. Population growth, immigration, urbanization, and technological advances changed the face of the country. The sewing machine, the light bulb, vulcanized rubber, the railroad, telegraphy, the camera, and innovations in printing revolutionized sports.

5. The development of intercollegiate sports, the creation of professional sport leagues, the development of the Amateur Athletic Union (AAU), and the reinstitution of the Olympic Games in 1896 were landmark events in the mid- to late 1800s.

6. Other landmark events include the crisis in American football that required the intervention of President Theodore Roosevelt in 1905, attacks on blue laws prohibiting Sunday sports and recreation, the revelation that American youth were far less fit than their European counterparts, the Civil Rights Act of 1964 and Title IX legislation of 1972 banning discrimination by race or gender, and the tremendous influence of the media on sports since 1970.

7. The physical education movement has had a profound impact on American life. In the mid- to late 1800s, books were written extolling the virtues of fitness, physical education courses were introduced in high schools and colleges, and prominent leaders in the field emerged.

8. Psychology as a science began in Leipzig, Germany, in the laboratory of Wilhelm Wundt in 1879. Five philosophical stances have dominated psychology: structuralism, functionalism, psychoanalysis, humanism, and behaviorism. Psychological testing also has had a profound influence on society and sport.

9. The first sport psychology experiment can be traced to Norman Triplett at Indiana University in 1898. The major force in sport psychology in the early 1900s was Coleman Griffith of the University of Illinois. He developed the first sport psychology laboratory in 1925 and wrote two important books relating psychology to coaching and athletics. He is considered the "father of sport psychology." The emergence of major sport psychology societies and organizations has been instrumental in the growth of the field.

KEY TERMS

Amateur Athletic Union (43)
blue laws (44)
"Camptown Races" (41)
Pierre de Fredy, Baron de Coubertin (43)
fives (41)
Coleman Roberts Griffith (50)
National Collegiate Athletic Association (44)
President's Council on Youth Fitness (44)
rounders (41)
rowing regatta (41)
shinny (41)
skittles (41)
Norman Triplett (47)

SUGGESTED READINGS

Higgs, R. (1982). *Sports: A reference guide*. Westport, CT: Greenwood Press.

The author provides a chapter on the history of sports and a chronology of important dates and events. Higgs also takes a look at the art and literature of sports. An appendix lists important research centers, collections, and directories within the United States and Canada. Though somewhat dated, this book is still useful.

Massengale, J. D., & Swanson, R. A. (eds.). (1997). *The history of exercise and sport science*. Champaign, IL: Human Kinetics.

Nine authorities explore the history of the disciplines making up the sport sciences: sport pedagogy, adapted physical education, sport sociology, sport history, sport philosophy, motor behavior, sport and exercise psychology, biomechanics, and exercise physiology. Massengale and Swanson also provide an introduction and their opinions concerning future directions in sport and exercise science. This is an excellent resource.

Sears, H. D. (1992). The moral threat of intercollegiate sports: An 1893 poll of ten college presidents, and the end of the "champion football team of the great west." *Journal of Sport History, 19,* 211–226.

In 1894—more than a decade before President Theodore Roosevelt met with college presidents concerned about football—a group of ministers in the Kansas Methodist Conference had a meeting about the situation at Baker University in Kansas. The school had somehow amassed a great pool of football talent through questionable recruiting practices and was known as the "Best in the West" among football teams of the era. The game itself and the way in which Baker went about winning seem to have offended the sensibilities of the Christian advocates who had helped create the Kansas Methodist Conference of which Baker University was a member. Sears says that pietists viewed the game as being "inextricably linked to alcohol, sabbath-breaking, gambling, de-civilizing public violence, and the sinful waste of youthful blood and time" (p. 211). Ultimately, football was banned in the conference in 1894 because of the opposition of the Kansas Methodist Conference ministers.

Twombly, W. (1976). *Two hundred years of sport in America: A pageant of a nation at play.* New York: McGraw-Hill.

Twombly divides the history of sport in America into four periods—Pastoral (1776–1865), Passionate (1866–1919), Golden (1920–1945), and Electronic (1946–1976)—and provides approximately 15 vignettes per page in both prose and pictures as a means of documenting the growth of sport.

 INFOTRAC COLLEGE EDITION

For additional readings, explore Infotrac College Edition, your online library. Go to:
http://www.infotrac-college.com/wadsworth
Hint: Enter these search terms: blue laws, Civil War, colonial period, Revolutionary War.

Behavioral Principles

CHAPTER 5

Classical Conditioning
Operant Learning
Cognitive Learning
Summary
Key Terms
Suggested Readings

Former New England Patriots head coach, Pete Carroll, shouts instructions to his team before their game with the Indianapolis Colts on September 19, 1999. The Patriots won 31–28, coming back from a three-touchdown deficit.

© AFP/CORBIS

An athlete rarely excels in a sport because of natural ability alone. Natural endowment surely plays a major role in athletic performance, but skill development is equally essential to the establishment of a competitive profile. Basic to the notion of skill development is the idea that the environment shapes, polishes, and directs the course of sport behaviors. In other words, what we learn about a sport often dictates how we perform, and ultimately determines our level of proficiency. In this chapter, we discuss some of the basic learning processes that underlie skill acquisition in athletics. As you will see, coaches and others can intervene to alter these processes, thus producing a more talented sport performer.

In psychology, *learning* is a generic term referring to a variety of environmental conditions that function to effect enduring changes in behavior through prior experience (Domjan, 1998). The discussion in this chapter focuses on three types of learning and their roles in sport: classical conditioning, operant learning, and cognitive learning. We provide examples of how each type of learning may be applied in the sport setting to enhance performance and reduce anxiety.

CLASSICAL CONDITIONING

Classical conditioning is a form of learning that is tied most closely with the work of Ivan Pavlov (1849–1936), a Russian physiologist (Pavlov, 1927). Traditionally the procedure shown in Figure 5.1 is used to describe the

---

Classical conditioning the type of learning that takes place when a conditioned stimulus alone elicits a desired response.
Unconditioned stimulus (UCS) a stimulus that elicits an involuntary (unconditioned) response.
Unconditioned response (UCR) an automatic response to a particular stimulus.
Conditioned stimulus (CS) a previously neutral event that elicits a response when paired with an unconditioned stimulus.
Conditioned response (CR) the response that is elicited by a stimulus that ordinarily would not elicit such a response.

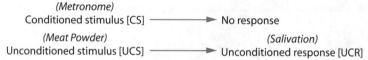

The Procedure for Obtaining Classical Conditioning

A. Before conditioning

(Metronome)
Conditioned stimulus [CS] ⟶ No response

(Meat Powder)
Unconditioned stimulus [UCS] ⟶ (Salivation)
Unconditioned response [UCR]

B. During conditioning

Metronome
conditioned stimulus [CS]
followed by

(Meat Powder)
Unconditioned stimulus [UCS] ⟶ (Salivation)
Unconditioned response [UCR]

C. After conditioning

(Metronome)
Conditioned stimulus [CS] ⟶ (Salivation)
Conditioned response [CR]

conditions necessary for learning to take place. First, a primary eliciting stimulus called an **unconditioned stimulus (UCS)** is presented. It reflexively evokes a response called an **unconditioned response (UCR).** Note that this relationship is biologically determined—that is, experience is not necessary for the behavior to occur. Subsequently a neutral event called a **conditioned stimulus (CS)** is paired with the UCS. After several such pairings, the CS produces a **conditioned response (CR)** that it did not previously trigger.

In Pavlov's original investigations using dogs as subjects, the introduction of a food pan containing meat powder (UCS) automatically elicited a flow of saliva (UCR) from the dogs' salivary glands. When a metronome (a device that marks exact time by emitting sounds at regular intervals) was presented repeatedly (CS) just prior to introducing the meat powder, the metronome came to elicit a salivation reaction (CR).

Despite the enormous popularity of classical conditioning as a subject area for experimental psychologists, there has not been widespread application of classical conditioning techniques in sport and physical education. When applications have been made, they generally have fallen into the area of alleviation of stress or other forms of discomfort associated with sport performance. For instance, it is not uncommon to find gifted competitors who become so acutely anxious before a big meet or a critical game that they lose sleep, experience nausea or vomiting, and so forth. Such reactions lower the physical and mental status of the athlete to the point at which his or her ability to perform is compromised. When this sort of misery occurs, a form of classical conditioning called **reciprocal inhibition** may prove helpful (Speigler & Guevremont, 1993). This counterconditioning technique involves training the athlete to think about the upcoming competition in a supportive, relaxed context. By pairing the stressful thoughts or cognitions with behavioral events that are incompatible with the anxiety reaction, the former anxiety-eliciting mental events elicit relaxation. For example, in gymnastics, a competitor who is worried about falling off the balance beam relaxes in a comfortable chair and imagines a perfect performance on the beam. Now, the thought or actual sight of the beam is associated with a comfortable state instead of stress. Such approaches have been used successfully to help many types of athletes (Cox, 1998).

Other possible uses of classical conditioning in sport include memory aids and cues that might facilitate recall of particular performance strategies. Along these lines, the importance of the learning context becomes apparent (Smith, 1984). For example, psychologists have known for years that we remember best when we recall information under the precise conditions under which it was learned. Trouble arises when we learn in one situation and perform in another. Perhaps this problem comes about because the requisite behaviors have been classically conditioned to relevant stimuli in the environment. When the stimuli are reinstated, performance improves because of the added benefits associated with multiple retrieval cues. For an athlete, this may translate into better execution and a more effective competitive posture. It follows that coaches would be wise to arrange for their athletes to engage in skill acquisition under fundamentally the same circumstance as their expected uses. This might mean practicing on the game field as opposed to in a remote practice area, working out with an audience present, and wearing the uniform that will be worn in actual game conditions.

OPERANT LEARNING

In contrast to classical conditioning, there has been considerable experimental work on the application of operant techniques in sport and exercise (for reviews see Donahue, Gillis, & King, 1980, and Leith & Taylor, 1992). **Operant learning** (or *operant conditioning,* as it is also called) is a set of principles set forth by B. F. Skinner. Unlike classical conditioning, for which the important feature for learning is temporal contiguity, for operant learning the consequences or outcome of responding dictates behavioral development (Domjan, 1998).

Basic Principles

Although operant behavior theory and research are exceedingly complex, the basic tenets of operant learning can be expressed rather simply (see Figure 5.2). First, there is the common reward procedure known as **positive reinforcement.** Positive reinforcers are events or stimuli that when produced by a response increase the probability of occurrence of that response. An example of positive reinforcement is giving praise or recognition for a task well done. **Negative reinforcement,** by contrast, is an operant procedure wherein behavioral probability increases when the response prevents or terminates an aversive stimulus. Performing well to avoid the wrath of an excessively harsh coach is one example of how negative reinforcement can lead to productive sport behavior. Another is the unhappy fellow who ran up to 100 miles a week not for the intrinsic joy of running but to escape from or to avoid the unhappiness that

---

Reciprocal inhibition a form of classical conditioning that promotes confidence by pairing stressful thoughts with behavior that is incompatible with an anxiety reaction.

Operant learning the type of learning that takes place in response to the application or withdrawal of rewards and punishments.

Positive reinforcement the use of rewards after a desired response in order to increase the likelihood that the response will be repeated.

Negative reinforcement the withholding of an aversive stimulus if a desired behavior occurs.

FIGURE 5.2

Four Basic Training Procedures Used in Operant Conditioning

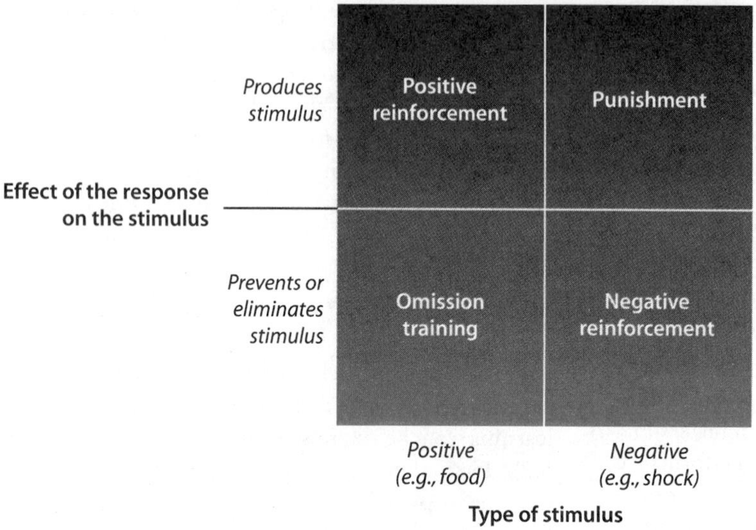

	Type of stimulus	
	Positive (e.g., food)	**Negative** (e.g., shock)
Produces stimulus	Positive reinforcement	Punishment
Prevents or eliminates stimulus	Omission training	Negative reinforcement

Effect of the response on the stimulus

he associated with his home life. Or how about the coach who gets his players to attend classes regularly with the threat of 6 A.M. wind sprints or running the steps at the football stadium?

Opponent processes to these reinforcement techniques are punishment and omission training, each of which operates to weaken behavior (see Figure 5.2). **Punishment** involves the delivery of aversive stimulation contingent upon some behavior. **Omission training** is said to have taken place when a response results in the loss of a scheduled reward. In either case, the effect is a negative one that is intended to diminish the strength of the response.

Punishment the use of an aversive stimulus in response to an undesired behavior.
Omission training the loss of a reward or a pleasant stimulus in response to an undesired behavior.
Effective behavioral coaching coaching techniques based on the identification of specific, targeted behaviors rather than on impressions and poorly defined training criteria.

Behavioral Coaching Techniques

Operant conditioning has been applied under a variety of labels. One of the more elaborate was introduced by Martin and Hrycaiko (1983)—**effective behavioral coaching (EBC).** They define EBC as "the consistent application of principles of behavioral psychology for the improvement and maintenance of athletic behavior" (p. 10). An essential component of EBC is the identification of target behaviors. In this case, this means the specific detailed measurement of selected athletic performances. Rather than rely on impressions and poorly defined criteria for evaluating the effectiveness of certain training strategies, a coach should prepare a preliminary list of behaviors that are the goal of the training manipulation. Such precision provides better clues to the validity of new techniques. Martin and Hrycaiko (1983, p. 11) suggest the following as an example list for a coach of age-group competitors:

I. Desirable behaviors by athletes at practices:

 A. Attendance at practice

 B. Good listening to instruction (in groups and individually)

 C. Practice of proper skill technique following instruction

 D. Practice of proper components of good technique during endurance training

 E. Continuous repetition of skills without frequent stopping

 F. Practice of skills with the intensity and speed at least equal to that required in the final desired performance

 G. Practice of relaxation techniques and imagery (so they might be used just prior to competition)

II. Desirable behaviors by athletes at competition:

 A. Muscle relaxation and imagery to prepare to compete

Shaping is a technique in which approximations of the desired behavior are reinforced. This swimmer will be reinforced by his coach for the use of proper arm strokes.
© Joseph Sohm; Chromosohm Inc./CORBIS

B. Good skill performance leading to measurable performance improvements (e.g., time, distance)

C. Good team spirit and mutual support of group members

D. Desirable sportsmanlike behaviors and minimal behavior problems (e.g., shaking hands, emotional control after losing or poor officiating)

Once the specific target behaviors have been identified, the appropriate reinforcement procedures should be implemented. It is the consequence of responding that is believed to regulate future response probabilities. Therefore, the coach should provide the appropriate positive or negative experiences consequent to the performance of desired or undesired athletic responses.

An elegant report demonstrating uses of behavioral coaching has been provided by Allison and Ayllon (1980). These researchers compared the efficacy of behavioral coaching and standard methods of coaching youth football. The behavioral coaching involved the use of verbal instructions and feedback in a systematic way with 4 players. When an athlete executed a blocking motion properly, the coach blew a whistle and told

the player, "Great, way to go." Incorrect blocking techniques were met with verbal reprimands while the player was in a frozen position. Furthermore, the player was given explicit instruction using the coach as a model and later was asked to imitate the proper techniques. This behavioral method contrasted with the standard method primarily in terms of consistency. Using the standard method, the coach did not often provide encouragement, and when verbal rewards were given, they were not enthusiastically offered.

Figure 5.3 shows the results of this attempt to apply an operant learning strategy. Obviously, the 4 players tested performed better when they received behavioral coaching as opposed to standard coaching. The praise following the desirable response can be interpreted as positive reinforcement. Similarly, the verbal reprimands can be viewed as punishment for the incorrect response. The idea is that these environmental events were contingently related to selected target behaviors.

The comparative effectiveness of positive reinforcement and punishment was assessed in a differential reinforcement study of coaching tennis skills (Buzas & Ayllon, 1981). Under one set of conditions, 3 female

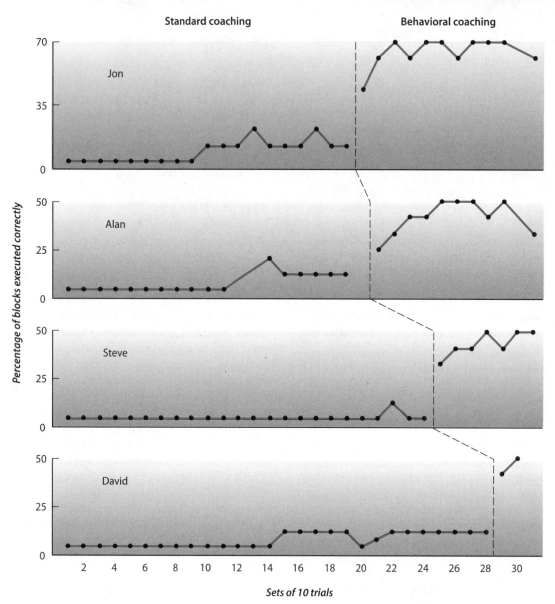

FIGURE 5.3

Percentage of Trials in Which Football Blocks Were Executed Properly as a Function of Standard Coaching and Behavioral Coaching Techniques

Standard coaching

Behavioral coaching

Jon

Alan

Steve

David

Percentage of blocks executed correctly

Sets of 10 trials

Source: Allison & Ayllon (1980).

Why Punish?

Jason R., a defensive end for a high school football team in the Midwest, was not a star, but he was a solid, reliable player with good judgment. During last Friday night's game against a team from a neighboring town, Jason did not play well. It was an absolutely horrid evening. Three days later, at the Monday afternoon practice, prior experience told Jason that he was going to pay a price for his Friday night shortcomings—missed assignments, poor tackling technique, and a profusion of penalties. He would suffer the abuse of his coach and the embarrassment of being singled out for punishment.

"You're worthless, kid," the coach screamed. "I might as well have stood a dummy out there. You let that jerk across from you beat you all night long. Do you know what it means to hit somebody? Try this sometime!" The enraged coach decked Jason.

"I'm warning you, son, you execute the way you did Friday night, and I'll execute you. I'll be on the sideline waiting for you. Count on it!" the coach snarled.

For anyone who has participated in athletics, this scenario is probably all too familiar. It is an example of a coaching strategy predicated on fear and intimidation. How many times have you seen a coach shout negative comments to a player when a mistake is made, only to look quietly past positive performances?

Little research has been conducted on this negative style of intervention (Donahue, Gillis, & King, 1980). In the one or two studies that include a negative condition approximating this approach, more desirable results were obtained from positive reinforcement. Why, then, do so many coaches use harsh motivational tactics? Perhaps years of modeling aggressive coaches who win have spawned a generation of coaches whose policy is "My way or the highway." Whatever the reason for their use, a serious scientific look into the widespread use of aversive conditioning techniques is badly needed.

Even if the gap between research and practice were lessened in the area of aversive control, we nonetheless should question the wisdom of continuing to use an approach that creates stress and negative self-images. How is Jason likely to feel about being disgraced in front of his teammates? Even if his performance does improve, he is not likely to forget the ridicule and open contempt heaped on him by his coach. B. F. Skinner himself (1971) cautioned against excessive use of punishment and negative reinforcement in controlling behavior, on the grounds that such procedures evoke unwanted emotional by-products. Along with control come anger and aggression. Although these traits may be only moderately destructive within the bracketed framework of certain sport environments, they clearly may have a more negative impact on society as a whole. To even the most ardent supporter of sport, aversive techniques that achieve the desired results would not likely appear useful when they sacrifice personal dignity and perceptions of self-worth. Perhaps coaches would be better advised to employ positive reinforcement techniques. As author/naturalist Henry David Thoreau remarked, "There are few exceptions where it is better to punish a sin than to reward a virtue."

SOURCES: Donahue, Gillis, & King (1980); Skinner (1971).

---

students ages 13 to 14 from a physical education class at a junior high school were corrected with routine criticism when they made errors in executing three tennis skills—the forehand, backhand, and serve. Performance under this correction procedure defined **baseline,** an operant term used to describe stable response rates when a specified set of conditions is employed. After a period of time, **differential reinforcement** was introduced— a procedure whereby the coach selectively ignored errors but systematically praised correct performance.

Baseline a measurement or set of data used as a basis for comparison.
Differential reinforcement reinforcement of behavior by consistently praising correct performance and selectively ignoring errors.

The results of this study revealed that all 3 girls increased their execution of appropriate tennis skills by two to four times the baseline rates when the coach used differential reinforcement. Positive reinforcement was a more desirable tactic than punishment. Although different findings might occur with older age groups or other special populations, it is doubtful that aversive training procedures ever are preferred over positive techniques, at least when they are used in isolation.

In another area of athletic competition, Shapiro and Shapiro (1984) extended the use of behavioral coaching techniques to include skill acquisition in track. Using the previously described procedures employed by Allison and Ayllon (1980), conditioning, form, and starts in the blocks improved for a group of high school track athletes. The end result was decreases in running times for the 100-meter and 200-meter races.

Elsewhere, the development of swimming skills has been the focus of attention for operant applications including behavioral coaching techniques. Shaping was used to modify an incorrect kicking motion in the front crawl stroke of a novice swimmer at Dalhousie University in Canada (Rushall & Siedentop, 1972). **Shaping** is an operant technique that involves the selective reinforcement of successive approximations of a goal behavior. When teaching an animal to press a lever to receive food, for example, it is most improbable that the animal will begin pressing the lever immediately after placement in the apparatus. Typically, the animal is given reinforcement (food) for simply moving toward the lever, then for touching the lever with some part of its body, and eventually the criterion for an actual lever press is introduced. Gradually, the animal is shaped into performing the desired response. Similarly, the young swimmer mentioned above was shaped into executing a more acceptable flutter kick. The specific operant procedure used to accomplish the intended result is described by Rushall and Siedentop (1972, p. 149) as follows:

> The desired terminal behavior was to effect an acceptable form of the flutter kick. The consequences used were (1) a light was shone in the swimmer's face every time he performed an incorrect kick, (2) only lengths performed to criterion were recorded on the swimmer's progress chart each being worth double the normal amount, and (3) the coach discussed the subject's performance after each session. The performance criterion was gradually made more stringent for the subject to record a satisfactory length. Initially, four [unacceptable] kicks per length were allowed to be deemed satisfactory. This was reduced to a complete absence of kicks in the fourth practice session. The most attention time required of the coach for the process was to observe 20 laps of swimming in each of the four sessions.

Along with shaping, there is another operant principle at work here. Recall that we said that omission training involves the removal of a scheduled positive reinforcer when an unwanted behavior occurs. Under such circumstances, reinforcement is given when the undesired response is not present—that is, when it is omitted. This is basically what was required of the swimmer. Reinforcement was not given for executing a certain number of correct actions; instead, it was given for the absence of incorrect actions. Such a modification procedure illustrates the uses and advantages of operant methods.

Elsewhere, it has been shown that music can be used to positively reinforce productive behaviors during swimming training sessions. Hume and Crossman (1992) played a tape of an athlete's favorite music when the athlete increased practicing a skill by as much as 15% above the previous baseline. When the opportunity to listen to music was taken away, practice dropped to baseline levels. In this simple demonstration of the effectiveness of positive reinforcement, we see how a minor, unobtrusive change by a coach produced real benefits for swimmers.

Another sport in which behavioral techniques have proved effective is gymnastics. Allison and Ayllon (1983) were able to identify 6 female gymnasts on a high school team who demonstrated either no proficiency or no higher than 20% proficiency on basic routines such as backward walkovers, front handsprings, and reverse kips. The format for teaching the gymnastic skills using behavioral coaching was very similar to the format that Allison and Ayllon used in their football study (1980).

Shaping selective reinforcement of successive approximations of a desired response.

Basically, executing the skill, judging correct position, describing the incorrect position, modeling the correct position, and imitating the correct position were emphasized. Each step was handled by the coach using his own words to shape behavior. Incorrect landings on the mat were met with the word "freeze" followed by corrective instruction. Properly executed landings were exempt from the "freeze" admonition. In the standard coaching condition, instructions on proper execution were given, skills were modeled by the coach or another gymnast, verbal feedback was given regarding errors, and praise and threats were used when deemed appropriate by the coach. As might be predicted, the behavioral coaching procedure was more effective in imparting all three skills to the young gymnasts.

In a later study with a slightly variant theme, Wolko, Hrycaiko, and Martin (1993) compared standard coaching versus standard coaching supplemented by behaviorally based self-regulation with 5 female gymnasts ages 10 to 13 years. Three experimental conditions were manipulated: a baseline condition with standard coaching only, a treatment condition (T1) that combined elements of standard coaching with public self-regulation, and a treatment condition (T2) that combined standard coaching with private self-regulation. Conditions T1 and T2 are important because there is controversy among psychologists as to the merit of public versus private self-regulation strategies such as self-monitoring, goal setting, and self-evaluation. Bandura (1977) is one advocate of the privacy point of view. Hays and associates (Hayes, Rosenfarb, Wulfert, Munt, Korn, & Zettle, 1985; Hayes, Munt, Korn, Wulfert, Rosenfarb, & Zettle, 1986) are convinced of the efficacy of a public component in self-regulation strategies. (We shall return to this point briefly when discussing public recordings.) In this context, Wolko et al. (1993) looked at private versus public self-regulation in an effort to improve balance-beam proficiency among the gymnasts in question. Setting performance goals, behavior recording, displaying the results, rewarding goal attainment, and providing frequent and immediate feedback about the desirable behavior were some of the techniques used to shape performance. In general, the T2 condition was the most effective of the three treatments, although the effect was not particularly pronounced. Overall, the Wolko et al. research did support the utility of adding a behavioral-based self-management component to standard coaching. The net effect of all this is supportive of the use of behavioral coaching procedures to enhance skill acquisition in gymnastics.

Public Recording

The performance of swimmers has also been studied using a public recording reinforcement procedure (Donahue et al., 1980). **Public recording** is the displaying of formal evaluations in such a way that how well an athlete performs, or how poorly, is apparent to all. When we do something well, generally speaking, we want someone to know about it, and athletics is most certainly no exception. Positive reinforcement comes from the satisfaction of publicly posting a good score.

An investigation by McKenzie and Rushall (1974) evaluated the impact of checking off completed work units on a program board that was presented publicly. Eight members of a swimming team were asked to record the number of laps they swam during successive 1-minute periods in a series of uninterrupted swims. When a certain level of output was achieved, the swimmers checked off the appropriate box on a program board located where the other swimmers could see it. In this particular investigation, the intervention strategy, or the public recording manipulation, was introduced after a baseline control period, and then it was discontinued. This design, called an **ABA design,** successively involves recording during an initial period of nontreatment (A), continued recording during a subsequent treatment period (B), and still further recording during a return to the initial conditions that were in place prior to treatment (A). Specifically, one would expect that to the extent to which the intervention (B) produced superior results relative to baseline conditions (A), then there should be a pattern of improvement under B but a subsequent decline under A. Otherwise, the improvement registered during the period of intervention might just reflect practice efforts or something else unrelated to the behavioral manipulation.

Public recording a reinforcement technique in which formal evaluations are publicly displayed.

ABA design a type of research design involving recording during nontreatment (A), a treatment period (B), followed by nontreatment conditions (A).

Regarding the findings reported by McKenzie and Rushall (1974), the results were in the expected direction. Specifically, all 8 swimmers had 20 to 30% more work output in the intervention phase than in the baseline period. Moreover, when the public recordings procedure was discontinued, the output of 7 of the 8 swimmers decreased substantially.

The use of public recording as an applied operant technique raises some interesting theoretical questions. Not the least of them relates to the very nature of reinforcement. Is the intervention grounded to positive reinforcement or to negative reinforcement? At first glance, the reinforcement appears to be positive, because athletes enjoy the satisfaction of showing everyone how well they perform. But there is also the possibility that a negative incentive is responsible for the performance improvement. Surely athletes do not want to risk the embarrassment or ridicule attendant to a poor showing. To avoid the possibility of such negative experiences, the athlete may perform at a high level not so much to gain recognition but to ensure acceptance among peers or competitors. This is clearly negative reinforcement, and many psychologists have suggested that this sort of control is stronger than that accompanied by positive means (Geen, Beatty, & Arkin, 1984).

Changing Coaching Behaviors

Operant procedures can be used to modify the behavior of coaches as well as athletes. Indeed, Dickinson (1977) has expressed forcefully the need to implement techniques for changing coaching behavior. Among the recommendations for change are increases in the frequency with which positive comments are offered and greater clarity with regard to specific sport behaviors that are required for excellence. In other words, coaches should use more positive reinforcement and provide better instruction.

Rushall and Smith (1979) attempted to show that the quality and quantity of feedback statements could be increased through self-recording techniques. The subject in the investigation was a 32-year-old male swimming coach. Self-recording of "reward and feedback behaviors" was accomplished through the use of sheets that contained columns indicating types of feedback (effort, skill, task execution, performer interaction) and 31 key words, all of which could be checked. During several coaching sessions, the subject was signaled at the end of successive 5-minute intervals to count the frequency with which he was giving verbal rewards and relevant feedback. This self-recording process, which in essence is reinforcing the coach for performing goal behaviors that define high-quality coaching, produced the desired result. The frequencies of emission of verbal comments and feedback increased dramatically over the course of the study.

An adjunctive element to the Rushall and Smith project bears mentioning. Realistically, one cannot expect a coach to continue to keep detailed personal records indefinitely. It is simply too time-consuming to keep track of the frequency with which specific verbal remarks are registered, and so forth. How, then, can we expect the target behaviors to survive when the intervention processes are removed? Fortunately, operant conditioners have perfected a procedure called **fading,** which ensures persistence even beyond the point at which the behavioral manipulation is discontinued. The fading strategy used by Rushall and Smith involved gradually "leaning" or stretching the reinforcement schedule so that the required 5-minute interval counts became less and less frequent. The high production of the target behaviors continues in such a case, but the control of the higher-quality coaching performance falls under the influence of other stimuli—witnessing improvement in the athletes themselves, greater camaraderie, and so forth. In effect, a temporary control device is exchanged for a more enduring one. A follow-up period of observation conducted by Rushall and Smith indicated that their fading techniques were successful in achieving the purpose of transferring stimulus control from the checklist to the performance of the swimmers.

Conditioned Reinforcement

Another operant procedure that may prove useful for training athletes is **conditioned reinforcement.**

Fading a procedure that ensures the persistence of desired behaviors after reinforcement is ended.

Conditioned reinforcement reinforcement that occurs when a previously neutral stimulus that has been paired with a primary reinforcer elicits the same response as the primary reinforcer.

Conditioned reinforcers are stimuli that, when paired with a primary reinforcer, come to possess the same control properties as the primary reinforcer (Martin & Pear, 1992). In a traditional laboratory setting, conditioned reinforcement occurs when a tone is paired with a primary reward object such as food and then the previously neutral tone acquires the ability to strengthen a behavior that produces it—that is, the subject works for the previously neutral event (the conditioned reinforcer) because it has been correlated with reward.

In applied situations, a common training rationale based on conditioned reinforcement is the **token system.** In such a system, an object of some sort is given to the subject when the appropriate behavior is executed. For example, a plastic disk might be given to a child suffering from a speech difficulty upon the successful production of a word phrase. At some point, the token (the disk) can be exchanged for a more meaningful object such as a toy or food. Research has shown that this form of conditioned reinforcement is an effective way to modify behavior, and it has the advantage of not physically satiating the subject (Martin & Pear, 1992).

Two investigations have indicated that a token system can be used to alter athletic skills. In a study by Jones and reported in Donahue et al. (1980), the subjects of the manipulation were participants in a basketball camp. Because the objective of most basketball coaches is to outscore the opponent, it seemed reasonable to select "points scored" as the target behavior. The staff employed three different training routines. First, all members of a given basketball team were rewarded with an "Olympic ring" each time their team scored 20 points. With 80 points in a single game, 4 rings were given to each player on the team. Later, these rings could be redeemed for food or other rewards. Second, the players were placed on the same token system, but it was predetermined that no rings would be dispensed. A third condition simply scored the games in the standard way, and no token system was even suggested. The findings from this study revealed that players scored more points under the Olympic ring contingency than did players in either of the other conditions. Evidently, the operant strategy of token reinforcement was an effective behavioral control device.

Nine members of a professional basketball team were subjects in a token system intervention that used money as the conditioned reinforcer (money, after all, is a sort of a token because it has value only when it can be exchanged for something of greater worth). The players were given financial rewards for efficient offensive performance. An efficiency average (EA) served as the target measure. In this study, an ABAB design was used in which the intervention following the initial baseline was discontinued but subsequently reinstated. Each time the token intervention was instituted, 3 players with the highest EAs received monetary payments. The results showed that 6 of the 9 players increased their offensive production during the first intervention, and 4 of these 6 decreased their offensive production during the return to baseline. All 4 players subsequently improved again when the final intervention was introduced. So, consistent with findings in other studies using token systems, conditioned reinforcers did have a positive influence on athletic performance.

Although it seems clear that token systems have a legitimate place in the development of athletic skills, the use of tangible rewards to control behavior is not without opposition. Concern over the use of such techniques stems from evidence indicating that, after the removal of a recently introduced reward, response rates decline to levels below those consistently maintained prior to the introduction of the reward (Lepper, Greene, & Nisbett, 1973). Consider what may happen with the use of rings to reinforce high point production in basketball games. How will the athletes react when their high point production no longer earns them a ring? Will they abandon the activity altogether because the payoff is no longer there? Unfortunately, there is a chance that they will.

Lepper and Greene (1978) suggested that such negative patterns following reward removal may relate to "overjustification." According to this view, the introduction of an external reward forces a person to review the value of the activity, and the amount of worth attached to the behavior often is defined according to the degree of extrinsic gain. Ultimately, when the external reward is taken away, the person concludes that

---

Token system a type of conditioned reinforcement in which a token that can be exchanged for something more meaningful, such as special privileges, is given as a reward for desired behavior.

the entire reason for responding is gone. What this may mean to a coach is that, if external reinforcement manipulations are to be used, some agenda should exist for shifting to a more realistic controlling stimulus. Earlier in this chapter, we talked about fading as a psychological principle. Here is another instance in which such a procedure could prove useful.

A specialized application of conditioned reinforcement is **chaining.** Chaining is a schedule condition that requires that several behaviors must be completed before a reward is given. According to Martin and Pear (1992), a stimulus–response chain is a series of stimuli and responses in which each response except the last serves as signal for the next response in a designated sequence. The last response in the chain is followed by a reinforcer. Accordingly, three kinds of chains are possible: total, forward, and backward. In the **total chain,** all behaviors are to be completed at once. The person attempts all steps from the beginning to the end on each trial and continues with total task trials until the entire chain is acquired. In the **forward chain,** behaviors are mastered step-by-step in a forward direction. The first step in a sequence is mastered, then the first and second steps, then the first, second, and third steps, and so forth, until the entire chain is mastered. In the **backward chain,** behaviors are mastered step-by-step in a backward direction. The last step in a chain is established, then paired with the next-to-last step, and so forth, with progression to the beginning of the chain.

Two sport-related examples of backward chaining have been used by Killian (1988) with swimmers and O'Brien and Simek (1983) with golfers. Killian's article is a how-to-do-it presentation and focuses on a backward-chain sequence for teaching the back float, the prone float, and the crawl stroke. Using the back float as an example, in step 1 the swimmer crouches in chest-deep water, lays the head back until the ears are submerged, and immediately recovers to a standing position. Step 2 in the chain begins with the ears submerged followed by rising on tiptoe and recovery to a standing position. Step 3 begins with the ears submerged followed by the extension of one leg off the bottom of the pool and recovery to a standing position. Step 4 begins in a crouch position with the ears submerged and one leg extended, followed by a gradual lifting of the support leg from the bottom of the pool and recovery to a standing position.

The utility of backward chaining was the focus of the O'Brien and Simek (1983) study. Its superiority over conventional or traditional coaching methods was demonstrated with 12 novice golfers divided into 2 groups of 6 for experimental purposes. Of particular interest were the scores of the golfers on their first competition following the chaining versus standard coaching sequences. The chaining group scored 17 strokes better than the traditionally coached group, or almost one stroke per hole for 18 holes.

In a separate study, Simek, O'Brien, and Figlerski (1994) applied their chaining-mastery approach outlined in *Total Golf* (Simek & O'Brien, 1981) in hopes of improving the performance of 14 collegiate golfers. Their initial goal was to make the experimental treatment a four-week training program. Week 1 was devoted to establishing a baseline of golf performance by having all subjects complete three rounds of play. Week 2 involved completing the first 9 segments of a backward-chaining sequence, primarily involving putting at ever-increasing distances. Also, three rounds of golf were played for purposes of later comparisons. Week 3 involved short iron play and represented steps 11 through 19 of the chain. Again, three more rounds of golf were played to check on progress. Team golf scores improved by 3.4 strokes per 18 holes during the three-week period of training. Unfortunately, at the end of the third week of the training period, the team coach was unable or reluctant to follow through on the reward system originally agreed upon (spots on the golf team for upcoming matches and/or new golf balls). As might be expected, performance deterioration occurred as a function of the extinction condition imposed by the coach. Steps 20 through 23, hitting long irons and woods, were never instituted. However, even after the unfortunate coaching decision was made (unfortunate at least in terms of re-

---

Chaining stimulus-response chain in which each response except the last serves as a signal for the next response.

Total chain a behavioral chain in which all behaviors are completed at once.

Forward chain a behavioral chain emphasizing step-by-step mastery in a forward direction.

Backward chain a behavioral chain in which behaviors are mastered in a backward direction; mastering golf by starting on the green and working sequentially to the tee box is an example.

search design), team performance remained above baseline achieved prior to the chaining-mastery program. Despite some limitations, the Simek et al. study lends additional support to the validity of chaining as a means of improving athletic performance.

Premack Principle

When tokens or other types of tangible rewards are not used for behavior modification, the opportunity to engage in a preferred activity can act as reinforcement. In learning circles, this approach is referred to as the **Premack Principle** (Premack, 1962). The idea is that any behavior that is independently more probable than some other behavior can be used as a reward to strengthen the lower-probability response. For example, a child presented with the task of completing an arithmetic assignment may be offered a chance to play with the classroom gerbil, subject to meeting the academic contingency. Another example presented by Kearney (1996) involved some graduate students who were laboriously working through a scholarly book by Albert Bandura (1969) entitled *Principles of Behavior Modification*. The enterprising students intermingled a chapter of Mario Puzo's bestseller *The Godfather* with each chapter of Bandura's book, thus allowing themselves to accomplish the lower-probability behavior of reading a difficult textbook by rewarding themselves with the higher-probability behavior of reading an engaging bestseller.

The potential effectiveness of a Premack training operation in the area of exercise is evident from a study by Kau and Fisher (1974). The purpose of this research was to demonstrate that engaging in various preferred social activities could be used as a reinforcement for the less probable activity of jogging for its health benefits. The result of the study indicated that over a four-week course, a sharp increase in jogging behavior was apparent. Interestingly, weight loss and other natural reinforcers took over, and the program was judged to be successful beyond the point of the intervention. At any rate, in at least some cases the opportunity to perform a response that is deemed desirable can be used successfully as a behavioral training method.

One of the great advantages of the Premack approach is that the program is individually tailored to meet each person's needs. Not all people enjoy doing the same things. Some people may find the opportunity to immerse themselves in a social context downright distasteful. Rather than be forced to engage in what might be viewed as trivial social interactions, a person may greatly prefer a private moment in a sauna. The point is that, according to the Premack Principle, targeted behavior rates can be increased in both types of individuals as long as the responses occasion the opportunity to do what they enjoy.

Response Cost

Another operant technique is response cost. **Response cost** is a procedure whereby undesirable behaviors are penalized by taking away a reward object already in the possession of the person. The rewards are gained when appropriate behaviors are exhibited. This approach differs slightly from omission training in that the response involves rewards that have already been obtained, whereas omission training involves scheduled rewards that are never dispensed. Wysocki, Hall, Iata, and Riordan (1979) successfully used a response cost procedure in getting 7 of 8 college students to increase aerobic exercising, and the benefits were still apparent at a 12-month follow-up.

Training Variables

SESSION LENGTH. Training variables that are known to affect performance have also attracted the interest of sport psychologists. One such variable with the potential for having profound impact on the acquisition of sport skill is the length and spacing of practice sessions. What are the optimal durations for teaching new skills? Should practice sessions occur close together, or should they be widely spaced with long rest intervals? These are a few of the questions taken under consideration in an article by Sanderson (1983). The psychology of learning literature would argue that **distributed practice**

Premack Principle the idea that the opportunity to engage in a preferred activity can be used as a reward for engaging in a less probable activity.

Response cost penalizing undesirable behavior by taking away a reward object previously gained for appropriate behavior.

Distributed practice practice sessions in which training trials are separated by long periods of rest.

(widely spaced training trials and long periods of rest) should be superior to **massed practice** (cramming training sessions into a short time frame). But as Sanderson notes, the only conclusion that can be drawn for the development of sport skill is that "somewhere between too little rest and too much lay off is the desired condition for practice" (p. 121). A great deal depends on the skill being developed and the nature of the instruction process. In general, it is safe to say that aspects of performance requiring gross motor skills, such as catching a baseball or blocking in football, survive over longer periods of time than do events that have mental components, such as reading keys in football or using appropriate cognitive strategies when participating in a variety of sports. Accordingly, coaches should be alert to the different types of training programs that may be most suitable for introducing a particular skill.

SCHEDULES OF REINFORCEMENT. Another variable that may influence the efficacy of athletic training operations is schedules of reinforcement. It is widely accepted that **intermittent reinforcement** occasions greater persistence than **continuous reinforcement** (Nation & Woods, 1980). This means that when a target response is rewarded on half the trials but is not rewarded on the other half (intermittent reinforcement), the response will continue for a greater time after the reward is no longer available than would be the case had the response been rewarded every time it occurred (continuous reinforcement). An example is the child who learns to get what he or she wants from a parent. If the parent is inconsistent—that is, occasionally he or she gives in but not on every occasion—the child has essentially been placed on an intermittent schedule of reinforcement. Rest assured that the parent will have greater difficulty extinguishing this behavior by finally ignoring it altogether than would have been the case

had the response been reinforced continuously (had the child always gotten his or her way).

To date only a few studies of sport behavior have examined the possible utility of intermittent reinforcement as a tool for ensuring response persistence (see Donahue et al., 1980). But there is little doubt that such schedules can serve the coach or training staff. An offensive lineman who learns that he will fail once in a while learns to keep trying nonetheless. A tennis player who learns that most but not all strategically placed serves will be winners acquires an attitude of perseverance. To be sure, intermittent reinforcement is, to some degree, a natural result of competition. But training experiences in this area need not be haphazard; rather, schedules can be judiciously programmed to produce the intended result.

Learned Helplessness

Perhaps one of the most exciting links between operant conditioning and sport rests with the concept of **learned helplessness.** Learned helplessness is said to occur when an organism previously exposed to an aversive non-contingency exhibits a deficit in the acquisition of a subsequent operant behavior (Maier & Seligman, 1976). This means that when animals or people are placed in situations over which they have no control over their successes or failures, they do poorly on other, unrelated tasks even though their chances for success might be good. An example from the animal laboratory is the rat that is exposed to shock and cannot turn it off regardless of its activity. Later, when this animal is exposed to shock in another environment in which the shock could be terminated by something as simple as a lever press, no responses are attempted (Seligman & Beagley, 1975). It is as if the rat has learned that it is helpless with respect to controlling the environment and carries this expectancy of uncontrollability with it into new learning situations even though the reward conditions have improved dramatically. Similarly, humans often show depression and other types of performance anomalies once they have experienced a series of failures due to circumstances they view as largely beyond their control (Abramson, Seligman, & Teasdale, 1978). The person comes to expect failure and, not surprisingly, does indeed fail.

Massed practice practice sessions in which training is crammed into a short time frame.
Intermittent reinforcement rewarding a desired response some of the time, not all of the time.
Continuous reinforcement rewarding a desired response every time it occurs.
Learned helplessness a sense of helplessness transferred from a situation in which a person has no control to new situations in which the individual might experience success with a little effort.

Dweck (1980) has written on the potential parallels between learned helplessness as a laboratory phenomenon and certain problem athletes. The issue seems to center on how sport participants react to encounters with failure. When a person becomes preoccupied with failure and assumes personal responsibility for it, chances for helplessness to occur are great. Dweck uses the example of former heavyweight boxer Dwayne Bobick, who at the time had a near-perfect record but eventually was knocked out in the first round of a fight. He lost every fight thereafter. According to helplessness theory (see Abramson et al., 1978), such a result in a "success only" person is not unexpected. Because there is no experience with failure and interpolated success, failure signals only more setbacks, and negative expectations build on themselves. Ultimately, a losing attitude (helplessness) emerges.

What is preferable may be a mastery-oriented attitude toward failure. When a person uses a personal disappointment or setback as a "psyching-up" mechanism, and struggles even harder, then the chances for an eventual triumph increase appreciably. It has been recommended that intermittent reinforcement schedules of the sort described earlier could help immunize individuals against feelings of helplessness (Nation & Massad, 1978). The belief is that failure experienced in the context of aggregate success builds an attitude of persistence, thus preempting helplessness. One has only to look at Dweck's example of Ben Hogan, the golfing legend, to appreciate what a positive perspective in the face of adversity can do for a competitor. Despite his relatively small size, years of struggling as a player, and a near-fatal automobile accident, a dedicated Hogan came back and established himself as one of the all-time golfing greats. Clearly, failure is perceived differently from person to person.

On a purely commonsense level, all of this points to the need to make players, especially young ones, feel as if they are winners. A young athlete constantly berated and criticized by a coach or parent will think only of losing and will feel helpless about winning. In Highlight 5.1 we addressed the issue of aversive control and concluded that, even though it may be effective at times, it is potentially destructive, both to the individual and to society. Rather than criticize, a better strategy might be to build real confidence by teaching children how to handle failure in a realistic fashion.

COGNITIVE LEARNING

Cognitive learning is learning that takes place at a purely mental level. In recent years, psychologists have been more accepting of concepts such as "mind," and processes such as imagery, rehearsal, and causal ascription have become fashionable topics for theory and research. Although such mental operations may be difficult to study, it is hard to deny that they are important to psychology in general and to sport psychology in particular. In this regard, one is reminded of the fascinating story of Major James Nesmeth, a prisoner of war for seven years in North Vietnam. In an effort to maintain his sanity while imprisoned in a tiny cage, Major Nesmeth mentally placed himself on his favorite golf course and played 18 holes every day. Every step was imagined; every aspect of his game reviewed; and when appropriate, mental corrections were made. Released at the war's end, Major Nesmeth set foot on an actual golf course for the first time in seven years and shot an astonishing 74—20 strokes below his average! Such phenomenal changes in sport performance have not gone unnoticed by sport psychologists. We look at cognitive learning in greater detail in our discussion of cognitive learning approaches to anxiety reduction in Chapter 8.

SUMMARY

1. Classical conditioning, operant learning, and cognitive learning are three types of learning that have relevance to sport and exercise psychology.

2. In classical conditioning, a primary eliciting stimulus called an unconditioned stimulus (UCS) reflexively produces a response called an unconditioned response (UCR). When a neutral stimulus, called a conditioned stimulus (CS), is paired with the UCS, the CS comes to evoke a conditioned response (CR) similar to the UCR.

3. Despite its considerable influence on psychology, classical conditioning has largely been overlooked in sport and exercise psychology.

4. In operant learning, positive reinforcement refers to the strengthening of behavior by presenting an event after a response. Conversely, negative reinforcement refers to the strengthening of behavior

by removing an event after a response. Punishment and omission training both weaken behavior. Different operations are involved with each procedure.

5. Behavioral coaching involves the application of learning principles to situations related to training athletic competitors. Differential reinforcement and shaping are two learning principles used in behavioral coaching.

6. Public recording is the displaying of formal evaluations so that how well an athlete performs, or how poorly, is apparent to all. There is some debate as to whether the procedure improves athletic performance through positive or negative reinforcement. Seeing one's name in a positive context can be positively reinforcing, but having one's name omitted from a desirable listing may accomplish the same thing through negative reinforcement.

7. Operant procedures can be used to make coaches more aware of their use of, or failure to provide, positive feedback, encouragement, and clear instruction to athletes.

8. Conditioned reinforcers are neutral stimuli that, when paired with primary reinforcers, come to produce much the same effect as the primary reinforcer. The token system and chaining in its various forms offer conditioned reinforcement and have been shown to be effective in shaping and maintaining athletic and fitness behaviors.

9. The Premack Principle suggests that a high-probability behavior can be used as a reward to strengthen the occurrence of a lower-probability response. Rewarding oneself by reading an interesting book after running three miles is an example of Premack training. An advantage of the Premack approach is its adaptability to the needs and interests of each individual.

10. Session length and schedules of reinforcement are training variables that affect behavior. Widely spaced training sessions are effective when gross motor skills are the training target. Massed training sessions are effective when activities call for cognitive strategies. Persistence in responding is greater when intermittent rather than continuous reinforcement is used.

11. Learned helplessness occurs when a general expectation of uncontrollability emerges after exposure to an aversive non-contingency. Many athletes fail because they anticipate failure; thus it is important for coaches or trainers to incorporate success experiences into the training program.

12. Cognitive learning theory involves the study of mental aspects of behavior and is a departure from the behavioral orthodoxy of the 1960s and early 1970s.

KEY TERMS

ABA design (61)
backward chain (64)
baseline (59)
chaining (64)
classical conditioning (54)
conditioned reinforcement (62)
conditioned response (54)
conditioned stimulus (54)
continuous reinforcement (66)
differential reinforcement (59)
distributed practice (65)
effective behavioral coaching (56)
fading (62)
forward chain (64)
intermittent reinforcement (66)
learned helplessness (66)
massed practice (66)
negative reinforcement (55)
omission training (56)
operant learning (55)
positive reinforcement (55)
Premack Principle (65)
public recording (61)
punishment (56)
reciprocal inhibition (55)
response cost (65)
shaping (60)
token system (63)
total chain (64)
unconditioned response (54)
unconditioned stimulus (54)

SUGGESTED READINGS

Martin, G., & Pear, J. (1999). *Behavior modification: What it is and how to do it* (6th ed.). Englewood Cliffs, NJ: Prentice-Hall.

This is an excellent text on behavior modification. The basics of conditioning and learning are presented in a comprehensive and readable fashion. Positive and negative reinforcement, token systems, conditioned reinforcement, punishment, chaining, and cognitive behavior modification are among the topics discussed. The occasional examples from athletics will be particularly interesting to sport psychology students.

Peterson, C., Maier, N. F., & Seligman, M. E. P. (1994). *Learned helplessness: A theory for the age of personal control.* New York: Oxford University Press.

This book extends and updates the work of Seligman on learned helplessness. Applications are made with regard to contemporary culture, and those who read Seligman's 1975 book on learned helplessness as well as this one will be well versed on the topic.

Seligman, M. E. P. (1975). *Helplessness.* San Francisco: W. H. Freeman.

This is a nonacademic account of learned helplessness as related to depression and the stresses of everyday life. The book is tied to research, but the reader does not have to be an experimental psychologist to understand it.

Sherman, C. (1995). Shaping and chaining motor skills. *Track Technique, 130,* 4148-4150.

The author provides a readable introduction to the behavioral concepts of shaping and chaining as applied to track. Shaping is applied to learning to run the hurdles, and chaining is demonstrated for the shot-put event. Also provided are a good review of the literature and pertinent references concerning shaping and chaining in a variety of sports and for developing various motor skills.

Skinner, B. F. (1971). *Beyond freedom and dignity.* New York: Knopf.

Skinner addresses the problems associated with the use of aversive techniques to shape human behavior. He calls into question the wisdom of using negative reinforcement and punishment when other, more desirable procedures are available. Skinner's recommendation is the substitution of positive reinforcement for negative reinforcement and omission training for punishment. This book is a must read for serious students of psychology.

 INFOTRAC COLLEGE EDITION

For additional readings, explore Infotrac College Edition, your online library. Go to:
http://www.infotrac-college.com/wadsworth
Hint: Enter these search terms: classical conditioning, experimental design, learned helplessness, punishment (psychology), reinforcement (psychology).

Anxiety and Arousal

CHAPTER 6

Determinants of Anxiety and Arousal

Effects of Anxiety on Competitive Performance

Effects of Arousal on Competitive Performance: The Inverted-U Hypothesis

The Measurement of Anxiety and Arousal

Summary

Key Terms

Suggested Readings

Things do not appear to be going very well for this baseball player. However, resiliency in coping with sport-related anxiety is the hallmark of the true competitor.

FIGURE 6.1

The Arousal Continuum

(low)   (high)

Stupor – **Elation**

Nearly every person who has been involved with sport recognizes the importance of motivational influences on athletic performance. Coaches and players alike attribute success to "being up" and failure to "being down." Intensity, commitment, and level of alertness often dictate the style and eventual outcome of sport performance.

Despite the obvious advantage of individual readiness and determination, the negative consequences of extreme excitement cannot be ignored. Gearing up for an athletic contest produces benefits up to a point, and then further increases in motivation may actually be counterproductive. To better understand this basic principle, one needs to focus on the subtle but exceedingly important difference between arousal and anxiety. **Arousal,** as it is commonly used, refers to an all-inclusive, broad-ranging continuum of physiological and psychological activation at any point in time (Weinberg & Gould, 1999) (see Figure 6.1). Arousal is not necessarily positive or negative. A person can be equally aroused by winning the lottery or by learning of the death of a parent or best friend. By way of contrast, **anxiety** is generally regarded as a negatively charged emotional state characterized by internal discomfort and nervousness. This is not to say that arousal and anxiety are completely independent states, but anxiety must be dealt with as a special case of activation. For example, the impact of anxiety in sport is apparent from empirical studies of wrestlers who reported they felt excessive stress prior to competition (Gould, Horn, & Spreeman, 1983), as well as numerous anecdotal accounts of the debilitating effects of tension.

In this chapter, we explore the determinants of arousal and anxiety and the effect of these variables on sport performance, and we examine some of the ways in which anxiety is measured in sport psychology.

DETERMINANTS OF ANXIETY AND AROUSAL

I'm scared when I play tennis. I fear failure at every corner, and until I rid myself of that attitude, I know I'll never attain my goals, winning a Wimbledon or U.S. Open.

(Pam Shriver, tennis great of the 1980s)

Because of the diverse nature of anxiety formation, both physiological and psychological causes must be considered. Each of these aspects of anxiety and arousal is important to the ultimate expression of the behavior—biological and mental events work in concert to produce changes in athletic performance. With a better grasp of this interaction, our understanding of how best to manipulate arousal increases.

Neurophysiological Mechanisms

Although a detailed description of the body components that compose the physiological substrate of anxiety is beyond the scope of this book, two of the major contributors can be specified: brain mechanisms and the autonomic nervous system. The cerebral cortex, the hypothalamus, and the reticular formation are the most critical brain structures related to arousal and anxiety (Johnstone, 1996). The **cerebral cortex** is the convoluted mass of neural tissues that make up the outer cov-

---

Arousal an all-inclusive, broad-ranging continuum of physiological and psychological activation at any point in time.
Anxiety a negatively charged emotional state characterized by internal discomfort and nervousness.
Cerebral cortex neural tissues making up the brain's outer covering; cortical activation determines the extent to which an arousal state, such as nervousness, becomes a relevant emotional phenomenon.

FIGURE 6.2

Human Brain Structures Important for Arousal and Anxiety

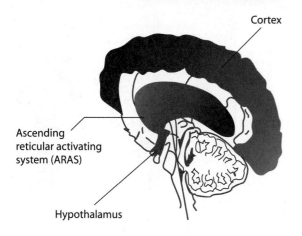

Cortex

Ascending reticular activating system (ARAS)

Hypothalamus

ering of the brain (see Figure 6.2). *Cortex* is a Latin word meaning "bark," and the cerebral cortex indeed has a rough, barklike appearance. Here, higher intellectual functions take place, and cognitive representations of anxiety are fashioned. When gymnasts mull over their nervousness prior to a vault, for instance, cortical activation determines how the arousal state is translated into constructive determination and focus. It is at the cortical level that the experience of anxiety is interpreted as a relevant emotional phenomenon.

The **hypothalamus** is another forebrain structure that has been linked to arousal (see Figure 6.2). When certain areas of the hypothalamus are surgically destroyed, a decrease in the level of behavioral action occurs and sleep often ensues. Conversely, electrical stimulation of discrete regions within the hypothalamic area has been shown to cause increased excitement (Benjamin et al., 1994). Few studies of the role of the hypothalamus in sport behavior have been conducted. However, the fact that this structure is very much involved in the control of the endocrine system (which prepares the body for both physiologically and psychologically demanding circumstances) seems to suggest that hypothalamic functions are vital determinants of athletic proficiency.

The **reticular formation** is a complex system of ascending and descending pathways that extend from lower brain regions throughout the midbrain area (see Figure 6.2). Although the precise function of the reticular formation is difficult to pinpoint, the available evidence suggests that it serves as an alarm system to awaken the rest of the brain (Cotman & McGaugh, 1980). When an incoming signal arrives at the level of the reticular formation, cortical centers are alerted that new information is on the way. Appropriately, when the reticular formation functions efficiently, new sensory information is processed attentively and arousal results (Delcomyn, 1998). But when the reticular formation is rendered dysfunctional, loss of attention or even sleep occurs. It follows from these observations that the reticular formation should be involved in any situation in which alertness is at a premium, as is the usual case in athletic participation.

The **autonomic nervous system (ANS),** which regulates involuntary action, such as the action of the heart and glands, is also very involved in arousal functions. It is largely through the ANS network of neural fibers that bodily reactions to environmental stressors are expressed. Of special interest is the interaction between the ANS and the **endocrine system,** which consists of glands, such as the adrenals, the thyroid, and the master controlling gland called the pituitary, that release their respective hormonal secretions into the bloodstream in order to prepare the body for emergency situations. The provocation for this hormonal discharge often comes from stress-mediated ANS activation. For example, immediately prior to a critical dive in an aquatics competition, a diver may feel anxious or nervous. Consequently, the ANS excites the adrenals, thus forcing the systemic distribution of the hormone epinephrine. Also known as adrenalin, epinephrine energizes the person and accents physical and

---

Hypothalamus a forebrain structure involved in the control of the endocrine system and thus linked to arousal.

Reticular formation midbrain pathways that seem to serve as an alarm system, alerting the rest of the brain to the arrival of new information.

Autonomic nervous system the part of the nervous system that regulates involuntary action, such as by the heart and glands.

Endocrine system the system that consists of various glands that secrete hormones directly into the bloodstream.

mental readiness. Accordingly, the interplay between the nervous and endocrine systems serves to enhance performance. In this instance anxiety and arousal increase the chances for success by triggering physiological reactions that contribute to positive performance.

Psychological Mechanisms

Although biological processes are central to the experiencing of anxiety, cognitive and behavioral aspects of stress reactivity also bear addressing. How athletes think about threatening events may determine both the level of felt discomfort and the course of action for alleviating the tension. Occasionally, people become so preoccupied with their negative thoughts that they are unable to resolve even routine life events. As a result, their confidence about handling stress diminishes. This process evolves into a negative circular spiral in which one disastrous encounter precipitates yet another, and on it goes. The ultimate outcome of these recurrent episodes is emotional debilitation that may require psychological intervention (see Chapter 7). With respect to coping strategies, it is important to distinguish between two types of anxiety, state and trait.

STATE ANXIETY. Spielberger (1972) defined **state anxiety** as a transitory form of apprehension that varies in intensity, commensurate with the strength of the fear-eliciting cue. When a young girl is required to perform a recital in front of a live audience for the first time, she may exhibit signs of nervousness such as trembling, perspiration, and high distractibility. Similarly, a professional tennis player who has never before played at Wimbledon may be overwhelmed by the crowds at center court, and performance may be adversely affected as a result. In instances such as these when highly skilled performers suffer bouts of anxiety, the emotional reaction is likely to be peculiar to that specific circumstance. The budding young pianist may have no difficulty performing in front of small groups of friends, and

---

State anxiety situational apprehension, the intensity of which varies with the strength of the fear-eliciting cue.
Cognitive state anxiety state anxiety characterized by worry and emotional distress.
Somatic state anxiety state anxiety manifested through physical symptoms such as rapid heartbeat.

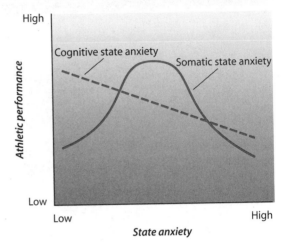

FIGURE 6.3
Effects of State Anxiety on Athletic Performance

surely the experienced professional tennis player feels at ease in more familiar surroundings. This sort of situational apprehension, which occurs in all of us at one time or another, is referred to as state anxiety.

Recent developments in the state anxiety literature focus on the multidimensional nature of the phenomenon. Specifically, it has been proposed that state anxiety actually consists of two subcomponents. **Cognitive state anxiety** is characterized by worry and emotional distress. **Somatic state anxiety** is more physiologically based and is manifested through physical symptoms such as rapid heartbeat, shortness of breath, and clammy hands.

In support of the notion that these two aspects of state anxiety are separate entities and differentially affect performance, studies by Burton (1988) with swimmers and Gould, Petlichkoff, Simons, and Vevera (1987) with pistol shooters are instructive. In both the Burton and the Gould et al. studies, performance was linear and inversely related when cognitive state anxiety was assessed, and performance was quadratically related (first increasing, then decreasing) when the somatic scale was assessed. Figure 6.3 shows a representation of these effects.

Figure 6.3 suggests that as cognitive anxiety increases, performance deteriorates. This means that even a little anxiety is not productive if it is of the cognitive variety. This suggestion flies in the face of conventional coaching wisdom suggesting that a bit of anxiety is good for the athlete. In contrast, if the anxiety is of the somatic variety, the coaching axiom is supported, but only up to an optimal and not always predictable level, which is suggested by the inverted-U relationship. Gould et al. (1987) believe that coaches and athletes need to distinguish between cognitive and somatic anxiety when dealing with anxiety and performance. An awareness of the differences between cognitive and somatic anxiety would help coaches and athletes deal with precompetitive anxiety symptoms. Self-doubt and worry, manifestations of *cognitive* anxiety, are detrimental to performance unless intervention is made by either the athlete or the coach. But optimal levels of *somatic* anxiety need to be encouraged because of its facilitative effects on performance.

In any event, the multidimensional relationship between state anxiety and sport performance is complex. Future work in this area should help clarify the issue.

TRAIT ANXIETY. Trait anxiety is more enduring than state anxiety (Spielberger, 1972). Persons with **trait anxiety** (A-trait persons) project a profile that reflects proneness to nonspecific anxiety. A broad range of life situations is perceived as threatening, and the individual's reaction to such events is commonly disproportionate to the actual fear properties of the stimulus. A person with this type of anxiety disturbance may be haunted by fears of the most trivial phenomena. In its most extreme form, the A-trait condition may render the individual dysfunctional and incapable of responding at all.

EFFECTS OF ANXIETY ON COMPETITIVE PERFORMANCE

What is the relationship between state and trait anxiety and competitive athletic performance? One theoretical formulation that has guided research in this area has been proposed by Martens, Gill, Simon, and Scanlan (1975). The theory posits that state anxiety registered by a person in a competitive situation is determined by the person's perception of the likelihood of success. The prediction is that when sport outcomes are con-

tingent on lower levels of anxiety, athletes who are uncertain about their ability and thus more likely to feel anxious are also more likely to perform poorly. Consistent with this prediction, Gerson and Deshaies (1978) examined batting averages of female varsity softball players participating in a national tournament and found that, indeed, higher precompetitive state anxiety was associated with a lower batting average. Perhaps the expectancy of performing poorly does in fact lead to poor performance.

Supporting evidence also comes from field investigations of golf performance (Weinberg & Genuchi, 1980). Because golf is a game that requires precision, coordination, and the integration of fine muscle movements, it is an especially appropriate venue for studying the effects of anxiety on athletic performance. Excessive levels of anxiety may interfere with the execution of golfing responses that must occur within a relatively narrow range of expertise. Weinberg and Genuchi found that golfers with high A-trait levels were more likely than golfers low in trait anxiety to experience elevated state anxiety on days 1 and 2 of a collegiate tournament. Further, it was shown that high levels of state anxiety and strong expectations of poor performance were related to how well golfers did in the tournament. Better performances were associated with low anxiety, and poorer performances were associated with high anxiety.

Additional evidence favoring the idea that competitive anxiety may be a principal determinant of athletic proficiency comes from studies of youth sport (Passer, 1983). When 316 male youth soccer players were evaluated with respect to competitive trait anxiety, it was discovered that players' performance expectancies, anticipated affective reactions to success–failure, and expectancies of criticism were all influential in determining how well each child played. The greater the anxiety (i.e., the more dismal the expectations for being successful), the less effective were the youth participants, at least as rated by their coaches with respect to overall ability. Moreover, failure seems to be potentially more psychologically devastating for youngsters who demonstrate high competitive trait anxiety. Such children worried

---

Trait anxiety disproportionate fear of a broad range of situations.

more about their performance and were more apprehensive about evaluations by peers than were children who registered low anxiety. The disturbing aspect of these findings, of course, is that a vicious cycle may form. The child who is anxious and expects to perform poorly does so and consequently experiences greater perceived ridicule, which leads to increased apprehensiveness about competitive situations.

Brustad and Weiss (1987) extended Passer's research on patterns of anxiety by examining female and male athletes in several sports. Interestingly, when male baseball players were evaluated, those who registered high on competitive trait anxiety reported lower levels of self-esteem and more frequent worries, in much the same manner as the youth soccer players mentioned earlier. For female softball players, however, no significant relationships were found between levels of competitive trait anxiety and selected cognitive variables. Apparently, competing in sport takes on different meanings for males and females, a point we shall return to in greater detail in subsequent chapters.

Two other variables that seem to be important with respect to modulating the intensity of anxiety reactions in children and adult competitors are skill level and relative time to competition (see Huddleston and Gill, 1981, for a review). In a study of parachutists, Fenz (1985) observed that highly skilled parachutists actually exhibited low levels of anxiety immediately prior to a jump. Conversely, parachutists who were not yet accomplished jumpers experienced extreme levels of anxiety just before making a jump. The studies discussed earlier, beginning with Martens et al. (1975), would lead us to believe that the high anxiety before the jump would prevent the less accomplished parachutists from gaining in skill development. Additional work by Fenz (1985) and Mahoney and Avener (1977) indicates that the discrepancies in skill level that foster differential anxiety reactions in athletes are particularly important as the person nears actual competition. However, Huddleston and Gill (1981) failed to confirm this idea. In their study involving track-and-field competitors, athletes did show greater levels of anxiety as their respective events drew nearer, but this was uniformly true for highly skilled athletes who had reached national qualifying standards during the season and for less skilled competitors.

At odds with the relatively large literature that argues that competitive trait anxiety negatively affects

One of the truly anxious moments in all of sports is in the start of the 100-meter dash.
© 1999 PhotoDisc, Inc.

athletic performance, Scanlan and Passer (1979a, 1979b) have shown that competitive performance expectancies, but not competitive trait anxiety, relate to athletic ability. In a field study involving 10- to 12-year-old female soccer players, intrapersonal factors affecting players' pregame personal performance expectancies were first identified. Subsequently, the impact on each player of winning and losing the game was determined, and the interaction of the game outcome with intrapersonal variables was assessed by determining each player's expectations for a hypothetical rematch, ostensibly with the same opponent. The results showed that winning players held higher expectancies for themselves and for their team than did losing players or players who had tied. Similarly, players with greater ability were higher

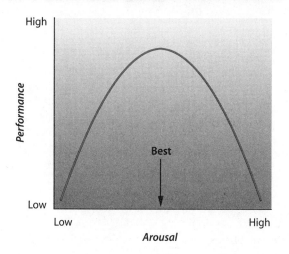

FIGURE 6.4

The Relation Between Arousal and Performance as Expressed by the Inverted-U Hypothesis

High

Performance

Best

Low

Low   High

Arousal

in self-esteem than were their less proficient counterparts. But players high or low in trait anxiety evidenced similar profiles with respect to performance expectancies. Performance expectancies and general attitudes about the self would appear to be more directly related to how well an athlete performs than are the anxiety events they supposedly mediate (Martens, 1974).

EFFECTS OF AROUSAL ON COMPETITIVE PERFORMANCE: THE INVERTED-U HYPOTHESIS

As long ago as 1908, Yerkes and Dodson described the relation between psychological arousal and performance as an inverted U (see Figure 6.4). According to the **inverted-U hypothesis,** there is an optimal level of arousal for every behavior, and values above and below that level are likely to create poor performance. It follows that in some cases intensely motivated performers are going to do well, but in other cases those same individuals are going to have trouble.

As it relates to sport, the inverted-U hypothesis predicts that athletes may become so psychologically

charged that they are unable to perform efficiently (Bunker & Rotella, 1980). Precompetition hype is a familiar tool used by coaches and others, ostensibly to get athletes "ready to play." Implicit in the message of the inverted-U formulation is the notion that such a strategy can be used excessively to the detriment of performance. When a high-jump competitor in track gets so psyched up that he or she ties up in approaching the bar, arousal is translated as anxiety and thus becomes counterproductive. A preferred approach would be to relax so that the appropriate response could be executed. This is not to say that motivational enhancement techniques are valueless, of course, because a moderate level of excitement may be needed to maintain attention and generate the best performance.

Because the basic tenet of the inverted-U hypothesis proposes that the optimum point of arousal varies as a function of task characteristics, different sports are likely to demand different levels of arousal to produce the best results. In a game such as golf in which the fine motor behaviors are at a premium, a lower point of optimal arousal is expected than in, say, wrestling, in which delicate actions are not deemed so critical. Even for the same sport, the nature of the requisite behaviors may dictate different levels of psychological activation for the best results. In football, a highly aroused defensive lineman attempting to sack the opposing team's quarterback is undoubtedly appropriately cast. But a quarterback who must make numerous instantaneous decisions may not be so well served by such high levels of arousal. The essential point here is that the individual demand characteristics of each sport may dictate, to a large extent, the optimal level of arousal necessary for good performance. Figure 6.5 shows this relationship.

Also, as graphically depicted in Figure 6.6, skill level is likely to dictate disparate points of optimal arousal. For a beginning athlete, the inverted-U hypothesis predicts a lower optimum range than would be the case for intermediate or advanced players. When a shooter in a rifle competition is new to the sport, high levels of excitation may exert a diverting influence and make it difficult to sustain a steady aim. For a more experienced

Inverted-U hypothesis a hypothesis about the relation between psychological arousal and performance—namely, that arousal above or below an optimal level is likely to create poor performance.

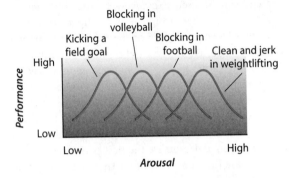

FIGURE 6.5

Optimal Arousal Levels Required for Various Sports

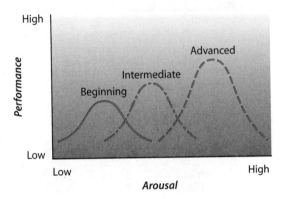

FIGURE 6.6

Application of the Inverted-U Hypothesis to Rifle Shooters of Differing Skill Levels

shooter, however, the same level of arousal may channel attention and contribute positively to the task.

In terms of explicit tests of the validity of the position taken by the inverted-U hypothesis in sport, Martens and Landers (1970) assigned high-, moderate-, or low-anxious male youths to a motor tracking task under conditions of high, moderate, or low stress. Supporting evidence from physiological measures (heart rate, palmar sweating) confirmed the differences in the three different stress conditions. The overall pattern of the results was highly favorable for the inverted-U model. Specifically, it was shown that the moderate stress condition was associated with better motor performance than either the low- or the high-stress condition. Further, Martens and Landers observed that boys with moderate A-trait scores performed better on the tracking task than did boys with either low or high A-trait scores.

Similar findings were reported by Klavora (1977) in a field study that used Canadian male high school basketball players as subjects. Precompetition state anxiety scores for 145 boys were obtained for each player throughout the second half of the season. After the completion of each game, the respective coaches were asked to rate the performance of each basketball player as poor, average, or outstanding. When the performance ratings were presented as a function of the individual athlete's level of state anxiety, a profile emerged that was of the general form of the inverted U: The rating of outstanding was most likely to be achieved when the player reported a moderate level of stress.

When players indicated either low or high levels of state anxiety, they were more likely to perform at a poor or average level.

Sonstroem and Bernardo (1982) wrote one of the more compelling articles related to the validity of the inverted-U hypothesis. In this study involving 30 female university basketball starters from six different teams, an athlete's lowest, median, and highest pregame state anxiety values across three games of a double elimination tournament held at Brown University were used to define low, moderate, or high anxiety levels. Also, the effects of trait anxiety were investigated. Performance during the competition was determined by total points scored and an overall value that was generated for each player by the linear combination of shot percentage, rebounds, points, assists, steals, fouls, and turnovers. As in the previous studies, the performance measures were examined as a function of registered anxiety. The intrasubject results appeared to be remarkably consistent with the inverted-U hypothesis. Not only did total points and game performance (see Figure 6.7) follow a quadratic trend (first increasing, then decreasing) as a function of state anxiety, but this general pattern held across comparisons of low, moderate, and high trait anxiety. Thus, the robustness of the effect of anxiety, and therein arousal, would seem to be substantial.

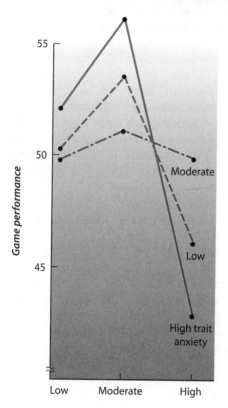

FIGURE 6.7

The Effect of Trait and State Anxiety on Individual Game Performance (Standard Scores)

SOURCE: Sonstroem and Bernardo (1982).

Although there has been considerable support for the viability of the inverted-U relationship between arousal and performance, it is not without its critics. Chief among them is Neiss (1988), who has raised objections on a number of fronts. First, Neiss objects to the inverted U itself because it is descriptive rather than explanatory. Second, he sees the inverted-U hypothesis as immune from falsification. Because of definitional and methodological difficulties inherent in most research involving the construct, almost any results could be interpreted or otherwise explained away as supportive. Thus, the construct is unfalsifiable. Third, Neiss suggests that even if the hypothesis were true, it is trivial in terms of explaining anything but the simplest of performance behaviors. Finally, Neiss believes the inverted-U hypothesis is an impediment to the attainment of a sound understanding of individual differences in performance.

Woodman and Hardy (2001) have noted that a major shortcoming of the inverted-U hypothesis rests with the characterization of arousal as a unidimensional construct that affects performance. As noted at the beginning of this chapter, arousal is distinctly different from anxiety and from other forms of activation that may contribute to athletic performance. For many researchers, this overly simplistic view of a complex relation limits the utility of the inverted-U hypothesis for sport.

Nevertheless, others suggest that the inverted-U hypothesis continues to be of value to the sport psychologist because it offers a way to conceptualize the arousal–performance relationship. Studies supportive of the construct have been numerous, as noted earlier. Studies by Anderson (1990) and Landers and Boutcher (1993) are among those supporting the inverted U. Landers and Boutcher base their case on two points. One is the apparent generalizability of the inverted U across field and experimental situations. The other is similarities in performance patterning for arousal that are induced either psychologically or physically through drugs, exercise, or muscle tension. In a rejoinder to the critical 1988 article by Neiss, Anderson (1990) argues for the credibility of the inverted-U hypothesis. She indicates that Neiss's arguments are unwarranted on both logical and empirical grounds. She sums up her views (and ours) as follows: "Although the ultimate value of the hypothetical, conceptual construct of arousal is as yet unresolved, substantial evidence does favor its pragmatic usefulness and hence its continued investigation" (p. 99). We expect to hear more about the inverted-U hypothesis in future deliberations in sport psychology.

THE MEASUREMENT OF ANXIETY AND AROUSAL

The measurement of arousal has typically been conducted through the assessment of physiological indicators or through psychological self-report questionnaires. Both approaches have been used extensively, and

Alternatives to the Inverted-U Hypothesis

Like most provocative theories, the inverted-U hypothesis has generated considerable interest among sport researchers. An outgrowth of this interest has been the emergence of alternative theories thought to offer better explanations of the arousal–performance relationship. Perhaps the most well developed and researched of these alternatives is the **individualized zones of optimal functioning (IZOF) theory** proposed by the eminent Russian sport psychologist, Yuri Hanin (1978, 1986).

Most of Hanin's work has been conducted with elite European and Asian athletes, and it departs from the inverted-U hypothesis in its emphasis on intraindividual responses to anxiety. IZOF theory does not assume that there is an optimal level of arousal for all athletes, as does the inverted-U hypothesis. Instead, IZOF theory predicts that some athletes will perform best when anxiety is high, others when it is moderate, and others when it is low.

Individualized zones of optimal functioning theory the theory that each athlete has his or her own optimal level of anxiety and his or her own zone of optimal functioning; an alternative to the inverted-U hypothesis.

Essential to Hanin's work has been the State–Trait Anxiety Inventory (STAI; Spielberger, Gorsuch, & Lushene, 1970). Hanin used the STAI to operationalize IZOF theory by finding the athlete's best level of performance, attaching a value derived from the STAI to it, and then adding plus and minus 4 points to that optimal anxiety score, thereby producing a zone of optimal functioning. Recent investigations of IZOF theory have been supportive; these include a study of female volleyball players (Raglin and Morris, 1994), Olympic-caliber soccer players (Hanin & Syrja, 1995), collegiate male and female distance runners (Gould, Tuffey, Hardy, & Lochbaum, 1993), and semi-professional cricketers (Thelwell & Maynard, 1998).

Some criticisms have been leveled at IZOF theory. Perhaps the most telling is criticism of its emphasis on a unidimensional assessment of anxiety, thus neglecting the important distinction between somatic and cognitive anxiety. This omission led Weinberg (1990, p. 235) to ask whether there should be "two separate IZOF's: one for somatic anxiety and one for cognitive anxiety." As has been suggested by Hackfort and Schwenkmezger (1993), future research on IZOF theory should stress the use of multidimensional measures of anxiety. They also suggest that future use of sport-specific measures would be an improvement on the past reliance on the more general STAI for assessing anxiety.

---

strengths and weaknesses are associated with each. Let us first look at the physiological measures.

Physiological Measures

Researchers have used at least six measures of physiological arousal:

1. **Electroencephalography (EEG).** The emphasis is on the assessment of brain waves. Alpha state is

---

Electroencephalography the recording and measuring of brain waves.
Electromyography the recording and measuring of muscle tension.

indicative of relaxation; beta state is suggestive of arousal.

2. *Electrical properties of the skin.* Skin conductance or resistance to an electrical current is measured. Arousal causes increased perspiration, which increases flow of the current.

3. *Heart rate (HR).* Increases in heart rate or changes in patterns may indicate arousal.

4. *Blood pressure.* Increases in blood pressure are associated with arousal.

5. **Electromyography (EMG).** Muscular tension is measured with EMG. Increases in tension are indicative of arousal.

Catastrophe theory, another alternative to the inverted-U hypothesis, has been proposed by L. Hardy (1990). From Hardy's perspective, *somatic* anxiety has the effect on performance predicted by the inverted-U hypothesis, but only in situations in which levels of *cognitive* anxiety are low. Hardy predicts that when both somatic and cognitive anxiety are present at high levels there will be a "catastrophic" decrement in performance. He suggests that his theory has important implications for coaches' pregame "psych-up" strategies and general anxiety management. Many athletes have high levels of both somatic and cognitive anxiety immediately prior to a competition, and Hardy warns that efforts to get them even more psyched-up may be counterproductive (i.e., catastrophic). Also, because somatic and cognitive anxiety coexist at varying levels within all athletes, coaches and sport psychologists should help them learn to control or manage both forms of anxiety.

Another interesting approach to the arousal–performance relationship is **reversal theory** (Kerr, 1985, 1990). Perhaps Kerr's major contribution to our understanding of the anxiety–performance relationship lies in his emphasis on how the individual athlete interprets anxiety, rather than its presence or absence: What may be an extremely unpleasant level of anxiety for one athlete may be quite positive for another; what is important is each individual's interpretation. Kerr also indicates that individual interpretations of anxiety-provoking situations are subject to change or reversal, and it is this shift in the interpretation of anxiety that gives the theory its name. Wann (1997) suggests that optimal performance as predicted from this model would occur when there is consonance between the athlete's preferred state of arousal (e.g., "I would like to feel relaxed") and actual state ("I am relaxed"). Although little in the way of research has been conducted on reversal theory, it does provide some provocative ways of viewing the interaction of anxiety and athletic performance.

SOURCES: Gould, Tuffey, Hardy, & Lochbaum (1993); Hackfort & Schwenkmezger (1993); Hanin (1978, 1986); Hanin & Syrja (1995); Hardy (1990); Kerr (1985, 1990); Raglin & Morris (1994); Spielberger, Gorsuch, & Lushene (1970); Thelwell & Maynard (1998); Wann (1997); Weinberg (1990).

Catastrophe theory the theory that high levels of both somatic and cognitive anxiety will produce a "catastrophic" decrement in performance; an alternative to the inverted-U hypothesis.
Reversal theory a theory that emphasizes the importance of each individual's reversible views of what constitutes his or her preferred levels of anxiety; an alternative to the inverted-U hypothesis.

---

6. *Levels of epinephrine, norepinephrine, or cortisol.* These biochemical agents are released during stress and can be measured in blood or urine samples.

Some advantages are associated with physiological measurement. One is its independence from verbal expressive ability. Another is its utility with almost anyone; the capacity for self–observation is not a prerequisite. Also, almost all of the physiological measures can be used while actual behavior is taking place.

As might be expected, there are also disadvantages to physiological measurement. One is that the measurements do not correlate highly with each other. Another is the difficulty of explaining why athlete A responds to stressful competitive situations with heart-rate changes and athlete B reacts to the same stress conditions with increased gastrointestinal activity. Also, some of the instrumentation necessary to measure physiological changes is expensive and at times cumbersome to use.

On the whole, it appears that there is much to be learned about how best to use physiological measurement in sport psychology. In our view, too little of this kind of research and application is being conducted in sport and exercise settings.

FIGURE 6.8

Items from the Sport Competition Anxiety Test—Form A

1. Competing against others is socially enjoyable.

2. Before I compete I feel uneasy.

3. Before I compete I worry about not performing well.

4. I am a good sportsman when I compete.

5. When I compete I worry about making mistakes.

6. Before I compete I am calm.

7. Setting a goal is important when competing.

8. Before I compete I get a queasy feeling in my stomach.

9. Just before competing I notice my heart beats faster than usual.

10. I like to compete in games that demand considerable physical energy.

11. Before I compete I am relaxed.

12. Before I compete I am nervous.

13. Team sports are more exciting than individual sports.

14. I get nervous wanting to start the game.

15. Before I compete I get uptight.

SOURCE: Martens (1977).

Psychological Measures

The measurement of sport-related anxiety has generated a great deal of interest. Much of this interest has its origins in the work of Spielberger (1972) and his conceptualization of state and trait anxiety, mentioned earlier in this chapter.

THE SPORT COMPETITION ANXIETY TEST. Borrowing from Spielberger's conceptualization, Martens and associates (Martens, 1977; Martens, Vealey, & Burton, 1990) created the **Sport Competition Anxiety Test (SCAT),** a sport-specific measure of anxiety that has been a pivotal part of the assessment of trait anxiety in sport since

its inception. The SCAT purports to measure competitive A-trait anxiety or what Rupnow and Ludwig (1981, p. 35) call "the tendency to perceive competitive situations as threatening and to respond to the situations with apprehension or tension." Martens's original work on the SCAT was driven by four overriding beliefs about anxiety theory and assessment:

1. An awareness that an interactive paradigm for studying personality is superior to trait or situational explanations

2. The recognition that situation-specific instruments are superior to general A-trait measures

3. The distinction between A-trait and A-state in the trait–state theory of anxiety

4. The desirability of developing a conceptual model for studying the social process of competition

The original work on the SCAT was instituted by modifying items from the Manifest Anxiety Scale (Taylor, 1953), the State–Trait Anxiety Inventory for Children (Spielberger, 1973a, 1973b), and the General Anxiety Scales (Sarason, Davidson, Lighthall, Waite, & Ruebush, 1960). After considerable refinement in line with the principles of test development and ethics advocated by the *Standards for Educational and Psychological Tests and Manuals* of the American Psychological Association (1974), two versions of the SCAT emerged. SCAT–C was to be used with children from 10 to 14 years old. SCAT–A was to be used with adults. Each version is made up of 15 brief statements that are answered "hardly ever," "sometimes," or "often." Items from SCAT–A are listed in Figure 6.8.

The SCAT has been an extremely popular assessment tool. It was used in at least 217 studies from its inception through 1990 (Martens, Vealey, & Burton, 1990). Based on results gleaned from available research on the SCAT, Martens and associates reached the following conclusions:

1. Research supports the reliability and concurrent, predictive, and construct validity of the SCAT as a measure of competitive trait anxiety.

2. Gender differences on the SCAT have been equivocal; however, it appears that the feminine gender role is associated with higher levels of A-trait and the masculine gender role is linked to lower competitive A-trait anxiety.

Sport Competition Anxiety Test a test intended to measure trait anxiety related to sport.

3. A-trait research looking at the age of the competitors is also equivocal; there is a trend, however, suggesting that younger athletes are lower in A-trait than older ones. In all likelihood, this difference is attributable to the increased emphasis on winning placed on youth sport participants as a function of age.

4. High-competitive A-trait individuals perceive greater threat in competitive situations than do low-competitive A-trait individuals.

5. Situational and interpersonal factors mediate the influence of competitive A-state anxiety on perception of threat.

6. The SCAT is a significant predictor of A-state anxiety.

7. The SCAT is a much better predictor of competitive A-state in athletes than are coaches. The same is generally true with regard to A-trait, though the effects are mediated by coaching experience and the gender of the athletes. Older coaches are better predictors of competitive anxiety than are younger ones, and competitive anxiety is easier to predict in female athletes.

8. The SCAT has been used as an assessment device in a variety of international settings, with translations into French, German, Japanese, Russian, and Spanish (Spain). It also has been used extensively in English-speaking countries such as Australia, Canada, and Great Britain.

THE COMPETITIVE STATE ANXIETY INVENTORY. A relative of the SCAT is another creation by Martens (1977), the **Competitive State Anxiety Inventory (CSAI).** Like the SCAT, the CSAI was adapted from Spielberger's earlier work in an effort to have a measure of state anxiety related specifically to sport.

Representative research with the CSAI includes that of Gruber and Beauchamp (1979) and Martens, Burton, Rivkin, and Simon (1980). The first study concluded that the CSAI is most suitable for repeated assessment of athletes in competitive settings. Gruber and Beauchamp based their conclusions on results obtained from 12 University of Kentucky female basketball players who were administered the CSAI on 14 separate occasions. Researchers concluded that the CSAI has high internal consistency, that state anxiety was significantly reduced after wins but remained high after losses, and that state anxiety varied from game to game depending on the game's importance. In the second study, Martens et al. (1980) reported reliability coefficients ranging between .76 and .97 for both the children and the adult forms. Concurrent validity was established by correlating the CSAI with Thayer's Activation–Deactivation Adjective Checklist (AD–ACL) (1967). Similarities were such that confidence in the CSAI as a measure of sport-related state anxiety was enhanced.

COMPETITIVE STATE ANXIETY INVENTORY–2. Unlike the original CSAI, which is a unidimensional measure of state anxiety associated with competition, the **Competitive State Anxiety Inventory–2 (CSAI–2)** (Martens, Burton, Vealey, Bump, & Smith, 1990) is a multidimensional scale that assesses somatic anxiety, cognitive anxiety, and state self-confidence. The CSAI–2 is composed of 27 items (three 9-item subscales) arranged in a 4-point Likert scale format. These items are listed in Figure 6.9.

A considerable literature supports the use of the CSAI–2 (see LeUnes, 2002), but some have questioned the structural validity of the scale. For instance, a factor analytic study by Lane, Sewell, Terry, Bartram, and Nesti (1999) revealed that none of the fit indices from the original CSAI–2 reached acceptable thresholds. This led Lane et al. to conclude that "Investigators of anxiety responses to sport competition cannot have faith in data obtained using the CSAI–2 until further validation studies have been completed and possible refinements to the inventory have been made" (p. 511). Yet, despite such admonitions, on the whole it seems that the CSAI–2 is a valuable assessment tool in sport, and its continued popularity is expected.

OTHER ANXIETY ASSESSMENT SCALES. Three other scales bear mentioning. The **Cognitive–Somatic Anxiety Questionnaire (CSAQ),** created by Schwartz,

---

Competitive State Anxiety Inventory a test intended to measure state anxiety related to sport.
Competitive State Anxiety Inventory–2 a test intended to measure somatic anxiety, cognitive anxiety, and state self-confidence related to sport.
Cognitive–Somatic Anxiety Questionnaire a test intended to measure both cognitive and somatic anxiety.

FIGURE 6.9

Items from the Competitive State Anxiety Inventory–2

1. I am concerned about this competition.

2. I feel nervous.

3. I feel at ease.

4. I have self-doubts.

5. I feel jittery.

6. I feel comfortable.

7. I am concerned that I may not do as well in this competition as I should.

8. My body feels tense.

9. I am self-confident.

10. I am concerned about losing.

11. I feel tense in my stomach.

12. I feel secure.

13. I am concerned about choking under pressure.

14. My body feels relaxed.

15. I'm confident I can meet the challenge.

16. I'm concerned about performing poorly.

17. My heart is racing.

18. I'm confident about performing well.

19. I'm concerned about reaching my goal.

20. I feel my stomach sinking.

21. I feel mentally relaxed.

22. I'm concerned that others will be disappointed with my performance.

23. My hands are clammy.

24. I'm confident because I mentally picture myself reaching my goal.

25. I'm concerned that I won't be able to concentrate.

26. My body feels tight.

27. I'm confident of coming through under pressure.

SOURCE: Martens, Burton, Vealey, Bump, & Smith (1990).

Davidson, and Goleman (1978), is composed of 14 items and, as the test title indicates, measures both cognitive and somatic anxiety. The **Sport Anxiety Scale (SAS),** created by Smith, Smoll, and Schutz (1990), is a variant of the cognitive–somatic theme: The cognitive scale is subdivided into two components, worry and concentration disruption. Smith et al. believe that their three-part assessment scheme allows for more precise measurement and more creative and effective treatment approaches for anxiety alleviation.

The **Endler Multidimensional Anxiety Scales (EMAS),** created by Endler, Parker, Bagby, and Cox (1991), is a factorial approach to anxiety assessment that is based on an interactional view of personality—namely, that anxiety is a multiplicative function of the person × situation interaction. The EMAS scales are composed of 60 items that measure trait anxiety and 20 that assess state anxiety. Data analysis by Endler et al. supports the distinction between trait and state anxiety, and the two EMAS scales appear to be psychometrically sound. Endler and his collaborators also make a case for the multidimensionality of both trait and state anxiety, thereby suggesting that each is actually made up of several subcomponents.

Advantages and Disadvantages of Psychological and Physiological Measures

As might be expected, there are advantages and disadvantages to the use of paper-and-pencil self-report psychological assessment devices. Chief among the advantages is ease of administration, scoring, and analysis. However, honesty in responding is always a concern, as is social desirability responding—the tendency

---

Sport Anxiety Scale a test intended to measure somatic anxiety and two components of cognitive anxiety—worry and disruption of concentration.

Endler Multidimensional Anxiety Scales scales intended to measure trait anxiety and to assess state anxiety.

of subjects to respond in image-enhancing ways when in doubt about a proper answer to a test item. This effect is particularly troublesome when an athlete feels that she or he should, for whatever reason, outguess the coach or sport psychologist administering the test. Another disadvantage of questionnaires at times is the need for large samples that enable the researcher to tease out the desired information. Athletic teams in many cases are small, and drawing conclusions based on testing small numbers of subjects is difficult.

There is a trend toward the use of more multidimensional arousal measures as well as measures with a more sport-specific orientation. Both of these advances can only assist the process of psychological assessment.

With regard to physiological measurement, the use of multiple indicators as opposed to a single marker may prove to be a fruitful way to proceed. The trend toward more sophisticated, more portable, and less expensive hardware eventually will facilitate physiological assessment.

SUMMARY

1. *Arousal* is an all-inclusive term referring to physiological and psychological activation. *Anxiety* is generally regarded as a negatively charged emotional state.

2. The cerebral cortex, the hypothalamus, and the reticular formation are brain structures important to the expression of anxiety.

3. State anxiety is a transitory form of apprehension that varies in intensity. Trait anxiety is a more enduring variable that reflects proneness to nonspecific anxiety.

4. According to the inverted-U hypothesis, all behaviors (low or high habits) will increase as arousal increases, up to a point; then further increases in arousal will result in performance deterioration. Research in sport has demonstrated that optimal arousal is not uniform across all sports; the level of arousal necessary to bench-press 350 pounds is very different from the level needed to sink a 6-foot putt.

5. Measurement of anxiety can be done with physiological and psychological assessment procedures.

6. Electroencephalography (EEG), electrical properties of the skin, heart rate, blood pressure, electromyography (EMG), and levels of epinephrine, norepinephrine, and cortisol measurement are all physiological assessment tools. They are independent of verbal expressive ability and do not require the capacity for self-observation, but they correlate with each other poorly, are not universally applicable to all subjects, and the instrumentation required is often expensive and cumbersome to use.

7. The Sport Competition Anxiety Test (SCAT), created by Martens, is the leading measure of A-trait anxiety related to sport competitive situations. Research has demonstrated the utility of the SCAT in assessing trait anxiety.

8. The Competitive State Anxiety Inventory (CSAI) was created in 1977 by Martens as a measure of sport-related state anxiety. It was expanded in 1990 and became known as CSAI–2. CSAI–2 measures two sport-related anxiety states, cognitive and somatic, and assesses sport self-confidence.

9. Three other anxiety assessment tools are the Cognitive–Somatic Anxiety Questionnaire (CSAQ), the Sport Anxiety Scale (SAS), and the Endler Multidimensional Anxiety Scales (EMAS). Their utility as measures of sport-related anxiety is less well demonstrated at this point in comparison with the SCAT and CSAI–2.

10. There are advantages and disadvantages to using paper-and-pencil self-report questionnaires as measures of anxiety. Ease of administration, scoring, and analysis are pluses. Questions of honesty and image-enhancing responses (conscious or subconscious) are drawbacks.

KEY TERMS

anxiety (72)
arousal (72)
autonomic nervous system (73)
catastrophe theory (81)
cerebral cortex (72)
cognitive state anxiety (74)
Cognitive–Somatic Anxiety Questionnaire (CSAQ) (83)

Competitive State Anxiety Inventory (CSAI) (83)
Competitive State Anxiety Inventory–2 (CSAI–2) (83)
electroencephalography (EEG) (80)
electromyography (EMG) (80)
Endler Multidimensional Anxiety Scales (EMAS) (84)
endocrine system (73)
hypothalamus (73)
individualized zones of optimal functioning (IZOF) theory (80)
inverted-U hypothesis (77)
reticular formation (73)
reversal theory (81)
Sport Competition Anxiety Test (SCAT) (82)
somatic state anxiety (74)
Sport Anxiety Scale (SAS) (84)
state anxiety (74)
trait anxiety (75)

SUGGESTED READINGS

Kleine, D. (1990). Anxiety and sport performance: A meta-analysis. *Anxiety Research, 2,* 113–131.

Kleine applied the statistical treatment called meta-analysis to 50 studies published between 1970 and 1988 relating anxiety and sport. The relationship between anxiety and performance was analyzed with regard to age, gender, anxiety inventories used, sport task characteristics, and the inverted-U hypothesis. In the 10 studies reviewed by Kleine that dealt with the inverted-U hypothesis in sport, it was concluded that evidence for the controversial hypothesis was scarce. Kleine was particularly intrigued by the fact that few of the inverted-U studies tested for or discussed the linearity versus curvilinearity issue.

Petruzello, S. J., Landers, D. M., & Salazar, W. (1991). Biofeedback and sport/exercise performance: Applications and limitations. *Behavior Therapy, 22,* 379–392.

The authors provide a good review of biofeedback procedures. They conclude that heart rate (HR), respiration, and slow potentials have been sufficiently researched and demonstrated to be effective tools for enhancing sport performance. In contrast, electromyography (EMG) and electroencephalography (EEG) (alpha feedback procedures) have been investigated the most but have produced the least convincing effects. This article does a good job of introducing the various physiological assessment tools used in sport psychology.

Singer, R. N., Hausenblas, H. A., & Janelle, C. M. (Eds.) (2001). *Handbook of sport psychology.* New York: Wiley.

This edited volume provides comprehensive coverage of important topics in skill acquisition, performance enhancement, motivation, life-span development, and health psychology. It is an excellent reference source and offers extensive coverage of the relevant literature in different areas of sport psychology.

 INFOTRAC COLLEGE EDITION

For additional readings, explore Infotrac College Edition, your online library. Go to:
http://www.infotrac-college.com/wadsworth
Hint: Enter these search terms: biofeedback, biofeedback training, cognitive anxiety, somatic anxiety, sport anxiety, Sport Competition Anxiety Test, State-Trait Anxiety Inventory.

Anxiety Reduction: Classical Conditioning and Operant Learning Applications

CHAPTER 7

Classical Conditioning Techniques
Operant Learning Techniques
Summary
Key Terms
Suggested Readings

Skydivers learn to cope with anxiety through repeated exposure to stressful events in their sport.
© PhotoDisc 2001

In Chapter 6, some of the biological and psychological mechanisms that are believed to be most important in the formation of anxiety were reviewed. In addition, it has been noted that anxiety viewed as a source of arousal can have a positive effect on sport performance. However, there is no dismissing the debilitating impact that intense stress and excessive emotional reactivity can have on performance. In this chapter, several intervention techniques used to alleviate anxiety and stress are discussed. Lowering and controlling anxiety within tolerable limits is one of the most important services the sport psychologist can provide to coaches and athletes.

Some sport competitors approach even the most stressful situations as they would approach a leisurely walk in the park. In a nationally televised college basketball game between two of the top-ranked teams, a point guard was observed yawning during a team time-out with three seconds left in regulation play. With his team leading by only one point, his seemingly relaxed style might seem somewhat unexpected, especially since this same player had to convert two free throws following the time-out to ensure a victory for his team. He promptly made both free throws and withdrew to the locker room without ceremony.

Such examples are commonplace in competitive athletics, but the truth is that a sizable number of highly skilled athletes are prone to bouts of anxiety that prevent them from reaching their full athletic potential. When a player chokes in a game situation, the effect may be to make it more difficult to freely execute when a similar circumstance presents itself. The resultant vicious cycle in which anxiety precludes success and failure increases anxiety may render the athlete dysfunctional unless something is done to break the cycle. In some types of treatment, conditioning techniques can be used that produce the desired behaviors independent of cognitive mediation. In some instances this intervention may take the form of a program designed to increase the player's mental toughness. In this chapter, we approach intervention strategies mainly from the viewpoints of classical conditioning and operant learning.

Extinction the process of repeatedly presenting the conditioned stimulus without the unconditioned stimulus in order to eliminate the conditioned response; the goal is to eliminate anxiety altogether.

Flooding The name given to *extinction* in therapeutic settings.

CLASSICAL CONDITIONING TECHNIQUES

One of the oldest and most widely accepted accounts of the causes of anxiety is predicated on the principles of classical conditioning (Mowrer, 1960). Recall from our discussion in Chapter 5 that classical conditioning involves the continuous association of an unconditioned stimulus (UCS) and a conditioned stimulus (CS). Regarding fear (anxiety) development, a CS is paired with a fear-eliciting UCS; consequently the CS acquires the ability to elicit a fear reaction (conditioned response [CR]). Fear, then, mediates performance by occasioning behaviors that are compatible with or in opposition to selected voluntary behaviors.

What does this conditioned fear mechanism mean in sport? Apprehensiveness is likely to be engendered when an athlete associates poor performance in pressure situations with peer disappointment and ridicule. Especially in sports like rifle shooting and golf, which require fine motor behaviors, the situation (the CS) evokes a level of anxiety (the CR) that in turn produces muscle tightness, nervousness, an unsteady hand, and other reactions that interfere with the synchronous flow of appropriate movements. Here, the fact that anxiety occurs at all runs counter to successful performance. What is necessary is a strategy aimed at disrupting the chain of events that produced the anxiety, or "conditioned fear," as it is more often referred to in the psychology literature.

Extinction

From the perspective of classical conditioning, one of the surest ways to reduce or eliminate conditioned fear is by the process of **extinction**—that is, by repeatedly presenting the eliciting cue (CS) without the threatening event (UCS). Because the CS is inherently neutral, repeated exposure with no UCS pairing will result in a diminution of the response strength of the CR. Simply stated, the CS cannot stand by itself. When this extinction approach is used in the therapeutic realm, it is called **flooding** (see Martin & Pear, 1992, for a more detailed discussion).

Flooding is used extensively in the treatment of phobias such as claustrophobia and fear of flying. A client with claustrophobia may be put in a closet for several hours, after which point the fear of closed places should subside. A client who is afraid of flying might be exposed to a real, aborted jet takeoff and subsequent flight (Serling, 1986). In both cases the idea is that the subject will experience a vivid terror response followed by gradual relaxation in the face of the fear-producing stimulus. Crafts, Schneirla, Robinson, and Gilbert (1938) reported an interesting case of a young woman with a phobic response to traveling in an automobile. The physician in the case ordered her to drive the 50 miles to his office. By the time she arrived, a cure had been effected. Though suffering intensely at first, she gradually calmed down and manifested little fear of riding in or driving the car.

One of the strengths of flooding is that it forces the person being treated to stay in a phobic situation while concurrently demonstrating that catastrophe does not result by doing so. In one study of the efficacy of flooding, Marks, Boulougouris, and Marset (1971) reported that 75% of a group of 70 phobics remained in an improved state four years after treatment by a flooding procedure. Carson, Butcher, and Mineka (1998), however, do issue a caution concerning flooding. They reviewed research on the procedure and concluded it may be useful for some people, neutral for others, and harmful in some cases. Nolen-Hoeksema (1998) issues a similar caveat, suggesting that it is difficult to get clients to agree to its use because of the fright element involved. One example in which flooding proved harmful involved a client with a fear of wide-open places (agoraphobia) who cowered in a cellar rather than face the 90 minutes of exposure dictated by the therapist as part of the treatment regimen (Emmelkamp & Wessels, 1975).

Because flooding is an intervention technique that is likely to provoke extremely high levels of anxiety, especially in the early stages of treatment, it must be used with caution (R. E. Smith, 1984). Consider what a 30- to 40-minute flooding session may involve. As a professional baseball player, you are asked to imagine that you are batting in the bottom of the ninth inning of an important game. Your team is trailing by one run. The count is three balls and one strike. You swing at the next pitch and miss. Fans shout derisive remarks about your character or ancestry, opposing players taunt you, and you sense the impending rejection of your team-

mates if you fail. Again you swing and again you miss the ball, which was actually out of the strike zone. The game is over, you have failed, and you are left alone with only your thoughts of failure.

The purpose of such forced exposure to unkindness and rejection, of course, is to permit the player to encounter such thoughts within the relatively safe confines of the treatment environment. Ultimately, the amount of fear and anxiety that such threatening images trigger should diminish. But in the initial treatment sessions, intense unpleasantness is going to be the rule, and judiciousness on the part of the therapist is essential.

Many psychologists prefer a variant of flooding called **implosive therapy** (Stampfl & Levis, 1967). This technique incorporates many features of flooding but also uses a hierarchy of fear-eliciting images that each person judges to reflect the aspects of his or her personal situation that are most and least threatening. The therapist systematically works through the list, extinguishing the anxiety associated with the items lower in the hierarchy before proceeding to the more tension-laden images. Combining this technique with clinical insights into the psychodynamic undercurrents contributing to the disorder, the practitioner can help alleviate stress symptoms (Foa, Grayson, Steketee, Doppelt, Turner, & Latimer, 1983) without producing undue felt anxiety.

Despite the widespread use of extinction procedures in applied settings in general, few attempts have been made to employ the treatment regimen in sport settings (R. E. Smith, 1984). Many sport psychologists are disinclined to use an approach that is so fundamentally geared to aversive conditioning. Nonetheless, flooding and implosion have on occasion produced real benefits when alternatives have failed to reduce anxiety, and they should be considered part of the many treatment approaches available to the applied sport psychologist.

Counterconditioning

A classical conditioning therapeutic procedure that is favored over extinction approaches, at least by sport

---

Implosive therapy a variant of flooding in which the therapist systematically extinguishes the anxiety produced by a series of fear-eliciting images.

psychologists, is **counterconditioning.** In this approach, there is no attempt to eliminate the anxiety evoked by the CS. Rather, the objective is to use an antagonistic UCS to condition competing responses to the CS that will interfere with the existing CR (i.e., fear, anxiety). If a person is given sufficient retraining, or counterconditioning, the newly acquired conditioned behaviors will replace the older fear reaction as the dominant response tendency. The basic components of counterconditioning are illustrated in Figure 7.1.

The aim of any counterconditioning initiative is redefining the behavioral consequences of anxiety. For the athlete, this means changing habits with respect to how stressful situations are handled. Consider the hypothetical case of Vernon Smith. Vernon is a 19-year-old member of a college track team. He is a talented high jumper with potential for developing into a national-class competitor in his event. However, his performance is erratic, and he especially has trouble in the meets that would bring him the most recognition. Closer inspection reveals that a major factor in Vernon's erratic performance record is stress. He suffers intense feelings of discomfort and tension in big meets. He imagines that he will embarrass himself by stumbling on his approach to the high-jump bar and that thousands of fans will see him as foolish and miscast. To ensure that he does not fall, he approaches the bar tentatively, thus avoiding shame but guaranteeing a substandard jump.

Treatment in this case involves **relaxation training,** which teaches a person to induce a series of physiological reactions that signal relaxation—decreased muscle tone, lowered heart rate, slower respiration, and an increase in the production of alpha brain waves. Once Vernon masters the art of relaxation, he is asked to think about a competitive scene that makes him anxious. When his anxiety is superordinate, Vernon is asked to switch off that scene and focus once again on relaxing. According to the basic tenets of countercon-

ditioning, the relaxation response eventually will bond to the stimulus events that Vernon associated with tension. When Vernon begins a jump at the next meet, thoughts of disaster that previously caused him to tighten up should evoke a relaxation response, thus resulting in an improvement in performance.

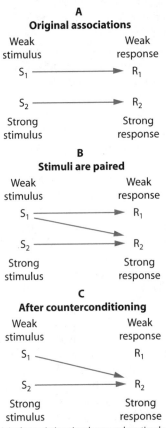

FIGURE 7.1

Basic Model of Counterconditioning Used in Behavior Therapy

NOTE: (A) The original associations involve a weaker stimulus–response connection (e.g., anxiety reaction) and a stronger stimulus–response connection (e.g., relaxation). (B) When the stimuli that cause each response are paired, the stronger of the two responses begins to connect to the weaker stimulus as well as the stronger stimulus. (C) Eventually, the originally weaker response is replaced with the new, stronger response (e.g., the previously anxiety-eliciting stimulus now evokes relaxation). SOURCE: Benjamin, Hopkins, & Nation (1994).

Counterconditioning the use of an antagonistic unconditioned response in order to condition competing responses to the conditioned stimulus that will compete with the existing conditioned response; the goal is to replace the conditioned anxiety reaction with a more tolerable alternative.
Relaxation training training that teaches a person to trigger a series of physiological reactions that signal relaxation.

Successful high jumpers come in all sizes, shapes, and descriptions. Here, a high jumper is successfully clearing the bar using the Fosbury Flop. The technique was popularized by former Olympian, Dick Fosbury.
© Richard Hamilton Smith/CORBIS

An assortment of relaxation techniques such as the one prescribed for Vernon are used in behavioral therapy, and are all variations of the progressive relaxation procedure originated by Edmund Jacobson (1938). **Progressive relaxation** begins with the patient/ athlete lying on his or her back with arms extended to the side. One by one, major muscle groups are first tensed and then slowly relaxed. The goal is to assist in the identification of the various muscle systems within the body and to teach how to discriminate between tense and relaxed muscle conditions. Most of each session is devoted to relaxation training, which is difficult to accomplish. Acquisition may be slow at first, but after a few months athletes learn to evoke a relaxation response in a few seconds (Nideffer, 1981).

A variant of counterconditioning that has been used successfully since the late 1950s is **systematic desensitization** (Wolpe, 1982). A unique feature of

systematic desensitization is the creation of a hierarchy of anxiety-arousing events, with low-anxiety items at the bottom and high-anxiety items at the top. R. E. Smith (1984) provided an example of the use of systematic desensitization in the case of a basketball player suffering from severe anxiety in pressure situations. An anxiety hierarchy for this player would look something like this:

1. Thinking about the fact that the game will be played in two days (low-anxiety scene)

Progressive relaxation a procedure in which a person learns to tense and then relax selected muscle groups in order to evoke a relaxation response.
Systematic desensitization a variant of counterconditioning in which the therapist systematically pairs anxiety-arousing events with relaxation or some other conflicting behavior.

2. Getting up from bed in the morning and thinking of the game that evening (moderately low-anxiety scene)

3. Walking around the arena where the game will be played (moderate-anxiety scene)

4. Sitting in the locker room before the game as your coach tells you how important this game is (moderately high-anxiety scene)

5. Preparing to shoot a free throw, with one second left in the championship game and your team trailing by one point (high-anxiety scene)

Treatment involves taking the lowest-anxiety scene and pairing it with relaxation, or an amusing idea, or some other conflicting behavior. Once the scene no longer evokes an anxiety response, and instead produces the desired counterconditioned behavior, treatment proceeds to the next step (moderately low-anxiety scene) and the process is repeated. Eventually, the client works upward through the list until completion. The advantage of such a strategy is that it makes counterconditioning easier to achieve. Because items low on the list necessarily evoke minimal fear and anxiety, they are more susceptible to disruption. In classical conditioning terms this means that the strength of the CR is likely to be low relative to the strength of the competing response elicited by the antagonistic UCS (see Figure 7.1). Further attempts at counterconditioning involving more intense fear-eliciting cues will be accomplished with greater ease because of gains made in the hierarchy.

To summarize the application of classical conditioning techniques in treating sport-related anxiety problems, one approach (extinction) is intended to eliminate anxiety altogether, whereas the other (counterconditioning) aims to replace the conditioned anxiety reaction with a more tolerable alternative. Regardless of the type of classical conditioning approach, athletic performance should be facilitated.

OPERANT LEARNING TECHNIQUES

In this section, we discuss the relevance of operant conditioning procedures for treating anxiety reactions that actively interfere with the execution of sport-related behaviors.

Reinforced Practice

The procedure known as **reinforced practice** (refer to Leitenberg, 1976) has been used with success in remediating anxiety-based problems. The central theme underlying this approach is that reinforcement can be administered in such a fashion that responses incompatible with the typical anxiety responses are strengthened. For example, a person who has a fear of snakes may be asked to approach a snake that has been placed in a glass enclosure at a set distance across the room. Numbered strips of tape on the floor denote steps toward the snake. A-1 may correspond to the first step, A-2 to the second, and so on up to, say, A-14, which is at the point of the enclosure containing the snake. Each time the client moves closer to the snake, he or she is rewarded with verbal praise or some tangible evidence of the therapist's approval. A record is kept of the patient's progress so that it can be seen visually. By learning to approach a feared object, the patient overcomes the phobic response.

Although this procedure has not been applied in any systematic way in the sport setting, it could easily be adapted to fit such demands. Rewarding mental approaches to a crowded area, for instance, could prove to be helpful for a gymnast who fears a large audience. Perhaps reinforcing a young baseball player who fears a pitched baseball for making increasingly more aggressive swings may decrease anxiety and thus increase hitting performance. Reinforced practice is a potentially rich area for research, and systematic data using reinforced practice within sport settings is needed.

Biofeedback Training

Perhaps the most common intervention technique based on principles of operant learning is **biofeedback training,** known in the experimental psychol-

---

Reinforced practice an operant technique that rewards a person for overcoming anxiety by approaching the anxiety-producing stimulus step-by-step.

Biofeedback training an operant technique that uses reward outcomes (feedback) to control autonomic responses such as heart rate and muscle tension.

ogy literature as "instrumental conditioning of autonomic behaviors." The origins of biofeedback are traceable to Neal Miller at Rockefeller University (Dicara, 1970; Miller, 1978). Challenging a long-standing axiom that operant techniques were restricted to voluntary and somatically controlled responses, Miller and several colleagues observed under a variety of experimental conditions that animals could learn to control their heart rate, digestive functions, salivary output, and other internal processes. Before long, practitioners were employing reinforcement techniques to treat everything from migraine headaches to excessive muscle tension caused by stress.

The popularity of biofeedback is due in part to the fact that the various procedures are by-products of sound experimental procedures in psychology and psychophysiology. Other factors contributing to its popularity include its applicability to conditions in which there is no medical or surgical alternative, its freedom from demonstrable toxicity, and its cost-effectiveness compared with many other alternative treatment modalities (Sandweiss, 1985). Sandweiss and Wolf (1985) point out three areas of application in sport have been identified by a task force supported by the Biofeedback Society of America: stress management for athletes, rehabilitation of sport-related injuries, and performance enhancement training.

Often biofeedback training involves the use of some sort of electronic gadgetry that signals the athlete that an appropriate autonomic response has occurred, and the use of such devices has produced convincing results. DeWitt (1979), for example, used an electromyographic (EMG) procedure to assist football players in learning to relax. The EMG is equipped with electrodes that can be placed at selected muscle sites. The electrodes sense the degree of muscle contraction, and the information appears on a display screen in either digital or analog form. By focusing on the feedback from the screen, players were able to decrease muscle tension and preempt excessive arousal.

In a subsequent investigation, DeWitt (1980) combined biofeedback with cognitive therapy in an attempt to lower stress among university football and basketball players. The cognitive approaches focused on restructuring thought processes and self-perceptions as well as mental rehearsal and were used in conjunction with EMG feedback. DeWitt was able to lower

A recreational distance runner is training for her first marathon. As part of her training regimen, she is using biofeedback as a relaxation technique.
© Arnold LeUnes

muscle tension in 6 football and 12 basketball players. Moreover, the players' performance efficiency improved dramatically following the intervention. Although this study provides no clues as to the differential contribution of cognitive therapy versus biofeedback training, it does provide evidence that performance increases parallel reductions in muscle tension brought about by biofeedback sessions.

Elsewhere, Daniels and Landers (1981) conducted a study of a squad of shooters who were given either auditory biofeedback training or verbal feedback about performance. The findings revealed that the shooters who were given biofeedback training improved more and maintained greater consistency than their counterparts who received only verbal statements concerning their performance. Additionally, the biofeedback groups exhibited greater control over the autonomic pattern, thus validating the relationship between internal autonomic control and enhanced shooting performance.

Despite forceful arguments by sport psychologists concerning the efficacy of using biofeedback procedures (Bird & Cripe, 1986; Zaichkowsky & Fuchs, 1989), only a few experimental demonstrations of the potency of the approach have occurred in actual field studies. Although supporting evidence from well-controlled laboratory investigations of motor performance are somewhat helpful (French, 1978), what is needed are experiments with athletes who are actually attempting to function under extreme stress.

A report by Dworkin and Miller (1986) called into question the appropriateness of biofeedback as an intervention technique in the broad field of psychology. These researchers ran more than 2,000 animals in a series of experiments designed to replicate some of the seminal biofeedback studies. The result was an inability to reproduce the earlier effects. The unreliability of biofeedback with human behavior disorders has also been an item for fiery debate.

Certain treatment specialists seem more likely than others to obtain positive results. Although differing techniques and varying levels of expertise may contribute to the discrepant results to some degree, it is most remarkable that many therapists never report improvement for their clients on a consistent basis. This has triggered a steady flow of accusations about fraudulent reporting and embellished accounts of biofeedback successes.

This controversy is no less heated in sport psychology. In a report on enhancing performance, quite negative conclusions were drawn with regard to the efficacy of biofeedback training techniques (Druckman & Swets, 1987). It seems that when a positive result is obtained, it often turns out to be a fluke. Because performance enhancement is noted in one instance or in one individual does not mean that it will be seen again in the same situation or with other performers. The lack of reliability from case to case has caused many treatment specialists to turn away from biofeedback and pursue other behavioral change strategies.

Still, it likely would be a mistake to presume that biofeedback is contraindicated as a sport performance intervention. Biofeedback training does appear to be useful in certain situations. Perhaps it would be a better idea to drop the indictment and focus on defining the boundaries and conditions under which the technique actually does work.

To this end, Zaichkowsky and Fuchs (1989) suggest that biofeedback alone or in conjunction with other self-control methods can be useful in teaching athletes how to self-regulate their psychophysiological stress responses and related athletic performance. They are quick to point out, however, that there are problems to be addressed. One has to do with the fact that elite athletes have not been the subject of biofeedback studies. Another shortcoming is that seldom has the mastery of self-regulation actually been demonstrated in the available research. Inferences made from small samples of athletes represent yet another difficulty. Zaichkowsky and Fuchs call this forcing of small numbers of subjects into traditional research designs that traditionally call for large sample sizes the "shoe-horn" procedure. As an antidote to the last criticism, they suggest the use of single-subject experimental designs with proper monitoring and careful follow-up. Finally, designers of future studies should be careful in specifying whether they are studying a particular biofeedback procedure or a combination of intervention modalities.

In this connection, Lehrer, Carr, Sargunaraj, and Woolfolk (1993) conducted a comprehensive review of the literature on stress management techniques to include certain types of biofeedback. It is their contention that cognitively oriented stress management techniques have specific cognitive effects, that specific autonomic effects arise from autonomically oriented methods, and that specific muscular effects are generated from muscularly oriented methods. Their conclusion that electromyographic (EMG) biofeedback is very effective with particular muscle groups may point to its efficacy as a biofeedback instrument of choice in a number of sport situations.

SUMMARY

1. Interventions in sport psychology have arisen from the three models of learning discussed in Chapter 5: classical conditioning, operant learning, and cognitive learning (the latter to be discussed in the next chapter).

2. Two classical conditioning approaches that have been used successfully in sport psychology are

flooding and implosive therapy. In each, extinction is used for anxiety alleviation.

3. A classical conditioning procedure favored over extinction is counterconditioning, in which the goal is to replace anxiety reactions to fear-eliciting cues with calmness, thus improving athletic performance. Systematic desensitization is a variant of counterconditioning.

4. Reinforced practice is an intervention based on the principles of operant conditioning. The idea is to reward a person for systematic approaches to dealing with an anxiety-provoking stimulus.

5. Biofeedback training, a popular method for treating anxiety, is based on operant conditioning principles. Ostensibly, this approach uses reward outcomes (feedback) to change the probabilities of autonomic behaviors. Much research remains to be done to clarify the utility of the various biofeedback procedures.

KEY TERMS

biofeedback training (93)
counterconditioning (90)
extinction (89)
flooding (89)
implosive therapy (89)
progressive relaxation (91)
reinforced practice (92)
relaxation training (91)
systematic desensitization (92)

SUGGESTED READINGS

Curry, L. A., Snyder, C. R., Cook, D. L., Ruby, B. C., & Rehm, M. (1997). Role of hope in academic and sport achievement. *Journal of Personality and Social Psychology, 73,* 1257–1267.
This article is a first in the study of hope in sport achievement. Using state and trait hope scales with college students, the authors found that male and female athletes were higher in trait hope than nonathletes. Also, trait hope was predictive of athletic outcome in female cross-country athletes. Overall, athletes scored higher in hope than nonathletes.

Field, T. M. (1998). Massage therapy effects. *American Psychologist, 53,* 1270–1281.
Though considered an alternative therapy in modern medicine, massage therapy has its advocates within sport circles. The procedure can be traced at least as far back as 400 B.C. to Hippocrates, who defined medicine as the "art of rubbing." Massage therapy became popular in the United States in 1940 and has achieved considerable popularity in Europe and Asia. Several studies of the use of sport massage are reported in this article; the results are equivocal. The author also provides a good discussion of research shortcomings related to the use of massage therapy.

 ## INFOTRAC COLLEGE EDITION

For additional readings, explore Infotrac College Edition, your online library. Go to:
http://www.infotrac-college.com/wadsworth
Hint: Enter these search terms: behavior modification, behavior modification techniques, habit breaking, research in behavior modification.

Anxiety Reduction: Cognitive Learning Techniques

CHAPTER 8

Imagery

Visuomotor Behavioral Rehearsal

Stress Inoculation Training

Cognitive Control

Hypnosis

Yoga, Zen, and Transcendental Meditation

Psych-Up Strategies

Summary

Key Terms

Suggested Readings

Successful free throw shooting utilizes imagery, deep breathing, and relaxation.

© Dimitri Iundt/CORBIS

Cognitive intervention strategies are designed to restructure the way athletes think about themselves in the context of competitive situations. Attitudes, impressions, and other covert mental operations not only are acknowledged to exist but often are the targets of change. Thus, rather than attempting to modify behavior, cognitive approaches aim to alter thought processes (cognition) and thereby influence responding (athletic performance).

In this chapter, some of the more contemporary approaches to anxiety reduction and performance enhancement that have arisen from cognitive psychology are discussed. One of the most often used of these procedures is imagery. Athletes are encouraged to use the technique, but its effects vary greatly from athlete to athlete. Some athletes swear by it; others find it ineffective. Research and practice with imagery is complicated by the fact that the concept is elusive and measurement devices are few in number and of dubious validity.

Akin to imagery is visuomotor behavioral rehearsal (VMBR), a technique proposed and promoted by Richard Suinn. As the name implies, it incorporates the best that imagery provides but emphasizes the behavioral practice component. A number of applied sport psychologists with a general interest in imagery have used VMBR with their athletes.

Another of the cognitive techniques that has received fairly wide acceptance is stress inoculation training (SIT), a procedure popularized by Donald Meichenbaum. SIT incorporates relaxation training, adaptive self-statements, and the reinforcement of desirable behavior. This procedure has seen its successes in practice with athletes.

Currently, a great deal of emphasis is placed on the power of positive thinking, and M. E. P. Seligman's work on learned optimism is important in this regard. To state things concisely, optimistic athletes perform better than athletes with a less positive outlook on life and sport. Closely related to this emphasis on positive thinking are the cognitive control techniques of thought stoppage, countering, and reframing. Each of

these techniques stresses replacing negative thoughts with positive and adaptive self-statements. Many applied sport psychologists today use these positive approaches to assist athletes in improving their sport performance.

Other approaches to be considered in the present discussion are hypnosis, transcendental meditation, yoga, and Zen. Each has its devotees, but they are not used as commonly among sport psychologists as are the others examined in this chapter. Finally, ten psych-up strategies that can be used to facilitate performance will be explored.

IMAGERY

Cognitive learning theory and its applications have gained visibility in the sport environment in recent years. One outgrowth of the cognitive approach is what Mahoney (1977) has called the cognitive skills of self-efficacy, arousal regulation, attentional focus, and imagery. The focus here is on imagery; the other skills Mahoney mentions are discussed elsewhere in the book.

According to Solso (1991, p. 267), **imagery** refers to "a mental representation of a nonpresent object or event." Moran (1993) adds to this definition by suggesting that the representation need not be confined to the visual sense but may actually be manifested in "hearing a favorite tune" or "feeling a favorite fabric." However, as has been pointed out by Porter and Foster (1988), the focus of attention within sport psychology has largely centered on the visual representation—the mind's eye.

Imagery has been of scientific interest for over 100 years. John Hughlings Jackson (1874/1932) wrote that "the posterior lobe of the right side of the brain . . . is the chief seat of the revival of images." Tippett (1992) identified case studies dating back to the nineteenth century in which imagery was used. In the realm of motor behavior and athletics, Woolfolk, Parrish, and Murphy in 1985 indicated that imagery has been used for almost 60 years (given that their study is over 15 years old now, we can make this figure 75-plus years).

A number of sports have been used in studies of imagery: baseball (Gough, 1989), basketball (Predebon & Docker, 1992), golf (Martin & Hall, 1995), ice skating (Rodgers, Hall, & Buckholz, 1991), racquetball (Gray, 1990), softball (Hecker & Kaczor, 1988), and

---

Imagery a mental preparation strategy in which the athlete concentrates on images in his or her mind's eye in an effort to counteract anxiety and enhance performance.

track and field (Machlus & O'Brien, 1988). Even earlier success stories involving the use of imagery in sport were reported for downhill skiing (Suinn, 1972), gymnastics (Meyers, Schleser, Cooke, & Cuvillier, 1979), volleyball (Schick, 1970), and weightlifting (Hale, 1982). These studies (and a number of anecdotal reports) make it clear that imagery has utility with a broad range of athletic events. A couple of anecdotes from professional athletes underscore this point.

Wayne Gretzky, considered by many to be the greatest hockey player of all time, was quoted as follows: "We taped a lot of famous pictures on the locker-room door; Bobby Orr, Potvin, Beliveau, all holding the Stanley Cup. We'd stand back and look at them and envision ourselves doing it. I really believe if you visualize yourself doing something, you can make that image come true. . . . I must have rehearsed it ten thousand times. And when it came true it was like an electric jolt went up my spine" (quoted in Orlick, 1998, p. 67). The great professional golfer Jack Nicklaus offered up a similar sentiment: "never hit a shot, not even in practice, without having a very sharp, in-focus picture of it in my head" (Nicklaus, 1974, p. 79).

The sport of basketball is one in which imagery training has been studied on a fairly frequent basis. For example, Meyers and Schleser (1980) used imagery training to facilitate the shooting performance of a collegiate player. In actual game situations, the following coping strategies were used: Coping statements patterned after Meichenbaum's stress inoculation training (SIT), to be discussed shortly, were implemented so that self-reinforcement statements were given for successful performances. At the same time, attributions for failure were shifted from self-blame to effort requirements and external demands, and so forth. Also, the athlete was taught to relax and imagine successful scenes in increasingly problematic situations. The player imagined failure situations as well but was able to cope with the setbacks during the imagery session. Those procedures were practiced first in a noncompetitive environment; later, pregame warm-ups and breaks in the action during the game itself were brought into play. Figure 8.1 shows the points-per-game record for the basketball player before the cognitive intervention (pretreatment) and after the intervention (posttreatment). Clearly, significant improvement in performance did occur. Though not reflected in Figure 8.1,

the field goal shooting percentage increased from 42 to almost 66%.

Other studies of imagery and basketball have focused on improving free throw performance. Wrisberg and Anshel (1989) noted that mental imagery played a substantial role in assisting young boys at a summer camp to improve free throw performance. Predebon and Docker (1992) obtained similar results in a study of 30 male basketball players in Australia. Their imagery-plus-preshot-routine group significantly outperformed physical-routine and no-routine groups, thus lending credibility to the use of both imagery and a preshot routine in helping athletes to deal with distracting performance influences.

Not all research is so supportive of the use of imagery. For example, Lamirand and Rainey (1994) failed to find any benefits from imagery in their study of 18 female collegiate basketball players. Lamirand and Rainey did go on to point out that small sample size and unforeseen methodological problems (i.e., failure to assess imagery ability of the subjects, lack of individualized interventions, no actual check on whether subjects were using imagery) were problematic in their study, thus lowering confidence in their results.

In a related study that also failed to demonstrate the efficacy of imagery training, this time with field goal shooting, Weinberg, Hankes, and Jackson (1991) introduced college students ($n = 105$) to a basketball task requiring a 15-foot perimeter shot. After a performance baseline was established, the subjects were randomly assigned to a 1-minute, 5-minute, or 10-minute mental preparation condition not restricted to, but most commonly employing, imagery. Also, the subjects were again randomly assigned to groups in which mental practice took place either prior to or after a 3-minute physical practice preparatory to the actual shooting task. Thus, six experimental conditions were created by combining the amount of mental preparation (1 minute, 5 minutes, 10 minutes) and the temporal location of the mental practice (either before or after a 3-minute physical practice period prior to performing the basketball shooting task). In addition, there was a seventh group that engaged in physical practice only. Interestingly, none of the mental-practice groups shot field goals any better than the practice-only group. Also, the temporal location of the mental practice was of no significance. Perhaps the

FIGURE 8.1

Points per Game for the 28-Game Season Before (Pretreatment) and After (Posttreatment) the Introduction of a Cognitive Intervention Technique

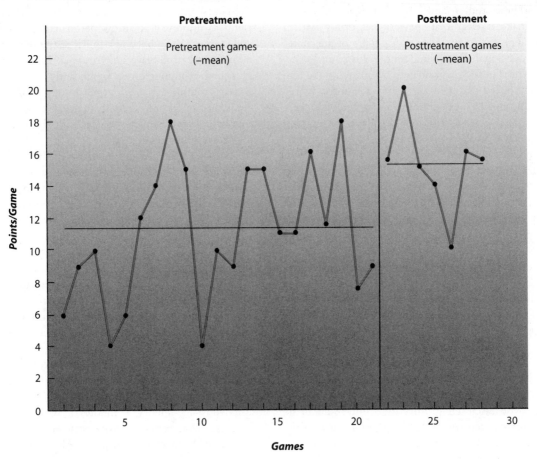

SOURCE: Meyers & Schleser (1980).

failure to achieve the desired results in this case is best explained by the fact that, in addition to imagery, the subjects were allowed to use other mental preparation strategies of their choice (i.e., attentional focus, relaxation, positive self-statements, preparatory arousal), thus diluting the imagery effects. This confounding of effects noted in the Weinberg et al. study is not unusual in the imagery literature because of the obvious overlap among the various mental preparation techniques. In this regard, Kendall, Hrycaiko, Martin, and Kendall

(1990) reported difficulties in teasing out the relative merits of imagery versus relaxation and positive self-talk in explaining the success of their intervention package in improving the defensive play of four female collegiate basketball players.

The merits and drawbacks of the use of imagery notwithstanding, there are a number of things to consider if the technique is to become more viable when used with athletic populations. Although elite performers and beginners may practice imagery training to some extent, few athletes develop this skill to the maximum degree possible. The fact that imagery is often self-taught is part of the problem. A second limiting factor is that imagery is often practiced in an unsystematic fashion. The effectiveness of sport imagery training would undoubtedly be enhanced if greater attention were directed toward the conditions that facilitate its cultivation. Among such considerations are the following:

1. *Vividness and controllability.* Images are likely to prove most beneficial when they are colorful, realistic, and involve the appropriate emotions. Actual recollections of previous performances provide an anchor for building comparisons, and they make images seem more believable. It may well be that vividness and controllability themselves are mediated by having the athletes use images that are personally meaningful to them, as has been noted by Hecker and Kaczor (1988) and Lee (1990). When a downhill skier, for example, really sees the slope, accompanying mental executions are more likely to result in real improvements in performance. Also, it is essential that the skier be able to control the presence of the image. For the image to be of use, the athlete must be able to turn it on or off. In certain instances, images may be distracting and divert the athlete's focus from the task at hand. Knowing when to use imagery is as important as knowing how to use it.

2. *Practice.* Imagery is a skill that can be learned. Although some people are better at visualizing events than others, everyone can improve mental functioning along these lines. This is not to say, however, that improvement is likely to come about quickly or without effort. Often, athletes must mentally practice for months before they become proficient in the use of imagery. Short sessions with long rest intervals are preferable, but repetition is an absolute necessity. Weinberg (1982) has advocated that imagery practice sessions should last at least a minute but never exceed five minutes. Suinn (1997) takes a more liberal view, and suggests that the main consideration is to avoid fatigue irrespective of time considerations.

3. *Attitude and expectation.* Imagery is most likely to benefit individuals who believe in its effectiveness

(Harris & Robinson, 1986). It is not likely to be of much value to an athlete who rejects the approach as nontraditional. If used at all, imagery should be approached with the awareness that it is a legitimate skill and, like any other skill, can be learned over time and with appropriate effort.

4. *Previous experience.* Some evidence shows that experienced athletes may gain more from imagery training than do beginners (Howe, 1991). The reason for this is not clear, but it may be due to the fact that the more experienced athlete has achieved a high level of mastery of physical skills and thus is able to allocate more attention to mental processes.

5. *Relaxed attention.* A relaxed state of mind during imagery training seems to facilitate its effectiveness (Lanning & Hisanga, 1983). A person who is fully relaxed is better able to attend to the integrity of an image, with resultant greater vividness and control.

6. *Internal versus external imagery.* The notion that an internal perspective results in more favorable images than an external one has been suggested by Suinn (1993, 1997) and by Whelan, Mahoney, and Meyers (1991). A meta-analysis of studies that was conducted by Hinshaw (1991) has lent support to the superiority of an internal frame of reference over an external one. To see someone else perform successfully is one thing; it is something else again to visualize oneself accomplishing the same feat. If for no other reason, the image should likely include oneself because it is desirable for the image to overlap as much as possible with the real-life situation.

7. *Age.* It is generally believed that older athletes are better able to use imagery, and not totally because of differences in levels of skill development. However, there is evidence that young children can in fact become good imagers. Partington (1990) demonstrated that young figure skaters ages 10 to 14 years and gymnasts ages 8 to 11 years could profit substantially from mental imagery training. Similarly, Li-Wei, Qi-Wei, Orlick, and Zitzelsberger (1992) reported significantly greater improvements in table tennis skills among Chinese children ages 7 to 10 who were trained in imagery when they were compared with nontrained

controls. Although studies such as these are encouraging and suggestive of a need for more research, it still appears that there is a positive correlation between experience and ability to profit from imagery training.

VISUOMOTOR BEHAVIORAL REHEARSAL

A modification of the basic imagery procedure has been developed by Richard Suinn (Suinn, 1972) and is called **visuomotor behavioral rehearsal (VMBR).** According to Suinn (1993, p. 499), VMBR is "a covert activity whereby a person experiences sensory-motor sensations that reintegrate reality experiences, and which include neuromuscular, physiological, and emotional involvement." The three major components to VMBR are relaxation training, imagery rehearsal of athletic performance under stress, and rehearsal of skill performance in a simulated environment. Unlike typical mental practice sessions, in which the athlete is told, "Close your eyes and try to imagine yourself making the free throw," VMBR seeks a full-dimensional experiencing of the event:

> Be there in the situation again . . . so that you are aware of where you are, what's around you, who's with you . . . you're actually on the basketball court again, the home court . . . score is all tied, the crowd is especially vocal, you have the ball in your hands, breathing a little shallowly . . . you bounce it several times, can feel the firmness . . . take a deep breath to settle down . . . focus on the rim. (Suinn, 1993, p. 449)

Suinn stresses that VMBR is not a random process but rather is a well-controlled copy of experience and is subject to conscious control. He further suggests that the strength of VMBR over many other mental practice strategies lies in the fact that it is a standardized training method that is subject to replication in both practice and research.

Visuomotor behavioral rehearsal a mental preparation strategy in which the athlete utilizes relaxation training, imagery, and skill practice in a simulated environment.

VMBR has in fact been the subject of considerable investigation. It is also efficacious because it does not require the sort of specialized training associated with the use of imagery through hypnosis. Perhaps the first study involving VMBR was reported by Titley (1976), who employed the technique with a football field goal specialist who had recently missed three crucial kicks from 35 yards, all of which resulted in a loss or tie. After VMBR, the kicker became more consistent and ended up setting 14 records at his university as well as kicking a personal best and NCAA record 63-yard field goal. Similar kinds of success using VMBR have been reported for baseball (Gough, 1989), bowling, tennis, and basketball (Winning Associates, 1978), golf (Kirschenbaum & Bale, 1980), and pistol shooting (Hall & Hardy, 1991).

VMBR has been used often in basketball. One such study was conducted by Schleser, Meyers, and Montgomery (1980) with two females. One player was a center with problems in shooting free throws and the other a forward who needed assistance with field goal shooting. Using VMBR in conjunction with several other mental skills techniques, Schleser et al. were able to improve the accuracy of free throw shooting by the center from a baseline of 41% to 55%; however, no perceptible change in field goal accuracy was noted. In the case of the forward, her field goal percentage rose from 37% to 52%, while her free throw average remained stable at 68%. Such real-life research with athletes is fraught with difficulties; in this case, the center withdrew from the treatment program after the 7-game baseline and the 13-game intervention period. The remaining 11 games offered a rare opportunity, methodologically, to follow up on the center. Interestingly, she hit 29% of her free throws during that time frame. Perhaps the performance decrement is not an indictment of the training but rather may be attributable to a motivational deficit for the last part of the basketball season. Regardless of interpretation, Suinn (1993) suggests that data such as these underscore the fact that compliance with mental training is as important as compliance with physical training in athletics.

In another basketball study, Hall and Erffmeyer (1983) employed VMBR in an attempt to enhance free throw accuracy among 10 highly skilled members of a collegiate team. In their research (rare in that an actual control manipulation was conducted), one group was trained to relax and visualize free throw shooting. A second group, the VMBR condition, viewed a color videotape of a model female basketball player executing 10 consecutive free throws with perfect form. Because the model was viewed from behind, it was relatively easy for each player to imagine that she was the person actually shooting the foul shots. After the tape, those in the VMBR condition were asked to close their eyes and again view themselves as shooting without errors in form or consequence.

The findings from this interesting study indicated that watching a tape had a more dramatic impact on performance than did imagery training alone (see Figure 8.2). Specifically, the percentage of successful free throws rose sharply during a five-day posttest period following treatment for the VMBR athletes, but there was no corresponding increase among the players who merely learned to relax and use visual imagery (no modeling). These findings are of special significance because they suggest that the use of more traditional imagery techniques may be of limited value. Certainly such approaches may be at a disadvantage without some sort of visual aid that may assist in the process of image formation.

On a slightly different tack, Lohr and Scogin (1998) were able to demonstrate the efficacy of VMBR with collegiate athletes in seven different sports. Lohr and her colleague created a VMBR manual in workbook form with the idea that athletes could learn to self-administer the procedure without external guidance. Thirty-six athletes took part in the self-administered VMBR program, and their respective sport performance standards were used to determine the success of the training. In brief, there was significant improvement in performance among the VMBR-trained athletes and a concomitant decrease in their competitive trait anxiety as measured by the Sport Competition Anxiety Test (SCAT). In addition to having potential anxiety-reducing qualities, Suinn (1996) suggests, imagery rehearsal can also contribute to character building through improving self-confidence and optimism.

To this point, we have reviewed a body of literature that is generally supportive of the utility of imagery and VMBR. It appears that imagery-based mental training techniques can be of use to sport psychologists, coaches, and athletes.

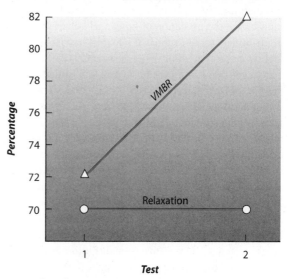

FIGURE 8.2

A Comparison of Pretest and Posttest Foul-Shooting Percentages of a Group Experiencing Visuomotor Behavioral Rehearsal (VMBR) and a Group Experiencing Intervention or Relaxation Training Only

SOURCE: Hall & Erffmeyer (1983).

STRESS INOCULATION TRAINING

Another cognitive strategy that is grounded in an empirical treatment framework is **stress inoculation training (SIT)** (Meichenbaum, 1977). With SIT the person learns an appropriate coping strategy for dealing with the negative emotional fallout that comes with anxiety. Typically, a person experiencing debilitating stress tends to become preoccupied with self-deprecating personal statements and the feeling that his or her defense systems are collapsing. In SIT, the idea is to get the person to recognize the pattern of events

Stress inoculation training an anxiety reduction technique in which causes and dynamics of anxiety are delineated, followed by practice of appropriate coping behaviors.

that characterizes the anxiety attack and then to use those cues as signals for making adaptive coping responses. Such a treatment is designed to redirect anxiety-mediated behavior and to formally teach the person how to deal with stress.

Three stages constitute this retraining process: (1) The experiential conditions of anxiety are clarified for the person so that the onset of the negative mood state is easier to identify. (2) Reeducation regarding the determinants and dynamics of the stress response is introduced. (3) Appropriate coping behaviors are practiced and then used when stress occurs. Thus, stress becomes a stimulus for the execution of functional behavior.

In athletics, the original SIT format has been altered slightly to produce four stages (see Long, 1980). In the first stage, discussions are held with the athlete about the particular feelings experienced in certain competitive situations. The therapist explains the impact that such feelings are likely to have on performance. The intent is to increase the athlete's awareness of the unique physical and mental reactions that constitute stress. In the second stage, the educational program is intensified, and the athlete learns about basic self-regulation skills. It is not unusual for the therapist to administer the training in small groups. During the third stage, specific coping behaviors are prescribed, and the athlete is taught to transform negative thoughts into positive self-statements. For instance, a player might be instructed to react to an image of choking under pressure with a private statement such as "Just relax, you can do this. You have handled tougher situations, so just get on with doing your job." By converting negative self-statements to positive verbal commands, the individual develops a more practical coping style. Finally, during the fourth stage, the athlete has a chance to implement the newly learned strategies in graded stress situations. Successively more threatening competitive circumstances are presented imaginally, and actual athletic situations are instated. Even though the athlete's fears may not subside, the reaction to them may be dramatically altered.

Learned optimism a positive outlook that results from focusing on the positive aspects of a situation and avoiding negative self-talk.
Cognitive control maintaining control of one's thoughts in order to keep a positive, confident perspective and avoid negative self-talk.

Another application of SIT to athletics has been highlighted in a series of reports by Mace and several colleagues. Mace, Eastman, and Carroll (1987) demonstrated the efficacy of SIT in remediating the performance difficulties of a male Olympic gymnast with concentration problems brought on by debilitating anxiety and self-doubt. Twelve SIT sessions involving relaxation, visualization, and positive self-statements were employed, and highly positive performance in subsequent gymnastics meets was reported. Other successes using SIT have been noted with squash players (Mace & Carroll, 1986).

Meichenbaum (1993), in a 20-year update of the use of SIT, cited a dozen studies from 1980 through 1989 in which SIT was successfully employed with athletes from at least five different sports. He further cited over 200 additional studies of the utility of using SIT in a variety of school, medical, psychiatric, and other treatment settings.

Meichenbaum sees SIT with athletes as an educational program in self-control, not as a form of psychotherapy. R. E. Smith (1984) refers to the kinds of things that are part and parcel of SIT as "mental toughness training." Perhaps the best way of summarizing what SIT has to offer is provided in the following quote from Meichenbaum (1993, p. 374):

> SIT is not a panacea. Rather, it is a heuristically useful way to conceptualize both the distress that individuals experience and the factors leading to their behavioral change, as well as a clinically sensitive way to provide help on both treatment and a preventative basis. SIT does not represent a treatment formula that can be routinely applied to distressed individuals; it is a set of general guiding principles and accompanying clinical procedures that must be individually tailored to the unique characteristics of each case.

COGNITIVE CONTROL

Successful athletes, in comparison with their less successful peers, are invariably more positive and confident in perspective. Part of this optimism, or what Seligman (1991) calls **learned optimism,** is attained because of **cognitive control:** The athletes are in control of their thought patterns relating to performance. Bunker, Williams, and Zinsser (1993, p. 225) sum up this proposition as follows:

> Confident athletes think they can and they do. They never give up. They typically are characterized by positive self-talk, images, and dreams. They imagine themselves winning and being successful. They say positive things to themselves and never minimize their abilities. They focus on successfully mastering a task rather than worrying about performing poorly or the negative consequences of failure. This predisposition to keep one's mind on the positive aspects of one's life and sport performance, even in the face of setbacks and disappointments, is a hallmark of the successful athlete. . . ." Critical to this control of cognitions is self-talk, and the key is always to accentuate the positive and not to engage in self-defeating cognitions. At the same time, it is important to realistically assess successful and unsuccessful behaviors without engaging in counterproductive cognitive attacks on the self. It is okay to be critical of poor performance, say on a classroom test: "I did poorly because I failed to grasp some key concepts" is far preferable to judgmental thoughts like "I am obviously stupid or I would have done better on the test." Again, keep the emphasis on assessing behavior and stay away from self-condemnation; nothing constructive comes from such ideation.

It is important to realize that too much thinking can be detrimental to performance. For example, when New York Yankee baseball legend Yogi Berra was asked what he thought about when he was preparing to hit, he replied: "I don't think 'cause I can't think and hit at the same time." As sport behaviors become more ingrained, less and less cognitive activity is necessary. Take learning to play golf as an example. Many youngsters pick up the game rather readily just by playing a lot. Their play has a huge trial-and-error component to it, but seldom do these young people think about what they are doing; they simply do it and work out most of their errors through continuous play. In contrast, the adult who is learning the game fixates on having the best equipment, the right grip, a correct stance, lining up properly to the hole, having a preshot routine, waggles, practice swings, and a never-ending list of other things to think and worry about. Many of these concerns detract from rather than enhance performance, as any beginning adult player (popularly known as a "duffer") can testify.

There are times when things go wrong and self-defeating thoughts arise. At this point, positive self-talk is essential. Self-talk can be used for a variety of purposes, including skill acquisition, changing bad habits, helping maintain proper focus, creating a positive mood state, change existing negative affective states, controlling effort, and building self-efficacy (Bunker et al., 1993).

Three effective methods of controlling self-talk are thought stoppage, countering, and reframing. **Thought stoppage** is the elimination of counterproductive or distracting thoughts through the use of mental or physical triggers such as uttering or thinking the word "Stop" or snapping the fingers. Each athlete should choose the trigger that is the least intrusive and most useful. Bunker and Owen (1985) report an interesting application of thought stoppage with a golfer. The golfer in question was asked to put 100 paper clips into her pocket prior to playing a round of golf. As a negative thought entered her mind, she was asked to move a clip to her back pocket. At the end of 18 holes, her score was 84 and she had moved 87 clips from one pocket to the other. This accumulation of paper clips served as a powerful reminder of how many negative thoughts she engaged in during that round of golf and how thought stoppage might help in dealing with the problem.

Countering is the use of an internal dialogue filled with facts and reasons to refute negative thinking. When using countering, it is important to remember that merely challenging negative thoughts may not be enough to build confidence. What may be needed to change a negative mind-set that has some basis in fact and thus is firmly entrenched are countering facts and additional information or data. Table 8.1 provides examples of self-defeating thoughts and useful counters.

Thought stoppage a cognitive control technique in which negative thoughts are eliminated through the use of mental or physical triggers.

Countering a cognitive control technique that uses an internal dialogue filled with facts and reasons to refute negative thinking.

TABLE 8.1

Examples of Countering

Self-Defeating Thoughts	Countering Thoughts
I can't hit her. She throws too hard!	Yes, she throws hard, but I have worked hard on my hitting. I will hit!
I wish they wouldn't use the off-colored balls, as I have trouble picking them up off of the bat.	The color of the ball is the same for everyone, and I'm as good as anyone else.
I can't stand the pressure. I'm about to choke, and that is a sign of failure.	Really, the pressure is a sign that I care about the match, and is merely a prelude to a peak performance.
If I walk this batter, things will go downhill from there.	Just throw strikes like you almost always do. And they won't banish you to Rwanda or Siberia if you fail.
The officiating stinks and we can't win because of it.	Officials almost never make a difference in who wins, so I'll play my best and let the chips fall where they may.
She runs the 100 in 11.3 seconds. There's no way I can beat her.	I am well trained in the sprints, and she's probably exaggerating her times anyway.
If I try to catch the fly and miss, I will look silly.	Looking silly is irrelevant; I owe it to myself and my teammates to give it my best effort.

Reframing is the creation of alternative frames of reference or ways of looking at the world (Gauron, 1984). Essentially, the athlete takes negative thoughts and reframes them as positives. Performance decrements, such as slumps in hitting in baseball or poor shooting in basketball, can be mentally reframed as periods of rest and renewed dedication. Feelings of arousal prior to competition, such as "butterflies" before the opening kickoff in football, can be reframed as excitement and readiness as opposed to tension and anxiety. As Bunker et al. (1993) have pointed out, reframing does not bring into play any denial or downplaying of expressed concerns. It does, however, involve a conscious awareness of reality and subsequent cognitive restatement that can be used to the advantage of the athlete.

HYPNOSIS

Hypnosis has been defined as an altered state of consciousness characterized by increased receptiveness to suggestion. Despite past associations with circus sideshows and suggestions of voodoo, mysticism, and deception, hypnosis has a lengthy history that suggests that it can be an effective method for controlling anxiety (Rotella, 1985). Scientists, however, remain uncertain about how this procedure benefits patients suffering from anxiety-related problems. Some argue that hypnosis is nothing more than increased concentration, whereas others maintain that trance states alleviate basic psychic conflicts. Some have proposed that the true strength of hypnosis rests with the athlete's belief that the procedure in fact works (Rotella, 1985).

Cox, Qiu, and Liu (1993) summarized the available literature from the 1960s and 1970s and arrived at the following conclusions about the hypnosis–performance relationship:

1. General arousal techniques are more useful than hypnotic suggestions in enhancing muscular strength and endurance.

2. Negative suggestions invariably work to the detriment of the performer.

3. Hypnosis can help a successful athlete, but it cannot make a good performer out of a poor one.

4. Hypnotizing athletes may do more harm than good. It is important for hypnosis to be conducted by a highly trained practitioner.

Reframing a cognitive control technique in which the athlete takes negative thoughts and reframes them as positives.
Hypnosis an altered state of consciousness characterized by increased receptiveness to suggestion.

A football player psychs up before a game by meditating. A well-known study gives credence to the idea that athletes who are permitted to use their own methods for getting themselves psyched up show dramatic increases in performance.
© Brian Drake/SportsChrome USA

5. The deeper a hypnotic trance is, the more likely it is that the trance will work to improve performance.

6. Dependency problems involving the therapist can be circumvented by the use of autohypnosis.

Along these same lines, Schwartz (1993) suggests that hypnosis is more effective with individuals who are high in hypnotic susceptibility, whereas EMG feedback and progressive muscle relaxation are more efficacious in subjects low in hypnotic susceptibility. Hypnotic susceptibility appears to be associated with responsiveness to treatment using most relaxation techniques, but this responsiveness apparently does not extend to biofeedback. Schwartz goes on to suggest that hypnosis and biofeedback may be incompatible when paired together, something that can be answered with further research.

How much use is made of hypnosis in sport psychology? The answer is not much, apparently. For example, Suinn (1985), in a summary of services provided by 11 different sport psychologists at the 1984 Olympic Games, found no mention of hypnosis. Similarly, Gould, Tammen, Murphy, and May (1989) surveyed the services provided by 44 sport psychologists at the 1988 Olympic Games and found that hypnosis was the least commonly used of 13 available intervention procedures. Certainly, these kinds of reports fly in the face of an image entertained in some circles that sport psychologists go around hypnotizing athletes for a living.

YOGA, ZEN, AND TRANSCENDENTAL MEDITATION

Potentially useful procedures for teaching relaxation are meditation procedures such as yoga, zen, and transcendental meditation. These approaches teach people to relax by excluding distracting images from consciousness. By narrowing the concentration of the individual and restricting the range of mental activity, task requirements are afforded greater attention and performance is thus enhanced, at least theoretically. Yet, because the precise goals of intervention are not clearly delineated in such procedures, gauging psychological growth during treatment is difficult at best. Consequently, it is nearly impossible to determine parallels between performance changes and mental progress. Not surprisingly, there has been a scarcity of empirical studies concerning the role that transcendental meditation and other meditation procedures may play in the alleviation of anxiety in athletes.

PSYCH-UP STRATEGIES

None of the intervention strategies that have their genesis in the traditions of cognitive psychology has received more attention, at least among coaches and athletes, than the so-called psych-up techniques. The term *psyching-up* is often used in athletics by coaches, players, and others as the time of the competition approaches. A player who "psychs up" achieves a state of mental readiness that supposedly affords her or him a psychological advantage.

Zaichkowsky and Takenaka (1993) have identified many different **psych-up strategies** that an athlete or coach might use to create a state of arousal or energy. Among these activities are the following:

1. *Breathing.* Increasing breathing rhythm and imagining with each breath that energy is being taken in may increase physiological activation or arousal.

2. *Stretching and exercise.* Stretching and exercise can assist performance by warming up the body and increasing blood flow.

3. *Precompetitive workout.* This workout may take place from 4 to 10 hours before an actual compe-

tition and should serve to reduce anxiety and optimize arousal. One example is an ice hockey player who goes for a mid-morning skate prior to an evening match.

4. *Music and video.* These modalities undoubtedly are powerful energizers, but their effects are probably quite different. Some athletes may react positively to music; others may react in quite an opposite fashion, thus generating an adverse reaction that is not conducive to optimum performance. Little research has been conducted to date on this potentially interesting relationship.

5. *Energizing imagery.* Having athletes focus on a machine image such as a locomotive or an animal image such as a tiger or greyhound can produce powerful states of arousal. The all-time-great heavyweight boxer Muhammed Ali's oft-quoted "Float like a butterfly, Sting like a bee" is an example of the use of **energizing imagery.**

6. *Energizing verbal cues.* Energizing verbal cues such as "explode," "charge," "blast," or "power" might be used effectively, particularly when used in conjunction with energizing imagery.

7. *Drawing energy from the environment.* For some athletes, environmental cues such as the venue itself, the sun, the flag, or the National Anthem are energizing sources.

8. *Transferring energy.* Many athletes, with practice, can learn to transform negative thoughts or emotions into positive action. The key is in practice, and rehearsal of these kinds of transfers from the negative to the positive is required.

9. *Pep talks.* Pep talks are a double-edged sword. They can be great energizers, but they also may fall flat. Long-winded, inane, trite, and oft-repeated pep talks are likely to have either no effect or a negative effect and should be avoided. So should performances such as the following, pulled from the memory of your senior author and epitomizing the worst in pregame pep talks by coaches: throwing chairs through dressing-room windows, biting the heads off frogs, wringing the neck of a chicken and letting the bird flop hopelessly around the dressing room, throwing a football helmet across the dressing room and watching

---

Psych-up strategy a strategy intended to create a state of energy and mental readiness that gives a competitor a psychological advantage.
Energizing imagery a psych-up strategy in which the athlete concentrates on images of powerful machines or animals.

it bounce around wildly, castrating bulls in front of the football team (yes, this actually happened at a major university in the South), writing down past mistakes and burying them in a coffin, and challenging the prowess or masculinity of male athletes (we don't challenge the femininity of female athletes, do we?).

10. *Bulletin boards.* How many times have coaches tried to energize their athletes with admonitions, slogans, favorite sayings, old saws, and newspaper barbs from the upcoming opponents? This strategy is probably effective within limits, although no research has been conducted to date to shed light on this issue. (For a brief list of coaching slogans, see Chapter 23.)

The validity of psych-up strategies in enhancing athletic performance in field settings has been documented by Caudill, Weinberg, and Jackson (1983), using collegiate sprinters and hurdlers from a varsity track team. Performance was evaluated for each of 16 competitors under both psych-up and control conditions. Their findings revealed that significantly better performance occurred for 15 of the 16 athletes under the psych-up as opposed to the control condition. Apparently, the increased effectiveness associated with psyching-up, assumed by the coaches and players, is genuine and amenable to confirmation.

SUMMARY

1. Cognitive learning theory focuses on the study of mental aspects of behavior, and provides a framework for the creation of a number of anxiety reduction and performance enhancement techniques in sport.

2. One of the more popular cognitive learning procedures is mental imagery, which is essentially a mental representation of a nonpresent object or event. Interest has been expressed in imagery for over 100 years. The imagery research in sport psychology has been equivocal, but the technique remains popular among athletes and sport psychologists.

3. A variant of imagery is visuomotor behavioral rehearsal (VMBR). VMBR combines relaxation

training, imagery, and behavioral practice under simulated conditions, and is also a popular procedure for reducing anxiety and improving performance.

4. Another popular technique is stress inoculation training (SIT). SIT involves the redirection of anxiety through the identification and clarification of causal factors combined with practicing of coping behaviors that are germane to reducing sport-related anxiety.

5. Cognitive control techniques include thought stoppage, countering, and reframing, all of which place heavy emphasis on positive self-talk in the face of competitive stress. These techniques have all been used successfully in helping athletes manage competitive anxiety.

6. A well-known but controversial cognitive procedure is hypnosis, used successfully with a variety of athletes. However, hypnosis does not work in every case and is not a big part of the repertoire of the sport psychologist.

7. Yoga, zen, and transcendental meditation are other well-known relaxation procedures, though their efficacy with athletes has not been demonstrated at this time.

8. Psych-up is a term used often in sport, and refers to a variety of techniques designed to increase arousal prior to competition. Included here are such things as stretching, listening to music, and increasing arousal through pep talks.

KEY TERMS

cognitive control (104)
countering (105)
energizing imagery (108)
hypnosis (106)
imagery (98)
learned optimism (104)
psych-up strategy (108)
reframing (106)
stress inoculation training (SIT) (103)
thought stoppage (105)
visuomotor behavioral rehearsal (VMBR) (102)

SUGGESTED READINGS

Lehrer, P. M., & Woolfolk, R. L. (Eds.). (1993). *Principles and practice of stress management* (2nd ed.). New York: Guilford.

Readings on progressive relaxation, yoga, meditation, hypnosis, autogenic training, biofeedback, cognitive approaches to stress management, stress inoculation training, music therapy, aerobic exercise, and pharmacology are included in this book. Comparisons are drawn concerning the effectiveness of these various stress management techniques. This is an invaluable reader for the sport psychologist or student interested in stress management.

Moran, A. (1993). Conceptual and methodological issues in the measurement of mental imagery skills in athletes. *Journal of Sport Behavior, 16,* 156–170.

Moran discusses one of the problematic issues related to imagery: its assessment. Mental imagery tests discussed here include the Questionnaire on Mental Imagery (QMI), a brief version of the QMI (SQMI), the Vividness of Mental Imagery Questionnaire (VMIQ), and the Movement Imagery Questionnaire (MIQ). The SQMI, the VMIQ, and the MIQ do have some history of usage in sport psychology. Moran suggests that the ephemeral nature of imagery itself contributes to validity problems with the various scales, thus creating a confused picture concerning mental imagery assessment.

Prapavessis, H., Grove, J. R., McNair, P. J., & Cable, N. T. (1992). Self-regulation training, state anxiety, and sport performance: A psychophysiological case study. *The Sport Psychologist, 6,* 213–229.

The efficacy of a cognitive–behavioral intervention with a small bore rifle shooter was assessed in this report. Relaxation, thought stoppage, refocusing, positive coping statements, and biofeedback were all used with the shooter. Decreases in cognitive and somatic anxiety and increases in confidence were noted over the course of the treatment regimen. Based on their results, the authors suggest that their multi-method approach is most likely to be successful with other athletes if (1) the athlete believes the anxiety is in fact detrimental to performance, (2) the procedures are individually tailored and administered individually rather than in group settings, and (3) the training sessions are carried out in a training environment that closely approximates the one in which the athlete must actually perform.

Suinn, R. M. (1997). Mental practice in sport psychology: Where have we been, where do we go? *Clinical Psychology: Science and Practice, 4,* 189–207.

Suinn, past president of the American Psychological Association, creator of visuomotor behavioral rehearsal (VMBR), and long-time consultant to elite athletes in downhill skiing, summarizes past research and theory related to mental practice. He also offers suggestions that he thinks will strengthen future research and practice in the area. Suinn suggests that training athletes in the use of imagery, increasing repetitions, using relaxation exercises, defining the content of imagery better, using more relevant details, and alternating physical and mental practice will result in better athletic performance where mental skills are used.

Tippett, L. J. (1992). The generation of visual images: A review of neuropsychological research and theory. *Psychological Bulletin, 112,* 415–432.

This is a high-level literature review for the serious student. Tippett provides a good view of the biological mechanisms thought to influence mental imagery. She concludes her article by stating that imagery is multidimensional as opposed to unidimensional and that mental images appear to be generated in the left side of the brain rather than the right. The latter assertion challenges conventional wisdom about imagery, thus opening up the issue for further scientific investigation.

Vealey, R. S., & Greenleaf, C. A. (2001). Seeing is believing: Understanding and using imagery. In J. M. Williams (Ed.), *Applied sport psychology: Personal growth to peak performance* (4th ed., pp. 247–275). Mountain View, CA: Mayfield.

The authors look at imagery from a number of theoretical perspectives, talk about key considerations in its usage, give guidelines for introducing the procedure to athletes, give insights into its many uses, and cite a number of prominent athletes who have used the technique successfully during their careers in a variety of sports. Also included is a sample imagery script that might be employed by someone using the procedure.

Zinsser, N., Bunker, L., & Williams, J. M. (2001). Cognitive techniques for building confidence and enhancing performance. In J. M. Williams (Ed.), *Applied sport psychology: Personal growth to peak performance* (4th ed., pp. 284–311). Mountain View, CA: Mayfield.

The authors have updated a previous paper and provide a nice discussion of optimism, confidence, self-talk, thought stoppage, countering, and other cognitive techniques for improving sport performance. This is an excellent starting point for the reader interested in these issues.

INFOTRAC COLLEGE EDITION

For additional readings, explore Infotrac College Edition, your online library. Go to: http://www.infotrac-college.com/wadsworth
Hint: Enter these search terms: guided imagery, Hatha yoga, hypnosis, imagery, imagery research, optimism, stress management, transcendental meditation, visuo-motor behavioral rehearsal, Zen Buddhism.

Motivation: Attribution Theory and Need Achievement

CHAPTER 9

What is Motivation?
Attribution Theory
Need for Achievement
Summary
Key Terms
Suggested Readings

Figure skater Michelle Kwan is seen after winning another competition. The need to achieve is extraordinarily high in athletes such as Kwan.

© Duomo/CORBIS

The behavioral perspective, as we noted in previous chapters, has intrigued psychologists for many years. However, interest in what motivates people to behave as they do, separate and apart from the interplay of reinforcement and punishment, has reemerged as a major focus of scientific inquiry. We say *reemerged* to emphasize the fact that theories of motivation were held in some disrepute in the psychology community, partially due to the prevailing fascination with the simplistic stimulus–response (S–R) thinking. However, as it became clear that many human behaviors fall outside a strict S–R interpretation, the role of internal, organismic, or cognitive intervening variables crept back into scientific respectability. Geen, Beatty, and Arkin (1984, p. 11) refer to this reemergence of the acceptability of consciousness and thinking as mediators of behavior as the "cognitive revolution."

In this chapter, motivation is defined, and two major approaches to motivation, attribution theory and need achievement, are discussed.

WHAT IS MOTIVATION?

There is no doubting the fact that motivation is of interest to us all, whether we are laypersons or scientists. At the international level, we are concerned that the average American student is not measuring up favorably with his or her counterpart in Japan or in some of the heavily industrialized countries of western Europe. Fitness experts have been concerned for over 50 years about the lack of fitness in young people in the United States in comparison with European children. The President's Council on Fitness and Sport has expended a great deal of effort (not to mention money) in hopes of altering this disconcerting picture. In the American business sector, management is always trying to find ways to inspire employees to produce more and be happy in the process. As a result, motivational speakers are much in demand. Also, educators at every level are deluged with academic instruction, in-service workshops, and parental pressures designed to make them more effective motivators of young people—a daunting task at times.

In the sports world, coaches are fascinated with motivation; they generate motivational slogans, deliver

motivational talks to their players, and sometimes become motivational speakers for a variety of audiences during the off-season. Roberts (1992) asserts that nowhere is motivation more poorly understood and misused than in sports. He goes on to say that coaches make three fundamentally erroneous assumptions about motivation. Perhaps the biggest is that motivation and arousal are synonymous. Delivering emotional pregame speeches, biting off the heads of chickens or frogs, throwing football helmets against lockers, castrating bulls in front of team members, and heaving chairs through locker-room windows are thought to be motivating by some coaches. In all likelihood, such absurdities will cause arousal, but whether they will motivate is another question. Athletes react in a number of ways to emotional approaches, but not always in the ways coaches would choose. A second misunderstanding is that "positive thinking" is always an answer to motivational problems. Clearly, realistic expectations have to prevail. Some difficulties are not overcome with effort or positive expectations, and the result is often frustration rather than improved performance. Finally, there is a tendency among coaches to view motivation as an innate entity—that is, they believe some people are born with motivation and some are not.

From the point of view of psychologists who make it their work to study motivation, the definition provided by Roberts (1992, p. 5) will serve to give us a better understanding of the construct. According to Roberts, "motivation refers to those personality factors, social variables, and/or cognitions that come into play when a person undertakes a task at which he or she is evaluated, enters into competition with others, or attempts to attain some standard of excellence." Roberts goes on to state that in sports we use language like "try harder," "concentrate," "pay attention," and "practice longer and harder" to describe achievement or motivational behavior.

Now that a framework for understanding **motivation** has been provided by Roberts, it seems appropriate to move on to a discussion of the major motivational models that have been generated to date in the broader field of psychology. We discuss each model in detail and provide sport applications. Two theoretical perspectives have dominated theory and research in psychology: attribution theory (with its many variants) and need achievement. Major reviews of the

---

Motivation psychological and social factors that impel a person to act and affect a person's levels of effort and persistence.

motivational literature by Biddle (1993) and Roberts (1992, 1993) serve as general guides for our discussion.

ATTRIBUTION THEORY

Attribution theory was first advanced by Fritz Heider (1944, 1958). Representing a move toward a more cognitive approach to psychology, **attribution theory** essentially deals with the "naive psychology" of the average person and how he or she interprets behavior. According to Heider, behavioral inferences may be causal attributions or dispositional attributions. **Causal attributions** are inferences about why something happened. For example, a tennis player playing on a doubles team may attribute success to his or her capacity for teamwork. **Dispositional attributions** are inferences about a quality or trait that an individual may possess. The athlete who plays at a level generally above his or her apparent ability is said to be a "winner" or an "overachiever." Both causal and dispositional attributions represent attempts by laypersons and professionals alike to explain their own behavior and the behavior of people around them. By engaging in such attributions, individuals achieve a measure of psychological closure, maintain integrity and self-esteem, and perceive a degree of order in their environment. Such is the function of continuous behavioral attributions.

According to Geen, Beatty, and Arkin (1984), attributions are subject to a number of biases, and these biases must be taken into account when dealing with related theory, research, or application. One source of error is **informational bias.** This comes about as the result of discrepancies between what is known about oneself, what we know about others, and what they know about us. As a result of these discrepancies, misunderstanding of motives and behavior takes place. A second error source is **perceptual bias.** Briefly stated, we cannot perceive ourselves as others perceive us because we cannot observe ourselves. As a result, we are prone to make external as opposed to personal attributions about life events. A final problem is **motivational bias,** and here we are dealing primarily with defensive attributions. Of particular interest has been the notion of the **self-serving attributional bias.** In this instance, the person involved assumes too much personal responsibility for success and too little for fail-

ure. We are all prone, in athletic events, to see victory or success as due to ability or effort and defeat or failure as attributable to poor officiating, faulty equipment, unfavorable weather conditions, and bad luck.

Three models of attribution theory have caught the fancy of psychologists: cognitive, social cognitive, and functional models.

The Cognitive Model

The **cognitive attributional model** is based on an integration by Weiner (1974, 1980) of Heider's work and that of Julian Rotter and his locus-of-control theory (to be discussed later). Weiner's formulation in its simplest form asserts that task outcome (O) in any achievement-related activity is a function of ability (A), effort (E), task difficulty (T), and luck (L):

$$O = f (A, E, T, L)$$

This formula allows for an assessment of success or failure through an evaluation of level of ability, the amount of effort expended, the difficulty of the task at hand, and the strength and direction of luck or chance factors (Weiner, 1980). To put it another way, these **causal antecedents for behavior** suggested by Weiner—that is, ability, effort, task difficulty, and luck—allow for inferences about achievement outcomes.

- *Ability antecedents.* According to Weiner (1980), ability antecedents are primarily drawn from past

---

Attribution theory theory that attempts to explain the underlying causes of a person's behavior.
Causal attribution an inference about why something happened.
Dispositional attribution an inference about a quality or trait that an individual may possess.
Informational bias bias resulting from discrepancies between self-knowledge, our knowledge of others, and others' knowledge of us.
Perceptual bias bias resulting from our inability to see ourselves as others see us.
Motivational bias bias resulting from a more negative set and designed to preserve a positive sense of self.
Self-serving attributional bias bias resulting from attributing success to internal factors (ability, effort) and failure to external events (task difficulty, luck).
Cognitive attributional model the idea that a person's success or failure is a function of ability, effort, task difficulty, and luck.
Causal antecedents for behavior ability, effort, task difficulty, and luck, all of which influence an outcome.

TABLE 9.1

Some Cues Utilized for Inferences Concerning the Causes of Success and Failure

Causes	Cues
Ability	Number of successes, percentage of success, pattern of success, maximal performance, task difficulty
Effort	Outcome, pattern of performance, perceived muscular tension, sweating, persistence at the task, covariation of performance with incentive value of the goal
Task difficulty	Objective task characteristics, social norms
Luck	Objective task characteristics, independence of outcomes, randomness of outcomes, uniqueness of event

SOURCE: Weiner (1980).

experience with success ("I can") or failure ("I cannot"). High academic achievement often leads to an inference that a person is "smart" or is "a brain" just as general speed and agility may lead to the conclusion that the person possessing these qualities is a "good all-around athlete."

■ *Effort antecedents.* The amount of effort put forth in order to achieve is an important variable, although there is not necessarily a one-to-one correspondence between effort and achievement (if there were, the student who studies the most would always make the highest grade). In the athletic realm, the black athlete is often perceived as successful because of natural or innate ability as opposed to hard work.

■ *Task antecedents.* If many succeed at a task, it is seen as easy, whereas the opposite is true when few succeed. For example, running the hurdles or pole vaulting without embarrassing or injuring oneself is seen as a major accomplishment; hence, task difficulty is considered high. The role of consensus information in assessing task difficulty is of paramount importance, although objective factors such as length, complexity, and novelty also enter into the overall process of judging task antecedents.

■ *Luck antecedents.* The flip of the coin, the luck of the draw, and various weather events in outdoor sports are examples of things that are perceived as chance or luck attributions contributing to success

or failure. It is all too easy to conjure up luck attributions to bear on losing efforts. For example, Mann (1974) asked spectators at a football game why the winning team had triumphed over its opponent. Ninety-three percent of the winner's fans cited superior play as the reason for victory, whereas the loser's fans in 50% of the cases cited bad luck as the cause of their team's defeat.

An expanded list of reasons for success and failure related to ability, effort, task difficulty, and luck is presented in Table 9.1.

Carrying this preliminary work a step farther, Weiner expanded beyond the elements of ability, effort, task difficulty, and luck to include stability and locus of causality in what then became a two-dimensional taxonomy, which is represented in Figure 9.1. As the figure shows, ability and effort are internal, and task difficulty and luck are external. At the same time, ability and task difficulty are seen as stable, whereas effort and luck are unstable or changing over time. A number of possible inferences can be drawn. Among them are the following:

1. The low-ability athlete who loses would expect to lose in future events because of his or her perception of ability as stable. Defensiveness could be expected to enter in here, thereby salvaging self-esteem by attributing failure to any of the other three causal antecedents—effort, task difficulty, or luck.

FIGURE 9.1

Dimensions and Elements of Weiner's Original Two-Dimensional Taxonomy (1972)

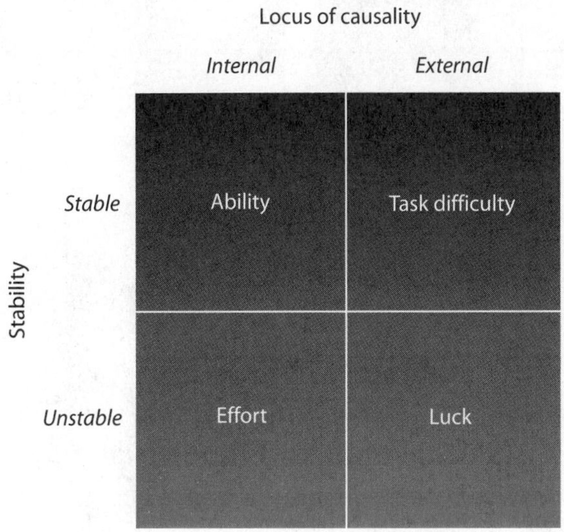

Locus of causality

	Internal	External
Stable	Ability	Task difficulty
Unstable	Effort	Luck

Stability

SOURCE: Biddle (1993).

2. Winning or losing attributable to changeable elements such as effort or luck offers something for both successful and less successful sport participants. The less successful may view more effort as a means of reversing losing. The successful may see that luck can change things in a negative way, so they, too, may expend more effort in order to neutralize chance events. The latter behavior is typified by the coach who pushes his already successful team to even greater effort with exhortations such as these: "The harder I work, the luckier I get," or "I believe in luck and the harder I work, the luckier I get," or "Good luck is what happens when preparation meets opportunity." Although in recent years Weiner expanded his model beyond the two-dimensional framework, that framework is the most influential in terms of creating research in sport psychology (Biddle, 1993).

In an effort to expand Weiner's work, Roberts and Pascuzzi (1979) created a sport-related attributional model (see Figure 9.2). Roberts and Pascuzzi arrived at their formulation through a study conducted at the University of Illinois using 346 male and female undergraduate students. Subjects were asked to respond to eight stimulus items aimed at determining causal attributions for success or failure as a player and as a spectator. Only 45% of the subjects' attributions fell into Weiner's four elements of ability, effort, task difficulty, and luck. On a related note, Frieze (1976), in a study of an academic environment, found that 83% of all attributions were within Weiner's four elements, leading Roberts and Pascuzzi to later conclude that perhaps the two-dimensional model is more applicable to academic than to sport environments.

Although all other factors reported by Roberts and Pascuzzi can be seen in Figure 9.2, it is interesting to note that psychological factors (such as motivation, anxiety, and arousal), practice, and unstable ability factors related to day-by-day performance variations were cited so often by the subjects in the study.

Roberts and Pascuzzi's work is an extension of the Weiner two-dimensional model, but **Weiner's three-dimensional taxonomy** has not gone unnoticed by sport researchers. The three-dimensional taxonomy (Weiner, 1979, 1980) adds to the stability and locus-of-causality dimensions a third component: controllability. Events are seen as either controllable or uncontrollable. Figure 9.3 shows the three-dimensional model.

Consistent with the addition to the earlier models, antecedents such as effort would be viewed as controllable, whereas ability has a strong element of uncontrollability. In terms of ability, effort, task difficulty, and luck—the originally stated causal antecedents of behavior—a perusal of Table 9.2 yields the following generalizations:

1. Individual ability is internal, stable, and uncontrollable.

2. Individual effort is internal, stable or unstable, and controllable.

Weiner's three-dimensional taxonomy a three-part classification of the perceived causes of success and failure: (1) stability, (2) locus of causality (i.e., internal or external), (3) controllability.

FIGURE 9.2

Dimensional Categorization of Sport-Relevant Activities

Locus of control

	Internal	External
Stable	Ability	Coaching
Unstable	Effort Psychological factors Unstable ability Practice	Luck Task difficulty Teamwork Officials

Stability

SOURCE: Roberts & Pascuzzi (1979).

This gymnast is demonstrating the form and balance necessary for success on the balance beam.
© Ales Fevzer/CORBIS

3. Task difficulty is external, stable, and uncontrollable.

4. Luck is external, unstable, and uncontrollable.

Generalizations also can be made about the contributions of others (teammates, opponents) with regard to the success–failure dichotomy. These, too, are revealed in Figure 9.3.

Considerable research has been generated in an effort to evaluate the three-dimensional taxonomy. Illustrative of an early attempt is the work of Gill, Ruder, and Gross (1982). Gill and her associates gathered a total of 352 open-ended attributions by simply asking their subjects, once they had completed actual field or laboratory competitions, to respond to the question "What is the most important reason for your team's winning or losing in today's match?" The preponderance of responses indicated an emphasis on internal, unstable, and uncontrollable attributions in team com-

petition. References to teamwork were the most frequent attributions, and the traditional attributional elements of ability, effort, task difficulty, and luck were not particularly salient. Partial substantiation of the point made by Gill et al. is provided by Roberts and Pascuzzi (1979); they found that the traditional foursome of ability, effort, task difficulty, and luck accounted for only 45% of the attributions made by undergraduate students taking part in their sport attribution experiment. This finding would suggest that a reliance on the basic four elements in sport attribution research would be overly restrictive (Biddle, 1993). As a caveat related to their work, Gill and associates have suggested that coding difficulties and psychometric weaknesses associated with the open-ended format were problematic.

FIGURE 9.3

A Three-Dimensional Taxonomy of the Perceived Causes of Success and Failure

| | Controllable | | Uncontrollable | |
	Stable	Unstable	Stable	Unstable
Internal	Stable effort of self	Unstable effort of self	Ability of self	Fatigue, mood, and fluctuations in skill of self
External	Stable effort of others	Unstable effort of others	Ability of others; task difficulty	Fatigue, mood, and fluctuations in skill of others; luck

Source: Weiner (1980).

Gill et al. recommended that the **Causal Dimension Scale (CDS)** of Russell (1982) might offer a productive way to deal with measurement problems in future attribution research. Simply stated, the CDS purports to assess the various attributional elements, including locus of causality and stability. McAuley has been at the forefront of the research efforts aimed at validating the CDS (McAuley, 1985; McAuley & Duncan, 1989; McAuley & Gross, 1983). In one study (McAuley & Gross, 1983), male and female undergraduates who were enrolled in a physical education skills class in table tennis served as subjects. Upon completion of matches between same-sex players, equal numbers of winners and losers of each gender were identified. All subjects were administered the CDS. Winners and losers alike made attributions that were internal, unstable, and controllable, but winners used more of them than losers. McAuley and Gross also reported high reliability coefficients for the dimensions of locus of causality and stability, but the controllability dimension had lower reliability than expected. As a result, reservations were expressed about the applicability of the controllability scale to sport research.

The second study by McAuley was conducted with women intercollegiate gymnasts as subjects. Each gymnast was judged on the traditional gymnastic events (vault, balance beam, uneven parallel bars, floor exercises). Prior to finding out her scores, each was asked how she felt she had done in each event, and all subjects then completed the CDS. Among the more salient findings were that high-success gymnasts made more internal, stable, and controllable attributions for their performance; made significantly more stable attributions on all four events; made more internal attributions on two events (vault, balance beam); and made more controllable attributions on all events except the floor exercise. Perceived success was seen as a more powerful predictor of causal attributions than actual performance scores. Impressions of success for all gymnasts were lowest for the balance beam, an event many believe to be the hardest of the group of exercises to accomplish successfully.

In the third study, McAuley and Duncan (1989) tested male and female undergraduates on a bicycle ergometer task operating in what they called "expectancy disconfirmation" conditions—that is, one group was high expectancy/failure and the other low expectancy/success. For the success group, no single attribution dimension predicted emotional responses to the experimental treatment conditions. However, all three dimensions predicted feelings of confidence. In the failure group, depressed emotion was related to the stability and locus dimensions. These results are again seen as supportive of the CDS.

The CDS does have critics, including Russell himself. Concerns about reliability and scale overlap are most often noted (Biddle & Hill, 1992; McAuley, Duncan, & Russell, 1992). In the case of reliability, low

Causal Dimension Scale a psychological assessment device designed to measure causal attributions.

FIGURE 9.4

Revised Causal Dimension Scale (CDSII)

Instructions: Think about the reason or reasons you have written above. The items below concern your impressions or opinions of this cause or causes of your performance. Circle one number for each of the following questions:

Is the cause(s) something:

1. That reflects an aspect of yourself	9	8	7	6	5	4	3	2	1	reflects an aspect of the situation
2. Manageable by you	9	8	7	6	5	4	3	2	1	not manageable by you
3. Permanent	9	8	7	6	5	4	3	2	1	temporary
4. You can regulate	9	8	7	6	5	4	3	2	1	you cannot regulate
5. Over which others have control	9	8	7	6	5	4	3	2	1	over which others have no control
6. Inside of you	9	8	7	6	5	4	3	2	1	outside of you
7. Stable over time	9	8	7	6	5	4	3	2	1	variable over time
8. Under the power of other people	9	8	7	6	5	4	3	2	1	not under the power of other people
9. Something about you	9	8	7	6	5	4	3	2	1	something about others
10. Over which you have power	9	8	7	6	5	4	3	2	1	over which you have no power
11. Unchangeable	9	8	7	6	5	4	3	2	1	changeable
12. Other people can regulate	9	8	7	6	5	4	3	2	1	other people cannot regulate

NOTE: The total scores for each dimension are obtained by summing the items, as follows:
1, 6, 9 = loss of causality; 5, 8, 12 = external control; 3, 7, 11 = stability; 2, 4, 10 = personal control.
SOURCE: McAuley, Duncan, & Russell (1992).

internal consistency of the controllability subscale is problematic. Also, the overlap of the controllability subscale with the locus-of-causality subscale is troubling.

In an attempt to remedy these shortcomings, McAuley et al. proposed a revised CDS that is called the CDSII. Data generated from four separate studies (introductory psychology students in studies 1 and 2, college students in a gymnastics class in study 3, and students volunteering to play one-on-one basketball in study 4) were analyzed through confirmatory factor analysis for the purpose of demonstrating the validity of CDSII. The authors concluded that CDSII is valid and reliable, but they make the obligatory and necessary call for more research. The items included on the CDSII can be seen in Figure 9.4.

Future research will undoubtedly focus on Weiner's three-dimensional model, and further utiliza-

tion and refinement of the CDSII can be expected. Also, self versus team attributions will be more intensively scrutinized in an effort to shed light on individual and team dynamics.

Social Cognitive Models

Social cognitive attributional models are those that represent a blend of social-psychological and recent cognitive psychology theories. Three social cognitive models of attribution have received considerable attention: self-efficacy, perceived competence, and the achievement goal approach.

SELF-EFFICACY THEORY. An explosion of interest in self-efficacy is evident in the sport psychology literature. **Self-efficacy theory** owes its origins to Albert Bandura (1977). This theory suggests that performance will be determined jointly by the strength of a person's conviction that he or she has the competency to execute the skills that the situation demands and by the responsiveness of the environment. One determinant of responding, which might be called "self-confidence," is efficacy expectation. A second variable is known as outcome expectation. The different effects on re-

Social cognitive attributional models models emphasizing the role of self-efficacy, mastery, and goal achievement in explaining behavior.

Self-efficacy theory a social cognitive approach to attribution suggesting that success or failure depends on a person's beliefs about his or her own ability and about the likelihood that a given behavior will lead to a specific outcome.

FIGURE 9.5

Relations of Efficacy Expectations and Outcome Expectations to the Individual, the Individual's Behavior, and Behavioral Outcomes

sponding that these two types of expectancy are likely to have are profiled in Figure 9.5.

The term **efficacy expectancy** refers to the person's belief about his or her own ability: "Can I even do this? Sure, other people are good at this sort of thing, but what am I capable of doing?" Because efficacy expectancies are integrated with the person's perception of self-worth, they often constitute the target for behavioral change in therapy. It really makes little difference that an individual possesses talent if that person is convinced of his or her inability to succeed. Remediation in this case must take the form of enhancing self-esteem and making clients believe they are winners, not losers. **Outcome expectancy** refers to a person's beliefs about the likelihood that a given behavior will lead or not lead to a given outcome. If the expectancy is negative in a given situation, self-efficacy may be lowered.

Feltz (1984) believes that efficacy expectancies may be of greater importance in the mediation of athletic performances than outcome expectancies. When a player loses confidence, his or her perceptions about the payoff ratio in the environment may be incidental. For example, a golfer may be acutely aware of the need to take the ball from right to left out on the fairway. However, questions about his or her ability to accomplish this feat may be intrusive, thus preventing the athlete from executing the swing appropriately. Feltz further notes that performance accomplishments (one's own mastery experiences), vicarious experience (information obtained by watching others), verbal persuasion (the opinions of others), and emotional arousal

(the person's perception of his or her anxiety status) all contribute to the formation of efficacy expectations.

Much literature on self-efficacy has centered on the relation between self-confidence and athletic achievement. Performance in competitive gymnastics, for instance, has been found to vary as a function of one's efficacy expectations (Lee, 1982). In this investigation of female gymnasts, expectations about how well they thought they could do in competition were found to be a better predictor of their actual performance than their previous competition scores. Curiously, the athletes' coach made predictions about the athletes' ultimate performance scores that were more accurate than were the athletes' own expectations or the coach's past records. This overall pattern was particularly apparent when the participants were more experienced and of greater natural ability.

In an empirical test of self-efficacy theory, Weinberg, Gould, and Jackson (1979) conducted a study of high and low self-efficacy men and women using a muscular leg endurance task. A confederate was said to be either a varsity track athlete who exhibited higher performance on a related task (the high self-efficacy condition) or an individual suffering from a knee injury who exhibited lower performance on a related task (the low self-efficacy condition). With the experiment rigged so that subjects lost to the confederates in

Efficacy expectancy a person's belief about his or her own ability.
Outcome expectancy a person's belief about the likelihood that a given behavior will lead to a specific outcome.

competitive trials, the findings revealed that subjects in the high self-efficacy manipulation maintained leg extensions for longer periods of time than subjects in the low self-efficacy manipulation. The results from self-report questionnaires administered after the experiment confirmed that confidence was a major factor in determining individual performance.

More recent experiments relating self-efficacy to performance have been concerned with induction procedures that may change efficacy expectations, thus moderating athletic outcome. Along these lines, Kavanaugh and Hausfeld (1986) examined the role of mood in optimal sport performance. They felt that elevations in mood might alter what athletes think they can achieve. Accordingly, competitive efficacy should be enhanced when athletes are made happy as compared to cases in which a sad state is induced. Using an audiotape that asked some subjects, but not others, to visualize winning $10,000 from a lottery, researchers found that performance on a handgrip (dynamometer) task was positively influenced by an elevated mood state. However, the increases in motor performance paralleling improvements in mood did not appear to be related to changes in efficacy expectations.

Although the relation of self-efficacy to anxiety is often implicitly stated in such basic research projects, serious attempts at documenting the assumed tie between these two phenomena are scant (see Duncan & McAuley, 1987). One such report is that of Lan and Gill (1984). In their experiment, subjects performed either easy or difficult tasks, and cognitive worry, somatic anxiety, self-confidence, and heart rate were measured concurrently. The easy task generated higher self-confidence (self-efficacy) and lower anxiety; the opposite pattern was produced by the difficult task. Such findings of an explicit link between anxiety reduction and a self-efficacy intervention forcefully argue for the validity of this cognitive strategy as a treatment device in the sport realm. What is needed, of course, are more systematic field studies.

It has been suggested that self-efficacy theory, for all of its surface appeal, reliably accounts for a modest amount of the variance in athletic achievement (Feltz, 1982; McAuley, 1985; Roberts, 1993). It appears that self-efficacy theory actually fares best in the area of exercise behavior, where it has reliably predicted exercise compliance, exercise adherence, and recovery from cardiac problems (McAuley, 1992). A study by Marcus, Selby, Niaura, and Rossi (1992) is also instructive in documenting the exercise/efficacy connection. Marcus and her associates looked at the relationship between stages of fitness and self-efficacy in 1,500 government and hospital employees in Rhode Island. All subjects were placed in one of four categories for analysis purposes: (1) precontemplation (having no interest in exercise and no intent to begin), (2) contemplation (not involved in exercise but thinking about becoming involved), (3) action (participates in occasional exercise), and (4) maintenance (actively participates in regular weekly exercise). A five-item self-efficacy measure was administered to all subjects, and scores on the scale successfully differentiated among the employees at most stages. The authors suggest that efficacy-related interventions are most useful at all levels of involvement, but most particularly early in the establishment of exercise behavior.

PERCEIVED COMPETENCE THEORY. Perceived competence theory has its roots in the work of Harter (1978, 1980). Harter uses a mastery approach to achievement situations, with much emphasis placed on the role of evaluation by significant others, such as parents, peers, and team leaders. In cases where the evaluation is positive, there should be a concomitant increase in feelings of mastery and internal well-being; these positive emotions should then result in escalations in achievement behavior. In the reverse instance, negative evaluations result in unhealthy attitudes about personal competence or mastery, thus causing anxiety and other mood disturbance accompanied by a concomitant decrease in motivated behavior. Figure 9.6 is a representation of Harter's theory.

Most of the sport psychology work with Harter's model has been conducted with children, but little support has been noted. It is likely that children participate in sports for a variety of reasons having little or nothing to do with mastery or competence (motivation to participate in youth sports is explored in greater detail in Chapter 21). Overall, as Roberts (1993)

Perceived competence theory a social cognitive approach to attribution that relates success or failure to positive or negative evaluations by significant others such as parents, peers, and team leaders.

Collective or Team Efficacy

One interesting contemporary application of self-efficacy theory has to do with collective or team efficacy (Bandura, 1990). As Bandura has noted, most self-efficacy research has been focused on individual success expectations, and little has been done concerning perceived efficacy involving the collective (or team). Bandura feels certain that successful teams are characterized by a strong sense of group efficacy and resiliency, which manifests itself in times of both prosperity and adversity. Conversely, average or inconsistent teams appear to be functioning in an inefficacious fashion, particularly in times of adversity.

Two studies, one specifically sport-related, attest to the emerging interest in **collective efficacy.** In the first instance, Whitney (1994) divided 108 introductory psychology students into 36 groups of 3 each; all groups were mixed-sex in composition, randomly assigned to one of six experimental treatment conditions, and given a problem-solving task designed to shed light on the interaction of group efficacy, goal setting, and cohesion. Whitney found that (1) groups assigned difficult goals performed better than groups with easier goals, (2) high-efficacy groups outperformed moderate-efficacy groups, and (3) more goal-committed and cohesive groups outperformed less committed and cohesive groups under difficult goal conditions. Whitney concluded that the cognitive and motivational mechanisms by which goals affect performance on a given task may operate similarly for individuals and groups, thereby providing support for the notion of collective efficacy.

In the second study, by Hodges and Carron (1992), a muscular endurance task involving 153 male and female high school students was used to test collective efficacy theory. The students were assigned to three-person, mixed-sex groups and assigned to a high- or low-efficacy condition involving bogus feedback on a hand dynamometer task. Irrespective of actual results on the dynamometer task, one group of students was told that its hand strength was greater than it actually was; conversely, the other group was fed bogus information in the opposite direction, thereby setting up the high- and low-efficacy groups. Both groups then participated in a medicine ball task supposedly emphasizing strength (the perception of which had already been manipulated in the dynamometer task). Results of assessing arm strength in both preferred and nonpreferred arms indicated no statistically significant differences in either of the expectancy groups. However, when competing against a supposedly stronger confederate, subjects in the low-efficacy group consistently handled failure poorly, whereas those in the high-efficacy condition responded to failure by improving subsequent performance. These results are seen by Hodges and Carron as demonstrating the transferability of self-efficacy from the individual to the group situation.

Clearly, these two studies are supportive of Bandura's collective or team efficacy idea, but one was not sport-related and both were essentially laboratory studies. More research in the laboratory and in actual sport settings is needed.

SOURCES: Bandura (1990); Hodges & Carron (1992); Whitney (1984).

Collective efficacy a team's beliefs about its ability and about the likelihood that a given behavior will lead to a specific outcome for the team.

---

clearly points out, the applicability of Harter's motivation theory leaves something to be desired in the context of sport.

GOAL ACHIEVEMENT MODEL. With origins in the work of Dweck (1986) and Maehr and Nicholls (1980), the **goal achievement model** examines the interaction of (1) task, learning, and mastery goals and (2) ego,

performance, and ability goals. An understanding of the role of these multiple goals in determining achievement behavior is at the heart of this approach. Success or failure is viewed as being driven by complex

---

Goal achievement model a social cognitive approach to attribution that relates success or failure to perceptions of what constitutes an appropriate goal in any specific situation.

FIGURE 9.6

Harter's Theory of Perceived Competence

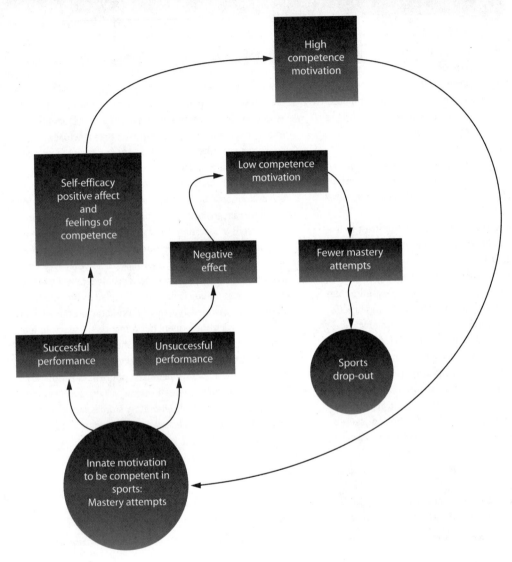

SOURCE: Harter (1978).

individual goals and interpretations of situations. For example, Roberts (1993) indicated that variations in achievement behavior may not be due to high or low motivation but rather may reflect different perceptions of what is an appropriate goal in a specific situation. To elaborate, Roberts uses the example of children who

are motivated to achieve in sports for social approval, as opposed to children who strive to excel for mastery or competence reasons. Individual interpretation or perception of goals drives them motivationally.

Goals in this model have been termed mastery goals (task involvement) and competitive goals (ego involvement), according to Roberts. The individual with mastery goals engages in motivated behavior for reasons that are largely internal, and demonstrating mastery or competence on a task becomes an end in itself. The individual with competitive goals engages in motivated behavior for reasons that are more external. Demonstrating ability in comparison with the abilities of others becomes important; perceptions of ability here are other-referenced and depend heavily on social comparisons in the competitive situation. Roberts goes on to say that little is known about the mechanisms that create one orientation instead of the other. Overall, the goal achievement approach to attribution has received good support in the sport psychology literature. Undoubtedly, additional research will be forthcoming.

The Functional Model

The **functional attributional model** posits that the motivation to maintain or enhance feelings of self-esteem is at the core of attributional efforts. As noted previously, this is the self-serving attributional bias whereby feelings of self-worth are maintained or enhanced through attributing success to internal factors (ability, effort) and failure to external events (task difficulty, luck).

Early studies by Iso-Ahola (1975, 1977) and Roberts (1975) were supportive of the existence of a self-serving attributional bias in Little League baseball players. Essentially, those studies indicated that evaluations of self and team are disparate. Players from unsuccessful teams tended to be rather critical of team ability and effort but did not view losing as an indictment of their own ability and work output. Conversely, players from successful teams made both self- and team-serving attributions (Bird & Brame, 1978; Roberts, 1975). Bird and Brame, however, in their study of female collegiate basketball players, found consistency between self- and team-serving attributions on effort but not on ability. Winners generally saw the team as possessing more ability than they themselves did individually. In a later study, Bird, Foster, and Maruyama (1980) introduced another variable into the process, namely, team cohesion. Cohesive teams in women's collegiate basketball demonstrated greater agreement on team- and self-attributions than did teams low in cohesion. However, there were no differences in either ability or effort at-

tributions between the two groups, although members of low-cohesive teams made greater luck and lesser task attributions for their performance than for the performance of the team.

Bukowski and Moore (1980), in a disclaimer, found little evidence for the existence of a self-serving bias in their study of Canadian youngsters who participated in a camp "Olympics" made up of a variety of physical activities. Two days prior to competing in the "Olympics," each contestant was asked to rate how important certain factors would be in terms of succeeding in the upcoming events. Ratings were on a 5-point scale ranging from 1 (important) to 5 (not important). A second rating was made one day after the camp competition was concluded. Results from the two administrations can be seen in Table 9.2.

In general, there is agreement between pre- and postcompetition evaluations. Overall, "trying hard" (effort), "being good athletes" (ability), "being interested in competing," and "good officiating" were seen as very important to success in the posttest condition. In contrast, "having lots of luck" (luck) and "perceiving the events as easy" (task difficulty) were viewed as less important to success.

Another failure to support the existence of the self-serving attributional bias is provided by Mark, Mutrie, Brooks, and Harris (1984). Mark et al. reported results from two studies, one with squash players in a national tournament and the other with racquetball players participating in an open tournament in Pennsylvania. In general, winners and losers in both situations did not differ in their attributions on locus-of-causality dimensions. Winners, as opposed to losers, did make more stable and controllable attributions, however.

An interesting slant on this locus-of-causality issue is that of Biddle (1993). He suggests that statistically significant differences may obscure real differences between winners and losers. Sometimes both winners and losers report internal attributions, but the strength of those reported by winners may simply outstrip those of losers. In short, what we may be seeing is not internal–external differences but merely differences in degrees of internality.

Functional attributional model a model that places much emphasis on maintaining and enhancing self-esteem.

TABLE 9.2

Mean Ratings of Attributions for Success and Failure

Attributions for Success	M
Trying hard	1.23/1.29
Good officiating	1.61/1.63
Being good athletes	1.61/1.66
Being interested in competing	1.67/1.58
Being in a good mood	1.80/2.06
Having good leaders	1.84/1.91
Being interested in winning	1.97/2.04
Having good equipment	2.44/2.76
Having lots of experience	2.55/2.67
Being smart	2.95/2.89
Perceiving the events as easy	3.68/3.79
Having lots of luck	3.66/3.81

Attributions for Failure	M
Not trying hard	1.84/1.84
Bad officiating	2.07/2.42
Not being interested in competing	2.08/1.98
Not being interested in winning	2.22/2.07
Being in a bad mood	2.30/2.55
Having bad leaders	2.32/2.52
Being poor athletes	2.52/2.27
Having poor equipment	2.77/3.25
Having no experience	3.30/3.28
Perceiving the events as hard	3.43/3.27
Not being smart	3.58/3.29
Having bad luck	4.00/3.79

The number to the left of the slash is the item's mean rating from the post-event evaluations; the number to the right of the slash is the item's mean rating based on the pre-event evaluations. Sixty-nine subjects provided post-event evaluations; 70 subjects provided pre-event evaluations.

SOURCE: Bukowski & Moore (1980).

It would appear that evidence for the existence of a self-serving attributional bias is inconclusive. Mark and his colleagues suggest that research in the area could profit from more real-life as opposed to con-trived, novel test situations in the laboratory, from better measures of attribution, such as CDSII, and from less emphasis on team as opposed to individual success. Despite these caveats, the self-serving attributional bias appears to be a viable concept because of its protective role with regard to self-esteem. Further research is needed.

Future Directions in Attribution Research

Excellent reviews containing suggestions for future work in the realm of attributions and sport are offered by Brawley and Roberts (1984); Mark, Mutrie, Brooks, and Harris (1984); and Rejeski and Brawley (1983). All parties show common concerns about such research, and their suggestions may be summarized as follows:

1. Let the athlete define the causal attributions, not the experimenter. Seldom has the relevance of subject definition been seen as important (Bukowski & Moore, 1980; Roberts & Pascuzzi, 1979). The biggest step toward subject definition of attributions has been the use of the Causal Dimension Scale; it clearly lets the subject define the causes of his or her achievement behavior.

2. Too much emphasis has been placed on winning and losing, and they have been equated with success or failure. Many an athlete has won yet viewed performance as a failure, and many losses have been seen as successes. The win/lose dichotomy offers too narrow a definition of success or failure.

3. Team versus individual attribution becomes blurred because of team mores, folkways, pressures, and concerns. Attributions for success and failure are complicated by team pressures to present oneself in ways that may or may not represent one's true feelings about things.

4. The role of perceived ability as a moderator of causal ascriptions has been studied fairly thoroughly but has not been exhausted.

5. There seems to be universal agreement that research in the area of youth sport represents a considerable gap in attributional research. How this

These relay team members are obviously reaping the benefits of their hours of hard work and dedication to the sport of track. They also exemplify teamwork and the camaraderie associated with sport participation.
© Copyright 1999 PhotoDisc, Inc.

deficiency might be rectified is problematic, given the tendency of young people to make few or relatively primitive attributions.

6. The original Weiner model is limited and should be replaced with updated models emphasizing elements far broader than ability, effort, task difficulty, and luck.

7. In past attributional research, too much reliance has been placed on the use of college students, and team sports have been studied far more often than have individual sports.

NEED FOR ACHIEVEMENT

Closely related to our discussion of attribution theory is the concept of need for achievement.

Murray's Contribution

Inquiry into the need to achieve began in the late 1930s with the work of the accomplished Harvard personality theorist Henry Murray. It was Murray's position that people differ in their need "to overcome obstacles, to exercise power, to strive to do something difficult as well and as quickly as possible" (Murray, 1938, pp. 80–81). He called this striving the **need for achievement,** often expressed as **n ach.** Murray devised the **Thematic Apperception Test (TAT)** (Murray, 1943) as a means of measuring variations in human motivation. Over the years, the TAT has become one of the most popular projective tests available to psychologists and psychiatrists working in clinical settings. The TAT consists of 20 stimulus cards into which subjects are asked to project hidden personality themes or dimensions through fantasy stories. These fantasy stories are analyzed by specialists in thematic analysis who categorize the various response themes. The TAT has undergone revision over the years and is still used in clinical work and research studies, though its use in research studies in sport psychology ranges from sparse to nonexistent.

The McClelland–Atkinson Model

Murray's pioneering efforts were advanced by David McClelland and associates in the early 1950s (McClelland, Atkinson, Clark, & Lowell, 1953). McClelland and his associates revised and added considerable sophistication to the scoring procedure of the TAT and greatly extended Murray's original premises. Although McClelland and Atkinson have engaged in several collaborative efforts, in much of their work they have proceeded independently of one another. The net effect of their independent efforts, however, led to their work being referred to as the McClelland–Atkinson model.

Basically, the **McClelland-Atkinson model** takes the position that motivation to achieve is a function of the relative strengths of the motive or tendency to

Need for achievement the need to set and achieve challenging goals.
Thematic Apperception Test a projective test of personality that has been used to measure the need for achievement.
McClelland–Atkinson model the idea that motivation to achieve is a function of the relative strengths of hope of success and fear of failure.

approach success and the motive or tendency to avoid failure. Atkinson (1957) calls these simply "hope of success" and "fear of failure." Goal-directed or achievement behavior is mediated by the joint action of the two motives regardless of the terminology used. Atkinson brought quantification to bear on the issue and suggested that three factors *must* be considered in making the determination of hope of success: (1) motivation to achieve success, (2) perceived probability of success, and (3) incentive value of success. Three factors also are salient to fear of failure: (1) motivation to avoid failure, (2) probability of failure, and (3) negative incentive value of failure. The additive interplay of all these forces allows for a mathematical prediction of total motivation, the details of which are beyond the scope of the present discussion.

Atkinson (1974) made an important extension to this model by incorporating the notion of **extrinsic motivation** to the motivational prediction formula. Money, verbal praise, pats on the back, medals, trophies, and other awards all constitute sources of extrinsic motivation, and their relevance to performance has not gone unnoticed.

Deci (1975) has suggested that the interplay of intrinsic and extrinsic motivation can be explained through his **cognitive evaluation theory.** Essentially Deci stated that **intrinsic motivation** is a function of the degree of competency, self-determination, and feelings of self-worth created by sport competition. In turn, these intrinsic qualities are lessened or enhanced by two external reward characteristics: control and information. In the control aspect, we are essentially dealing with a locus-of-causality artifact—that is, the extent to which a sport participant views his or her rewards as residing internally greatly determines how much an activity is enjoyed. Briefly stated, when a player perceives that a sport is no longer played for the intrinsic enjoyment but rather for a trophy or medal, intrinsic motivation may decrease. How often have the fans and the sports writers decried the performance decrement in the first year after a professional athlete has signed a secure and financially lucrative contract? Although these decrements may vary from performer to performer, they do serve notice that internal motivation can decrease when external rewards become more powerful.

Insofar as the informational aspect is concerned, participation that increases feelings of self-worth and self-determination because of the message it transmits to the player is seen as facilitating intrinsic motivation. When these coveted qualities are not created, external rewards decrease intrinsic motivation. A player who is voted Most Valuable Player (MVP) on his team is being afforded information about his worth and competence; this information should lead to considerable intrinsic motivation. In contrast, a player who wins a trophy as part of a championship team to which he or she frankly contributed little is getting a very different message about worth and competence. Further athletic participation for this competitor may be a function of the extrinsic reward associated with the activity.

The controlling and informational aspects of rewards are not mutually exclusive; they do interact to effect intrinsic motivation. For example, the high school football player who participates because of his father's expectations and peer pressures but who is doing well at the task may feel that he is getting positive information about himself even though he is primarily playing to please others. It might be expected that his intrinsic motivation would be lessened, thereby giving increased importance to external rewards. Weinberg (1984, p. 182) succinctly summarizes the issue: "If the controlling aspect is more salient, rewards will decrease intrinsic motivation whereas if the informational aspect is the more salient aspect and provides positive information about one's competence, rewards can enhance intrinsic motivation."

Two additional concepts that add to our understanding of internal and external motivation are the overjustification hypothesis (Lepper, Greene, & Nisbett, 1973) and the discounting principle (Kelley, 1972). The following example helps in defining the overjustification hypothesis: Jane, a 12-year-old, plays slow-pitch softball because, in her words, "It's fun." Then overzeal-

---

Extrinsic motivation external factors, such as money, medals, and pats on the back, that affect a person's levels of effort and persistence.

Cognitive evaluation theory Deci's theory of intrinsic motivation (IM) that suggests that IM is a product of competency, self-determination, and feelings of worth in competitive situations.

Intrinsic motivation internal factors, such as competency, self-determination, and feelings of self-worth, that affect a person's levels of effort and persistence.

ous parents decide that the season would be more successful for everyone if trophies were made available to all players. According to the **overjustification hypothesis,** Jane is already playing the game because it is enjoyable, and playing for a trophy may actually decrease her enjoyment and intrinsic motivation to compete. At the same time, enjoyment of the game for its own sake has been stripped away or discounted, at which point the **discounting principle** becomes operational in lowering intrinsic motivation. The trophy, rather than the game, becomes the goal of participating in softball. Parents, coaches, and youth league administrators need to be alert to this caveat about external rewards for activities that might well survive as a function of their own internally reinforcing properties.

Enjoying sport and physical activity for internal reasons is preferable to engaging in them for external ones. This is not to downplay the role of external rewards; they are real, sometimes very powerful, and likely to continue to serve as sport motivators. Weinberg (1984) offers five ways to enhance intrinsic motivation:

1. Coaches and others involved in physical activity should structure their activities in ways that guarantee a certain amount of success. People are not successful in everything they do every time they do it, and such should and will not be the case in sport. But some success should be assured. Weinberg cites the example of the 10-foot-high basket for very young basketball players. For these vertically challenged competitors, few successes can be achieved with the 10-foot goal, whereas lowering the goal a few feet creates a situation that is conducive to success.

2. Athletes should be allowed more of a role in goal setting and decision making. This granting of responsibility coincides with the locus-of-causality concern of Deci (1975). Athletes who take an active role in the decision-making process should feel more in control, which should, in turn, help develop and maintain intrinsic motivation.

3. Praise is a facilitator of intrinsic motivation. Players whose roles on the team are of a smaller magnitude need just as much praise as do the team stars. Role players or substitutes need to feel that they also contribute to overall team goals. We can recall a high school experience in which this

principle was brutalized. A third-team linebacker named Hall who never played in any of the games made a bone-jarring tackle in a midweek scrimmage. Excitedly, Hall awaited the expected praise. Once the pile was sorted out and the coach could identify the involved parties, his response was "Oh, hell, it was only Hall!" This remark, of course, was devastating to Hall and was a source of considerable bitterness some six years later when he graduated from college. All players need periodic reinforcement for desirable behavior.

4. Realistic goals feed players' feelings of competence, thus facilitating intrinsic motivation. Despite what many would mistakenly have us believe, winning is not everything. Playing well, improving on previous skill levels, and furthering social development are desirable goals and need to be stressed. Everyone cannot win; there will be losers on the scoreboard. But win/loss statistics are far from the only standards with which success should be measured.

5. Variation in content and sequence of practice drills helps generate intrinsic motivation. Boredom is an enemy of sport participation. When practice is not fun, people drop out or stay on only for extrinsic rewards. Practices do not have to be repetitious or exercises in stamina or drudgery. The mark of a good practice is not measured by the amount of time, repetition, or drudgery involved. One highly successful high school football coach in Texas was known to take his team fishing once or twice during the season instead of engaging in the usual practice activities. Everyone fished, food was cooked on the beach, camaraderie was enhanced, and boredom and drudgery were alleviated or avoided.

Clearly, there are a number of ways to create, maintain, and enhance intrinsic motivation. A little creativity coupled with a lot of knowledge of human

---

Overjustification hypothesis process whereby reinforcement is provided beyond what is minimally necessary, thus causing a person to question the justification for responding in the first place.
Discounting principle process whereby internal reward is stripped of its meaning, thus discounting the value of a behavior or activity.

motivation can be a significant force in creating a positive atmosphere for competition at all levels.

SUMMARY

1. Two major motivational theories have dominated research in psychology over the past 50 years: attribution theory and need achievement theory. Two psychological constructs that exert an effect on motivation are locus of control and self-esteem.

2. The topic of motivation is fascinating to professionals and laypersons alike. According to Glyn Roberts (1992, p. 5), "motivation refers to those personality factors, social variables, and/or cognitions that come into play when a person undertakes a task at which he or she is evaluated, enters into competition with others, or attempts to attain some standard of excellence."

3. Attribution theory owes a considerable debt to the impetus provided in the 1940s and 1950s by Fritz Heider. Causal attributions are inferences about why something happened. Dispositional attributions are inferences about some trait an individual may possess.

4. The cognitive, social cognitive, and functional models represent three ways of looking at attributions.

5. The cognitive approach to attributions owes much to Julian Rotter, whose work in locus-of-control theory has been significant. Another key figure has been Bernard Weiner, who initially suggested that causal attributions for behavior could be conceptualized along four dimensions: ability, effort, task difficulty, and luck. Later theorizing by Weiner added stability–instability and controllability–uncontrollability to the formulation.

6. The assessment of attributions of late has centered around Russell's Causal Dimension Scale (CDS) and an updated version, CDSII.

7. Three variants of Weiner's work are in the social cognitive realm: self-efficacy, perceived competence, and the goal achievement approach.

8. Self-efficacy owes its origins to the work of Albert Bandura. Emphasis in the model is placed on efficacy expectations and outcome expectations. The former deals with a person's belief about his or her own ability; the latter involves outcome perceptions as they interact with efficacious responding. A relatively new application of efficacy theory has to do with collective or team efficacy.

9. Perceived competence is associated with Harter, who emphasized a mastery approach to achievement situations.

10. Dweck, Maehr, and Nicholls have been at the forefront of research in the goal achievement approach. Achievement behavior, according to these theorists, is driven by complex goals and situational interpretations. Much is made of (1) task, learning, and mastery goals and (2) ego, performance, and ability goals.

11. The functional model takes the position that maintenance of self-esteem is at the heart of attributional efforts. This notion has led to the emergence of what is known as the self-serving attributional bias, whereby success is attributed internally (ability, effort) and failure is attributed externally (task difficulty, luck).

12. Future directions in attribution research: The athlete, not the researcher, should define causal attributions. Winning and losing have too long served as the only indices of success or failure; future research should look more at performance. Team versus individual attributions need to be viewed separately. Perceived ability as opposed to actual ability as a moderator of attributions bears additional scrutiny. Youth sport suffers from a dearth of research. The original Weiner model seems limited and needs expansion. Basing attributional generalizations on studies largely conducted with college students seems narrow in scope.

13. Henry Murray introduced to the psychological literature the concept of the need to achieve. He also devised a projective test, the Thematic Apperception Test (TAT), to measure the construct.

14. McClelland and Atkinson advanced a model for need for achievement that has been scrutinized continually in the sport psychology literature. Intrinsic versus extrinsic motivation has played a big part in the total picture of unraveling the need for achievement in athletics and physical activity.

KEY TERMS

attribution theory (115)
causal antecedents for behavior (115)
causal attribution (115)
Causal Dimension Scale (CDS) (119)
cognitive attributional model (115)
cognitive evaluation theory (128)
collective efficacy (123)
discounting principle (129)
dispositional attribution (115)
efficacy expectancy (121)
extrinsic motivation (128)
functional attributional model (125)
goal achievement model (123)
informational bias (115)
intrinsic motivation (128)
McClelland–Atkinson model (127)
motivation (114)
motivational bias (115)
need for achievement (127)
outcome expectancy (121)
overjustification hypothesis (129)
perceived competence theory (122)
perceptual bias (115)
self-efficacy theory (120)
self-serving attributional bias (115)
social cognitive attributional models (120)
Thematic Apperception Test (TAT) (127)
Weiner's three-dimensional taxonomy (117)

SUGGESTED READINGS

Hawkins, R. M. F. (1995). Self-efficacy: A cause of debate. *Journal of Behavioral Therapy and Experimental Psychiatry, 26,* 235–240.

This paper is one of 14 articles appearing in a special edition of the journal devoted entirely to self-efficacy. Hawkins takes the position that self-efficacy is not a cause of behavior, as Albert Bandura suggests. Rather, it is useful as a descriptive metaphor for predicting behavior. Bandura gives his own opinions in an earlier paper in the same volume. The reader with a serious interest in self-efficacy will find much to digest in this special edition.

Roberts, G. C. (Ed.). (1992). *Motivation in sport and exercise.* Champaign, IL: Human Kinetics.

Nine articles by authorities in motivation theory in sport psychology such as Duda, Feltz, McAuley, Nicholls, and Roberts are included in this excellent reference for the sport psychology student or professional. Part 1 has six readings on definitions, achievement motivation, goal setting, and self-efficacy. Part 2 has three readings designed to illustrate applications of several theories of motivation.

Stajkovic, A. D., & Luthans, F. (1998). Self-efficacy and work-related performance: A meta-analysis. *Psychological Bulletin, 124,* 240–261.

The authors review 114 studies of self-efficacy in the work-related context. Their results showed a positive significant correlation between self-efficacy and work-related performance. They conclude by pointing to other arenas where self-efficacy has been successful, including vocational choice and career pursuit, health behavior, sport psychology, sports medicine, educational settings, and human adjustment.

Weiner, B. (1990). History of motivational research in education. *Journal of Educational Psychology, 82,* 616–622.

Bernard Weiner traces the history of motivational research in education from 1941 to 1990. He arrives at the following conclusions: (1) The grand formal theories of the early days—namely, drive, psychoanalytic, cognitive, and associationistic theory—have largely faded into obscurity. (2) Achievement strivings remain at the center of motivation research, and goal theory is one of the bright stars in this regard. (3) Efficacy beliefs, causal cognitions, and learned helplessness are increasingly being used in explanations of success and failure in achievement settings. (4) There is a lack of cross-situational generality among most of the motivation theories. (5) There is an increasing interest in the interplay of emotions and motivation. Weiner predicts a bright future for motivation theory and research but suggests that studying motivation primarily in educational settings is limiting.

INFOTRAC COLLEGE EDITION

For additional readings, explore Infotrac College Edition, your online library. Go to:
http://www.infotrac-college.com/wadsworth

Hint: Enter these search terms: attribution theory, causal attributions, collective efficacy, fear of success, research in self-efficacy, self-efficacy.

Motivation: Locus of Control and Self Theory

CHAPTER 10

Locus of Control

Self Theory

Some Final Thoughts on Motivation

Summary

Key Terms

Suggested Readings

The sport of soccer is popular all over the world, and some players in Europe now earn salaries in excess of $50 million.

© Copyright 1999 PhotoDisc, Inc.

Two additional theoretical areas merit our attention because of the significant moderating effects they play with regard to motivation: locus of control and self theory. It is difficult to discuss motivation without mentioning these important moderators. Also, sport self-confidence, setting performance goals, and explanatory style are germane to the present discussion because of their significant impact on motivation.

LOCUS OF CONTROL

Closely related to attribution theory and need for achievement is the concept of **locus of control.** Rotter (1966), a social learning theorist with a cognitive bent, gave initial impetus to the conceptualization. Evidence of the popularity of the construct is seen in reports by Throop and MacDonald (1971), who put together a bibliography of locus-of-control research that contained 339 studies for the period 1966 to 1969 alone, and Rotter (1975), who located more than 600 such studies prior to 1975. Rotter conceived of locus of control as a generalized expectancy to perceive reinforcement as contingent on one's behavior **(internal locus of control)** or as the result of forces outside one's control and related to luck, chance, fate, or powerful others **(external locus of control).**

Rotter's I–E Scale

To measure the internal (I) and external (E) dimensions of locus of control, Rotter (1966) developed a scale that is made up of 29 items, 6 of which are used as fillers. Subjects are asked to respond to each of the 29 items by choosing between two alternative statements. Scores range from 0 to 23. Higher scores denote externality. Here are some sample items from **Rotter's I–E scale:**

a. In the case of the well-prepared student, there is rarely if ever such a thing as an unfair test.

b. Many times exam questions tend to be so unrelated to course work that studying is useless.

and

a. There is too much emphasis on athletics in high school.

b. Team sports are an excellent way to build character.

The first locus-of-control study utilizing the I–E Scale in sport was conducted by Lynn, Phelan, and Kiker (1969). They administered the Rotter scale to equal numbers of basketball players (group sport), gymnasts (individual sport), and nonparticipants in sport. Group sport participants were significantly more *internal* than were members of the other two groups. Finn and Straub (1977) used the I–E Scale in a study of highly skilled female softball players from the Netherlands (N = 35) and the United States (N = 44). Statistically significant differences (.01) were noted. The Dutch players were more *external* than their American counterparts. Further analyses also showed that American pitchers and catchers were significantly more *internal* than the Dutch battery-mates as well as groups of Dutch infielders and outfielders. Analyses of the relationship of locus of control to height, weight, years of playing experience, playing position, and position in the batting order failed to produce significant differences. As a caveat, Finn and Straub point to potential problems in translating the I–E Scale to the Dutch language. Hall, Church, and Stone (1980) used the Rotter scale with nationally ranked weight lifters. Firstborn lifters were more *external* than later-borns, but all were basically *internal* when compared to overall norms reported by Rotter. More recently, studies of football players, gymnasts, and track athletes by Bleak and Frederick (1998) and studies of risk sport participants by Schrader and Wann (1999) attest to the robustness of the I–E Scale as a measure of locus of control.

Conversely, at least four studies have failed to support the validity of the I–E Scale. Celestino, Tapp, and Brumet (1979) found no differences between finishers and nonfinishers in male marathoners in New York.

Locus of control individuals' beliefs about how much control they have over the situation they are in and over what happens to them.
Internal locus of control belief that ability and effort give individuals some control over the situation they are in and over what happens to them.
External locus of control belief that outside forces such as luck and fate determine what happens.
Rotter's I–E Scale a scale that measures the extent to which a person has an internal or external locus of control.

They did find, however, a small (.28) but significant correlation between internality and order of finish. Di Giuseppe (1973) divided high school freshmen into four groups: participants in team, individual, and intramural sports, and persons with no athletic involvement. No significant differences were noted among the four groups. Gilliland (1974) divided college males and females into five groups related to sports involvement. Again, various analyses by sex and by athletic activity or nonactivity revealed no differences in locus of control. Finally, McKelvie and Huband (1980) studied various college athletes and nonathletes and concluded that no systematic relationship exists between athletic participation and locus of control.

As with nearly every paper-and-pencil instrument, there are dissenting views about various psychometric issues. Nevertheless, Rotter's I–E Scale has been used in at least four dozen published studies in sport and exercise since its publication, and it continues to be a useful instrument in investigations of the locus-of-control concept.

Levenson's Multidimensional Approach

Another popular measure of locus of control is **Levenson's IPC Scale** (1973). Levenson believed that Rotter's externality dimension was confounded by the fact that individuals could be "externals" on the I–E Scale yet arrive at that point from greatly different avenues. For example, a person who views external causation as a function of chance or luck is probably very different from someone who perceives causality as a function of powerful others in the environment. Reacting to criticisms of Rotter's original conceptualization (e.g., Collins, 1974; Gurin, Gurin, Lao, & Beattie, 1969; and Mirels, 1970), Levenson arrived at a multidimensional locus-of-control measure that taps into internality (I) and two dimensions of externality: powerful others (P) and chance (C).

The IPC Scale is made up of 24 items, 8 of which load respectively on the internal, powerful others, and chance dimensions. A 7-point Likert scaling procedure is used to score responses. All scores range from 0 to 48. Here are some representative items for each dimension:

1. *Internal:* "When I make plans, I am almost certain to have them work."

2. *Powerful others:* "In order to have my plans work, I make sure that they fit in with the desires of people who have power over me."

3. *Chance:* "It's not wise for me to plan too far ahead because many things turn out to be a matter of good or bad luck."

Levenson (1981, p. 18) offers an interpretive caution with regard to her scale: High scores on each subscale are interpreted as indicating high expectations of control by the source designated. Low scores reflect tendencies not to believe in that locus of control. A low *internal* score should not be interpreted as indicating that a subject believes in chance; it can only be said that this subject does not perceive himself or herself as determining outcomes. In actuality, one could score high or low on all three scales—that is, a person could say he or she was personally in control yet also say that life is a random series of events controlled by powerful others. Rarely has such a profile been obtained, however. Before interpreting such a seemingly inconsistent profile, one would have to give serious consideration to the presence of confounding factors (e.g., acquiescence response set or random responding).

Among the first sport studies using the IPC Scale were those made by LeUnes, Nation, and Daiss (Daiss, LeUnes, & Nation, 1986; LeUnes & Nation, 1982; Nation & LeUnes, 1983a, 1983b). Summing across these four studies of major university football players and two groups of college students not playing football, the following results were reported:

1. College football players scored significantly higher on the *powerful others* dimension (.05) than did a group of college students who had played football in high school and a group of nonathletes. It is highly likely that these athletes were acutely aware of the *powerful others* nature of their coaches.

2. In looking at differences across playing positions within the team, no significant findings were noted.

3. In terms of racial differences, black defensive linemen were significantly more *internal* than white

---

Levenson's IPC Scale a scale that measures the extent to which a person has an internal (I) or external locus of control but divides externality into two categories: powerful others (P) and chance (C).

Putting a golf ball is a fine motor task with a substantial mental component. Confidence is essential to successful putting.

© Copyright 1999 PhotoDisc, Inc.

offensive linemen, and black players were significantly more *chance*-oriented than white players.

4. In a five-year follow-up of the players who were tested only once prior to their freshman year in 1980, 16 had stayed with the football program for either four or five years, and 18 had departed. The *chance* score of the "stayers" was 19.39 while "leavers" scored 11.65, a difference that is significant at the .001 level. Before they ever played a

---

Nowicki–Strickland Scale a locus-of-control scale used with children.

down of college football, players who stayed appeared to have an early realization of the role *chance* factors might play (e.g., coaching decisions, academic difficulties, injury, or other bad luck) in determining their ultimate success.

More recent research using Levenson's IPC Scale has been reported by Van Raalte, Brewer, Nemeroff, and Linder (1991). They were interested in the relationship between Levenson's *chance* scale and the development of sport-related superstitious behavior. They hypothesized that there would be a significant negative correlation between IPC *chance* scores and the development of superstitious behavior associated with a putting task. Subjects were introductory psychology students with little or no golfing background who were chosen so as to control for already developed superstitions often found in golfers (and other athletes, for that matter). Subjects completed a putting task using golf balls of four different colors, and superstitious behavior was defined as using the same colored ball immediately after a successful putt (i.e., the "lucky ball"). Subjects scoring low on *chance* orientation chose the lucky ball significantly more often for ensuing putts than did high scorers, thus confirming the original hypothesis. The authors concluded that low-*chance* subjects believed they could take control of events by use of the so-called lucky ball.

Levenson's scale has been shown to be psychometrically sound (Blau, 1984; Levenson, 1974; Ward, 1994), as has Rotter's I–E Scale. The two scales should continue to be used as the primary measures of locus of control in the future.

Locus-of-Control Measurement With Youth

Nowicki and Strickland (1973) created a scale for measuring locus of control in children. Although their work has been applied rather widely with children in general, its use in youth sport has been relatively sparse. Anshel (1979), Lufi, Porat, and Tenenbaum (1986), and Morris, Vaccaro, and Clarke (1979) represent three such studies. Anshel used the **Nowicki–Strickland Scale** with fifth and eighth graders in Florida. Subjects were assigned by age and internality–externality scores to one of four groups of 16 each. Older subjects were more *internal* than their younger peers. In general, Anshel's work supported previous locus-of-control work with youth in settings of a nonsport nature.

In the Lufi et al. study, boys ages 7 to 11 were selected for a one-year study of psychological variables and gymnastic potential. Based on tests of physical skills, the boys were divided into two equal groups, one considered high in potential, the other average. After a month of training, a battery of psychological tests, including the Nowicki–Strickland, was administered. Briefly put, the high-potential boys were significantly more *internal* than the average ones. The authors suggest that coaches would be well advised to take into account psychological variables, such as direction of locus of control, in talent identification and selection.

Morris et al. administered the Nowicki–Strickland Scale to competitive swimmers, ages 7 to 17. When their scores were compared with applicable norms published by Nowicki and Strickland (1973), the swimmers were significantly more *internal* than their nonathletic age-mates.

Recent studies such as that of Kerr and Goss (1997) and Lambert, Moore, and Dixon (1999), both with youth gymnasts, attest to the continuing interest in the Nowicki–Strickland measure and the study of locus of control in young sports participants. Clearly, however, more work is needed to get a better perspective on locus of control in young athletes.

Current Status of the Locus-of-Control Construct

The majority of the locus-of-control research in sport was conducted in the 1970s and 1980s. Activity slowed a bit in the 1990s. Part of the problem may center on questions of interpretation of what locus-of-control scores mean. For example, there has been some intimation in the literature that being a high "internal" is the optimal state of adjustment (i.e., Chalip, 1980; Rotter, 1971). However, there may well be legitimate instances in which a *powerful others* orientation is adaptive. For example, it is likely that an athlete who played basketball for Bobby Knight at Indiana or one who played football for Paul "Bear" Bryant at Alabama in his heyday would be best served by a *powerful others* orientation. Both coaches used an exaggerated "my way

or the highway" approach to player selection and retention. It is also conceivable that a high *chance* orientation is essential to performance excellence, as was suggested earlier in the LeUnes et al. football research.

According to Lefcourt (1992), another obstacle to locus-of-control research is that the conceptualization has been assimilated into the burgeoning literature of related constructs. We mentioned some of these in Chapter 9, such as Bandura's self-efficacy, Weiner's causal attribution, and Harter's perceived competence. Other variants of locus-of-control theory include perceived control (Langer, 1983), personal causation (DeCharms, 1968), and explanatory style (Seligman, 1975). Like locus-of-control theory, these theories deal with aspects of perceived causality and control. Lefcourt goes on to point out that these authors insist on the unique properties of their respective theories, but the overlap is obvious. The end result, says Lefcourt, is "convergent findings obtained with widely divergent methodologies" (p. 413).

Locus-of-control theory and research will continue to be important. The fact that 18 different locus-of-control scales are available (Lefcourt, 1992) and that foreign versions have appeared in Argentina (DeMinzi, 1991) and Holland (Finn & Straub, 1977) attests to the robustness of the concept and its assessment.

SELF THEORY

After a while you learn the subtle difference between holding a hand and chaining a soul,
And you learn that love doesn't mean leaning and company doesn't mean security,
And you begin to learn that kisses aren't contracts and presents aren't promises,
And you begin to accept your defeats with your head up and your eyes open, with the grace of an adult not the grief of a child,
And you learn to build all your roads on today because tomorrow's ground is too uncertain for plans.
After a while you learn that even sunshine burns if you get too much.

So plant your own garden and decorate your own soul, instead of waiting for someone to bring you flowers.

And you learn that you really can endure ... that you really are strong,

And you really do have worth.

ANONYMOUS

Like many conceptualizations in psychology, the self is a hypothetical construct. We cannot see the self any more than we can view electrical current. But we can infer the existence of the self from behavior in much the same way that we can define electricity by its effects. Essentially, self theory includes such constructs as self-concept, self-esteem, self-actualization, and aspects of the self-serving attributional bias discussed earlier.

According to Hamachek (1987), the awakening of interest in **self theory** can be traced to the works of the French mathematician and philosopher René Descartes (1596–1650). Descartes's notions, in turn, were scrutinized in the 17th and 18th centuries by the likes of Leibnitz, Locke, Hume, and Berkeley. By the twentieth century, interest in the self was primarily vested in the works of the American psychologist William James (1842–1910), who summarized his feelings about the self through the following personal vignette:

> I am not often confronted by the necessity of standing by one of my empirical selves and relinquishing the rest. Not that I would not, if I could, be both handsome and fat and well-dressed, and a great athlete, and make a million a year, be a wit, a bon-vivant, and lady-killer, as well as a philosopher, a philanthropist, statesman, warrior, and African explorer, as well as a "tone-poet" and saint. But the thing is simply impossible. The millionaire's work would run counter to the saint's; the bon-vivant and the philanthropist would trip each other up; the philosopher and lady-killer could not keep house in the same tenement of clay . . . to make any one of them actual, the rest must more or less be suppressed. . . . So the seeker of his truest, strongest, deepest self must review the list carefully, and pick out the

one on which to stake his salvation. All other selves thereupon become unreal, but the fortunes of this self are real. Its failures are real failures, its triumphs real triumphs, carrying shame and gladness with them. . . . I, who for the time have staked my all on being a psychologist, am mortified if others know more psychology than I. But I am contented to wallow in the grossest ignorance of Greek. My deficiencies there give me no sense of personal humiliation at all. (1890, p. 91)

With the advent of the behavioral movement in the late 1800s and the early 1900s, it became unfashionable or unscientific to devote time to studying what might be viewed as mystical imponderables, so self theory temporarily became passé. However, much has been made of various aspects of self theory in the past 40 years, and the self, self-concept, self-esteem, and self-actualization have become prominent topics of discussion in both professional and lay circles.

The Self

In a tone reflective of an earlier time, Jersild (1952) tells us that a person's self "is the sum of all he can call his. The self includes, among other things, a system of ideas, attitudes, values, and commitments. The self is a person's total subjective environment; it is the distinctive center of experience and significance. The self constitutes a person's inner world as distinguished from the other world consisting of all other people and things." Calhoun and Acocella (1983, p. 38) also define the self: "The self may be defined as a hypothetical construct referring to the complex set of physical processes of the individual." These authors go on to describe five aspects of the self:

1. The physical self (the body and its biological processes)
2. The self-as-process (the perception, response, problem-solving, and action component of the self)
3. The social self (people and roles—father, student, Republican, industrious worker, leader, wife, and so on)
4. The self-concept (what Calhoun and Acocella call the "mental self-portrait")
5. The self-ideal (what the person could be if all barriers were down)

Self theory an all-encompassing term that includes self-concept, self-esteem, self-actualization tendencies, and other aspects of the self.

Of all of those structures, perhaps the most understood and most widely researched is the self-concept.

The Self-Concept

Martens (1975a, 1975b) tells us that the **self-concept** has three important components: cognitive, affective, and behavioral. The cognitive component refers to descriptive terms that we apply to ourselves—*bright, attractive, slow, athletic,* and so forth. The affective component, also known as self-esteem, refers to how we feel about the cognitive ascriptions we have made about ourselves. The behavioral component refers to our tendencies to behave in ways consistent with the cognitive and affective components. The behavioral component was expressed by Jourard (1974), who defined the self-concept as a self-fulfilling prophecy:

> When a person forms a self-concept, thereby defining himself, he is not so much describing his nature as he is making a pledge that he will continue to be the kind of person he believes he is now and has been. One's self-concept is not so much descriptive of experience and action as it is prescriptive. The self-concept is a commitment. (p. 153)

Self-Actualization

Related to the present discussion is the self-actualization motive described by Abraham Maslow. It seems only natural that sport and physical activity would be an important part of what Maslow considers **self-actualization:** "man's desire for self-fulfillment, namely, to the tendency for him to become actualized in what he is potentially" (1970, p. 46). Carrying this definition a step farther, Maslow (cited in Gundersheim, 1982, p. 187) says:

> We may define it as an episode or a spurt in which the powers of the person come together in a particularly efficient and intensely enjoyable way, and in which he is more integrated and less split, more open for experience, more idiosyncratic, more perfectly expressive or spontaneous, or fully functioning, more creative, more humorous, more ego-transcending, more independent of his lower needs, etc. He becomes in these episodes more truly himself, more perfectly actualizing his potentialities, closer to the core of his Being, more fully human.

It seems that sport would be a perfect forum for the manifestation of self-actualizing behavior. The available research, however, is sparse and has shown little relationship between actualization and sport. Gundersheim (1982), in the introduction to a research report, cited eight references prior to 1980, none of which found any relationship between the two variables. Gundersheim also reported on a study he did with male and female university athletes and nonathletes. Numerous cross-sport, cross-sex, and sport and nonsport comparisons were made based on results from the **Personal Orientation Inventory (POI)** (Shostrom, 1963), for many years the most popular measure of self-actualization. The only significant difference found was between male and female athletes: The females scored higher on actualization. In a second study, Ibrahim and Morrison (1976) found a tendency for male and female high school and college athletes to be average or above on self-actualization. Interestingly, and symptomatic of the confused self theory literature in sport psychology, the athletes they studied scored significantly lower than their nonathletic peers on 8 of the 15 dimensions of the **Tennessee Self-Concept Scale (TSCS)** (Fitts, 1965), used to measure the self-concept.

One line of supportive self-actualization research has been that of Sherrill and colleagues (i.e., Sherrill, Gench, Hinson, Gilstrap, Richir, & Mastro, 1990; Sherrill, Gilstrap, Richir, Gench, & Hinson, 1988; Sherrill & Rainbolt, 1988; Sherrill, Silliman, Gench, & Hinson, 1990; and Silliman & Sherrill, 1989) with a variety of handicapped athletes. Another research effort by Leclerc and associates (i.e., Leclerc, Lefrancois, Dube, Hebert, & Gaulin, 1998; Leclerc, Lefrancois, Dube, Hebert, & Gaulin, 1999; Lefrancois, Leclerc, Dube, Hebert, & Gaulin, 1997; and Lefrancois, Leclerc, Dube, Hebert, & Gaulin, 1998) has been directed at adapting the earlier work on the POI and creating a more contemporary and relevant measure of self-actualization.

Self-concept the mental image one has of oneself.
Self-actualization Maslow's term for the full realization of one's potential.
Personal Orientation Inventory a device used to measure self-actualization.
Tennessee Self-Concept Scale a device used to measure various aspects of the self-concept.

Maslow's Concept of Self-Actualization

Abraham Maslow devoted most of his professional life to an in-depth analysis of normal personality, undoubtedly in response to the dominant focus in psychology: psychopathology. His optimistic view was in sharp contrast to the pessimism of the Freudians' psychoanalytic model.

Among Maslow's major contributions to our understanding of human behavior is the concept of self-actualization. Maslow considered a self-actualized person to be someone who achieves a sense of personal harmony or unity and maximizes his or her potentials across a broad spectrum. Before self-actualization can occur, the individual must satisfy a range of needs that motivate behavior. Maslow discussed these needs in terms of a hierarchy. The accompanying pictorial representation of **Maslow's need hierarchy** tells us much about motivation.

At the bottom of the hierarchy are the most compelling needs, *physiological needs*—the need for food, water, and warmth. When these basic needs are met, *safety needs* come into play. The realization that we are generally safe from harm gives us the freedom to satisfy *love and belongingness needs,* the need to be loved and accepted by whatever indi-

Pyramid diagram:
- *Actualization* reaching potential — Self-actualization needs
- *Esteem needs* competence, achievement, approval, recognition — Psychological needs
- *Belongingness and love needs* affiliation, acceptance, belonging — Psychological needs
- *Safety needs* security, safety — Fundamental needs
- *Physiological needs* hunger, thirst, sex drives — Fundamental needs

vidual standards we use to gauge acceptance. Out of this acceptance grows a feeling of *esteem,* a belief that we are not only accepted or loved but also respected for our capabilities. If all of those needs have been satisfied, we are free to achieve the maximization of potential—*self-actualization.*

It would be easy to assume that the needs in the hierarchy are satisfied in a step-by-step, predictable progression. But the process actually is ongoing and dynamic and not predictable. Sudden regressions in service of fundamental needs can sidetrack the achievement of psychological needs and self-actualization. Maslow's work—his emphasis on growth and on the capacity for change, and his positive perspective in general—has had a major impact on psychology.

SOURCES: Hamachek (1987); Suinn (1984).

Maslow's need hierarchy a model that explains motivation in terms of the satisfying of five types of needs: physiological, safety, love and belongingnéss, esteem, and self-actualization. Needs at the lower levels of the hierarchy must be satisfied before higher-level needs can be met.

Status of Research on Self Theory

Several conclusions about the status of research on the self in sport psychology are readily deducible: (1) There is precious little of it, and the available research may be generously summarized as scattered. (2) There is little or no theory driving the research, and the result is the limited generalizability of results. (3) The measurement of self-concept has not been particularly precise. As stated earlier, the most commonly used assessment device is the Tennessee Self-Concept Scale (TSCS). According to McInman (1992), 33% of all self-concept studies in the area of aerobic fitness used the TSCS. In the case of weight-training studies, the figure is 80%.

Critics of the TSCS are not kind. Berger and McInman (1993) take the TSCS to task for being too broad, having too much overlap with other psychological constructs, having high subscale intercorrelations, possessing low convergent validity, and being plagued by broad problems of reliability and validity as a function of the other shortcomings. Berger and McInman feel that future researchers would be better served by using more recent and psychometrically promising scales such as the Physical Self-Perception Profile (PSPP) (Fox & Corbin, 1989) or the Self-Description Questionnaire series: SDQI (primary school students), SDQII (early adolescents), and SDQIII (later adolescents and adults) (Marsh, 1990a, 1990b, 1990c).

The PSPP is strictly a measure of the physical self in terms of five subscales: body, strength, condition, sport, and global physical self-worth. Each subscale has six Likert-type formatted items. The authors report satisfactory psychometric documentation for their scale. As for the SDQ series, 7, 11, and 13 dimensions of self-concept (corresponding to versions I, II, or III) have been identified by Marsh and various colleagues through the use of factor analysis (Marsh, 1987, 1990a, 1990b, 1990c). There seems to be little subscale overlap, and the overall psychometric properties of the SDQ series appear to be acceptable.

There is a healthy awareness of the methodological and assessment problems that have plagued studies of the self in sport psychology to date. The creation of improved assessment tools is particularly encouraging, and it is to be hoped that this line of research in sports and fitness will continue to improve in both numbers and methodological sophistication.

SOME FINAL THOUGHTS ON MOTIVATION

Four other topics are also germane to the subject of motivation and sport psychology. They are sport self-confidence, sport motivation, goal setting, and explanatory style.

Sport Self-Confidence

Vealey (1986) has been at the forefront of research on **sport self-confidence** with the creation of three sport self-confidence measures: the Trait Sport-Confidence Inventory (TSCI), the State Sport-Confidence Inventory (SSCI), and the Competitive Orientation Inventory (COI). SC–Trait refers to the belief or degree of certainty individual athletes possess about their ability to succeed in sports. In the case of SC–State, emphasis is placed on a "right now" orientation that stresses the degree to which an individual believes or expresses certainty at one particular moment. As for the COI, it was developed to deal with problems inherent in the distinction between performance and outcome orientations to competition. Athletes may publicly endorse an "I'd rather perform well than win" sentiment yet engage in behavior of a completely different sort (i.e., "win at all costs") in the heat of battle. The COI forces athletes to choose one or the other approach to competition, thus resulting in either a performance orientation (COI–Performance) or an outcome orientation (COI–Outcome) to competitive situations. In Vealey's initial report in 1986, five separate studies of high school, college, and adult athletes demonstrated that the three scales are psychometrically sound. Additional support for the scales and for the theoretical model was reported in a later study by Vealey (1988).

Partial substantiation of Vealey's efforts has been reported from at least two sources. Gayton and Nickless (1987) administered the TSCI and SSCI to male and female runners competing in the Casco Bay marathon in Portland, Maine. Both scales correlated significantly with the runners' predicted and actual finishing times. Martin and Gill (1991) administered

---

Sport self-confidence a research topic pertaining to athletes' beliefs about their ability to succeed in sports and their views of winning versus performing well.

the Vealey scales to male high school middle- and long-distance runners; these athletes were more performance than outcome oriented and were high in trait and state self-confidence.

As is so often the case with new scales, there are detractors. Feltz (1988), for one, has been critical of the inventories. She indicates that the only thing the trait scale actually predicts well is SC–State, thereby rendering the SC–Trait score redundant and, ultimately, unnecessary. Feltz goes on to say that determining SC–State may be more fruitful than assessing dispositional aspects of self-confidence. Data from the Gayton and Nickless study also raised questions about the necessity for conceptualizing sport self-confidence in terms of a trait–state dichotomy.

Feltz also has criticized the COI, primarily because of the measurement difficulties inherent in assessing something so situationally fleeting as competitive orientation. This criticism has led Feltz to conclude that a measure of dispositional competitive orientation is of little value, a point echoed in the Martin and Gill study.

Despite these criticisms, it appears that Vealey's work is important. Certainly, the trait–state distinction problem and the situational variability in competitive orientation are troublesome and will undoubtedly undergo changes over time. However, additional research into and refinement of these scales could still be fruitful. There is still much to be learned about sport self-confidence, and Vealey as well as her critics have been instrumental in providing direction for future work.

Sport Motivation

A second line of research offering promise is that of sport motivation from the perspective of Willis (1982; Willis & Layne, 1988). Borrowing from the McClelland–Atkinson model of achievement motivation discussed in Chapter 9, Willis created a sport motivation scale designed to measure motive to achieve success (MAS), motive to avoid failure (MAF), and motive to achieve power (MAP). The initial psychometric work on **Willis's sport motivation scale** was done in 1982

Willis's sport motivation scale a scale designed to measure motive to achieve success (MAS), motive to avoid failure (MAF), and motive to achieve power (MAP).

using male and female subjects, all of whom were members of organized sport teams ranging from junior high through college. Seventeen sports and 22 schools were represented in the original Willis sample. The end result of this preliminary research was a 45-item scale arranged on a 5-point Likert-like format. Each of the three subscales (MAS, MAF, MAP) is assessed by 15 items. Initial psychometric work indicated satisfactory alpha and test–retest reliability, adequate content, criterion-related, and construct validity, and relative freedom from social desirability bias. In the 1988 paper, additional construct and concurrent validity was demonstrated in a study of high school football players.

Recent preliminary and as yet unpublished research involving well over a thousand subjects has convinced your authors of the utility of the Willis measure. Of particular interest is the consistent relationship noted between the motive to achieve power and positive constructs from other psychological tests. Athletes at all levels strongly endorse MAP as a sport motivation. At the same time, these athletes score in the positive direction on psychological constructs thought to be desirable, such as psychological vigor, internal locus of control, and positive traits measured within what is known as the Personality Big Five (discussed in Chapter 15). Based on the early work of Willis and the results that have emerged strongly and consistently in our own work, we are convinced that additional research in sport motivation as conceived by Willis is warranted.

Setting Performance Goals in Sport

A popular means of motivating people to perform more effectively is goal setting, and much of its popularity is due to the efforts of Locke and Latham and their collaborators (Locke, 1968; Locke, Shaw, Saari, & Latham, 1981). Locke's original exposition on goal setting in 1968 was followed by a strong substantiation in the 1981 Locke et al. piece. In brief, the research team found that 99 of 110 studies they reviewed substantiated their major hypothesis that specific but difficult goals, if accepted, are more facilitative of performance than are easy, vague, or no goals. Subsequent meta-analyses by Mento, Steel, and Karren (1987) and Tubbs (1986) strongly supported the validity of the goal difficulty/specificity proposition of Locke and associates. In 1985, Locke and Latham extended their goal-setting work to sport psychology and arrived at five conclusions they feel are applicable to sport settings:

1. Specific, difficult goals lead to better performance than vague, easy goals.

2. Short-term goals can facilitate the achievement of long-term goals.

3. Goals affect performance by affecting effort, persistence, and direction of attention, and by motivating strategy development.

4. Feedback regarding progress is necessary for goal setting to work, and

5. Goals must be accepted if they are to affect performance. (p. 205)

Using these five general conclusions as a point of departure, Locke and Latham elaborated on 10 specific hypotheses of their own, all generated with the overall unifying hypothesis that **goal-setting theory** is as applicable to sport as it is in business or research laboratory settings. Chief among their suggestions was the use of goal setting in the practice and competitive environments. For example, Figure 10.1 contains a suggested list of goals for the development of certain skills within a variety of sporting contexts. Specific suggestions for skill attainment are made; all are clear-cut and, at the same time, attainable. The suggestions also serve as specific feedback sources to coaches and athletes. The results of the goal setting are measurable, and thus the goals are far superior to the sort of general advice so often given: "Let's go hard for ten or fifteen minutes" or "Work on your free throws. You've had trouble with them lately."

Another way to look at this set of conclusions from Locke and associates is provided by Smith (1994), who talks about **SMART goals** when he talks to coaches and athletes: Goals must be specific (S) or spell out clearly what is to be accomplished. Goals must be measurable (M) or quantifiable in some sense. Goals should be action oriented (A) and indicative of something germane to the activity at hand that needs to be accomplished. Goals must be realistic (R), sensible and capable of being carried out. Goals must be timely (T), able to be accomplished in a reasonable time frame. Bringing all this together, then, results in SMART goals.

Table 10.1 offers concrete ways of assessing goal-setting performance in football and basketball. Players are provided with measurable and attainable goals that push them to greater performance. This goal setting, in turn, translates into better overall team performance, an obvious goal of coaches of team sports. Crucial to the success of goal setting is the concept of reinforcement (see Chapter 5). In brief, reinforcement must convey to the athletes that it is contingent on very specific behavior by them. Reinforcement should be used to accurately portray degrees of skill acquisition.

Before moving on to explanatory style, it should be noted that all is not utopian in the goal-setting literature. Tenenbaum, Pinchas, Elbaz, Bar-Eli, and Weinberg (1991) and Weinberg, Fowler, Jackson, Bagnall, and Bruya (1991) cite a number of difficulties with the Locke and Latham work—namely, equivocal results with regard to the goal difficulty/specificity issue. Tenenbaum and his associates feel that the research findings are sufficiently equivocal to call into serious question the generalization of goal-setting results from industry to the sport and exercise setting. In the Weinberg et al. research, subjects in two separate motor tasks showed no decrement in performance irrespective of goal difficulty—that is, subjects placed in unrealistic-goal conditions, while admitting the difficulty of the assigned task, did not show any motivation decrements. This finding, as is intimated by both the Tenenbaum and the Weinberg research teams, is suggestive of the fact that much is yet to be done in understanding the role of goal setting in sport performance. Both groups also propose that personality variables probably moderate the effects of goal-setting strategies, and additional research of this nature is warranted.

Explanatory Style

Considerable interest has emerged of late about differences in what is known as **explanatory style.** Seligman,

Goal-setting theory the idea, found applicable not only in business but also in sport, that specific but difficult goals that are agreed to, and feedback about goal achievement will facilitate performance.

SMART goals Smith's acronym for goals that are simultaneously specific (S), measurable (M), action oriented (A), realistic (R), and timely (T).

Explanatory style the way in which a person accounts for positive and negative happenings; a negative, pessimistic style sometimes correlates with poorer performance than does a positive, optimistic style.

FIGURE 10.1

Examples of Goals for Subcomponents of Skilled Tasks

Tennis

10 backhands in a row down the line

10 volleys in a row alternating left and right corners

5 first serves in a row in left third of service court; 5 in middle third; 5 in right third

5 returns of serve in a row deep to the add court

Football

Wide receiver:

5 over-the-head catches in a row of a 40-yard pass

5 one-handed catches in a row of a 15-yard pass

Defensive back:

5 interceptions in a row with receiver using preannounced route

2 or fewer completions allowed out of 5 tries with receiver running unknown route

Kicker:

10 field goals in a row from 40-yard line

Baseball

Infielder:

10 hard grounders in a row fielded without error, 5 to left and 5 to right

Outfielder:

20 fly balls caught on the run without error, 5 to left, 5 to right, 5 in back, 5 in front

Hitter:

5 curve balls in a row hit out of infield

Wrestling

6 takedowns using at least two techniques against an inferior but motivated opponent in (?) minutes

6 escapes using at least 3 different techniques in (?) minutes against same opponent

Basketball

20 foul shots in a row

30 uncontested lay-ups in a row

10 jump shots in a row from 10 feet

dribbling 2 minutes man-on-man against best defensive player without losing ball

Soccer

10 shots into left corner of goal from 30 feet with goalie not moving from center of goal

5 goals out of 10 shots from 20 feet with goalie free to move

Hockey

Goalie:

stops 10 of 15 shots from 20 feet

stops 5 of 10 one-on-one situations

Forward:

passes successfully 8 out of 10 times to open man in front of net with one defender in between

Lacrosse

Similar to soccer and hockey

Golf

6 drives in a row over 200 yards and landing on fairway

15 putts in a row of 12 feet

10 nine-irons in a row onto green from 75 yards

SOURCE: Locke & Latham (1985).

Nolen-Hoeksema, Thornton, and Thornton (1990) suggest that some people habitually attribute *bad* life events to factors that are stable in time, global in effect, and internal, and *good* happenings to factors that are unstable, specific, and external. Seligman et al. regard this explanatory style as pessimistic and hypothesize that it results in poor performance in achievement situations, generalizes across behavioral domains and lowers performance, and likely leads to lowered behavioral resiliency in the face of failure.

TABLE 10.1

Concrete Ways of Assessing Performance in Football and Basketball

A. Sample Point System for Defensive Lineman in Football

Point value	Action
20	Touchdown
10	Interception or fumble recovery
5	Cause fumble
5	Sack
3	Block pass
3	Pressure passer (e.g., within 3 feet of passer when ball released)
5	Tackle runner for 5 yard loss or more
4	Tackle runner for 1 to 4 yard loss
3	Tackle runner after gain of 0 to 3 yards
2	Tackle runner after gain of 4 to 5 yards
3	Tackle after lineman runs more than 10 yards
1	Any other tackle
—	Assist on any of above: one-half the number of points indicated
—	Bonus points (0 to 20): Any key 4th-quarter play in a winning effort: judgment of coaches

Possible comparison standards for setting goals:

1. Own performance (number of points in previous game and/or against same opponent last time played)
2. Own best previous performance (same season)
3. Performance of other team's best lineman in previous week
4. Average of all defensive linemen on same team in previous week

B. Sample Point System for Basketball Players

Point value	Action
2	Field goal
1	Assist
1	Foul shot
1	Rebound
1	Steal
1	Blocked shot
Number of points held below average	Hold opposing player to less than season average (one-on-one defense)

Possible comparison standards for setting goals:

1. Own season average
2. Own performance against same opponent that year
3. Own performance in last 3 games

SOURCE: Locke & Latham (1985).

Applications of Goal Setting in a Variety of Settings and Circumstances

Goal Area	Goal
Psychological skills training	A high jumper imagines successful completion of a personal best and engages in appropriate self-reinforcement statement.
Physical fitness	A 60-year-old woman with high blood pressure sets a goal of reducing her heart rate from 210 to 180 in one month of relaxation training and yoga.
Individual skills	An 11-year-old golfer sets a goal for the summer of reducing the average number of putts required to complete nine holes of competitive golf from 22 to 18.
Team skills	A Little League team of 12-year-olds sets a season goal of reducing errors in the field from 3 at the start of the season to 1 by the end.
Physical health	A recent heart attack victim with a weight problem sets a goal of losing 3 pounds a month for 12 months through an exercise regimen, rewarding himself every 3 months with new clothes reflective of his weight loss.
Personal satisfaction	A middle-aged but competitive softball player sets a goal of at least 3 self-statements each game during the season reflective of the notion that the game is fun and not World War Three.

To measure explanatory style, Seligman and his colleagues created the **Attributional Style Questionnaire (ASQ)** (Peterson, Semmel, von Baeyer, Abramson, Metalsky, & Seligman, 1982; Seligman, Abramson, Semmel, & von Baeyer, 1979). Scores for good and bad explanatory styles are derived from responses to items assessing three causal dimensions: stable versus unstable, global versus specific, and internal versus external. A composite score is derived for bad events by adding scores on the three dimensions for bad events. Good-event scores are derived in essentially the same way—by adding responses to good events. A composite score can also be obtained by subtracting good from bad scores.

Seligman et al. (1990) investigated explanatory style and performance in swimmers from two college

teams by administering the ASQ to members of the University of California–Berkeley men's and women's swimming teams prior to the start of the 1987–1988 season. Four major findings resulted from the study:

1. Swimmers with a pessimistic explanatory style were more likely to perform poorly during the season than were swimmers with an optimistic style.

2. Pessimistic swimmers rebounded from a simulated defeat situation less well than did optimistic swimmers.

3. Swimming ability was a less powerful predictor of success than was explanatory style, thereby suggesting that actual performance is jointly determined by an interaction between talent and habitual belief patterns about causes of events.

4. Female swimmers expressed a significantly more negative explanatory style than did males, though

Attributional Style Questionnaire a device for measuring explanatory style.

their scores were very similar to the scores for college women in general. The males, in contrast, were as optimistic in explanatory style as any group the experienced investigators had ever seen other than life insurance agents.

A recent study reported by Higgins, Zumbo, and Hay (1999) lends further support to the utility of the ASQ. Using confirmatory factor analysis on data from over 1,300 respondents, Higgins et al. found solid support for the three-factor model of the ASQ. In summary, the preceding reports are supportive of explanatory style and the ASQ, and indications are that both the theory and the assessment device will continue to be of interest to sport researchers.

SUMMARY

1. Locus of control continues to be a salient personality variable in sport research. Rotter's I–E Scale has been a very popular instrument for the measurement of internal or external locus of control.

2. In response to Rotter's early work, Levenson developed a multidimensional scale of locus of control. The primary difference in the two scales has to do with the external dimension, which Levenson divides into *powerful other* and *chance.*

3. The measurement of locus of control in youth has been largely the province of Nowicki and Strickland. The inability of the young athlete to make a variety of attributions has hampered locus-of-control research in youth sport.

4. Interest in the locus-of-control construct has lessened, but it is an area of interest that will continue to grow though perhaps at a slower rate than in the 1970s and 1980s.

5. The relatively sparse, confused, and atheoretical research in the area of self-esteem and self-concept has hampered efforts to arrive at a better understanding of the role sport and exercise play in enhancing feelings of worth.

6. William James, among others, made significant literature contributions to self theory.

7. Definitions of what constitutes the self are varied. Dimensions such as the physical self, the self-as-process, the social self, the self-concept, and the self-ideal have generally received some degree of universal acceptance.

8. Maslow's conceptualization of the self-actualization motive has been most significant in psychology. However, no consistent relationship between sport and exercise and self-actualization has been noted.

9. Research on self-concept or self-esteem has largely been atheoretical, methodologically flawed, and beset by measurement problems. Much of the research conducted thus far has used the Tennessee Self-Concept Scale (TSCS), and its use has been called into question because of problems of validity, reliability, and subscale overlap. It has been suggested that more promising scales, such as the Physical Self-Perception Scale and the Self-Description Questionnaire series, should be used in future sport psychology research on self theory.

10. Four additional motivational topics of interest include Vealey's work in the area of sport self-confidence; sport motivation measurement as viewed by Willis, involving the motive to achieve success, the motive to avoid failure, and the motive to achieve power; Locke and Latham's work in the area of goal setting; and Seligman's explanatory style, which is measured with the Attributional Style Questionnaire (ASQ).

KEY TERMS

Attributional Style Questionnaire (ASQ) (146)
explanatory style (143)
external locus of control (134)
goal-setting theory (143)
internal locus of control (134)
Levenson's IPC Scale (135)
locus of control (134)
Maslow's need hierarchy (140)
Nowicki–Strickland Scale (136)
Personal Orientation Inventory (POI) (139)
Rotter's I–E Scale (134)
self-actualization (139)
self-concept (139)
self theory (138)

SMART goals (143)
sport self-confidence (141)
Tennessee Self-Concept Scale (TSCS) (139)
Willis's sport motivation scale (142)

SUGGESTED READINGS

Dweck, C. S. (1992). The study of goals in psychology. *Psychological Science, 3,* 165–167.

Dweck discusses the resurgence of interest among psychologists over the past several years concerning motivation. She also reviews a considerable body of literature. Dweck concludes the article by making a case for her own work in goals and their attendant behavior–cognition–affect patterns as a primary motivating force in human behavior.

Klein, H. J., Wesson, M. J., Hollenbeck, J. R., & Alge, B. J. (1999). Goal commitment and the goal-setting process: Conceptual clarification and empirical synthesis. *Journal of Applied Psychology, 84,* 885–896.

This meta-analysis of 83 studies updates much of the earlier research on goal setting. The authors provide an excellent synthesis of the existing theories and explanations for goal setting. Key to this article is the role of goal commitment in goal setting. There are some who say that goal commitment is not of great importance in goal setting, but these authors see it as central to the whole process.

Lefcourt, H. M. (1966). Internal versus external control of reinforcement: A review. *Psychological Bulletin, 65,* 206–220.

A summary of the literature concerning the locus-of-control construct is presented by Lefcourt, one of the leading authorities in the area. Of particular interest is Lefcourt's review of his own early work as well as that of other prominent locus-of-control researchers, including Rotter and Levenson.

Seligman, M. E. P., & Csikszentmihalyi, M. (2000). Positive psychology. *American Psychologist, 55,* 5–14.

These eminent psychologists guest-edited 15 articles on optimism for the *American Psychologist.* Though not sport psychologists, Seligman and Csikszentmihalyi are two major contributors to the sport psychology literature on optimism and flow, respectively. Both advocate a movement in psychology toward a more positive perspective, and they reveal interesting anecdotes that have guided their interest in optimism. Seligman's personal revelation on page 6 about his conversion to optimism is particularly noteworthy.

 ## INFOTRAC COLLEGE EDITION

For additional readings, explore Infotrac College Edition, your online library. Go to: http://www.infotrac-college.com/wadsworth *Hint:* Enter these search terms: Abraham Maslow, emotional intelligence, explanatory style, goal setting, motivation, self-actualization, self-perception, self theory.

Social Psychology of Sport:
Leadership and Group Cohesion

CHAPTER 11

Leadership
Group Cohesion
Summary
Key Terms
Suggested Readings

Helping a teammate from the playing field is an act of good sportsmanship.
© Michael Newman/PhotoEdit

The social psychology of sport comprises a number of interesting areas, including leadership, group cohesion, and audience effects. Few would question the role of players or coaches as leaders. It is widely believed that cohesive teams are going to be the most successful ones. It is usually the coach (or leader) who is expected to forge these cohesive and successful units. Athletic performance is also moderated by audience effects. Being around other participants, being evaluated by coaches, parent, and peers, and being cheered on by friendly supporters all fall under that rubric. The first two items in this threesome from the social psychology literature are discussed in this chapter. Audience effects is the subject of Chapter 12.

LEADERSHIP

The urgency of the hour calls for leaders of wise judgment and sound integrity—leaders not in love with money, but in love with justice; leaders not in love with publicity, but in love with humanity; leaders who can subject their egos to the greatness of the cause.

Martin Luther King, Jr.

Leadership is getting someone to do what they don't want to do in order to achieve what they want to achieve.

Tom Landry, former coach of the Dallas Cowboys

Leadership is the assertion of a vision and not simply the exercise of a style.

A. Bartlett Giamatti, former commissioner of major league baseball

The ancient Chinese and Egyptians wrote of leadership. Homer's *Iliad* provides early Greek examples of leadership qualities: the fairness of Agamemnon, the wisdom of Nestor, the shrewdness of Odysseus, and the valor of Achilles. According to Bass (1981), discussion of leadership dates back to the time of Plato, Julius Caesar, and Plutarch.

Psychologists have studied the concept of leadership for nearly 100 years. Much has been learned, but there are still as many definitions and ideas of what constitutes leadership as there are experts to generate

them. Burns (1978, p. 2) states unequivocally that "leadership is one of the most observed and least understood phenomena on earth."

Although leadership has always been recognized as an important part of sport, it has been scientifically addressed for only about 25 years (Danielson, 1976; Danielson, Zelhart, & Drake, 1975). Everyone is familiar with individuals in sport who have established a winning tradition through their leadership capabilities. Football fans from the 1970s can attest to the leadership of Roger Staubach in making the Dallas Cowboys a power for many years. He refused to believe that the Cowboys would lose, and the effect of his tenacity on his teammates was highly positive.

At one time Staubach's ability to play in the National Football League was widely questioned because as a graduate of the U.S. Naval Academy he had a five-year active-duty military obligation. Near the end of Staubach's five years in the Navy, your senior author expressed concern about the effects of Staubach's long hiatus. An acquaintance who had played with Staubach at the Naval Academy took exception, insisting that Staubach would become a force in the NFL primarily but not exclusively because of his leadership ability. As the ex-teammate said, "If Roger wanted you to do it, it was simple. You did it! We knew he was right, and we would have done anything he asked. He's the greatest leader I have ever seen." Obviously, Staubach's former teammate knew what he was talking about. Many football fans—not all supporters of the Cowboys—thrilled to his last-ditch efforts and exhortations in snatching victory from apparent defeat. Staubach rallied his mates to wins on 23 occasions after trailing in the fourth quarter, and 14 of those comebacks came in the last 2 minutes of regulation play or in the overtime period.

A more recently retired player, John Elway of the Denver Broncos, exemplifies many of the same leadership qualities attributed to Hall-of-Famer Staubach. According to an article in the *Austin* (Texas) *American Statesman,* during his 16-year career with the Denver Broncos, Elway rallied his team to wins in the fourth quarter on 40 occasions (Game Winning Drives, 1999). Part of this success can undoubtedly be attributed to his athletic ability, but some surely can be explained by leadership. Kip Corrington (1994), a defensive back and teammate of Elway's, said in a conversation with your senior author: "John raised his

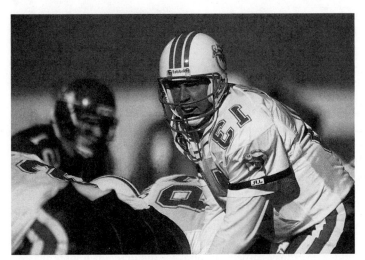

Future Hall of Fame quarterback Dan Marino exuded the kind of confidence that brought out the best in himself and his teammates. "Players have to feel that you're the kind of guy who can make it happen when you're called on," he said.
© Rob Tringali, Jr./Sportschrome USA

game to another level in pressure situations, and the rest of the team seemed to do the same thing. He led more by example than anything else, but he got the job done." Whether this ability to perform at a peak level when the outcome of a competition hangs in the balance is really a function of leadership is open to conjecture. However, Corrington strongly suggests that during his five years with the Broncos, Elway's leadership in game situations was clearly a major factor in the team's numerous come-from-behind wins. In a *USA Today* interview, Elway somewhat humorously responded to all the hoopla associated with the comebacks by stating: "There's a reason I was always making those come-from-behind victories; we were always behind" (Weiner, 1999, p. C2).

Examples such as Staubach and Elway have fueled interest in the relationship between sport and leadership. Before examining the topic of sport leadership in depth, however, a review of general theories and research is in order.

Leadership studies in the United States probably began around the turn of the twentieth century (Bass, 1981). These early efforts generated interest that has continued unabated. Several general theories or models have been proposed over the years, and brief accounts of six of them follow on the next several pages.

General Theories of Leadership

TRAIT THEORY. The earliest theory of leadership is **trait theory** (also known as the "great man" theory), which views leadership from the vantage point of the leader. In its simplest form, trait theory suggests that a person who is a leader in one situation will be a leader in any circumstance because he or she possesses the traits that make for excellence in leadership. The typical paradigm for testing trait theory is to select effective and ineffective leaders through some subjective judgment and measure both types of leaders on a variety of personal, psychological, and demographic variables. Then, appropriate statistical procedures are applied to the data to see whether there are differences between the two groups on any of the assumed-to-be relevant dimensions. Assuming that the theory is correct and all of the preceding conditions have been met satisfactorily, critical traits distinguishing leaders should then emerge.

One variable that has received mild support in the literature on trait theory is intelligence. Bass (1981) cites 23 studies supportive of the position that leaders are intellectually brighter than so-called followers. Bass cites five references to the contrary and also mentions five more indicating that large disparities in the intelligence of leaders and others can actually militate against successful leadership. Research has revealed little of note about the personality traits of leaders, although many variables have been advanced as relevant. To sum up the problems inherent in trait theory, a quote by Brown (1954, p. 219) may be appropriate: "The longer and more comprehensive the list of qualities, the more obvious it must be that their possession would be of no use to a junior leader in industry, for he would inevitably be in demand elsewhere as a Prime Minister, or maybe as an Archangel."

BEHAVIOR THEORY. Like trait theory, the behavioral approach to leadership focuses attention on the leader as

---

Trait theory an approach to the study of leadership based on the assumption that certain traits distinguish leaders from nonleaders.

opposed to situational variables. However, the two theories differ considerably in emphasis. **Behavior theory** stresses what a leader actually does. Researchers using the behavioral approach study leaders, categorize their behaviors, and create a checklist of effective leadership behaviors. The evaluation of leader effectiveness is based on the checklist and external criteria such as employee turnover, group productivity, morale, and work absences. The seminal study of leadership behavior was conducted at Ohio State University in the early 1950s. Several scales for assessing leadership were created, and two types of behavior that leaders use to influence their subordinates were isolated: consideration and structure. Consideration is behavior that indicates trust, rapport, concern for subordinates, and an interest in maintaining two-way communication. Structure is behavior that leaders engage in to make sure that things get done—for example, planning, deciding on a course of action, role assignment, and motivating subordinates to perform well.

The Ohio State research team created the **Leader Behavior Description Questionnaire (LBDQ),** which is filled out by subordinates to obtain information about how leaders behave in a variety of situations. The LBDQ has been used in several sport-related leadership studies. Danielson, Zelhart, and Drake (1975) tested adolescent hockey players to see how they viewed coaching leadership behavior. Coaches were seen as much more communication oriented and less involved in dominance kinds of behavior. Neil and Kirby (1985) administered a version of the LBDQ to elite and novice male and female competitive rowers. Statistical analyses indicated that younger and lesser skilled rowers exhibited a decided preference for open communication with their coaches and for individual consideration to a greater extent than did the older, more experienced rowers.

Snyder (1990) was able to demonstrate the utility of the LBDQ in a study of male and female collegiate coaches from 17 colleges and universities in California. Each coach was asked to respond to the consideration and structure components of the LBDQ for purposes of assessing the coaches' perceptions of their respective athletic directors (i.e., leaders). Male coaches were more likely to show a preference for highly considerate athletic directors. Female coaches preferred athletic directors with a structure orientation. It is not clear why males preferred consideration and females preferred structure. Gender-related socialization practices may partially account for the different responses.

FIEDLER'S CONTINGENCY MODEL. A person who is an effective leader in one situation might not be an effective leader in another. For example, an effective army drill sergeant might not be an effective fencing coach. Fiedler believed that effective leadership depends on—is contingent on—characteristics of both the leader and the situation.

Fiedler's contingency model (1967, 1978) takes into account both traits and situational variables as predictors of effective leadership. Styles of leadership receive much emphasis in Fiedler's model. Fiedler identifies two styles: task-oriented, autocratic leadership and relationship-oriented, democratic leadership. The other key aspect of Fiedler's theory is how favorable a situation is for one leadership style or the other. Three factors determine the favorableness of the situation: leader–member interactions, task structure, and the power position of the leader. According to Fiedler's theory, task-oriented leadership works best in either of two situations: (1) when task structure is loose and unfavorable and (2) when task structure is rigid and favorable. And relationship-oriented leadership works best in situations neither too loose nor too rigid and of intermediate favorableness.

Fiedler uses a questionnaire known as the **least preferred coworker (LPC) scale** to measure leadership style. Respondents—leaders—are asked to think of the one person they would *least* like to work with— this person is the LPC, the least preferred coworker. The respondent then describes the LPC by marking up

---

Behavior theory an approach to the study of leadership based on the assumption that the behavior of leaders differs from the behavior of nonleaders.

Leader Behavior Description Questionnaire a questionnaire used to gain information from subordinates (such as team members) about the behavior of their leaders (such as coaches).

Fiedler's contingency model an approach to the study of leadership that takes into account characteristics of both the leader and the situation.

Least preferred coworker scale a questionnaire that asks leaders to describe the one person they would *least* like to work with. Relationship-oriented leaders generally have high LPC scores; task-oriented leaders, low LPC scores.

the LPC scale. The questionnaire consists of 16 or more items describing extremes of behavior or style—for example:

Boring   1 2 3 4 5 6 7 8   Interesting
Friendly 8 7 6 5 4 3 2 1   Unfriendly
Efficient 8 7 6 5 4 3 2 1   Inefficient

The total score is called the LPC score. A high LPC score indicates that the respondent can separate competence from personality in coworkers. A low LPC score indicates an inability to make this distinction. A low score would be tantamount to telling a coworker, "You are an inefficient worker, and you are a boring, unfriendly person." Relationship-oriented leaders describe their least preferred coworker in a relatively favorable way. Task-oriented leaders describe their LPC in more negative terms.

In evaluating the contingency model, Muchinsky (1987) indicated that Fiedler was successful in elevating the importance of situational factors to the level of traits. As a result, Fiedler's contingency model has been the most widely researched and criticized of the modern theories of leadership (Berry & Houston, 1993).

In the 1970s some attempts were made to apply the contingency model to sport. Inciong, in his 1974 study of high school basketball teams, found correlations between performance effectiveness and situation favorableness to be sufficiently low to warrant rejection of the theory. Danielson (1976) studied minor league hockey coaches and concluded that leadership in hockey may have peculiar properties that make it different from leadership in business and industry, where the Fiedler model may be more applicable. Bird (1977) studied female intercollegiate volleyball coaches and players and found no support for Fiedler's formulation.

PATH–GOAL THEORY. House (1971) popularized a situation-specific leadership model known as **path–goal theory,** which focuses on what a leader can do to motivate subordinates to achieve goals. According to this theory, an effective leader is a catalyst and a facilitator. House and Mitchell (1974) indicated that the basic function of a leader is to provide a "well-lighted path" for subordinates. House and Dessler (1974, p. 31) state: "The motivational function of the leader consists of increasing personal pay-offs to subordinates for work-goal attainment, and making the path to these [pay-offs] easier to travel by clarifying it, reducing road blocks and pitfalls, and increasing the opportunities for personal satisfaction en route." Path–goal theory is a contingency model, because it is concerned with situational factors that affect leadership. Situational variables of significance include (1) the characteristics of subordinates (i.e., personality, ability) and (2) environmental constraints (e.g., the task itself, the formal structure of the organization) that impinge on subordinates' job effectiveness and needs.

Though appealing in a common-sense way, path–goal theory has not generated much research in the sport domain. One exception in sport is reported by Chelladurai and Saleh (1978). Their study was conducted with 160 physical education students, and partial support for path–goal theory was gained. Members of team sports had a preference for leaders who would improve their individual performances through training, as well as facilitate improvement through clarification of the relationships among team members. Another test of path–goal theory has been reported by Vos Strache (1979), who investigated the leadership style of coaches as perceived by female basketball players from 29 universities. Players from winning teams perceived their coaches to be high in the more technical aspects of coaching (e.g., persuasion, production emphasis). Players from losing teams perceived their coaches as high on tolerance. Vos Strache interpreted these results as supportive of the path–goal theory notion that the main role of the coach is as a catalyst or facilitator.

LIFE CYCLE THEORY. Life cycle theory, or what Carron (1980) prefers to call situational theory, is a situation-specific approach to leadership that places greater emphasis on subordinates' behavior than on the behavior of the leader (Hersey & Blanchard, 1977; Hersey, Blanchard, & Hambleton, 1980). According to this theory,

---

Path–goal theory an approach to the study of leadership that proposes that effective leaders motivate subordinates to achieve goals by making rewards available, keeping the path to goal achievement free of obstacles, and being mindful of subordinates' levels of personal satisfaction.

Life cycle theory an approach to the study of leadership that focuses on the "maturity" (i.e., the motivation, experience, and competence) of followers. Changes in the maturity of followers prompt changes in the leader's task behavior and relationship behavior.

the effectiveness of the leader depends on three factors: the maturity of the followers, task behavior, and relationship behavior.

Maturity may be viewed in terms of motivation, competence, and experience. Levels of maturity vary from situation to situation. Task behavior is the extent to which a leader engages in one-way communication to explain what to do, when to do it, and how to do it. Relationship behavior is the extent to which a leader engages in two-way communication through social support, psychological "stroking" of followers, and other facilitative behaviors. Thus, life cycle theory explores the interplay of the amount of direction (task behavior) provided by the leader, the amount of social–psychological support (relationship behavior) provided, and the maturity level exhibited by followers with regard to group or leader goals.

According to Hersey, Blanchard, and Hambleton (1980), four styles of leadership are identified by their model:

1. *Low task/high relationship leader behavior.* The term "telling" is applicable to this style of leadership. The leader is very assertive and communication is one-way.

2. *High task/high relationship leader behavior.* The leader engages in "selling" behavior. Two-way communication and social psychological support are of paramount importance.

3. *High task/low relationship leader behavior.* "Participating" is the key term. Shared decision making and two-way communication characterize this leadership style.

4. *Low task/low relationship leader behavior.* "Delegating" is the trademark. Because of followers' maturity, much freedom for decision making is left in the hands of followers.

The application of the model to a sport-related context is well illustrated by the progression from beginning youth sport to competition at the elite level. In the low-task/high-relationship condition, athlete immaturity would dictate a lot of high-task/high-

---

Functional model an approach to the study of leadership that proposes that effective leaders attend to both the instrumental and the expressive needs of subordinates.

relationship leadership from coaches and other youth leaders. As the athlete progresses to the elite amateur or professional level, low-task/low-relationship leadership would probably be effective because of the athletes' maturity, ability to accomplish tasks independently, and willingness to learn and make progress toward personal or group goals.

Partial support for this formulation is provided by Neil and Kirby (1985). These investigators asked 128 elite and 77 novice Canadians (average age 20.3 years) involved in rowing, canoeing, and kayaking to respond to a leadership questionnaire. Overall, differences indicated that the novices preferred a coach who explained how each athlete fit into the total picture, helped new members adjust, did not place unnecessary barriers between him- or herself and team members, did little things to facilitate player satisfaction, and could rule in a decisive fashion when necessary. No gender differences were noted.

THE FUNCTIONAL MODEL. Another model of leadership worthy of consideration is the **functional model,** as proposed by Behling and Schriesheim (1976). Though tested little in sport, the face validity of the functional model is appealing for future sport applications. Essentially, the functional model proposes that the success of any group depends on the satisfaction of expressive and instrumental functional needs. Expressive needs are interpersonal, social, and emotional. Instrumental needs are task related. A leader who is trying to meet the expressive needs of subordinates is concerned with how they interact, with cohesion, and with factors affecting morale. A leader focused on the instrumental function is concerned with task achievement.

An application of the functional model to coaching is as follows: The instrumental, task-oriented head coach selects an expressive assistant, who will relate well to the players, monitor the psychological pulse of the team, and round off any rough edges that are created in the pursuit of skill acquisition (i.e., the instrumental function). Here is an example of the functional model at the player level: The individuals selected as team co-captains in some way strike a balance between the instrumental and expressive functions. Most certainly, some player-leaders are task oriented and others are better at meeting the social–psychological needs of their teammates.

FIGURE 11.1

Multidimensional Model of Sport Leadership

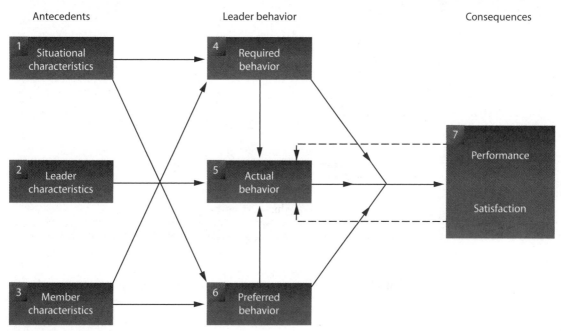

SOURCE: Chelladurai (1990).

One test of the functional model has been made by Rees (1983). Twenty-three collegiate intramural basketball teams answered questionnaires designed to measure leadership development in their respective organizations. In general, Rees found moderate correlations between both functions, thereby failing to lend support to the theory. Rees also found integration of the two roles to be more the norm than was differentiation. These results are further supported by work done by Rees and Segal (1984) with varsity football teams.

Chelladurai's Multidimensional Model of Sport Leadership

In a series of papers, Chelladurai proposed a **multidimensional model of sport leadership** that has been at the forefront in sport leadership research for the better part of 25 years (Chelladurai, 1984a; Chelladurai & Carron, 1978). Figure 11.1 shows an updated version of this model.

The model proposes three types of leader behavior: actual, preferred, and required. *Actual* leader behavior is behavior that is engaged in irrespective of norms or subordinate preferences. *Preferred* leader behavior is behavior that subordinates would like to see in the leader. *Required* leader behavior is behavior expected of the leader on a more formal basis, such as organizational demands. In any athletic situation, but particularly in advanced and formalized situations, the organization expects a leader to behave in certain ways. The leader/coach is expected to select players, organize practices, create a disciplined atmosphere, meet the press and public, and engage in a host of other leadership behaviors. Players, too, have expectations about their leader/coach, for competence, fairness, and humane treatment. The coach in turn has to

---

Multidimensional model of sport leadership an approach to the study of leadership in sport that proposes that congruence among actual, required, and preferred leader behavior determines levels of performance and satisfaction.

TABLE 11.1

Dimensions of Coaching Leadership Behavior on the LSS

Dimension	Description
Training and instruction behavior	Coaching behavior aimed at improving athletes' performance by emphasizing and facilitating hard and strenuous training; instructing athletes in the skills, techniques, and tactics of the sport; clarifying the relationship among the members; and structuring and coordinating the members' activities
Democratic behavior	Coaching behavior that allows greater participation by athletes in decisions pertaining to group goals, practice methods, and game tactics and strategies
Autocratic behavior	Coaching behavior that involves independent decision making and stresses personal authority
Social support behavior	Coaching behavior characterized by a concern for the welfare of individual athletes, positive group atmosphere, and warm interpersonal relations with members
Rewarding (positive feedback) behavior	Coaching behavior that reinforces an athlete by recognizing and rewarding good performance

Source: Chelladurai (1989).

lead in a way that is consistent with his or her own goals, ability, and personality, which will dictate much of his or her actual leadership.

Chelladurai proposed that the antecedents of leader behavior are (1) leader characteristics, (2) subordinate characteristics, and (3) situation (see Figure 11.1). The interaction of these antecedents with the various leader behaviors results in performance and satisfaction at varying levels. According to Chelladurai (1990), the major proposition of the model is that performance and satisfaction are ultimately determined by the degree of congruence among the three types of leader behavior.

To test the theory, Chelladurai developed the **Leadership Scale for Sports (LSS)** (Chelladurai & Saleh, 1978, 1980). The 1980 version is a 40-item scale with five dimensions of coaching behavior. A total of 485 subjects from various Canadian universities (in both studies) responded to the scale. Roughly half of the participants were physical education students of both sexes; the other half were male athletes in basketball, rowing, track and field, and wrestling. The physical education students were asked to indicate their favorite sports; the

athletes were also asked to indicate the actual behavior of their coaches. Statistical analyses yielded five dimensions of coaching leadership behavior: training and instruction, democratic behavior, autocratic behavior, social support, and positive feedback (see Table 11.1). Chelladurai and Saleh (1980) categorized the five dimensions as one direct task factor (training and instruction), two decision-style factors (democratic behavior and autocratic behavior), and two motivational factors (social support and positive feedback).

Efforts aimed at validating the Chelladurai and Saleh measure have been steady. At least 40 published studies have been devoted to the LSS since its creation (LeUnes, 2002). Chelladurai and Carron (1981) have attempted to extend the LSS to youth sport. High school wrestlers (N = 54) and basketball players (N = 193) were administered the LSS. With the exception of the autocratic behavior dimension, the applicability of the LSS to high school sport was supported (incidentally, the autocratic behavior scale was not particularly salient in the 1980 work of Chelladurai and Saleh).

Chelladurai and Carron (1983) had high school and university basketball players complete the "preferred leader behavior" version of the LSS. The goal of the research was to assess the relationship between (1) maturity as defined by level of competition and

Leadership Scale for Sports a questionnaire used to assess leader behavior in sport in terms of task, decision-style, and motivational factors.

preferences for training and instruction (task oriented) and (2) social support (relationship-oriented) approaches to leadership style. In general, findings with regard to training and instruction and to social support were the opposite of what was predicted—that is, preference for both increased rather than decreased with maturity. Several methodological problems are raised by this study. One has to do with maturity. The definitional range from high school to the university level is quite narrow and may not accurately reflect increases in maturity. A second relates to sport as a mechanism for fostering maturity. Chelladurai and Carron (1983) point out that sport is largely an autocratic enterprise that may run counter to the development of maturity.

Another effort by Chelladurai (1984a) bears on the issue of congruence mentioned earlier. Canadian university athletes (basketball players and track-and-field athletes) took part in the study. The LSS was used to assess leadership behavior by coaches. Both the "preferred" and the "perceived" variants of the LSS were used. Training and instruction and positive feedback were the most prevalent dimensions of leadership behavior that bear on athlete satisfaction. To quote Chelladurai (1984b, pp. 338–339):

> The discrepancy between athletes' perception of coaching behaviors and their preferences for specific behaviors was significantly correlated with their satisfaction with leadership, team performance, and overall involvement. Although the pattern of relationships between the discrepancies in the five dimensions of leader behavior and the satisfaction measures varied in the three sport groups studied (basketball, wrestling, and track and field), the relationship between discrepancy in training and instruction and satisfaction with leadership was similar in all three groups. That athletes' satisfaction with leadership increased as the coach's perceived emphasis on this dimension also increased was considered to be consistent with the task oriented nature of athletics. Another finding of their study highlights the effects of situational differences. Basketball players were satisfied even when the coach's positive feedback exceeded their preferences (linear relationship), while the wrestlers were dissatisfied with discrepancy in either direction (curvilinear relationship). Such dis-

crepancy did not have any effect in the track and field group.

In another study, Chelladurai (1986) administered the LSS to collegiate and other adult athletes in India in an effort to establish its utility in other countries. Though limited by the fact that only Indian athletes proficient in the English language were able to participate in the study, the reliability of the LSS was demonstrated.

Yet another study by Chelladurai (Chelladurai, Haggerty, & Baxter, 1989) involved male and female university basketball players and coaches in Canada. Consistent with theory and previous research, considerable congruence among coaches and players was noted in their decision-style choices. Interestingly, both male and female players demonstrated a preference for more autocratic versus participative leadership styles.

The popularity of the LSS is further attested to by the fact that it has been translated into a number of languages: Finnish (Liukkonnen, Salminen, & Telama, 1989), French (Lacoste & Laurencelle, 1989), Japanese (Chelladurai, Imamura, Yamaguchi, Oinuma, & Miyauchi, 1988), Portuguese (Serpa, Pataco, & Santos, 1991), and Swedish (Isberg & Chelladurai, 1990).

In a review paper, Chelladurai (1990) indicated that the multidimensional theory and the LSS have been successful for the most part. He does, however, indicate that there are problems to be addressed in future research, particularly concerning the relationship between leadership and group performance. Chelladurai suggests that the problem may lie in the scale itself, or it could be an artifact of the fragile outcome measures often employed in sports (i.e., win–loss records), which are potentially contaminated by a number of external factors such as the opponents or game officials. In an attempt to address some of the potential psychometric shortcomings of the LSS alluded to by Chelladurai, Zhang, Jensen, and Mann (1997) have created a revised LSS (RLSS). Using factor analysis, Zhang et al. feel that they have demonstrated the utility of the RLSS, and a subsequent effort by Jambor and Zhang (1997) further demonstrated the reliability and validity of the RLSS. Undoubtedly, similar efforts by these and other researchers will extend the utility of the LSS. Research to date is most positive with regard to the multidimensional model and the LSS, and it is anticipated that

Chelladurai's work will be driving leadership research in sports in the foreseeable future.

Player Leadership

An often overlooked aspect of leadership in sports is leadership demonstrated by the players themselves. Good player leadership may transcend bad coaching and, in turn, add much when the coaching leadership is superb. The late-in-the-game heroics of Roger Staubach and John Elway, mentioned at the beginning of this chapter, exemplify this point.

One effort in this area has been offered by Yukelson, Weinberg, Richardson, and Jackson (1983) in a study of collegiate baseball and soccer teams. Though limited in scope and more correlational than causal, preliminary support is generated for the notion of player leadership. Significant correlations were found between leadership status and coach ratings of performance, eligibility, and locus of control. Leaders in both sports were generally viewed as excellent performers by the coaches, were more experienced, and tended to be more internal than external on Rotter's I–E Scale.

In a study of collegiate football players, Garland and Barry (1988) found team leaders to be more group-dependent, tough-minded, extroverted, and emotionally stable. In research conducted with female soccer athletes, Glenn and Horn (1993) separated the players into central (i.e., center forward, center midfielder, center back, sweeper, and goalkeeper) or noncentral (all other player positions), and found self-ratings and coaches' ratings of leadership to be significantly associated with centrality of position. Player leaders also exhibited significantly higher levels of competitive trait anxiety than nonleaders on peer evaluations, perhaps indicating highly competitive or highly motivated behavior on the part of leaders, at least in the view of their teammates. Much more work needs to be done in the neglected area of player leadership.

Evaluation of Leadership Research

Despite the fact that leadership has been the subject of much theorizing and research, only "partial truths" (Muchinsky, 1987, p. 525) have emerged. The trait approach has a certain appeal but lacks comprehensiveness. Behavioral approaches have their applicability, but a leader in one situation may not be a leader in an-

other. Contingency theories are appealing, but the number of leadership factors to be considered appears to be unlimited. Muchinsky suggests that future research may move away from the content of leadership to a more organizational approach emphasizing practices that produce functional or dysfunctional consequences. This transformation would render leadership more of a means than an end.

In sport psychology, little research of consequence has been conducted on most of the models borrowed from industrial/organizational psychology. However, the sport-specific adaptation of a number of these models by Chelladurai shows promise as a potentially viable mechanism for sport scientists to conduct leadership research in the future.

GROUP COHESION

"I am successful because I play my best eleven rather than my eleven best."

KNUTE ROCKNE, NOTRE DAME COACHING LEGEND

Shaw (1976, p. 11) defines a group as "two or more persons who are interacting with one another in such a manner that each person influences and is influenced by each other person." Carron (1980, p. 233) states that "a group is not simply a crowd of people—a group is characterized by purposive interaction in goal directed and/or interpersonal behavior." Carron and Chelladurai (1981) further assert that the factors that most saliently distinguish a group from a random gathering of individuals is the degree of attraction, commitment, and involvement of the individual members related to the collective totality. This triumvirate—attraction, commitment, and involvement—is the essence of cohesion.

The term *cohesion* is derived from the Latin word *cohaesus,* which means "adhering or sticking together" (Carron, 1984). The resistance of the group to disruptive forces (Gross & Martin, 1952) and the total field of forces causing members to remain within a group (Festinger, Schachter, & Back, 1950) are examples from the psychology literature that buttress the theme of sticking together. Carron (1984, p. 341) views cohesion in sport as a "dynamic process that is reflected in the group's tendency to stick together while pursuing its goals and objectives."

The joys of winning a competition are expressed in several ways. Winning also is widely believed to contribute to team cohesion in athletics.
© Reuters NewMedia Inc./CORBIS

In the eyes of coaches and players at all levels of sophistication, team cohesion seems both highly desirable and extremely necessary to ultimate team success. Coaches are expected to forge cohesion among their players, and this expectancy has not gone unnoticed by members of the coaching profession. Silva (1982), in a national survey, found that the issue of how to create and maintain cohesion in sport teams was the most frequently cited concern among the coaches he polled. Players also point to cohesion as a necessary condition for excellence. For example, quarterback Danny White, now retired from the Dallas Cowboys, undoubtedly spoke for many an athlete when he said: "This is not a game you can be successful at on nothing but raw talent. Sooner or later, the team that works together and supports each other is going to come out on top" (Stowers, 1985, p. 20).

The issue of team unity also extends to the fans. A particularly noteworthy example is seen in the baseball World Series championship team of 1979, the Pittsburgh Pirates. Led by the team leader, Willie Stargell, the Pirates generated excitement and unity seldom seen in the annals of sport. To quote Dickey (1982, p. 264):

The "Family" was the big news in the National League in 1979, and one of the great stories in baseball history. It started one rainy spring day in Pittsburgh. The Pirates had been in the habit of playing the Sister Sledge record, "We Are Family," in the clubhouse before and after games. During a rain delay that day, the song was played over the public address system and the fans started singing it. The song became the team's anthem and it forged a bond between fans and players. No team ever deserved the family nickname more.

The examples given here notwithstanding, the relationship between cohesion and team success remains unclear. The popular literature is filled with examples of teams that appeared to be disharmonious but successful. Members of the Oakland A's teams of the early 1970s fought among themselves and with their controversial owner, Charles O. Finley, who was no shrinking violet when it came to a fight with superiors or subordinates. Yet the A's won three consecutive World Series—in 1972, 1973, and 1974. The New York Yankees of 1978 were reputedly a group of malcontents yet won the World Series that year. Recently retired NBA Hall-of-Famer Charles Barkley, somewhat cynically perhaps, summed up his view of the cohesion/team success issue as follows: "Harmony isn't important. The only thing that matters is winning and getting paid" ("The Last Word," 1989, p. 6C).

On a more scientific level, a study by Lenk (1977) is instructive. Lenk worked with a 1960 Olympic champion rowing team from Germany. By most standards, the team was highly successful, but team unity was minimal according to Lenk. In summing up his observations, Lenk (p. 12) says: "The strength of achievement of the crew even increased in the two years in which the crew existed, parallel with the strength of conflict in its increase. The crew was not beaten at all and won the Olympics in 1960. Sports crews can, therefore, perform top athletic achievements in spite of strong internal conflicts." To put it another way, Lenk (p. 38) said: "Even fierce social internal conflicts in top performance rowing crews need not noticeably weaken their achievement strength and capacity if these conflicts do not really blow up the crew."

These examples of both positive and negative reflections on cohesion only serve to illustrate its complex and controversial nature. And the issue of whether to-getherness is really necessary for athletic success only touches the tip of the iceberg insofar as the issue of cohesion is concerned. Let us now address some of the more relevant issues related to team cohesion.

Models of Team Cohesion

Carron (1984) has proposed three cohesion models. The **pendular model of cohesion** suggests that forces affecting team cohesion operate like a pendulum. This idea can be illustrated with an example from high school basketball. During the initial tryout period, a sense of cohesion comes from merely being part of what all team members expect will become a well-oiled machine capable of winning most if not all of its games. Also, the mental and physical demands made on all participants to perform well are cohesive forces. After a short time, however, athletes are divided into subgroups—guards, forwards, centers—for certain parts of the overall workout. Drills and skills somewhat unique to each group are stressed, and competition for a starting spot on the team begins to intensify. At this point, team identity and cohesion are lessened. As skills develop, as players are selected, and as the team is put back together to form a whole, cohesion among team members should again increase. This increase in to-getherness will be particularly evident as actual game competition begins and feelings of "we" are heightened. During the course of the season, events may arise that lessen the team's cohesion and the pendulum may again swing in the direction of disunity.

The **linear model of cohesion** suggests that cohesion progresses in a linear fashion as teams go through various developmental stages, which Tuckman (1965) identified as forming, storming, norming, and performing. According to Tuckman's formulation, cohesion progresses from its most primitive state (forming), to conflict and polarization (storming), to

conflict resolution and a more cooperative stance (norming), to the final stage, in which goal attainment is paramount (performing).

The **life cycle model of cohesion** offers a cradle-to-grave approach to group formation. In this model, initial formative efforts or encounters are followed by a period in which limit testing predominates. This testing process is followed by the creation of a system of expected behaviors or norms, which, in turn, lead to a phase in which goal attainment is emphasized. Finally, the group faces its eventual death through separation or dissolution.

The similarities in the three models appear to be considerable, and none has emerged as superior to the others. Carron (1984) is quick to point out that, regardless of the model preferred, dynamism pervades each of them. Cohesion is definitely not a static, lock-step sort of phenomenon.

Factors Affecting Team Cohesion

Inasmuch as cohesion is a dynamic process, a number of forces must be at work in its creation. Four factors of note are group size, the task, team tenure, and satisfaction.

GROUP SIZE. One of the correlates of cohesion is group size. As is intuitively obvious, the problems of handling a collegiate golf team are very different from the problems associated with managing a university football team that is allowed by NCAA rules to award 85 scholarships to players. In football, much reliance is placed on individual assistant coaches as catalysts for cohesion within the various offensive or defensive domains. As a group becomes larger, communications problems almost certainly arise. Also, it is easy to get lost in the shuffle. Coaches (as well as player-leaders) must be alert to both communication difficulties and feelings of depersonalization. Another negative outgrowth of too much size is the feeling that the individual can slack off because the group will collectively make up the difference. It may be tempting, perhaps because of laziness or fatigue, to go at half speed for a few plays in football on the assumption that the other 10 players will pick up the slack. In this regard, Hoeksema–van Orden, Gaillard, and Buunk (1998) have noted that fatigue does in fact serve as an impediment to group cohesion and productivity. To

---

Pendular model of cohesion the idea that forces swing team members back and forth between cohesion and disunity.
Linear model of cohesion the idea that cohesion progresses in a predictable way through a series of stages: forming, storming, norming, and performing.
Life cycle model of cohesion the idea that the life cycle of a group is similar to the human life cycle.

combat this problem in their study, Hoeksema–van Orden et al. used individualization of collective tasks and providing public individual feedback as countermeasures to the deleterious effect of fatigue.

Related to slacking off are two social psychological concepts: the Ringelmann effect and social loafing. The **Ringelmann effect** is named after a French agricultural engineer (C. J. Hardy, 1990) who observed many years ago that average effort decreases with an increase in group size. Ringelmann watched individuals and groups of two, three, and eight persons engaged in a rope-pulling task. Eight-person groups pulled only 49% of the average individual force. Three-person groups pulled 85% of the average individual force; two-person groups, 93%.

Ingham, Levinger, Graves and Peckham (1974) resurrected Ringelmann's work and found essentially the same results as Ringelmann. However, Ingham et al. noted an important difference between their findings and those of Ringelmann. Their research outcomes replicated those of Ringelmann in instances where group size increased from one to two and two to three, but the effect diminished with the addition of a fourth, fifth, or sixth member. Nonsignificant performance decrements were noted in the latter three situations. This finding led Ingham et al. to conclude that the Ringelmann effect is not linear, as long supposed, but curvilinear.

Social loafing is a decrease in individual effort due to the presence of coworkers (Latane, Williams, & Harkins, 1979). Essentially, what produces social loafing is a decrease in group motivation as group size increases. Social loafing has been tested in such diverse situations as shouting and clapping, rowing and hand grip, running, swimming, pumping air, cognitive tasks, brainstorming, maze solving, song writing, evaluation and judgment tasks, signal detection tasks, pulling a tug-of-war rope, and making paper moons (C. J. Hardy, 1990; Shepperd, 1993). In addition, social loafing research has been conducted in a variety of countries, including the United States, France, India, Japan, Poland, and Taiwan (Harkins & Syzmanski, 1987). This documentation of interest led C. J. Hardy (1990, p. 312) to conclude, "Social loafing is a robust phenomenon, threatening the actual productivity of a variety of collective endeavors."

Williams and Karau (1991) offer an example of social loafing in academic life. The teacher divides a class into small groups and asks students to work together on an assigned task. In general, this scenario opens the door to social loafing and hard feelings. At the conclusion of the group effort, a final product is expected to emerge, and individual grades reflecting group effort are thus assigned. Invariably, some members contribute substantially to the group effort, others contribute a little, and others add nothing.

At least two factors moderate social loafing: identifiability of individual effort and evaluation of individual effort (Latane, 1973; Latane, Williams, & Harkins, 1979; Williams, Harkins, & Latane, 1981). When groups are large, evaluation potential drops as each individual contribution becomes obscured within the totality. The origins of glitches in the system are unclear because of the inability to correctly identify the sources of poor group performance. Latane et al. (1979) conducted group research in a number of situations, and one particularly relevant to our concerns within sport is most intriguing. Through a creative series of experimental manipulations, Latane, Harkins, and Williams (1980) were able to deal effectively with the identifiability issue in a study of intercollegiate swimmers. Latane and his colleagues asked 16 swimmers to take part in both individual and relay swimming events. All swimmers participated in two 100-meter freestyle events as individuals and then swam one lap in each of two 400-meter freestyle relay races. Identifiability was manipulated by announcing or not announcing individual lap times. In the low-identifiability condition, individual times were faster (61.34 seconds) than were the corresponding relay times (61.66 seconds), all of which is suggestive of social loafing. However, under the high-identifiability condition, individual times were slower (60.95 seconds) than were the relay times (60.18 seconds). The announcing of individual times evidently did much to eliminate social loafing. Also, the high-identifiability condition served as a social incentive to perform.

Some researchers take the counter position on the social loafing phenomenon. Research conducted by Worchel, Hart, and Butemeyer (1991) and by Zaccaro (1984) indicates that individual effort can actually

---

Ringelmann effect the tendency of the average effort of group members to decrease with an increase in group size.
Social loafing a decrease in individual effort due to the presence of coworkers.

increase in instances where task relevance, intergroup competitiveness, partner effort, and personal involvement are salient. Kerr and Bruun (1981) labeled this phenomenon **social striving.**

Based on an analysis of pertinent research and theory, C. J. Hardy (1990) arrived at a set of implications for sport psychologists and coaches from the social loafing literature. Among Hardy's recommendations are:

1. Keep individual effort and subsequent evaluation identifiable.

2. Increase individual responsibility to the group by increasing group interaction, task commitment, and level of task cohesion.

3. Seek to make tasks personally involving, with an emphasis on collective identity.

4. Employ systematic goal-setting procedures for both the team and individual members.

5. Keep lines of communication open to prevent and/or treat emerging social loafing.

6. Allow for uniqueness and creativity in individual contributions to the total team effort.

7. Keep in mind that temporary or situational decrements in motivation may actually be adaptive.

8. Where feasible, rotate athletes to other playing positions; this allows for better assessment of the likelihood of social loafing as well as assessing its impact on the collective.

9. Provide breaks in the intensity of preparation to perform athletically. No one can perform at peak intensity at all times, and breaks provide for balance and regeneration.

10. Finally, somxonx will notice of you don't do your bxst! [sic]

Inasmuch as sport teams are highly susceptible to social loafing, it behooves researchers to continue

looking into this phenomenon, as it is a potential source of performance decrements within sport.

THE TASK. The task at hand for sport teams is another correlate of cohesion. Obviously, all sports do not require the same degree of cooperative effort among and between members. Cox (1990) refers to an interactive–coactive continuum to explain this relationship. **Interactive sports** are sports in which close teamwork is required for success. **Coactive sports** require little individual interaction. In turn, Cox talks of low means interdependence and high means interdependence, a conceptual framework created by Goldman, Stockbauer, and McAuliffe (1977). Coactive tasks exemplify low means interdependence; interactive tasks personify high means interdependence. Sports such as golf and riflery require little team interaction, and interdependence is therefore low. In contrast, basketball and volleyball require that all players depend on each other for success, and interdependence is high. As is almost always the case, the coaction–interaction dichotomy is not steadfast. Some sports (softball and rowing) involve aspects of both coaction and interaction and involve a moderate amount of interdependence. Table 11.2 provides a summary of the coaction–interaction and means-interdependence relationship.

Research in the area of task interaction and cohesion is scant. Cratty (1989) has intimated that sports such as hockey require a positive cohesiveness–performance effect, whereas this relationship may be less apparent and necessary among successful shooters (Widmeyer, Brawley, & Carron, 1992). Clearly, much remains to be done in the area of task characteristics as they relate to group cohesiveness.

TEAM TENURE. The length of time that a team stays together is an important aspect of cohesion. Donnelly (1975) talks of a **team half-life** (Donnelly, Carron, & Chelladurai, 1978). Donnelly analyzed data on six major league baseball teams from 1901 to 1965 and concluded that a half-life of five years was most desirable for success, thereby suggesting that cohesion does not take place instantaneously but requires time and nurturance. In Donnelly's study, a half-life was considered to be the amount of time it took for the starting roster of a particular team to turn over by 50%. From this, Donnelly arrived at the five-year figure by studying win–loss records and player turnover rates. Though

---

Social striving an increase in individual effort due to factors such as intergroup competitiveness and partner effort.
Interactive sports sports such as soccer and volleyball in which close teamwork is required for success.
Coactive sports sports such as bowling and wrestling that require little individual interaction.
Team half-life the amount of time it takes for the starting roster of a particular team to turn over by 50%.

TABLE 11.2

Coaction–Interaction and Means–Interdependence Relationship

Coacting teams	Mixed coacting–interacting	Interacting teams
Low means-interdependent tasks	Moderate means-interdependent tasks	High means-interdependent tasks
Archery	American football	Basketball
Bowling	Baseball/softball	Field hockey
Field events (track)	Figure skating	Ice hockey
Golf	Rowing	Rugby
Riflery	Track events	Soccer
Skiing	Tug-of-war	Team handball
Ski jumping	Swimming	Volleyball
Wrestling		
Degree of task cohesion required		
Low	Moderate	High

SOURCE: Cox (1990).

caveats are necessary about the relevance of this finding to other teams and sports, Donnelly's work is suggestive of a temporal force in team cohesion. More work needs to be done in this aspect of team tenure.

A related phenomenon is team stability. Keeping players together for reasonable periods of time would seem to be a necessary first step in creating a cohesive atmosphere. Some evidence indicates that stability does in fact contribute to performance success. In a study of 18 German soccer teams, Essing (1970) found that successful teams made fewer lineup changes than did less successful ones (correlation of .62 between winning and lineup stability). Essing also found that successful teams used their better players more on average and that newly acquired players were put into action less on winning teams.

Zander (1976) adds another perspective on the team stability. In discussing reactions of the management of losing teams, Zander (pp. 974–975) says: "Poorly performing organizations typically release more members than do organizations that are succeeding—this is demonstrated at the end of a professional sports season when losing teams rid themselves of

managers and players, while winning teams leave well enough alone."

None of the preceding assertions address the circular nature of the stability–cohesion issue: Are stable teams more cohesive, or are cohesive teams more stable? Perhaps future research efforts will shed light on this question.

SATISFACTION. A decided circularity is seen in cohesion and individual or team satisfaction. Satisfaction could either be a cause or an effect of group cohesion. Also of relevance here is performance success. There are two noteworthy models for viewing the interaction among satisfaction, success, and cohesion. An early model by Martens and Peterson (1971) posits a circular relationship, with performance success leading to satisfaction, which, in turn, leads to team cohesion. A second model, from Williams and Hacker (1982), hypothesizes that performance success leads to both satisfaction and team cohesion, that team cohesion can lead to satisfaction, but that satisfaction in and of itself leads nowhere in terms of either success or cohesion. Figure 11.2 is a representation of both of these models.

FIGURE 11.2

Two Models of the Relationship Among Performance, Satisfaction, and Cohesion

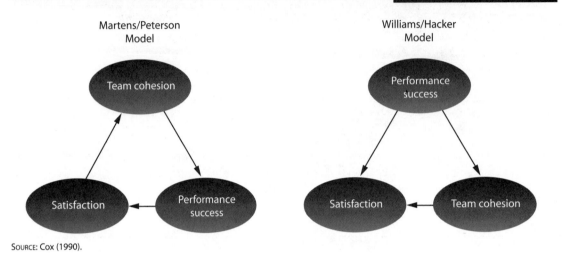

Martens/Peterson Model

Williams/Hacker Model

SOURCE: Cox (1990).

In brief, the two models agree that a relationship exists between performance success, satisfaction, and team cohesion, but the direction of causality constitutes a fundamental point of departure between them. Based on the Williams and Hacker model in particular, Cox (1990) urges continuation of efforts aimed toward maintaining team cohesion on the part of coaches. Cox also urges researchers to continue to study this interrelationship and suggests that the Group Environment Questionnaire (Carron, Widmeyer, & Brawley, 1985) may provide the most effective way to measure team cohesion.

Measures of Team Cohesion

Two of the more prominent instruments that have emerged to measure cohesion in sport are the Sports Cohesiveness Questionnaire (SCQ) and the Group Environment Questionnaire (GEQ). The SCQ has been a popular measure in sport cohesion research,

Group Environment Questionnaire a questionnaire that measures four dimensions of sport-related cohesion: group integration–task, group integration–social, individual attractions to the group–task, and individual attractions to the group–social.

having been a part of at least 12 published studies (Widmeyer, Brawley, & Carron, 1985). It consists of seven questions. The first five load on social cohesion; the final two are more task related. Even though the SCQ is not the instrument of choice in cohesion research today, R. Martens (personal communication, June 9, 2000) reports that he still receives 20 or 25 requests a year for his scale.

The most-referenced sport-related measure of cohesion is the **Group Environment Questionnaire** (Carron, Widmeyer, & Brawley, 1985; Widmeyer, Brawley, & Carron, 1985). The GEQ represents the soundest integration of cohesion theory and research to date. Widmeyer and his colleagues have been critical of other measures of cohesion, primarily because they are largely atheoretical. Widmeyer et al. also argue that, in addition to theory problems, too little has been done to validate the psychometric properties of cohesion measures used up to this time. Widmeyer and his associates go on to state unequivocally that the lack of conceptual clarity and inadequate measurement procedures add up to equivocal results.

The GEQ is derived from Chelladurai's multidimensional model of sport leadership and places em-

FIGURE 11.3

Items from the Group Environment Questionnaire

Individual attractions to the group–social

"I do not enjoy being part of the social activities of this team."

"I am not going to miss the member of this team when the season ends."

"Some of my best friends are on this team."

"I enjoy other parties more than the team parties."

"For me this team is one of the most important social groups to which I belong."

Individual attractions to the group–task

"I am not happy with the amount of playing time I get."

"I am unhappy with my team's level of desire to win."

"This team does not give me enough opportunities to improve my personal performance."

"I do not like the style of play on this team."

Group integration–social

"Members of our team would rather go out on their own than get together as a team."

"Our team members rarely party together."

"Our team would like to spend time together in the off-season."

"Members of our team do not stick together outside of practices and games."

Group integration–task

"Our team is united in trying to reach its goals for performance."

"We all take responsibility for any loss or poor performance by our team."

"Our team members have conflicting aspirations for the team's performance."

"If members of our teams have problems in practice, everyone wants to help them so we can get back together again."

"Our team members do not communicate freely about each athlete's responsibilities during competition or practice."

SOURCES: Hogg (1992); Widmeyer, Brawley, & Carron (1985).

phasis on social and task aspects of group behavior. It was created in response to the perceived inadequacies of other measures. It is an 18-item questionnaire responded to along a 9-point continuum ranging from "strongly agree" to "strongly disagree." Four dimensions of cohesion are measured: group integration–task, group integration–social, individual attractions to the group–task, and individual attractions to the group–social. **Group integration** represents the perceptions of the group as a total unit (or team). **Individual attractions to the group** refers to each member's attraction to the group. Those two basic dimensions are subdivided into task and social orientations to yield group integration–task (GI–T), group integration–social (GI–S), individual attractions to the group–task (ATG–T), and individual attractions to the group–social (ATG–S). To summarize the GEQ, Brawley (1990, p. 365) says, "The four related dimensions concerning various perceptions of cohesion are likely a product of complex person–environment attraction." Figure 11.3

Group integration the perceptions of the group as a total unit, or team; the GEQ measures task (GI–T) and social (GI–S) aspects of this dimension of cohesion.

Individual attractions to the group each member's attraction to the group, or team; the GEQ measures task (ATG–T) and social (ATG–S) aspects of this dimension of cohesion.

FIGURE 11.4

Conceptual Model of Group Cohesion

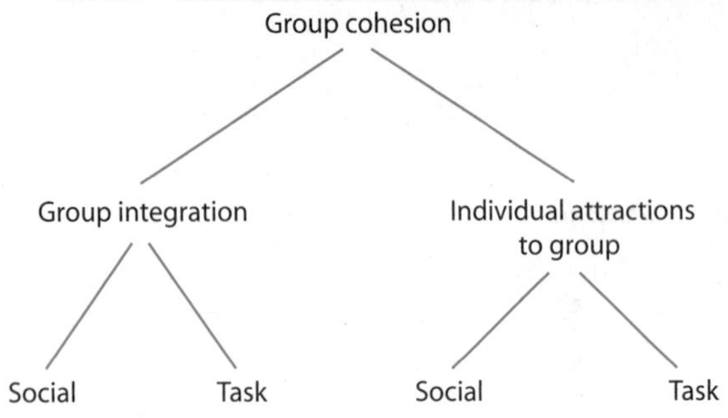

SOURCE: Carron, Widmeyer, & Brawley (1985).

shows sample items from the GEQ that load on each of the four dimensions.

Several tests of the utility of the GEQ have been conducted since its creation in 1985 (Brawley, Carron, & Widmeyer 1987; Carron et al., 1985). The purpose of the 1985 Carron et al. paper was to introduce the GEQ to the sport psychology literature. In essence, it outlined the conceptual model on which the GEQ was based. At the same time, psychometric soundness of the scale was satisfactorily demonstrated. Figure 11.4 shows the conceptual model in its simplest form.

From the psychometric viewpoint, the authors generated a 354-item pool from which the final 18 items were ultimately derived. Various statistical procedures were used to satisfactorily demonstrate the reliability and validity of the instrument. At that point in the infancy of the GEQ, the authors issued the customary call for additional research. That is precisely what has taken place.

The 1987 paper by Brawley et al. was a summary of three separate validity studies designed to support the utility of the GEQ. Chief among the conclusions from their 1987 work was that the GEQ correlated well with other measures of cohesion while not correlating with other constructs such as affiliation and personal motivation. The second study further demonstrated the validity of the GEQ; task cohesion scores were predictive of membership in either team or individual sports, and

team tenure predictions could be made based on social cohesion scores. The third study dealt with attributions of responsibility; the authors concluded that cohesion moderates the self-serving attributional bias in sport outcomes. The research team viewed all of the preceding results as supportive of the validity of the GEQ.

Additional confirmatory research has been reported by Spink (Carron & Spink, 1992; Spink, 1990; Spink & Carron, 1992). In the 1990 study by Spink, the relationship between team cohesion and collective efficacy in elite and recreational Canadian volleyball teams was analyzed. All participants in the study were asked two efficacy questions related to their expectations with regard to personal and team performance in a volleyball tournament. These expectations were then compared statistically with responses to the GEQ. Consistent with previous research, high- and low-efficacy players differed on the ATG–T and GI–S scales. The finding that ATG–T was related to high collective efficacy among the elite players suggests that high task orientation characterizes successful teams. Though not predicted by Spink, the GI–S finding indicates that social factors may also play a significant role in team cohesion.

In the two 1992 studies by Spink and Carron, the GEQ was modified for use in exercise settings. Carron and Spink (1992) reported basic psychometric data supporting the use of the GEQ in the exercise environment; Spink and Carron (1992) followed up on this modification and were able to show differences in measures of exercise adherence. Specifically, they found that exercisers who were absent less often than a comparable group gave a stronger endorsement to the ATG–T and ATG–S dimensions of the GEQ. Additionally, exercisers who were late less often than their counterparts endorsed the ATG–T dimension more strongly.

Two additional studies have lent support to the use of the GEQ in exercise settings. Estabrooks and Carron (1999) looked at exercise intentions, attitudes, and behaviors of older adults in an exercise group. In general, both task and social cohesion were high among these exercisers, and both were generally predictive of attitude and attendance. Annesi (1999) tested the efficacy of a brief warm-up/cool-down instructional procedure on group cohesion, attendance, and dropout rates. Adult exercisers were placed in one of four experimental groups receiving from a fitness instructor warm-up/cool-down instruction that was to be an adjunct to their regular exercise programs. A waiting-list control group was made up of people who had agreed to continue exercising but to defer receiving the warm-up/cool-down instruction to a later date. Both groups responded to the GEQ, and it was demonstrated that the experimental groups had a significant rise in the ATG–T over the course of the experiment and also attended on a more regular basis and had fewer dropouts than did the control group. Once again, the efficacy of the GEQ in assessing group cohesion was demonstrated.

Results from studies of several sports have been favorable with regard to the GEQ. Rainey and Schweickert (1988) administered the GEQ to 37 collegiate baseball players prior to a 10-day road trip. Twenty-two players made the trip, and 15 remained on campus. Players making the trip reported higher social and lower task scores than did the others upon their return home. It would appear that traveling as a team for an extended period created a socially cohesive effect, though it is not clear why the task orientation was less pronounced. In another study, Williams and Widmeyer (1991) looked at cohesion in a coactive sport, golf. Specifically, they administered the GEQ to 83 female collegiate golfers from 18 teams and compared team scores with cohesion responses. Cohesion significantly predicted performance (i.e., golf scores). Task cohesion was the best predictor. Finally, in an international application, Kim and Sugiyama (1992) tested 114 Japanese high school athletic teams with regard to the cohesion/performance relationship; these researchers again found strong support for the GEQ.

On a less supportive note, a recent study calls into question the factor structure of the GEQ (Schutz, Eom, Smoll, & Smith, 1994). Schutz et al. administered the GEQ to large numbers of male and female high school athletes. A confirmatory factor analysis indicated that there were different factor structures depending on gender, and neither group conformed to the structure hypothesized to exist by the authors of the GEQ. Also, they were not able to produce the four-factor structure said to exist in the scale. The Schutz et al. findings are provocative and serve as a reminder that the GEQ, like most paper-and-pencil tests, is a work in transition.

Despite the foregoing disclaimer, Widmeyer and his colleagues assert that the GEQ is an improvement over existing measures because it incorporates group cohesion theory from social psychology with sound psychometric properties. Whether the authors of the GEQ are correct in their assertion will be answered by research conducted over the next several years, but the instrument looks promising.

Two Final Notes

Two additional issues related to group cohesion warrant discussion. One is the issue of circularity, particularly as it relates to the cohesion–performance distinction. Perhaps the ultimate question is, Does cohesion facilitate performance, or does performance dictate cohesion? Studies within sport by Landers, Wilkinson, Hatfield, and Barber (1982), Ruder and Gill (1982), and Williams and Hacker (1982) all support the notion that the direction of causality is likely to be from performance to cohesion rather than the reverse. If these researchers are correct, team cohesion may have been traditionally overrated as a cause of success. Nevertheless, coaches and leaders of exercise groups should strive for cohesive units, but also maintain an awareness of the significance of task success in shaping the coveted spirit of togetherness.

The other issue is potentially negative aspects of cohesion. If overdone, cohesion may lead to conformity and lessened task success. Individuality may be suppressed, self-deception may become more likely, and cliques may form. The Klein and Christiansen (1969) and Fiedler (1967) studies, which showed that basketball players who are close friends tended to pass more often to each other to the detriment of the collective effort, demonstrate the dangers of cliques within a team.

SUMMARY

1. Leadership, group cohesion, and audience effects are three variables of interest to sport psychology.

2. The trait theory of leadership takes the position that a person who is a leader in one situation will be a leader in any situation, because he or she possesses certain personal, psychological, and demographic traits associated with leadership.

3. Behavior theory emphasizes what a leader does, not what traits he or she possesses. Research on leadership behavior was conducted at Ohio State University in the 1950s. One result of this work was the Leader Behavior Description Questionnaire, which has been used in several sport-related studies of leadership.

4. Fiedler's contingency model takes into account both traits and situational variables as predictors of effective leadership. Styles of leadership and how favorable a situation is for one style or another receive much emphasis in Fiedler's theory. Research within sport has been sparse and not especially supportive of Fiedler's approach.

5. Path–goal theory suggests that the leader is a catalyst for group success and satisfaction. Research in sport has been scant, and the efficacy of path–goal theory has not been determined.

6. Life cycle theory is a situation-specific approach that emphasizes the importance of the motivational and maturity levels of subordinates to attaining the goals of the group. There is some support within the sport literature for the life cycle formulation.

7. A model with little research support so far, but with intuitive appeal, is the functional approach. Instrumental needs and expressive needs are emphasized. The former are task related, and the latter are social and emotional. The model proposes that effective leaders attend to the instrumental and expressive needs of their subordinates.

8. Chelladurai's multidimensional model of leadership is at the forefront of sport leadership research. It proposes that performance and satisfaction are ultimately determined by the degree of congruence among three types of leader behavior: actual, preferred, and required.

9. Despite its obvious importance to team success, player leadership is a largely neglected area of inquiry in sport psychology.

10. The study of leadership is an evolving enterprise, and much speculation exists about where the field is going. Chelladurai's multidimensional model looks promising to leadership researchers in sport psychology.

11. Group cohesion is generally but not universally considered to be essential to success in sport.

12. Three cohesion models—pendular, linear, and life cycle—are suggested by Carron as representative of current thinking about team cohesion.

13. Group size is a correlate of cohesion. Cohesion generally lessens as group size increases. The Ringelmann effect and social loafing are performance decrements associated with increases in group size.

14. The task at hand greatly affects group cohesion. Cox refers to an interactive–coactive dichotomy to partially explain differences in task demand across sport. Coactive sports, such as archery and golf, require little individual interaction. Interactive sports, such as soccer and volleyball, require close teamwork.

15. The length of time that a team stays together has an effect on cohesion. Research by Donnelly suggests that there is an optimal length of time for cohesion to develop and subsequently dissolve.

16. Two models, one by Martens and Peterson and the other by Williams and Hacker, explore the relationship among success, cohesion, and satisfaction.

17. Two prominent measures of team cohesion are the Sport Cohesiveness Questionnaire and the Group Environment Questionnaire. The GEQ has been used widely in sport studies, and it may supplant other instruments. The GEQ is derived from Chelladurai's multidimensional model of sport leadership and places emphasis on social and task aspects of group behavior.

18. The circularity of the cohesion–performance relationship is troublesome, but the available evidence supports the performance-to-cohesion direction rather than the reverse.

19. If overdone, cohesion may lead to conformity and lessened task success.

KEY TERMS

behavior theory of leadership (152)
coactive sports (162)

Fiedler's contingency model (152)
functional model (154)
Group Environment Questionnaire (GEQ) (164)
group integration (165)
individual attractions to the group (165)
interactive sports (162)
Leader Behavior Description Questionnaire (LBDQ)
    (152)
Leadership Scale for Sports (LSS) (156)
Least Preferred Coworker (LPC) scale (152)
life cycle model of cohesion (160)
life cycle theory (153)
linear model of cohesion (160)
multidimensional model of sport leadership (155)
path–goal theory (153)
pendular model of cohesion (160)
Ringelmann effect (161)
social loafing (161)
social striving (162)
team half-life (162)
trait theory (151)

SUGGESTED READINGS

Cota, A. A., Evans, C. R., Dion, K. L., Kilik, L., & Longman, R. S. (1995). The structure of group cohesion. *Personality and Social Psychology Bulletin, 21,* 572–580.

A review of the literature on group cohesion is provided, and an alternate way of conceptualizing cohesion is suggested. Both unidimensional and multidimensional models are discussed. The authors conclude that cohesion is a multidimensional concept with primary and secondary dimensions. In the case of primary dimensions, applicability to describing virtually all groups is implied. As for secondary dimensions, applicability to specific groups is intended. The group cohesion literature within sport psychology, particularly the work of Carron and his colleagues, is discussed at length.

Eagly, A. H., Makhijani, M. G., & Klonsky, B. G. (1992). Gender and the evaluation of leaders: A meta-analysis. *Psychological Bulletin, 111,* 3–22.

Eagly and her coauthors review literature relevant to gender and leadership using the statistical technique known as meta-analysis. Surprisingly, there has been a fair amount of research related to women in leadership roles despite the limited number of leadership positions traditionally open to them. Sixty-one studies from the years 1966 to 1988 were analyzed. Results of the meta-analysis indicated that women in leadership positions were not viewed particularly negatively in comparison with males in similar positions. However, female leaders who carried out their duties in a more stereotypically male style were devalued, as were women in male-dominated situations in which men were conducting the evaluations.

Evans, C. R., & Dion, K. L. (1991). Group cohesion and performance: A meta-analysis. *Small Group Research, 22,* 175–186.

A computer search of the Educational Research Information System (ERIC) and the Psychological Abstracts databases produced 317 published and unpublished studies on group cohesion, 27 of which addressed the issue of cohesion and performance. Meta-analytic procedures indicated a relatively strong and positive correlation of .419 between group cohesion and performance. These analyses support the contention that cohesive groups are more productive than noncohesive ones. Caveats to the study and research in cohesion and performance were also discussed.

Janssen, J. (1999). *Championship team building: What every coach needs to know to build a motivated, committed and cohesive team.* Tucson, AZ: Janssen Peak Performance, Inc.

Jeff Janssen works with athletes in a variety of sports at the University of Arizona, and this book captures the essence of the team-building procedures that he uses in his work there. It is a hands-on book with a number of team-building exercises, strategies for evaluating team strengths and weaknesses, and Janssen's "seven C's" formula for building a championship team. The book has ringing endorsements from prominent coaches such as Gary Barnett of the University of Colorado football team and Mike Krzyzewski of the Duke basketball program.

Weese, W. J. (1994). A leadership discussion with Dr. Bernard Bass. *Journal of Sport Management, 8,* 179–189.

This report is a synopsis of an interview with Bernard Bass, Distinguished Professor Emeritus of Management and director of the Center for Leadership Studies at the State University of New York at Binghamton, who Weese calls "arguably the most prolific writer in the leadership field" (p. 180). The paper gives glimpses of the current perspectives of one of the pioneers in the area of leadership theory and research. Weese also attempts to relate information gathered through the interview with Dr. Bass to the field of sport management.

INFOTRAC COLLEGE EDITION

For additional readings, explore Infotrac College Edition, your online library. Go to:
http://www.infotrac-college.com/wadsworth
Hint: Enter these search terms: Group Environment Questionnaire, group cohesion, leadership, social loafing.

Social Psychology of Sport: Audience Effects

CHAPTER 12

Social Facilitation
Other Drive Theories
An Evaluation of Drive Theory
Alternative Nondrive Models
Interactive Audience Effects
on Sport Performance
Summary
Key Terms
Suggested Readings

Texas Ranger Alex Rodriguez is booed by Seattle Mariner fans in Seattle on April 18, 2001. Former Mariner Rodriguez signed a $252 million contract with the Rangers during the off season, making him the highest paid player in baseball. The Rangers defeat the Mariners, 8–6.
© AFP/CORBIS

Anyone who has participated in any form of athletics is acutely aware of what it is like to be evaluated by others. We strive to perform well because of a personal desire to excel and other internal factors, but we also strive to succeed because of pressures generated by the presence of other persons: coparticipants, coaches, and audiences. Also, as Cratty (1981, p. 191) pointed out: "Even a solitary workout may be accompanied by an unseen audience, a group of people residing psychologically and socially in the mind of the performer. This audience, the athlete knows, stands ready to judge his or her performance at some future time, harshly or with kindness and praise."

The interaction between internal motivational and external evaluative forces is complex and intriguing, and a number of theorists and researchers have tried to shed light on the tangled web of **audience effects** on human performance. This fascination with audience effects owes a great debt to research on what is known as **social facilitation**—the effects that the presence of others has on individual performance.

SOCIAL FACILITATION

The earliest research on social facilitation dates back to the work of Norman Triplett (1898), who studied bicycle racers under a variety of conditions and concluded that the mere presence of others actually facilitated performance. In the same study, Triplett also showed that adolescents could spin a fishing reel–like device more rapidly when working with another individual than when working alone. In 1933, the **mere presence hypothesis** received its first significant challenge as a result of research reported by Pessin (1933).

Audience effects the effects of spectators on individual performance.
Social facilitation the effects that the presence of other people have on individual performance.
Mere presence hypothesis the theory that individual performance is facilitated by the presence of either a passive audience of spectators or an active group of coparticipants.
"Futile caution" the name given to the performance style generally adopted by an individual performing a skill-based task in front of a supportive audience; the person who works slowly in a futile attempt to ensure accuracy.

Pessin noted that college students learned nonsense syllables better when alone than in the presence of others. In 1935, Dashiell proposed that there is no such thing as a pure alone or a pure coactive situation because of the intrusion of internal psychological mediators. Also, Dashiell observed that the presence of others tended to speed the rate of performance but not increase the accuracy of response. The latter point served as a precursor to the substantial contribution of Zajonc some 30 years later.

In 1965, Zajonc published a pivotal paper in which he outlined his approach to social facilitation. According to Zajonc (1965, p. 269), social facilitation "examines the consequences upon behavior which derive from the sheer presence of other individuals." Borrowing heavily from Hull–Spence drive theory, Zajonc suggests that the mere presence of an audience increases physiological arousal, which in turn enhances the likelihood that the individual will emit his or her dominant response in social situations. To quote Zajonc (1965, p. 270), "The emission of these well-learned responses is facilitated by the presence of spectators, while the acquisition of new responses is impaired." This formulation means that the presence of others enhances performance but hinders learning. Given these predictions, it should follow that audiences would have differential effects on sport performance as a function of the athletes' skill levels. Young athletes would be most adversely affected by audiences, highly skilled athletes least affected. Figure 12.1 is a visual representation of this hypothesis.

Butler and Baumeister (1998) suggested that audience effects are also affected by whether the audience is positive, neutral, or negative. To test their notion, Butler and Baumeister devised a series of experiments using college students as subjects. Subjects were assigned to three groups and were requested to perform a difficult, skill-based task in front of supportive, neutral, or hostile audiences. Consistently, the favorable audience proved detrimental to performance. While offering a number of intriguing explanations for their results, Butler and Baumeister concluded that the detrimental effects of a supportive audience are mediated by some combination of unfavorable expectations (i.e., fear of failure) and adopting a less-than-desirable performance style, which they labeled **"futile caution."**

FIGURE 12.1

Audience Effects on Athletes at Varying Skill Levels

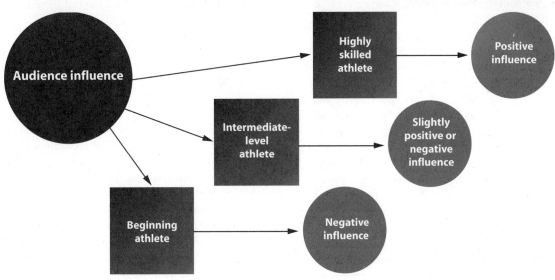

SOURCE: Cox (1990).

Futile caution involves trade-offs between speed and accuracy. Subjects in the study worked more slowly in front of supportive audiences in an effort to preserve accuracy. This trade-off proved futile, for slowing down did not necessarily guarantee accurate performance on the skill-based task.

There has been some support for Zajonc's model in the motor learning area (e.g., Hunt & Hillery, 1973; Landers, Brawley, & Hale, 1978; Martens, 1969). However, studies such as those reported by Paulus and associates (Paulus & Cornelius, 1974; Paulus, Shannon, Wilson, & Boone, 1972) present a less rosy view of his work. College gymnasts served as subjects in the two Paulus studies, and in both instances it was found that the presence of spectators resulted in findings directly opposite to the Zajonc model's predictions. As Paulus and associates note, it may be that naturalistic performance situations cannot be directly compared with laboratory manipulations of audience effects. The comparability problem, of course, is not unique to this area of scientific inquiry.

As a result of equivocal findings both within and external to sport-related research, there has been considerable interest in developing competing models to explain audience effects on performance.

OTHER DRIVE THEORIES

Cottrell (1972) took exception to the mere presence hypothesis and suggested that drive is facilitated by **evaluative apprehension** generated by the presence of someone who can evaluate performance. Through socialization experiences, the individual comes to anticipate positive or negative outcomes as a result of the presence of evaluative others. This emphasis on the critical audience is a point of separation between Cottrell's work and that of Zajonc. Zajonc suggests that the

---

Evaluative apprehension uneasiness or fear generated by the presence of a critical audience.

uncertainty created by the presence of an audience would increase arousal. Cottrell emphasizes evaluative apprehension as the cause of an increased drive state. As is the case with the Zajonc model, some support for the Cottrell approach has been generated in the area of motor behavior (e.g., Haas & Roberts, 1975; Martens & Landers, 1972). All in all, however, research on the Cottrell model has been equivocal and rather scant.

Other drive theories of note include those of Sanders, Baron, and Moore (1978) and Guerin and Innes (1982). Sanders and colleagues view attentional conflict as the cause of drive—that is, the presence of people who can provide social comparison data that will conflict with attention to the task at hand serves as a source of generalized drive. Guerin and Innes suggest a social monitoring theory, which posits that the presence of others who cannot be visually monitored or the presence of others who are unfamiliar, unpredictable, or threatening increases drive. According to Bond and Titus (1983, p. 266), "Drive will not be increased by the mere presence of innocuous others if those others can periodically be monitored. According to this social monitoring theory, the individual should be less affected by the presence of coactors than by the presence of spectators because coactors are more predictable."

AN EVALUATION OF DRIVE THEORY

Wankel (1984) suggests that drive theory has been dominant in social facilitation research partially because of its generally parsimonious nature. But Wankel maintains that the various drive theories are too mechanistic to be of value in trying to explain complex human behavior. Sanders (1981) indicates that the various drive models have much overlap and generally are not comprehensive enough to explain socially facilitated behavior. Cox (1990) raises objections to drive theory on relevancy grounds: Although important from a research viewpoint, the noninteractive audiences used in drive theory studies are far less relevant to sport than are interactive audiences. Most athletic situations are characterized by interactions between coaches and athletes and spectators.

Because of the preceding charges, calls for other approaches to explaining social facilitation have been made (Geen & Gange, 1977; Landers, 1980; Wankel, 1984). Each of these authorities has issued a call for more cognitive explanatory models. Several models, however incomplete, have been advanced in response to the challenge.

ALTERNATIVE NONDRIVE MODELS

Duval and Wicklund (1972) have suggested a model that stresses objective self-awareness. In theory, a performer who is self-aware should be motivated to reduce discrepancies that arise from the disparities between actual and ideal task performance. Another formulation is that of Bond (1982), who proposes a self-presentational model. Bond contends that the motivation to project an image of competence in the presence of others will facilitate performance. Whereas the drive theorists equate drive with physiological arousal, Bond sees possible embarrassment as the source of arousal (Bond & Titus, 1983).

An arousal-cognitive information-processing model is a third approach. Within sport, Landers (1980) and Wankel (1984) are proponents of the model because it represents a step away from the mechanistic drive theory and places emphasis not only on the energizing effects of social factors but also on the informational or cognitive aspect.

Although these cognitive models are intuitively appealing, little has been done to test them within the sport context. Perhaps future efforts will be directed toward confirming or disconfirming these cognitive approaches, thereby shedding light on the complex issue of social facilitation.

INTERACTIVE AUDIENCE EFFECTS ON SPORT PERFORMANCE

Most sport interactions are with an active audience, not the passive audience so prominent in social facilitation research. The effects of supportive versus nonsupportive audiences, audience size, and viewer sophistication are only a few of the interactive forces at work in shaping athletic behavior. Of the preceding

TABLE 12.1

Percentage of Games Won by the Home Team in Four Sports

| Home Team Outcome | Professional | | College | | |
	Baseball (1971)	Football (1971)	Football (1971)	Hockey (1971–1972)	Basketball (1952–1966)
Win	53% (989)	55% (100)	59% (532)	53% (286)	82% (290)
Lose	47% (891)	41% (74)	40% (367)	30% (163)	18% (64)
Tie	—	4% (8)	1% (11)	17% (93)	—
Total	100% (1,880)	100% (182)	100% (910)	100% (542)	100% (354)

SOURCE: Schwartz & Barsky (1977).
Number of games in parentheses.

factors, far more is known about the supportive audience than about the other variables. This supportive audience generally is viewed in athletics as constituting the home advantage, a topic of considerable interest to spectators, athletes, coaches, sport announcers, and sport scientists. The remainder of this chapter is devoted to the home advantage, to the phenomena known as basking in reflected glory (BIRG), and to choking under pressure.

The Home Advantage

Much is made in the media of the so-called **home advantage.** A rule of thumb in basketball, according to some experts, is that the home court is worth from three to seven points to the home team. In major league baseball, the goal often seems to be to win big at home and break even on the road. Although one can speculate that, for the visitors, the demands of travel, disrupted schedules, and unfamiliar surroundings give rise to the home advantage, fans typically believe that their support of the home team is at the heart of the edge enjoyed by their beloved players.

Schwartz and Barsky (1977) conducted the first major study of the home advantage. They analyzed data from 1,880 major league baseball games played in 1971, 182 professional football games played that same year, 542 National Hockey League games from the 1971-1972 season, and 1,485 college basketball games played from 1952 through 1966 by the big five in

Philadelphia (LaSalle, Penn., St. Joseph's, Temple, and Villanova). Table 12.1 shows the percentage of games won by the home teams in each sport. Clearly, a home advantage is evident. The edge is greatest in basketball. Also, hockey teams profit from playing at home, particularly if tie games are excluded (in Table 12.1, the winning percentage for the home team in hockey would become 64). Schwartz and Barsky concluded that the source of this advantage was social support from a friendly audience.

In another early study, Varca (1980) lent support to the idea of the home advantage. In arriving at his conclusions about why the home advantage exists, Varca used game statistics for all men's basketball games in the Southeastern Conference for the 1977–1978 season. Varca's main hypothesis was that differences in aggressive play between the home team and visitors could account for the advantage. Simply stated, **functionally aggressive play** by the home team and **dysfunctionally aggressive play** by the visitors accounts for the edge afforded the home team. Functionally aggressive play, according to Varca, included rebounding, stealing the ball from opponents, and blocking shots, whereas

---

Home advantage the advantage enjoyed by the home team competing in front of a supportive audience.
Functionally aggressive play aggressive play that results in the scoring of points.
Dysfunctionally aggressive play aggressive play that results in personal fouls and not in the scoring of points.

TABLE 12.2

Representative Studies of Home Advantage in Sports

Authors	Participants	Results
Courneya & Carron (1990)	360 slow-pitch softball players	No win–loss advantage to batting first or last by gender, playing position, or time of season
Courneya & Carron (1991)	26 Double-A professional baseball teams	Significant home advantage; winning percentage of 55% in home games
Gayton & Coombs (1995)	4 high school basketball teams	3 of 4 had significant home advantage
Gayton & Langevin (1992)	Wrestlers	Significant home advantage; winning percentage of 61% in home matches
Glamser (1990)	Soccer matches in England	Significant home advantage
Irving & Goldstein (1990)	No-hitters in major leagues since 1900	111 of 175 no-hitters (63%) and 7 of 9 perfect games pitched at home
Leonard (1989)	Summer Olympics, 1896–1988; Winter Olympics, 1924–1988	Host teams won more medals than they did at previous or ensuing games
Leonard (1998)	529 baseball World Series games from 1903 to 1993	Eventual series winner more likely to win at home and less likely to lose on the road
McAndrew (1992)	High school wrestlers	Home wrestlers won 1,422 matches, visitors 964
Nelson & Carron (1991)	4 men's and 4 women's teams in 5 Division I college sports	68.6% of home games won over 5-year period; 48% of games won by same teams when on the road

dysfunctionally aggressive play was limited to personal fouls, a generally detrimental force in basketball. As predicted, the home team was superior in all three of the functional behaviors, and the visitors were guilty of more fouls (dysfunctional aggression) than were the home teams. It was Varca's opinion that arousal states generated by the friendly, supportive audiences at the various home courts was at work. The home team channeled the arousal positively; the visiting team channeled it negatively.

More recently, Courneya and Carron (1992) reported data in which the home team won as few as 53% and as many as 72% of home games in professional baseball, basketball, cricket, ice hockey, and soccer. In a study of the National Hockey League involving a 20-year period, Bray (1999) found that when ties are excluded, the home team won 60% of the time. In an interesting twist, Bray also noted that the home advantage is not universal across the NHL; a small percentage of

teams win equally at home and on the road. A home advantage in individual sports such as alpine skiing (Bray & Carron, 1993) and wrestling (McAndrew, 1992) has also been demonstrated. Other studies demonstrating the home advantage are listed in Table 12.2.

Given the results of these various pieces of research, it seems that a home advantage in a number of fairly advanced sport settings is a reality. Collegiate and professional teams as well as some individuals seem to profit from playing at home. However, a study by Baumeister and Steinhilber (1984) adds a provocative caveat to this assumption. These researchers looked at major league baseball's World Series from 1924 through 1982 and the National Basketball Association championship playoff games from 1967 through 1982 in an effort to see whether the home audience is in fact a positive force in the final or deciding games. In both instances, they found the home field or home court advantage to be valid for early games in the playoffs but not for the games that actually determined the ultimate winner. Of particular interest to Baumeister and Steinhilber was the source of this effect. Was the home team manifesting the phenomenon known as **choking,** or

Choking failure to perform effectively because of intense pressure to perform well.

University of Southern California marching band performs during halftime at a football game in the Los Angeles Coliseum. The noise generated by 100,000 fans is deafening, but the athletes seem to be able to tune it out and perform well.
© Nik Wheeler/CORBIS

were the visitors merely playing unusually well? In baseball, they chose fielding errors to analyze because their low mutual determinacy makes them a relatively pure measure of choking—failure to perform well under pressure. In the first two games of the series, the visiting team made the most errors. In the seventh game, the home team committed the most errors. The difference in errors noted in the seventh game is significant at the .01 level of confidence. These data are reflected in Table 12.3.

In basketball, Baumeister and Steinhilber analyzed the NBA semifinal and championship series, again from 1967 through 1982. In games one through four, the home team won 70.1% of the contests; in series decided in the seventh game, the home court advantage dropped to 38.5%. Clearly, a **home disadvantage** appears to exist in critical games at the highest levels of professional basketball. Free throw shooting was also

chosen for analysis. In games one through four of a seven-game playoff, the home team shot about the same as the visitors, but the tables again turned in game seven, with the visitors having an edge that was statistically significant. These data are available in Table 12.4. These findings, along with those in baseball, are highly suggestive of a home disadvantage in at least some professional sports.

In a most interesting interchange, Baumeister and Steinhilber were taken to task by Schlenker, Phillips, Boniecki, and Schlenker (1995a, 1995b); in turn, Baumeister (1995) was afforded the opportunity to respond to the critics. All three papers were published as a package in volume 68, number 4, of *Journal of*

Home disadvantage the disadvantage of playing at home in the decisive seventh game of a championship series.

TABLE 12.3					
Fielding Errors in World Series Games, 1924–1982					
	Errors per Game		**Errorless Games**		
Games	**Home**	**Visitor**	**Home**	**Visitor**	
1 and 2	0.65	1.04	33	18	
7	1.31	0.81*	6	12**	

SOURCE: Baumeister & Steinhilber (1984).
*p = <.01
**p = <.02

TABLE 12.4		
Free Throw Performance in NBA Playoffs, 1967–1982		
Performance	**Home**	**Visitor**
Games 1–4		
Success (scored)	3368	3412
Failure (missed)	1303	1266
Scoring percentage	.72	.73*
Last (7th) game		
Success	873	937
Failure	391	328
Scoring percentage	.69	.74**

SOURCE: Baumeister & Steinhilber (1984).
*p = not significant
**p = <.01

Personality and Social Psychology. Schlenker and associates (1995a) presented their disagreements with the 1984 Baumeister and Steinhilber research, followed by a rebuttal by Baumeister, and concluding with a rejoinder by Schlenker and associates (1995b) (hereafter referred to merely as Schlenker for purposes of brevity and avoidance of repetition).

Through clever methodological controls and statistical analyses, elaborate and compelling arguments are made by Schlenker and associates that there is not a disadvantage to playing at home in the decisive seventh game of a series. It was important to note that the era from 1950 through 1968 did in fact show a huge home disadvantage, whereas the effect was not there for the other two time periods. Eleven series went to seven games in the 1950–1968 era, and the visiting team won nine of the eleven. Schlenker contends that any analysis of the home advantage/disadvantage that makes major use of the period 1950–1968 is going to yield biased results indicating a home field choke. Otherwise, there was little evidence for the home choke. Fielding errors were used in the original work as a validation of the home field disadvantage; this relationship was shown earlier in Table 12.3.

Schlenker found those errors to be salient only when the home team falls behind in the decisive seventh game. Perhaps anxiety, self-consciousness, and pressing too hard become operational at that point, thereby creating a favorable environment for failure. Based on the preceding analyses and others too numerous and complex to mention here, Schlenker concludes

that Baumeister and Steinhilber were simply wrong, theoretically, methodologically, and interpretively.

Schlenker also found fault with the data-gathering process used by Baumeister and Steinhilber, suggesting a failure to properly sample the archival data used for analyzing the home choke. Like Baumeister and Steinhilber, Schlenker used all baseball World Series since the institution of the seven-game series in 1924, excluding four-game sweeps (Schlenker did have an additional eleven World Series to consider beyond Baumeister and Steinhilber's stopping point of 1982). Unlike Baumeister and Steinhilber, Schlenker chose to exclude the years 1943 through 1945 because of the significant changes in baseball brought about by World War II. Another difference between the two pieces of research was that Schlenker analyzed all divisional playoffs since the start of the seven-game format in 1985, using this data as a moderator for some of his subsequent analyses. Other points of departure included analyzing *when* fielding errors occurred and choking across eras (three eras were identified: 1924 through 1949, 1950 through 1968, and 1969 through 1993).

The rebuttal by Baumeister points out a variety of problems with the Schlenker work. He also points to the larger issue of social psychology research employing archival data. It is Baumeister's contention that science proceeds best by research under laboratory controls not present in "real world" archival data. Baumeister does admit, however, that the Schlenker finding concerning the timing of fielding errors represents a breakthrough in our understanding of the literature on home team advantage/disadvantage and choking under pressure.

Gayton, Matthews, and Nickless (1987) took the work of Baumeister and Steinhilber to the Stanley Cup playoffs in the National Hockey League for the years 1960 through 1985 and obtained very different results. They found no support for a significant home ice disadvantage at any level in the NHL playoffs. Additionally, the choking phenomenon alluded to by Baumeister and Steinhilber did not occur in those series that went to a seventh game. Of the 12 playoffs that went to a seventh and deciding game, the home team won 7. Kornspan, Lerner, Ronayne, Etzel, and Johnson (1995) also did not find a home team disadvantage in their study encompassing 23 years of National Football League conference championship games.

The home advantage is perhaps more clearly understood than other facets of audience effects. Audience size, audience sophistication, gender effects, team identification factor, and audience density are also important aspects of the overall audience issue. Much work remains to be done in clarifying these and other parameters that impinge on the audience effects issue.

Basking in Reflected Glory

Everyone likes to be associated with a winner, and a 1976 report of three studies conducted by Robert Cialdini and his associates (Cialdini, Borden, Thorne, Walker, Freeman, & Sloan, 1976) has added an element of scientific verification to the notion. In the first of the three studies, Cialdini and associates sought support for the existence of a phenomenon known as **basking in reflected glory (BIRG)** by covertly observing the apparel worn to introductory psychology classes by students from seven universities with major football programs. Essentially what the observers did was look for the wearing of various paraphernalia (buttons, T-shirts, jackets, sweatshirts) that displayed the school name, team nickname or mascot, or university insignia on Mondays after football games. Students clearly tended to wear more school-related paraphernalia on Mondays after wins than after losses, a finding that was interpreted as lending support to BIRG.

In the second experiment, an examination of pronoun usage served as the mechanism for studying BIRG. It was hypothesized that students would respond to wins with increased use of the pronoun *we* and to losses with greater use of the pronoun *they*. In order to test this notion in a covert fashion, students were contacted by telephone, the investigators identified themselves as employees of a "Regional Survey Center," and subjects were asked to respond to six general questions about campus life. Students were placed in success or failure groups irrespective of how well they actually had done on the six questions. They were then asked to respond to questions about their teams' recent football games, half of which had been won and half lost.

Two hypotheses were generated by the experimental manipulations just described. One was that team wins would result in more uses of *we* than would losses. The second hypothesis was that the effect of the first hypothesis would be greater for those who had "failed" the test from the so-called Regional Survey Center. The latter supposition was based on the idea that those who had "failed" the campus events test would want to enhance themselves in the eyes of the investigators by associating themselves with positive entities, such as a team victory the previous Saturday. Clear support for BIRG was found in both instances. There was strong support for the use of the pronoun *we,* and an even stronger relationship was noted when the respondents' public prestige was in jeopardy.

The third experiment arose out of the results of the previous manipulations of BIRG. Specifically, the investigators were curious about how the students would respond when they were told that the phone calls were from either a University Survey Center or a Regional Survey Center. The idea here was that the students would demonstrate a stronger BIRG response to the regional than to the local center. The rationale for this

---

Basking in reflected glory associating oneself with a winner in order to enhance one's self-esteem and social image; also called BIRGing.

hypothesis rested in the supposition that BIRG would be stronger when the respondent had a stronger link to the prestigious object than did the observer. The likelihood that a local caller would have a reasonably similar degree of identification was thought to be quite high. An outsider, however, would not be so likely to have the same emotional investment in the admired object, and identifying with the source of prestige would enhance students' perception in the eyes of the more geographically and presumably emotionally remote caller. By way of paraphrasing the authors, little prestige is to be gained from bragging about the virtues of California weather to another Californian; relating the same message to someone from a state with more severe weather conditions might be more image enhancing. As expected, confirmation for BIRG was again demonstrated.

Overall, support for BIRG in all three studies was evident, and the results were viewed as providing support for the importance of perceived esteem of others. Alternatively, however, an explanation for the results that is couched in terms of enhancing the self-concept might also be a viable one. Cialdini and his associates contend that BIRG is best explained in terms of its enhancing effects on social image, but the interplay between social image and self-image cannot be ignored.

Additional support for the BIRG phenomenon has been provided by other sources (e.g., Hirt, Zillman, Erickson, & Kennedy, 1992; Murrell & Dietz, 1992; Wann & Branscombe, 1990). Of particular salience is the Hirt et al. research, in which a series of studies was conducted with university students with the intent of assessing the interplay of social image and self-identity and mood as they relate to BIRG. Strong support was found for the role of self-esteem in image maintenance; mood appeared to have less explanatory value. Hirt and his associates concluded, "BIRGing is a strategic impression management technique whereby individuals raise their esteem in the eyes of others" (p. 724). The authors were also quick to point out that BIRGing is not confined to fans at athletic events; they are convinced that it would also manifest itself in any social context (such as national identity, political party, ethnic group) involving strong personal allegiances.

Cutting off reflected failure distancing oneself from a loser in order to protect one's self-esteem and social image; also called CORFing.

A phenomenon related to BIRGing that has received less attention but is of interest is **cutting off reflected failure (CORF)** (Snyder, Higgins, & Stucky, 1983). CORFing is an image protection tactic that allows individuals to avoid negative evaluation from others by distancing themselves psychologically from unsuccessful people, teams, or other entities (Hirt et al., 1992; Wann, 1993). As such, BIRGing represents an image enhancement technique and CORFing is an image protection mechanism, a subtle but important difference (Hirt et al., 1992).

Given the tremendous importance of spectators at athletic events in terms of economics and social psychological dynamics, research on BIRGing and CORFing is likely to continue in an attempt to better understand this important aspect of audience effects.

Choking Under Pressure

Choking is a compelling topic of conversation among fans and sport talk show hosts. It is also one of the greatest fears that athletes have in the performance arena. How many times have we, as sports competitors, seen an opponent grab his or her neck and make the all-too-familiar choking noise in critical competitive situations? Perhaps a quote from professional golfer Scott Hoch, known at one time as a choker because he missed a two-foot putt that would have won the 1989 Master's, provides an interesting personal glimpse concerning choking: "It will always be Hoch as in choke until I do otherwise" (Hershey, 1989).

Baumeister defined *choking* as "performance decrements under pressure circumstances" and *pressure* as "any factor or combination of factors that increases the importance of performing well on a particular occasion despite incentives for optimal performance" (1984, p. 610). In his 1984 paper, Baumeister reported the results of six separate studies where particular emphasis was placed on the role of self-consciousness as a cause of choking. Baumeister suggests that increases in self-consciousness are accompanied by deteriorations in the lawfulness or predictability of behavior. Counterintuitively, individuals who are habitually self-conscious should handle pressure situations that engender self-consciousness because they are so accustomed to dealing with it on a daily basis, but individuals low in self-consciousness when under pressure may suffer incremental escalations in self-

Reprinted by permission of Newspaper Enterprises Association, Inc.

consciousness that interfere with performance. Thus, greater choking under pressure may be expected from individuals low in self-consciousness, instead of from highly self-conscious individuals. Schlenker and associates (1995a, 1995b) suggested that Baumeister and Steinhilber had taken a kind view as opposed to a dark view of the mechanism at work in choking. Baumeister and Steinhilber said that choking arises because of poorer-than-usual task performance produced by anticipation of success in front of a supportive audience (the kinder view). Schlenker's contention was that self-doubt, self-consciousness, and unwanted and aversive self-attention are at the heart of choking under pressure (a more negative, darker view of the process).

An alternate view of choking is that of Brant (1988), who linked the problem to physiological processes related to the interplay of the sympathetic and parasympathetic nervous systems. He asserts "the choking response itself begins in the middle of the brain, at the hypothalamus, the so-called governor of the autonomic nervous and endocrine systems" (p. 23).

In short, we choke because of bodily sabotage. Again, Brant says, "our circuitry and chemistry couldn't give a fig how we perform in the clutch; they want us (and thereby themselves) to survive" (p. 24). Perhaps the Brant view is simplistic, but it does bring into play the role of physiological processes in choking that more psychosocial models tend to ignore or downplay.

SUMMARY

1. Audience effects on athletic performance is an area of considerable scientific interest, getting its impetus from early social facilitation research.

2. Triplett, in 1898, was the first to study social facilitation.

3. A reawakening of interest in social facilitation took place in 1965, prompted by a pivotal paper by Zajonc. According to Zajonc, the mere presence of others increases arousal that facilitates well-learned responses and hinders the acquisition

of new ones. Zajonc's ideas sparked controversy and generated additional research as well as the creation of alternate theories.

4. Agreeing with Zajonc on some points, Cottrell disagreed with his mere presence formulation and suggested that evaluative apprehension generated by the presence of a critical audience is at the heart of audience effects. Other recent theories have been advanced by Sanders, Baron, and Moore and by Guerin and Innes.

5. Critics of the various drive theories claim that they are too mechanistic to explain complex human behavior. Also, much of the research on drive theory is inapplicable to sport psychology, because the typical research in the area of drive theory deals with noninteractive audiences but the typical sport situation involves an interactive audience.

6. Alternative theories take a more cognitive approach to social facilitation. Though little used so far, these newer approaches are appealing to sport scientists.

7. Studies involving professional hockey, baseball, and basketball teams and collegiate basketball teams indicate the existence of a home advantage. Research by Baumeister and Steinhilber suggests that this advantage does not extend to championship games in the baseball World Series or the National Basketball Association playoffs.

8. Fans are susceptible to the effects of BIRGing (basking in reflected glory) and CORFing (cutting off reflected failure), because both mechanisms cut right to the core of individual and group esteem. Individuals like to be associated with a winner to build esteem (BIRG) and choose to distance themselves psychologically from losers in order to preserve their sense of well-being (CORF).

9. Baumeister (1984) defined *choking* as "performance decrements under pressure circumstances" and *pressure* as "any factor or combination of factors that increases the importance of performing well on a particular occasion despite incentives for optimal performance." Critical to Baumeister's view is the role of self-consciousness. He suggests that habitually self-conscious individuals should handle pressure situations that engender self-consciousness, because they are accustomed to dealing with it

daily, and individuals low in self-consciousness may experience performance decrements due to a concomitant increase in their respective levels of self-consciousness. Thus, greater choking under pressure may be expected from athletes low in self-consciousness instead of from highly self-conscious athletes. Schlenker and associates suggest that this is the kinder view of the phenomenon and suggest that self-doubt, self-consciousness, and unwanted and aversive self-attention are at the heart of choking under pressure. Brant proposed a theory that emphasizes neural functioning as the cause of choking under pressure.

KEY TERMS

audience effects (172)
basking in reflected glory (BIRG) (179)
choking (176)
cutting off reflected failure (CORF) (180)
dysfunctionally aggressive play (175)
evaluative apprehension (173)
functionally aggressive play (175)
"futile caution" (172)
home advantage (175)
home disadvantage (177)
mere presence hypothesis (172)
social facilitation (172)

SUGGESTED READINGS

Butler, J. L., & Baumeister, R. F. (1998). The trouble with friendly faces: Skilled performance with a supportive audience. *Journal of Personality and Social Psychology, 75,* 1213–1230.
      This article provides an excellent review of the literature on supportive, neutral, and hostile audiences, the home advantage/disadvantage, basking in reflective glory (BIRG), choking under pressure, and the concept of futile caution, which Butler and Baumeister use to explain part of their results from three experiments they conducted.

Lewis, B. P., & Linder, D. E. (1997). Thinking about choking? Attentional processes and paradoxical performance. *Personality and Social Psychology Bulletin, 23,* 937–944.

In an experiment designed to test the two explanatory mechanisms often used to account for choking under pressure—distraction and self-focus—the authors concluded that self-focus-mediated misregulation was the mechanism most related to choking, thus disconfirming the distraction hypothesis. A good discussion of the literature relevant to the two points of view is provided.

Moore, J. C., & Brylinsky, J. A. (1993). Spectator effects on team performance in college basketball. *Journal of Sport Behavior, 16,* 77–83.

This brief paper presents an interesting slant on the audience effects literature. A measles epidemic during the 1988–1989 basketball season dictated that Siena and Hartford play 11 games without spectators and afforded the authors a unique opportunity to investigate crowd effects in a natural setting. Analyses were conducted of Siena away games and Hartford home games; each team played a number of games with and without spectators during the season. The performance of both teams improved in the no-spectator condition as measured by total points, field goal percentage, and free throw percentage. Though very interesting, the results are not easily explained in terms of the usual social facilitation, audience arousal, or audience evaluation theories.

Nevill, A. M., & Holder, R. L. (1999). Home advantage in sport: An overview of studies of the advantage of playing at home. *Sports Medicine, 28,* 20–26.

The primary purpose of this paper was to review the available literature on the home advantage in sport. Four factors were identified as potentially accounting for the effects noted in the home advantage: game location factors, learning/familiarity factors, travel factors, and rule factors. Additional discussion was devoted to critical psychological states and critical behavioral states that might also impinge on the home advantage. Analyses of four sports since 1992 yielded home advantage percentages of over 54% for major league baseball, 61% for major junior–A ice hockey, 64% for college basketball, and 60% for soccer.

INFOTRAC COLLEGE EDITION

For additional readings, explore Infotrac College Edition, your online library. Go to:
http://www.infotrac-college.com/wadsworth
Hint: Enter these search terms: home advantage, peer pressure, self-evaluation, self-preservation.

Aggression: Dimensions and Theories

CHAPTER 13

Aggression Defined

Dimensions of Aggression

Biological Theories of Aggression

Psychosocial Theories of Aggression

Sociological Explanations of Aggression in Sport

The Measurement of Aggression

Factors Promoting Aggression

Critical Sport-Related Variables Affecting Aggression

Summary

Key Terms

Suggested Readings

The player making the tackle is engaging in sport assertive behavior consistent with the spirit and the rules of the game of football.

PhotoDisc © 2001

185

Dancing is a contact sport. Football is a collision sport.

Vince Lombardi, football coach

A nice quiet person who lifts weights and sometimes separates people's heads from their shoulders.

Sports Illustrated (1977) description of Kermit Washington of the Los Angeles Lakers shortly before he did exactly that to Rudy Tomjanovich of the Houston Rockets

If you have hate, you have good NFL football.

Phil Simms, retired NFL quarterback and television sports announcer

If I hit an opponent and his eye fell out . . . I would eat it before he would get it back.

Bobby Czyz, former light-heavyweight boxing champion

We most certainly live in a world filled with acts of violence. Violent events of major proportions occurred in the 1990s in Bosnia, Rwanda, and Somalia, to name only a few places. In the United States, according to statistics from the Federal Bureau of Investigation (Uniform Crime Reports, 1993), there is a property crime every 3 seconds and a violent crime every 21 seconds.

Particularly disturbing crime statistics are those for domestic violence, including child and spousal abuse. Corby (1993) reports that approximately 652,000 instances of child abuse occur annually in the United States. Whitcomb (1992) indicates that the figure could be as high as 6.9 million if the definition of child abuse were expanded to include hitting with a belt or stick. Child sexual abuse by parents or caregivers endangers the welfare of 155,000 young people annually (Whitcomb, 1992). In the case of spousal abuse, or what Zawitz (1994, p. 1) calls "violence between intimates," statistics from the National Crime Victimization Survey of the U.S. Department of Justice for the years 1987 through 1991 indicate that intimates committed over 621,000 rapes, robberies, or assaults. Of this number, 90% were committed against females by spouses, ex-spouses, or boyfriends. White and black females were abused at the same rates; this ratio was maintained

when Hispanic females were compared with non–Hispanics. There was an inverse relationship between abuse and educational attainment; women who had earned college degrees reported the lowest abuse rates. The same relationship existed with regard to income; women earning less than $9,999 were abused at a rate of 11 per 10,000, while women earning over $30,000 were abused at a rate of 2 per 10,000. Divorced or separated women were 10 times more likely to be victims of violence by an intimate than were their married counterparts (Bachman, 1994; Zawitz, 1994). By any measure, it appears that domestic violence is an unfortunate reality of American life. As will be noted later in this chapter, domestic violence involving high-profile athletes is a problem of major proportions.

Wars on other continents seem to be driven by class conflicts, tribal rivalries, religious conviction, racial or ethnic hatred, and dreams of geographical expansionism. In addition to hearing about aggressive and violent acts abroad, we are besieged by the sounds of everyday discontent or disagreement. Angry lovers having a verbal spat, teenage gangs verbally jousting with their rivals, harried taxi drivers shouting among themselves over traffic snarls, and angry sports enthusiasts filling the air with epithets hurled in the direction of a player or coach are constant reminders that violence is never far away. The sports world is not exempt from the effects of aggression gone awry, and the brief chronology of recent violent events in sports listed in Figure 13.1 serves to remind us that the behavior of fans and players can be volatile, unpredictable, unmanageable, and violent.

AGGRESSION DEFINED

Aggression is ubiquitous. On the one hand, aggressiveness is an admired trait in American society. A person who overcomes urban or rural poverty, gets an education, and works hard to become a success, or a highly motivated young business school graduate with lofty ambitions, is thought to be appropriately aggressive. Captains of American industry are held in esteem for their aggressive qualities. The language of the workplace is filled with commonplace expressions with aggressive themes (Rohrlich, 1998): "That broker doesn't have the killer instinct." "This memo doesn't have

FIGURE 13.1

A Chronology of Sports Violence

1968   A riot at a soccer match in Buenos Aires, Argentina, kills 74 and injures at least 150 more.

1971   Celebration over the World Series triumph of the Pittsburgh Pirates leaves two dead; an additional dozen rapes are linked to the "celebration."

1971   Soccer rioting in Kayseri, Turkey, kills 400 and injures 600.

1971   Soccer riot in Glasgow, Scotland, kills 66 and injures 140.

1973   Paul Smithers, a 17-year-old hockey player, is convicted of manslaughter after killing an opposing player in a Toronto, Canada, parking lot after a hockey game.

1975   David Forbes of the NHL Boston Bruins is charged with aggravated assault by use of a dangerous weapon after attacking an opponent during a hockey match. After more than a week of testimony and 18 hours of jury deliberation, Forbes is acquitted.

1975   *Nabozny v. Barnhill* lawsuit is lodged when a youth soccer goalie is kicked in the head by an opponent.

1976   *Hogensen v. Williamson* lawsuit is filed when a junior high football player suffers a neck injury when assaulted by his coach at practice.

1977   Rudy Tomjanovich of the NBA Houston Rockets suffers critical facial and skull injuries during a brawl when attacked by Kermit Washington of the Los Angeles Lakers.

1978   Daryl Stingley of the NFL New England Patriots is left quadriplegic after sustaining a crippling blow from Jack Tatum of the Oakland Raiders.

1982   Twenty-five policemen are hospitalized in Tallahassee, Florida, after fights erupt at the end of the Florida–Florida State college football game.

1984   Celebration over the World Series triumph of the Detroit Tigers leaves 16 injured and much related property damage to stores, businesses, and police cars.

1985   Soccer rioting in Brussels, Belgium, kills 38 and injures 437 others.

1989   Soccer rioting in Sheffield, England, kills 94 and injures 170 fans of Liverpool soccer club.

1991   Soccer rioting in Orkney, South Africa, kills 40 and injures 50 others.

1994   Andres Escobar, soccer star from Colombia, is gunned down in his hometown of Medellín for accidentally scoring a goal for the United States in the 1994 World Cup.

1995   Eighty-four people are killed and hundreds injured in a soccer riot prior to a match between Guatemala and Costa Rica.

1999   Tony Limon, a high school basketball player in San Antonio, Texas, intentionally elbows an opponent in the face, fracturing his nose and causing him to have plastic surgery to repair facial damage. Limon is sentenced to five years in prison for aggravated assault.

2000   Millions of dollars' worth of property damage is done by out-of-control fans after the Los Angeles Lakers win the National Basketball Association title over the Indiana Pacers.

2000   Michael Costin, a single father of four children, is beaten to death by Thomas Junta over what Junta thought was excessively rough play in a hockey league for 10-year-olds in Reading, Massachusetts.

---

enough punch." "We made a killing on the stock market last year." "It was a great show; I knocked 'em dead." These are expressions of prosocial aggression.

On the other hand are aggressive acts that result in pain and suffering—aggression gone awry. This antisocial aggression is of considerable interest to social scientists because of the emotional and monetary tolls it exacts.

According to *Webster's New Twentieth Century Dictionary* (1983), *aggression* is derived from the Latin *ad* (meaning "to" or "toward") and *gradi* ("to step," "to go") or from *aggredi* ("to attack," "to go toward"). Taking these etymological roots and putting them into a psychological context, we can then define **aggression** in terms of four properties: aversiveness, intent, and victim unwillingness (Geen, Beatty, & Arkin, 1984), plus expectancy of success (Cox 1990). Aggression begins with the delivery of an *aversive stimulus* to another person. The aversive stimulus might take the form of a verbal insult, a punch in the nose, or a bullet in the back. The person who is being aggressive must *intend* to harm the victim. The thief who hits you over the head in order to steal the contents of your wallet or handbag is being aggressive; his intent is to harm. (In contrast, physicians often inflict pain on their clients, but the intent is to cure or heal rather than harm.) Aggression involves an *unwilling victim*. Most acts of aggression are perpetrated in the *expectation of success*. By way of summary, aggression is the infliction of an aversive stimulus on an unwilling victim with the intent to do harm and with the expectation that the act will be successful.

DIMENSIONS OF AGGRESSION

Provoked and Unprovoked Aggression

Years ago, Hakeem Olajuwon of the Houston Rockets and Mitch Kupchak of the Los Angeles Lakers were ejected from a National Basketball Association playoff game for exchanging punches, a fracas that led to both benches coming to the aid of their respective teammates. Olajuwon said, "He threw the first punch and I could not help it" ("Sampson Answers a Prayer," 1986, p. 3B). If we assume that he has the facts straight, we can say that his aggressive act was generated by the actions of Kupchak and was an example of provoked aggression. If a vandal randomly selected the automobile of either of these athletes for an act of vandalism, the aggression would be considered unprovoked aggression. The latter sort of aggression is less likely to occur in the sport world than is the provoked variety. Many acts of aggression in sport result from verbal or physical provocation.

Direct and Indirect Aggression

If a vandal broke the windshield, snapped off the radio antenna, or slashed the tires of Olajuwon's automobile during the game because of general frustration with life, the aggression would be indirect. This variety of aggression is also called **displaced aggression**—that is, aggression directed at a source other than the source that created it. However, if the villain was a spectator at the Rockets–Lakers game who became incensed at Olajuwon for hitting Kupchak and then left the arena early and sought out Olajuwon's car (on the basis of prior knowledge of its make and whereabouts), we would have a clear-cut case of direct aggression.

Physical and Verbal Aggression

Singling out Olajuwon and Kupchak for further analysis, we note that their altercation attained physical proportions. In all likelihood, verbal exchanges had preceded the outbreak of physical aggression. More of the verbal than the physical type of aggression probably occurs in sport. Fortunately, we tend to talk more than we fight.

Adaptive and Maladaptive Aggression

In some cases, aggression in sport may be adaptive. An athlete in activities such as basketball, football, or hockey probably could not function without establishing the fact that he or she will not be pushed around and intimidated. This is not to condone the kinds of borderline sportsmanship and rules infractions that take place, but to merely point out that, given the way the games are played today, an athlete simply must be aggressive. However, blatant high-sticking in hockey and fistfights on the basketball court have little adaptive value and should be considered counter to the spirit of sport.

Hostile Aggression, Instrumental Aggression, and Sport Assertiveness

Aggression also may be viewed in terms of the reinforcement that is sought. For example, it is generally agreed among slow-pitch softball players that the pitcher

---

Aggression the infliction of an aversive stimulus on an unwilling victim with the intent to do harm and the expectation of success.
Displaced aggression aggression that is not directed at the person or situation that sparked aggressive feelings but is instead diverted to some other target.

A Longitudinal Study of Prosocial and Aggressive Behavior

In 1987, Leonard Eron reported results of a 22-year study of prosocial and aggressive behavior that began in 1960. More than 600 third graders (ages 7 to 9) from one county in New York were interviewed and tested along with 75% of their parents. Aggressive behavior was assessed through peer nominations by asking questions such as "Who pushes or shoves children?" Prosocial behaviors were gathered in the same way with questions such as "Who says 'excuse me' even if they have not done anything bad?" and "Who will never fight even when picked on?" Three salient correlates of aggression were identified through the testing and parent interviews: (1) The less nurturant and accepting the parents were, the higher were the levels of aggression displayed. (2) The more a child was punished for aggression, the more aggressive he or she was at school. (3) The less a child identified with the parents, the higher was the aggression displayed.

At the end of 10 years, a follow-up was conducted through interviewing 427 of the original subjects. The major conclusion reached at that juncture in the study was that those who were aggressive in the third grade were three times more likely to have police records at age 19 than were those not so rated.

Twenty-two years after the original study, 414 of the original subjects were again interviewed. The correlation between aggression in the third grade and aggression displayed in the intervening 22 years was .46, a hefty figure. Prosocial third graders strongly tended to be prosocial adults as exemplified by educational and occupational attainment, low levels of antisocial acts, and overall good mental health. Aggression at age 8, unfortunately, predicted social failure, psychopathology, aggression, and low educational and occupational attainment.

Clearly, Eron's results add to the literature that points to early childhood antecedents of both prosocial behavior and aggression in adults.

SOURCE: Eron (1987).

---

is inordinately vulnerable to being hit by the batted ball because of the pitcher's physical proximity to home plate and the ample force applied to the ball by a strong and skilled hitter. Some players try to take advantage of this vulnerability by hitting the ball directly at or near the pitcher. Such an act is **hostile aggression** if the batter truly enjoys hitting the pitcher and seeing the person in physical pain. Such an act is **instrumental aggression** if the batter hits the pitcher not to inflict pain or injury but to promote a winning effort. The goal of instrumental aggression, simply stated, is something other than the infliction of harm or injury. In either case, deviance is rewarded, which of course increases the likelihood that the aggression will recur.

It is possible to distinguish hostile and instrumental aggression in sport from **sport assertiveness** (see Figure 13.2). The intent of both types of aggression is to harm, but that is not the intent of assertive behavior. The three concepts can further be separated on the dimension of winning versus harming: The goal of hostile aggression is to harm; the goal of instrumental aggression is to win; and the goal of sport assertiveness is to play with as much enthusiasm, force, and skill as possible. Also, a hostile assertive athlete feels much anger, but an athlete using instrumental force does so without anger, and anger is not an issue in sport assertiveness. Unusual effort and energy

---

Hostile aggression the infliction of an aversive stimulus in order to cause harm or pain.
Instrumental aggression the infliction of an aversive stimulus not to cause harm or pain but to promote a winning effort.
Sport assertiveness assertive behavior not intended to cause harm or pain and characterized by the use of legitimate force and unusual effort and energy expenditure and by observance of the formal rules of the game.

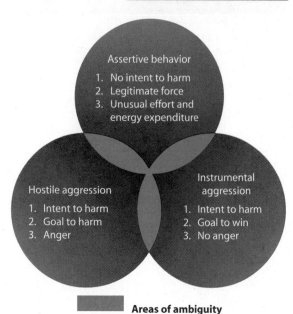

FIGURE 13.2

Relationship Among Hostile Aggression, Instrumental Aggression, and Sport Assertiveness

Assertive behavior

1. No intent to harm
2. Legitimate force
3. Unusual effort and energy expenditure

Hostile aggression

1. Intent to harm
2. Goal to harm
3. Anger

Instrumental aggression

1. Intent to harm
2. Goal to win
3. No anger

■ **Areas of ambiguity**

SOURCES: Cox (1990); Silva (1979).

expenditure are issues in sport assertiveness, however. The constitutive or formal rules (Silva, 1981) of the game matter in assertiveness; they are violated, at least in spirit, by acts of aggression, regardless of type.

To illustrate how assertiveness might differ from the two types of aggression, let us return to our slow-pitch softball example. A batter who is being assertive rather than aggressive realizes when he enters the batter's box that hitting at or near the pitcher will give him several distinct advantages well within the rules and the spirit of the game. For one thing, the pitcher is very close to home plate. For another, the pitcher is often the poorest fielder in the infield. Also, infielders are called upon to cover a lot of ground in the middle of the diamond. These facts indicate that a well-hit drive in the vicinity of the pitcher would be a good play. The pitcher might get hit by the ball a couple of times, but those are the breaks of the game.

As this illustration indicates, there are ambiguous areas of overlap among hostile and instrumental aggression and sport assertiveness; the three are not completely distinct. For example, the forceful but clean and legal tackle in football could be viewed as assertive because there was no intent to harm; but, given the generally violent nature of football, it might be argued that all tackles are acts of aggression. With regard to goals sought, it is probably true that most football players hold winning in higher regard than hurting their opponents. As for the third area of overlap, the anger seen in hostile aggression and the force and expenditure of energy in assertion are hard to distinguish. Players of collision sports, such as football, possess a certain amount of controlled anger, which Kiester (1984) says can be put to constructive use. He cites the example of Conrad Dobler, a one-time offensive lineman for the then St. Louis Cardinals, who achieved notoriety through his borderline violation of the rules coupled with constructive use of anger. Dobler attributed much of his success to being able to do things verbally and physically that greatly angered his opponents and thereby distracted them from playing well. John McEnroe, the tennis great of the 1980s, was also a master at turning anger to his advantage through distraction of the opposition.

Inferring whether aggressiveness or assertiveness has taken place in any particular event is a judgment call. Football and other collision sports offer many legitimate opportunities to injure yet stay within the rules. Certain kinds of blocks, such as the crackback, can be applied legally yet be intended to injure; a number of serious knee injuries owe their genesis to the crackback block. In baseball, the legal brushback pitch and the illegal and potentially life-threatening beanball are very difficult to distinguish. Often, such plays are labeled "aggressive" or "assertive" on the basis of subtle cues. Stares, glares, hand gestures, and verbal exchanges are often used to determine whether a behavior was aggressive or assertive.

Aggression and Violence: One and the Same?

In defining aggression, it is appropriate to look at the relationship between aggression and violence. There is a reasonable continuum ranging from sport assertiveness to instrumental aggression to hostile aggression and, finally, to **sport violence.** Terry and Jackson (1985, p. 27) provide a good working definition of sport violence: "Violence is defined as harm-inducing behavior bearing no direct relationship to the competitive goals of sport, and relates, therefore, to incidents of uncontrolled aggression outside the rules of sport, rather than highly competitive behavior within the rule boundaries." Because of the definitional overlap between aggression and violence, we shall use the terms interchangeably in the remainder of this chapter.

BIOLOGICAL THEORIES OF AGGRESSION

Biological explanations of aggression have taken many forms. One emphasizes the role of genetics. There is some evidence for a genetic hypothesis from the animal world—the breeding of fighting cocks and fighting dogs—but little substantiation exists in the human domain. Perhaps the closest example in humans is the XYY chromosomal theory of aggression and criminality. In the 1960s, it was hypothesized that this chromosomal abnormality partially explained male criminality. The theory was chromosomal factors predisposed some males to a life of crime. Evidence gathered since then has cast much doubt on this simplistic explanation for complex human behavior.

A second biological approach to understanding aggression has been to examine the role of various neurological structures, such as the hypothalamus, the limbic system, and the temporal lobe. An interesting case involving temporal lobe pathology is that of Charles Whitman, who in 1966 killed his wife, mother, and 14 other people while perched atop the tower of the administrative building at the University of Texas in Austin. Whitman's lack of a history of violence, coupled with an autopsy finding of what appeared to be a brain tumor, led authorities to suspect temporal lobe pathology as a likely etiological factor in his aggressive acts. All things considered, however, there is plenty of room for alternative explanations for Whitman's acts of violence.

A third viewpoint is that the interaction of certain hormonal agents and learned or cognitive factors produces aggressive acts. Chief among the suspected hormonal culprits is testosterone, the male sex hormone

(which is 10 times higher in males than females). Dabbs and Morris (1990) conducted a particularly interesting investigation of the testosterone/aggression relationship. They studied over 4,000 male military veterans, comparing the top 10 percent with the remaining 90 percent on blood testosterone levels. The males with high testosterone levels reported more trouble with authorities and peers, more frequent assaultive behavior, more absent without leave (AWOL) violations, and more frequent abuse of drugs than did those in the other group. Because of the size of their sample, Dabbs and Morris feel that their study produced compelling evidence for the testosterone/aggression relationship.

As an aside, Baron and Richardson (1994) suggest that the relationship between testosterone and aggression is most likely a bidirectional one—that is, high levels of testosterone may produce aggression and, conversely, aggressive acts may increase the production of testosterone. The potentially bidirectional nature of the testosterone/aggression relationship gives some indication of how complicated the study of hormonal influences on behavior is.

In the case of females, the estrogen/progesterone ratio has been a focus of some research. Imbalances in the ratio have been known to cause irritability or hostility, particularly around the menstrual period. Dalton (1961, 1964) linked this hormonal imbalance to criminal acts outside and behavior problems inside the prison environment among incarcerated females.

In addressing the necessarily interdisciplinary approaches to the study of hormones and behavior, Baron and Richardson (1994, p. 253) succinctly summarized the issue: "Regardless of the research approach or the disciplinary affiliation of the investigator, the results are similar and inconclusive."

PSYCHOSOCIAL THEORIES OF AGGRESSION

Cathartic Approaches

The notion that aggression is reduced through allowing its expression is neither novel nor unappealing. All

---

Sport violence uncontrolled hostile aggression that is unrelated to the competitive goals of sport and ignores the rules of the game.

FIGURE 13.3

Bandura's Social Learning Theory

Aggression is acquired through:

Biological factors (e.g., hormones, neural systems)

Learning (e.g., direct experience, observation)

Aggression is instigated by:

Influence of models (e.g., arousal, attention)

Aversive treatment (e.g., attack, frustration)

Incentives (e.g., money, admiration)

Instructions (e.g., orders)

Bizarre beliefs (e.g., delusions of paranoia)

Aggression is regulated by:

External rewards and punishments (e.g., tangible rewards, negative consequences)

Vicarious reinforcement (e.g., observing others' rewards and punishments)

Self-regulatory mechanisms (e.g., pride, guilt)

SOURCE: Baron & Richardson (1994).
Note: This theory explains the acquisition, instigation, and regulation of aggressive behavior.

---

of us at times have probably subscribed to the idea that "letting off steam" is a constructive way of dealing with pent-up emotion. The release felt at these times is often referred to as catharsis, which comes from the Greek *kathairein,* meaning "to cleanse." A number of theorists, including Freud, Lorenz, Ardrey, and Dollard and Miller and their associates, have generated scholarly explanations that are in line with the **catharsis hypothesis.**

Catharsis hypothesis the theory that the expression of aggressive tendencies prevents the buildup of harmful levels of aggression.

Frustration–aggression hypothesis the theory that frustration—the blocking of motivated behavior—always precedes aggression.

Social learning theory the theory that the expression of aggression reinforces (rather than alleviates) tendencies toward aggression.

INSTINCT THEORY. Instinct theory has its origin in the work of Sigmund Freud. Freud hypothesized that we are all possessed of a powerful life wish (Eros) and a potent death wish (Thanatos), the former manifesting itself in the sex drive and the latter in the need to aggress. According to Freud, the death wish involves self-destructiveness, but harm to oneself may be avoided by aggressing against others. Freud viewed the tendencies toward self-destruction and harm avoidance as instinctual, and he believed that aggression is dissipated by its expression.

Ethologists such as Ardrey (1966) and Lorenz (1966) proposed alternative instinct theories. Both posit that human beings have the same need to aggress as other animals. According to Lorenz, aggression is an instinctive behavior that persists because it facilitates survival of the species. Because of its innate nature, it does not have to be learned. Ardrey talks in terms of territoriality, the tendency of all animals to drive intruders out of their chosen territory. Territoriality is easily seen in the behavior of animals but is less obvious in human behavior. However, the way we construct our dwellings, our locks, our fences, and our "beware of the dog" and "no trespassing" signs all indicate a desire to defend our territory.

FRUSTRATION–AGGRESSION HYPOTHESIS. Another cathartic approach is the **frustration–aggression hypothesis,** first proposed by Dollard, Doob, Miller, Mowrer, and Sears (1939). Though having similarities with the other cathartic models, the theory of Dollard and colleagues differs from them in its emphasis on learned experiences rather than instinctive tendencies. Their hypothesis is that frustration, or the blocking of motivated or goal-directed behavior, leads to aggression and that aggression is always preceded by frustration. This provocative hypothesis sparked a great deal of research but has fallen on hard times because it greatly oversimplifies the issue.

Social Learning Approach

A point of view that seriously calls into question the basic tenets of the cathartic theories is **social learning theory,** of which Bandura (1973) is a major proponent. Figure 13.3 presents a brief description of the social learning position, which emphasizes reinforcement and modeling. Essentially, proponents assert that aggression is reinforced rather than alleviated or lessened by aggression. Instances in which aggressive behavior is reinforced increase rather than reduce the likelihood of its future occurrence. Aggressive acts that are reinforced by tacit approval or by a coach's or parent's failure to punish may be seen as acceptable. As for modeling, parents are usually the first models for a child. A parent who displays aggression serves as a model for aggressive acts by the child. A Little League coach who verbally attacks the umpires is modeling aggression for his young players. Also, an aggressive athlete serves as a negative model for youthful admirers.

Catharsis or Social Learning?

Does the expression of aggression reduce aggression or make aggression more likely? No easy answers are at hand. The complexity of the issue is illustrated by the furor over violence on television, whether in sport or elsewhere. If the cathartic school of thought is correct, viewing violence on television will decrease the incidence of violence in the real world. If the social learning people are correct, viewing aggression on television will promote rather than discourage aggression. The issue is far from resolved, and heated debate is likely to continue for quite some time. Russell (1993), however, conducted a comprehensive review of the literature and concluded that there is little support for a cathartic view and substantial evidence for the social learning position.

Our personal view is that the impact of learning on the development of human behavior cannot be dismissed, and its relationship to aggression and violence is no exception. Perhaps our viewpoint is best expressed by Montagu (1975, pp. 438, 449):

> No matter who or what was responsible for making us into what we have become, that does not for a moment relieve us of the responsibility of endeavoring to make ourselves over into what we ought to be . . . . To suggest that man is born ineradicably aggressive, warlike, and violent is to do violence to the facts. To maintain that he is innately already "wired" or "programmed" for aggression is to render confusion worse confounded, to exhibit a failure to understand the pivotally

most consequential fact about the nature of man. That fact is not that man becomes what he is predetermined to become, but that he becomes, as a human being, whatever—within his genetic limitations—he learns to be.

SOCIOLOGICAL EXPLANATIONS OF AGGRESSION IN SPORT

Sport sociologists look at violence in sport in a number of ways. Snyder and Spreitzer (1983, 1989) identified four perspectives: contagion theory, convergence theory, emergent norm theory, and value-added theory.

Contagion Theory

Critical to an understanding of **contagion theory** is milling, the process whereby tension, uneasiness, and excitation are manifested by fans or players. As tensions mount, the tendency to react in impulsive or counterproductive ways escalates, and a psychological contagion may emerge that can manifest itself in collective violence. Inherent in all of this is a tendency toward circularity of response—that is, the restlessness and irritability serve to influence others through what amounts to modeling. As Snyder and Spreitzer (1989, p. 242) put it: "The mutual interstimulation results in a circular spiral of feelings and action."

Convergence Theory

Convergence theory emphasizes common interests and goals in a highly divergent group of people whose emotions are brought to a fever pitch by the sporting event. The behavior of soccer hooligans in Britain (discussed later in this chapter) serves as an exemplar for the convergence model. The soccer matches become a forum for ruffians and ne'er-do-wells to engage in ritualistic misbehavior that is fueled by the sport and the fever pitch of the action.

Contagion theory a theory of fan violence emphasizing "milling," whereby tension and excitation create an atmosphere of psychological contagion.
Convergence theory a theory of fan violence emphasizing the coming together of divergent groups as a result of the fevered pitch of a sporting event.

Emergent Norm Theory

Emergent norm theory suggests that group interaction creates a situation-specific set of standards that emerge over time among spectators at a sports event. The emphasis here is on the collective response emerging as a function of the crowd interaction that is situation-specific. It may be that the politeness of the typical golf gallery or of tennis fans is an emergent norm with a long history, one in stark contrast to the behavior often seen at hockey games or soccer matches.

Value-Added Theory

Value-added theory owes its genesis to Smelser (1962). It is inclusive of aspects of the other three models and more comprehensive. Crowd behavior, according to Smelser, can escalate in healthy or unhealthy ways as a function of six steps:

1. Structural conduciveness, which is a function of fans' and players' personal and social characteristics, avenues or lack of avenues for expression of emotion, proximity of targets for verbal or physical attack, and physical setting characteristics.

2. Structural strain, which represents a dissonance between what fans want to happen and what actually transpires; the larger the gap, the more unpredictable behavior becomes.

3. Dissonance reduction, which dictates that there must be some attempt to deal with the dissonance created in item 2. Poor officiating, an antagonistic fan for the opposition, or a dirty player may serve as a source of resolution of the dissonance state. At this point, there may be an escalation in psychological contagion.

4. A specific precipitator of violence must present itself, such as a particularly rough play or a decidedly bad officiating decision.

5. Mobilization for action characterizes the next step in the process. The interaction between the crowd, the physical surroundings of the sports facility, and the emergence of a leader to force the action are at work here.

6. A breakdown in the physical and/or psychological mechanisms for social control to keep behavior within reasonable bounds further contributes to the problem.

Each stage adds its respective value to the totality, thus increasing the likelihood of collective violence in sports fans.

THE MEASUREMENT OF AGGRESSION

Aggression has been measured from a variety of angles:

1. *Naturalistic observation,* such as observation of violence in hockey or soccer.

2. *Laboratory research.* Manipulation of aggression variables under laboratory conditions has great appeal, although critics argue that much may be lost in translating laboratory findings to the so-called real world.

3. *Archival analysis.* This involves the collection of data from public sources, such as police files or FBI crime statistics.

4. *Questionnaires.* Asking people to engage in self-disclosure about their own use of aggression has been done with some success.

5. *Projective tests of personality,* such as the Rorschach Inkblot Test, the Thematic Apperception Test (TAT), and various sentence completion techniques. In the case of the Rorschach, the subject is shown 10 inkblots. The guiding assumption is that the person being tested will generate enough responses to the 10 cards to allow for inferences about his or her personality. In the case of the TAT, subjects are shown a series of real pictures about which they are to tell detailed stories. Emerging themes (e.g., aggression) are then identified and analyzed. In the case of sentence completion tests, subjects are presented with fragments

---

Emergent norm theory a theory of fan behavior emphasizing the development of normative expectancies over extended periods of time.
Value-added theory a complex theory of fan behavior drawing upon other models that emphasizes six steps leading to violence.

of sentences, and it is anticipated that personality traits, such as aggressiveness, will emerge as subjects create complete sentences.

6. *Objective tests of personality.* These instruments employ a variety of forced-choice formats—such as true–false, yes–no, choose A or B—to assess personality. Of particular interest is the Aggression Questionnaire (Buss & Perry, 1992), which measures four factors: physical aggression, verbal aggression, anger, and hostility. Factor analytic studies by Bernstein and Gesn (1997) and by Harris (1995) are supportive of Buss and Perry's four-factor structure. Felsten and Hill (1999) conducted an investigation using only the anger and hostility scales and found support for the latter but not the former. In a sport-related study, Bushman and Wells (1998) looked at the physical aggression scale in a sample of high school hockey players and found a significant relationship between physical aggression measured during a preseason administration and aggressive penalty minutes imposed during the season.

Given widespread fascination with aggression, it is striking that so little has been done in sport psychology to unravel its many nuances. Little has been done in sport-specific measures of aggression. The Bredemeier Athletic Aggression Inventory (BAAGI) (Bredemeier, 1978) and her Scale of Children's Action Tendencies in Sport (SCATS) (Bredemeier, 1994) represent two attempts to create sport-specific measures of aggression, but they have not met with great success thus far.

FACTORS PROMOTING AGGRESSION

A nearly unlimited number of factors may cause or facilitate aggression. Physical factors include temperature, noise, and crowding. Psychological factors include modeling, reinforcement, and deindividuation. An interesting sociological phenomenon is hooliganism. Also, no discussion of aggression and violence would be complete without a look at another sociological phenomenon, the media and their role in promoting such misbehavior.

Physical Factors

Three physical factors that contribute in a complex fashion to create or promote aggressive acts are temperature, noise, and crowding.

TEMPERATURE.

> I pray thee, good Mercutio, let's retire;
> The day is hot, the Capulets abroad,
> And, if we meet, we shall not 'scape a brawl,
> For now, these hot days, is the mad blood stirring. (III.1.1–4)

This quotation from Shakespeare's *Romeo and Juliet* serves as a reminder that temperature can exert a negative influence on behavior.

There are two theories about the temperature–aggression relationship. According to one, the relationship is linear; according to the other, it is curvilinear. Anderson's general affective model (Anderson, Deuser, & Deneve, 1995; Anderson, Anderson, & Deuser, 1996) suggests that the relationship is linear—that is, as temperature rises, there will be concomitant increases in aggression. Anderson and Anderson state: "Research consistently shows higher rates of aggression during hotter time periods in daily, monthly, quarterly, and yearly time period studies" (p. 22). Anderson, Bushman, and Groom (1997) looked at crime statistics and temperature data in the 50 largest cities in the United States over a 45-year period and found a positive correlation between temperature and serious and deadly assaults. No relationship between temperature and property crime was found.

Proponents of the other side of the **linear–curvilinear debate** suggest that the relationship between temperature and aggression is curvilinear, not linear. According to this model, aggressive episodes will be predictably low in frequency at the temperature extremes; temperatures too high or too low will limit the kinds of arousal and human interaction that lead to violence. This model suggests that there may be an

---

Linear–curvilinear debate the debate about whether the temperature–aggression relationship is linear (As temperature rises, will there be an increase in aggression?) or curvilinear (Is there an optimal temperature for aggressive acts?).

FIGURE 13.4

Relationship Between Ambient Temperature and Riots

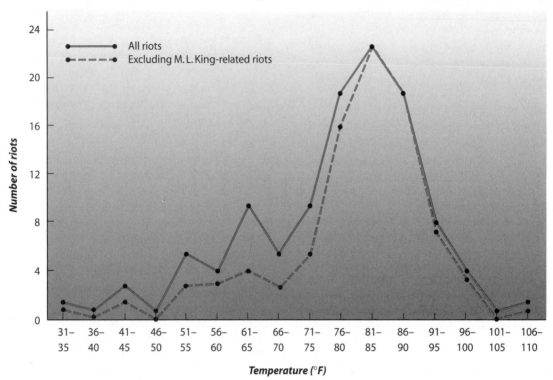

Source: Baron & Ransberger (1978).

optimal temperature at which aggressive acts would flourish. Baron (1977) was among the first researchers to suggest that the curvilinear model is the correct one. Baron and Ransberger have substantiated this curvilinear relationship (1978) in a study of temperature and the incidence of riots in large U.S. cities, and this relationship can be seen in Figure 13.4. Obviously, riots are linked to temperature in a curvilinear fashion in this case. Riots are infrequent below a temperature of 55 degrees and above a temperature of 95 degrees.

In this connection, Cohn and Rotton studied aggression in Minneapolis, Minnesota and Dallas, Texas (Cohn & Rotton, 1997; Rotton & Cohn, 2000). These researchers concluded that there is general support for the curvilinear model, but they do grant that the temperature–aggression relationship is highly com-

plex. For example, in the Dallas study they found an inverted-U (i.e., curvilinear) relationship between the two variables during the daylight hours and in spring months but a linear relationship during the nighttime hours and in other seasons. The fact that comparisons between a cooler northern city (Minneapolis) and a city that can be unbearably hot for long periods of time (Dallas) are difficult to interpret in terms of the existing theories substantiates how complex the issue is. In addition, there is a nearly endless number of other variables to take into account—beyond the scope of this discussion—when trying to unravel the mystery of the temperature–aggression relationship.

How all this relates to sport violence is unclear because of a paucity of research on temperature and its effects on players and fans. However, hot baseball and

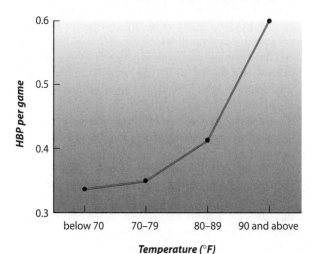

FIGURE 13.5

Number of Batters Hit by Pitchers as a Function of Game Temperature

Note: Mean number of players hit by a pitch (HBPs) in games played below 70° F (N = 176), between 70° F and 79° F (N = 315), between 80° F and 89° F (N = 224), and at 90° F and above (N = 111).
Source: Reifman, Larrick, & Fein (1991).

soccer venues and steamy, sweaty basketball arenas must in some way contribute to the instances of player or fan aggression that occur from time to time.

One sport-related test of the temperature–aggression relationship is that of Reifman, Larrick, and Fein (1991). In their research, they looked at archival data from the 1986, 1987, and 1988 major league baseball seasons. Their methodology was to relate game temperature to number of batters hit by the pitchers in 826 games over those three seasons. A positive and significant relationship was found between game temperature and number of hit batters. Interestingly, in light of our previous discussion, the relationship between hit batters and temperature in this study was linear (see Figure 13.5).

Two additional points merit mention. First, methodological controls over potential confounding variables having nothing to do with aggression per se were factored into the Reifman et al. study. For example, walks, wild pitches, passed balls, errors, home runs,

attendance, and home versus visiting ballpark were analyzed statistically and deemed to be of minimal influence in their effects on the overall results. Second, as a check on their results for 1986–1988, Reifman et al. found a similar linearity effect when they analyzed archival data from the 1962 season.

NOISE. There is little research in the area of noise and sport violence, but the roar of the crowd is likely to be a factor in increasing arousal. Concomitantly, the likelihood of aggression is greater in heightened states of arousal. Part of the home advantage discussed in Chapter 12 may be attributable to the noise factor. Basketball coaches intentionally place the visitors' bench behind the home team's band, and football cheerleaders exhort the home crowd to drown out the opponent's signals. Although the intent in these instances is not to stir aggression, such noisy outbursts can intensify already existing hostile feelings or emotions.

Donnerstein and Wilson (1976) demonstrated a link between noise and aggression, though not in a sport setting. They exposed students to either 55- or 95-decibel bursts of noise while the students were administering electric shocks to a confederate of the researchers. Students exposed to the high noise level delivered more shock to the confederate than did students exposed to the lower noise level. If we can extrapolate from the results of this research to the world of athletics, we can infer a possible relationship between noise and aggression. Perhaps Franken (1982, p. 290) said it best: "Noise does not seem to evoke aggression by itself. Rather, noise simply facilitates this behavior if it has already been evoked." Obviously, more sport-related research linking noise and aggression needs to be conducted.

CROWDING. Information arising from the 1994 International Conference on Population and Development held in Cairo, Egypt, indicated that it took well over 100 years for the world population to grow from 1 billion to 2 billion but only 13 years to grow from 4 billion to 5 billion. Left unchecked, the world population is projected to become 12.5 billion by the middle of the 21st century (Ambah, 1994). In and of itself, this increase does not signal a problem of crowding, according to Berkowitz (1986), but more one of density. Density is the relationship between the amount of physical space available and the number of people occupying it; crowding is a psychological stress response created by problems of density. How all of this relates to aggression is not clear. After reviewing the available research, Freedman (1975) concluded that crowding itself is not a causative factor in aggression but is most definitely a facilitator when the propensity for hostility already exists.

The conclusion that emerges from the research in temperature, noise, and crowding is that they are more facilitators than causes of aggression. They interact with other variables to produce aggression in situations in which the propensity for hostile action already exists. One does not have to look far in the world of sport to find applications for this generalization. The heat generated by the sun and by lots of warm bodies, coupled with the roar of the crowd and accentuated by a shoving mass of people, has undoubtedly contributed to more than one act of sport violence.

Psychological Factors

A number of psychological variables are related to the expression of aggression. Modeling and reinforcement, mentioned earlier in this chapter, merit additional discussion. Also important are external rewards, deindividuation, and inurement to violence.

VICARIOUS REINFORCEMENT AND MODELING OF AGGRESSION. According to Silva (1984a, p. 268), one of the main promoters and maintainers of aggressive behavior in sport is **vicarious reinforcement,** or what he calls "the tendency to repeat behaviors that we observe others rewarded for performing." A related concept is **vicarious punishment.** In defining the latter term, Silva says: "We are less likely to perform a behavior that we have seen another individual being punished for doing."

According to Bandura (1973), the acquisition of behavior through either vicarious reinforcement or vicarious punishment is greatly mediated by model and

---

Vicarious reinforcement reinforcement that results from observing other individuals being rewarded for performing a specific behavior.
Vicarious punishment imagined punishment that would result from some behavior for which other individuals have been punished.

observer similarity, by reward and punishment intensity, by setting similarity, and by the status of the model being observed. As might be expected, the greater the similarity between the model and the observer, the greater is the likelihood of any given behavior being repeated. Reward value is rather obvious in this context: Something meaningful to an individual is likely to be pursued with vigor. Also, the greater the similarity between the setting in which a behavior is performed and the circumstances in which the behavior was originally observed and vicariously reinforced, the greater the transfer will be. Finally, the status of the model for the observer is critical. Young aspiring athletes emulate their heroes—this is one of the reasons why positive role models should be promoted and negative ones downplayed.

The relationship of these variables advanced by Bandura to aggression in sport is reasonably obvious. Youngsters viewing aggressive models with whom they strongly identify are prone to believe that aggression in athletics is acceptable behavior.

DIRECT EXTERNAL REWARDS FOR AGGRESSION. Bandura (1973) identified four types of external reward that are operative in human interactions: (1) tangible rewards, (2) status rewards, (3) expression of injury, and (4) alleviation of aversive treatment. Their applicability to sport is undeniable.

Perhaps the most powerful tangible reward is money. If being aggressive means more money in the personal coffers, then aggression it shall be. In a highly publicized incident from the football world of the 1970s, coaches at a major university in the now defunct Southwest Conference offered various amounts of money to players on the specialty teams for tackles, breaking up wedges, kicks into the end zone, and so forth. Behavior that was particularly assertive (if not aggressive) was highly prized and rewarded accordingly. This system of external rewards met with disfavor among the various organizations that govern the conduct of intercollegiate athletics, and the university in question was given the most severe penalty (i.e., the "death penalty") in NCAA history.

In many sports, aggressiveness earns an athlete a certain amount of status—respect and recognition among peers. Aggressive behavior also gives rise to the use of nicknames connoting and reinforcing aggression

(Assassin, Dr. Death, Enforcer, Hammer). This somewhat deviant form of recognition fosters aggression as the nicknames become a sort of self-fulfilling prophecy. An athlete cannot be "the assassin" without working hard at it!

The relationship of Bandura's third type of external reward, expression of injury, to sport is less clear. Hurting an opponent may promote aggression, but it seems equally plausible that injury infliction may inhibit displays of aggression. Research has not sufficiently established what the effects may be. For some athletes—a minority, we hope—the sight of an opponent bleeding is probably reinforcing because it is evidence that the aggressive act worked. Boxing, in which intent to hurt is so manifest, serves as a prime example of the reinforcing properties of injury infliction.

The fourth type of external reward is alleviation of aversive treatment. Aggression that reduces aggression by an opponent is reinforcing. Establishing one's territory is important here, and failure to be aggressive in defending it is likely to be frowned on. Self-esteem and status in the eyes of others are also at issue. An example is the case of Paul Mulvey, a National Hockey League player who refused his coaches' order to take part in a brawl between his team, the Los Angeles Kings, and the opposition, the Vancouver Canucks. Mulvey's reticence to fight was poorly received by his peers and by the team management. Because of his violation of the eye-for-an-eye norms of hockey, he soon found himself out of the league altogether. Such violations of the aggressive norm simply are not tolerated in contact sports.

DEINDIVIDUATION. Another contributor to aggression, and one unstudied but not unrelated to sport, is deindividuation, a concept introduced by Festinger, Pepitone, and Newcomb in 1952 and highlighted in research conducted by Zimbardo (1969). According to the researchers, **deindividuation** is a psychological state that occurs when a person who is a member of a group loses his or her sense of individuality and increasingly conforms to the dictates of the group. The loss of identity or sense of belonging, coupled with the loss of a sense of personal accountability, serves to promote aggression. When an individual can no longer be separated from the mass, and individual responsibility for proper behavior has been diluted, it can be said that deindividuation has taken place.

Although deindividuation is an intriguing concept, Postmes and Spears (1998), using meta-analysis, reviewed 61 studies but found little support for deindividuation as a cause of antinormative behavior. Unfortunately, no research has attempted to relate deindividuation to aggression in sport. As has been the case with so many other variables, to make a case for singular causation is difficult because most human behavior is dictated in a complex fashion. Nevertheless, loss of personal responsibility for behavior would appear to offer an explanation of sport aggression in at least some cases.

INUREMENT TO VIOLENCE. Some would say that violence has become so commonplace that we are accustomed to it. The media report numerous acts of individual and group violence daily, often highlighting incidents of sport aggression to boost ratings or sell newspapers. Exposure to violence on a continual basis tends to inure us to aggressive acts, thereby raising our tolerance for such behaviors.

Sociological Considerations

One of the more interesting phenomena associated with sport is soccer violence, popularly known as hooliganism. From all appearances, hooliganism has a substantial social class component and merits further attention. Another significant sociological consideration is the role of the media in fostering and promoting aggression.

HOOLIGANISM. According to *Webster's New Twentieth Century Dictionary,* a hooligan is "a young ruffian, especially a member of a street gang; hoodlum"; and hooliganism is "the behavior or character of a hooligan; rowdiness; vandalism." The term **hooliganism** often refers to the behavior of soccer fans in Europe, particularly in England (Dunning, 1983; Dunning, Maguire, Murphy, & Williams, 1982; Marsh, Rosser, & Harre, 1978). Dunning indicates that hooliganism, in

---

Deindividuation the loss of a sense of individuality coupled with an increase in willingness to conform to group norms.
Hooliganism rowdy, violent behavior, especially by soccer fans in Europe.

Soccer hooliganism in Europe has become such a problem that an increasing number of control measures are being implemented by the agencies with jurisdiction over the game.
© AFP/CORBIS

the eyes of its participants, has become an accepted, almost normal part of professional soccer. Hooliganism's central feature, the characteristic that marks it most, is physical violence. Hooligan violence is directed toward players, toward officials, and, more often than not, toward rival fan groups. The violence may take the form of hand-to-hand combat, the use of weaponry, or aerial bombardment from a distance. The fact that darts, coins, beer cans, and petrol bombs have been used as weapons brings to mind our previous discussion of the intention to do harm as an integral part of aggression. As Curry and Jiobu (1984, p. 250) observe: "For the soccer hooligan, the soccer stadium is a battlefield, not a sports field."

In an effort to curb some of these hostilities, officials have resorted to segregating various fan groups by penning them together in separate areas within the stadium. Dealing with these people is complicated by the fact that many hooligans do not buy tickets to the events and engage in their violence on the streets before and after the games (Lopez, 1998). The hooligan problem has led international soccer spokesperson Keith Cooper to state: "the mindset of these guys is a puzzle. England seems to have invented it, exported it. England seems to be intent on remaining world champions at this particular problem" (Lopez, 1998, p. 9B).

Dunning's opinion is that the behavior of soccer hooligans demonstrates a misplaced attempt to demonstrate masculinity, with an exaggerated emphasis on toughness and willingness to fight. He further asserts that the rival groups are recruited principally from the rougher segments of the working-class populace. Dunning also believes that the soccer games may merely serve as a forum for rival gangs to conduct their long-standing feuds—that is, fighting appears to be more important than watching the soccer match. A final noteworthy observation by Dunning concerns the conformity to group dictates that characterizes the various hooligan gangs. Hooligans tolerate little individuality among gang members, and they reinforce group identification and conformity through ritualized songs and chants that they engage in at the matches. One of the more benign of these chants is provided by Marsh, Rosser, and Harre (1978, p. 66):

In their slums,
In their Nottingham slums,
They look in the dust bin for something to eat,
They find a dead cat and think it's a treat,
In their Nottingham slums.

The theme of most of these incantations is enhancement of masculinity.

A major instance of hooliganism occurred in 1985 in Brussels, Belgium, when 38 people were killed and 437 injured by a group of young Britishers. Severe sanctions were sought against these people; 26 British participants were prosecuted for manslaughter ("Soccer," 1988). Some suggestions for controlling these hooligans are entertained later in this chapter as a part of some recommendations for curbing sport violence.

THE MEDIA. Much ado has been made about the role of the media in the glorification of violence. Of particular concern has been the sex and violence issue as it relates to young, impressionable children. However, the role of the media in promoting violence through their handling of sport has most certainly not gone unnoticed. Bryant and Zillman (1983, p. 197) get right to the heart of our ambivalence with regard to portrayals of violence in sport with the following questions: "Why does the public tolerate such extensive violence in its favorite spectator sports? Or is it the wrong question? Better, perhaps, why do people *desire,* why do they *demand* so much violence in their spectator sports?"

In answer to their query, Bryant and Zillman offer three theories about why people enjoy aggression in sports. One possible clue has to do with the catharsis hypothesis. Scientific support for the catharsis view is not strong, but its popular appeal is considerable. The catharsis hypothesis has been received for the most part with open arms by the various media. From catharsis theory it follows that engaging in or viewing aggression lessens aggression; if this is the case, then the more violence we observe, the more cathartic the effect will be. The media therefore provide as much blood and gore as they think we can tolerate, all the while assuring us that our aggressive needs will be ameliorated by those mega-doses of violence.

A second explanation for our enjoyment of violence in sports has to do with assertive dominance over others. Adler (1927) hypothesized that the need to be assertive and to dominate others is among the strongest of human motivations. Opportunities for the expression of these strivings for assertion and dominance abound in sports such as basketball, football, hockey, and soccer, and the vicarious viewing of these dominance acts might account for some of our enjoyment of sport aggression. And, as noted earlier, according to catharsis theory, the greater the dominance displayed within the rules, the greater the enjoyment should be for the fans.

A final theory focuses on competition, or the enjoyment of drama. As Bryant and Zillman have said, the catchphrase "the human drama of athletic competition" captures the essence of this theory. In this context of human drama, aggression is seen as exemplifying the ultimate in competition. The athlete who aggresses is only trying to win, and aggression is proof positive of that fact. Part of the fascination with extreme or high-risk sports in which the contestants face serious injury or death may lie not in our perversity but in the realm of high drama. Participants who are willing to wholeheartedly tempt the fates may represent the ultimate in intensity (i.e., competitiveness) for the spectators. An alternative view is that people enjoy

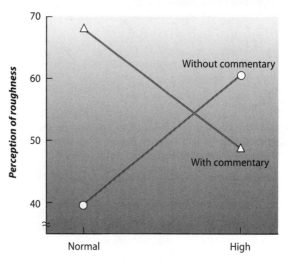

FIGURE 13.6

Viewers' Perceptions of Roughness of Play in Ice Hockey as a Function of Broadcast Commentary

SOURCE: Bryant & Zillman (1983).

the risk sports because of the opportunity to view the serious injury or death of the participants. To this point, a local sports talk show host with a dislike for professional football recently (and we hope facetiously) spent 30 minutes making a case for his returning to watch the sport if the league would judiciously place land mines throughout the playing field.

No consensus about the validity of the three theories is available, but there appears to be general agreement with the notion that sport violence has entertainment value. Three studies by Jennings Bryant and various colleagues have lent credibility to the supposition that spectators like violence in sports. In the first study, Comisky, Bryant, and Zillman (1977) looked at the sport of ice hockey because of its rough-and-tumble nature. In the Comisky et al. research, the effect of color commentary on viewer enjoyment was studied. As can be seen in Figure 13.6, enjoyment of play was a function not of actual roughness but rather

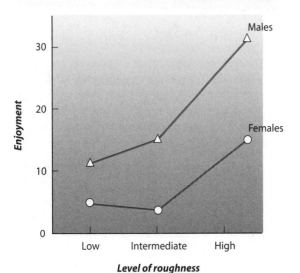

FIGURE 13.7

Viewers' Enjoyment of Plays of Televised Football as a Function of Degree of Roughness and Violence Involved

SOURCE: Bryant, Comisky, & Zillman (1981).

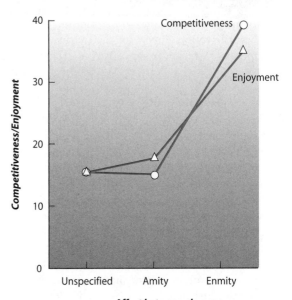

FIGURE 13.8

Viewers' Enjoyment of Tennis as a Function of Perceived Affect Between the Players

SOURCE: Bryant, Brown, Comisky, & Zillman (1982).

of perceived roughness. Color commentary emphasizing how rough play was when it actually was not very rough and the downplaying of very rough play greatly affected spectator enjoyment.

In the second study (Bryant, Comisky, & Zillman, 1981), professional football was the sport under scrutiny. Male and female viewers were asked to rate their enjoyment of selected plays from National Football League games. As can be seen in Figure 13.7, enjoyment increased as a function of concomitant increases in rough play. This was true for both sexes but was statistically significant for males only. Apparently, football fans like aggressive play by their beloved warriors.

The third study (Bryant, Brown, Comisky, & Zillman, 1982) was done with the less violent sport of tennis as target, and the variable manipulated was how much or how little tennis players were perceived to like each other. Enjoyment of a tennis match was clearly a function of perceived enmity. When players were per-

ceived as intensely disliking each other, enjoyment was high. Such was not the case when the tennis adversaries were thought to be friends. Competitiveness was also seen as much more intense when supposed enemies were playing each other (see Figure 13.8).

Collectively, these three studies suggest that fans really do like violence in their sports fare. However, there does appear to be a limit to this affinity for violence. Russell (1986) suggests that the acceptance of violence is curvilinear—that is, fans enjoy aggression within limits but are not willing to endure excessive violence. Perhaps future research will answer this question, despite the logistical and ethical problems inherent in such an undertaking. Manufacturing violence under laboratory conditions to see how far people would go before they draw the line is impractical. Also, it is hoped that sport violence would not escalate to the point that we would have a real-world laboratory for the viewing of injurious or sadistic acts in sports reminiscent of the spectacles that entertained the ancient Romans.

Bryant and Zillman (1983) suggest that the media exploit violence in three ways:

1. *In their coverage of violent plays.* How many times can you recall seeing replays of a bone-jarring and injurious tackle in football or a savage knockout in boxing? One encouraging development, however, is the general policy of the various television networks not to give coverage to fights and other misbehavior by players or fans at sporting events.

2. *By giving printed articles the status of features.* Many articles in the print media focus on violence. It is difficult to pick up a newspaper or any of the popular sport magazines without encountering a featured article on sport violence.

3. *By using exploitative television promotions.* The filming of deaths in various high-risk sports, such as automobile or power boat racing, and using the footage later to promote upcoming events in those sports appears to be pandering, as Bryant and Zillman so aptly put it, to some rather base human emotions.

CRITICAL SPORT-RELATED VARIABLES AFFECTING AGGRESSION

A number of game-related variables have an impact on the expression of aggression. Summing across a number of studies, Bird and Cripe (1986) and Cox (1990) identified five that affect aggression in sport.

Point Spread

When the score is close, aggressive acts will be relatively rare because a penalty at a critical juncture in a game can be decisive in determining the eventual winner. Also, when there is a substantial disparity in the score, aggression tends to be less noticeable because arousal is not so salient. Aggression is most likely to occur at a point midway between the two extremes.

Home/Away Factor

As discussed in Chapter 12, a case can be made for the existence of a home advantage in some sports. One of the more provocative hypotheses used to account for this supposed edge has been advanced by Varca (1980), who found that home basketball teams were more assertive in terms of rebounds, blocked shots, and steals, whereas the visitors were charged with more fouls. These results from Varca's work suggest some sort of dysfunctional use of assertion (if not aggression).

Outcome

Winning or losing makes a difference in frustration level, needless to say. Winners tend to display less aggression than losers. Temperamental outbursts by losing players are reasonably common occurrences. They lend some support to the frustration–aggression hypothesis discussed earlier if one can assume that losing is in fact frustrating.

League Standing

Although there are some areas of disagreement about league standing, consensus exists on the point that first-place teams commit fewer aggressive acts than do their competitors. The point of contention concerns the other teams. For example, Volkamer (1971) found in a study of soccer teams that the lower a team was in the standings, the more likely it was to engage in aggression. Russell and Drewry (1976), studying Canadian hockey teams, found that the teams trailing the league leader most closely were actually the most aggressive. The two studies, however, are in agreement about lower levels of aggression by the first-place teams. In a related study, Engelhardt (1995) found an inverse relationship between assessment of penalty minutes for major fights and final league standings. His analysis of over 4,000 NHL game summaries from the late 1980s and early 1990s showed that the greater the number of fighting penalties, the lower the team was likely to finish in the league standings.

Period of Play

Cullen and Cullen (1975) studied hockey players and found that aggression increased in a linear mode for winning teams and in a curvilinear mode for losing teams. To put the issue another way, losing teams were lowest in aggression at the beginning and end of play, and most of the aggression occurred in the middle of the match. Winning teams, in contrast, displayed more aggression as the game wore on. The last finding drew support from Russell and Drewry (1976) in their study of hockey teams.

Clearly, critical events and junctures in various sports partially determine the frequency and intensity of aggression. However, their relationship to sport aggression is far from understood, and more research on these situational variables is needed. Also, broadening the sports studied beyond hockey and soccer, which have dominated so far, would be most interesting.

SUMMARY

1. We live in a violent world with numerous examples of aggression within and external to sport.

2. Aggression is defined as the infliction of an aversive stimulus on an unwilling victim with the intent to do harm and with the expectation that the act will be successful.

3. Aggression may be provoked or unprovoked, direct or indirect, physical or verbal, adaptive or maladaptive, and hostile or instrumental.

4. Hostile aggression, instrumental aggression, and sport aggression are differentiated by intent or lack of intent to do harm, by the nature of the goal that is valued, and by the presence or absence of anger or unusual effort and energy expenditure. In many sport situations, the distinctions among the three behaviors can be quite blurred.

5. Because of the overlap in their definitional properties, we use the terms *aggression* and *violence* somewhat interchangeably.

6. Biological theories of aggression emphasize genetics, neurological structures, and hormonal influences.

7. Psychosocial models of aggression include cathartic approaches—instinct theory, the frustration–aggression hypothesis—and the social learning approach.

8. Cathartic explanations of aggression emphasize the release of aggressive tendencies through their expression. The instinctive theories advanced by Freud, Lorenz, and Ardrey, as well as the frustration–aggression hypothesis of Dollard and Miller, are examples of cathartic theories.

9. Bandura challenged catharsis theory with his social learning approach, which emphasizes reinforcement and modeling. According to the social learning approach, aggression is made more likely by its expression.

10. Our personal view is that the social learning approach has more to offer in terms of understanding aggression than do the cathartic approaches.

11. Sociological explanations of aggression include contagion theory, convergence theory, emergent norm theory, and value-added theory.

12. Aggression has been measured in a variety of ways: naturalistic observation, laboratory research, archival analysis, questionnaires, projective tests of personality, and objective tests of personality. One of the more promising objective tests is the Aggression Questionnaire of Buss and Perry. Little of note is taking place in the area of sport-specific measures of aggression.

13. Physical, psychological, and sociological factors promote aggression.

14. Temperature, noise, and crowding are three physical factors affecting aggression. Although there is much research in the general effect of these variables on the human condition, little has been done in the sport realm, and their respective roles in sport-related aggression are poorly understood.

15. Vicarious reinforcement and modeling of aggression, external rewards for aggression, deindividuation, and becoming inured to violence are four psychological variables that have been studied as they relate to aggression.

16. A person who has been reinforced for aggression or who has seen aggression work for other people, particularly role models, is likely to try it to see whether it works for him or her.

17. External rewards of significance include tangible rewards (money), status rewards (aggressive nickname), expression of injury, and alleviation of aversive treatment (evading coaches' wrath by

being aggressive). Each type of external reward is likely to facilitate aggression.

18. Deindividuation is a process whereby individual conformity to group dictates increases as personal identity and personal accountability decrease.

19. Inurement to violence may be occurring because we are so inundated with violence by the media. The ramifications for sport are considerable.

20. Interesting sociological forces at work creating and promoting violence are hooliganism and the media.

21. Hooliganism is a term used for the rowdy, violent behavior of some European fans at soccer matches. Misplaced displays of masculinity are the source of much of the fan violence there; the hooligans are members of working-class gangs more intent on fighting than on watching soccer.

22. The media have been criticized for glorifying sport violence. Why American sports fans appear to thrive on a steady diet of descriptions of violence is not known. Theories include the catharsis hypothesis, the assertion of dominance, and the enjoyment of drama.

23. The media have been described as exploiting violence by giving excess coverage to violent plays, featuring stories that glorify violence, and using promos depicting violence to sell future sporting events.

24. Five sport-related variables influence the way violence is expressed: point spread, the home/away factor, outcome, league standing, and period of play.

KEY TERMS

aggression (188)
catharsis hypothesis (192)
contagion theory (193)
convergence theory (193)
deindividuation (199)
displaced aggression (188)
emergent norm theory (194)
frustration–aggression hypothesis (192)
hooliganism (199)
hostile aggression (189)
instrumental aggression (189)
linear–curvilinear debate (195)

social learning theory (192)
sport assertiveness (189)
sport violence (191)
value-added theory (194)
vicarious punishment (198)
vicarious reinforcement (198)

SUGGESTED READINGS

Bushman, B. J., & Anderson, C. A. (2001). Is it time to pull the plug on the hostile versus instrumental aggression dichotomy? *Psychological Review, 108,* 273–279.

The authors make the case that categorizing human aggression as either hostile or instrumental has outlived its usefulness and is hampering advances in gaining an understanding of and controlling human aggression. Aggression is defined, and a timely discussion of the interplay of goals, anger, and intent in determining whether aggression is hostile or instrumental serves to reinforce definitional issues elaborated on in this chapter. This short article, written in a highly readable style, tackles an important issue in the aggression literature.

Bushman, B., & Bertilson, H. (1985). Psychology of the scientist: Frequently cited research on human aggression. *Psychological Reports, 56,* 55–59.

Bushman and Bertilson reviewed seven major journals in social psychology and personality over a three-year period (1980–1982) to identify the books and articles that other authors most often cited when writing about aggression. Bushman and Bertilson selected 35 references for discussion in their paper on the basis of the frequency with which they were cited. Most often cited in books was Baron's 1977 text, *Human Aggression,* followed by Bandura's *Aggression: A Social Learning Analysis* and Buss's *The Physiology of Aggression.* Berkowitz (40), Baron (37), Zillman (32), and Bandura (31) were the most frequently cited authorities in all types of publications. This article is a good starting point for anyone interested in reviewing some of the early work done in aggression.

Rainey, D. (1986). A gender difference in acceptance of sport aggression: A classroom activity. *Teaching of Psychology, 13,* 138–140.

Rainey gave three psychology classes examples of six sport competition situations and asked the students to rate the acceptability or unacceptability of each. Substantial gender differences were noted: Males endorsed nearly twice as many of the aggressive acts depicted. This exercise can easily serve as a springboard for discussing aggression in sport and in society as a whole.

Widom, C. S. (1989). Does violence beget violence? A critical examination of the literature. *Psychological Bulletin, 106,* 3–28.

Widom takes a protracted look at seven aspects of the idea that violence breeds violence. Areas explored include child abuse, delinquency, violent and homicidal offenders, aggression in small children, and the effects of viewing aggression. Widom concludes that much is yet to be learned about abusive home environments and subsequent violence.

INFOTRAC COLLEGE EDITION

For additional readings, explore Infotrac College Edition, your online library. Go to: http://www.infotrac-college.com/wadsworth
Hint: Enter these search terms: aggression, Albert Bandura, antisocial personality disorder, hooliganism, violence in children, violence in sports.

Aggression: Violence in Selected Sport Populations

CHAPTER 14

Boxing

Football

Hockey

Smith's Violence Typology

Violence Among Female Athletes

Violence Against Females by Male Athletes

Violence Against Sports Officials

Recommendations for Curbing Violence in Sport

Summary

Key Terms

Suggested Readings

These two featherweights are seen fighting for the world championship. Boxing raises an interesting ethical question for sport psychologists. Is it ethical to provide psychological skills to an athlete in a sport where the avowed purpose is to inflict pain or injury on the opponent?

© Reuters NewMedia Inc./CORBIS

Many athletic events possess a propensity for violence by players, coaches, or spectators. This chapter focuses on three: boxing, football, and hockey. Also to be discussed are violence among female athletes, violence directed at females by male athletes, and violence directed toward sports officials. Finally, recommendations for curbing sports violence will be entertained.

BOXING

The avowed purpose of boxing is the infliction of harm on one's opponent—rendering the other person in the ring unconscious. Skill, artistry, and the ability to outsmart an opponent are important, but there is an overriding desire in boxing to pummel the opponent into submission or unconsciousness. Dr. George Lundberg, editor of the *Journal of the American Medical Association,* summed up the goal of the boxer as follows: "The intention in professional boxing is to damage your opponent's brain. What counts is a knockout, a blow to the head"(Gavzer, 1990, p. 5).

Boxing has been and probably always will be the subject of controversy and public outcry. Lobbying directed toward cleaning up or abolishing boxing is conducted by the powerful American Medical Association, and protests by members of that organization have not fallen on deaf ears at the national level of politics. Given that boxing has long been viewed as a brutal, barbarous spectacle, the present uproar is unlikely to change much of anything.

As noted in Chapter 3, pugilists in ancient times went to great lengths to subdue the enemy. They tried to gain an advantage by doing such things as wrapping their hands in rawhide and adding lead weight or metal spikes to their gloves. One legendary figure, Theagenes of Thasos, reputedly won 1,400 championships and killed as many as 800 opponents during a 20-year career. The modern era of boxing began in the 1800s in Great Britain and the United States. The first matches were bare-knuckle brawls. Fights generally lasted until someone quit or was beaten into bloody submission. Contemporary boxing is slightly more humane, but boxing remains a brutal sport. The violence is well summarized by a remark made by an anonymous boxer: "I don't want to knock him out. I want to hit him, step away, and watch him hurt. I want his heart" (Yeager, 1979, p. 124).

Psychologists know little about the psychological makeup of boxers. Armchair speculation abounds, but very little substantial data is available. One attempt to bring applied sport psychology to the understanding of boxing is provided by Butler, Smith, and Irwin (1993). Butler and colleagues applied a performance profile (Butler, 1989, 1991; Butler & Hardy, 1992) to an analysis of three amateur boxers. They asked boxers to produce the attributes of an elite boxer on the assumption that these attributions would yield insights into their performance needs. One amateur boxer identified 22 attributes, which the authors subsumed under six headings: physical, defense, punches, technical work, attitude, and psychological. Various needs within each category were expressed and served as focal points to work on for the athlete and his coach. According to Butler, performance profiling has utility as a means of exploring and assessing an athlete's perception of his or her performance needs. Though interesting, the work of Butler and colleagues shed little light on the personality makeup of boxers.

As a final note, boxing raises some interesting ethical questions for sport psychology practitioners. How does one justify providing performance enhancement skills or anxiety reduction procedures for athletes involved in such a tawdry enterprise?

FOOTBALL

Just bring along the ambulance.
And call the Red Cross nurse,
Then ring the undertaker up,
And make him bring a hearse:
Have all the surgeons ready there,
For they'll have work today,
Oh, can't you see the football teams
Are lining up to play.
J. R. Betts (1974, p. 244)

Betts aptly describes the nature of football. Although the game is not as controversial as boxing, it is not without its detractors, and there is undoubtedly some validity to the criticisms. Take, for example, injury statistics from high schools and colleges. According to Mueller and Schindler (1984), 893 deaths between 1931 and 1983 were directly attributable to football (that is, due to head injury); and of that total, 572 occurred at the high school level. Another 465 deaths occurring during that same time period were attributable to indirect causation (that is, systemic failure due to coronary problems or heat stroke). In another study involving data analysis for the years 1977 to 1987, Mueller, Blyth, and Cantu (1989) indicated that there were 105 catastrophic cervical cord injuries; of these, 86 occurred in high school, 14 in college, and 5 in semi-pro or sandlot football. Seventy-five percent of those injured were defensive players, most commonly defensive backs (a third of the total).

Fortunately, there has been a continuous diminution in the number of catastrophic injuries each year. In the five years beginning with 1977, there were 58 such injuries. From 1984 through 1987, there were 24 cervical cord injuries. Gorman (1992) indicates that permanent cervical cord injuries plummeted from 34 reported in 1976 to 1 in 1991. Improvements in football headgear and changes in tackling techniques undoubtedly contributed to this improving picture. Also, advances in the treatment of spinal cord injuries, especially in the first hours and days after their occurrence, have greatly improved the treatment picture for all victims of spinal cord injury, football or otherwise (Gorman, 1992).

As for minor head injuries, Wilberger (1993) estimates that there are a quarter of a million such occurrences annually in all contact sports including football. In a disclaimer, Clarke and Braslow (1978) put together a response to critics of football in which they showed that deaths attributable to football in 1964 among high school and college players occurred at about the same rate as non-football-related fatalities in the age group under consideration. In all likelihood, most of these football fatalities and injuries were inflicted within the limits of the rules and spirit of the game and were tragic outcomes of assertive rather than aggressive actions.

The National Football League (NFL) exemplifies the worst in the area of football injuries, though catastrophic injuries are rare. The NFL projects its injury rate each year at 100%: It is anticipated that all 1,200 players will be injured to some degree during each season. The following statistics also indicate the magnitude of the injury problem in professional football (King, 1992):

- Twenty-seven quarterbacks and 47 running backs, players the fans most often want to see in action, missed from one to twelve games during the first 12 weeks of the 1992 season. Five quarterbacks and 8 running backs missed all twelve games.

- Eleven weeks into the 1992 season, 213 players were on the injured reserve list, down from 219 for the same time period in 1991.

- As of December 1, 1992, 482 pro players had missed at least one game. This represents 17 players per team.

- Based on the above, and given that in 1992 the average player salary was $480,000, nearly 3,000 games were missed at a loss of nearly $84 million.

Joe Jacobi, upon retirement from the Washington Redskins at age 35, summed up his feelings: "You just get tired of hurting . . . and I'm not even talking about the major injuries . . . my body can't do it anymore" (Bell, 1994, p. 7C). In line with Jacobi's sentiments about the injury situation in professional football, Table 14.1 illustrates the nagging injuries reported by a retired professional defensive back.

Quotations about the propensity for violence among professional players abound. Dave Peurifory of the Green Bay Packers made the following observation:

> It's vicious and barbaric. They try to make it safe, but they can't. It's like playing tag on a highway. You can try to make it safe, but sooner or later, it's going to get you. They draft the biggest, meanest, nastiest players they can find and line them up. Nice guys can't play this game. There is no way a nice guy can make it. Smart guys can't play this game. You have to be on a low mentality. It's like butting your head into a brick wall. . . . I'm no different. I'm just as bad as the rest. I'm on a different level during the season as opposed to the off-season. Football is not conducive to a good vocabulary and being articulate. I'm a degenerate, just like the rest. ("Page Three," 1985)

One of the all-time greats, Jerry Kramer, also of the Green Bay Packers, wrote the following in his autobiography:

> Forrest Gregg tackled Andrie just as he crossed the goal line, and I was only a step or two behind

TABLE 14.1

Injuries Sustained by a Professional Defensive Back Over Two Seasons

1989	07/25/89	Right hip flexor strain
	08/03/89	Right hand first metacarpal contusion
	08/12/89	Right thumb thenar laceration
	09/18/89	Right knee patella contusion
	09/24/89	Right posterior lateral ankle sprain and contusion
	10/01/89	Left hip contusion
	11/26/89	Mild acute cerebral concussion
	11/26/89	Right brachial plexus compression
	11/26/89	Left shoulder glenohumerous joint subluxation
	12/16/89	Right superior knee contusion, quadricep tendon
	01/07/90	Right upper arm contusion, biceps brachii
	01/14/90	Right quadriceps contusion
1990	09/17/90	Right knee pre-patellar bursae contusion
	09/23/90	Right shoulder posterior rotator cuff irritation
	11/18/90	Left wrist sprain

SOURCE: K. A. Corrington (personal communication, November 15, 1994, College Station, TX).

Forrest, and I suddenly felt the greatest desire to put both my cleats right on Andrie's spinal cord and break it. We had been victimized by these stupid plays—scooped up fumbles, deflected passes, blocked kicks, high school tricks—so many times during the season that I felt murderous. I'd never in my career deliberately stepped on a guy, but I was so tempted to destroy Andrie, to take everything out on him, that I almost did it. A bunch of thoughts raced through my mind—I'd met Andrie off the field a few times and I kind of liked him—and, at the last moment, I let up and stepped over him. (Kramer & Schaap, 1969, p. 257)

Such expressions of aggressive tendencies are indicative of how violent football can be. Little is being done about this precarious situation. Like boxing, football operates with many critics but few restraints.

HOCKEY

Headlines from newspapers and magazines (e.g., *USA Today* and *Sports Illustrated*) document violence in hockey and frequently express concern about its effect on the future of the sport:

"Some Fans Rate Fisticuffs Integral Part of Big Picture"

"Probert, Wilson at Top of Heap in Scrapping"
"Hockey's Top Ice Warriors"

"Fighters Aren't Always Winners"

"Gretzky Has Good Hands—Not Fists"

"Horror Show: Galloping Goons and Gratuitous Gore Marred the Dramatic Opening Round of the NHL Playoffs"

"Players Join Game's Furor Over Fighting"
"Gretzky: We Have to Stop the Fights"

"McSorley is out for the season: Longest suspension in history of NHL doled out for slash"

It is widely accepted that ice hockey is a violent sport. Stand-up comedian Rodney Dangerfield once wisecracked, "I went to a fight the other night and a hockey game broke out." To the casual observer, the sport seems unusually rough. The players look haggard, most are missing several teeth, speed of movement is breathtaking, sticks seem to be flying everywhere, and bodies are sacrificed with reckless abandon. The resulting impression is one of institutionally condoned mayhem. Penalty calls would seem to support this perception. Penalties for the 1989–1990 season were up by 1,330 near the end of the season. In the 1991 NHL playoffs, the Detroit and St. Louis teams were assessed a total of 298 minutes of violence-related penalties in game five alone (Greenberg, 1991).

SMITH'S VIOLENCE TYPOLOGY

M. Smith (1986) devised a typology with which to analyze sport violence. Though based on material drawn

The comedian Rodney Dangerfield has remarked that he once went to a boxing match and a hockey game broke out. Clearly, the officials are trying to restore order in this game.

© Reuters NewMedia Inc./CORBIS

in two players dropping their gloves and letting a little steam escape. I think that's a lot better than spearing somebody. I think it's an escape valve because you know yourself pressure builds up and there's no other way to release it and if fighting is not allowed then another violent act will occur." Players involved might be fined, but legal involvement is unlikely. The legal community tends to stay away from acts of this type within sport because there is no public mandate to do anything about it. This reluctance was evident after the vicious stick attack by Marty McSorley of the Boston Bruins on Vancouver Canucks player Donald Brashears during an NHL game (Allen, 2000). The incident was so violent that McSorley was given a 23-game suspension, the longest suspension in NHL history, and was fined $72,000. The league, however, asked that McSorley be spared criminal prosecution. The NHL's chief legal officer said: "We firmly believe this is an incident that occurred in the context of the game. It's been handled decisively and harshly, and we would hope in this case they (the Vancouver police) would defer to our judgment" (p. 6C). Despite this plea from the NHL front office, a Canadian court eventually heard the case, and McSorley was convicted of assault with a weapon and sentenced to eighteen months of probation ("Feedback," 2000).

from the legal area, **Smith's violence typology** has relevance to hockey. Smith distinguished among four types of violence: body contact, borderline violence, quasi-criminal violence, and criminal violence.

Body contact—body blocks, checks, and blows—is integral to the sport and the risks it poses are accepted as part of the game. In legal terms, the players are consenting to receive such blows.

Hockey, of course, is filled with a variety of physical acts that fall under the game rules but border on violence. The frequent fistfights in hockey are an example of what Smith terms borderline violence. Potentially serious injuries could result from these altercations but seldom do. If such injuries were to occur, they would be regarded as part of the game in all likelihood. M. Smith (1982, p. 294) quoted an unidentified NHL player on this issue: "I don't see any violence

Quasi-criminal violence violates both the formal rules and the informal norms of the game. Serious injury is likely to be involved, and the legal authorities are likely to step in and impose penalties beyond any the league might levy. A notable case of quasi-criminal violence in hockey involved David Forbes of the Boston Bruins and Henry Boucha of the Minnesota

Smith's violence typology a typology that distinguishes among four types of violence: body contact, borderline violence, quasi-criminal violence, and criminal violence.

North Stars. During a particularly heated match, both players were sent to their respective penalty boxes simultaneously and they exchanged verbal unpleasantries while waiting for the penalty to expire. Upon reentering the ice, Forbes assaulted Boucha with his hockey stick, causing extensive damage to Boucha's vision in one eye. Forbes was fined and barred from play for a short period and later was charged by a Minnesota grand jury with assault with a deadly weapon. After much testimony and 18 hours of jury deliberation, a mistrial was declared. In an interesting postscript, Boucha filed a civil suit against the Boston Bruins and the NHL, and an undisclosed amount of money was awarded to him in an out-of-court settlement (M. Smith, 1986).

The fourth category identified by Smith is criminal violence—a violation of such proportions that it transcends the usual league sanctions and the courts become involved. A case reported by Runfola (1974) remains a legal classic in sport violence. Paul Smithers, a 17-year-old youth league player, became so upset with game-related events that he carried the hostilities with him to a Toronto parking lot after a game. An opposing player was killed and young Smithers was convicted of manslaughter as a result of the melee.

It is apparent that there are gradations of violence as indicated by Smith's typology. What is less clear is why these kinds of behavior have become such an integral part of hockey. Various authorities have advanced a number of possible explanations. Not surprisingly, the mass media are implicated, because they tend to promote violence in hockey. A prominent example is an article in which the writer perhaps unwittingly extolled violent actions in a tribute to one of the all-time greats, Gordie Howe, on the occasion of his 50th birthday:

> It's not as if he played some Caspar Milquetoast game, shying away from the corners, relying on speed and finesse. He is of the generation that disdains the now accepted protection of helmets and he never was one to skate from a fight. After he was nearly killed from a check into the boards by Ted Kennedy of the Toronto Maple Leafs—a skull operation saved his life—he returned as one who knows it is better to give than to receive, that retribution is best administered quickly and deci-

sively. With Lou Fontinato of the New York Rangers he participated in what many regard as the greatest hockey fight in the history of the NHL. Fontinato was the terror of the league then, intimidating everyone, pulverizing even the mighty Rocket Richard, but Howe destroyed him in that fight. He broke his nose, splattered Fontinato's blood over his face and jersey, and Fontinato never was as terrifying again. (O'Malley, 1977, p. 40)

More troublesome than this gratuitous glorification of violence involving adults is the impact of this point of view on children, who are supposed to be learning sport skills and sportsmanship. Research from a number of sources indicates that youth players admire aggressive players and learn a lot about illegal or violent play from these role models. M. Smith (1982) listed things young players learn from watching violent behavior by their role models who perform on television (see Figure 14.1). A second substantive explanatory mechanism for the learning of violence is the role of significant others, such as parents, coaches, and peers. Parents are often intensely involved in the activities of their children, and their approval of violence, tacit or otherwise, is positively related to the incidence of violent behaviors in their children (Clark, Vaz, Vetere, & Ward, 1978; M. Smith, 1979). Players also translate coaches' approval into aggression. Vaz and Thomas (1974) found a statistically significant relationship between insistence by coaches on being rough and aggressive and youth participants' subsequent willingness to resort to unusual aggression. As for peer influence, youth hockey players live in an increasingly aggressive subculture in which masculinity and defense of territory are valued highly. To demonstrate this point, Smith (1979) reported the extent to which players agree with violent statements as a function of increasing age; these data are presented in Table 14.2. It is apparent that the approval of violence in this instance is linear, with an increase in acceptance as a function of increasing age.

Rough play, aggressiveness, and violence are part and parcel of play in the NHL. Terry and Jackson (1985) report that more than 31 player minutes per game over a 10-year period in professional hockey were spent in the penalty box as a result of rule violations. The figure for the years 1981 through 1983 averaged nearly 35 minutes. This sort of violation of the

FIGURE 14.1

Illegal Actions That Young Players Learn From Watching Professional Hockey

I learned spearing and butt-ending.

You sort of go on your side like turning a corner and trip him with a skate.

Charging. You skate toward another guy who doesn't have the puck and knock him down. Or coming up from behind and knocking him down.

Sneaky elbows, little choppy slashes Bobby Clarke style.

Hitting at weak points with the stick, say at the back of the legs.

Coming up from behind and using your stick to hit the back of his skates and trip him.

Butt-end, spearing, slashing, high sticking, elbow in the head.

Put the elbow just a bit up and get him in the gut with your stick.

Along the boards, if a player is coming along you angle him off by starting with your shoulder then bring up your elbow.

The way you "bug" in front of the net.

Clipping. Taking the guy's feet out by sliding underneath.

Sticking the stick between their legs. Tripping as they go into the boards.

I've seen it and use it: When you check a guy, elbow him. If you get in a corner you can hook or spear him without getting caught.

Giving him a shot in the face as he's coming up to you. The ref can't see the butt-ends.

How to trip properly.

Like Gordie Howe, butt-ends when the ref isn't looking.

SOURCE: M. Smith (1982).

rules is reinforced by findings of Widmeyer and Birch (1984) in a study of 1,176 professional hockey games over a four-year period. Among other things, they found a correlation of .48 between games won and penalties in the first period of play. These data suggest that setting an aggressive tone early would be a productive strategy. Also, Russell (1974) reported a correlation of .43 between hockey assists and acts of hostile aggression, and this finding sends a message to players that violence works.

Two final points are worthy of mention. First, there is actually some evidence that hockey violence may be counterproductive. In analysis of data from the 1989–1990 NHL season in which league standing was correlated with fighting penalties, a small but negative correlation was noted: Fighting and winning were actually at odds with each other ("Fighters Aren't Always Winners," 1990). Perhaps information such as this can be used with management to stem the tide of violence

in the NHL. Second, the economics of violence are compelling and provide some interesting if unsettling data to ponder. Jones, Ferguson, and Stewart (1993) compared NHL attendance figures with a variety of violence indicators and found that violence is positively related to attendance; in short, violence sells. In the words of Jones and his colleagues, "hockey is show biz, hockey is blood sport" (p. 74). Jones and his colleagues, all economics professors, also reported that American fans have an even greater appreciation for violence than do their Canadian counterparts. In Canada, attendance is actually negatively related to the more extreme acts of violence, whereas the relationship is a positive one for fans in the United States. In this connection, it is interesting to note that North American players in the NHL accounted for over 80% of the penalty minutes for the 1995–1996 season, whereas European players accounted for only 20% (Grossman & Hines, 1996).

TABLE 14.2

Acceptance of Violence as a Function of Age

	Minor Midget Through Juvenile (N = 169)	PeeWee Through Bantam (N = 313)	Junior B and Junior A (N = 122)
If you want to get personal recognition in hockey it helps to play rough. People in hockey look for this.	52	70	88
Roughing up the other team might mean getting a few penalties, but in the long run it often helps you win.	51	64	74
Most people in hockey don't respect a player who will not fight when he is picked on.	31	42	59
To be successful, most hockey teams need at least one or two tough guys who are always ready to fight.	43	57	84

Source: M. Smith (1982).

VIOLENCE AMONG FEMALE ATHLETES

The psychology literature strongly indicates that women are less prone than men to resort to physical aggression when provoked. The literature in sport psychology relevant to this issue is practically nonexistent. Female involvement in the sports most likely to evoke aggression (e.g., boxing, hockey, professional football) is either nonexistent or limited. As a consequence, female athletes are spared being involved in activities in which spectators or players are likely to lose control over their emotions. Generalizations about female athletes and aggression are therefore difficult to make. Simply put, if females are not confronted with the stimuli most likely to evoke aggression, they will not display it. As more and more women move into the competitive realm, there might be an increase in aggression among them. The issue remains unresolved at this time.

VIOLENCE AGAINST FEMALES BY MALE ATHLETES

It is an unusual day when the sports headlines do not focus on an athlete who has committed some sort of violent act against a spouse, a girlfriend, or some other female. Rae Carruth, Warren Moon, Lawrence Phillips, O. J. Simpson from football, Sugar Ray Leonard and Mike Tyson from boxing, Will Cordero and Daryl Strawberry from baseball, John Daly from golf—the list of high-profile athletes with incidents or histories of abuse of females is long. Carruth, for example, was implicated in the murder of his pregnant girlfriend and sentenced to 19 years in prison (Nowell, 2001).

Although some cases of violence involve recent acquaintances (i.e., first dates, women picked up after a party or from a bar), the preponderance of the cases involve someone with whom the athlete is intimate. The U.S. Bureau of Justice defines intimate violence as "those murders, rapes, robberies, or assaults committed by spouses, ex-spouses, boyfriends, or girlfriends" (Zawitz, 1994). According to 1998 Bureau of Justice statistics, 876,340 women were victims of one or several of these acts of violence (Tjaden & Thoennes, 2000). It is only slightly reassuring to note that these numbers are actually improvements over those reported for 1993, when 1.1 million victims were noted. In 1998, 72% of the murder victims were females and 85% of the nonlethal violent acts were perpetrated against females. Women between ages 16 and 24 were most likely to be the victims of intimate violence. In the case of sport, one seldom hears of acts of violence perpetrated against males by females, though undoubtedly the frequent reports of spousal abuse are probably not completely one-sided.

A Glossary of Sports Violence

Beanball. A baseball thrown deliberately by the pitcher at a batter's head.

Board checking. In ice hockey, throwing an opponent violently against the "boards," the wall that forms the boundary around the rink.

Brushback. A baseball deliberately aimed by the pitcher at a batter's body, ostensibly to force the batter back from home plate.

Butt-ending. Poking an opponent with the butt end of a hockey stick.

Chop block. An especially vicious football technique in which one player, usually a lineman, straightens an opponent up while a teammate blocks down on his knees.

Clothesline. A football tackle in which the ball carrier is hooked from one side or behind by an arm around the neck.

Crackback. A football block in which an offensive player, usually a receiver feigning movement away from his own backfield, doubles back and at the last moment throws himself in front of the charging defensive player.

Crosschecking. Using the hockey stick with both hands to block across the upper body of an opponent.

Earholing. In football, a player's deliberate aiming of the top of his helmet at the hole in the side of an opponent's helmet.

Enforcer. A term used in arena sports such as ice hockey and basketball to describe a player skilled in intimidating or, if need be, actually fighting with opponents.

Giving the bone. In football, using the outside of the forearm to smash an opponent, usually in the head, as he runs toward the aggressing player.

Hand checking. In basketball, using hand contact to control the movement of an opponent.

Head slap. In football, using the open hand to hit the side of an opposing player's helmet.

High-sticking. In ice hockey, striking an opponent with the stick carried above shoulder height.

High tagging. In baseball, purposely trying to hit a base runner in the head while tagging him out.

Leg whipping. In football, a lineman uses his leg to trip an oncoming rusher from the side or behind.

Rake blocking. In football, a technique in which a lineman jerks up his head from an opponent's chest, raking his face mask into the opponent's chin.

Raking. In rugby, deliberately running over a fallen opponent with cleated rugby shoes.

Rip-up. In football, a forearm uppercut usually administered by either an offensive or a defensive lineman with the intent of catching an opponent under the chin.

Spearing. In ice hockey, poking an opponent with the point of the stick; in football, driving the top of the helmet into a player who is down.

Spikes high. In baseball, trying to avoid being tagged out by aiming the spikes high while sliding into a base.

SOURCE: Yeager (1979).

Some would say that participation in sport encourages people to define their relationships with others in terms of domination (Miedzian, 1991). Sanday (1981) writes of a rape culture, drawing from her anthropological study of tribal communities. She noted that cultures that display a high level of tolerance for violence and male domination have a greater incidence of rape. Welch (1997) talks in terms of narcissism and a sense of entitlement to account for episodes of antisocial behavior by some athletes. Toch (1984), in his book *Violent Men*, devised a **typology of violent men** with 10

Typology of violent men a typology that identifies types of aggressors found in sports: self-image promoters, self-image defenders, rep defenders, self-indulgers, and bully-sadists.

distinct types of aggressors; at least 5 of those types are applicable to sports:

1. *Self-image promoters,* who seek situations in which they can reduce their sense of inadequacy and enhance their fragile self-image through acts of aggression

2. *Self-image defenders,* who are always on the lookout for slights or challenges from others

3. *Rep defenders,* athletes from sports such as hockey or football who assume a violent or aggressive role on their respective teams (i.e., "gorillas," "hit men," "enforcers")

4. *Self-indulgers,* who look at life from a selfish, infantile perspective that suggests that others exist to fulfill their needs

5. *Bully-sadists,* who derive their pleasures from pain and suffering inflicted on others

No definitive study has been conducted to date that unequivocally proves that athletes are more violent than nonathletes of similar backgrounds and circumstance. However, high-profile athletes certainly make headlines when they do step out of bounds socially. This creates the impression that athletes as a group are prone to aggressive acts, most particularly against females in their lives. These acts of violence have led Ellin (1995, p. 44) to say: "It seems that professional athletes and sexual assault are as common as apple pie and Chevrolet."

VIOLENCE AGAINST SPORTS OFFICIALS

In an email addressed to all of the viewers of the sport sociology Website, Roizen (1996) captured the feelings of many who have officiated sports:

> Without having been there though, how could they have any gut feel for the molten hostility coaches, that is some coaches, can direct at officials? How could they know, for instance, what it's like to face the wrath of a full-grown, fully steamed, vermilion-faced coach, neck veins standing out like gardenhose, haranguing you (expletives often deleted) over an unending string of alleged blown calls, early whistles, late whistles, etc.? What the

heck do coaches actually think? That we officials get together before games to scheme how we're going to inflict injustice upon the contest? . . . that we go out after the game for pizza just to recall and celebrate all the havoc we sowed?

Sports officials also experience violence at the hands of individuals other than coaches. For example, results of a survey of 721 basketball referees by Rainey and Duggan (1998) indicated that 13.6% of the respondents had been assaulted at least once while officiating. In over half of these instances, the referees had been punched or choked or had had objects thrown at them. Players were the most common offenders (41%), followed by parents (20%), coaches (19%), and other fans (15%). In 55% of the cases, there was no penalty for these acts. The preceding data led Rainey and Duggan to conclude that assaults on referees are common, some of the assaults are serious, and consequences for these offenses are inconsistent. In a study by Rainey and Hardy (1999) of 682 Rugby Union referees from England, Scotland, and Wales, 47% reported being punched or choked on at least one occasion. Once again, players were the most common assailants and punishment was meted out in an inconsistent fashion. Rainey and Hardy concluded their study by noting that assaults against Rugby Union officials occurred at a lower rate than assaults against the baseball and basketball officials they had surveyed.

A troubling report on youth soccer suggests that assaulting officials is all too common in that sport. Individual suspensions reported in *STYSA Shootout,* the official publication of the South Texas Youth Soccer Association, were 49 in number ("STYSA Discipline and Suspension Report," 1998). Twenty-nine involved referee assault. Of those assaults, 12 were by players, 10 by parents, and 7 by coaches. Most of these suspensions were for an indefinite period of time. When one considers how many regional, state, and local soccer associations there must be in the United States that sponsor youth soccer, the magnitude of the problem of violence against officials in soccer alone takes on staggering proportions.

In an effort to deal with the kinds of problems reported above, officials and sports organizations are increasingly adopting a policy of zero tolerance for the harassment of officials. Much of the emphasis in this regard is being placed on parents controlling their own behavior at youth sporting events. Underscoring this point, Rick Reilly, a writer for *Sports Illustrated,* wrote an article on how to make youth sports more enjoyable for all. One of his recommendations concerned officiating: "I'll realize that the guy behind the umpire's mask, whom I've been calling 'Jose Feliciano' and 'Coco, the talking ape' is probably a 15-year old kid with a tube of Oxy 10 in his pocket, making $12 the hard way. I'll shut up" (Reilly, 2000, p. 88).

RECOMMENDATIONS FOR CURBING VIOLENCE IN SPORT

Many recommendations have been made to curtail violence in all athletic events. The ensuing discussion integrates the suggestions of a number of authorities: Bird and Cripe (1986), Coakley (1994), Cox (1990), Mark, Bryant, and Lehman (1983), Miller (1997), and Snyder and Spreitzer (1989). The recommendations presented here are broad based because the solution to the problem of sport violence must be a systems approach involving all interested parties: management, the media, game officials, coaches, and players.

Management

At the highest level of intervention is the management structure of sport. There are at least five innovations that management can implement in an effort to slow the pace of violence:

1. **Abolish or control the use of alcoholic beverages at sporting events.** Use of alcohol interferes with good judgment. The enjoyment of sporting events often is lessened by overconsumption of alcohol by one or more fans. Alcohol abuse has been repeatedly linked with acts of sport-related vandalism in the United States and with hooliganism in Europe.

   American baseball represents a case in point. Dewar (1979) analyzed factors associated with fights among spectators at professional baseball games. Dewar's analysis of 40 games included 39 fights that occurred in 19 of the 40 games. Chief among the findings: 33 of the 39 fights took place on week-ends, primarily at night, mostly in the cheaper seats, usually when attendance was above 80% of capacity, most often in the hottest months of the year, usually late in the game, and particularly when the home team was making a rally. Dewar had no data on alcohol sales and fights but surmised that the late-innings effect was probably related to alcohol consumption. In analyzing fights at major league baseball games, Gammon (1985) arrived at conclusions nearly identical to those of Dewar.

   Major league owners have tried to combat this problem by creating nondrinking sections in 10 stadiums ("Alcohol-Free," 1987). Certainly, this move is in line with results of a poll conducted by *USA Today* in which 42% of the respondents voted for the creation of nondrinking sections ("Yes Beer," 1987). In a later survey by *USA Today,* 28% of the respondents favored banning alcohol sales at sporting events ("Fans Say," 1991). Other measures used to deal with the problem of alcohol consumption include training staff members to recognize the danger signals of impending inebriation, providing designated driver programs, stopping alcohol sales an hour before the games end, and monitoring consumption when drinks are provided free of charge.

2. **Deal swiftly and firmly with acts of spectator aggression.** Management should take a firm stand. Players and nonaggressive fans should be protected from individuals who would interfere with their right to take part in or watch sport. Cox (1990) suggested that barring the flagrant first-time or chronic offender would not be a bad course of action.

3. **Make sports more of a family affair.** Perhaps professional baseball has done as much in this area as any sport with its sponsorship of family nights, cap or travel-bag nights for children, and similar promotions. Certainly, bringing more of a family orientation to baseball and other sports should reduce aggressive behavior. This idea might be facilitated by reducing the price of tickets for families and by offering promotions attractive to adults and children alike.

4. **Monitor the behavior of coaches.** Management should hold coaches accountable for their actions

Sports Officials

There is no doubt that sports officials play a big role in controlling the expression of potentially aggressive behaviors by players, fans, and coaches. But what do we know about the men and women who officiate sports? We know that officials will most likely be young, well-educated, first-born, politically conservative males who are involved in professional or managerial occupations (Furst, 1989; Quain & Purdy, 1988). They have variously been reported as gregarious, outgoing, and practical (Spurgeon, Blair, Keith, & McGinn, 1978) and as self-sufficient, self-assured, self-reliant, and socially sensitive (Fratzke, 1975). Professional baseball and hockey officials have been shown to view their jobs as challenging and rewarding, and they see themselves as major and integral parts of their sport. At the same time, they are not terribly fond of the travel and the diminished family life associated with their profession and are generally suspicious of the fans (Mitchell, Leonard, & Schmitt, 1982).

Psychologically, little is known about sports officials. One line of preliminary research has focused on sources of stress that affect these key individuals. Anshel and Weinberg (1995) studied 132 basketball referees, 70 from the southwestern United States and 62 from Australia. As part of their study, the authors created an assessment scale arranged on a 10-point continuum known as the Basketball Official's Sources of Stress Inventory (BOSSI). The top five sources of stress for these basketball officials were, in order of importance, making a wrong call, verbal abuse by coaches, threats

of physical abuse, being in the wrong place when making a call, and experiencing injury. Easily the least stressful of the 15 stress situations on the BOSSI was the presence of media. With regard to cross-cultural comparisons, there were more similarities than differences noted.

In a related study, Rainey (1995) adapted a scale used to measure stress in Canadian soccer officials and mailed it to 1,500 baseball and softball umpires in one state; 782 umpires properly completed the scale and served as subjects for subsequent scrutiny. Exploratory and confirmatory factor analyses yielded four noteworthy factors: fear of failure, fear of physical harm, time pressure, and interpersonal conflict (i.e., personality clashes with players, coaches, or fans, dealing with abusive players, and so forth). It is important to note, however, that although these perceived sources of stress were the most salient for this sample of umpires, they were viewed as "mild" contributors. Also, these results are in line with previous research by Goldsmith and Williams (1992) with football and volleyball officials and by Taylor and Daniel (1987) with soccer officials. Stress, then, appears to be a fact of life for sports officials, but its effects are viewed as manageable.

In examining actual skills related to officiating, Rainey and various associates have conducted several studies of baseball umpires. Studies have focused on the "phantom tag" at second base (Rainey, Larsen, Stephenson, & Olson, 1991), first base calls (Larsen & Rainey, 1991), ball and strike

(or inaction, as the case may be) when they encourage or fail to penalize their players for aggressive acts. Athletes who are convinced that aggression on their part will meet with censure from the coaches are less likely to engage in aggressive acts. Coaches are powerful others in the eyes of players, and they should act the part insofar as acceptance of sport violence is concerned.

5. **Monitor the behavior of players.** Managers should make players aware of the fact that violence will not be condoned at the upper levels of

the organization, whether peewee or professional. Penalties for violating institutional policy should fit the crime. A $1,000 fine for a professional player who makes $3 million per year hardly serves as a deterrent to future misbehavior.

The Media

The role of the media in promoting sports violence is a continuing source of interest for social and behavioral scientists. Although media effects are subject to argu-

calls (Rainey & Larsen, 1988; Rainey, Larsen, & Stephenson, 1989; Rainey, Larsen, & Williard, 1987), and fan evaluations of umpires (Rainey & Schweickert, 1991; Rainey, Schweickert, Granito, & Pullella, 1990). A major and consistent finding running throughout the Rainey efforts is that normative rules of officiating seem to dictate umpire behavior more than do the actual rules. Perhaps this normative effect is most salient with the "phantom tag," where an infielder is given the benefit of the doubt on tagging the bag on force plays at second base. Other instances in which a normative rule may be more salient than the actual rule are the close or "tie" call at first base and ball and strike calls behind home plate. With regard to the latter, it is interesting to note that umpires were more prone to call marginal pitches strikes for pitchers who were labeled as wild than they were for pitchers with a reputation for extremely fine pitching control, again probably due to a normative rule. In theory, marginal pitches by throwers of either reputation should get the same treatment from the umpires, but such does not appear to be the case.

Fan evaluations of umpires were interesting. In the Rainey and Schweickert study, players and coaches believed that umpires perform below acceptable and expected standards. For example, players and coaches believed that umpires miss 16 calls per 200 in a seven-inning game (mostly on balls and strikes), for an error rate of 8% of all calls. Conversely, umpires' certainty about their calls was quite high, an expected finding.

How should umpires be treated by players or coaches? The most popular response noted by Rainey and colleagues was "Question Politely." "Argue Heatedly" got some support. Little endorsement was given to "Do Nothing" and "Yell and Swear." Ninety-eight percent of the sample of 159 men chose "Never" or "Rarely" with regard to "Physically Attack"; 96% of the 52 women chose those two alternatives. Apparently, the time-honored refrain "Kill the ump" is endorsed by fans in a figurative but not a literal sense.

A final note: In several of the studies, matched samples of males with no officiating experience were as good as, or in some cases better than, the baseball officials at making the various calls mentioned here. It is only fair to say, however, that most of the Rainey studies did employ laboratory manipulations as opposed to real-life ones, and the results may not be generalizable to an actual baseball game. Also, generalizations about officials in other sports based on a study of baseball umpires can be made only with extreme caution. Nevertheless, the emerging literature on the sports official is intriguing and offers food for thought with regard to future research efforts in the area.

SOURCES: Anshel & Weinberg (1995); Fratzke (1975); Furst (1989); Goldsmith & Williams (1992); Larsen & Rainey (1991); Mitchell, Leonard, & Schmitt (1982); Quain & Purdy (1988); Rainey (1995); Rainey & Larsen (1988); Rainey & Schweickert (1991); Rainey, Larsen, & Stephenson (1989); Rainey, Larsen, & Williard (1987); Rainey, Larsen, Stephenson, & Olson (1991); Rainey, Schweikert, Granito, & Pullella (1990); Spurgeon, Blair, Keith, & McGinn (1978); Taylor & Daniel (1987).

ment, the media collectively could assist in at least three ways in defusing potentially violent episodes in sports.

1. **Do not glorify aggressive athletes for children, and, conversely, provide as much coverage of counter examples to aggression as possible.** There are many sensitive and humane athletes, and every attempt should be made to present them in as favorable a light as possible to young people. Conversely, athletes who openly espouse aggression should be given as little media visibility as possible. Watching some oversized professional football player threatening to break someone's head if he does not purchase a certain product or subscribe to a particular sports magazine surely serves no healthy purpose. Such unadulterated nonsense provides a poor example for young players (as well as for those of us a bit older).

2. **Refrain from glamorizing violence.** Progress has been made, particularly in refusing to give airtime or print space to fan misbehavior. The same restraint should apply in cases of player-against-player aggression. The 1994 World Cup soccer

match between the United States and Brazil, in which an American player got his skull fractured from deliberate elbowing by a Brazilian opponent serves as a case in point. The celebrated altercation was replayed over and over on television and rehashed for days. Little of value is accomplished by such media sensationalism.

3. **Do not attempt to promote hostility between teams.** There is already plenty of healthy rivalry in sports and more than enough ego and money riding on the outcome. The media need not feed into the system. Sport is not war, but it can be made to appear that way with a little assistance from the various media.

Game Officials

Umpires, referees, and line judges play important roles in sport events. They are charged with the responsibility for making important split-second decisions and rule interpretations that can greatly affect game outcomes. As a result, these people can be a catalyst for arousing emotions conducive to player or spectator violence. Two procedures for improving officiating are suggested.

1. **Eliminate perceived officiating injustices.** Mark and his associates (1983) indicate that officials get themselves into difficulty with players or spectators because of the perception that they committed an injustice, either by applying a rule inaccurately or unfairly or as a result of a perception that the game itself is unfair, irrespective of officiating excellence. In the first case, judgment calls and decisions about rule infractions are predominant. Certainly, blown calls or misapplied rule interpretations can trigger violence. In the second case, judgments and interpretations are secondary to the fact that the rules of the game itself are seen as unfair. Sometimes an official can be dead right about a call and still inflame the players or audience because they perceive the overall situation as unfair. Mark and his colleagues suggest that the incidence of rules infractions can be reduced and the resultant violence lessened through proper implementation of two types of penalties: equity based and deterrent based. Equity-based punishment follows the principle "an eye for an eye." For example, a basketball player fouled while in the act of shooting would be awarded not one but two shots. This is equity. The probation for illegal recruiting in intercollegiate sports is an increasingly prominent example of deterrent-based penalties. The hope is that these penalties will deter further excesses. With the proper use of both equity and deterrent-based penalties, perhaps violence in sports can be brought within acceptable limits.

2. **Take part in workshops on aggression and violence in sport.** Clinics would be especially useful for people who are officials in the sports in which aggression is most likely to occur. Intuitively, it is recognized that some officials exercise more control over games than others. There always will be gradations of control over game play, but all officials can be better schooled in the anticipation, recognition, and control of potentially explosive situations.

Coaches

Coaches are important determinants of the course of violence in sports. Coaches who espouse notions such as the one expressed by a prominent college basketball coach ("Defeat in sports is worse than death because you have to live with defeat") or that of an equally esteemed professional football coach ("To play this game you must have fire in you, and there is nothing that stokes the fire like hate") are partially to blame for setting a tone for violence in sport. However, ways exist to improve on the current situation.

1. **Encourage athletes to engage in prosocial behavior.** There is much to be said for the athlete who treats the opponent with respect. Verbal give-and-take or a friendly handshake before and after a game can only serve to reduce violence. The coach should reinforce nonviolence, as when an athlete takes a very assertive blow without resorting to very aggressive types of retaliation. As Cox (1990, p. 295) says: "Acts of great self-control *must* be identified and strongly reinforced."

2. **Participate in workshops on aggression and violence.** Like officials, coaches should acquire an

awareness of the counterproductive nature of sport violence, not only in their own immediate situations but also in society as a whole. As the proponents of social learning theory would say, "Violence begets violence."

Players

Ultimately the individual player must assume much of the responsibility for reducing aggressive behavior. It is the responsibility of each player to remain under control. To try to sell anything less than that is to abrogate each person's responsibility for emotional self-governance. We are all too quick to project blame on our provocateurs, and such projections should in no way be accepted or reinforced. Accordingly, players should volunteer to take part in programs aimed at helping them cope with aggressive feelings and actions. Visual imagery and mental practice are two techniques that should be valuable in learning greater emotional control.

Overall, a carefully orchestrated effort generated by management, the media, spectators, coaches, and players could effect a substantial reduction in sport violence. However, as long as social conditions that transcend sport are in effect, the task will be difficult. Sport cannot do it alone, but those of us working in sport should willingly do our part. We can have an impact on violence in sport and hope that our efforts generalize to society as a whole.

SUMMARY

1. Boxing, football, and hockey are three sports in which violence is common.

2. The avowed purpose of boxing is to inflict intentional harm on the opponent. In other sports, that intent is at least hidden behind sport assertiveness. Little is known of the psychological makeup of boxers.

3. Injury data suggests that football is a dangerous sport at the high school and intercollegiate levels. At the professional level, manifestations of hostile thoughts and violent actions abound.

4. Ice hockey has been researched more than most sports, thanks primarily to Canadian sport psychologists.

5. Using a typology suggested by M. Smith (1986), hockey can be analyzed for four types of violence: body contact, borderline violence, quasi-criminal violence, and criminal violence.

6. Media coverage and encouragement from significant others are viewed as prime contributors to violence in hockey.

7. Little is known about aggressive sport behavior by female athletes.

8. Violence against females is nearly a daily topic of media coverage. Several theories have been advanced to account for it, including preservation of masculinity, the rape culture, narcissism and a sense of entitlement, and various aggression typologies.

9. Violence against sports officials occurs at a relatively high rate and, somewhat surprisingly, is most likely to come from players themselves. Coaches, parents, and other fans are other sources of aggression.

10. Changes in the way the games are viewed by management, the media, game officials, coaches, and the players themselves might curb violence.

11. Management needs to control alcohol use at sports events, deal swiftly and firmly with fan violence, try to make sports more of a family affair, more effectively monitor coaching behavior with regard to the encouragement of aggression, and monitor players to reduce aggressive acts.

12. The media need to stop glorifying violence. Children, in particular, need to see more prosocial and less antisocial behavior from their sport heroes. Violence by players and fans should never be played up, and stoking the fires of hostility between players or teams is to be avoided.

13. Game officials play important roles in the controlling of sport violence. Useful goals include making the rules fairer and clearer to eliminate perceived injustices; training officials in rule interpretation and application; and having officials attend clinics on the anticipation, recognition, and control of violence.

14. Coaches should encourage prosocial behavior by their athletes, and exceptional cases of emotional control in adverse circumstances should be reinforced. Coaches, too, should attend clinics on violence management.

15. Ultimately, individual players must assume much of the responsibility for aggressive behavior.

KEY TERMS

Smith's violence typology (211)
typology of violent men (215)

SUGGESTED READINGS

Benedict, J., & Yaeger, D. (1998). *Pros and cons: The criminals who play in the NFL.* New York: Warner Books.

The authors examined the records of 509 of the approximately 2,500 NFL players from the 1996–1997 season. Of the 509, 109—21%—had been arrested for one or more serious offenses, for a total of 264 arrests. Included were 2 murders, 7 rapes, 45 instances of domestic violence, and 42 cases of aggravated assault or assault and battery. The NFL has chastised Benedict in particular for what the league regards as his continuing efforts to stereotype or stigmatize NFL athletes (Benedict authored an earlier volume on sports violence entitled *Public Heroes, Private Felons*). A listing by name and offense of the 109 with criminal charges pending or resolved makes interesting reading.

Frank, M. G., & Gilovich, T. (1988). The dark side of self- and social perception: Black uniforms and aggression in professional sports. *Journal of Personality and Social Psychology, 54,* 74–85.

The authors examined whether professional football and hockey teams that wear black uniforms are more aggressive than those wearing other colors. In general, teams wearing black uniforms appear to be more aggressive. Also, they are apparently perceived as more aggressive by game officials, which may contribute to their being penalized more often than other teams.

Goldstein, J. H. (Ed.). (1998). *Why we watch: The attractions of violent entertainment.* New York: Oxford University Press.

The essays in this collection examine the appeal of violence in sports and other forms of entertainment. Included is an essay by Allen Guttman, an authority on violence in general, on why sports-related violence takes place and has such appeal.

Kirker, B., Tenenbaum, G., & Mattson, J. (2000). An investigation of the dynamics of aggression: Direct observations in ice hockey and basketball. *Research Quarterly for Exercise and Sport, 71,* 373–386.

The authors point out that methodological and definitional problems have plagued past research in sport aggression. Of particular interest was the relationship between hostile and instrumental aggression. Hockey was chosen for study because of its popularity in past research, and basketball because of a relative lack of aggression studies in that sport. Intrapersonal, interpersonal, intergroup–intragroup, and environmental factors contributing to aggression were identified and discussed. An experimental analysis of two hockey and two basketball games revealed that aggression occurred much more frequently in hockey than it did in basketball and that negative verbalization by players in both sports was the most frequent type of aggressive behavior.

Tenenbaum, G., Stewart, E., Singer, R. N., & Duda, J. (1997). Aggression and violence in sport: An ISSP position stand. *The Sport Psychologist, 11,* 1–7.

The authors review some of the literature on violence in sport and make nine recommendations that constitute the International Society of Sport Psychology (ISSP) stand on the issue. The ISSP recommendations closely parallel those made in this chapter and serve to reinforce the idea that the ultimate responsibility for controlling sport violence rests with the individual athlete, although the media, management, game officials, and coaches also have important roles to play in curbing violence in sports.

 INFOTRAC COLLEGE EDITION

For additional readings, explore Infotrac College Edition, your online library. Go to: http://www.infotrac-college.com/wadsworth
Hint: Enter these search terms: football fans, football violence, hockey violence, soccer fans, sport spectator.

Personality and Psychological Assessment

CHAPTER 15

Personality Defined

Theories of Personality

Problems in Sport Personality Research

Psychological Assessment

What Is a Test?

Validity, Reliability, and Norms

Sources of Error in Testing

Test Ethics and Sport Psychology

Summary

Key Terms

Suggested Readings

These college students are filling out a series of personality tests as part of a psychology experiment. Psychological assessment is a big part of sport psychology research and application.

© Arnold LeUnes

The study of personality has intrigued psychologists for well over a century, and sport psychologists have been no exception. According to Ruffer (1975, 1976a, 1976b), almost 600 studies of the personality/sport performance relationship were conducted prior to the mid-1970s alone. Fisher (1984) set the figure at well over 1,000. More recent estimates are not available, but it is certain that the number is substantially larger at this date.

Though skepticism has been expressed about the type and quality of inquiry done in many of those investigations, the quest for the link between sport and personality continues unabated. This interest arises out of a desire to find better answers to questions of importance to sport scientists, such as:

1. What personality variables are at work in producing the choking response in the face of competitive pressure?

2. What personality variables make for good leadership in coaches and players?

3. Can personality tests be used to identify elite youth athletes at an early age so that they can be given the best of training for future athletic development?

4. Does sex role orientation relate in any way to performance among female athletes?

5. What unique features, if any, compel people to seek new experiences by jumping out of airplanes or diving into oceans, seas, bays, and lakes?

6. Are there personality predictors that might be useful in promoting fitness and exercise adherence?

These questions represent a scant few of the many that might be asked about the personality–sport performance relationship. Before attempting to answer some of them, we would like to anchor the chapter discussion to a definition of personality, various theories of personality that have guided theory and research, and suggestions for improving research in sport. We will then examine in Chapter 16 what is known

about personality assessment and, finally, attitude measurement in sport.

PERSONALITY DEFINED

Lazarus and Monat (1979, p. 1) define personality as "the underlying, relatively stable psychological structure and processes that organize human experience and shape a person's activities and reactions to the environment." Essentially, what Lazarus and Monat refer to is the notion that a basic personality or **psychological core** exists and is more or less the "real you." In other words, we all possess core components of personality by which we know ourselves and are known by others, and these are generally quite stable and unchanging. For the most part, a healthy self-concept is stable and unchanging, just as being aggressive is. Similarly, being warm and friendly and trusting of others are core traits. These traits may be buffeted by life events, but generally they will withstand such trials and tribulations with little alteration. The psychological core, simply put, is not subject to much change once it is set. Think of your parents or grandparents as examples; how much are they changing or likely to change their basic patterns of reacting to life? Not much, we suspect.

Explaining behavior based on a set psychological core has clear limitations. Many years ago, Allport (1937) suggested that in addition to these core traits, behavior is also determined by **peripheral states.** Some aspects of our personalities, in other words, appear to be in a constant state of flux. For example, our responses to religious, political, moral, or racial issues are subject to variability. Daily events also take their toll on adjustment in such areas as depression, anxiety, and other related mood states. The dynamic interaction between the core (trait) and peripheral (state) portions of each of us composes the essence of what is known as **personality.**

A slightly different way to look at these issues has been provided by Hollander (1967) who talks of a psychological core, typical responses, and role-related behaviors (see the schematic representation in Figure 15.1). Hollander has maintained the core as conceptualized earlier in this discussion and broken the peripheral portion into typical responses and role-related behaviors. We respond to ordinary daily events with fairly pre-

---

Psychological core a person's basic personality, composed of core traits, stable and unchanging over time, by which we know ourselves and are known by others.

Peripheral states aspects of a person's basic personality that are constantly in flux.

Personality dynamic interaction between core traits and peripheral states that makes up the complete personality.

dictable behaviors, but these **typical responses** are more amenable to change than are the core traits. In other words, typical responses operate at a level slightly less entrenched than the core. **Role-related behaviors** are the most superficial, and therefore malleable, aspect of the personality. Each of us is called upon daily to fulfill a number of different roles, and we accomplish them in ways that get us by but are not always representative of our true core selves. How many times have you had to refrain from stating your real opinion about a life event because role expectations did not allow for honest expression?

One final point about Hollander's proposal must be made. The social environment is a constant source of pressure on adjustment. Role-related behaviors are the most susceptible to the influence of the social environment, whereas typical responses and the psychological core are increasingly less affected. This relationship is diagrammed in Figure 15.1.

THEORIES OF PERSONALITY

Theories of personality are numerous, all striving to explain why the human organism behaves as it does. These various theories have guided our thinking about personality, and we will examine six of them.

Biological Models

One model advanced to account for behavior is the **constitutional theory** of William Sheldon (Sheldon, 1940, 1942). Sheldon says that *somatotypes,* or basic body types, predict personality. For instance, Sheldon's *ectomorph,* characterized by leanness and angularity of build, responds behaviorally with a high level of activity, tension, and introversion. His classic *mesomorph* is likely to be very muscular and athletic and responds to environmental stimuli with aggression, risk taking, and leadership. It follows logically that team leaders would be likely to belong to the mesomorph somatotype. Finally, the *endomorph* has a rounder body type than the others and reacts behaviorally with joviality, generosity, affection, and sociability. Jolly Old Saint Nick most closely serves as the prototype for the endomorphic individual. Clearly, the three somatotypes are stereotypes, and as such they suffer from all of the shortcomings of

FIGURE 15.1

Hollander's Model of Personality Structure

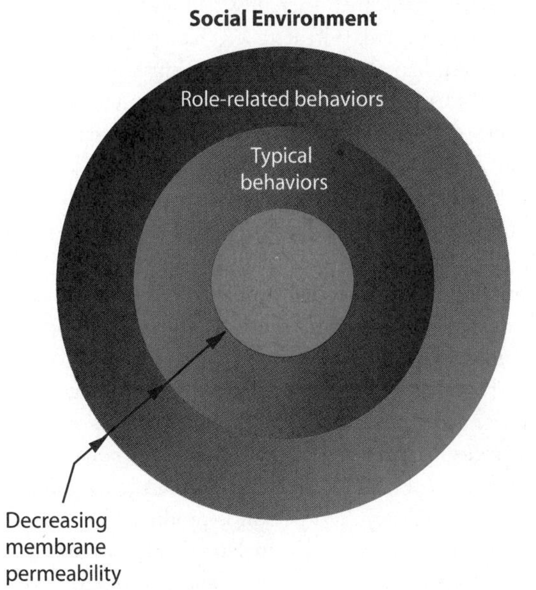

Social Environment

Role-related behaviors

Typical behaviors

Decreasing membrane permeability

SOURCE: Hollander (1967).

this kind of conceptualization. The reader is referred to Eysenck, Nias, and Cox (1982) for a review of Sheldon's theory as it relates to sport.

More closely related to sport is **psychobiological theory** (Dishman, 1984), which has gained some acceptance as a means of predicting exercise adherence. Dishman's contention is that biological factors, such as body composition, interact with psychological variables, such as motivation, to produce an index of exercise compliance.

Typical responses predictable behaviors in response to daily events that are slightly less entrenched than core traits.
Role-related behaviors the most superficial, and therefore malleable, aspect of the personality.
Constitutional theory Sheldon's theory of somatotypes, or basic body types, that predict personality.
Psychobiological theory Dishman's theory that biological factors interact with psychological variables to produce an index of exercise compliance.

The Psychodynamic Model

One of the more complex and controversial theories about human behavior is the **psychoanalytic theory** of Sigmund Freud. The cornerstone of Freud's theory is that humans are inherently bad and, if left to their own devices, will self-destruct. This pessimism has fueled Freudian thought since its formative days in the late 1800s and early 1900s. Psychoanalytic theory is based on an **intrapsychic model** of internal conflict; that is, the psyche or self is made up of an id, an ego, and a superego, with the id and the superego in a constant state of conflict over control of the whole psyche. The arbiter of this eternal dispute is the ego, and its strength is a prime determinant of psychological adjustment. The person whose id wins the intrapsychic conflict will be a hedonistic thrill seeker in constant search of pleasure; the person whose superego dominates, a dogmatic moralist. When the ego is able to arbitrate a healthy rapprochement between the pleasure-seeking id and the moralistic superego, a healthy, well-adjusted person is produced.

Unfortunately, psychoanalytic theory has focused almost exclusively on pessimism and pathology, and this preoccupation with abnormality has served to limit its applicability to normal behavior. Inasmuch as sport participants, on the whole, appear to have no more and no fewer psychological problems than other people do, the Freudian model has limited utility for the sport psychologist. On a broader scale, however, psychoanalytic thought has served as an impetus for a mammoth amount of research and a number of competing theories.

The Humanistic Model

A view counter to the Freudian model is that of **humanism.** Beginning in the eighteenth century with the writings of the French philosopher Jean Jacques Rousseau, and continuing into the twentieth century with the works of American psychologists Abraham Maslow and Carl Rogers, humanists have adopted a stance that is diametrically opposite to that of the psychoanalysts. To the humanist, our nature is basically good and behavior, rather than being determined by deep, dark psychic forces, is based on free choice. The capacity for growth and change lies at the heart of this personal freedom. In the psychoanalytic model, bad impulses must be kept in check by laws, rules, mores, and customs if the person is to adjust properly. Thus, when a person turns out bad, it is because society has failed. To the humanist, society with all its strictures is seen as a potential corrupting force; a person turns out bad because society interfered in some way with this natural expression of goodness.

Rogers posits maximum adjustment in his concept of the fully functioning person. In Maslow's terminology, the person who maximizes his or her potentials across a broad spectrum of human endeavors has achieved self-actualization. (Recall the discussion of self-actualization in Chapter 10.)

The Behavioral Model

A view counter to the previous models is that of **behaviorism.** Behaviorism owes its origins to the work of Pavlov in Russia in the late 1800s and of Watson in the United States in the early 1900s. Contemporary behaviorists believe that behavior is inherently neither good nor bad; rather, it is the product of an interaction between genetic endowment and learned experience. This position relegates the goodness–badness issue to its proper place, in the eyes of the behaviorist—to the realm of philosophy. On the issue of freedom versus determinism, behaviorists are somewhat similar to the psychoanalysts in believing that behavior is determined. However, they differ on the mechanism by which behavior becomes engrained. Traumatic childhood events are crucial to the psychoanalyst; to the behaviorist, reinforced early experiences are critical. Behaviorists also differ from psychoanalysts in their views of the extent to which these childhood experiences are changeable later in life. In the behaviorists' view, if a behavior can be learned, it can be unlearned, though not without some difficulty at times.

Psychoanalytic theory Freud's theory that human behavior is basically unregulated and self-destructive.

Intrapsychic model Freud's separation of the personality into three components—id, ego, and superego—that constantly compete for power over the psyche.

Humanism belief that human nature is basically good and based on free choice rather than the domination of the instincts.

Behaviorism human nature is neither good nor bad but the result of genetic endowment interacting with learned experience.

Big Five Personality Traits

One of the more exciting concepts in the study of personality to come along in years has been proposed by Costa and McCrae (1985). Summarizing a number of studies and many different methodologies, McCrae and Costa offered the essential **big five personality traits:** Extraversion, Agreeableness, Neuroticism, Conscientiousness, and Openness to Experience. *Extraversion* is comprised of such elements as sociability, activity, and the tendency to experience positive emotional states. Evidence from the sport personality literature suggests that athletes as a group would score high on the Extraversion dimension. *Agreeableness* relates to interpersonal style; high-A individuals are cooperative and establish rapport easily. Low-A people, on the other hand, tend to be negative and more unapproachable. We might hypothesize that coachable athletes would be high-A people. *Neuroticism* is identified by a clinically related scale pertaining to poor coping mechanisms and resulting psychological distress. Where athletes might fall in this trait dimension is speculative; our hunch is that they would be no more or less represented than the population at large. The fourth trait composite, *Conscientiousness,* contrasts well-organized, scrupulous, and diligent people with those who are lax, disorganized, and lackadaisical. The application of this trait to sport personality research is unclear, though the argument could be made that successful athletes may differ from less successful ones in terms of their organizational skills. The final trait, *Openness to Experience,* relates to creativity, sensitivity, and behavioral flexibility. Costa and McCrae (1992) stress that clinical psychologists probably regard this trait as an indicator of good mental health, but they are not so confident that such is always the case. They suggest that conformity and conventionality are also viable paths to good adjustment. In terms of sport, it could be argued that conformity and conventionality would be more productive avenues for expression than creativity and imagination. Admittedly, all of these hypotheses are speculative.

Costa and McCrae have created an assessment device, the NEO Personality Inventory (NEO-PI), to measure the big five personality traits (Costa and McCrae, 1985, 1992). Fifteen years of their research and development has resulted in the current 181-item version of the NEO-PI, which has two forms: S for self-reports and R for observer ratings. All items are arranged on a five-point Likert scale from "strongly agree" to "strongly disagree," and the scales are balanced to control for acquiescent response patterns. Reliability and validity studies conducted thus far are supportive of the NEO-PI (Hogan, 1989; Mount, Barrick, and Strauss, 1994). The authors have developed a number of features to assist the test user, one of which is a 60-item abbreviated scale known as the NEO Five Factor Inventory (NEO-FFI).

The utility of both the big five trait theory and the scale derived from it remains to be demonstrated in psychology generally and sport psychology specifically. Further study may well prove to be a very interesting chapter in personality theory and research as well as in sport personality research.

Sources: Costa & McCrae (1985, 1992); Hogan (1989); Mount, Barrick, & Strauss (1994).

Big five personality traits Costa and McCrae's summary of the essential elements of human personality: Extraversion, Agreeableness, Neuroticism, Conscientiousness, and Openness to Experience.

The behavioral approach has been warmly embraced by sport psychologists. The behavioral coaching procedures discussed earlier represent one contribution from the behaviorists; the emphasis on modeling and social reinforcement as espoused by Bandura is a second. The performance enhancement and anxiety reduction strategies so integral to improving sport performance have had considerable impact on sport psychology practice and research. Finally, reinforcement principles have been widely used as a means of facilitating exercise adherence. In brief, the behavioral model, with its emphasis on learning new productive behaviors and unlearning old counterproductive ones, has had a major and positive influence on the field of sport psychology.

Trait Theory

Much sport research has been triggered by the trait (or factor) approach to personality as advanced by such psychologists as Gordon Allport, Raymond Cattell, and Hans Eysenck. **Trait theory** contends that personality is best understood in terms of enduring traits or predispositions to respond in similar ways across a variety of situations. This is not to say that behavior is invariable; however, a strong tendency exists to respond in persistent, predictable, and measurable ways. A host of psychometric instruments has been created to measure these theoretically predictable traits. Trait theory has generated much research (and controversy) in sport psychology.

The Interactional Model

To bring some clarity to the issue of personality within sport, researchers have developed an **interactional model** that suggests that behavior is the product of the interaction between the person and the environment. The interactive model is summed up by a single formula advanced more than sixty years ago by Kurt Lewin (1935), as follows: $B = f(P,E)$; that is, behavior is a function of the person and the situation or environment. A significant point here is that traits are still viewed as relative determinants of behavior, but they are not regarded as nearly so powerful as trait psychology purists would have us believe.

A major elaboration on the interactional model has been made by Endler and Hunt (1966). These investigators studied the responses of nearly three hundred college students from three universities to the S–R Inventory of Anxiousness (Endler, Hunt, & Rosenstein, 1962). After considerable statistical manipulations of the data as well as in-depth interpretive effort, Endler

and Hunt concluded that the question of whether individual traits or situational differences explain behavior is a pseudo-issue. Their statistical analyses indicated that thirteen percent of response tendencies to the S–R Inventory of Anxiousness were explained by traits. The remaining 87% were accounted for by seven different sources of behavioral variance suggested by the Endler and Hunt model. These seven sources were: Person (P); Situation (S); Modes of Response (M–R); P × S; P × M–R; S × M–R; and Residual, which is a function of a three-way interaction involving P × S × M–R. A visual representation of these relationships can be seen in Figure 15.2.

Similar results were reported by Fisher, Horsfall, and Morris (1977) in a study of male collegiate basketball players using a sport-specific variant of the S–R Inventory of Anxiousness. These investigators were able to link 19% of the performance variation in their sample of 147 athletes to Person (P) and Situation (S).

As a final note on the interactional model and its relationship to trait and/or situational explanations of behavior, Endler and Hunt (1966, pp. 344–345) conclude: "Human behavior is complex. In order to describe it, one must take into account not only the main sources of variance (subjects, situations, and modes of response) but also the various simple interactions (Subjects with Situations, Subjects with Modes of Response, and Situations with Modes of Response) and, where feasible, the triple interaction (Subject with Situations and Modes of Response). Behavior is a function of all these factors in combination."

PROBLEMS IN SPORT PERSONALITY RESEARCH

The utility of personality measures in sport personality research has been limited by a number of factors, some conceptual, some methodological, and others interpretive.

Conceptual Problems

Conducting research in the absence of a sound conceptual framework has led to at least two difficulties that affect the quality of sport research and the reliance that can be placed on resulting conclusions. One of the problems concerns the dearth of theory-driven research

---

Trait theory personality is composed of enduring traits or predispositions that respond in similar ways across a variety of situations.
Interactional model human behavior is the product of the interaction between the person and the environment.

FIGURE 15.2

Endler and Hunt Interactional Model of Behavior

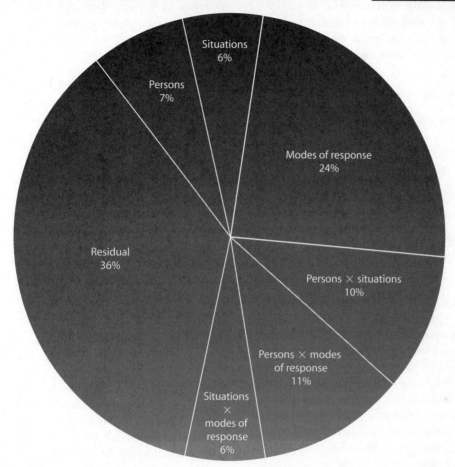

SOURCE: Endler & Hunt (1966).

and the second a failure to operationalize or properly define terms used in the various investigations.

THEORETICAL VERSUS ATHEORETICAL RESEARCH. Much of the research in sport has proceeded in the absence of any underlying theoretical framework. All too frequently, psychological assessment devices have been selected for a variety of reasons, some defensible and some not, and administered to the most available captive audience of athletes. From this shaky research design have emerged published studies purporting to be descriptions of the personality of the athlete. The

problems inherent in such a shotgun approach to data collection, analysis, and reporting are numerous. Ryan (1968, p. 71) aptly characterized this chaotic situation more than 30 years ago:

> The research in this area has largely been of the "shotgun" variety. By this I mean the investigators grabbed the nearest and most convenient personality

---

Theoretical versus atheoretical research much research in sport psychology is conducted without a sound theoretical framework, producing questionable and conflicting conclusions.

test, and the closest sport group, and with little or no theoretical basis for their selection fired into the air to see what they could bring down. It isn't surprising that firing into the air at different times and different places, and using different ammunition, should result in different findings. In fact, it would be surprising if the results weren't contradictory and somewhat contrary.

Cox (1985, p. 20) sums up the situation this way:

> A large percentage of the sports personality research has been conducted atheoretically. That is, the researchers had no particular theoretical reason for conducting the research in the first place. They just arbitrarily selected a personality inventory, tested a group of athletes, and proceeded to "snoop" through the data for "significant" findings.

That so few answers about personality research in sport have emerged from so many studies is therefore not surprising. Gill (1986, p. 34) tersely sums up the state of the art as follows: "If researchers do not ask meaningful questions, their efforts cannot produce meaningful answers."

FAILURE TO OPERATIONALIZE. Another reason for the conflicting results within sport personality research undoubtedly is the sheer inconsistency with which terms are defined from study to study, which we call a **failure to operationalize.** For example, what does the term *elite athlete* really mean? Equally problematic in the research have been terms like *athlete, nonathlete, nonparticipant, youth athlete, sportsman,* and so forth. Careful and consistent definition of terms warrants greater attention in the design of future studies.

Methodological Problems

A host of methodological shortcomings have also plagued sport personality research, and each will be addressed in turn.

Failure to operationalize a tendency in sport psychology research to omit the proper definition of terms, leading to flawed results.

Faking good/faking bad when subjects of a psychological assessment test manipulate their responses either for self-enhancement or self-denigration, skewing test results.

SAMPLING PROBLEMS. Many studies, for example, have used college athletes and nonathletes from the United States as subjects for a variety of comparisons. The problems of defining the terms *athlete* and *nonathlete* notwithstanding, there is little assurance that college athletes and nonathletes from different universities going to school in different geographic locations are similar in personality makeup. The probability that the varsity athlete and nonathlete from Stanford (or Slippery Rock), for instance, are representative of all college students is low. Limits in generalizing results in these situations are present; we shall examine the implications of the generalization problem shortly.

FAULTY METHODS OF DATA ANALYSIS. A second methodological problem has to do with data analysis. Too much reliance has been placed on univariate analysis of results and too little on multivariate approaches. Essentially, univariate approaches to data analysis compare two or more groups on one variable and, as such, are useful. However, they provide what Silva (1984, p. 65) calls a "snapshot" of subjects without capturing the interactions that take place between or among the variables under study. Consequently, a fuller picture of the relationship between or among events is portrayed through multivariate methods.

RESPONSE DISTORTION. *Response distortion* represents a third methodological problem in sport personality research. A number of issues must be addressed in administering psychological assessment devices to sport participants, not the least of which is response distortion. Sports participants, like other groups of people, respond to psychological assessment in a variety of ways. It would be naive to think that all responses to psychological inventories are completely honest and void of distortion. Careless responding, **faking bad,** and **faking good** are but a few of the possible ways in which a subject may distort data gathered from trait, state, or sport-specific inventories. The serious researcher should employ, wherever possible, measures to detect these various response distortions. Trait, state, and sport-specific assessment techniques, as well as one of the possible sources of response distortion, will be discussed later.

FAILURE TO USE THE INTERACTIONAL MODEL. Too few studies have been made of the interactional model, which incorporates traits, states, and situations, and this omission represents a fourth methodological difficulty. As the earlier discussion of the various models of personality indicated, the interactional approach offers the best long-term results in sport personality research.

ABSENCE OF LONGITUDINAL RESEARCH. A fifth methodological consideration is the absence of virtually any *longitudinal research* in sport psychology. The problem is bad enough in psychology generally, though the recent work of Eron (1987) on aggression mentioned in Chapter 13 represents a heartening exception. Unfortunately, sport psychology is virtually devoid of research that examines sport populations over extended periods of time. Youth sport and the sport for all movement, just to name two areas of inquiry, lend themselves beautifully to such an approach.

OVERRELIANCE ON "ONE-SHOT" METHODS. Finally, the **"one-shot" research method** of data collection merits mentioning. At times, collecting data on a one-time basis may be useful. In most cases, however, conducting intensive investigations of sport samples is preferable. The benefits to the discipline, the investigator(s), and the sport participants being sampled will undoubtedly be greater in most cases with the in-depth approach.

Interpretive Problems

Two prime areas of concern that interfere with proper communication of research findings in the area of interpretation include *faulty generalizations* and *inferring causation from correlation.*

FAULTY GENERALIZATIONS. As mentioned earlier, generalizing from one study to another has been problematical in sport personality research. For example, generalizing about sport participants in team activities based on data collected from those involved in individual sports is treacherous at best; the same can be said for generalizing from the reverse situation. Equally shaky are generalizations made between various age groups, different genders, and participants from different countries, to name just a few. Another common source of error in sport personality research is generalizations made among the various assessment devices. Tests such as the Eysenck Personality Inventory (EPI) (Eysenck &

Eysenck, 1963) and the Minnesota Multiphasic Personality Inventory (MMPI) (Hathaway & McKinley, 1943), have little in common philosophically and yet are often used for comparative purposes.

INFERRING CAUSATION FROM CORRELATION. A persistent problem in all of psychology (and life in general) is inferring causation from correlated events. A high correlation between two or more variables does not per se imply a cause-and-effect relationship between or among them. Almost everyone eats pickles, for example, and everyone eventually dies, thus implying a high correlation. To infer that the eating of pickles causes death, however, is a blatant misinterpretation of the data. In the same way, to infer that the existence of a personality trait affects the quality of sport performance is also fraught with danger. The causes of sport performance are multiple and complex; to attribute too much to a certain personality trait may be stretching the data. This is not to say that traits do not have some relevance; rather, it is an admonition to be careful in attributing too much to any given trait and underscores the need for multivariate analysis in sport research.

PSYCHOLOGICAL ASSESSMENT

Psychological testing is big business in the United States; the role of testing in athletics is also substantial. Tests may be administered to individuals or groups and cover such diverse aspects of human behavior as intelligence, aptitude, achievement, personality, and interests. One test for academic aptitude is administered to well over 2 million people annually (Kaplan & Sacuzzo, 1989). Of that number, 1.8 million take the Scholastic Aptitude Test (SAT), another 120,000 the Law School Admission Test (LSAT), and 75,000 a special test for admission to business school. Coupled with the widespread use of other aptitude and interest tests in public high schools and colleges and the use of personality tests in our employment/clinical psychology/criminal justice networks, psychological testing represents a multibillion dollar enterprise of considerable significance.

"One-shot" research methods collecting data from a study population on a one-time basis instead of over an extended time period, less desirable than longitudinal studies.

Important, sometimes critical, decisions are made about people based on test results. Children with intellectual deficits are assigned to special education classes or schools for the mentally retarded; other children are placed in gifted and talented classes to capitalize on their mental abilities; individuals are classified as schizophrenic or psychopathic because of test results that substantiate their behavioral idiosyncrasies. Tests have been with us for most of the twentieth century and will continue to play an important role, despite their controversial status, in the foreseeable future.

Testing is, by and large, an American enterprise. However, Kaplan and Sacuzzo (1989) tell us that four thousand years ago the Chinese had a reasonably sophisticated system of testing that was used in work evaluation and job promotion decisions. Subsequent developments extended into many facets of Chinese life and included examinations to determine who was qualified to serve in public office, a precursor of our civil service testing program in this country. Kaplan and Sacuzzo point out that the Western world probably learned about testing through interactions with the Chinese in the nineteenth century.

Though rudimentary attempts at testing were made in the late 1800s and considerable theorizing about individual differences was starting to emerge, the first major breakthrough came at the turn of the twentieth century with the work of two Frenchmen, Alfred Binet and Theodore Simon. Initially, Binet was commissioned by the French ministry of education to design a paper-and-pencil test to separate the mentally fit from the intellectually subnormal. Out of this initial effort the two men developed the Binet-Simon Scale, which was published in 1905 and revised in 1908 and in 1911. A Stanford psychologist, Lewis Terman, adapted the scale for use in the United States in 1916, and the testing movement became a major force in psychology. World Wars I and II intensified interest in mass testing and led to many important improvements.

On another front, personality testing was given its initial impetus by events surrounding World War I. These first efforts led to a proliferation of paper-and-pencil instruments designed to measure both global and isolated traits of personality. Of these tests, none has achieved the stature of the Minnesota Multiphasic Personality Inventory (MMPI). The impact of the MMPI across a number of areas of personality research and application extends to sport psychology, as we shall see shortly. A brief history of the testing movement is provided in Table 15.1.

Psychological tests remain one of the cornerstones of psychology. They have not been without critics, however, and some of the criticisms are justified. Tests have many uses and, as a consequence, are susceptible to abuse. Proper selection, use, and reporting of tests represents a challenge for all psychologists, sport psychologists among them.

WHAT IS A TEST?

To Cronbach (1970, p. 26), a psychological test is "a systematic procedure for observing a person's behavior and describing it with the aid of a numerical scale or a category-system." The emphasis here is on avoiding unsystematic, spur-of-the-moment procedures for evaluation, such as casual conversation. To Anastasi (1988, p. 23), a psychological test is "essentially an objective and standardized measure of a sample of behavior." Emphasis in this case is placed on the use of objective measurement and on the important notion that test responses are merely a sample of a person's overall behavior. It is hoped, of course, that the sample will be representative of the totality; this is the essence of creating a valid testing instrument. A third definition is that of Kaplan and Sacuzzo (1989, p. 4): "A psychological test is a device for measuring characteristics of human beings that pertain to behavior." Kaplan and Sacuzzo add that these behaviors include the overt, or observable, and the covert, or internal and unobservable (feelings and thoughts). They also point out that tests can be used to measure past, present, and future behaviors. For example, a test on this portion of the text might identify how much you have studied (i.e., the past), measure your level of current functioning, and make some predictions about your future performance. (We suspect your professors will be aiming for all three of these goals with their tests!) In any event, the emphasis on the objective study of behavior that is implied in all three definitions will serve as our guide for the rest of the material in this chapter.

TABLE 15.1

Significant Events in the History of Psychological and Educational Measurement

2200 B.C.	Mandarins set up civil service testing program in China.
1219 A.D.	First formal oral examination in law held at University of Bologna.
1575	J. Huarte publishes a book, *Exámen de Ingenios,* concerned with individual differences in mental abilities.
1869	Scientific study of individual differences begins with publication of Galton's *Classification of Men According to Their Natural Gifts.*
1905	First Binet-Simon Intelligence Scale published.
1916	Stanford-Binet Intelligence Scale published by L. Terman.
1916	Army Alpha and Army Beta, first group intelligence tests, constructed and administered to U.S. army recruits; R. Woodworth's Personal Data Sheet, the first standardized personality inventory used in selection of military personnel, introduced.
1920	H. Rorschach's Inkblot Test first published.
1921	Psychological Corporation, first major test publishing company, founded by Cattell, Thorndike, and Woodworth.
1938	Buros publishes first *Mental Measurements Yearbook.*
1942	Minnesota Multiphasic Personality Inventory (MMPI) published.
1949	Wechsler Intelligence Scale for Children published.
1985	*Standards for Educational and Psychological Testing* published.
1986	Ninth edition of *Mental Measurements Yearbook* published.
1989	MMPI–2 published.

VALIDITY, RELIABILITY, AND NORMS

Three critical dimensions of any psychological test are validity, reliability, and norms: that is, does a given test measure what it is designed to do, does it do so in a consistent fashion, and is it based on an appropriate reference group? If these three conditions are met, it is likely that this test will be a useful psychological assessment tool.

Validity

The generally accepted definition of **validity** is determined by the degree to which a test measures what it is created to measure. There are several methods for determining the validity of a test, and a summary of them is provided by Aiken (1982, p. 80):

Among the methods for studying the validity of a test are analyzing its content, relating scores on

the test to scores on a criterion of interest, and investigating the particular psychological characteristics or constructs measured by the test. All of these procedures for assessing validity are useful to the extent that they increase understanding of what a test is measuring so that the scores will represent more accurate information on which to base decisions.

This elaboration sets the stage for a discussion of the three dimensions of validity: content, criterion, and construct. Before undertaking our discussion of these types of **empirical validity** (i.e., data-based determinations) however, we must first examine a factor relevant to any discussion of psychological assessment: face validity.

Validity the degree to which a test measures what it is created to measure.
Empirical validity the three-part data-based determination of validity: content, criterion, and construct.

FACE VALIDITY. Face validity is the extent to which an assessment device appears to measure what it is intended to assess. In other words, does the test look valid to its evaluators as well as to its subjects? This issue underlies the call for more sport-specific tests, ones that athletes can readily identify with because they seem to have some bearing on athletic competition. The abstractness of many of the traditional personality measures has been criticized by athletes for lack of relevance. To put it in a different context, think of a classroom exam that seemed to get right to the heart of the subject matter, whereas another exam seemed to have been pulled from thin air by the professor. The first test has face validity, the second does not. All in all, face validity is important in psychological assessment because it motivates test-takers to perform well.

CONTENT VALIDITY. *Content validity* refers to the degree to which a group of test items are representative of the totality, or universe, of items that could be asked. Obviously, there is a practical limit to how many questions we might ask an athlete at any point in time, so we settle for a sample that we hope is representative. If this goal is achieved, we can then say that the test has content validity. For instance, your professor in sport psychology will not be able to ask you every possible question on the subject because of time and other practical limitations. Therefore, he or she will settle for a sample of 50, 75, or 100 representative items from the hypothetical pool of all possible questions related to the course content. The extent to which these items are representative of the course content determines the exam's content validity.

CRITERION VALIDITY. In making a judgment or decision, some standard for doing so must be generated, and this standard is known as a *criterion*. Operationally, a criterion can be just about anything: success in selling insurance, ability to fly an airplane, a time in the 100-meter dash, or your score on your upcoming exam in the sport psychology class. Subtypes of criterion validity are concurrent and predictive. *Concurrent validity* refers to statements or inferences about an individual's present standing on a criterion. An example is found in psychodiagnostic work, where an individual's test scores are validated against a criterion of previously and similarly diagnosed clients. *Predictive validity* refers to comparing one set of test scores with a set of criterion scores at a later juncture. The classic example, and one that is well known to college students, is the use of Scholastic Aptitude Test (SAT) scores and high school grades to predict college achievement. For many, the relationship of the SAT test scores to the criterion of grades in college is not particularly strong. In sport psychology, William Morgan's work with "successful" and "unsuccessful" Olympic athletes, to be discussed shortly, represents an example of predictive validity. Scores on a set of tests administered by Morgan differentiated the two groups of athletes, thereby allowing for some predictions about athletic performance based on psychometric results.

CONSTRUCT VALIDITY. A *construct* is a conceptual device used in psychology for inferring the existence of something that is essentially hypothetical or unobservable. For example, "intelligence" and "locus of control" are two of the innumerable constructs common to psychology, and a number of assessment devices have been generated to validate their existence. To illustrate *construct validity,* suppose that three measures of locus of control were administered to a group of aspiring Olympic cyclists and the result from the tests converged. Suppose further that the scores from the three tests were similar and thus supportive of the "locus of control" construct. At this point, we can conclude that construct validity of the concept has been established with some degree of confidence.

Reliability

Reliability means that a test yields consistent results, or to quote Aiken (1982, p. 72):

> To be useful, psychological and educational tests, and other measuring instruments, must be fairly consistent or reliable in what they measure. The concept of the reliability of a test refers to its relative freedom from unsystematic errors of measurement. A test is reliable if it measures consistently

---

Face validity the degree to which both evaluators and subjects agree that a test measures what it is intended to measure.
Reliability the extent to which a test yields results.

TABLE 15.2

Methods of Assessing Reliability and Some Related Caveats

Method	Procedure	Caveats/Problems
1. Test–Retest	Same test administered at two points in time	Length of time between tests and effects of memory and/or practice effects must be taken into account
2. Parallel Forms	Two forms of same test administered to same subjects	Difficult to construct equivalent forms; potentially expensive procedure; virtually unheard of in sport psychology
3. Internal Consistency		
a. Split–Half	Correlations between odd and even or first and last half of items require further statistical analysis to be computed	Yields reliability of half the test; requires further statistical analyses to get reliability of full test
b. Kuder–Richardson	Statistical formula applied to test responses	Useful when responses are dichotomous; that is, yes or no, true or false
c. Coefficient Alpha	Statistical formula applied to test responses	Applicable when multiple responses are used, as in Likert scaling

under varying conditions that can produce measurement errors. Unsystematic errors affecting test scores vary in a random, unpredictable manner from situation to situation; hence, they lower test reliability. On the other hand, systematic (constant) errors may inflate or deflate test scores, but they do so in a fixed way and hence do not affect test reliability. Some of the variables on which unsystematic error depends are the particular sample of questions on the test, the conditions of administration, and the internal state of the examinee at testing time.

Psychologists generally use three methods of determining reliability: test–retest, parallel forms, and internal consistency. Simply stated, the *test–retest* format requires the same group of examinees to respond to a given test on two separate occasions. In *parallel forms,* two equivalent forms in terms of content and difficulty are administered to the same subjects. The *internal consistency* method consists of several statistically based procedures in which the internal properties of tests are scrutinized. These procedures are known as the *split-half method, Kuder–Richardson reliability,* and *coefficient alpha.* The nuances of each procedure are beyond the scope of the present discussion, but the serious student can find readable discussions in a number of standard reference works on psychological assessment. A summary of these methods of assessing reliability and related caveats or problems is presented in Table 15.2.

Norms

Norms are detailed summaries of the characteristics (i.e., age, gender, vocation, years of education, and so forth) of those individuals composing the sample on which the test was originally used. Implicit in this situation is an understanding that future application of the test will be best served if it is administered to subjects similar to those in the normative sample. The Minnesota Multiphasic Personality Inventory (MMPI) was originally normed on mental patients but has been used with graduate students, medical students, law enforcement officers, and athletes; the violation of the norms inherent here has not gone unnoticed or uncontested. As we will note later, the publication of an updated version of the MMPI using a new normative group represents an attempt to remedy this criticism. In any event, the applicability of either form of the MMPI to sport remains suspect.

Norms detailed summaries of the characteristics of individuals in the test sample.

Selecting valid, reliable, and properly normed psychological tests is an immensely important part of psychological assessment in any context, and sport psychology is no exception.

SOURCES OF ERROR IN TESTING

An implicit assumption about tests in general is that the subjects involved are cooperative and honest respondents. Sport psychologists tend to compound this error by assuming that athletes will be even more cooperative and honest than other test populations, even though there is little if any evidence to support this notion. As test givers, we must be aware of possible sources of error related to the people we are testing.

No test, moreover, is perfect. Compounding this problem is the tendency of subjects to enhance themselves through their responses or, conversely, to look as bad as possible. Other problems include a conservative response style, defensiveness, fear, ignorance, and misinformation about testing in general. We will explore three of these problems here.

Faking Good

We are all probably guilty of trying to project a self-enhancing image in social situations, and this phenomenon of **faking good** is not unusual in psychological assessment of athletes. They may try to outguess the test, and one way to do this is always to answer troublesome questions in a manner that will project the most positive image. Tests may also vary considerably in their transparency. In cases where it is obvious what quality or trait a test is assessing, subjects show a tendency to answer in a self-enhancing manner, thus potentially accentuating measurement error.

Faking Bad

Faking bad on a personality test is typically an aberrant response pattern; it is hard to comprehend why anyone would want to project a poor or maladjusted image. In reality, the sport psychologist is probably not nearly as likely to see this effect as is the psychologist working in a clinical setting. When faking bad does occur, Nideffer (1981) suggests that it should be interpreted as a cry for help. Another interpretation might be that the sport psychologist has created an improper testing climate. Obviously, care should be exercised to generate an atmosphere of cooperation so that faking-bad protocols are avoided or, if they do occur, are not a function of hostility or rejection by the athlete.

Conservative Response Style

Nideffer suggests that the **conservative response style**—the tendency to respond to tests in the most conservative, middle-of-the-road, pedestrian way possible—is largely a function of rejection of the situation, the coach, the sport psychologist, or a combination thereof. An alternative interpretation is that the athlete who responds in this way approaches all life situations in the same way, always staying within the so-called white lines, never venturing too far from the middle in life or test taking. Obviously, scores that cluster near the mean for the test are going to render decisions inconclusive or useless.

TEST ETHICS AND SPORT PSYCHOLOGY

The AAASP guidelines on psychologists' testing of sport populations are aimed at maintaining quality control in situations where assessment devices are used. These guidelines address such issues as validity, reliability, proper test manual development in the case of new instruments, user qualifications, conditions of administration, and the use of proper norms. Sport psychologists who are conducting psychological assessments of athletes or others involved in physical activity must be familiar with the AAASP guidelines. Many errors in the past could have been prevented by a greater awareness of the relative strengths and weaknesses of psychological tests and their ethical usage both within sport psychology and outside it.

Nideffer (1981) indicates that sport psychologists are generally required to accomplish two basic tasks in psychological assessment: selection and/or screening decisions and program development and/or counseling. He further suggests that sport psychologists should consider the following factors when they administer tests:

1. Their own ability to determine the relevance of a test to the assigned task

2. Their ability to evaluate test validity and reliability

3. Their awareness of ethical considerations related to testing

4. Their test interpretation skills, aided by the use of other available information, such as case histories

5. Proper establishment of a testing climate that fosters cooperation

6. Sensitivity in reporting of test results to individuals or organizations so as to minimize misunderstanding and maximize effective use of the information communicated

SUMMARY

1. The study of the relationship between personality and sport performance is a dynamic component of sport psychology.

2. Personality is composed of core traits and peripheral states, which Hollander further breaks down into typical responses and role-related behaviors. The social environment constantly exerts pressure on each of these facets of the personality.

3. A number of competing theories, some biological and others psychological, attempt to explain human behavior.

4. Biological theories include Sheldon's somatotype theory, which classifies people according to body type and temperament, and Dishman's psychobiological model, which is used to account for exercise adherence.

5. Sigmund Freud's psychodynamic or psychoanalytic model is a detailed though pessimistic framework for explaining human behavior. This model emphasizes intrapsychic conflict, inherent badness, and determined behavior.

6. The humanistic model, most closely identified with Carl Rogers and Abraham Maslow, stands counter to the psychoanalytic approach. Key concepts in the humanistic model include the inherent goodness of the organism and freedom of choice. Rogers' fully functioning person and Maslow's self-actualized individual account for superior adjustment.

7. The behavioral model suggests that the goodness/badness issue is best left to philosophers. However, behaviorists partly agree with psychoanalysts on the deterministic nature of behavior, though they suggest a very different explanation for how behavior becomes entrenched. The behavioral approach has been warmly embraced by sport psychologists because of its utility in improving sport performance.

8. Trait theory spawned both research and controversy in sport psychology because many researchers believe that sport performance can be explained by trait dispositions.

9. The interactional perspective, which posits that behavior is a function of both personality and environment, has become increasingly popular in sport psychology.

10. Limitations in applying the results of sport personality research have centered around conceptual, methodological, and interpretive shortcomings.

11. Conceptual problems in sport research include the tendency to conduct too much atheoretical as opposed to theoretical investigation and the failure to properly and consistently define terms, such as *elite athlete.*

12. Sampling inconsistencies, an overreliance on univariate analysis at the expense of multivariate techniques, failure to control for response distortion, too little use of the interactional model, and the use of one-shot studies have all been methodological limitations in sport research.

13. Interpretive problems include making faulty generalizations and inferring causation from correlational data.

14. Testing in the United States is a big business, involving millions of people and billions of dollars.

15. Testing seems to have originated in China some 4,000 years ago. The two world wars of the 1900s served as potent forces in test development.

16. Definitions of what constitutes a psychological test vary, but they emphasize systematic, objective measurement of behavior.

17. Reliability, validity, and norms are three critical components of a good psychological test. A test must measure what it is designed to measure,

it must do so consistently, and its content and form must be based on sound standardization procedures. There are three major types of validity: content, criterion, and construct. Tests must also possess face validity; they should appear to measure what they are meant to assess. Reliability can be established through test–retest, parallel forms, and internal consistency procedures. Norms are useful when they are pertinent to the sample being surveyed in a testing situation.

18. Honesty in responding to test situations is often assumed. However, response style can generate a number of sources of error, including faking good, faking bad, and conservative response style.

KEY TERMS

behaviorism (226)
big five personality traits (227)
conservative response style (236)
constitutional theory (225)
empirical validity (233)
face validity (234)
failure to operationalize (230)
faking good/faking bad (230)
humanism (226)
interactional model (228)
intrapsychic model (226)
norms (235)
"one-shot" research methods (231)
peripheral states (224)
personality (224)
psychoanalytic theory (226)
psychobiological theory (225)
psychological core (224)
reliability (234)
role-related behaviors (225)
theoretical versus atheoretical research (229)
trait theory (228)
typical responses (225)
validity (233)

SUGGESTED READINGS

Cronbach, L. J., & Meehl, P. E. (1955). Construct validity in psychological tests. *Psychological Bulletin, 52,* 281–302.

In the November 1992 edition of *Psychological Bulletin,* Robert J. Sternberg reports on the 10 most frequently cited articles over the past 40 years from that premier journal in the field of psychology. Frequency of citation was determined through counts made from the *Science Citation Index* and the *Social Sciences Citation Index,* two reputable sources for determining the impact of specific articles in science or the social sciences. The Cronbach and Meehl article on construct validity of psychological tests was the second most frequently cited, amassing some 900 citations by other authors. Given that the two indexes mentioned cite many but not all of the journals in science and the social sciences, it is clear that this figure is an underestimate. (Cronbach is also a co-author of four of the top 10 articles cited by Sternberg.) This article provides an historical perspective on psychometrics.

Moreland, K. L., Eyde, L. D., Robertson, G. J., Primoff, E. S., & Most, R. B. (1995). Assessment of test user qualifications. *American Psychologist, 50,* 14–23.

In 1950, the American Psychological Association (APA) instituted guidelines for the ethical distribution of psychological tests. The APA arrived at a three-level classification system based on the complexity of the test and the qualifications of the test administrator. Level A tests (e.g., educational achievement tests) could be administered by public school or business personnel, whereas Level C tests (projective tests of personality) require that the administrator be a licensed psychologist. Although the three-level system is no longer formally used, it serves today as a rule of thumb for the ethical distribution and use of tests. The authors maintain that the three-level system is antiquated and difficult to apply and has created what they believe to be a more workable system for governing test distribution. Essentially, their system calls for assessing test user competencies, identifying factors related to potential misuse of tests, and identifying characteristics of the tests themselves.

Pope, K. S. (1992). Responsibilities in providing psychological test feedback to clients. *Psychological Assessment, 4,* 268–271.

This is actually an introduction to an entire volume of *Psychological Assessment* devoted to test feedback that provides the latest professional thinking on test feedback. Pope sets the stage for longer discussions of assessment and feedback as a dynamic as opposed to a pro forma process, test feedback goals, and the possibility of crisis intervention based on test results. Other topics include informed consent and feedback of test results, acknowledgment of test (and test administrator) fallibility, misuse of test results, the place of records and documentation in the feedback process, how to ensure that the person receiving feedback really understands what was being communicated, and a look at the future of testing. This article and series present state-of-the-art perspectives from a variety of experts on psychological testing.

Rupert, P. A., Kozlowski, N F., Hoffman, L. A., Daniels, D. D., & Piette, J. M. (1999). Practical and ethical issues in teaching psychological testing. *Professional Psychology: Research and Practice, 30,* 209–214.

Perhaps the greatest contribution of this article is its discussion on protecting the rights and well-being of subjects undergoing assessment. Seventy-nine tests were identified as commonly taught in psychological testing courses, with intelligence measurement taking center stage. The most commonly taught personality measure was the Minnesota Multiphasic Personality Inventory (MMPI); ranking second and third were the Rorschach Inkblot Test and the Thematic Apperception Test. Of all psychological tests reported in this study, the various Wechsler tests of intelligence were the most popular.

INFOTRAC COLLEGE EDITION

For additional readings, explore Infotrac College Edition, your online library. Go to: http://www.infotrac-college.com/wadsworth *Hint:* Enter these search terms: Big Five Personality Traits, character, factor analysis, humanism, meta-analysis, personality, personality assessment, phenomenological psychology.

Psychological Assessment in Sport Psychology

CHAPTER 16

Tests of Enduring Personality Traits

State Measures Used in Sport Psychology

Sport-Specific Tests

Attitude Measurement in Sport

Summary

Key Terms

Suggested Readings

USA Olympic sprinter Marion Jones holds up the gold medal she won in Australia in 2000. She is widely regarded as one of the greatest female athletes of all time.

© AFP/CORBIS

241

In the broadest sense, assessment can include structured interviews, systematic behavioral observations, and a host of other techniques. The remainder of our discussion, however, will be restricted to paper-and-pencil self-report measures and primarily to those dealing with personality traits and states as opposed to intelligence, aptitude, and other characteristics.

Among the specific types of tests used in sport research and practice, we will first examine measurement of personality variables, both enduring and temporary. Next we will look at sport-specific tests, an area of increasing interest to sport psychologists. Finally, we will briefly discuss attitude measures used in sport.

TESTS OF ENDURING PERSONALITY TRAITS

Enduring traits are those that have developed and been established over many years, and are thus thought to be most descriptive of a person. Three standardized measures of **enduring personality traits** have dominated sport research for the past 50 years, beginning with the Minnesota Multiphasic Personality Inventory (MMPI) in 1943 (Hathaway & McKinley), followed by the Sixteen Personality Factor Questionnaire (16PF) (Cattell, 1949) and the Eysenck Personality Inventory (EPI) (Eysenck & Eysenck, 1963). Each test will be discussed in terms of its original purpose and its application to sport.

Minnesota Multiphasic Personality Inventory (MMPI)

The **Minnesota Multiphasic Personality Inventory (MMPI),** 550 items long and answered "yes," "no," or "cannot say," was created by S. R. Hathaway, a psychologist, and J. C. McKinley, a physician, in 1943. The original purpose of the test was to differen-

---

Enduring personality traits those traits that are most enduring and thus most descriptive of a person.

Minnesota Multiphasic Personality Inventory (MMPI) the most commonly used standardized measure of enduring personality traits, criterion based and consisting of 550 items in eight clinical categories.

---

tiate among various psychiatric categories. No one theoretical approach characterizes the MMPI; rather, it represents an example of criterion keying. The criterion groups ($n = 50$ per group) used in its development were psychiatric inpatients at the University of Minnesota Hospital. The eight clinical scales resulting from the original research were:

1. *Hypochondriasis:* patients with exaggerated concerns about their physical health
2. *Depression:* unhappy, depressed, and pessimistic patients
3. *Hysteria:* patients tending to convert psychological stress into physical symptomatology
4. *Psychopathic deviate:* patients with histories of antisocial behavior
5. *Paranoia:* suspicious, grandiose, persecuted patients
6. *Psychasthenia:* anxious, obsessive-compulsive, guilt-ridden patients
7. *Schizophrenia:* patients with severe thought disturbances
8. *Hypomania:* patients displaying mood elevation, excessive activity, and unusual distractibility

The 400 criterion individuals were then compared to approximately 700 control subjects consisting of relatives and friends of the criterion cases. Critics of the MMPI have not let this point go unnoticed.

In addition to the eight clinical scales, two others were subsequently added: the masculinity–femininity (MF) scale and the social-introversion (SI) scale. The MF was designed to assess male–female differences, the SI to assess the tendency to be (or not to be) outgoing. Finally, scales to measure test-taking abilities, honesty in test taking, carelessness, misunderstanding, malingering, or the operation of special response sets were created; these were called the L (Lie), F (Frequency or Infrequency), and K (Correction) scales.

The MMPI is easily the most commonly used personality test in clinical psychology research, having been the subject of approximately 6,000 studies in its first 45 years (Kaplan & Sacuzzo, 1989). In addition, it has been translated into all European languages (Blaser & Schilling, 1976), the only personality instrument having such a distinction.

Predictably, the MMPI has its shortcomings. Charges have been leveled that the size and biased nature of the normative sample is detrimental. Other criticisms include item overlap among the various scales, imbalance in true–false keying, high scale intercorrelations, relatively weak reliability, and generalizability problems across demographic variables (Kaplan & Sacuzzo, 1989). Despite these weaknesses, the MMPI enjoys immense popularity in clinical psychology.

Perhaps the first sport study using the MMPI was conducted by LaPlace (1954), who administered the MMPI to samples of major and minor league baseball players. As hypothesized, the major league players demonstrated a generally healthier profile, with significantly lower scores on the schizophrenia and psychopathic deviate scales. A subsequent study by Booth in 1958 gave further credibility to the MMPI. Using freshman and varsity athletes, team and individual sport participants, and athletes rated as good or poor performers, Booth obtained results that led her to conclude: "The MMPI has demonstrated merit as an instrument of measurement of personality traits of participants in programs of physical education and athletics" (p. 138). Not everyone agreed with Booth, but research using the MMPI continued to be popular.

Studies continued into the 1970s on a variety of athletes. Williams and Youssef (1972), looking at the relationship of personality variables to personality stereotypes based on position played, administered the MMPI to football players from four colleges in Michigan. No differences were found across thirteen positions that the authors used to categorize football players. In a series of studies of gifted athletes, Morgan and various associates demonstrated the efficacy of the MMPI in the personality assessment of athletes. Beginning with a study of collegiate wrestlers over a five-year period, Morgan (1968) found that successful wrestlers (those who entered as freshmen and went on to win two or three letters) demonstrated superior adjustment when compared with their less successful peers (freshmen going on to win one or no letters). In a similar vein, Morgan and Johnson (1978) followed up on 50 college oarsmen after four years of competition and found again that the successful competitors (two or three varsity letters) had a more favorable MMPI profile than the less successful oarsmen (one or no letters). All eight clinical subscales yielded a more desirable profile for the successful oarsmen.

Another study was conducted by Johnsgard, Ogilvie, and Merritt (1975) with elite sports parachutists, race drivers, and football players. All parachutists had made at least 1,000 free-fall jumps. The race drivers were considered to be among the top 30 participants in the world at that time, and the football players were all professionals with five or more years of experience with at least one selection as an All-Pro performer. MMPI differences among the three groups were relatively small. According to Johnsgard and his associates, there were no differences between parachutists and race drivers on any of the scales. Football players did score significantly higher on the psychasthenia (Pt) scale than either of the other two groups. The differences on the hypochondriasis (Hs) scale between football players and parachutists was interpreted to indicate that football players are more concerned with physical health and body functions than are parachutists. The difference between football players and race drivers on the psychopathic deviate (Pd) scale is interesting, possibly suggesting authority concerns among football players. Finally, the paranoia (Pa) difference between football players and parachutists may be suggestive of football players' greater social awareness. More recently, Geron, Furst, and Rotstein (1986) administered the MMPI to 273 male athletes and 379 male nonathletes. In general, the utility of the MMPI in discriminating among various groups of athletes was upheld by the research by Geron and his colleagues.

All in all, the MMPI has an interesting history within sport research, but there is no groundswell of movement at this time to suggest that it is the premier instrument for sport research. The broad issue of validity, the usefulness of tests whose norms are based on nonsport samples, and the highly clinical nature of the instrument are all problematical. It seems safe to say that the MMPI has seen its better days in sport psychology assessment, but the instrument served an important historical function in promoting interest in personality assessment with athletes.

Sixteen Personality Factor Questionnaire (16PF)

As opposed to the criterion-based approach found in the MMPI, the **Sixteen Personality Factor Questionnaire (16PF)** (Cattell, 1949) represents an attempt to develop a personality test using the sophisticated statistical technique known as factor analysis. Cattell began his work with nearly 18,000 adjectives found in the dictionary by Allport and Odbert (1936). By consistent refinement, Cattell arrived at 180 items that measure sixteen factors he thought were descriptive of personality.

Early on, the 16PF had many advocates in sport research work. One such study was conducted with Olympic athletes by Heusner (1952). A substantial number of studies followed in the 1950s and 1960s, and Hardman (1973) has provided an extensive review of the results of 42 studies through 1969 involving sports such as cross-country running, swimming, gymnastics, climbing, tennis, riflery, golf, judo, wrestling, karate, association football, rugby football, American football, and basketball. Hardman found a great deal of variability in the results of these works.

Interest in the 16PF continued well into the 1970s. For example, Williams, Hoepner, Moody, and Ogilvie (1970) studied national-class female fencers. In general, compared with national collegiate norms, the subjects could be described as intelligent, experimenting, self-sufficient, independent, and creative. Straub and Davis (1971), in a study of football athletes playing at four different levels of competition (Ivy League, small private school, small state-supported college, Big Ten university), found considerable differences within their samples. These investigators concluded that football players involved in major college football are very different from those playing football at a less competitive level. In a similar vein, Rushall (1972) studied the 1966, 1967, and 1968 football teams at Indiana Uni-

versity using the 16PF. Rushall isolated few differences among the squads from those three years even though performance varied considerably over time (the 1966 team was 1–8–1, the 1967 team 9–1, and the 1968 team 6–4). In a separate study reported in the same article, Rushall administered the 16PF to five college and six high school football squads. Again finding few personality differences, he concluded that no football player personality exists. A third study, again included in the same 1972 report, generally supported Rushall's previous conclusions.

Studies from the mid-1970s include King and Chi (1974) and Foster (1977). In general, King and Chi found track athletes to be most similar to nonathletes, football players to be least similar to nonathletes, with swimmers and basketball players generally falling in between the extremes. Foster studied athletes from four sports—football, baseball, basketball, and track. His six-part groupings of athletes (successful–unsuccessful, outstanding–other, successful–unsuccessful baseball, successful–unsuccessful basketball, successful–unsuccessfull football, and successful–unsuccessful track) yielded few significant differences on the 16PF.

Many studies were conducted using the 16PF in the late 1970s. In a study of outstanding Indian table tennis and badminton players, Bhushan and Agarwal (1978) found considerable differences between outstanding international competitors and low-achieving participants as well as between outstanding male and female participants. In a study of physical education majors and nonmajors, Gruber and Perkins (1978) concluded that the 16PF is not effective in discriminating among various categories that they had created. In a 1979 report, Renfrow and Bolton (1979a) compared 16PF responses of 23 adult male exercisers with an equal number of nonexercisers and found differences on six factors. In a related study, the same authors (1979b) report data in which they compared adult female joggers with female nonexercisers. In contrast to their study of males, only two factors achieved statistical significance. The authors defend these differences with the arguable point that "there appears to be a substantial divergence between males and females in the motivational factors that lead to the adoption of an aerobic jogging program" (p. 507).

Use of the 16PF as a research tool continued in the 1980s. For example, Williams and Parkin (1980) stud-

---

Sixteen Personality Factor Questionnaire (16PF) a standardized measure of sixteen enduring personality traits based on factor analysis. The factors are: warmth, reasoning, emotional stability, dominance, liveliness, rule-consciousness, social boldness, sensitivity, vigilance, abstractedness, privateness, apprehension, openness to change, self-reliance, perfectionism, and tension.

ied male field hockey players in New Zealand and found the 16PF to be useful in discriminating among three groups of varying ability and experience. In India, Pestonjee, Singh, Singh, and Singh (1981) compared male and female athletes with nonathletes and found consistent personality differences. Also in India, Thakur and Ojha (1981) administered the 16PF to badminton, soccer, and table tennis players and found the soccer players differ from the other two groups, who were rather similar in personality. Finally, Evans and Quarterman (1983) compared successful black female basketball players (*n* = 20) with unsuccessful basketball players and nonathletes. Evans and Quarterman found only two significant differences among all comparisons.

All things considered, the 16PF has been a popular psychometric device for sport psychology researchers. However, the literature generates a picture of inconsistent results for a multiplicity of reasons involving statistical treatments, widely varying athletic groups, definitional inconsistencies, interpretative error, and a host of more subtle problems. Critics of the 16PF also point out that it is easily faked (Irvine & Gendreau, 1974; O'Dell, 1971; Winder, O'Dell, & Karson, 1975).

In the 1990s the 16PF has been infrequently used in sport. The publishers of the test have come out with a fifth edition, which incorporates the best features of the original and subsequent work while streamlining and updating the 185 items now in use (WPS 1995–96 catalog, 1995). The scales included in the most current version are subsumed under five global factors: Extraversion, Anxiety, Tough-Mindedness, Independence, and Self-Control. It may be that this updated and streamlined version will reawaken an interest among sport psychologists in the 16PF.

Eysenck Personality Inventory (EPI)/Eysenck Personality Questionnaire (EPQ)

The **Eysenck Personality Inventory (EPI)** made up of 57 yes–no items, emerged in 1963 after many years of work by the Eysencks. While it was similar in etiology to the 16PF, the EPI was considerably more parsimonious in attempting to measure only two personality dimensions, neuroticism–stability and introversion–extraversion. As a validity check, a third scale made up of

eight MMPI Lie items was included. The following examples are representative of Lie items:

1. Have you ever been late for an appointment or work?
2. Do you sometimes gossip?
3. Do you sometimes talk about things you know nothing about?
4. Are all your habits good and desirable ones?

The transparency of these questions is obvious, but it is less so when they are embedded in other items designed to measure neuroticism or extraversion. EPI results obtained from subjects scoring 4 and above on the eight Lie items are considered suspect.

The EPI has not been as popular a research instrument as the MMPI or the 16PF, but sport researchers have made some use of it. Morgan's research with wrestlers at the 1966 World Tournament (Morgan, 1968) was perhaps its first application in athletics. Morgan found a significant correlation (*r* = .50) between extraversion and success at that event. Though a correlation of .50 only accounts for 25% of the variance, Morgan (1980) asserts that the coupling of this data with other sources of psychological or physical data can make a significant contribution to the prediction of sport performance. Brichin and Kocian (1970) found support for this finding in their research on accomplished female athletes in Czechoslovakia. These researchers found a significant difference in extraversion between their sample of accomplished athletes and a sample of female performers of lesser interest and accomplishment. Delk (1973) found a significant difference between experienced male skydivers and the norms reported in the manual on extraversion. Kirkcaldy (1980) found similar results in a study of German sportsmen. On the other hand, researchers such as Reid and Hay (1979) and Fuchs and Zaichkowsky (1983) failed to find this difference in their studies. Nevertheless, Eysenck, Nias, and Cox (1982) conclude that sportsmen and sportswomen, regardless of level of expertise, do tend to be characterized by an extraverted temperament, but they emphasize that the relationship

---

Eysenck Personality Inventory (EPI) a standardized measure of two enduring personality dimensions, extraversion and neuroticism.

is a tendency and not an incontrovertible fact. Eysenck and his associates also point to a tendency for athletes, particularly outstanding ones, to score low on the EPI neuroticism measure. In summary, the EPI measured two traits, extraversion and neuroticism, that were predictive of athletic participation and success in cases where the former was high and the latter was low.

The EPI has been supplanted by the EPQ and the EPQ–R, with the major change being the addition of a fourth scale, Psychoticism, on the EPQ. The EPQ–R contains six new items and an Addiction scale. Some recent sport and exercise-related research has made use of one or both of these scales. Examples include Arai and Hisamichi (1998) with Japanese exercise classes and Francis, Jones, and Kelly (1999) and Francis, Kelly, and Jones (1998) with female hockey players. Perhaps the EPQ will renew interest in measuring extraversion, neuroticism, psychoticism, or addiction. The new Addiction scale, in particular, might prove to be relevant given the drug problem in sport (and society) today. Little has been done in assessing drug problems from the aspect of personality.

STATE MEASURES USED IN SPORT PSYCHOLOGY

As opposed to enduring traits, other tests measure more transient or temporary aspects of personality. Foremost among these **measures of temporary states** are the Profile of Mood States (POMS) (McNair, Lorr, & Droppleman, 1971) and the State–Trait Anxiety Inventory (STAI) (Spielberger, Gorsuch, & Lushene, 1970).

Profile of Mood States (POMS)

One psychometric instrument that measures transient states is the **Profile of Mood States (POMS).** The POMS, made up of 65 words or phrases, measures six mood states: Tension–Anxiety, Depression–Dejection,

Anger–Hostility, Vigor–Activity, Fatigue–Inertia, and Confusion–Bewilderment. By subtracting the Vigor–Activity score from the sum of the other five subscale totals, a Total Mood Disturbance (TMD) score can be computed, though the authors urge caution in its use and interpretation.

The original intent of the POMS was to assess mood states and mood changes in psychiatric outpatients, and its usefulness in that area has been demonstrated (McNair et al., 1971). Further testimony on its utility is found in sport psychology. Morgan has been at the forefront in demonstrating the validity of the POMS in sport research. Morgan, who served as a consultant to the U.S. Olympic Committee in 1972 and 1976, was able to test 56 contenders for positions on the Olympic wrestling team. From the results, he was able to differentiate successful from less successful team candidates; individuals who made the team scored lower in tension, depression, anger, confusion, and fatigue and higher on vigor (Morgan, 1968, 1980). This configuration of scores represents the **Iceberg**

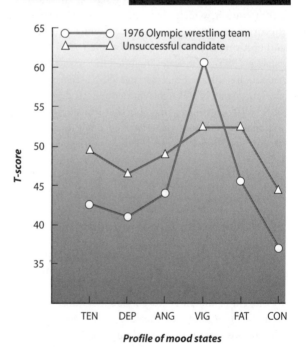

FIGURE 16.1
The Iceberg Profile

SOURCE: Morgan (1980).

Measures of temporary states standardized tests that measure transient or temporary aspects of personality.
Profile of Mood States (POMS) a psychometric instrument that measures six temporary aspects of mood.
Iceberg Profile a configuration of scores derived from the Profile of Mood States applied to sports research to distinguish successful from less successful athletes in terms of transient personality states.

According to data from the research of Dr. William P. Morgan, these Olympic wrestlers should demonstrate the Iceberg Profile so common to elite athletes.
© Reuters NewMedia Inc./CORBIS

Based on the success of Morgan and others, much research featuring the POMS has been generated. One study of college football players was initiated to see if the POMS and the Iceberg Profile would hold up in exceptional university level athletes (LeUnes & Nation, 1982). Sixty varsity football players at Texas A&M University were compared with 60 individuals from the same university who had lettered in football in high school and 60 peers who had never won a high school letter in any sport. In general, findings lent support to the POMS and Morgan's concept. The college athletes exhibited significantly less depression, fatigue, and confusion than the other two groups while scoring significantly lower on total mood disturbance; they also had a significantly higher vigor score.

An interesting outgrowth of the college football study was reported some five years after the original data were collected by LeUnes, Daiss, and Nation (1986). It is widely known in sport circles that the regulations of the National Collegiate Athletic Association (NCAA) allow college athletes five years to complete their four years of eligibility. We returned to the original data when the freshmen in our sample had completed their athletic eligibility. Out of 33 freshmen in the sample, 16 stayed with the program to the end of their eligibility ("stayers") and 17 dropped out at some point during the five years ("leavers"). Analysis of the data from the POMS and Levenson's locus of control scale, discussed at length in Chapter 10, was revealing. Using a statistical technique known as multiple discriminant analysis, we were able to accurately place 86% of the football players in the correct group—that is, "stayer" or "leaver." In other words, the administration of two brief psychometric instruments, one a trait measure and the other a state one, before the *beginning* of these players' athletic careers allowed us to predict with considerable accuracy which football players stayed with the program and which did not. Replication of this research could have important implications for the recruitment and retention of college athletes. In addition, the validity of the POMS as a research tool was again enhanced through this research.

Profile shown in Figure 16.1. Further efforts by Morgan have shown that Olympic oarsmen and top marathoners have the same Iceberg configuration (Morgan, 1978; Morgan & Pollock, 1977).

Subsequent studies of elite male distance runners by Morgan, Ellickson, O'Connor, and Bradley (1992) and of their female equivalents by Morgan, O'Connor, Sparling, and Pate (1992) have further substantiated the existence of the Iceberg Profile. The males in the first study were recruited from the Elite Distance Runner Project of the U.S. Olympic Training Center (USOTC). To qualify for the project, runners had to have times of 3:37 for 1,500 meters, 8:26 for the steeplechase, 13:42 for 5,000 meters, 28:14 for 10,000 meters, or 2.15 for the marathon; 14 subjects met these stringent requirements. The runners were observed by Morgan et al. to possess the Iceberg Profile. Among the elite female runners, 27 subjects were subdivided into elite ($n = 15$) and near elite ($n = 12$) based on previous performances. All members of both groups possessed the Iceberg Profile; this finding shows some discrepancy from results from the original Olympians upon whom the Iceberg Profile idea was based. However, the distinction between elite and near-elite runners in this case may well be an artificial one. In any event, the runners in this study differed from the normative group reported in the POMS manual in the expected direction; that is, they scored lower on the negative mood states and significantly higher on psychic vigor.

Dissociative Strategies in Distance Running

In 1977, Morgan and Pollock described elite runners in considerable detail on dimensions other than those generated from psychometric sources. Morgan had originally hypothesized that runners used **dissociative running strategies** while competing in order to cope with the painful demands inherent in long distance running. A few of the various dissociative strategies they identify include the following:

> Prior work conducted by the senior author revealed that marathon runners characteristically attempt to "dissociate" sensory input during competition. Previous interviews with twenty marathoners, as well as more recent interview data from long distance runners, revealed that these athletes are "cognitively active" during competition, but this cognitive activity seldom, if ever, relates to the actual running. Also, this general finding has since been observed for long distance swimmers and cyclists as well. The cognitive strategy employed by these athletes can best be regarded as "dissociative cognitive rehearsal." Many runners reconstruct images of past events throughout the 42.2 km run. For example, one of the first marathoners interviewed routinely rehearsed or reconstructed his entire educational experience during

each marathon. During the run he would age regress himself to first grade and attempt to recall as much as possible about the experience (e.g., the teacher's name and face, the names and faces of other boys and girls in the class, various experiences such as learning to read, print work with crayons, and paste, playing an instrument in the rhythm band, recess, and so on). After a while he would proceed to second grade, recall salient "chunks" of information, and then proceed to third grade. This continued throughout grade school, high school, college, his oral defense, receipt of the Ph.D., as well as his current postdoctoral experiences. This marathoner always reconstructed his educational experience during the marathon; it was always somewhat unique, however, in that he would remember different people, events, and activities each time. In other words, the theme was always the same, but the content varied. Suffice it to say that another runner always builds a house when he marathons; another writes letters to everyone he owes a letter to; another listens to a stack of Beethoven records; another participates in extremely complex mathematical exercises; another steps on the imaginary faces of two co-workers she detests throughout the marathon; another repeatedly sings the Star Spangled Banner in crescendo fashion; another age regresses and becomes a steam locomotive at the base of heartbreak hill; and so on. The various rehearsal themes

---

Dissociative running strategies strategies employed by distance runners to distract them from the pain and stress of running.

Overall, the POMS has proven to be an effective state measure with considerable utility in sport research. For example, there have been over 300 published studies between 1971 and early 2000 in which the POMS has been used in a sport or exercise context (LeUnes & Burger, 1998; LeUnes, 2000). Another indication of the influence the POMS has exerted on research in sport and exercise is found in an entire volume of the *Journal of Applied Sport Psychology* published in early 2000 devoted to historical, current, and future issues related to the scale. Further testimony to

the broad appeal of the POMS is found in a bibliography amassed by the publisher totaling 1,994 citations (Updated POMS Bibliography, 1995).

State–Trait Anxiety Inventory (STAI)

Spielberger and his associates make a distinction between anxiety that is relatively enduring (trait) and that which is more a function of recent events (state). Spielberger et al. attempt to measure each dimension of anxiety through responses to brief statements, twenty

are rather different but they all seem to be directed toward the same end—dissociating the painful sensory input. As a matter of fact most of these runners have reported that use of these techniques helps them negotiate various pain zones and particularly the proverbial (or mythical?) wall. (pp. 390–391)

Morgan and Pollock later recanted the dissociative idea because of additional work with other elite runners. They found that they used associated strategies as follows:

Dissociation of sensory input did not represent the principal "cognitive strategy," but rather, these elite marathon runners were found to utilize an associative strategy. These runners reported that (1) they paid very close attention to bodily input such as feelings and sensations arising in their feet, calves, and thighs, as well as their respiration; (2) whereas they paid attention to time ("the clock"), pace was largely governed by "reading their bodies"; (3) they identified certain runners they would like to stay with during a given run if possible, but they did not typically employ a "leeching" strategy; (4) during any given marathon they constantly reminded or told themselves to "relax," "stay loose," and so forth; and (5) they typically did not encounter "pain zones" during the marathon, and most of these elite runners dismissed the phenomenon referred to as "the wall" as simply a myth—that is, they did not "come up against the wall" during the marathon run. (p. 390)

More recent research by Morgan and his associates (Morgan, O'Connor, Ellickson, & Bradley, 1992; Morgan, Sparling, O'Connor, & Pate, 1992) has added yet a third interpretation of cognitive strategies used by elite distance runners. These two studies by Morgan and his associates involved male and female elite runners as defined by very stringent standards. It was noted that runners of both genders relied heavily on dissociative strategies during training but shifted to pure associative strategies or a mix of the two when competing. For example, 43% of the males used dissociative strategies when training; another 36% used both approaches. However, when it came time to compete, 72% used association only and the remaining 28% used a mixture. Obviously, highly competitive male runners dissociate little when competing. Results for the elite females were generally consistent with those of the elite male runners.

Perhaps the best conclusion to be drawn at this juncture on associative and dissociative strategies is that both are training tools for use by elite runners. The dissociative approach may help ease the pain of monotonous training, but seems to be of limited utility to runners during competition.

SOURCES: Morgan (1978); Morgan & Pollock (1977); Morgan, O'Connor, Ellickson, & Bradley (1992); Morgan, Sparling, O'Connor, & Pate (1992).

for state and twenty for trait. The fact that the **State–Trait Anxiety Inventory (STAI)** has been used in 2,000 archival publications in its first 10-plus years attests to its popularity (Spielberger, 1983). Spielberger, Gorsuch, Lushene, Vagg, and Jacobs (1983) also reported research on such diverse populations as the learning disabled, psychiatric patients, psychosomatic sufferers, coronary patients, and neurotics.

Klavora (1975) conducted an early STAI study with high school football and basketball players. In response to competitive stress, all subjects showed significant increases in state anxiety. High trait subjects exhibited significantly higher elevations than did low trait competitors. The STAI also discriminated between practice and game conditions and overall lent support

---

State–Trait Anxiety Inventory (STAI) a standardized measure widely used in sport psychology that distinguishes between transient (state) and enduring (trait) anxiety.

Short Forms of the POMS

While the original POMS contains only 65 items, there are occasions in which an abbreviated form of the scale may be useful. Examples include the assessment of mood states in athletes nearing competition, people in pain who are candidates for pain reduction procedures, or those who for whatever reason are unwilling to undertake the longer version.

The Shacham Version

The initial attempt to create an abbreviated form of the POMS was made by Shacham (1983), who deleted anywhere from two to seven items for each of the subscales, thereby creating a 37-item POMS. Correlations between the original and shortened scales ranged from .951 on Tension–Anxiety to .979 on Fatigue–Inertia. Shacham also found that the terminal cancer patients in the study reduced the time needed to complete the POMS from 15 to 20 minutes to three to seven minutes.

The EDITS Version

The Educational and Industrial Testing Service (EDITS), the original and current publisher of the POMS, created its own shortened version of the instrument in 1990. Their abbreviated POMS consists of 30 items distributed equally across each of the six subscales. Preliminary data reported from EDITS indicates that the reliability coefficients range from .75 on Confusion–Bewilderment to .95 on Fatigue–Inertia.

Only one study assessing the psychometric properties of the EDITS scale has been conducted, and it was by Fleming, Bourgeois, LeUnes, and Meyers (1992). Fleming and associates tested 665 subjects from a variety of sport and nonsport samples and reported correlations between each POMS subscale and its abbreviated equivalent ranging from .901 on the Anger–Hostility subscale to .980 on the Fatigue–Inertia scale. Fleming et al. also report that the EDITS abbreviated version is less susceptible to social desirability effects than is the original POMS, a definite plus.

The Grove and Prapavessis Version

Grove and Prapavessis (1992) adopted Shacham's basic format in creating their shortened POMS. They modified Shacham's work by dropping two items of the 37 in that scale and adding five new items aimed at assessing self-esteem. This modification resulted in a 40-item scale that was administered to 45 netball players in Australia. Reliability coefficients for the subscales ranged from .664 on Depression–Dejection to .954 on Fatigue–Inertia. Some evidence of subscale validity was demonstrated through differences between winning and losing teams, all in the expected direction with the exception of fatigue.

These three scales suggest that abbreviated forms of the POMS could have utility in sport research with little or no loss of psychometric soundness. It makes sense from the standpoint of parsimony to use 35 or 40 items if they will yield results as dependable as those garnered from a 65-item version.

SOURCES: Fleming, Bourgeois, LeUnes, & Meyers (1992); Grove & Prapavessis (1992); Revised Edition of the Manual for the POMS (1990); Shacham (1983).

to Spielberger's state–trait distinction. Since that early effort by Klavora, the STAI has been used in the sport or exercise context in over 100 published papers (LeUnes, 2002). Most of the research is supportive of the STAI and involves such diverse groups as exercisers (Ekkekakis, Hall, & Petruzzello, 1999), intramural participants (Carter & Kelley, 1997), judoists (Myung Woo, 1996), soccer players (Brunelle, Janelle, & Tennant, 1999), swimmers (Starek & McCullagh, 1999), and wheelchair athletes (Fung & Fu, 1995). The continuing popularity of the STAI in sport research is further demonstrated by the fact that it has been used in four dozen published studies during the period 1990–1999 alone (LeUnes, 2002).

SPORT-SPECIFIC TESTS

Global tests of personality measuring relatively stable traits may have problems of applicability to athletes because of the ever-changing nature of sport performance. None of the commonly used test batteries in psychology discussed earlier (the MMPI, 16PF, EPI, POMS, and STAI) were standardized on or intended for use with athletes, and the results have been mixed when these tests have been used in sport. Because of these mixed results, a call has been made for assessment devices developed with and for athletes, or what are known as **sport-specific tests.** Among the more notable are the Athletic Motivation Inventory (AMI), the Test of Attentional and Interpersonal Style (TAIS), the Psychological Skills Inventory for Sports (PSIS), the Athletic Coping Skills Inventory (ACSI), the Test of Performance Strategies (TOPS), the Competitive State Anxiety Inventory (CSAI; CSAI-2) and the Sport Competition Anxiety Test (SCAT) that were discussed in Chapter 6.

Athletic Motivation Inventory (AMI)

Tutko, Lyon, and Ogilvie developed the first major sport-specific test, the **Athletic Motivation Inventory (AMI),** in 1969. The sport-specific nature of the AMI is accentuated by the following statement by the authors (1969, p. 3) in their test manual: "The inventory assesses only athletic behavior and attitudes. Its use should be confined to those directly involved in athletics, and its results should not be generalized to other areas of the athlete's life." The initial AMI reference groups were literally thousands of professional, college, and high school athletes of both genders.

The AMI, 190 items long, is answered in a "true," "in between," "false" or "often," "sometimes," and "never" format. Sample questions include:

1. When I was young, I thought about breaking a sports record.

2. Sometimes I feel like I just don't give a damn about anybody.

3. I try to think about unexpected things that might come up during competition.

4. I rarely think that training rules inhibit my personal freedom.

5. Hustle is important, but it can't compensate for lack of talent.

6. One problem with athletics is that the individual athlete has so little to say in what happens.

7. I am sometimes hurt more by how the coach says things than by what he says.

8. If asked to follow a rigid off-season training schedule, I would stick to it religiously.

9. I need the encouragement of the coach.

10. I seldom stay after practice to work out.

The 190 items fall into three categories (Ogilvie, Tutko, & Lyon, 1973) as follows: (1) desire to be successful in athletics; (2) ability to withstand the emotional stress of competition; and (3) dedication to the coach and sport. Preliminary validity data on the AMI presented by Lyon (1972) indicated that college athletes and nonathletes differed significantly on all subtests of the AMI. Fosdick (1972), in a study of collegiate swimmers, found two significant correlations between the AMI and two subscales of the 16PF. In research comparing starting athletes with substitutes, Hammer and Tutko (1974), Hightower (1973), Hirst (1972), and Stewart (1970) all found consistent differences between the two groups. Similarly, Ogilvie (1974a) and Tombor (1970) both found differences among professional, college, and high school athletes. Morris (1975), in a study of highly skilled female field hockey players in Canada, found them to be significantly more aggressive, more seeking of the role of leadership, and mentally tougher than their counterparts not selected to represent their country in international play.

Despite this early burst of enthusiasm about the AMI, it had many critics and lapsed into a long period of disuse. Ogilvie responded to a decade-long period in which few, if any, published papers on the AMI were generated by calling for its resurrection (Straub, 1986). Two papers emerged in response to this call. Davis (1991) studied hockey players who were eligible for the National Hockey League (NHL) draft. Hockey

---

Sport-specific test standardized assessment measures developed with and for athletes.
Athletic Motivation Inventory (AMI) the first major sport-specific test to assess athletic behavior and attitudes.

scouts were asked to generate a global estimate of the psychological strength of each of these competitors. Subsequent comparison of the AMI scores with the scout ratings of psychological strength revealed that four percent of the variance in scout ratings of these hockey players was accounted for by AMI scores. This finding led Davis to conclude that the AMI has limited utility in predicting on-ice hockey behaviors regarded by scouts as representing psychological strength. Davis' data do little to support the validity of the test, but the AMI remains the psychometric instrument of choice with the NHL.

A second study by Klonsky (1991) reports data from male baseball and female softball players in which high school coaches rated their athletes on a number of variables using an adaptation of the AMI. Though Klonsky's adaptation met with some success, little can actually be inferred concerning the utility of the AMI itself.

Sport Competition Anxiety Test (SCAT)

As was discussed in considerable detail in Chapter Six, two well-received sport-specific instruments is the **Sport Competition Anxiety Test (SCAT)** of Martens (Martens, 1977; Martens, Vealey, and Burton, 1990). Based on the work of Spielberger and his associates, the SCAT is an attempt to measure competitive A-Trait or what Rupnow and Ludwig (1981, p. 35) call "the tendency to perceive competitive situations as threatening and to respond to the situations with feelings of apprehension or tension."

Martens bases the SCAT on four factors: (1) an awareness that an interactive paradigm for studying personality is superior to trait or situational explanations; (2) the recognition that situation-specific instruments are superior to general A-trait measures; (3) the distinction between A-trait and A-state in the trait-state theory of anxiety; and (4) the desirability of developing a conceptual model for studying the social process of competition.

The original work on the SCAT began by modifying items from a variety of existing paper-and-pencil anxiety measures including Spielberger's STAI. After considerable refinement, which was guided by the *Standards for Educational and Psychological Tests and Manuals* of the American Psychological Association ("Standards," 1974), two forms of the instrument emerged.

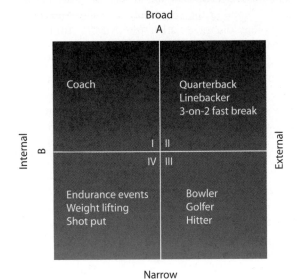

FIGURE 16.2

Nideffer's Model of Attentional Focus

Broad
A

Internal ← B | Coach | Quarterback Linebacker 3-on-2 fast break | → External

I | II

IV | III

Endurance events Weight lifting Shot put | Bowler Golfer Hitter

Narrow

SOURCE: Nideffer (1976b).

One, the SCAT-C, is intended for use with children from ten to fourteen years. The other, the SCAT-A, is the adult form for fifteen years and up. Each of them is made up of fifteen brief statements that are answered "hardly ever," "sometimes," or "often."

There has been a lot of interest in the SCAT, and this is reflected in the frequency with which it is used in research. For example, Martens et al. (1990) reported that the SCAT was cited 217 times between its original publication date and 1990; included in this figure are eighty-eight published papers and thirty-five doctoral dissertations. Martens and his associates have arrived at a number of what they feel are well-supported conclusions about the SCAT as a result of the preceding research:

1. Research supports the reliability and concurrent, predictive, and construct validity of the SCAT as a measure of competitive trait anxiety.

2. Gender differences on the SCAT have proven to be equivocal. However, it appears that the femi-

nine gender role is associated with higher levels of competitive A-trait and the masculine gender role is linked to lower competitive A-trait.

3. A-trait research looking at age differences is equivocal; there is a trend, however, toward younger athletes being lower than older ones in A-trait. In all likelihood, this difference is related to increasing pressure placed upon winning as a function of age.

4. High competitive A-trait individuals perceive greater threat in competitive situations than do low competitive A-trait participants.

5. Situational and interpersonal factors mediate the influence of competitive A-trait on perception of threat.

6. The SCAT is a significant predictor of competitive A-state.

7. The SCAT is a much better predictor of competitive A-state in athletes than are coaches. The same is generally true with A-trait, though the effects are mediated by coaching experience (older coaches are better predictors) and gender of athletes (competitive anxiety is easier to predict in female athletes).

8. The SCAT has been used in a variety of international settings as a research tool. Included are SCAT translations in France, Germany, Hungary, Japan, Russia, and Spain as well as English-speaking countries such as Canada, Great Britain, and Australia.

Support for these conclusions by Martens is repeatedly found in the literature where the SCAT remains immensely popular. For example, the SCAT has been used in well over 120 studies since its creation, and slightly over half of these were published in the 1990s (LeUnes, 2001).

Competitive State Anxiety Inventory (CSAI)

Related to the SCAT is another creation of Martens, the **Competitive State Anxiety Inventory (CSAI)** (Martens, 1977). As with the SCAT, the CSAI has been adapted from Spielberger's work in an effort to have a measure of state anxiety related specifically to sport.

Representative early research with the CSAI includes Gruber and Beauchamp (1979) and Martens, Burton, Rivkin, and Simon (1980). The first study concluded that the CSAI is most suitable for repeated assessment of athletes in competitive settings. Gruber and Beauchamp based their conclusion on results with twelve University of Kentucky female basketball players who were administered the CSAI on sixteen separate occasions. Gruber and Beauchamp found high internal consistency on the instrument, noted changes before and after competition, revealed that state anxiety was significantly reduced after wins but remained high after losses, and found differences in state anxiety among games varying in importance. In the second study, Martens et al. reported reliability coefficients ranging between .76 and .97 for both the adult and children's forms. Concurrent validity was established for the CSAI by correlating it with the *Activation-Deactivation Adjective Checklist (AD-ACL)* of Thayer (1967). Similarities were such that confidence in the CSAI was furthered.

Competitive State Anxiety Inventory-2 (CSAI-2)

Unlike the CSAI, which is a unidimensional measure of state anxiety associated with competition, the **CSAI-2** (Martens, Burton, Vealey, Bump, and Smith, 1982; Martens, Vealey, and Burton, 1990) is a multidimensional scale that purports to assess somatic anxiety, cognitive anxiety, and state self-confidence. The CSAI-2 is composed of twenty-seven items (three nine-item subscales) arranged on a four-point Likert scale.

The CSAI-2 has held up well under research scrutiny. For example, Burton (1988) reports strong support for the instrument in a study of two samples of swimmers at the national caliber and intercollegiate levels. Similar support has been provided by Bird and Horn (1990) with high school softball players, by Jones, Swain, and Cale (1990, 1991) with elite intercollegiate distance runners and a sample of male university athletes from England and Wales, by Swain and Jones (1992) with collegiate track and field competitors, by

Hammermeister and Burton (1995) with triathletes, and Maynard, Hemmings, and Warwick-Evans (1995) with semiprofessional soccer players. A Spanish version of the CSAI-II has been shown to have validity and reliability in a study conducted with Uruguayan soccer players (Rodrigo, Lusiardo, and Pereira, 1990).

As is the usual case, there are critics. Lane and his colleagues (Lane, Sewell, Terry, Bartram, and Nesti, 1999) conducted an evaluation of the factor structure of the CSAI-2. Based on their results with 1213 subjects, Lane et al. question the validity of the scale as a measure of competitive state anxiety. In an oft-cited paper, Swain and Jones (1996) also have raised reservations about the CSAI-2; these researchers concluded that the scale may well be measuring cognitive and physiological symptoms that, for lack of a better explanation, have been labeled as anxiety by the test creators.

Despite these reservations, research using the CSAI-2 continues at a hectic pace; the scale has been used on nearly 200 published studies with 120 occurring in the decade of the 1990s. Of this number, 76 were published in the time period 1995–1999 alone (LeUnes, 2002). It does appear that the CSAI-2 will remain a popular scale for the assessment of state anxiety and sport confidence.

Test of Attentional and Interpersonal Style (TAIS)

Yet another measure that has been applied to sports is the **Test of Attentional and Interpersonal Style (TAIS)** (Nideffer, 1976a), a 144-item test designed to assess 17 different attentional and interpersonal variables. Nideffer's contention is that athletic performance is closely related to attentional style or focus and, once this style is isolated, predicting athletic performance in a variety of situations becomes possible. Nideffer suggests that attention can be viewed in terms of both width and direction. Width, in turn, exists on a broad to narrow continuum; athletes with a broad focus will probably be quarterbacks, linebackers, or point guards, all positions that require a wide perspective. Narrow focus, on the other hand, is required for driving a golf ball or hitting a baseball; here the athlete must be able to shut out distractions and focus narrowly on the task at hand. Nideffer talks of directionality in terms of internal and external focus. Internals, such as world-class distance runners, are thought to be wrapped up in their own thought processes (see Morgan, 1978). Externals, of course, are more tuned-in to forces outside themselves. Nideffer believes that a balance between internality and externality is the optimal state. A visual representation of Nideffer's model using examples from sport can be seen in Figure 16.2.

De Palma and Nideffer (1977) demonstrated the versatility of the TAIS in an early study of psychiatric patients who were compared with control subjects. In general, the TAIS has acquitted itself quite nicely. In the area of sport, Richards and Landers (1981), in testing elite and subelite shooters, found that the TAIS was capable of discriminating among a number of conditions involving types of shooters (pistol, rifle, trap, skeet), gender (male and female), and experience (experienced and inexperienced). Molander and Backman (1994) studied highly skilled miniature golf players over four age groups ranging from adolescence through an older group ages 58–73 and found that the TAIS was capable of making distinctions among their groupings.

In an interesting variant, Van Schoyck and Grasha (1981) devised a tennis-specific version of the TAIS (the T-TAIS) and found it to be more related to tennis performance than the parent TAIS. In a similar vein, Albrecht and Feltz (1987) developed a baseball/softball batting version known as the B-TAIS. As was the case with Van Schoyck and Grasha, Albrecht and Feltz found their sport-specific variant of the TAIS to be more psychometrically sound than the original version. A basketball-specific version of the TAIS has been generated by Bergandi, Shryock, and Titus (1990).

The TAIS is not without critics. For example, Vallerand (1983) related the TAIS to decision-making processes. Using male basketball players as subjects who were either junior college or university competitors, Vallerand asked judges to place them in three groups based on their ability to properly decide what to do on a decision-making task, in this case repeated three-on-

---

Test of Attentional and Interpersonal Style (TAIS) a standardized measure that assesses the relation of athletic performance to attentional and interpersonal variables.

FIGURE 16.3

Training Procedures for Attentional Control

1. Athletes need to be able to engage in at least four different types of attention.

2. Different sport situations will make different attentional demands on an athlete. Accordingly, the athlete must be able to shift into different types of concentration to match changing attentional demands.

3. Under optimal conditions, the average person can meet the attentional demands of most sport situations.

4. There are individual differences in attentional abilities. Some of the differences are learned, some are biological, and some are genetic. Thus, athletes have different attentional strengths and weaknesses.

5. As physiological arousal begins to increase beyond an athlete's own optimal level, the athlete tends initially to rely too heavily on the most highly developed attentional ability.

6. The phenomenon of *choking,* of having performance progressively deteriorate, occurs as physiological arousal continues to increase to the point of causing involuntary narrowing of an athlete's concentration and internal focusing of attention.

7. Alterations in physiological arousal affect concentration. Thus, the systematic manipulation of physiological arousal is one way of gaining some control over concentration.

8. Alterations in the focus of attention will affect physiological arousal. Thus, the systematic manipulation of concentration is one way to gain some control over arousal (e.g., muscle tension levels, heart rate, respiration rate).

SOURCE: Nideffer (1990).

two or two-on-one fast breaks. The players were placed in good, average, or poor decision-making groups. It was hypothesized that good decision makers, as compared to the other groups, would display a more positive scan factor (higher BET, BIT, INFP) and a more adequate focus factor (low OET, OIT, high NAR). Analysis of variance results showed no differences. A later analysis of good and poor decision makers using functional discriminant analysis also yielded no clear results. Vallerand believes that the TAIS may not be sensitive enough to pick up attentional differences in athletic situations but calls for additional research.

Vallerand's reservations are shared by Dewey, Brawley, and Allard (1989) and Summers and Ford (1990). Dewey and her colleagues have raised serious questions about both the predictive and factorial validity of the TAIS. These researchers related a visual detection task administered to undergraduate kinesiology majors to TAIS scores and were not able to substantiate the overall validity of the instrument. Similar results were reported by Summers and Ford in their study of cricket, fencing, and basketball performers in Australia; they suggest that the utility of the TAIS as a measure of attentional style is questionable. In a later study

using 210 first-year psychology students, Ford and Summers (1992) again expressed serious reservations about the factor structure of the TAIS.

In an in-depth rejoinder, Nideffer (1990) points to methodological and interpretive errors that were made by his critics. Nideffer also cites evidence that he and others had gathered for a number of years with nearly 2,000 athletes at the Australian Institute for Sport (AIS), that country's training site for elite athletes, as further testimony to the validity of his creation (Nideffer & Bond, 1989). In general, the TAIS differentiated among athletes by type of sport with that large and elite sample.

The validity of the TAIS remains unsubstantiated; future research will undoubtedly provide answers to this empirical issue. Nideffer (1986), of course, is sold on the utility of the TAIS, and has developed a set of training procedures based on his model, known as attentional control training. These procedures are shown in Figure 16.3.

The utility of Nideffer's training regimen has been demonstrated with four collegiate soccer players (Ziegler, 1994). Subjects for the study were selected based on multiple criteria, one of which was a low score on the Martens (1989) test of attentional shift. Two of the subjects scored at the low end of the average range set by Martens, and the other two were below average. A series of attentional shift drills spaced over 24 sessions were used with the four players, and all players were able to significantly improve their attentional focus.

Other Sport-Specific Measures

A number of relatively recent sport-specific measures show promise in assessing various aspects of personality as they relate to performance. Two of the more prominent are the Psychological Skills Inventory for Sport, The Athletic Coping Skills Inventory, and the Test of Performance Strategies.

PSYCHOLOGICAL SKILLS INVENTORY FOR SPORTS (PSIS). An instrument with considerable face validity in the sporting context is the **Psychological Skills Inventory for Sports (PSIS)** (Mahoney, Gabriel, and Perkins, 1987). The PSIS is a 45-item test with a five-item Likert format ranging from "strongly agree" to "strongly disagree" (PSIS R–5) (Mahoney, 1989). The original psychometric work on the PSIS involved administering the scale to several hundred elite, pre-elite, and nonelite collegiate athletes as well as 16 sport psychologists who were asked to respond as an elite athlete might. Six subscales emerged from this analysis: concentration, anxiety management, self-confidence, mental preparation, motivation, and team emphasis.

Mahoney (1989) introduced the PSIS R–5 in a study of competitive weight lifters and cautiously endorsed the PSIS R–5 based on data gathered from this sample. Others have been less enthusiastic about the PSIS R–5. For example, Tammen, Murphy, and Jowdy (1990) conducted various psychometric analyses of the responses of nearly 1000 athletes ranging from elite to recreational and concluded that the factor structure of the PSIS R–5 was suspect. They asserted

---

Psychological Skills Inventory for Sports (PSIS) a sport-specific standardized test composed of six subscales measuring concentration, anxiety management, and other factors.
Athletic Coping Skills Inventory (ACSI) a sport-specific standardized test measuring seven types of coping skills during athletic performance.

that the subscales were not measured very well by the instrument, and the possibility existed that it taps subscale domains other than the six originally proposed by Mahoney. In a later study, Chartrand, Jowdy, and Danish (1992) report serious psychometric problems with the PSIS R–5, including poor internal consistency of the items and questionable factor structure involving the six subscales. Chartrand et al. contend that additional research should be conducted before the PSIS R–5 is used for either research or applied purposes. The position of Chartrand and colleagues is one that we also advocate. The face validity of the PSIS R–5 and its potential applicability to sport psychology practice and research indicates that continuing research is needed to deal with its psychometric shortcomings and to improve its utility.

ATHLETIC COPING SKILLS INVENTORY (ACSI). In 1988, Smith, Smoll, and Schutz created the **Athletic Coping Skills Inventory (ACSI),** a 28-item scale that measures seven coping skills: Coping With Adversity, Peaking Under Pressure, Goal Setting/Mental Preparation, Concentration, Freedom From Worry, Confidence and Achievement Motivation, and Coachability (Smith, Schutz, Smoll, & Ptacek, 1995). As with all good psychometric instruments, the authors were careful to demonstrate the factorial, construct, and predictive validity as well as the reliability of the ACSI. A subsequent study by Smith and Christensen (1995) with 104 minor league baseball players in the Houston Astros organization (Smith was a consultant with the team at the time) further demonstrated the utility of the scale. Players filled out the ACSI before the season started, and these results were analyzed in conjunction with the manager/coach evaluations of various baseball skills of each athlete. The utility of the ACSI to make important distinctions was upheld. One of the more noteworthy findings was that the ACSI results were predictive of survival in professional baseball two and three years after the original testing was conducted. Another finding was that the ACSI was a better predictor of pitchers' earned run average than were coaches' ratings of physical skills. In an interesting variant on this theme, Guarnieri, Bourgeois, and LeUnes (1998) tested aspiring baseball umpires at the three professional umpire training schools in Florida. Concurrently, Guarnieri et al. conducted a mail-out survey to all the umpires officiating in the minor leagues at that time. In both studies, an adaptation of the ACSI was used (very minor wording changes were employed where needed to make the test more umpire specific). It was found that the more experienced umpires (i. e., the minor leaguers) used these athletic coping skills more effectively than did umpires undergoing training in the three schools. The minor league officials were also similar to the baseball players in the Smith and Christensen study in their use of these ACSI mental skills. Good umpires, like good athletes, apparently peak under pressure, prepare mentally, set goals, and are team players, among other things.

Little has emerged recently in the literature concerning the ACSI other than the development of a Greek version (Goudas, Theodorakis, and Karamousalidis, 1998). However, the scale is potentially a very effective research tool with much to commend it for practitioners as well.

TEST OF PERFORMANCE STRATEGIES (TOPS). The most recent of the sport-specific tests is the **Test of Performance Strategies (TOPS)** of Thomas, Murphy, and Hardy (1999). After reviewing the literature on the PSIS and ACSI, Thomas et al. were convinced that the ACSI was the best available instrument but felt that it stopped short of measuring all of the mental skills necessary for peak performance—hence the TOPS. The TOPS was subjected to the requisite test development statistical treatments, and eight scales emerged from their various analyses: attentional control, goal setting, imagery, relaxation, activation, self-talk, emotional control, and automaticity. The last scale was defined as acting without having to think much about it, a skill thought to be essential, for instance, in superior golf play. Given the relative infancy of the TOPS coupled with the fact that its norms were based on athletes from Australia, most particularly from the Australian Institute for Sport (AIS), there is much work to be done in demonstrating the broad utility of the scale. It does, however, seem to show promise.

A Final Note

We would be remiss in our discussion of sport-specific measures to omit the Competitive State Anxiety Inventory–2 (CSAI–2) and the Sport Competition Anxiety Test (SCAT) of Martens and colleagues. However,

given the detailed discussion that the two instruments received in Chapter 6, it would be redundant to say much more here. Certainly, the contributions to the sport literature from research using the CSAI–2 and the SCAT are significant. For example, the SCAT has been used in over 120 published studies and the CSAI and the CSAI–2 in nearly 200 studies, with 120 conducted in the decade of the 1990s. Of this number, 76 were published in the time period 1995–1999 alone (LeUnes, 2002). The two scales appear likely to remain popular in the assessment of state and trait sport-related anxiety.

ATTITUDE MEASUREMENT IN SPORT

In addition to personality assessment, there has been strong interest in **measures of attitudes** in sport. Two of the more prominent examples include the Attitudes Toward Physical Activity Scale (ATPA) (Kenyon, 1968) and the Physical Estimation and Attraction Scales (PEAS) (Sonstroem, 1978).

A major conceptual framework for looking at attitudes has been proposed by Triandis (1971), who believes that attitudes can be viewed as having three dimensions: cognitive, affective, and behavioral. The cognitive dimension deals with beliefs, the affective with feelings, and the behavioral with intended behavior toward the attitude object. Attitude measurement in sport psychology has taken three paths, drawn from the works of Likert (1932), Osgood, Suci, and Tannenbaum (1957), and Thurstone (1928). A sport-related summary of these assessment procedures is presented in Figure 16.4.

Likert Scales

In response to the difficulties associated with the Thurstone method, Likert (1932) created a somewhat

---

Test of Performance Strategies (TOPS) most recent sport-specific standardized test with eight scales, based on a study population of Australian athletes.
Measures of attitudes standardized tests that measure personal attitude during athletic performance in three dimensions: cognitive, affective, and behavioral.

similar but simpler procedure that bears his name. In the **Likert scales,** judges are not necessary and the determination of scale item values is not made. Basically, subjects are asked to respond to a pool of items arranged on a five-point scale, and those items that discriminate most effectively between subjects scoring high or low are retained for the final Likert scale.

Semantic Differential Scales

Osgood and his associates (1957) developed a most popular technique known as the **Semantic Differential Scale.** The ATPA of Kenyon, mentioned earlier, is a prominent scale in sport based on the semantic differential method. Subjects in this procedure are asked to respond to a series of bipolar adjectives on a five- or seven-point scale. To Osgood et al., attitudes have evaluative (good–bad), potency (strong–weak), and activity (active–passive) components. In practice, only the evaluative component is used in much of the existing attitude research.

Despite the sophisticated nature of the attitude measurement techniques, their popularity of late has been greater in the larger area of psychology than in sport psychology. Because of the multitude of attitudinal issues surrounding athletics and exercise behavior, we should see continued use from time to time of Thurstone's, Likert's, and Osgood's procedures.

Thurstone Scales

Ratings provided by judges lie at the heart of the **Thurstone scale** procedure. Initially, the judges are provided with a large pool of items related to an issue from which the final scale will be forged. Once the pool of items is shrunk through these judgments, the remaining statements are assigned numerical weights that are reflective of various attitudinal dispositions along a continuum from favorable to unfavorable. It is

---

Likert scale an attitude assessment procedure in which subjects are asked to respond to preselected items along a continuum, usually from 1 to 5 or 1 to 7.
Semantic Differential Scale a technique for attitude assessment using a series of bipolar adjectives.
Thurstone scale a technique for assessing attitudes in which the ratings of judges are critical in scale construction.

FIGURE 16.4
Sport-Related Summary of Various Attitude Measures

One-Item Rating Scale

How much do you like jogging for exercise?

not at all - - - - - - - - very much
(1) (2) (3)　　(4)　　(5) (6) (7)

Thurstone Scale

(The scale values in parentheses are contrived for this example.)

Check the statements with which you agree.

_____ 1. Jogging is the best way to start a day. (10.7)

_____ 2. Jogging helps a person stay fit and healthy. (7.3)

_____ 3. Jogging is unnecessary and a waste of time for most people. (3.4)

_____ 4. Jogging is distasteful and unpleasant. (2.3)

Likert Scale

For each statement, check the extent to which you agree.

1. Jogging is a good activity for most people.

_____ strongly agree (+2) _____ moderately agree (+1)
_____ neutral (0) _____ moderately disagree (−1)
_____ strongly disagree (−2)

2. Jogging is boring.

_____ strongly agree (−2) _____ moderately agree (−1)
_____ neutral (0) _____ moderately disagree (+1)
_____ strongly disagree (+2)

Semantic Differential Scale

Rate how you feel about jogging for exercise on each of the scales below:

foolish- - - - - - - wise
(−3) (−2) (−1) (0) (+1) (+2) (+3)

good- - - - - - bad
(+3) (+2) (+1) (0) (−1) (−2) (−3)

beneficial- - - - - - harmful
(+3) (+2) (+1) (0) (−1) (−2) (−3)

unpleasant- - - - - - pleasant
(−3) (−2) (−1) (0) (+1) (+2) (+3)

valuable- - - - - - worthless
(+3) (+2) (+1) (0) (−1) (−2) (−3)

Source: Gill (1986).

Test Information Sources

Though testing is a dynamic and ever-changing area, a number of resources provide up-to-date information. Foremost is the series of **Mental Measurement Yearbooks (MMY),** a compendium of information compiled by Buros beginning in 1938 and continuing up to the most recent volume in 1992. Included in the MMY are such things as price, forms, and age of persons for whom each test is intended as well as expert reviews and a list of studies of each. The MMY reviews over 2,000 commercially produced tests and is updated every six months through a computerized program that can be accessed at http://www.silverplatter.com/catalog/mmyb.htm

Another significant source of test information has been compiled by Robinson, Shaver, and Wrightsman (1991). Their intent is to provide a source of test information in the social sciences useful not only to psychologists but to sociologists and political scientists. Included in the work by Robinson and associates are separate chapters on the measurement of self-esteem and related constructs, locus of control, alienation and anomie, authoritarianism and dogmatism, so-

ciopolitical attitudes, values, general attitudes toward people, religious attitudes, and several scales of a methodological nature (e. g., social desirability).

A third significant source of information about tests is the individual test manual. Information about usage, norms, relevant studies, reliability and validity data, and other subjects is included in any good test manual. Prospective users are strongly urged to consult this invaluable source.

Many of the tests listed in these various sources are not relevant to sport. Many others are, however, and the test user in sport research and application is well advised to refer to as many of them as possible. As time goes on, an increasing number of global and sport-specific tests of demonstrated validity and reliability may find their way into these volumes.

SOURCE: Robinson, Shaver, & Wrightsman (1991).

Mental Measurements Yearbook the number one reference work for professionals interested in information concerning published psychological tests.

---

hoped that the numerical weights assigned to each of the possible responses will be reasonably equally distributed along the favorable–unfavorable continuum. In general, the Thurstone scales have proven a popular procedure despite being cumbersome to develop.

SUMMARY

1. Psychological tests in sport are generally used for two purposes: selection and/or screening decisions or program development. The sport psychologist should therefore be alert to a variety of concerns related to test selection, reporting of results, and ethics in general.

2. Tests of enduring traits have been an integral part of sport psychology research. Chief among them have been the Minnesota Multiphasic Personality Inventory (MMPI), the Sixteen Personality Factor

Questionnaire (16PF), and the Eysenck Personality Inventory (EPI).

3. Personality traits of a more temporary or transient nature also have a rich if recent heritage in sport psychology. Chief among these are the Profile of Mood States (POMS) of McNair, Lorr, and Droppleman and the State–Trait Anxiety Inventory (STAI) of Spielberger and associates.

4. There has been made a move away from enduring traits or broadly conceived tests of temporary states to assessment techniques that are sport-specific. The first of these was created in 1969 by Tutko, Lyon, and Ogilvie and was called the Athletic Motivation Inventory (AMI). Subsequent efforts include the Test of Attentional and Interpersonal Style (TAIS) of Nideffer, the Sport Competition Anxiety Test (SCAT), and the Competitive State Anxiety Inventory–2 (CSAI–2), all of which are sport-related modifications of

Spielberger's work by Martens. Also, a number of more recent sport-specific instruments offer promise for sport psychology.

5. Attitude measurement in sport has given rise to such instruments as Kenyon's Attitude Toward Physical Activity Scale (ATPA) and Sonstroem's Physical Estimation and Attraction Scales (PEAS). According to Triandis, attitudes have cognitive, affective, and behavioral components.

6. The Thurstone scale, the Likert scale, and the semantic differential technique of Osgood and associates represent three different methods for the assessment of attitudes.

KEY TERMS

Athletic Coping Skills Inventory (ACSI) (256)
Athletic Motivation Inventory (AMI) (251)
Comprehensive State Anxiety Inventory-2 (CSAI-2) (253)
dissociative running strategies (248)
enduring personality traits (242)
Eysenck Personality Inventory (EPI) (245)
Iceberg Profile (246)
Likert scale (258)
measures of attitudes (257)
measures of temporary states (246)
Mental Measurements Yearbook (259)
Minnesota Multiphasic Personality Inventory (MMPI) (242)
Profile of Mood States (POMS) (246)
Psychological Skills Inventory for Sports (PSIS) (256)
Semantic Differential Scale (258)
Sixteen Personality Factor Questionnaire (16PF) (244)
Sport Competition Anxiety Test (SCAT) (252)
sport-specific test (251)
State–Trait Anxiety Inventory (STAI) (249)
Test of Attentional and Interpersonal Style (TAIS) (254)
Test of Performance Strategies (TOPS) (257)
Thurstone scale (258)

SUGGESTED READINGS

Eysenck, H. J., Nias, D. K. B., & Cox, D. N. (1982). Sport and personality. *Behavior Research and Therapy, 4,* 1–56.

Eysenck and his associates have taken an in-depth look at nearly 300 studies related to sport personality. Topics discussed include measurement of personality in sport; developmental aspects of personality; the relationship of personality to sport; differences among athletes in various sports; the state–trait distinction; sexuality, exercise and personality; somatotype theory; and strategies for learning physical skills.

LeUnes, A. (2002, in press). *Journal citations of psychological tests used in sport and exercise psychology research.* Lewiston, NY: Mellen Press.

Sixty-seven different tests measuring a wide assortment of traits, temporary states, and sport-specific skills were used in this compilation, and approximately 2,300 citations of relevance have been isolated. Citations are listed by test, author, and sport (i.e., baseball, soccer, or wrestling). This resource should prove invaluable for teachers, researchers, or practitioners in sport and exercise psychology.

Osipow, A. C. (1990). *Directory of psychological tests in the sport and exercise sciences.* Morgantown, WV: Fitness Information Technology.

Osipow has compiled a thorough listing of over 175 tests developed by various sport researchers that are specific to sport and exercise situations, and a brief description of each is provided. Areas covered include achievement orientation, aggression, anxiety, attention, attitudes toward fitness and exercise, attitudes toward sport, attributions, body image, cognitive strategies, cohesion, confidence, imagery, leadership, life adjustment, locus of control, exercise motivation, sport motivation, sex roles, and two sets of miscellaneous tests. Also included is a code of ethics section on test usage. One important feature of Osipow's work is the fact that virtually none of the tests he mentions are discussed anywhere else in our text, thereby providing a comprehensive listing of possible tests that might be employed in sport or exercise research or practice.

Speaking with Dr. Charles D. Spielberger. (1998). *1998 PAR Spring Update Catalog.* Odessa, FL: Psychological Assessment Resources.

The PAR spring catalog features an interview with Charles Spielberger, the creator of the

State–Trait Anxiety Inventory and its many variants. Professor Spielberger served as the hundredth President of the American Psychological Association and has written over 350 professional publications. In this interview, he traces some of the history of his interest in anxiety and its assessment, the role of anger in disease, the significance of the state–trait distinction, and other contributions he has made to the field of psychology.

INFOTRAC COLLEGE EDITION

For additional readings, explore Infotrac College Edition, your online library. Go to:
http://www.infotrac-college.com/wadsworth
Hint: Enter these search terms: anxiety research, Eysenck Personality Inventory, Eysenck Personality Questionnaire, Likert Scale, Minnesota Multiphasic Personality Inventory, mood psychology, State–Trait Anxiety Inventory.

Special Populations: Minority and High-Risk-Sport Athletes

CHAPTER 17

The Minority Athlete
The High-Risk-Sport Participant
Summary
Key Terms
Suggested Readings

Former Seattle Mariner shortstop Alex Rodriguez smiles during a news conference announcing his 10-year, $252 million deal with the Texas Rangers at the ball park in Arlington, Texas, December 12, 2000. The deal is the world's richest sports contract for a single player.

© Reuters NewMedia Inc./CORBIS

Considerable interest has been generated over the past 50 or 60 years on minority participation in sport. Much information and at least as much misinformation has been advanced in an effort to unravel the nuances of African-American involvement in sport, but much less is known about Hispanics, Asians, and Native Americans. The literature in sport psychology on these athletes is sparse, though some aspects of the African-American experience have been studied fairly well.

Many of the same statements can be made about risk-sport participants. Little research of a systematic nature has been done with skydivers, hang gliders, scuba divers, rock climbers, and other thrillseekers. Two prominent psychological constructs that have emerged are anxiety and sensation seeking, and these topics and others will be covered in the second part of this chapter.

THE MINORITY ATHLETE

The African-American Athlete

The overrepresentation of African-American athletes in many sports (e.g., basketball, boxing, football, track) has generated a great deal of interest among professionals and laypersons alike. What factors seem to account for this seeming dominance in some sports (and it is clear that the dominance is limited to a relatively small number of sports)? Is it true that black athletes are physically superior to their white competitors, or do the answers lie in sociocultural and/or psychological explanations? We will attempt to answer these and other questions in our treatment of this provocative area.

The first contingent of Africans in North America arrived in 1619 at the English colony of Jamestown, Virginia. Initially, they were brought not as slaves but as indentured servants who were theoretically free at the end of their agreed-on period of servitude. In practice, however, most were made slaves, initially on a more or less informal basis and later through legislation. This formal enslavement began in the mid-1600s and continued until the Emancipation Proclamation of 1862. The value of these African immigrants to the economy of the United States, and particularly of its southern regions, was a significant force in the creation and maintenance of slavery.

Wiggins (1977) has provided an extensive literature review of the recreation of African Americans living on southern plantations prior to 1860. The form and substance of this recreation varied greatly depending on the personality and philosophy of the individual plantation owners. Wrestling, boxing, footraces, cockfights, hunting, fishing, boat races, and dancing were all popular pastimes. Related to dancing and music was an activity described by Wiggins as "patting juba," a rhythmic patting or clapping of the hands as a substitute for musical instruments when none were available. All in all, much of the sport and recreation of the pre–Civil War period was tied to rural life and the work circumstances that prevailed.

After the Civil War, African-American athletes emerged in the sports of baseball, horse racing, and boxing. Chu (1982) states that the first African American to play professional baseball was John (Bud) Fowler, who played for New Castle, Pennsylvania, in 1872. Following the lead of Fowler was Moses Fleetwood Walker, who played for the Toledo (Ohio) Mudhens in 1883 and was the first African American to play in the major leagues. Eitzen and Sage (1978) note that Fleetwood was joined by his brother, Weldy (also cited by some sources as Weldey and Welday) Wilberforce Walker, and together they were the first to play major league baseball. Rader (1983) indicates that Moses preceded his brother Weldy by several months, with Weldy joining the team very late in the season. As one might suspect, the presence of the Walkers did not go unnoticed. As Peterson (1970, p. 3) recounts, members of a team in Richmond, Virginia, sent the following message to the Toledo, Ohio, manager prior to a game between the two teams:

> We, the undersigned, do hereby warn you not to play Walker, the negro catcher, the evening that you play in Richmond, as we could mention the names of 75 determined men who have sworn to mob Walker if he comes on the grounds in a suit. We hope you *will* listen to our words of warning, so that there *will* be no trouble; but, if you do not, there certainly *will* be. We only write to prevent much bloodshed, as you alone can prevent.

Peterson provides us with additional insight into the difficulties faced by black ballplayers with another quote from a white player in 1888:

While I myself am prejudiced against playing on a team with colored players, I still could not help pitying some of the poor black fellows that play in the International League. Fowler used to play second base with the lower part of his legs encased in wooden guards. He knew that every player that came down to second base on a steal would head for him and would, if possible, throw the spikes into him. About half the pitchers try their best to hit these colored players when at bat. (p. 41)

Though these vignettes suggest that much remained to be done in race relations and sport, baseball stayed integrated, however troubled, until the 1890s. At that time, it became totally segregated and remained so until 1945, when Jackie Robinson joined the Montreal Royales, a farm club of the parent Brooklyn Dodgers (which he later joined in 1947).

Curry and Jiobu (1984) indicate that perhaps 20 to 30 African Americans formed an elite cadre of post–Civil War jockeys, with one of them riding in the first Kentucky Derby in 1876. Another, Willey Sims, eventually won both the Belmont Stakes and the Kentucky Derby. Another prominent name of the era was Pike Simms, a winner of the Futurity. Coakley (1982) cites a number of factors that led to the elimination of black jockeys toward the end of the nineteenth century. Chief among these factors were the discriminatory Jim Crow laws that supposedly guaranteed separate but equal rights or protections, a white jockeys' union, a racist press, and assignment to slower horses. In a short period of time, the black jockey found himself relegated to less prestigious positions, such as trainer or stable boy. By 1900, the elite black jockey was effectively a historical footnote.

Boxing was, and remains, a somewhat different story. Beginning with Tom Molineaux in 1800, African Americans have fared relatively well, at least when compared with other sports. Though discriminated against, they have competed on a relatively continuous basis in boxing. The controversial Jack Johnson won the heavyweight championship of the world in 1908 by defeating the white champion, Tom Burns. Refusing to fit into the white man's predetermined mold for African Americans, Johnson lived life in the

Jackie Robinson (left) and heavyweight boxing great Joe Louis (right) appear to be trading inside secrets about their sports. These two men were instrumental in paving the way for full minority participation in sport in the U.S.
© Bettmann/CORBIS

fast lane. He had a penchant for expensive clothes and flashy women; had a succession of girlfriends, generally white; and married two different white women. These interracial relationships created many difficulties for Johnson, and he eventually fled the United States. Following Johnson as a great black boxer was the legendary Joe Louis, blessed with great ability, outstanding character, and a lifestyle that was more acceptable to the white establishment. To underscore the point about Joe Louis's reputation, Bontemps (1964) reports the following exchange between two people talking on the streets of Harlem:

"If we had more Negroes like Joe Louis, things would be better for us," one speaker said.

"True," the other answered, "but if we had more white people like Joe, things would be better still."

Joe Louis did much to change the image of the black American at that time, and he became a world ambassador of good will during his competitive and postcompetitive days. Louis has been succeeded by a series of African-American champions who have reigned for the better part of the past six decades. Only occasionally has there been a white champion or serious contender for the crown, at least in the heavyweight division of boxing.

With the integration of Jackie Robinson into the baseball major leagues in 1947, African Americans became more and more a part of the athletic scene. They entered the National Basketball Association in 1950; Althea Gibson embarked on the professional tennis circuit in 1959; Bill Russell became the first black head coach in professional basketball in 1966; in 1968, professional baseball hired its first black major league umpire in Emmit Ashford; and Frank Robinson became the first black manager in the major leagues in 1975.

According to the U.S. Census Bureau (The Black Population, 2001), African Americans represent 14% of the U.S. population. Blacks reached that same figure in professional baseball in 1957, basketball in 1958, and football in 1960. Since that time, they have been proportionately overrepresented to the point that they presently hold 79% of the professional basketball positions, while their numbers in football and baseball are 65% and 18% respectively (Leonard, 1997).

The Success of African-American Athletes

At least three possible explanations exist for the increasing numerical superiority and performance dominance of African Americans in the more visible sports. They are genetic, social/cultural, and psychological.

GENETIC OR OTHER BIOLOGICAL EXPLANATIONS. It has long been suggested that the apparent superiority of African Americans in sport results from genetic or other biological influences. Coakley (1982, p. 265) offers an excellent summary of these supposed differences:

1. Compared to whites, blacks have longer legs and arms, shorter trunk, less body fat, more slender hips, more tendon and less muscle, a different heel structure, wider calf bones, more slender calf muscles, greater arm circumference, and more of the muscle fibers needed for speed and power and fewer of those needed for endurance.

2. Compared to whites, blacks mature more rapidly, their lung capacity is lower, they are more likely to have hyperextensibility (be "double jointed"), they

dissipate heat more efficiently (they sweat more), they tend to become chilled more easily in cold weather, and they have superior rhythmic abilities.

As Coakley as well as Chu (1982) and Leonard (1984) point out, a number of problems are associated with these conclusions. First, most of what we know about African athletes has been gathered from studies, both controlled and anecdotal, of relatively superior athletes; seldom are blacks with average, limited, or no athletic ability taken into account. Second, what the designation *black* means scientifically is subject to interpretation. It is likely that a fair number of African Americans have white ancestors, particularly in light of some of the practices on the plantations of pre–Civil War America; by the same token, a number of people labeled as white undoubtedly have African ancestors. While the concept of black has relatively clearcut political overtones, its scientific validity is suspect. As Coakley so acutely states: "The notion that 'a black is a black is a black' has created enough problems on the street without letting it guide scientific research in the laboratory" (p. 265).

A third problem is the likelihood that there may be as many differences within "black" and "white" groups as there are between the two groups. One example of differences within a single race is that of Bobby Morrow and Bill Woodhouse, Olympic-caliber white sprinters of the late 1950s and early 1960s and college teammates at Abilene Christian University in Abilene, Texas. Morrow was relatively tall, lean, and graceful. Woodhouse, perhaps aptly named, was short, stocky, and powerful. How could these two diverse body types be so closely paired in terms of excellence? A second example: How could Curtis Dickey and Rod Richardson, both black sprinters at Texas A&M University during the late 1970s, have claimed so many indoor NCAA sprint titles between them, given their physical diversity? Dickey, at 6 feet, 2 inches and 215 pounds (and eventually a running back in the NFL), and Richardson, at 5 feet, 8 inches and 150 pounds, had relatively little in common except skin color and speed. Alternatively, how could Jimmy Howard, for years the American record holder in the high jump (white, 6 feet, 5 inches and 175 pounds), and Franklin Jacobs (black, 5 feet, 8 inches and 150 pounds), have had so much in common as world-class high jumpers? Interestingly, African Americans are known as "leapers" and European Americans are supposedly afflicted with "white man's disease," yet there are a number of examples where the stereotypes fail. A prominent and relatively recent one comes from statistics from the world of track and field; of the top 10 high jumpers in the world in 1985, nine were white and the tenth was Asian (High Jump, 1985).

A fourth problem arises from making generalizations about all sports based on a select few. The disproportionate representation of African Americans in basketball, boxing, football, and track obscures the fact that many sports are dominated by other groups of athletes. For instance, Japanese Americans, who constitute less than 1% of our total population, comprise in excess of 20% of the top AAU judo competitors (Phillips, 1976). No one has really come forth with a genetic explanation for this overrepresentation. As Robertson (1981, p. 91) beautifully notes:

> Nobody proposes genetic factors, for example, to explain why East Germany has produced so many excellent swimmers, why Canadians do well at hockey, why Japanese Americans are disproportionately represented in judo—or, for that matter, why the British are hopeless at baseball, while white Americans are equally inept at cricket. In each case, it is easy to see cultural factors, not genetic ones, are at work.

Coakley (1994, pp. 245–246) carries this line of thought a step farther by suggesting that the Swiss, with a population one-thirtieth the size of that of the United States, have won 10 times as many World Cup Championships in skiing and therefore should undergo screening for a skiing gene:

> Similarly, there have been no studies looking for a weight-lifting gene among Bulgarian men, or a swimming gene among East German women, or a cross-country skiing gene among Scandinavians, or a volleyball jumping gene among Californians who hang out on beaches. There have been no claims that Canadians owe their success in hockey to naturally strong ankle joints, or instinctive eye-hand-foot coordination, or an innate tendency not to sweat so they can retain body heat in cold weather. Nobody has looked for or used genetic

explanations for the successes of athletes packaged in white skin.

But as soon as athletes with black skin excel or fail at a certain sport, regardless of where they come from in the world, many people start looking for "race-based" genetic explanations. They want to explain the successes and failures of black athletes in terms of "natural" or "instinctive" qualities or weaknesses. They assume white skinned athletes succeed because of tradition, training opportunities, dedication, and personal sacrifice, not the genetic heritage of the entire white population of a region, a country, or the world.

To the preceding point, in an essay on racism in baseball, Poff (1995, p. 20) says:

> I believe we want to establish a genetic basis for the success of black athletes. This is a two-fold agenda. First, it dehumanizes blacks, emphasizing their physicality. Secondly, while surveys show that half of us at any given moment don't know who the Vice President is or when World War II was fought, it seems to me that almost all white people are aware we outperform blacks in IQ tests. We will give blacks an inherent physical superiority, which both demeans them and gives us a good excuse for not being able to make a dunk, while we will retain for ourselves an innate intellectual superiority.

Kane (1971) advanced an interesting genetic/biological explanation for African-American sport superiority in a *Sports Illustrated* article. Kane took the position that survival of the fittest and selective breeding among slaves while en route to the United States from Africa and thereafter is the best explanation for this athletic superiority. Kane's Social Darwinian hypothesis presupposes that the survivors of the admittedly brutal trip from Africa to America were physically stronger than the ones who died, thereby creating a superior gene pool among the survivors. In turn, this physical superiority has been transmitted genetically to subsequent generations of blacks. This rather myopic survival of the fittest notion does not take into account the fact that intelligence, character, and cunning may have been critical contributors to survival, thus greatly exaggerating the role of physical variables as significant influences.

Perhaps the best summation of what we know about genetic explanations for African-American superiority is provided by Eitzen (1989, p. 270): "we do not know whether African-American athletes actually possess physical traits superior to those of whites or not. Even if it were finally proved that African-Americans do have genetic advantages over whites, we believe that genetic differences will likely be less important than the social reasons for African-American dominance."

SOCIAL/CULTURAL INFLUENCES. Black superiority in sports (or more appropriately, some sports) appears to be best explained in terms of social influences. One such explanation is the **sport opportunity structure** (Eitzen & Sage, 1978) which has its roots in past discriminatory practices such as indentured servitude, slavery, and Jim Crow laws; Moses Fleetwood Walker felt their effects, Jackie Robinson felt them, and athletes of today feel them. In the past, the sport opportunity structure was an impediment to success of African-American athletes. Racial prejudice and lack of opportunity prevailed, but these barriers are coming down and the opportunities for success are thus increasing.

In the world of sports, discrimination has been and continues to be manifested in the form of **stacking,** a phenomenon whereby black players are relegated to certain peripheral positions in sports such as football and baseball while white players occupy the more central positions. For example, many quarterbacks are white, whereas most flankers or wide receivers are black. Yet another example comes from baseball, where pitchers are predominantly white, whereas outfielders are often black.

Pioneers in this area of research were Loy and McElvogue (1970), who found that 83% of major league infielders (central) in 1967 were white, whereas 49% of the outfielders (peripheral) were black; 96% of all catchers and 94% of pitchers were white. A reexamination of stacking in 1975 found few changes (Eitzen & Sage, 1978). Ninety-six percent of pitchers

and 95% of catchers were white, data almost identical to the 1967 findings; 49% of the outfielders were black and 76% of infielders were white, the latter being the only area of change but still overwhelmingly white. In a recent update using statistics from 1983 and 1993, Lapchick and Benedict (1993) indicate that there have been some slight shifts away from stacking. For instance, 86% of pitchers were white in 1983 as opposed to 82% in 1993. In the case of catchers, 93% were white in 1983 as opposed to 87% in 1993. The largest changes were among infielders and outfielders. Infielders (excluding first basemen) were 73% white in 1983 and 58% in 1993; outfielders were 45% white in 1983 and 33% 10 years later.

In football, the data look amazingly similar to those for baseball. Despite the influx of African Americans since 1960, central positions remained largely white in 1975. According to Eitzen and Sage (1978), in professional football 84 of 87 quarterbacks, 69 of 70 punters, and 26 of 26 placement holders were white in 1975. Best (1987), using data from the 1982 season, found a similar effect: 78 of 80 quarterbacks, 56 of 56 kickers, and 45 of 47 offensive centers were white. In 1991, Lapchick and Brown (1992) found that 92% of quarterbacks, 88% of kickers, and 89% of centers were white. These data are reflective of 7%, 10%, and 8% changes in the direction of fewer whites from 1983 to 1991 in these three central positions.

The intimation has been that African Americans, for a host of vague and unverified reasons, are just not suited for these varied duties. On the other hand, running back, wide receiver, and defensive back positions are regarded as particularly suited to the black athlete; 55% of running backs, 65% of wide receivers and 67% of defensive backs in the NFL in 1975 were black. By 1991, these figures were 90%, 89%, and 94%, respectively (Lapchick & Brown, 1992).

The sport of professional basketball, in which 77% of the players are African American, also has a form of stacking in the center or post position; 55% of National Basketball Association (NBA) centers are black, an underrepresentation in terms of the total picture. This point is accentuated when we consider that 83% of the guards and 80% of the forwards are black.

Unsubstantiated biases have indeed become fact, causing coaches to select athletes for some positions and discouraging them from even aspiring to others.

Sport opportunity structure a form of discrimination whereby minorities are denied access to the opportunities for success in athletics.
Stacking peripheral positioning of minority players in sports such as football and baseball.

How many white track athletes in this country have been charmed (coerced?) into middle distance or field events because the sprints belong to the blacks? Conversely, how many blacks have been discouraged from running distances because of the perception that they are sprinters, not distance runners? Evidence from Africa suggests that blacks in fact can excel at distance running. Why is it that we have no great black pole vaulters other than the 2000 Olympian, Lawrence Johnson? Surely speed, upper body strength, and gymnastic ability are not restricted to white athletes. Our own biases have led us into a self-fulfilling prophecy stance that validates them. If we don't have blacks running distances and if they continue to excel in the sprints, there will always be ample reason to suspect that they are not good at longer distances. Perhaps Harry Edwards (1973, p. 322) sums it up best: "The white athletes who do participate in sports operate at a psychological disadvantage because they believe blacks to be inherently superior as athletes. Thus, the white man has become the chief victim of his own lie."

An interesting by-product of this tendency to stack and stereotype is that few African-American athletes are groomed for positions of leadership, such as coaching or administration, when their playing days are over. Another by-product of the sport opportunity structure is lower earnings for the black athlete because of their shorter careers compared to those of whites. Shorter careers also mean that many do not qualify for the relatively lucrative retirement benefits associated with professional sports. This latter point has been substantiated by results from research on professional football by Best (1987).

Also at work is the belief that sport is the ticket to success for the black person in America. African Americans are generally underrepresented in most vocational areas, and role models for young people in the broad work arena are quite limited. In contrast, while black role models in sport are abundant, job opportunities in sport are quite limited. In sports to which blacks have traditionally gravitated—football, baseball, and basketball—jobs are scarce. According to Leonard (1996), NFL football employs 1,400 people per year, NBA basketball 400, and major league baseball approximately 700, yielding a total of about 2,500 available jobs. Given that white athletes will fill nearly 50% of these slots, job opportunities in professional sport are few. According to Gates (1991) there are 1,200 black athletes in all of professional sport. He further points out that there are 15 times as many black physicians and 12 times more black attorneys as black professional athletes. Harry Edwards has suggested that the likelihood that a black youth will be struck by lightning while walking down the street is greater than his or her chances of being a part of the glamour of professional sport. To put it another way, Leonard (1996) places the odds of a male between the ages of 15 and 39 achieving professional athletic status in the NBA, NFL, NHL, or major league baseball as 1 per 16,000. Leonard and Reyman (1988) indicate that the odds of entering professional sports in the United States are 4 per 100,000 for a Caucasian male; 2 per 100,000 for an African-American; and 3 per million for a Hispanic male. For females of any race taking part in a professional sport, Leonard and Reyman (1988) place the odds at 1 per 250,000. Professional sports are clearly for the chosen few—black, white, or otherwise.

The rather paradoxical result of discrimination, stacking, and the expectancy that sport can serve as a mechanism for social mobility is that a large number of exceptional African-American athletes have emerged. This excellence has been labeled as black superiority but in no way addresses the problem of what happens to those who do not excel and are left in the lurch with no sport career and few vocational opportunities elsewhere.

PSYCHOLOGICAL EXPLANATIONS. Precious few investigations have dealt with the black athlete or differences in psychological composition between blacks and whites. However, an excellent summary of a study conducted by Tutko in the early 1970s reported by Chu (1982) is most interesting. According to Chu, 300 coaches were asked to rate black and white athletes on five dimensions: orderliness, exhibitionism, impulsivity, understanding, and abasement or humility. Most coaches indicated that they expected African Americans to be low on orderliness, understanding, and abasement and high on exhibitionism and impulsivity. Similarly, Williams and Youssef (1975) found that college football coaches stereotyped blacks as possessing physical speed and quickness and excelling in achievement motivation, whereas white players were viewed as more reliable, more mentally facile, and possessing superior thinking ability.

Proportional Racial Representation Across Different Sports

Although there is considerable supportive evidence for the numerical and performance superiority of black athletes in several of the more visible sports, the picture is not so distorted if one takes the larger perspective. Snyder and Spreitzer (1989) have given us a schematic representation of African-American involvement across a number of types and levels of sports. The following figure is borrowed from the earlier Snyder and Spreitzer work, amended by data presented by Lapchick and Benedict (1993) and Yetman and Berghorn (1993).

Skewed groups are those in which black or white domination is at or near 100%; gymnastics and golf for whites and boxing and track sprints for blacks are representative. The ratio for **tilted groups** is about 65:35, with professional baseball loading in favor of whites and professional basketball for blacks. Interestingly, there is a subtle but continual trend over time showing these two sports potentially moving from tilted to skewed. Professional football is another good example of this trend; it has actually gone from balanced to tilted over the past decade. College basketball offers an interesting picture. According to data from the period 1985–1990 presented by Yetman and Berghorn, 47% of men's collegiate basketball teams are black (balanced), whereas 22% (tilted) are composed of women. Overall, the visibility of certain sports such as football, basketball, boxing, and the sprints in track tends to give a distorted image of African-American domination in sport.

SOURCES: Lapchick & Benedict (1993); Snyder & Spreitzer (1989); Yetman & Berghorn (1993).

Skewed groups in terms of racial representation in sports, groups in which black or white domination is near 100%.
Tilted groups in terms of racial representation in sports, groups in which the ratio of black or white majority is 65:35.

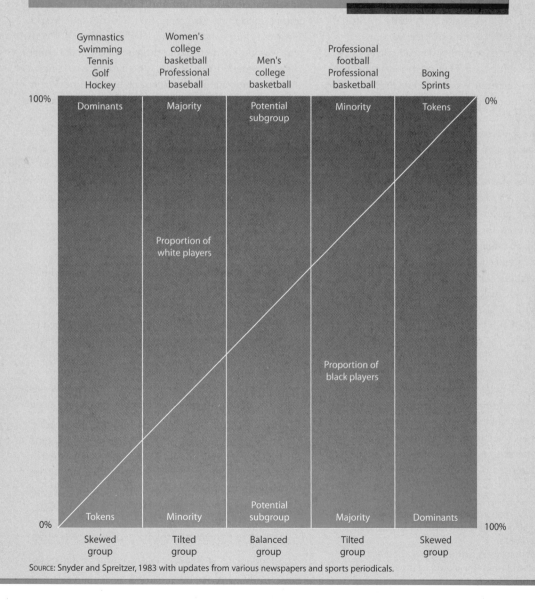

FIGURE 17.1

Proportional Black/White Representation in Selected Sports

Gymnastics Swimming Tennis Golf Hockey	Women's college basketball Professional baseball	Men's college basketball	Professional football Professional basketball	Boxing Sprints
Dominants	Majority	Potential subgroup	Minority	Tokens

Proportion of white players

Proportion of black players

Tokens	Minority	Potential subgroup	Majority	Dominants
Skewed group	Tilted group	Balanced group	Tilted group	Skewed group

SOURCE: Snyder and Spreitzer, 1983 with updates from various newspapers and sports periodicals.

Similarly, Sailes (1993) asked a sample of white and black college students to rate the intelligence, academic preparation, athletic style of play, competitiveness, physical superiority, athletic ability, and temperament of black and white collegiate athletes. Results indicated that white subjects rated black athletes as lower in intelligence and academic preparation but also more temperamental. Black subjects rated white athletes as less competitive and possessed of less athletic style. Sailes interpreted these results as supportive of the belief that black athletes are seen as physically superior but intellectually inferior to white athletes. In a study by Stone, Perry, and Darley (1997), white subjects were asked to evaluate the play of a collegiate basketball player as reported on a radio broadcast. Half were led to believe that the player in question was black and half that he was white. It was made clear to all that the player had performed quite well throughout the broadcast. These subjects, all white, perceived the black target as exhibiting less court smarts and less hustle but having more natural athletic talent. The white target was seen as possessing lots of court smarts, as a hustler, but not as especially talented. When the two targets were analyzed together, the black player was thought to be the better basketball player even though identical radio accounts were given for both targets.

To approach this issue from another angle, Stone, Lynch, Sjomeling, and Darley (1999) conducted a series of experiments with male and female college students in an attempt to look at racial stereotypes. Through a series of experimental manipulations, Stone et al. were able to demonstrate that black subjects performed significantly worse than controls on a golf task when the task was presented as diagnostic of "sports intelligence." On the other hand, white subjects performed significantly less well when the task was framed as diagnostic of "natural athletic ability." The results were seen as supporting the idea that blacks and whites alike perform less well when operating in a context of performance expectations influenced by racial stereotypes.

Self-paced activities sport activities such as pitching a baseball or games such as golf or bowling that focus on an individual player's self-initiated tasks.
Reactive tasks sport activities such as hitting a baseball or sports such as boxing in which the individual player reacts to another player's initiated task.

Worthy and Markle (1970) took an interesting slant on the issue of psychological differences with their study of self-paced versus reactive activities within sport. They theorized that whites would excel at **self-paced activities,** such as golf or bowling or pitching a baseball, and blacks would star at **reactive tasks** such as boxing, tackling in football, or hitting a baseball. Using athletes from college basketball and professional football, baseball, and basketball, Worthy and Markle concluded that blacks did excel at reactive tasks and whites at self-paced tasks. Dunn and Lupfer (1974), studying young soccer players, supported Worthy and Markle. However, Jones and Hochner (1973) criticized Worthy and Markle on methodological grounds, and Leonard (1984) suggested that if the Worthy and Markle position does not adequately account for the underrepresentation of blacks in clearly reactive activities, such as tennis, squash, fencing, auto racing, and skiing.

Other than the works reported earlier, one of the few studies aimed at black-white differences was conducted by Nation and LeUnes (1983). In a study of 55 college football players, significant differences were found on several dimensions, including the following:

1. As measured by the Profile of Mood State (POMS), white players were significantly higher in vigor ($<.05$).

2. On the California F-Scale, blacks tended to be more authoritarian than whites, though differences were not particularly pronounced.

3. In locus of control, black football players scored higher on the chance dimension ($<.05$). In view of obvious racism in both society and sport, this finding should not be particularly surprising. African Americans, athlete or nonathlete, may well be justified in their belief that life is a chance event.

4. Black football players as seen from the perspective of the Sport Mental Attitude Survey (SMAS) tend to impute responsibility for mental preparation to the coaching staff ($<.05$), feel confident about performing well even when depressed ($<.01$), are able to overlook poor past performances ($<.05$), and view physical, not psychological, factors as paramount in explaining athletic performance ($<.05$).

Given the lack of data on the validity of the SMAS, these findings must be regarded as tentative. In any event, it does appear that there may be psychological differences between white and black football players. How these possible differences translate into performance, however, remains an unanswered question.

In summary, we have only scratched the surface in our inquiry into the psychological makeup of the African-American athlete. The stark paucity of research in this area is most noticeable. Genetic or biological theories make it convenient to assert that black excellence in sport is "in the genes," but we never explain Nordic skiing superiority or Japanese gymnastics excellence in terms of a race-related gene. The overall effect of this persistent notion is to create a form of discrimination that never views African-American achievements as the product of intelligence, dedication to excellence, and long hours of arduous practice. From the sociocultural view, it appears that much of the superior performance of black athletes in selected sports can be attributed to the job opportunity structure and, often but not always, subtle discrimination that forces them into certain roles that have largely been predetermined by the long-term effects of racism. Success in these predetermined roles, in turn, reinforces the mutual perception that the black athlete is indeed superior to the white. Psychologically, much work remains in dealing with racial stereotyping in sport. It is clear that widespread stereotyping exists, and the challenge remains to identify strategies for lessening and eradicating its effects.

The Hispanic Athlete

According to Leonard (1996), *Latin, Latino* (male), and *Latina* (female) are terms referring to people from regions colonized by the Spanish and/or Portuguese to include South and Central America, the Caribbean, and Southern California, Arizona, and Texas, whereas *Hispanic* is a term referring to a diverse group of people to include Mexicans, Cubans, and Puerto Ricans. Leonard indicates that either term is acceptable but believes that *Latino* is a sensitive descriptor for this group of people. Sabo, Jansen, Tate, Duncan, and Leggett (2000) prefer the term *Hispanic* and include Hispanic Europeans (Spanish), South American, Central American, Mexican, and Latino athletes from the United States in their definition. We will adopt the stance of Sabo et al. and use the term *Hispanic* in our discussion.

Census figures indicate the Hispanic population in the United States is over 32 million and growing (Projections, 2001). Hispanic buying power is expected to triple to around $1 trillion dollars in the next few years (Weir, 1997). This sort of population growth and buying power has significance for sports organizations. Increasingly, professional sports organizations, and most particularly major league baseball, are expending greater effort to attract Hispanic athletes to their teams. The remainder of our discussion will center primarily on baseball, the sport in which Hispanics have had by far their greatest impact. By way of substantiating this point, in his study of four major league sports, Leonard (1996) had Hispanics in his sample as follows: NBA (0), NHL (7), NFL (14), MLB (112).

Clearly, there are marketing advantages to putting a winning team on the field. There is also a marketing edge in finding and employing talented Hispanic players given the population dynamics cited in the preceding paragraph. This edge is most notably true with the Florida teams, particularly the Florida Marlins, which is more than 50% Hispanic. To better serve their Hispanic clientele, a number of major league teams now spend as much as $1 million annually in Caribbean baseball academies, which are devoted to finding and training talented Hispanics (Weir, 1997). Obviously, putting a winner on the field will be attractive to fans of other racial and ethnic backgrounds as well.

In 1997, Hispanics accounted for approximately 16% of the players on opening day rosters in the major leagues (Weir, 1997). Among these players were Edgar Renteria of Colombia, Rafael Palmeiro of Cuba, Manny Ramirez and Moises Alou of the Dominican Republic, Marvin Benard of Nicaragua, Mariano Rivera of Panama, Roberto Alomar and Bernie Williams of Puerto Rico, and Wilson Alvarez of Venezuela. Altogether, the Dominican Republic had 57 players out of a total of 774 on opening day rosters in 1997. For a small country of 8 million people, producing almost 8% of the total number of major leaguers is quite a testimony to the dedication of their athletes. It is also a testimony to what good coaching, hard work, and year-round agreeable weather can accomplish.

Esteban Bellan, a Cuban, of the Troy Haymakers is generally accorded the status of being the first Hispanic to play major league baseball, in 1871. Another Cuban,

The Disappearance of the White Male Sprinter in the United States

George (1994) has written a provocative article on the diminishing role of the white male track sprinter in the United States (he chose not to deal with white female sprinters primarily because there has not been one of any consequence in this country since the late 1930s). To make his point, he provides a historical review of sprinting from the 1930s up to the mid-1990s. Most of George's conclusions were arrived at after interviewing 40 knowledgeable individuals, a veritable "Who's Who" of track and field for the last half century. Chief among his findings were:

■ Top black sprinters first emerged in the 1930s and included Eddie Tolan, Ralph Metcalfe, Jesse Owens, and Mack Robinson (brother of baseball great Jackie Robinson).

■ White sprinters such as Hal Davis, Grover Klemmer, Hubie Kerns, and Mel Patton set the standard in the 1940s. Patton ran one 100-yard dash in 1949 in which he was timed at 9.1, 9.1, and 9.0 seconds by the three timers.

■ Whites continued to dominate in the 1950s, led by runners such as Bobby Morrow, Dave Sime, Glenn Davis, Eddie Southern, J. W. Mashburn, and Thane Baker. Interestingly, Baker continued to compete well into his fifties, setting world records at all age levels in the process.

■ Dave Sime competed in the 1960 Olympics, winning a silver medal in the 100-meter race. He was the last white sprinter to represent the United States in an Olympics or World Championships in the 100 meters. Mike Larrabee won the 400-meter event in the 1964 Olympics and tied the world record in the event when he was past 30 years of age (44.90 seconds). No white American has come close to his time in the intervening 30-plus years.

■ There were a few world-class white sprinters outside the United States in the 1970s and 1980s, most notably Russian sprinter Valery Borzov and Italian sprinter Pietro Mennea, who held the world record for 200 meters at 19.72 until 1996. Marion Woronin of Poland ran 10.0 during the 1980s, and Alan Wells of the United Kingdom became the only man to run 10.30 in the 100 meters past age 35.

■ Explanations for the decline/disappearance of the white sprinter in the United States vary. Only two of the 40 experts interviewed thought the shift to be a function of black physical superiority. The phenomenon might be better explained in terms of the decline in importance of track in the white teenage subculture. Other possible factors include the fact that coaches, parents, and peers overtly and covertly push blacks toward the shorter distances and whites toward the longer ones and the apparent willingness of young blacks to "pay the price" in terms of training. The latter phenomenon appears to fly in the face of racial stereotypes that have long held that black runners are naturally fast and do not have to train hard in order to excel.

■ Two other points of interest: (1) Rick Wolhuter ran 800 meters in 1:43.4 in 1971. The fastest time for an American in that event in 1990 was 1:46.39, or 3 seconds slower. In view of advances in training, diet, footwear and other equipment along with the improved quality of track surfaces, this discrepancy is hard to explain. (2) No one is able to explain why African countries such as Kenya, Morocco, and Ethiopia produce great distance runners but few if any great sprinters whereas Ghana, Gold Coast, and Nigeria have produced largely accomplished sprinters. In five distance events ranging from 800 to 10,000 meters run at the World Championships for 1987, 1991, 1993, 1995 and the 1988 and 1992 Olympics, six African countries have accounted for two-thirds of the possible medals won; Kenya and Morocco alone account for almost one-half (44 of 90).

SOURCE: Burfoot (1992); George (1994); Patrick (1996).

Mike Gonzalez, became the first Hispanic field manager, with short stints in 1938 and 1940 as manager of the St. Louis Cardinals. In the mid-1940s, Joe Cambria, a scout for the Washington Senators, possibly changed the course of history when he informed a promising young Cuban pitching prospect that he just did not have a good enough arm to make a career in baseball; that prospect was Fidel Castro. Orestes (Minnie) Minoso, Chico Carrasquel, Luis Aparicio, Orlando Cepeda, Juan Marichal, and Roberto Clemente made an indelible impression on baseball with their accomplishments in the 1950s, 1960, and 1970s. Clemente was posthumously voted into the Hall of Fame in 1973, Marichal in 1983, Aparicio in 1984, and a newcomer with the non-Hispanic name of Rod Carew was added in 1991. A Hispanic star of the old black leagues, Martin Dihigo, was named to the Hall in 1977. Interestingly, Marichal now holds a cabinet position in the government of the Dominican Republic—that of minister of sports, physical education and recreation (Duarte, 1998).

Three prominent Hispanic families have emerged to make their mark on baseball. Brothers Felipe, Matty, and Jesus Alou all played together with the San Francisco Giants in 1963. Felipe currently manages the Montreal Expos and his son, Moises, is an All-Star, most recently with the Houston Astros. Another set of brothers, Hector, Jose, and Cirilo (Tommy) Cruz, all played major league baseball at one time or another. The most accomplished was Jose, a coach with the Houston Astros. His son, Jose, Jr., plays for the Toronto Blue Jays; another son, Enrique, is a promising prospect. Finally, Santos (Sandy) Alomar played and coached in the major leagues; his sons, Roberto and Santos, Jr., are All-Stars and play together in MLB's American League.

Mention must also be made of professional golfers Lee Trevino and Chi Chi Rodriguez, who have thrilled generations of fans with their outstanding play and showmanship. Eduardo Najera, drafted out of the University of Oklahoma by the NBA Dallas Mavericks, is already a national hero in Mexico because of his stellar play in collegiate basketball, with equally stellar play anticipated at the professional level. In professional football, now retired Anthony Munoz of the NFL Cincinnati Bengals is considered one of the greatest offensive linemen in league history. His son, Anthony, Jr., is also a highly regarded football prospect. All these athletes serve to remind us of the broad contributions Hispanic athletes have made to sport.

Little psychological research has been conducted on Hispanic athletes. The authors of this text are not aware of a single article in the professional literature that addresses the psychology of the Hispanic athlete; we do, however, know that stereotypes abound. For example, Mexico has a long and storied history in baseball, yet as of 1993 only 58 players made the major leagues, and half of those were pitchers (Beaton and Myers, 1993). Comments from scouts abound:

> There are two things that are rare in Mexicans— running speed and power. That's why the majority of Mexicans who reach the major leagues are pitchers.

> Mexicans, because of the Indian blood, can run to New York and not stop—just not fast.

> A lot of Mexicans have bad foot speed. It's a genetic-type thing. They have a different body type. Most all have good hands and good rhythm. That's why they dance so well. Rhythm is important in baseball; it means agility.

On a more positive note, in a study of American television and racial or ethnic stereotyping, Sabo et al. (2000) found that Hispanic athletes were generally described in positive terms by sports commentators at international sports events. There was a slight tendency, however, to call more attention to the physical characteristics of Hispanic athletes than was the case with African Americans and Anglos.

Recent concern has been expressed about the underrepresentation of Hispanics on U.S. Olympic teams. Menard (1996) reports data from Antonio Rios-Bustamente, a University of Arizona historian, who indicates that only 50 U.S. Hispanics have competed for the United States in Olympic competition since its reinstitution in 1896. The first was a boxer, Jose Salas, who represented the United States in the 1924 games. One barrier to Hispanic involvement is the sometimes substantial expenses associated with competing at the elite level. Another barrier, not unrelated to the first, is that many teams rely on collegiate athletes to become their team members. Hispanic underrepresentation in universities is well documented and a source of concern to college recruiters apart from athletics. Even in sports attractive to Hispanics, representation is low. For example, only one Hispanic, Augie Ojeda of the University of Tennessee, was invited to the Olympic tryouts in baseball. One other Hispanic, Lisa Fernandez, arguably the best player in the world, made the Olympic softball team. Only two were given a chance to make the 1996 Olympic soccer team. Yet another barrier to Hispanic participation in the Olympics is the absence of role models in a variety of sports, and this problem will be difficult to address if Hispanics do not participate in increasing numbers over the years.

All things considered, it appears that Hispanic athletes offer a potentially rich field for research. We know a bit about their history and culture, but virtually nothing about the psychology of this fascinating and increasingly important segment of society and sport.

The Asian-American Athlete

Sports enthusiasts are undoubtedly familiar with the accomplishments of Asian-American athletes such as gymnast Amy Chow, ice skater Tiffany Chin, tennis star Michael Chang, or figure skaters Michelle Kwan and Kristi Yamaguchi. Perhaps a less familiar name is that of Dr. Sammy Lee, a physician and the first Asian American to win an Olympic gold medal. Dr. Lee won a gold at the 1948 games in London in the 10-meter platform diving event; four years later, he won a gold in the 10-meter dive and a bronze in the 3-meter springboard. Lesser names of considerable talent represented the United States in a host of individual sports at the 1996 Olympics in Atlanta, including badminton, fencing, judo, shooting, table tennis, and weightlifting. Others were members of teams in baseball, women's soccer, women's softball, and women's volleyball. Even the young golf legend, Eldrick (Tiger) Woods, shows up on lists of Asian-American athletes because his mother was from Thailand. This said, virtually nothing has been done to examine the Asian-American sport experience from a psychological viewpoint.

Popular stereotypes of Asians have been upheld in results of a report by Sabo et al. (2000). In their analyses of how ethnic minorities are depicted in televised international sports events, Sabo and his colleagues concluded that Asians were viewed more negatively than African Americans or Anglos by sports commentators. Asians were portrayed as "obsessive hard workers, conformists, and extremely self-disciplined." A competition featuring two Asian weight lifters, promoted as the "Battle of the Asian Stars," was introduced as follows: "The serenity, the calm, that is the East. The mystique of the Orient with its mysterious inner strength. That strength today transformed into the brutal power of Olympic weightlifting where Asian strong men dominate the bantamweight division" (p. 6). Asian athletes were also represented as unemotional or reluctantly emotional. Though many of the competitors in the Sabo et al. study were Asian as opposed to Asian-American, it is likely that the stereotypes are equally applicable.

Native Asians are becoming much more a part of the American sport scene with the increasing visibility of baseball players from Japan and Korea, pitchers such as Chan Ho Park, Hideo Nomo, and Hideki Irabu. Shigeki Maruyama and Isao Aoki of Japan are top professionals in golf. Asian women are represented in professional basketball by Zheng Haixia of the Los Angeles Sparks at 6 feet, 8 inches, and Se Ri Pak from Korea is annually a leader on the women's golf tour. Professional football has Dallas Cowboy linebacker Dat Nguyen, the first person of Vietnamese extraction to play in the NFL. In addition to Nguyen, a sizable constituency of Pacific Islanders play in the NFL. All of these athletes highlight Asian involvement in sport. In alliance with the outstanding Asian Americans mentioned earlier, these athletes will help elevate sport to new heights among the Asian-American population in the United States. Sport psychology should be marching alongside, trying to arrive at a better understanding of the Asian-American sport experience.

The Native American Athlete

Despite a wonderful and illustrious history, the Native American has not had much impact on sport in the United States. Certainly, the accomplishments of the great Jim Thorpe of the Sac and Fox tribe are legendary. Thorpe was a great Olympian in track and an outstanding player in the NFL and major league baseball, and his accomplishments led to his being named the top athlete of the first 50 years of the twentieth century by the Associated Press. Another outstanding athlete in the early 1900s was Tom Longboat, an Onandaga. Longboat, among other accomplishments, won the Boston Marathon in 1907, setting a record for the event of 2:24.24. In hockey, George Armstrong, an Ojibway with an Irish-Scottish father, had an outstanding 21-year career with the Toronto Maple Leafs of the NHL. Currently, Notah Begay, who played collegiate golf at Stanford with Tiger Woods, is perhaps the most visible Native American on the sport scene. Begay, a mix of Navajo, San Felipe, and Isleta tribal blood, is one of the leading money winners on the PGA tour and a spokesperson for the "Sport Warrior Golf Program," which is dedicated to furthering the representation of Native American youth in the game of golf. Little if any mention is made in the literature about a Native American female with a major impact on the sport scene.

A major contribution to sport is found in Native American history. The increasingly popular game of lacrosse owes its origins to the tribes in the Great Lakes area as well as along the Saint Lawrence River. In its original form, as described by early settlers in North America, lacrosse was played with as few as 100 and as many as 1,000 players on a field 500 yards to a half-mile long with no sidelines. Games lasted two or three days with players roaming far afield. Jesuit missionaries from France and white settlers in Montreal took up the game and popularized it. The first collegiate lacrosse championship was sponsored by the NCAA and was held in 1971. Now over 500 colleges and 1400 high schools sponsor the sport for men and 100 colleges and 150 high schools do so for women.

One group attempting to propel Native Americans into the mainstream of U.S. sport is the Native American Sports Council (NASC), whose mission is to promote athletic excellence and wellness in Native American communities through sports and wellness programs. Much of its work is done in conjunction with the U.S. Olympic Committee. In 1996, NASC supported eight Native Americans in their pursuit of positions on various U.S. Olympic teams. One, Cheri Becerra, represented NASC and her country by winning a bronze medal in the 800 meters in track, thus becoming the first Native American female to win an Olympic medal.

Consistent with what has been reported concerning other minorities in this chapter, little research has been conducted on the Native American sport experience. It is hoped that this situation will change in the near future.

THE HIGH-RISK-SPORT PARTICIPANT

Another fascinating area of sport competition is the arena in which high risks of injury or death play an integral part. **Hish-risk sport** includes sport parachuting (skydiving), hang gliding, rock climbing, and scuba diving. Some would argue that football and boxing should be included as high-risk sports in view of the injuries and deaths associated with them. Granting that any classification system is arbitrary, we shall confine our discussion to the four activities of sky diving, hang gliding, rock climbing, and scuba diving. These sports were chosen because there is consensus that they are risky pursuits and at least some literature exists about them.

One way of conceptualizing high-risk activities is to ask professionals to rate a given set of risk sports. One such ranking is provided by Tangen-Foster and Lathen (1983). These investigators sent a questionnaire to chairs of 120 physical education departments, primarily in large universities, asking a number of questions about their involvement in courses that would be considered a part of the "risk revolution" going on in America; 73 responses were returned and analyzed. Ninety-six percent of the respondents viewed parachuting as "high" or "extraordinary risk," followed by 92 percent for hang gliding, and 64 percent for rock climbing. Scuba diving was viewed as risky by 32 percent of the respondents.

Another way to measure the relative perception of a sport's dangerousness is to ask potential participants. Pedersen (1997) did just this, asking 444 college men and women to rate eight risk activities. The order of perceived dangerousness isolated in the Pedersen study

---

High-risk sport sports such as skydiving, hang gliding, and rock climbing in which the high risk of injury or death plays a prominent role.

was: motorcycle racing first, followed by cliff jumping, hang gliding, sky diving, bungee jumping, rock climbing, scuba diving, and skiing. Pedersen also asked his subjects to rate the appeal of each of the activities and their likelihood of taking part in one or more of them. Likelihood of participation turned out to be directly rated to appeal and inversely related to perceived risk.

Sport Parachuting/Sky Diving

USPA Secretary Killed While Making Stunt Jump

On Friday, Jan. 14 [1983], Joe Svec, 35, secretary of the United States Parachute Association, was killed in a tragic skydiving accident during filming of a stunt sequence for *The Right Stuff*, a film version of Tom Wolfe's best-selling novel about test pilots and astronauts.

Skydiving cameraman Rande Deluca of Big Sky Films was jumping with Svec at the time, and reported seeing no problems. Deluca quit filming at approximately 3500 feet and turned and tracked away to open a distance away from and above where Svec planned to open. Svec was seen by Doc Johnson, an experienced jumper, to turn face-to-earth (he had been facing upward, flying on his back during the filming sequence) and fall flat and stable until impact. Despite very careful analysis and medical tests, no explanation has been found for the accident. The sequence being filmed depicts famed test pilot Chuck Yeager (first man to break the sound barrier) ejecting from an experimental aircraft. During the fatal jump, however, Svec was wearing no particularly cumbersome or otherwise "odd" gear (except perhaps his helmet) which might have inhibited his movements or reactions.

Svec had achieved meteoric success during his six years as a skydiver and USPA Board member. He began as a well-known figure in the Houston area, at the Spaceland Center and other Texas drop zones. He was elected as a write-in candidate for Conference Director in 1978 and published the very popular *Southwest Swooper* newsletter, which featured "Don DePloy" who had an opinion about almost every subject in the skydiving world, cleverly drawn and cleverly written. Svec became a National Director in 1980 (when Eric Pehrson succeeded him in the Conference Director slot) and was elected USPA's secretary that same year.

RW meet director of the National Championships in 1980, Svec also competed on various teams and served as Leader of the U.S. National Skydiving Ram which won gold medals "across the board" at the World Meet in Zephyrhills in 1981.

As his friends would tell you, Joe Svec was truly a "Renaissance man," with a tremendous collection of skills and achievements. Little known, for example, was his generosity: he funded other people's skydiving teams when they ran out of money in order to permit them to compete in the Nationals and in world competitions. He was a true hero—he held some sort of record as Vietnam's luckiest combat veteran, having returned to combat repeatedly (with and without the Army's permission) after having acquired seven Purple Hearts that the government knew about and a total of more than 20 battle wounds. He served with the Special Forces in their most secret and difficult assignments, where he operated almost exclusively behind the enemy lines for months at a time.

When finally his wounds got to him, he was MED-EVAC'ed to Tripler General Hospital in Honolulu, where he stayed after his recovery and became a successful political cartoonist for the *Honolulu Star Bulletin*. His interest in politics and his wry humor combined to help him create a series of memorable cartoons and satirical articles, some of which appeared in the pages of *Parachutist*.

Joe was principally involved in making El Capitan jumping legal (briefly, in 1980) and led the first Park Service-approved jump off the famed cliff. Perhaps one of his greatest disappointments was when a short time later actions by others caused Yosemite's policy to declare cliff jumping out of bounds. More recently Svec became a stunt jumper for the "Fall Guy" television show and this led directly to his commitment to "stand in" for one of the actors in the dangerous sequences to be filmed for the cinema version of Wolfe's best-seller.

Joe was buried by family and friends in a somber ceremony on a wind-swept afternoon on Tuesday, Jan. 18 in Houston.

(Ottley, 1983, p. 35)

USPA President Larry Bagley led a delegation of USPA officials who joined with hundreds of friends at the ceremony in the cemetery chapel. "This is one of the biggest services we've ever had," was the comment of one of the officials present.

The preceding account points out the perils of parachuting. If an experienced jumper like Joe Svec is at risk, what do the statistics tell us about the novice in the sport? Unofficial data (Skydiving Fatalities, 2000) indicates that fatalities involving skydivers for the past five years were as follows: 1996 (39), 1997 (33), 1998 (48), 1999 (29), and the first part of 2000 (18). Of the 18 fatalities for the first part of 2000, one jumper had over 5,000 jumps. His death was attributed to equipment failure. Another jumper with over 500 jumps apparently lost track of altitude while trying to fix a malfunction and did not get his parachute open in time (at 2,000 feet a jumper only has 11 seconds until impact with the ground). A third fatality came about when one jumper collided with another in a team practice. He was knocked unconscious and died of cardiac arrest.

Overall, one estimate drawn from statistics reported from 35 countries including the United States (Skydiving Statistics, 2000) indicates that there is one fatality per 65,000 jumps worldwide each year. One thousand more people are killed each year in boating accidents or by bee stings than die in skydiving (Skydiving Statistics, 2000). While these sorts of data are reassuring, there is no question that risk is involved in skydiving. Given the danger, what makes skydiving attractive to so many people? The ensuing discussion attempts to shed light on at least some aspects of this perplexing and difficult question.

Physiologically, there is no question that the jumper is in a state of arousal. Fenz and Epstein (1967), Fenz and Jones (1972), Hammerton and Tickner (1968), and Powell and Verner (1982) have variously reported elevations in heart rate (HR), galvanic skin response (GSR), respiration rate, anxiety, and self-reports of fear responses in both novice and experienced parachutists. In the Powell and Verner research, 20 naive college-level parachutists were studied. Using the State–Trait Anxiety Inventory (STAI) as a means of measuring anxiety, Powell and Verner found a correlation of .78 between performance as first-time parachutists and fear rating, heart rate change, and state and trait anxiety, thereby accounting for 61 percent of the variance in performance. These novice parachutists were well below the mean on trait anxiety when compared with 484 undergraduate students reported on in the test manual. Heart rate change between control and jump conditions rose 81%, similar to the 96% increase reported by Fenz and Epstein. Additionally, Powell and Verner found that low state anxiety is associated with better performance than is high anxiety. Finally, they make a case for good training methods as a means of reducing both competitive anxiety and, more important, injuries and deaths.

Beaumaster, Knowles, and MacLean (1978), in a study of the sleep patterns of 27 skydivers, found differences in anxiety of experienced versus novice jumpers, with the latter scoring higher on an anxiety measure. No differences between the two groups on the Neuroticism and Extraversion scales of the Eysenck Personality Inventory (EPI) were found, nor were either of the groups dissimilar to student sample norms reported in the test manual.

On the psychological dimension, parachutists are viewed variously as sensation seekers (Zuckerman, 1971; Zuckerman, Kolin, Price, and Zoob, 1964), as "spontaneous dissociaters" (Cancio, 1991), or as stress seekers (Johnsgard, Ogilvie, & Merritt, 1975). A study by Hymbaugh and Garrett (1974) lends support to the sensation-seeking notion. Twenty-one skydivers were compared with 21 nondivers on the Zuckerman Sensation Seeking Scale (SSS); the divers scored significantly higher than did the nondivers. In a similar vein, Johnsgard et al. studied 43 male members of the USPA, all of whom had made at least 1,000 jumps. Data gathered from the Edwards Personal Preference Schedule (EPPS), the Minnesota Multiphasic Personality Inventory (MMPI), and the Sixteen Personality Factor Questionnaire (16PF) were analyzed. On the EPPS, parachutists demonstrated high needs for achievement, dominance, exhibition, courage, and heterosexual expression. Conversely, they had little need for deference or order. This psychometric composite gives us a picture of the parachutist as achievement oriented, desirous of being the center of attention, needing change with little concern for orderliness, and being independent and unconventional. MMPI results showed mild elevations on the Mania and Psychopathic Deviate Scales, findings similar to those of Fenz and Brown (1958). These MMPI elevations would suggest that parachutists are highly motivated and unconventional individuals, both of which also came out in the EPPS data. Results from the 16PF showed the USPA members tested to be quite intelligent, happy-go-lucky, expedient, and not particularly influenced by group dictates.

Overall, Johnsgard et al. create an image of the parachutist as an intelligent, independent, achievement-oriented, and generally well adjusted individual, an image contrary to that provided but not necessarily supported by Ogilvie (1974b), who summarizes some psychologically unhealthy stereotypes of skydivers and other stress seekers. According to these stereotypes, sensation seekers do the things they do as a means of fear displacement, as supermasculinity ploys, or because of an unconscious death wish. The available data simply do not support such assertions.

Hang Gliding

The following obituary serves to illustrate the risk involved in the sport of hang gliding.

Obituary: Ian Middleton Pryde

Ian Pryde died as the result of a Gliding accident on the Dunstan Mountains range, 24th January, 1984, whilst competing in the New Zealand National Championships. Ian was an achiever, and only recently expressed the opinion that one must live each day as if it were a bonus. That is exactly how he lived his life.

Dedicated to Gliding from the early sixties, Ian in his younger days was an Olympic yachtsman of world renown.

His extreme competitiveness, developed in yachting, was carried on into Gliding. He flew for New Zealand in the 1972 and 1976 World Championships, was New Zealand Open Champion in 1976 and winner of the N.Z. 15 Metre class in 1981.

He first crewed for a New Zealand pilot at a World Championship in Poland in 1968, and was a consistent supporter for New Zealand at almost every World event since.

An extremely successful businessman, Ian was a Papakura City Councillor for 20 years, was Chairman of the St. Stephens Maori Boys' and Victoria Maori Girls' Colleges for 12 years. A Rotarian and a member of the Masonic Lodge.

One of the instigators of the Matamata Soaring Centre, he steered that Gliding Organisation into a very strong position. As President of the Auckland Gliding Club, and by his very inspiration in land and other deals, he directed the club into its own debt free airfield, almost in the middle of the city. He lifted the morale of the club to the point where it is now the strongest in New Zealand, and the Drury airfield will always be a living tribute to his drive, energy, ability and dedication.

Many a New Zealand Sailplane owner has Ian to thank for rebuilds to accident damaged sailplanes. His ability with his hands and his knowledge of fibre-glass construction will truly be missed. He was always very willing to help an owner in trouble. At his own time and expense he went to Germany to learn how to do it. Many who now have the skills in New Zealand have been taught by Ian.

Always outspoken, always making reasoned sense, he had a failing in not dotting all the "i's" and crossing the "t's" but we all accepted this, a small price for the magnificent "plus's" he scored for New Zealand and its Gliding fraternity.

He would achieve most things. I think he had vague dreams of sailing off into the sunset in a great ocean racer, but that was not to be. His great ambition was for a New Zealander to turn in an exceptional performance at a World Gliding Championship.

The whole New Zealand movement extends their sympathy to his wife Ruth and to Philip and Annette. We all share your loss.

(Finlayson, 1984, p. 21)

This obituary notice, taken in 1984 from the *New Zealand Gliding Kiwi*, the official publication of that country's hang-gliding association, serves as a reminder of the dangers inherent in the sport. Further substantiation of this point is seen in the fact that *Kiwi,* in addition to its periodical obituary column, also routinely contains separate sections known as "Safety Officers Column" and "Sailplane Accident Briefs." The most prominent American publication for gliding enthusiasts, *US Hang-Glider,* is similar to *Kiwi* in many respects but has discontinued the routine reporting of accidents and deaths for fear of alienating or scaring potential enthusiasts.

Brannigan and McDougall (1983) painted a less than rosy picture of the hazards involved in hang gliding, pointing out that the risk of death in the sport probably exceeds the suicide rate for all ages in Canada and the death by automobile rate of young American males. Brannigan and McDougall point to a death rate in hang gliding of 65 per 100,000 and also are of the opinion that hang gliding accident statistics are undoubtedly understated. Another report suggests that there is one death per 2,308 hang gliding flights (Skydiving Statistics, 2000).

As with sport parachuting, a strong positive correlation exists between experience and accident rates. Even so, some notable participants feel that hang gliding is misrepresented in terms of risk. For example, D. G. M. Yuill, a neurologist and a member of the British Hanggliding Association, is quoted as follows: "I believe this sport is no more dangerous than horse riding, rock climbing, potholing, or motorcycle racing, and with training may probably be rendered less hazardous than any of these sports" (Willard, 1978, p. 26).

Outside the observational data reported by Brannigan and McDougall, little psychological research has been done with hang gliders. Brannigan and McDougall observed seven groups of hang gliders from southern Ontario and upper New York and Pennsylvania in an effort to better understand what motivates hang gliders. Several tentative conclusions were drawn, including the following:

1. Hang gliders tend to be single male Caucasians in their mid-twenties.

2. They tend to come from every walk of fife, though students seem to be most frequent participants.

3. Most get into the activity through a friend.

4. Being a member of the subculture is a powerful force in maintaining their involvement.

5. Most believe that hang gliding has its risks, but they do not view it as a dangerous activity.

Rock climbing justifiably has a spot as a risk sport. The various risk sports are becoming increasingly popular worldwide.
© Copyright 1999 PhotoDisc, Inc.

6. "A rush," "a blast," "visceral pleasure," and "a high" are often used to describe the experience.

7. A number of participants are able to turn their interest into a vocation as manufacturer, teacher, dealer, designer, test pilot, photographer, or writer.

8. People who give up the sport do so primarily because of accidents and secondarily because of job demands or marital considerations.

Rock Climbing

Fatalities on Mount Everest, 1992

Doug Hansen, a postal worker from Renton, Wash., died sharing a snow hole with Rob Hall, a

The Exhilaration of Hang Gliding

The exhilaration of hang gliding is captured in the words of one devotee, as quoted in Dedera (1975, pp. 10, 14):

> Forcing an aluminum and Dacron wing that's twenty feet wide into a stiff breeze is work. I heave my body weight into the shoulder harness, and trot heavily toward the cliff edge. Two, three . . . four. The sharp red point of the kite that forms my protective awning dips with my final lunge. I stagger over the cliff, carrying my glider awkwardly. And suddenly, without warning, I materialize as a graceful swan. I rotate my hips back on the swing seat, stretch my arms forward and attempt to trim the kite. Up comes the nose, centers on the horizon and stays there. Fifty feet off the ground, and like a fledgling sparrow, I'm flying. Me. An uncoordinated humanoid, blessed with only a rudimentary aptitude the dumbest pelican takes for granted. I'm flying. Leonardo da Vinci would be proud of me. So would Kent Fraunenberger who lived on my block and broke his hand when we were twelve by jumping off the garage roof with a yellow Hi-Flier tied under each arm. Like every other kid who ever dreamed of escaping the mundane by just flying away from it all, I'm serenely gliding over the Southern California landscape, lost in euphoria. A twist of the hips rolls me right. A twitch of the arms, and I yaw left slightly. Pull back, and we dive alarmingly for the earth, sacrificing height for necessary speed. Aims forward, nose up, and we climb into a stall condition. . . . To fly, with no protective layer between you and the elements. To fly, really, like a bird. Dependent solely upon your own instincts, your own reflexes, your own skills to sustain effervescent flight. It's something you can't ever give up . . . natural, innocent, cleansing flight. You, and the kite, the wind and the sun, and the soft gray hills. And far away down the valley floor, Lake Elsinore, beckoning for you to fly to her once more.

guide who led a team from New Zealand; they were found beyond the reach of rescuers. Scott Fischer, a veteran guide from Seattle, trailed his party down from the summit, sat down exhausted, and was trapped by the storm. Yasuko Namba, an experienced Japanese climber died before reaching a camp's shelter; guide Andy Harris wandered from camp and died. Three members of the Indo-Tibetan Border Police, Tsewang Paljor, Dorjee Morup and T. Samania, disappeared after climbing the sheer northern face.

Excerpt from 1996 *Newsweek* article detailing fatalities associated with climbing Mount Everest

Five other climbers in this party survived, though not without repercussions. Seaborn Beck Weathers, a physician, paid $65,000 to make the climb but lost most of his right hand and suffered severe frostbite on his face and elsewhere. In response to why anyone would pay $65,000 to put his life on the line on Mount Everest, Gates and Miller (1996, p. 58) state: "It's chic now to say you're a mountain climber. For the fitness-obsessed, it's a quantum leap beyond the New York Marathon; for corporate Napoleons in search of new worlds to conquer, it is the ultimate hostile takeover."

A true test of the limits to which the human body and spirit can be pushed is found among those who have tried to conquer Mount Everest, the world's tallest peak. In searching for the universal reason for such a risky undertaking, the famous British mountaineer, George Mallory, uttered succinctly, "Because it's there." Though undoubtedly unrepresentative of the totality of rock climbers, those who have been on Everest can give us insights into the thrill and the dangers of such an undertaking. Accounts from elite rock climbers, or mountaineers as they sometimes refer to themselves, remind us of the awe and wonderment as well as the dangers of a very perilous enterprise:

A climber's memory is a golden sieve through which harsh realities slip away. Today, five months later, I vividly recall beautiful sunrises, but stormy days seem as distant as my childhood. (Rowell, 1983, p. 102)

I was on Mount Everest for 50 days before I felt real fear. It came suddenly while climbing a stretch I'd already been up and down eight times. Blood rushed through my head as I looked between my legs down a white wall that dropped thousands of feet to a glacier.

Looking down in itself didn't bother me. Twenty-seven seasons of mountaineering has conditioned me against freaking out simply because I am in the middle of a sheer wall. Just under my skin, however, I have the instinctive fear that all humans share: not a direct fear of heights as many of us wrongly suppose, but it is a more basic fear of being out of control in any potentially dangerous place. Confidence in technique and equipment assuages my fear on Everest, just as confidence in pilot and craft calms most people's fears in a 747 at an altitude even higher than the mountain's 29,028 feet. (Rowell, 1983, p. 90)

I came face to face with Everest three times in four years. I saw the sun rise from the gates of heaven, and I survived. I feel good about my future and glad for the camaraderie I experienced on Everest with my friends. Even the sunrise pictures turned out beautifully. As Anderson recently wrote, "I never knew footsteps or a friendship meant so much." (Webster, 1989, p. 74)

Mountaineers say that descending a mountain is harder and more dangerous than going up. Nowhere is this more true than on Everest. We stumbled back down to our tents at South Col. Even here there was absolutely no chance of our being rescued; our support team was too far away to reach us, we had no radio and rescue helicopters cannot function above 21,000 feet. Nor did we have Sherpas to make tea and soup, carry our packs or otherwise assist us. We were utterly exhausted and very much alone. We had existed for two days in what climbers call the Death Zone—any elevation above 26,200 feet.

For the first time I wasn't sure I would survive the climb. Oxygen deprivation, tiredness and the lack of food, water and sleep made us feel incredibly lethargic. We began to live in slow motion. . . . We were ready to head for home. The question was, Could we still get there? (Webster, 1989, p. 71)

In an article in *Sports Illustrated*, Rowell (1983, p. 99) has suggested that the popular conception of mountain climbers is that they are often loners but indicates that the team with which he ascended Mount Everest in 1983 was made up of rather gifted athletes:

Either the aura that surrounds the world's highest mountain attracts competitive types, or in our selection process we unconsciously looked for the strong drive inherent in athletes. . . . Craig had been a nationally ranked skier until he shattered a leg. Graber, who played tailback in college for Claremont-Mudd, was the team's most valuable player as a senior in 1973. Momb had been a top freestyle skier and a nationally ranked motocross racer. Harold Knutson had won masters-class marathons. Tackle had been an all-state football player. Jon Reveal had been a nationally ranked ski racer at thirteen. Steve McKinney had held the world's speed record on skis for seven of the last nine years.

Demographically, climbers in one study were predominantly Anglo, male, and professionals in their vocation (Freischlag & Freischlag, 1993); the last finding was also supported in a study of elite climbers by Levenson (1990). Interestingly, Freischlag and Freischlag found their subjects, 102 climbers from California, to be unremarkable in terms of physical attributes. Their climbers were 70 inches tall, weighed 163 pounds, and had 15.8 percent body fat, all measurements well within the average for males in general.

In a study of 57 rock climbers from Montana and Washington, Feher, Meyers, and Skelly (1998) were able to isolate a psychological profile of their subjects that indicated that they were similar for the most part to individual and team athletes in a variety of sports. Of particular significance is the fact that they demonstrated an Iceberg Profile reminiscent of Morgan's conception of the elite athlete discussed in Chapter 16. There is also evidence to suggest that mountain climbers (and other risk athletes) are sensation seekers, and we shall entertain that discussion in some detail shortly.

Scuba Diving

The following accounts from *Undercurrent,* a publication for serious divers, underscore the risky nature of scuba diving, a sport that has averaged 78 deaths annually in the United States during the 1990s. It is only fair to point out, however, that the sport averaged 130 deaths per year during the 1970s. Clearly, better training and improvements in diving equipment have been instrumental in making scuba diving less dangerous.

A U.S. Navy cruiser, the *San Diego,* sunk by the German Navy during World War I off Fire Island, New York, is one of the most popular wreck diving sites in the Northeast. A double fatality occurred there in October of 1989. The two male victims were both twenty-nine years of age. One was a diving instructor with many hours of wreck diving experience, and the second had a considerable amount of diving experience on wrecks in shallower water. Their bodies were found deep within the wreck in separate compartments and it can only be guessed that they were the victims of silt obscuring their vision and preventing them from finding the way out of the ship. Two more deaths occurred in 1990, bringing the number of deaths on this wreck since 1975 to seven.

In Jamaica, two U.S. citizens died while scuba diving with their Jamaican divemaster and six other Americans. The group intended to go no deeper than 70 feet on a drift dive. Missing the intended ledge, the entire dive party reached a depth of 160 feet. Inexperience and nitrogen narcosis resulted in three divers continuing to well over 200 feet. An experienced member of the dive group rescued one diver who had lost consciousness. The other two divers apparently continued to sink and were never recovered. The Jamaican divemaster died, as well.

Again, as we noted in parachuting, hang gliding, and rock climbing, the dangers of high-risk-sport participation are ever present. Much of the research on scuba diving, a sport involving some 2 million enthusiasts, has centered on the relationship between anxiety and various aspects of scuba training and performance.

Griffiths and his associates (Griffiths, Steel, & Vaccaro, 1978, 1979, 1982; Griffiths, Steel, Vaccaro, & Karpman, 1981) have provided us with a fair amount of information. Summing up all four of the Griffiths et al. studies, the following conclusions seem warranted:

1. The subjects were college students or YMCA divers, and all were novices.

2. The State–Trait Anxiety Inventory (STAI) was used in every case.

In the 1978 work, 29 beginning divers (college students) had resting trait and state anxiety scores significantly below college norms for the scale, but moderate increases in state anxiety were noted during the testing phase. The authors did note that anxiety levels were not sufficiently elevated to yield a meaningful indicator of stress that could ultimately prove to be life threatening in an underwater crisis situation. Related to this, Egstrom and Bachrach (1971) indicate that most underwater deaths are caused by panic. In their second study, Griffiths and associates used 62 beginning scuba divers from the YMCA training program. Four performance indicators were used, and no relationship was found between performance and anxiety on simple tasks. Such was not the case on more complex tasks, however, thereby indicating that anxiety does in fact interfere with satisfactory performance of complex activities.

The 1981 study was conducted with 50 college scuba divers who were subsequently broken into three groups, one receiving biofeedback ($n = 19$), one performing meditation ($n = 14$), and a control group ($n = 17$). Each group was asked after receiving the treatment condition to undertake an underwater assembly task borrowed from the U.S. Navy. Neither treatment group performed better than the control group, but state and trait anxiety as measured by the STAI were both significantly related to performance. In the 1982 research, the investigators chose to use the S–R Inventory of General Trait Anxiousness (Endler and Okada, 1975); the STAI subjects were beginning scuba students. Based on results obtained, the authors concluded that the S–R Inventory is more useful than the STAI trait measure in predicting anxiety prior to underwater testing. It was also determined that respiration rate is an effective measure of underwater stress in beginning divers, something also suggested by Bachrach (1970).

Two other studies have attempted to look at personality variables other than anxiety. One, by Weltman and Egstrom (1969), looked at personal autonomy as measured by the Pensacola Z-scale in scuba trainees at the University of California at Los Angeles. The Z-scale failed to differentiate trainees from two other campus groups (engineering students and Peace Corps volunteers), nor did it separate successful trainees and dropouts.

In the second study by Heyman and Rose (1979), male and female college divers were administered the STAI, the Sensation-Seeking Scale, Rotter's I–E Scale, and the Bem Sex Role Inventory (BSRI) (Bem, 1974). Overall, scuba participants were lower on trait anxiety, more adventurous, more internal, and more masculine in sex role orientation than student norms for these dimensions. Also, state and trait anxiety was not related to performance, internals made more dives than externals, and, surprisingly, there was an inverse relationship between sensation seeking and depth of dives. Intuitively, one might expect sensation seekers to dive deeper, but such was not the case.

Correlates of High-Risk-Sport Participation

At least two other correlates of participation in parachuting, hang gliding, rock climbing, and scuba diving deserve attention, and they are sensation seeking and birth order effects.

Sensation seeking is a construct first advanced by Zuckerman and associates (Zuckerman, Kolin, Price, & Zoob, 1964). Zuckerman et al. believed that psychological theories proposing that the human organism is basically a drive or tension reducer were limited; rather, they proposed "optimal stimulation," which takes into account large individual variations in the need for stimulus reduction—thus, the concept of sensation seeking.

The fifth revision of Zuckerman's test came out in 1984 (Zuckerman, 1984). The various editions of the

Sensation Seeking Scale (SSS) seek to measure four subdimensions of sensation seeking. They are:

1. *Thrill and Adventure Seeking (TAS):* the desire to engage in thrill seeking, risk, adventurous activities such as parachuting, hang gliding, mountain climbing, and so forth

2. *Experience Seeking (ES):* seeking arousal through mind, sense, and nonconforming lifestyle

3. *Disinhibition (Dis):* release through partying, drinking, gambling, and sex, generally regarded as more traditional sensation-seeking outlets

4. *Boredom Susceptibility (BS):* aversion to repetition, routine, and boring people; restlessness when escape from tedium not possible

The SSS has been linked to any number of psychological constructs outside sport (Zuckerman, 1971), and it has generally been a valid assessment tool within the sporting context, particularly in studies of risk athletes. As stated earlier, Hymbaugh and Garrett (1974) found skydivers to score significantly higher in sensation seeking than a matched sample of nondivers. Straub (1982) studied male athletes who participated in hang gliding, automobile racing, and bowling. As might be expected, the bowlers scored significantly lower (.01 level) on the total score and two of the four subdimensions of the SSS when compared with the other two groups. In response to the question, "Do you consider your sport to be a high-risk activity?" 67% of the hang gliders, 50% of the auto racers, and none of the bowlers said yes, though 63% of the hang gliders and 41% of the auto racers reported having been injured at some point in their careers. Similarly, Zarevski, Marusic, Zolotic, Bunjevac, and Vukosav (1998) reported significant differences on three of the four SSS subscales in their comparison of high-risk participants (parachuting, diving, gliding, speleology, and alpinism) with low-risk athletes (rowing, bowling, and table tennis).

Sensation seeking a channel by which the human organism seeks to reduce tension via "optimal stimulation."
Sensation Seeking Scale (SSS) Zuckerman's standardized test that measures four subdimensions of sensation seeking: thrill and adventure seeking, experience seeking, disinhibition, and boredom susceptibility.

Several studies have been conducted with rock climbers. Robinson (1985) contrasted sensation-seeking scores of 30 elite rock climbers (ERCs) with SSS normative data reported by Zuckerman; the ERCs were significantly higher in total Sensation Seeking (SS), Thrill and Adventure Seeking (TAS), and Experience Seeking (ES) than were the normative subjects. Similarly, Rossi and Cereatti (1993) compared four kinds of mountain athletes (free climbers, alpinists, speleologists, and ski jumpers) with control samples of nonathletes and high school physical education students. Significant differences in the predicted direction were found between mountain athletes and controls on all SSS scales except Boredom Susceptibility (BS). Interestingly, all mountain athlete groups scored significantly higher than rock climbers on TAS. A third and novel approach to examining sensation seekers was undertaken by Levenson (1990), who studied antisocial risk takers (drug offenders), adventurous risk takers (rock climbers), and prosocial risk takers (policemen and firemen). The rock climbers scored significantly higher on TAS than did the other two groups. Levenson further concluded that the SSS results along with other measures used seem to suggest that the three groups studied are characterized by different psychological composition and differing approaches to risk taking. A more recent study of Everest climbers by Breivik (1996) lends support to previous research in finding that the climbers scored significantly higher on three of the four SSS scales when compared to scores from samples of sports performers drawn from a university in Norway and military recruits.

Another correlate of risk sport is **birth order effects.** The relationship of birth order to a variety of human behaviors has been a popular area of investigation, and sport has not been exempt from this line of research. When Nisbett (1968) asked a group of judges to rank the most dangerous sports offered at Columbia University, football, soccer, and rugby were so designated. He then asked nearly 3,000 undergraduates from Columbia, Yale, and Penn State (about 2,400 were from Columbia) and a sample of professional athletes from the New York Mets

(baseball) and the New York Giants (football) to respond to a questionnaire on birth order. Firstborns were over-represented in all cases, but they were less likely to have participated in high-risk sports. Nisbett says: "The under-representation of firstborns in the dangerous sports is not a pronounced effect but it is a consistent one. In high school, college, and professional athletics, firstborns are less likely to play the high-risk sports" (p. 352).

In a similar vein, Longstreth (1970) asked students enrolled in two semesters of child development to respond to a seven-point continuum question in which Response 1 was "Physically very conservative at age 12; tended to avoid dangerous activities and rough games; preferred sedentary activities" and Response 7 was "Physically very daring at age 12; never turned down a physical challenge; always ready for rough and tumble with plenty of bruises and cuts to show for it." Like Nisbett, Longstreth found firstborns overrepresented in his classes but underrepresented at the "rough and tumble" end of the continuum; 59% of firstborns rated themselves at the conservative end of the scale. Sex differences were noticeable, with 62% of the males and 41% of the females scoring a 5, 6, or 7 on Longstreth's question.

Yiannakis (1976) compared 67 firstborn college students with 99 laterborns concerning their preference for such sports as judo, football, lacrosse, skydiving, ski jumping, and motorcycle racing. In general, firstborns tended to avoid the high-risk activities. Casher (1977), in a study of 127 Ivy League varsity athletes, lends strong support to previous findings with her observation that participation in dangerous sports is significantly related to birth order. In addition to the general underrepresentation of firstborns, Casher found a statistically significant number of thirdborns in dangerous sports. Nixon (1981, p. 12), in a study of Vermont collegians, found a "weak tendency for male firstborns to be less attracted than male laterborns to playing risky sports." Nixon also found that males showed a pronounced preference over females for participating in or watching risky sports.

One study finding no relationship between birth order effects and risk sport participation was conducted by Seff, Gecas, and Frey (1992). Seff et al. analyzed results of a mail survey of 436 members of the United States Parachute Association and found no relationship between the two variables whatsoever. Demographi-

---

Birth order effects in high-risk sport, the relationship of birth order to an individual's inclination to engage in dangerous sports.

cally, their sample was middle class, white (95%), male (87%), young (35 years), and college educated (45% had at least some college and 28% had graduated). Half were married and two-thirds had no children.

Despite the preceding disclaimer, birth order effects appear to have relevance for our understanding of risk sports; firstborns consistently appear to be underrepresented. Most of the writers mentioned here account for this apparent underrepresentation in terms of childrearing practices, the consensus being that firstborns are often treated differently from subsequent children within the family. Firstborns may have their needs met in more conventional ways, whereas laterborn children might be forced to resort to nontraditional activities in order to achieve a measure of success and parental and peer approval. Though speculative, this seems to be the implication of the most accepted explanation.

There is some indication that the risk experience is different for females than for males. Byrnes, Miller, and Schafer (1999) conducted a meta-analysis of 150 studies of risk behavior and concluded, in general, that males are more likely to engage in risky behaviors than are females. Byrnes and his colleagues looked at more conventional risk behaviors such as unprotected sex, excessive speed while driving, drug use, and so forth, but it is likely that their conclusions have relevance for the sport context. A second study of gender differences among adolescent males and females by Kerr and Vlaminkx (1997) indicated that staring down a sheer rock face was a more stressful experience for females than for males. These researchers indicated that the gender differences in perception of risk experience might be explained by a biological predisposition arising from evolutionary origins or, alternatively from peer pressure and socialization practices that encourage males to take more risks and report less pressure or stress in the process.

SUMMARY

1. The minority athlete and the high-risk-sport participant are of considerable interest to professional researchers and theorists.

2. Africans were brought to America as indentured servants in 1619 and were enslaved until the Emancipation Proclamation of 1862. After the Civil War, African Americans became involved extensively in baseball, boxing, and as jockeys in horse racing.

3. Moses Fleetwood Walker and his brother Weldy Wilberforce Walker were prominent baseball players of the late 1800s, though their acceptance by whites was very poor. Tom Molineaux was the first black heavyweight boxing champion of the world, and African-American dominance of boxing continues largely unabated. Willey Sims was an early leader in jockey circles, and blacks dominated the sport of horse racing until 1900, when they were relegated to lesser roles in favor of white jockeys.

4. The success of African-American athletes in certain sports—mainly football, basketball, baseball, track, and boxing—is difficult to explain. Genetic or biological superiority theories abound but are hard to substantiate. Social/cultural influences that arise out of prejudice, misguided preconceptions, and superstition probably constitute a more viable hypothesis for explaining black superiority in certain sports. Psychological explanations are sparse and shed very little light on the issue.

5. The Hispanic athlete has made a significant impact on sport, particularly in recent times and in professional baseball. Erroneous stereotypes about these athletes abound, but little psychological research has been conducted.

6. Asian Americans figure prominently in a fairly wide variety of sports. Again, stereotyping is common, but little research has been done with these athletes.

7. Native Americans are significantly underrepresented in the sport world. The Native American Sports Council, in conjunction with the U.S. Olympic Committee, is undertaking projects aimed at getting Native Americans into the sports mainstream.

8. Sport parachuting, hang gliding, scuba diving, and rock climbing are popular components of the modern "risk revolution," and the psychological makeup of the participants has proved intriguing to sport psychologists.

9. Twenty-nine U.S. sport parachutists died while participating in their sport in 1999, down from 48 in 1998. Deaths in sport parachuting are strongly related to inexperience. Physiologically, parachutists experience heightened arousal as well as elevated anxiety and self-reports of fear associated with jumping but are generally low in state and trait anxiety when compared with reported test norms. Parachutists are also above average in intelligence and are nonconformist sensation seekers with a low need for order and rigidity.

10. Hang gliding is a highly dangerous activity with a death rate exceeding that of suicide for people of all ages in Canada and automobile fatalities among youth in the United States. Based on highly preliminary observational data, hang-gliding participants are likely to be single, Caucasian college students who are "tuned in" to the hang-gliding lifestyle. They are not unrealistic about the dangers of their sport but do not see it as overly hazardous. Reasons for leaving the sport generally center around injuries, family concerns, or career issues.

11. Rock climbers, like other risk-sport athletes, are generally unconventional sensation seekers. Mount Everest climbers receive a lot of mention because of the particularly hazardous nature of that undertaking.

12. Scuba diving, while hazardous, appears to be a relatively safe activity when conducted properly. Overall, scuba participants appear to be relatively unremarkable in personality makeup except in the area of anxiety, where they appear to be generally low. Some evidence exists that these participants are also more internal in terms of locus of control and more masculine in sex role orientation.

13. Two correlates of risk taking have spawned a fair amount of research: sensation seeking and birth order effects. Clearly, risk-sport participants are sensation seekers; they are unconventional, bored by routine, and seekers of stress through more unconventional means. As for birth order effects, high-risk-sport participants are more likely to be laterborns than firstborn children. Apparently, firstborns have their needs met in such a way that

"proving" behavior through more unconventional means is not necessary for them.

KEY TERMS

birth order effects (286)
high-risk sport (277)
reactive tasks (272)
self-paced activities (272)
sensation seeking (285)
Sensation Seeking Scale (285)
skewed groups (270)
sport opportunity structure (268)
stacking (268)
tilted groups (270)

SUGGESTED READINGS

Chalk, O. (1975). *Pioneers of black sport*. New York: Dodd, Mead.

Chalk reviews the history of African-American athletes in four sports: baseball, basketball, boxing, and football. Pictures, historical chronicles, and game records of the early days of black sport serve as useful mechanisms to promote interest. This book is a must for the sport historian.

Dedera, D. (1975). *Hang gliding—The flyingest flying*. Flagstaff, AZ: Northland Press.

This book attempts to capture the essence of the hang-sliding sport through prose and a large number of color pictures. The beauty, the lifestyle, and the danger are all chronicled for the reader in a highly readable way. The photography is particularly compelling, with many of the pictures provided by the author.

Entine, J. (2000). *Why black athletes dominate sport and why we're afraid to talk about it*. New York: Public Affairs.

Entine, an award-winning journalist, has written a provocative and controversial book about racial differences and sport participation. Racial differences are real, he states, and the rapid ascent of the black athlete can indeed be traced to biology and ancestry. At the same time, Entine rejects the idea that opportunity, hard work, and the channeling of blacks into certain sports serve as explanatory mechanisms for this superiority. There is also a nice coverage of related history. Entine's book will be a source of heated debate among athletes and laypersons for years to come.

Lapchick, R. E. (1991). *Five minutes to midnight: Race and sport in the 1990s.* New York: Madison Books.
Richard Lapchick, outspoken critic of racism in sport (and the broader societal context), has followed up on his very successful book, *Broken Promises: Racism in American Sports,* with another outstanding effort. The first 11 chapters are extracted directly from the previous book, with six completely new chapters added. The end result is a highly readable and cogent discourse on racial relations in sport and society. Lapchick contends that sport can and should serve as a model for better human relations in all facets of society.

 ## INFOTRAC COLLEGE EDITION

For additional readings, explore Infotrac College Edition, your online library. Go to: http://www.infotrac-college.com/wadsworth
Hint: Enter these search terms: discrimination in sport, extreme sports, Jim Thorpe, race and sports, risk taking (psychology), rock climbing, sensation seeking, skydiving.

Special Populations: Elite, Disabled, Injured, or Drug-Abusing Athletes

CHAPTER 18

The Elite Athlete

The Athlete With Disabilities

The Injured Athlete

The Athlete Who Uses or Abuses Drugs

Summary

Key Terms

Suggested Readings

These wheelchair basketball players are part of a growing movement to provide sport and exercise opportunities for athletes with disabilities. For those handicapped athletes who excel, the Paralympic Games are held every four years in conjunction with the regular Olympic Games.

© Hulton-Deutsch Collection/CORBIS

In addition to minority and risk athletes, a number of other special athletic populations merit our attention. One group is composed of elite athletes, those who function at an exceptionally high level in Olympic or professional sports. Another group is made up of disabled athletes, and they are receiving more and more attention in the world of sport and fitness. Injury to athletes is all too common at every level of performance, and the psychological consequences are of considerable importance. Finally, the race to gain the competitive edge takes many forms, and abusing drugs and engaging in questionable practices of a related nature are all too common in sport, and much concern is expressed societally and within the scientific community about these abuses of sportsmanship. We will explore each of these four athletic groups in turn.

THE ELITE ATHLETE

Research on exceptional or elite performance in sport has been unfocused at best. Access to elite populations where much is at stake for the athlete is understandably limited. Nevertheless, some information about top-flight performers is available.

Kroll's Personality Performance Pyramid

One way of conceptualizing the relationship between personality and performance is provided by Kroll (1970). His formulation is summarized by Silva (1984b) in terms of the **personality performance pyramid,** which can be seen in Figure 18.1. Kroll's model predicts a great deal of heterogeneity among athletes at the entry level and considerable homogene-

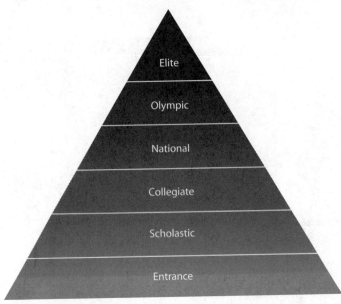

FIGURE 18.1

Kroll's Personality Performance Pyramid

- Elite
- Olympic
- National
- Collegiate
- Scholastic
- Entrance

Source: Kroll (1970).

ity at the elite level, though differences would still exist at any and all levels. Part of Kroll's similarity effect could be attributable to preselection variables for sport, and some of it would certainly be a function of the demands inherent in proceeding from the entry to the elite level. Kroll calls the latter phenomenon the **modification and attrition theory** for personality similarity in elite performers; that is, their own behaviors and personality have been modified by experience. Athletes who for whatever reason drop out of the process at some point only accentuate this homogeneity of personality. In effect, their attrition takes variability out of the formula.

Kroll's Personality Performance Pyramid a model of the relationship between athletic performance and personality that predicts heterogeneity among athletes at the entry level and homogeneity at the elite level.
Modification and attrition theory Kroll's explanation of personality similarity in elite athletes as a function of preselection and modification of traits while proceeding from the entry to the elite level.

Research on Exceptional Performance

One way of looking at the exceptional performer is through a series of studies conducted on Olympic athletes who are generally recognized as exceptional performers.

OLYMPIC/USA NATIONAL CHAMPIONSHIP FIGURE SKATERS. A fair literature has emerged on elite figure skaters, primarily through the efforts of Gould and Scanlan and their respective associates (Gould, Finch, & Jackson, 1993; Gould, Jackson, & Finch, 1993a, 1993b; Scanlan, Stein, & Ravizza, 1989, 1991). Scanlan et al. focused their research on sources of enjoyment and sources of stress among elite skaters. Interviews were conducted with 26 former national championship competitors in the United States. From these interviews, a large number of subject statements emerged that were subsequently analyzed for sources of both fun and stress. In the case of sources of enjoyment, skaters focused on four categories, which were summarized by the research team as follows:

- Social and Life Opportunities (friendship opportunities, broadening experiences afforded by competition, family/coach relationships)

- Perceived Competence (mastery, competitive achievement, demonstration of athletic ability)

- Social Recognition of Competence (peer recognition, recognition from fans and others)

- The Act of Skating (movement and sensory stimulation, self-expression, athleticism expression, flow or peak experience)

Sources of stress, on the other hand, were placed in five categories:

- Negative Aspects of Competition (worries, failure, preparation, importance of competing)

- Negative Significant-Other Relationships (skating politics, psychological warfare, interpersonal conflict)

- Demands or Costs of Skating (financial, time, personal costs)

- Personal Struggles (physical and mental difficulties, self-doubt, perfectionism, dealing with fears of becoming gay)

- Traumatic Experiences (family problems, death fears involving the 1961 plane crash that killed the entire USA national team)

Gould and his colleagues found similar sources of stress in their study of 17 elite American skaters who had won a national championship between 1985 and 1990.

Specifically, they identified dominant sources of stress to be (1) competitive anxiety and self-doubt; (2) financing, media, and time constraints and demands; (3) high performance expectations/standards; and (4) significant-other relationship issues. While categorized somewhat differently, there appears to be quite a bit of overlap in Gould's and Scanlan's findings on sources of stress.

OLYMPIC GYMNASTS. Mahoney and Avener (1977) administered a questionnaire to American men gymnasts at the 1976 Olympic trials. Subsequent comparisons between those who made the team and those who did not revealed that the better gymnasts tended to be more self-confident ($r = .57$), reported a higher frequency of gymnastic dreams ($r = .45$), thought more about gymnastics in everyday situations ($r = .78$), tended to downplay the role of officiating in influencing their performance ($r = .59$), and did not rate mental attitude as greatly influencing their success ($r = -.59$). The more successful participants also reported slightly more anxiety prior to competition, though the pattern reversed itself when competition actually began.

OLYMPIC TRACK AND FIELD ATHLETES. Vernacchia, McGuire, Reardon, and Templin (2000) have reported results of their study of 15 Olympic track and field competitors; one held two world records, four others were Olympic medallists, three were U.S. record holders in their event, and seven were present or past U.S. track and field champions. Prominent among their findings based on 30-minute interviews with these athletes was the role of mental imagery and visualization in preparing for competition. Having to overcome serious injury at some critical point in their career was another common factor among many of these competitors. Six of the athletes identified spirituality/religion/prayer as very important to them. Asked for advice they would give young people aspiring to Olympic goals, much emphasis was placed on having fun and maintaining a good work ethic. In the words of one athlete:

> I'd say your time as a kid, everything should be fun, at least through junior high and middle school . . . you should go out, try things out, give it your best when you try something, pick a few sports that you want to pursue. I think the main key is to have fun, enjoy the time that you have. . . . (p. 17).

OLYMPIC WEIGHT LIFTERS. Hall, Church, and Stone (1980) were primarily interested in birth order effects, though Hall and her collaborators did take into consideration achievement motives, locus of control, and anxiety in elite weight lifters. Overall, they found a very strong relationship between birth order effects and achievement motivation as measured by the Mehrabian Need Achievement Scale (Mehrabian, 1969). Firstborns had a very strong need to approach success, whereas laterborns had a tendency to avoid failure. On Rotter's locus of control measure, firstborns and others were generally internal, though the firstborns were more external than those born later. Both comparison groups were relatively low on trait anxiety as measured by the STAI. Mahoney (1989) compared nationally ranked lifters with a sample of nonelite competitors, and found the elite competitors to be more psychologically healthy as measured by several psychometric instruments. The elite lifters were also more motivated to compete as indicated by self-report.

OLYMPIC WRESTLERS. Gould, Eklund, and Jackson conducted intensive interviews with the 20 wrestlers (10 freestyle, 10 Greco-Roman) who represented the United States in the 1988 Olympic Games (Eklund, Gould, & Jackson, 1993; Gould, Eklund, & Jackson, 1992a, 1992b, 1993). Their primary aim was to ascertain precisely how these athletes prepared themselves mentally for competition. Of special interest were the differences in preparation that characterized winning and losing performances. In the case of winning performances, wrestlers followed a mental game plan routinely, were extremely confident and focused, and were optimally aroused. In losing matches, wrestlers deviated from their mental preparation strategies, were less confident, entertained negative thoughts, and were less attentive to the task at hand. With regard to mental preparation, a number of strategies were employed as opposed to a specific approach. In a more detailed look at the six wrestlers who eventually won medals in the 1988 Games, it was noted that they all used mental preparation strategies, but the content and focus of these approaches varied considerably. The study described here clearly illustrates the importance of self-confidence, performing at a near maximum capacity, and attention to the task at hand in determining elite wrestling performance.

To summarize, a synthesis across sports indicates that elite athletes believe self-confidence to be a big factor in determining success. Also, the ability of elite competitors to perform at a level that is consistent with their view of their potential appears to be a solid discriminator. Top-flight competitors are not prone to blame poor performance on practice inadequacies or officiating foibles; they tend to see themselves as the source and focus of success. Finally, elite athletes are not exempt from the effects of stress inherent in intense competition. They do, however, appear to find constructive ways of dealing with stress while maintaining a high level of competitive performance.

Our understanding of elite performers is, to quote Silva, Shultz, Haslam, and Murray (1981), "embryonic." Methodological shortcomings have been considerable; the definition of who is elite is highly variable, sample sizes are quite small in many cases, inconsistencies created by the use of a diversity of instruments are frequent, and variability in data analyses has contributed to the existing cloudy picture. It is hoped that increasing sophistication can be brought to bear on this important area in the future so that identification and development of exceptional performance can be fostered.

THE ATHLETE WITH DISABILITIES

Estimates are that 43 million people in the United States have a physical disability of one kind or another. Of this number, probably 2 to 3 million actually take part in sport or fitness activities (Carfagno, 1998). At times, there is confusion about what to call these athletes, and terms such as *disabled, impaired, handicapped,* and *physically challenged* are used. The National Collegiate Athletic Association (NCAA) refers to these athletes as "impaired student-athletes" and defines them as "those who are confined to a wheelchair, those who are deaf, blind, or missing a limb; those who have only one of a set of organs; or those who may have behavioral, emotional, and psychological disorders that substantially limit a major life activity" (Carfagno, 1998). The last portion of the NCAA definition is important in that it

---

Athlete with disabilities according to the National Collegiate Athletic Association, an athlete with a major physical or psychological disability.

Ericsson's View of Exceptional Performance

K. Anders Ericsson has made a career of investigating expert and exceptional performance by studying exceptional performers in bridge, chess, dance and music, juggling, medicine, physics, psychology, sports, and other activities, he is convinced that expert performance in any of these areas depends somewhat on inherent ability and greatly on deliberate practice, which is the rallying call for his theory of exceptional performance. To Ericsson (1996, pp. 278–279), the term **deliberate practice** means "individualized training activities especially designed by a coach or teacher to improve specific aspects of an individual's performance through repetition and successive refinement." Ericsson argues that anatomical or physiological determinants of performance (i.e., innate talent) are modifiable if deliberate practice is engaged in for a minimum of four hours per day

for a period of 10 years. Across all the talent domains he studied, Ericsson has found deliberate practice to be the key to expert or exceptional performance.

It is unlikely that elite athletes reach this level of excellence without many hours of deliberate practice. The notion that professionals and Olympians are simply blessed with superior innate ability tends to diminish the role of hard work in the creation of excellence.

SOURCE: Ericsson (1996).

Deliberate practice the cornerstone of K. Anders Ericsson's theory of exceptional performance, which emphasizes the role of hard work over superior innate ability.

---

broadens our perspective on disabilities by including those people with psychological problems or deficits.

The U.S. Olympic Committee recognizes seven National Disabled Sports Organizations (DSOs):

- The American Athletic Association of the Deaf
- The Dwarf Athletic Association of America
- Disabled Sports USA
- Wheelchair Sports USA
- Special Olympics International
- The United Association for Blind Athletes
- The U.S. Cerebral Palsy Athletic Association

Each of the DSOs seeks to provide meaningful sport and fitness activities for their clientele in order to foster fitness, greater self-confidence, independence, a more positive self-image, and friendships. At the same time, they hope to educate the rest of the population about these athletes and their disabilities.

For those elite athletes with disabilities, the ultimate sport experience may well be the Paralympic Games, which originated in England in 1951. These games, equivalent to the Olympics for athletes without handi-

caps or disabilities, are held every four years just after the Summer and Winter Olympic Games and at the same venues. The 2000 Summer Olympics in Sydney, Australia, welcomed almost 300 of its own Paralympians, who competed in 18 sports. In the 1996 Olympic Games in Atlanta, Australia finished second in medal tally to the United States and ahead of the next three contingents from Germany, the United Kingdom, and Spain. The 2002 Winter Paralympics are scheduled for Salt Lake City, Utah.

Research has been on disabled athletes, conducted for over 20 years, and has centered for the most part on the measurement of anxiety, mood states, and self-actualization. According to an extensive review of the literature on psychological research related to individuals with disabilities (Porretta & Moore, 1996/1997), the research on anxiety has been equivocal. For mood, the assessment tool has been the Profile of Mood States, and the mood profiles of athletes with disabilities closely parallel those of able-bodied athletes. Some confirmation of the Iceberg Profile has also been noted. In the self-actualization research findings, the disabled athletes again look very similar to their able-bodied counterparts.

Poretta and Moore call for more emphasis on enhancing the performance of these individuals, particularly in the areas of goal setting, self-regulation, visual rehearsal, relaxation training, and identification of participation motives.

THE INJURED ATHLETE

Injuries associated with sport and exercise are a common source of irritation for all concerned. They put the athlete temporarily out of commission, and coaches, trainers, orthopedists (sometimes), and supportive friends, parents, and teammates are worried about or affected by the consequences. Statistically speaking, Powell and Barber-Foss (1999) indicate that 6 million U.S. high school youth from some 20,000 schools take part in interscholastic sports each year. Of this number, more than 2 million will be injured, resulting in 500,000 visits to physicians and 30,000 hospitalizations. Based on their survey of 300 certified athletic trainers, Powell and Barber-Foss point out that football has the most injuries among the nine sports in their study, with an injury rate of 8.1 per thousand. Volleyball had the lowest injury rate at 1.7. Boys' and girls' soccer was the only sport reporting more game than practice injuries. Three-fourths of the reported injuries sidelined the athletes for less than eight days. Knee injuries were highest for girls' soccer and lowest in baseball. Of the sports requiring surgery, 60% involved the knee. Data from NBA basketball team trainers for the years 1988–1997 indicated that almost 90% of the athletes in the NBA suffered an injury or illness during the report period. As might be expected, ankle sprains were the most common injury (9.4%), followed by patello-femoral inflammation (8.1%), lumbar strains (5%), and knee sprains (2.3%). The greatest number of days missed because of injury was attributable to patello-femoral inflammation. Also, the injury rate in the NBA is twice that of collegiate basketball, partially because of an arduous schedule and the disproportionate number of injuries incurred by NBA players over the age of 30. In that older age group, inflammatory injuries are a substantial problem. While these reports are only the tip of the iceberg, they underscore the fact that sports injuries are a fact of life.

Many theories have emerged on the causes and treatment of sports injuries from the psychological perspective. One, the **affective cycle theory** of responses to athletic injury of Heil and Fine (1993), argues that reactions to injury are a function of three different responses: distress, denial, and determined coping. *Distress* is the negative response to the injury and may involve emotions such as guilt, anger, and a feeling of helplessness. *Denial* relates to a failure to accept the fact that an injury has actually occurred. This response could be positive in temporarily keeping the athlete from responding with debilitating negative emotion. Alternatively, denial can be negative in its effects on rehabilitation. The third response, *determined coping,* is the stage at which realism sets in; that is, the athlete admits the seriousness of the injury and sets up realistic coping procedures. Obviously, the point of intervention by the physical therapist, athletic trainer, and/or sport psychologist should be aimed at extending the determined coping stage.

Brewer (1994) has proposed a second approach, the **cognitive appraisal theory** of responses to athletic injury. In this model, the athlete's response to injury is a function of the interaction between personality and situational factors. In turn, the emotional response to the injury and the resultant behavioral response are salient. One important behavioral response is adherence to the rehabilitation regimen.

A third and perhaps more comprehensive approach is the **Andersen and Williams theory (1988),** which can be seen in its entirety in Figure 18.2. Clearly, it is the view of Andersen and Williams that personality variables (i.e., hardiness, locus of control, competitive trait anxiety, and achievement motivation) interact with situational variables (i.e., everyday life events and daily hassles) to determine the nature and extent of the stress response. At the same time, many intervention strategies are proposed in the model, most of which have been discussed in other contexts throughout this book.

Affective cycle theory Heil and Fine's theory that a sport injury produces three responses in athletes: distress, denial, and determined coping.

Cognitive appraisal theory Brewer's theory that the athlete's response to injury is a function of the interaction between personality and situational factors in producing first an emotional and then a behavioral response.

Anderson and Williams theory a comprehensive model of reaction to sports injury based on interaction of personality with situational variables that also proposes a range of intervention strategies.

FIGURE 18.2

The Andersen and Williams Theory

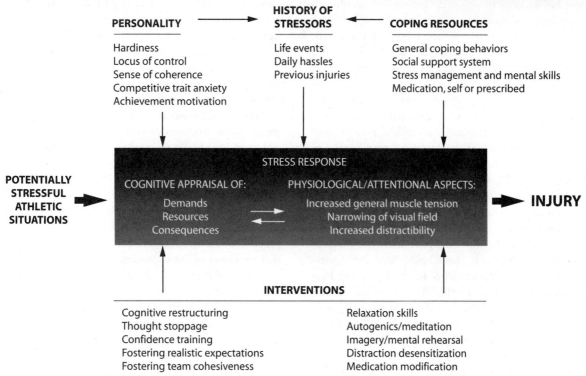

SOURCE: Andersen & Williams (1988).

For the most part, personality traits and states have produced a murky picture of the relationship between personality and injury. This situation is partially attributable to the fact that research on this relationship is plagued by the same problems that characterize much of the personality research discussed earlier in the text. It is likely, however, that personality variables do contribute to injury, as suggested by the Brewer and Andersen and Williams models. No doubt they also play an important role in injury rehabilitation.

Daily hassles and stressful life events are also pertinent to an understanding of athletic injury. Holmes and Rahe (1967) created a scale to assess stress in everyday life, suggesting that stresses could be quantified in terms of severity and that the total score made on their scale would be predictive of illness. Several adaptations of the original Holmes and Rahe scale have been made for use in sport. One, the Social and Athletic Readjustment Rating Scale (SARRS) (Bramwell, Minoru, Wagner, & Holmes, 1975), has been used with college football players, and a strong correlation was found between life stress and football injury. Coddington and Troxell (1980) modified the SARRS for use with high school football players and obtained essentially the same results as did Bramwell et al. A third study by Cryan and Alles (1983) of collegiate football players yielded results similar to the 1975 and 1980 studies. Other studies have not supported these findings, but the hypothesis that daily stresses and hassles contribute to injury seems a tenable one.

As for treatment of injury using psychological procedures, many have been discussed earlier and are applicable in the sport injury context. These procedures include biofeedback, a host of cognitive behavioral procedures, imagery, and meditation.

One outgrowth of injury is pain, a stimulus to which people respond quite differentially. Given that pain is part and parcel of everyday living, pain management has become an important topic within the health psychology and sport psychology literature. Pioneering work in the area was conducted by Melzack (1975, 1987), who created the McGill Pain Questionnaire (MPQ). This instrument was designed to assess pain along a number of dimensions he labeled sensory–discriminative, affective, motivational, and cognitive–evaluative. Melzack's work has spawned much research in psychology and medicine, but precious little in sport psychology. One takeoff on Melzack's work is that of Meyers and his colleagues (Meyers, Bourgeois, Stewart, & LeUnes, 1992), who created the **Sports Inventory for Pain (SIP),** a sport-specific attempt to gauge how different athletes respond psychologically when in pain.

Construction of the SIP began by borrowing a number of items from general pain inventories such as the MPQ of Melzack, the Coping Strategies Questionnaire (CSQ) (Rosenstiel & Keefe, 1983), the Pain and Impairment Relationship Scale (PAIRS) (Riley, Ahern, & Follick, 1988), and the Controlled Repression–Sensitization Scale (CRS) (Handal, 1973). Next, the SIP was administered over time and at various phases in the research design to injured athletes and college students with athletic backgrounds ranging from none to very extensive. The final SIP is composed of 25 items arranged in a five-point Likert scale designed to assess which psychological strategy (coping, cognitive, avoidance, catastrophizing, body awareness) an athlete might choose in an effort to cope psychologically with pain.

Preliminary psychometric analyses indicate satisfactory reliability, both in terms of test–retest and internal consistency measures, as well as promising predictive and factorial validity. Also, the SIP seems to be largely immune to the effects of social desirability as measured by the Marlowe Crowne Social Desirability Scale (Crowne & Marlowe, 1964). One of the more interesting preliminary findings from Meyers et al. is that general samples of males scored significantly

higher (i.e., more desirably) on coping and cognitive strategies for dealing with pain, while females scored significantly higher on the catastrophizing scale. When these comparisons were restricted to male and female athletes, there were no differences within the genders in the tendency to catastrophize pain.

Two investigations by Bartholomew (Bartholomew, Brewer, van Raalte, Linder, Cornelius, & Burt, 1998; Bartholomew, Edwards, Brewer, van Raalte, & Linder, 1998) have been less supportive of the SIP. In the Bartholomew, Brewer et al. study, three separate experiments were conducted, two with college students and one with individuals recovering from anterior cruciate ligament surgery. Summing across the three studies, only marginal support was found for the subscales of the SIP. Questions were raised about the utility of the SIP as a predictor of pain response. In the Bartholomew, Edwards et al. study, confirmatory factor analysis failed to support the factor structure of the SIP. It was suggested that a revision of the scale might be in order. Based on the work of Bartholomew and his colleagues coupled with their own analysis of SIP data over the past ten years, Meyers et al. (1992) are in the process of revamping what they believe to be a valuable sport-specific test relevant to the pain response literature.

THE ATHLETE WHO USES OR ABUSES DRUGS

We live in a drug-oriented society; prescription drugs, over-the-counter medications, and illegal substances are commonplace aspects of our daily lives. We seem to have a tacit "better life through chemistry" orientation to personal well-being, and athletes are certainly no exception. Documenting the extent of drug use is a difficult task at best, but an epidemiological review by Mottram, Reilly, and Chester (1997) placed the prevalence among children at 3–5% and 15–25% in adults.

The elite athlete is particularly prone to look for any competitive edge, and the various performance-enhancing substances available are all too often viewed as providing that coveted advantage. Track and field athletes and swimmers are often implicated in using banned or illegal substances to enhance performance. World record holders such as Javier Sotomayor of Cuba in the high jump and Randy Barnes of the

---

Sports Inventory for Pain (SIP) a sport-specific standardized test that attempts to measure athletes' psychological responses to pain.

United States in the shot put were stripped of Olympic medals and/or banned from participation in the 1990s because of steroid use. Florence Griffith Joyner, women's record holder in the 100 and 200 meter dash, has been the subject of much controversy about probable steroid use; many believe that Joyner's premature death at age 38 may well have been linked to this problem. Many other world-class runners, such as Linford Christie, Merlene Ottey, Dennis Mitchell, Ben Johnson, and Mary Decker Slaney, have been accused or found guilty of steroid abuse. In swimming, Chinese females are constantly being banned from competition for failing drug tests at international competitions.

Athletes also function at times in the presence of considerable pain or discomfort, and they may seek relief in pain-killing or ameliorative drugs. This sort of abuse has been widely chronicled in both the professional and popular literature.

Finally, the pressures of competition, particularly at the elite amateur or professional levels, are such that drugs, including alcohol, marijuana, and cocaine, are viewed as tension reducing, and their abuse is not at all unusual. Hardly a day goes by without some media report of a prominent athlete with a drug or alcohol problem. Darryl Strawberry and Dwight Gooden in baseball, Leon Lett in football, and John Daly in golf are only a few of many examples of professional athletes who have fallen prey to cocaine or alcohol abuse.

One way of looking at the various substances and performance-enhancement methods is from the perspective of the International Olympic Committee (IOC). This governing body classifies substances and methods as follows:

1. Prohibited classes of substances (stimulants, narcotics, anabolic agents, diuretics, and peptide and glycoprotein hormones and analogues)
2. Prohibited methods (blood doping and pharmacological, chemical, and physical manipulation)
3. Classes of drugs subject to restriction (alcohol, marijuana, local anesthetics, corticosteroids, beta-blockers)

Space does not allow for a protracted discussion of all of these agents, so discussion here will be confined to one or two of the more prominent examples within each category.

Prohibited Classes of Substances

These are substances aimed at performance enhancement, and they are often called ergogenic aids. Pate, Rotella, and McClenaghan (1984, p. 268) define an **ergogenic aid** as "any substance or treatment that improves, or is thought to improve, physical performance." The phrase "thought to improve" highlights the fact that the performance-enhancing effects of these various drugs may rest as much in the psychology of the individual as in the chemical properties of the various ergogenics. Chief among the prohibited substances are amphetamines and the anabolic steroids.

AMPHETAMINES. Pate and his associates suggest that **amphetamines,** particularly Dexedrine and Benzedrine, are among the ergogenics most commonly used by athletes. Amphetamines are drugs manufactured in a laboratory, and are used in sports to provide excitation or sudden bursts of energy. Their use has been documented in professional baseball (Kirschenbaum, 1980), professional football (Mandell, 1975), and track (Leonard, 1984). Leonard also reports that nine of twelve medalists in the 1970 world weightlifting championships were disqualified after urinalysis revealed the presence of amphetamines. In football, Mandell found their use widespread in the professional ranks, and he cited data to suggest that approximately 50% of NFL players were using amphetamines. The effects of amphetamines on one professional football player are thought provoking: "I'm not about to go out there one-on-one against a guy who is grunting and drooling and coming at me with big dilated pupils unless I'm in the same condition" (Mandell, 1975, p. 43). Jim Bouton, in his bestseller *Ball Four,* suggests that amphetamine use was widespread in major league baseball during his playing days. One player poignantly describes the amphetamine problem in baseball as follows: "At first they might take them before a big game. Then it was before every game. Then they had to take them to practice. As the players get older, they forget about

---

Prohibited classes of substances substances that enhance, or are thought to enhance, an athlete's physical performance; also known as **ergogenic aids.**
Amphetamines stimulant drugs manufactured in the laboratory and used by athletes to obtain sudden bursts of energy.

Anabolic-androgenic steroids (AAS), which are analogues or derivatives of testosterone, have anabolic effects such as bone growth, increases in muscle development and strength, greater blood cell production and protein synthesis, and decreases in body fat. Any of these may improve athletic performance and give the user an advantage over his or her competitors. Use of performance-enhancing drugs has been declared illegal in international competition, so all participating athletes are given a drug test. Occasionally, some fail the test and are eliminated from competition. The name Ben Johnson has become equated with the abuse of performance enhancing drugs. He was stripped of his gold medal in the 100-meter dash at the 1988 Olympics after testing positive for steroids.
© Bettmann/CORBIS

Anabolic-androgenic steroids (AAS) synthetic analogues or derivatives of the male sex hormone testosterone, ingested to enhance muscular development.

Adonis complex the pumped-up "Greek god" look of athletes who have used anabolic-androgenic steroids to enhance their muscular development.

how to get energy naturally and start getting it through amphetamine pills" (Oliver, 1971, p. 65). In addition to the dependency problem mentioned by Oliver, the amphetamines may produce rage, unwarranted fearlessness, and irrational feelings of omnipotence, all of which can be potential health detriments to the athlete both on and off the field.

Over time, effective tests for most of the commonly used stimulants have been developed and have, at least on the surface, curtailed their use. However, to get around the detection problem, a number of athletes have resorted to the use of legal over-the-counter (OTC) drugs that contain many of the same chemical agents as the banned substances. As might be expected, this situation has led to a confusing enforcement picture and has opened the door for athletes to claim "inadvertent use" whenever they are detected using stimulants (Catlin & Murray, 1996).

ANABOLIC-ANDROGENIC STEROIDS (AAS). The **anabolic-androgenic steroids** (**AAS**), include more than 100 synthetic compounds that are analogues or derivatives of the male sex hormone, testosterone (Riem & Hursey, 1993). The AAS are used by athletes and fitness buffs because they promote muscle development and strength. According to Strauss and Yesalis (1991), the AAS have been around since 1935 and were introduced to sports by Soviet-bloc weight lifters in the 1950s. By the 1980s, it became clear that the AAS were revolutionizing many aspects of the way we view sports. Initial AAS testing was instituted by the Olympic Games in 1976.

AAS use appears to be rising among both athletes and young people interested in what Toufexis (1989) calls the "Rambo Look." Toufexis cites statistics indicating that a half million adolescents nationwide have used steroids, many in search of a Mr. Universe or Hulk Hogan appearance. This look has also been referred to as the **Adonis complex,** so-named for the gorgeous half-man, half-god of Greek mythology by psychologists Harrison Pope of Harvard, Katherine Phillips of Harvard, and Roberto Olivardia of Belmont, Massachusetts (Cloud, 2000). A recent headline from *Time* magazine also underscores this point in an article about testosterone and the upcoming availability of a prescription drug AndroGel: "Are you man enough? Testosterone can make a difference in bed and at the gym. And soon you'll be able to get it as a gel" (Lacayo, 2000, p. 59).

Also driving the misuse of the various performance-enhancing drugs, and most particularly the AAS, is the willingness of some athletes to do almost anything to gain the proverbial competitive edge. This win-at-all-costs mentality is called the athlete's **Faustian philosophy** by Dr. James Puffer (Drug Testing in Sports, 1985), a sports medicine specialist. In 1990 are telling: 14% of the respondents to a "Speak Out Poll" by *USA Today* indicated that they would still take a pill that would make them a world-class athlete even if they knew that the medication would kill them in 10 years. Perhaps more gratifying, only 3% responded positively to the same question when the proposed time line was five years (Speak Out on Sports, 1990).

The AAS get their name from their masculinizing (androgenic) effects and tissue-building (anabolic) properties. The **androgenic effects of AAS,** in brief, refer to growth and maintenance of the male reproductive system and the development of secondary sex characteristics. **Anabolic effects of AAS** include bone growth, increases in muscle development and strength, deepening of the voice, increases in red blood cell production and protein synthesis, and a decrease in body fat. Steroid users who talk in terms of "dirty" and "clean" drugs are referring to the androgenic–anabolic ratio (Riem & Hursey, 1993). An example of a "dirty" steroid would be testosterone cypionate, with its 1:1 ratio; a "clean" steroid would be Anavar, with its 13:1 composition. The fact that AAS vary so much in androgenic–anabolic ratio should serve as a reminder that AAS really refers to a range of drugs with very different effects and side effects. Lombardo, Longcope, and Voy (1985) have provided us with a representational view of various AAS plotted by androgenic–anabolic ratio, shown in Figure 18.3.

The appeal of the AAS is obvious in view of the gains to be made in size, strength, and outward manifestations of masculinity. Drawbacks to the AAS, however, include negative effects on endocrinal and reproductive functioning, virilization and feminization, cardiovascular and hematologic functioning, hepatic disturbances, musculoskeletal development, dermatological conditions, risk of AIDS and other infections, and behavioral disturbances. Among the latter are withdrawal effects, depression, escalations in aggressive behavior, and rage responses ("roid rages"). With regard to rage responses or aggression, a former professional foot-

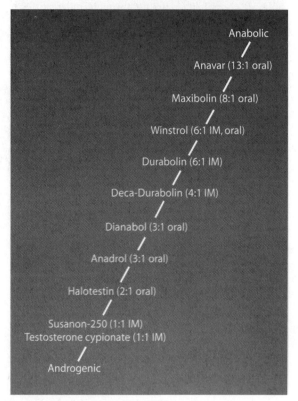

FIGURE 18.3

Anabolic-Androgenic Steroids Plotted by Anabolic to Androgenic Ratio

Anabolic
/
Anavar (13:1 oral)
/
Maxibolin (8:1 oral)
/
Winstrol (6:1 IM, oral)
/
Durabolin (6:1 IM)
/
Deca-Durabolin (4:1 IM)
/
Dianabol (3:1 oral)
/
Anadrol (3:1 oral)
/
Halotestin (2:1 oral)
/
Susanon-250 (1:1 IM)
Testosterone cypionate (1:1 IM)
/
Androgenic

SOURCE: Lombardo, Longcope, & Voy (1985).

ball player, Dean Steinkuhler, a steroid user in college and during some of his earliest years in the National Football League (NFL), said his drug regimen "made me real moody, violent, I wanted to kill somebody"

Faustian philosophy the win-at-all-costs philosophy of competitive athletics.
Androgenic effects of AAS masculinizing secondary sexual characteristics enhanced by taking steroids.
Anabolic effects of AAS tissue building enhanced by taking steroids, including bone growth, increases in muscle development and strength, deepening of voice, increases in red blood cell production and protein synthesis, and decrease in body fat.

(Former Husker, 1987, p. 24). Darren A. Chamberlain, a young ex-user for so-called aesthetic purposes, said: "I was doing everything from being obnoxious to getting out of the car and provoking fights at intersections. . . . I couldn't handle any kind of stress. I'd just blow. You can walk in my parents' house today and see the signs— holes in doors I stuck my fist through, indentations in walls I kicked" (Toufexis, 1989, p. 78).

In a related note, Steve Courson, an eight-year veteran of the NFL and an admitted hardcore AAS user, upon finding out that he was in need of a heart transplant because of dilated cardiomyopathy (a weakening of the heart muscle) said, "There's no glory dying for a sport" (Telander, 1989). Courson would probably agree that his abuse of AAS was driven by Puffer's Faustian philosophy. The death from brain lymphoma of ex-pro football star Lyle Alzado has been attributed to his more than 20 years of AAS abuse (Alzado, 1991). Here some would say that the win-at-all-costs mentality claimed another victim (though the relationship between AAS and cancer is far from proven).

In addition to efforts of the USOC/IOC to control drug abuse in sport, other agencies such as the NCAA are working toward the same goal. Based on data provided by their own records for the year 1989–1990, over 3,200 drug tests were conducted under NCAA jurisdiction, 19 of which turned up positive, or 0.6% (Houlihan, 1997). According to Yesalis (1990), in the past the NCAA has budgeted between $1.6 and $3.2 million to identify one or two dozen violators, figures that Albrecht, Anderson, and McKeag (1992) consider to be exorbitant in terms of return on the dollar.

Many states have taken measures to restrict the dispensation of AAS by physicians (Sounding Board, 1989). Congress undertook steps to curb AAS distribution through the mail, thereby cutting into one important supplier of AAS (Congress Considers, 1989). The Anabolic Steroids Control Act (ASCA) of 1990 instituted penalties for illegal steroid distribution of up to five years' imprisonment and fines of up to $250,000

(Getting Tougher on Steroids, 1991). Professional organizations within sports such as the American College of Sports Medicine (ACSM) and the International Society for Sport Psychology (ISSP), have taken firm stances against AAS utilization by athletes. The ISSP (Position Statement, 1993, p. 76) position is as follows:

> The use of AAS is potentially dangerous, both psychologically and physically, and should not be a part of sport and physical activity. An emerging body of medical literature suggests that the prolonged AAS intake may reduce the quality and longevity of life. Therefore, the ISSP recommends that all possible preventive measures be taken to eliminate AAS use in sport and physical activity around the world.

Similarly, the ACSM takes a dim view of AAS use; their position statement is presented in Figure 18.4.

Two final issues merit mentioning. One is raised by Yesalis (1990) and Albrecht, Anderson, and McKeag (1992), who separately suggest that the aforementioned Faustian emphasis on winning lies at the heart of AAS and other abuse by athletes. They recommend a soul-searching analysis of our misguided values with regard to winning and losing as a partial solution to the problem. Second, Riem and Hursey (1993), among many, have suggested that much of what is known about the effects of AAS is reasonable supposition as opposed to demonstrated fact. Anecdotal evidence, questionable case histories, subject credibility, subject unwillingness to participate in studies, inappropriate sampling strategies, inadequate control groups, failure to control dose type and length of administration, and other experimental errors have plagued research on AAS. These sorts of lingering problems have made it difficult to make confident generalizations about the effects of AAS.

Prohibited Methods of Administering Drugs

Blood doping and using drugs to mask the detection of banned substances in the urine fall into this category. Our discussion here will deal only with blood doping.

Blood doping or **boosting** was all but unheard of until 1972, when Dr. Bjorn Ekblom of Sweden announced that his research revealed significant increases in endurance through a procedure he had developed in his

---

Prohibited methods of administering drugs blood doping or boosting and using drugs to mask the presence of banned substances.
Blood doping withdrawing blood from an athlete for approximately one month and then reinfusing it to create enhanced performance; also known as **blood boosting.**

American College of Sports Medicine Position Statement on Steroid Use: Use of Anabolic-Androgenic Steroids in Sports

Based on a comprehensive literature and a careful analysis of the claims concerning the ergogenic effects and the adverse effects of anabolic androgenic steroids, it is the position of the American College of Sports Medicine that:

1. The anabolic-androgenic steroids in the presence of an adequate diet can contribute to increases in body weight, often in the lean mass compartment.

2. The gain in muscular strength achieved through high-intensity exercise and proper diet can be increased by the use of anabolic-androgenic steroids in some individuals.

3. Anabolic-androgenic steroids do not increase aerobic power or capacity for muscular exercise.

4. Anabolic-androgenic steroids have been associated with adverse effects on the liver, cardiovascular system, reproductive system, and psychological status in therapeutic trials and in limited research on athletes. Until further research is completed, the potential hazards of the use of the anabolic-androgenic steroids in athletes must include those found in therapeutic trials.

5. The use of anabolic-androgenic steroids by athletes is contrary to the rules and ethical principles of athletic competition as set forth by many of the sports governing bodies. The American College of Sports Medicine supports these ethical principles and deplores the use of anabolic-androgenic steroids by athletes.

SOURCE: The Use of Anabolic-Androgenic Steroids (1987).

laboratory. In his original study, Ekblom withdrew approximately a quart of blood from four subjects, removed the red blood cells, and put the samples in cold storage for a month. When their red blood cells were reinfused, all subjects were able to run on a treadmill to exhaustion for a much longer time than before. The theory behind blood doping is that the red blood cells carry more of the oxygen so essential to the muscle tissue involved in endurance sports. Though tests of the efficiency of blood boosting have been equivocal, its use has continued, culminating in the revelation that seven of the 24-member 1984 U.S. Olympic cycling team had engaged in blood boosting prior to competition. The resulting furor over the doping disclosure and others involving additive drugs led to sanctions against blood boosting in April 1985 by the International Olympic Committee (IOC) and the U.S. Olympic Committee (USOC) (Ethics of Blood Doping, 1985). Prior to 1985, blood boosting was against USOC policy but not its rules. As a consequence, blood boosting was a matter of individual physician, coach, or athlete conscience, and abuses such as the one involving the Olympic cycling team have occurred.

The advantages of blood boosting have not been satisfactorily demonstrated, but the dangers inherent in the practice (risks of infection, possibility of disease transmission) are well documented (Ethics of Blood Doping, 1985; Gledhill, 1982; Rostaing & Sullivan, 1985). Lemonick (1998) reports that some two dozen heart attack deaths have been linked to the practice, probably because an excess of red cells in the heart turn the blood gelatinous, thus making the heart work harder. As a result of these kinds of reports, testing has been instituted to detect blood boosting, though many problems remain in the area of test accuracy (Mottram, 1999; "New Techniques," 1986) as well as the ethics of blood testing (Birkeland & Hemmersbach, 1999; Browne, Lachance, & Pipe, 1999).

Classes of Drugs Subject to Restrictions

This category includes alcohol, marijuana, local anesthetics, corticosteroids, and beta-blockers. Much has been made about the abuse of marijuana and cocaine in our society, while alcohol gets off lightly at times despite its incredible popularity and potential for abuse.

Classes of drugs subject to restriction alcohol, marijuana, local anesthetics, corticosteroids, and beta-blockers.

Miscellaneous Drugs and Agents Used as Ergogenic Agents

Anti-Asthma Drugs
Salbutamol, salmeterol, and terbutaline are often prescribed to control asthma but have been banned because of their performance-enhancing effects. Whether the athlete is taking these drugs to legitimately deal with asthma or to enhance performance is at the heart of the issue here and has led to a listing of drugs and conditions allowable for use by asthmatic athletes.

Beta-Blockers
Anti-anxiety drugs used to control tremors and heart palpitations, **beta-blockers** are used in sports where anxiety reduction, heart rate, and control of tremors are important. As such, they could be most useful to archers, bowlers, and shooters. Conversely, they would be of little use in anaerobic and aerobic sports requiring endurance and power.

Caffeine
A legal drug so long as the dosage remains below 12 micrograms per milliliter in the blood, caffeine is a stimulant that may be of value to elite endurance athletes, though the research is equivocal. In general, caffeine is safe, socially acceptable, and for the most part legal, given that massive doses are required to reach the IOC illegal level.

Creatine
Creatine, an amino acid, was first discovered in 1835 and was first used in sport by British track and field athletes in the 1992 Olympics. Most recently, its popularity has been linked with the prodigious home run production in major league baseball by Mark McGwire of the St. Louis Cardinals. Its overall use is widespread among baseball and football players, sprinters, and weight lifters. Recreational softball players also extol its virtues. Creatine is a nutritional supplement as opposed to a drug, is not banned by any regulatory agency, and has produced conflicting results in studies aimed at demonstrating its efficacy in power production. Side effects remain unproven but might have long-term effects on muscles, the heart, and the kidneys.

Diuretics
These drugs are misused in sports requiring precise weight management, such as boxing, gymnastics, and wrestling. They can also be used to reduce the amount of other drugs that might be found in the urine, thus facilitating avoidance of detection through drug testing.

Human Growth Hormone (HGH)
Technically known as human chorionic gonadatropin, **human growth hormone (HGH)** has been highly controversial. HGH, naturally secreted by the pituitary gland, has substantial anabolic properties. Its effects on muscle mass, fat-free mass, and strength as well as its reputation as being tough to detect through testing have made this a popular and often-abused substance. HGH is thought to have serious side effects, one of which may be Creutzfeldt–Jakob Disease, a highly infectious and fatal affliction involving brain deterioration and death. Obviously, for a number of reasons, the use of HGH in sport is strongly discouraged.

Beta-blockers anti-anxiety drugs used to control tremors and heart palpitations; useful in sports where anxiety reduction, heart rate, and control of tremors are important.

Creatine an amino acid marketed as a nutritional supplement rather than a drug; thought to improve physical strength.

Human growth hormone (HGH) a hormone secreted by the pituitary gland that enhances muscle mass, fat-free mass and strength; side effects may include brain disease.

SOURCES: Clarkson & Thompson (1998); Demant & Rhodes (1999); Mottram (1999); Wirth & Gieck (1996).

Such is also the case in athletics. Studies conducted by Blood (1990), Evans, Weinberg, and Jackson (1992), and Issari (1998) support this position. In all three reports, alcohol was a runaway first-place finisher in use by athletes. In the Blood study at a small liberal arts college, 81% of a group of athletes ($n = 85$) and a group of nonathletes ($n = 154$) had used alcohol during the semester in which Blood administered his questionnaire. Marijuana use during the same time period was approximately 12% for both groups, while no use of cocaine was reported by athletes and in only two instances among the 154 nonathletes. In a more ambitious survey, Evans et al. sent a questionnaire to 377 male and 167 female athletes from Division I athletic programs. Alcohol users in their study numbered 88%; marijuana, 15%; and cocaine slightly over 4%. Interestingly, 34.5% of the alcohol group were considered high users based on frequency, intensity, and duration of usage. High users also scored significantly higher on the Profile of Mood States subscales of Anger and Fatigue than did the low users in the study. Results for Issari's study of 486 male and female athletes, representing 21 athletic teams from a Division I collegiate sports program, again indicated that alcohol use was widespread. Beer, liquor, and wine consumption far outstripped use of marijuana, cocaine, and other drugs. Ninety percent of the males and 73% of the females reported using alcohol at one time or another. Clearly, results of these three surveys strongly suggest that alcohol is the drug of choice among college athletes.

SUMMARY

1. Kroll's conceptualization of the personality performance pyramid is an intriguing way to view the elite athlete. However, the model is not supported by any hard evidence from the available research.

2. Olympic athletes have been a fertile source of data on the exceptional performance characteristic of elite athletes. Figure skaters, gymnasts, track and field athletes, weight lifters, and wrestlers have been the most common sources of data on elite performers. In general, elite athletes are most commonly distinguished by self-confidence and concentration on the task at hand. Performing at a level that is close to what they regard as their maximum potential is also a prominent trait of elite performers.

3. Studies of elite athletes are hampered by a host of methodological shortcomings, such as sample availability, sample size, definitional problems centering around the definition of *elite*, instrumentation selection, and data analysis variations. Nevertheless, research will continue in the hopes of shedding more light on the identification and training of elite athletes.

4. An estimated 2 to 3 million people with disabilities take part in sport and exercise on a regular basis. The USOC recognizes seven National Disabled Sports Organizations (DSOs) who represent their various clientele in order to foster fitness, greater self-confidence, and friendships. Psychological research on disabled athletes has focused mostly on anxiety, mood, and self-actualization and has demonstrated psychological profiles for disabled athletes similar to those of able-bodied performers.

5. The injured athlete is a serious problem in sport and exercise because of lost participation time, damaged sense of well-being, and so forth. Of the 6 million youth participating in interscholastic sport, one-third will suffer an injury each season. The rate of injury in professional sport is substantial. Theories used to explain injury susceptibility and rehabilitation include the affective life cycle theory, the cognitive appraisal theory, and the Andersen and Williams theory. Pain assessment and treatment go hand in hand with sport injuries.

6. The drug-oriented society in which we live has influenced the world of sport, and the abuse of a wide variety of drugs is a major problem for sport psychologists, physicians, and others with a stake in the future of athletics. The International Olympic Committee (IOC) classifies the various substances and methods used to enhance performance as prohibited classes of substances, prohibited methods, and classes of drugs subject to restriction.

7. The prohibited classes of substances include the stimulants and the anabolic agents, among others. They are also referred to as ergogenic aids.

8. The stimulant drugs were heavily abused by athletes in the 1970s and 1980s, but drug detection

programs are successful in detecting the stimulants. Over-the-counter drugs (OTCs) make this area problematic for enforcement because many contain banned stimulant agents.

9. The anabolic agents or anabolic–androgenic steroids (AAS) have been present in sports for over 50 years and have done much to alter the way we think about elite performance. The anabolic effects of the AAS have to do with masculinizing, whereas the androgenic effects are related to tissue-building properties. Because steroids are suspected to have a number of adverse side effects for both male and female athletes, their use is discouraged.

10. The second IOC category is banned methods, of which blood doping is most prominent. Blood doping involves the removal and storage of red blood cells for reinfusion just prior to competition. Though controversy exists about whether the procedure really works or not, it is popular with endurance athletes. The dangers of blood doping make it suspect, and the IOC has banned the practice.

11. Classes of drugs subject to restrictions include alcohol, marijuana, beta-blockers, and others. Alcohol by far is the drug of choice among athletes at all levels, from high school and beyond.

KEY TERMS

Adonis complex (300)
affective cycle theory (296)
amphetamines (299)
anabolic-androgenic steroids (AAS) (300)
anabolic effects of AAS (301)
Anderson and Williams theory (296)
androgenic effects of AAS (301)
athlete with disabilities (294)
beta-blockers (304)
blood doping (boosting) (302)
classes of drugs subject to restrictions (303)
cognitive appraisal theory (296)
creatine (304)
deliberate practice (295)
Faustian philosophy (301)

human growth hormone (HGH) (304)
Kroll's Personality Performance Pyramid (292)
modification and attrition theory (292)
prohibited classes of substances (ergogenic aids) (299)
prohibited methods of administering drugs (302)
Sports Inventory for Pain (SIP) (298)

SUGGESTED READINGS

Davenport, J. (1994). A double-edge sword: Drugs in sport. In P. J. Graham (Ed.), *Sport business: Operational and theoretical aspects* (212–222). Dubuque, IA: Brown & Benchmark.
A particularly nice feature of this brief, highly readable article is its focus on the history of steroid abuse in sports, beginning with the isolation of the male hormone, testosterone, in 1935. The abuse of steroids at the various Olympic Games since 1952 also receives thorough coverage, with statistics and prominent case histories.

Ericsson, K. A. (1990). Peak performance and age: An examination of peak performance in sports. In P. B. Baltes & M. M. Baltes (Eds.), *Successful aging: Perspectives from the behavioral sciences.* New York: Cambridge University Press.
This is a scholarly treatise on the effects of age on elite performance. Gender differences, the age of peak performers by event in the Olympics, the role of practice in shaping exceptional performance, and a comparison of current master athletes with record holders from the 1896 Olympics are all given an interesting treatment. Master track and field athletes placed by age into five-year groupings from ages 50 through 69 bettered the winning 1896 Olympic times in five, three, two, and one instances—a finding that attests, among other things, to the durability of exceptional performance if regularly engaged in with deliberate practice over many years. The serious reader interested in exceptional performance is strongly encouraged to read the many works of K. Anders Ericsson.

Karch, S. B. (Ed.) (1998). *Drug abuse handbook.* Boston: CRC Press.
Chapter 9 of this substantial volume discusses in rather complex detail the many nuances of the sub-

stances and methods listed in the International Olympic Committee (IOC) classification system. Pharmacology, effects, detection, and ethics are all discussed at length. Though heavy on biochemistry at times, this edited collection should prove most useful for the reader interested in substance abuse in sports and fitness.

Pargman, D. (Ed.). (1993). *Psychological bases of sport injuries.* Morgantown, WV: Fitness Information Technology.

This edited collection is broken down into four major subareas: conceptual and practical approaches to sport injuries, psychological perspectives, counseling injured athletes, and counseling athletes with permanent disabilities. Within this fourfold framework, discussion centers on such topics as the prevention and treatment responsibilities of the athletic trainer, ethics, injury assessment, malingering athletes, mental strategies used in treatment, and considerations in dealing with permanently injured or disabled competitors. All 15 of the readings are written either by sport psychologists and other mental health professionals with expertise in athletic injuries or by experienced athletic trainers, and they have much to offer the reader interested in psychological aspects of athletic injury.

Stainback, R. D. (1997). *Alcohol and sport.* Champaign, IL: Human Kinetics.

A readable treatment of the use of alcohol in sport. Statistics about alcohol use and abuse, the effects of alcohol on performance, alcohol dependence among athletes, prevention, and treatment of the problem drinker are all presented in this abbreviated but informative work.

 INFOTRAC COLLEGE EDITION

For additional readings, explore Infotrac College Edition, your online library. Go to:
http://www.infotrac-college.com/wadsworth
Hint: Enter these search terms: anabolic steroids, drugs and athletics, ergogenic aids, Olympic athletes (drug use), psychological aspects of pain, sports for the handicapped, sports injuries, Wheelchair Sports, USA.

The Female Sport Experience: Historical Roots and Physiological Concerns

CHAPTER 19

A Brief History

The Physiological Dimension in Women's Athletics

Summary

Key Terms

Suggested Readings

Champion figure skater Sonja Henie does a twirl during a performance at the Rockefeller Center Ice Rink. Known as the "First Lady of the Ice," Henie placed eighth as a 12-year-old in the 1924 Olympics. She added first place medals in 1928, 1932, and 1936.

© Lucien Aigner/CORBIS

I am strong. I am invincible. I am woman.

HELEN REDDY, "I AM WOMAN" (1972)

They are women; they are getting strong; and they feel damn near invincible.

SALLY B. DONNELLY, TIME (1990)

What are little boys made of? Frogs and snails and puppy dog tails; That's what little boys are made of. What are little girls made of? Sugar and spice and everything nice; That's what little girls are made of.

ANONYMOUS

Come on son, you throw like a girl!

ANONYMOUS

Women in sport have indeed come a long way, and much progress has been made in carving out a genuine niche in sport and society. A great deal of work remains to achieve the total integration of women into the fabric of sport and everyday life.

The prevailing view of women as the so-called weaker sex and, as such, subservient to men has had a long history. The French philosopher Jean Jacques Rousseau (1712–1778) said, "Woman was made especially to please man. . . . If woman is formed to please and live in subjugation, she must render herself agreeable to man instead of provoking his wrath; her strength lies in her charms" (quoted in Spears, 1978, p. 7). A time line of similar sentiments about women is given in Highlight 19.1.

A BRIEF HISTORY

Other than events and personalities of the late twentieth century, there is little history of female involvement in sport and physical activity to report. To put it another way, female involvement in sport is relatively recent.

Ancient Greece

Women engaged in some sport activities in early Greece, but they were barred from participating in

---

Heraean Games competitive games for female athletes held in ancient Greece, counterpart to the male-only Olympic Games.

Olympic events and faced the death penalty for attempting to be spectators at the games. Nevertheless, they had an outlet for their athletic energies in the form of the **Heraean Games,** named in honor of Hera, the wife of Zeus. Like the Olympics, these Heraean Games were held every four years and consisted of races for unmarried girls (Mouratidis, 1984). The games were held in Olympus beginning in what Spears (1984) calls the Archaic Period (800 B.C.–500 B.C.). In summarizing the overall influence of sports on early Greek women, Spears has written: "The history of women's sport in ancient Greece must be viewed in the perspective of men's sport of the same period. Throughout the ancient literature any suggestion of sport-like activity for women becomes evidence because of its rarity" (p. 44).

Little of significance took place in women's athletics in modern Western societies until the inclusion of females in the Olympic Games in 1900. Prior to that time, female participation in physical activity was neither expected nor condoned. However, the modern Olympics ushered in a new era in women's athletics.

The Modern Olympics

The founder of the modern Olympics, Baron Pierre de Coubertin, reinstituted the games in 1896. Women began to participate in 1900, though de Coubertin was adamant in his view that they should not be allowed to do so (Emery, 1984; Gerber, Felshin, Berlin, & Wyrick, 1974). Over his considerable protests, two events for women, tennis and golf, were added to the 1900 games. Archery followed in 1904, though it had unofficial status at that time. In 1908, women's figure skating was made an official event, and unofficial competition was staged in gymnastics, swimming, and diving. Track and field events were added in 1928, though the debut was inauspicious. Emery (1984) reports that several runners fell upon completing the 800-meter run, which led the opponents of female participation to conclude that women were indeed not up to the challenge of strenuous athletics. The extent of the setback is reflected in the fact that the event was discontinued until the 1960 Olympics. Perhaps the ultimate strenuous running event, the marathon, was not added to the female events until 1984.

Female competitors are now an integral part of the Olympic process, and their presence is reflected in the

A Time Line of Older Sentiments Concerning Women in Sports

External stimuli such as cheering audiences, bands, lights, etc., cause a great response in girls and are apt to upset the endocrine balance. Under emotional stress a girl may easily overdo. There is widespread agreement that girls should not be exposed to extremes of fatigue or strain either emotional or physical.

Agnes Wayman, President of the American Physical Education Association, speaking at their annual meeting (Loggia, 1973, p. 64)

I hear they're even letting w-o-m-e-n in their sports programs now [referring to Oberlin College]. That's your Women's Liberation, boy—bunch of goddam Lesbians.... You can bet your ass that if you have women around—and I've talked to psychiatrists about this—you aren't gonna be worth a damn. No sir! Man has to dominate ... the best way to treat a woman ... is to knock her up and hide her shoes.

Woody Hayes, legendary Ohio State University football coach (Vare, 1974, p. 38)

We tried to organize a girls' sports program but it hasn't worked out very well.... Unfortunately, the girls didn't show a lot of interest. Only twelve came out for the team. There were two big tomboyish girls who remained quite enthused, but the others have not been faithful about practice. I'm not blaming them because I think a normal girl at that age is going to be more interested in catching a boy than catching a basketball.

High school athletic director (Gilbert & Williamson, 1973b, p. 47)

There is hardly a real mother in this nation who would not prefer to see her daughter dressed in a cute outfit, attracting boys and getting voted the most popular girl in her class and maybe marrying a football star after she graduates, rather than growing big muscles and looking like a man in some sport.

Anonymous South Carolina woman (Michener, 1976, p. 182)

Sports is a male sanctuary; therefore any woman who tries to invade it is not really a woman.

Anonymous (Lipsyte, 1975, p. 217)

---

wide range of sports in which they participate and also in their numbers. According to data from the U.S. Olympic Committee, 10,310 men and 3,513 women (36% of the total) participated in the 1996 Olympic Games at Atlanta, up almost 8% from the 1992 games in Barcelona (Closed Doors, 1996). With the addition of soccer and softball in 1996, the number of sports for women reached 25.

Eitzen and Sage (1982) provide additional information concerning the continuing development of women in the Olympics. They noted that in 1976 the time of a 15-year-old East German girl in the 400-meter freestyle swimming event was a full 3 seconds better than American Olympian Don Schollander's winning time in the same event for men only 12 years earlier. The Olympic Games have served a valuable function as a vehicle for promoting feminism in general and female sport involvement in particular.

Title IX Legislation

Another significant landmark in the development of women's athletics in the United States was the Higher Education Act of 1972 and its **Title IX Provision.**

Title IX Provision section of the Higher Education Act of 1972 that prohibits exclusion from educational programs, including physical education and sports, on the basis of sex.

The Heraean Games

The Heraean Games represented a formalized outlet for athletic skills among young women in ancient Greece. However, evidence suggests that the games were actually limited to a footrace, as Pausanias describes (Robinson, 1955, p. 9):

> The games consist of footraces for maidens. These are not all of the same age. The first to run are the youngest; after them come the next in age, and the last to run are the oldest of the maidens. They ran in the following way: Their hair hangs down, a tunic reaches to a little above the knee, and they bare a right shoulder as far as the breast. These too have the Olympic stadium reserved for

their games, but the course of the stadium is shortened for them by about one-sixth of its length. To the winning maidens they give crowns of olive and a portion of the cow sacrificed to Hera. They may also dedicate statues with their names inscribed upon them.

There is some evidence that the Heraean Games actually predated the Olympic Games and continued well into the first century A. D.

Source: Robinson (1955); Spears & Swanson (1983).

Title IX states: "No person in the United States shall, on the basis of sex, be excluded from participation in, be denied the benefits of, or be subjected to discrimination under any education program or activity receiving federal financial assistance." To achieve compliance with the provision's intent, a university must pass a three-part **Title IX Compliance Test,** shown in Table 19.1.

Though its effects were not immediately felt, some equalization of opportunity in sport at the high school and college level has come about through the provision of separate but equal women's teams, athletic scholarship opportunity, and other perquisites previously available only to male athletes. Though the battle for equality has not been a smooth one, the net effect of Title IX legislation so far is that women have achieved more equity in terms of facilities, coaching, fairness in scheduling, equipment, and selection of sports.

Title IX Compliance Test three-part test that U.S. universities must pass to demonstrate that they meet the standards set by this provision of the Higher Education Act.
Unintended consequences of Title IX male and female coaches receive increasingly disparate salaries; women's sport receives far lower budget allotments; male administrators govern women's sport; money allocations by gender are disproportionate.

A most significant challenge to Title IX was lodged in 1984 in the landmark legal case known as *Grove City v. Bell*. In this case, the court ruled that athletics did not come under the Title IX umbrella because athletics did not receive federal financial assistance. Fortunately, the Civil Rights Restoration Act of 1988 overrode *Grove City v. Bell* and mandated that universities and colleges receiving federal funding for *anything* were bound by the Title IX legislation (Tallant, 1997).

While the overall effect of the legislation has been a positive one for women's sports, there have been a number of **unintended consequences of Title IX** along with potentially harmful side effects. First, coaching salaries have become increasingly disproportionate in the years of Title IX. For example, statistics for the academic year 1997–1998 reveal that the average salary for a male basketball coach in Division I-A is $121,000; for female coaches, the figure is $74,000 (Wieberg, 1999). Looking at salaries from a slightly different perspective, Wong (1998) reported results of a *USA Today* survey of average salaries at Division I-A universities fielding football teams. In these universities, the average male coach across all sports made $135,000, whereas the average female coach made $99,000, a discrepancy of $36,000. Average salaries, of course, are skewed by the disproportionate money paid

Title IX Compliance Test

1) *Demonstrate that sport participation opportunities for each gender are substantially proportionate to its full-time undergraduate enrollment.* For example, if the undergraduate enrollment at a particular university is 50% female, 50% of the athletes there should be women. As of 1997, nine NCAA Division I programs met the proportionality test, and they were, in order of degree of compliance, Air Force, Navy, Army, Georgia Tech, Washington State, Virginia Tech, Kansas, Utah, and Washington. Schools with the greatest disparities in terms of proportionality, again in order, were Arkansas State, Southern Mississippi, Southwest Louisiana (now University of Louisiana–Lafayette), Texas Christian University, and Northeast Louisiana—Monroe (Brady & Weiberg, 1997).

2) *Demonstrate a history and continuing practice of expansion in its women's athletics program.* To this provision, Sabo (1998) reports results of a survey of 637 NCAA-affiliated universities for the years 1978 to 1996. Overall, women's sports programs increased by a total of 1,658 programs, while men netted 74 across all NCAA divisions. When only Division I-A and II-A are considered, there was a net loss of 152 men's programs. Some would say that these programs for men were sacrificed so that women's programs could be added. An alternative interpretation suggested by Sabo is that the shortchanging of men may be more an artifact of overspending in other areas of the men's athletic program operating budget. You don't suppose Sabo had the collegiate cash cow football in mind, do you?

3) *Demonstrate that the interests and abilities of members of the underrepresented sex have been fully accommodated.* This is a more nebulous standard, and a recent clarification from the U.S. Department of Education's Title IX enforcement wing, the Office of Civil Rights (OCR), has helped clarify matters. Essentially, the university athletic department must ask itself if there is enough ability and unmet interest to field a team and if enough competition exists to make it worthwhile.

to male coaches in the high-profile sports of football and basketball.

Second, only 22% of all expenditures in Division 1-A sports were allocated to women as of 1997–1998. The average Division 1-A school was 53% female, yet only 37% of females were athletes (Wieberg, 1999).

Yet another unintended consequence of Title IX is that males have taken over the administration of women's sports. In 1972, 90% of all women's programs across all divisions were administered by women; in 1992, that figure was 16.8%. In addition, only 15% of all women's programs in Division 1-A had at least one woman involved in athletic administration, Division I-AA had 39% and Division 1-AAA had 32% (Gender Equity Survey, 1992).

A fourth problem is concerned with the so-called bottom line, money allocations by gender. In Division 1-A athletic programs, 64% of the scholarship money, 78% of the operating expenses, and 76% of recruiting dollars were spent on men's programs in 1995–1996. At the same time, 65% of Division I athletes were female (Wieberg, 1997).

Another forum for expression of athletic interest by females in universities is intramural sports. Tharp (1994) surveyed 65 directors of intramural programs and found that participation by women had noticeably increased since the passage of Title IX. However, 16 of the 65 directors responding to Tharp's survey reported reductions in the number of activities offered for women. The money saved from program reductions was then used to fund intercollegiate sports for women attending these 16 universities. Also noted was a decrease over time in the number of women intramural directors, obviously an unintended consequence. Concerning this point survey data from Pufahl (1987) indicates that 81% of all intramural program directors are male.

The picture is not altogether a negative one; recent evidence from Berg (1995) points to an ever-so-slight reversal of the unintended consequences theme and offers a note of optimism for the future. R. Vivian Acosta and Linda Jean Carpenter at Brooklyn College have observed women's collegiate sports since 1978, serving as monitors of the progress (or, at times, the lack

A Modern Time Line of Historic Moments in Women's Sports

1894   Women are allowed to participate at Wimbledon, the premier tennis event in the world. According to Hargreaves (1990, p. 17), the first all-female match was described as "a leisurely affair, all the more so as the distinguished charmers participating were weighed down by heavy dresses over multi-petticoats, and were permitted to simper, to take a rest if their service broke down—in a final which provided more titters than jitters."

1896   The Olympic Games are reinstituted, but women are barred from participating. Melpomene, a female runner from Greece, is an unofficial entrant in the marathon.

1912   Tennis and swimming are the only two Olympic events for women. However, the American women are not allowed to take part because of the scanty nature of the swimwear; the American tennis players boycott their event in a sympathy gesture to the swimmers.

1928   Sonja Henie, arguably the best female figure skater of all time, wins the first of her three Olympic medals.

1930   A Czech, Zdena Koublova, wins the 800-meter run at the Third World Women's Games. Czech officials later admit that Koublova is male, and this admission eventually leads to the institution of gender testing for females in sports.

1936   Women are barred from Hitler's new Olympic Village during the 1936 Olympiad.

1948   Fannie Blankers-Koen, a Dutch woman and mother of two, wins four Olympic gold medals in track.

1964   The first team sport for women, volleyball, is added to the Olympic Games in Tokyo.

1969   Gender testing is implemented at the Olympic Games.

1971   Billie Jean King, of professional tennis fame, wins $117,000 during the year, marking the first time a woman has earned a six-figure income in any sport.

1972   Olga Connolly, a five-time Olympian in track and field, is named captain of the U.S. team, a fact that did not merit mentioning in the Olympic Games book of 1972. The East German women win 20 of 28 possible gold medals in swimming and track and field, raising the specter of illegal use of banned substances in competition.

1977   Janet Guthrie becomes the first woman to drive in the Indianapolis 500, qualifying with a four-lap average of 188 miles per hour.

1982   Judy Mable Lutter founds the Melpomene Institute, named in honor of the Greek marathon runner in the 1896 Olympic Games, to foster a greater awareness of women's issues both inside and outside the field of athletics.

1988   Dorothy Harris is the first woman to receive a Fulbright fellowship specifically for conducting research in sports.

1990   Rick Pitino of the University of Kentucky appoints Bernadette Locke as the first female assistant coach of a Division 1-A men's basketball team. (Locke took over as head coach of the Kentucky women's basketball team in 1995.)

1991   Judy Sweet, athletic director at San Diego State University, becomes the first female president of the National College Athletic Association (NCAA). Terry Taylor, age 40, is named sports editor for the Associated Press, a rarity in sports writing.

1995   Kendra Wecker becomes the first female to qualify for the national finals in the National Football League Punt, Pass, and Kick Competition.

1997   The National Basketball Association (NBA) hires its first two female officials.

1997   The Women's National Basketball Association (WNBA) kicks off its inaugural season.

1998   Ila Borders becomes the first female to pitch and win a game in men's professional baseball.

SOURCES: *Houston Chronicle, Inside Sports, Sports Illustrated, Time, USA Today.*

thereof) of the Title IX legislation. Data from their 1994 report *Women in Intercollegiate Sport: A Seventeen-Year Update* are encouraging. Chief among the findings: (1) the percentage of female coaches has edged closer to 50% than it has in eight years; (2) the number of athletic programs with no female administrator dropped below 25% for the first time in 10 years; (3) 49.4% of women's teams in 1994 were coached by females, up from the 48.1% figure in 1993; (4) NCAA schools offered 7.22 sports for women in 1994, up from 7.02 in 1993 and 5.61 in 1978; (5) there were 6,371 head-coaching jobs with women's teams, a gain of 653 since 1990; the number of assistant coaching jobs held by women has grown by 411 since 1990; (6) there were 2,533 athletic administration jobs in women's sports programs, a gain of 659 since 1990; (7) 21% of women's programs were headed by women, up from 16.8% in 1992.

Acosta and Carpenter summarize: "This year's summary brings with it good news on several fronts. Participation rates are up. The percentage of females serving as head coaches is up. The number of programs administered by women is up, and the number of schools including a woman's voice somewhere within their athletic administrative structure is up" (Berg, 1995, p. 9). Much work remains to be done in bringing about the equity of participation and money allocations that was the intent of the Title IX legislation. In all likelihood, the same thing can be said for the broader issue of women's rights across the societal spectrum.

Contemporary Forces in Women's Athletics

In addition to the historical antecedents, a few contemporary forces have been at work in propelling women's efforts to the athletic forefront. Over and above the Title IX legislation, Coakley (1982) cites four reasons why there has been a demonstrable increase in female participation in sport. One is simply an *increase in opportunity*. Greater numbers of teams in a broader array of sports are highly noticeable today. Also, the fallout created by what might be called *the women's movement* has most certainly touched women's sport. Yet a third force is the *fitness boom* of the past decade. It has become fashionable for women to work out and fully participate in

the fitness revolution. Finally, the *presence of role models* for aspiring young female athletes is a refreshing addition. Young girls are increasingly being afforded worthy role models in track and field, golf, tennis, swimming, the marathon, and other sports. As Coakley points out, professional athletes are important role models, but they are surpassed in impact by real-life neighborhood or school athletes with whom younger girls can identify.

Now that we have a historical and contemporary perspective on women's sports, we can consider the physiological dimensions of female sport participation.

THE PHYSIOLOGICAL DIMENSION IN WOMEN'S ATHLETICS

The scientific community at times has questioned the ability of women to compete because of a variety of physiological concerns including menstrual function, reproduction, and the breasts and genitals. Some researchers have proposed that involvement in strenuous physical activity is damaging to these various structures and/or functions. To this point, Dr. Geoffrey Theobald (1936, p. 871) stated over six decades ago: "I am convinced of two things: (a) that physical activity is as good for women as it is for men; (b) that excess exercise is more harmful to women than to men. . . . It must of course be axiomatic that nothing can be good for a girl's body which renders her less capable of motherhood."

Menstrual Functioning

There has been an ongoing debate on the effect of physical activity on the menstrual cycle. Arnold (1924), a prominent physical educator of the early 1900s, discouraged female involvement in sport because of the deleterious effects of physical exertion on the frequency and extent of menstruation. It was widely believed that physical exertion during the menses would endanger the reproductive capabilities of female participants. Another prominent physical educator of that era, Mabel Lee, conducted surveys in 1923 and 1930 in which 60% of her respondents echoed Arnold's concern with the dangers of disrupting the menstrual process (Lee, 1924, 1931). Lee was, incidentally, the first woman president of the American Alliance for Health, Physical Education, Recreation and Dance (AAHPERD) and at age 96 wrote a book on the history of sport and physical activity (Lee, 1983).

EARLY STUDIES. Despite early skepticism, evidence that ran counter to the prevailing skepticism about the interactive effects of exercise on menstruation and reproduction began to accumulate. Landmark studies by Erdelyi (1962) and Zaharieva (1965) did much to demonstrate that strenuous exercise did not negatively affect the menstrual cycle nor did menstruation significantly affect physical performance in a negative way. Erdelyi conducted an intensive study of 729 Hungarian female athletes, and Zaharieva's work was with 66 female Olympians from ten different countries taking part in four different sports (gymnastics, swimming, track and field, and volleyball). Much of the early scientific data on the exercise–menstruation issue has come from their combined works. Major conclusions drawn from their efforts are:

1. Some female athletes do in fact suffer a performance decrement during the menses, but the majority of subjects reported similar or improved performance as the norm.

2. Of Zaharieva's subjects, 46% reported that they felt no differently during the menses; 32% reported feeling weaker at the time.

3. Ninety-two percent of Zaharieva's subjects were rhythmic in their menstrual periods. Length of menses was not adversely affected, and blood flow was generally normal. Among those who were irregular (6.1%), most were young enough for their irregularity to be more likely a function of youth than of sport participation. Erdelyi found similar results with his Hungarian athletes, with 83.8% reporting no change in menstrual cycle throughout training and competition. Eleven percent reported irregularity.

Further elaboration on these results comes from research by Astrand, Eriksson, Nylander, Engstrom,

Karlberg, Saltin, and Thoren (1963) and Ingman (1952). Astrand et al. studied 84 Swedish swimmers and found that 15.5% reported menstrual problems while training, though the complaints ceased at the end of competition. Ingman, in a study of 107 top Finnish athletes, reported unfavorable changes in 18% of his subjects. Overall, it would appear that these papers from the 1960s did much to dispel misconceptions about menstruation and performance.

LATER STUDIES. Given that some research (Webb, Millan, & Stolz, 1979) has shown higher rates of menstrual disturbance than reported by earlier authorities, as well as concern with menstrual difficulties associated with overtraining (Erdelyi, 1976), the exercise–menstruation debate continues unabated. For instance, Webb et al. reported a 59% rate in menstrual difficulties in a group of 56 Olympic athletes (basketball, gymnastics, track and field, swimming, and rowing). Primary among the complaints were "missing my period" ($n = 17$) and "delay in onset of period" ($n = 16$). Foreman (see Bloomberg, 1977), in a study of the women's AAU cross-country championships in 1971 and 1973, found 43% of the runners to be either irregular or very irregular in menstrual functioning. Lutter and Cushman (1982) found, in a study of 35 distance runners, that 19.3% of these women reported irregular menstrual periods and 3.4% reported having no period for the previous year.

A link seems to exist between strenuous physical activity and disruptions in the menstrual cycle. Why this relationship exists and what the consequences are in terms of the total health picture of the participants are subjects of considerable speculation.

CAUSES OF MENSTRUAL DIFFICULTIES. A number of theories have been advanced to explain why sport participation causes menstrual difficulties. One theory is that of Frisch (Frisch, 1976; Frisch & McArthur, 1974). **Frisch's hypothesis** centers around the relationship between body mass and percentage of body fat. The theory is that once body fat percentage drops below a certain point, a chain reaction of biochemical changes takes place, causing a cessation of menstrual periods.

Though the argument has a certain amount of surface appeal, evidence does not universally support Frisch's hypothesis. For example, Plowman (1989) cites

---

Frisch's hypothesis lowering of a woman's body fat below a certain point (i.e., during athletic training) produces biochemical changes leading to a cessation of menstrual periods.

PART FOUR *Personality, Assessment, and Special Athletic Populations*

three areas of criticism, the first of which is methodological, particularly a failure to use standard methods for assessing percentage of body fat. Second, Plowman points to problems in statistical interpretation. Third, Plowman cites experimental evidence from a dozen pieces of research in which the conclusions run counter to those of Frisch. It appears that Plowman is correct in her assertion that there are methodological, statistical, and evidentiary concerns that call the Frisch hypothesis into serious question.

Another possible source of menstrual difficulties has been advanced from an endocrinological perspective, pointing to hormonal changes within female athletes (Loucks, 1990). Also implicated as possible etiological agents have been heavy exercise training, most particularly in runners who log many miles per week (Feicht, Johnson, Martin, Sparkles, & Wagner, 1978); stress (Sasiene, 1983); diet (Sanborn, 1986); and engaging in strenuous physical activity prior to menarche (Frisch, Gotz-Welbergen, McArthur, Albright, Witschi, Bullen, Birnholz, Reed, & Hermann, 1981).

CONSEQUENCES OF MENSTRUAL DIFFICULTIES. Several sources point to disruption of the normal menstrual cycle and the effects of strenuous training as possible causes of difficulties associated with pregnancy. However, the preponderance of the data bearing on this issue does not support such a stance. Erdelyi (1962) and Zaharieva (1965), in a combined study of more than 740 female athletes, showed that the athletes had shorter labor periods, fewer instances of toxemia, fewer premature deliveries, and a lower rate of Caesarean sections than did a comparable nonathletic sample. Astrand et al. (1963) obtained similar results in their study of 84 elite swimmers. Gerber, Felshin, Berlin, and Wyrick (1974) attribute this finding to superior conditioning in fit females. The fitness associated with athletics does in fact appear to be conducive to a good pregnancy and delivery. However, is pregnancy a handicap when an athlete is trying to perform? Anecdotal reports would have us believe that the answer is no. Juno Stover Irwin won an Olympic medal in diving (10-meter board) during her fourth month of pregnancy (Kaplan, 1979); Sue Pirtle Hays successfully competed in world championship rodeo as a bareback bronco rider when she was eight months pregnant (Kaplan, 1979); three medal winning divers in the 1952

Olympics were pregnant at the time they competed (Dyer, 1982); 10 of 20 Russian medal winners in the 1956 Olympics were pregnant at the time (Dyer, 1982). Reports such as these certainly give the impression that pregnancy and top-level performance are not incompatible. In particular, evidence from Erdelyi supports these anecdotal observations. She found that two-thirds of 172 Hungarian female athletes with children continued normal sport functioning in the early phases of pregnancy, though performance decrements were typically visible beyond the third or fourth month, at which time most of these athletes stopped serious competition.

Athletes appear to return to top form rather quickly after childbirth. Zaharieva and Sigler (1963), in a combined effort involving 207 Spanish and Hungarian athletes, found that all had between one and four children and over 75% of them bettered their Olympic results within two years after delivery, most in the first year. Bloom (1986) interviewed the world-class American distance runner, Mary Decker Slaney, and reported that she was back on the track six days after giving birth and was running almost normally at one month. Brownlee (1988) cites personal records achieved following childbirth in such world-class athletes as Valerie Brisco, Ingrid Kristiansen, and Tatyana Kazankina (track); Nancy Lopez (golf); Karen Kania (speed skating); Pat McCormick (diving); and Steffi Martin Walter (luge). Gwen Torrance won the 1992 Olympics 200-meter dash three years after giving birth to son Manley Waller, Jr.; she continued to be the top 200-meter runner in the world through 1994 (Patrick, 1994). Cheryl Swoopes of Texas Tech University found out that she was pregnant shortly after helping the United States win the Olympic basketball championship in 1996; she has gone on from there to become what many regard as the best basketball player in the Women's National Basketball Association (WNBA). A not so well known but elite performer, Kathy Hughes, has completed three Ironman triathlons in Hawaii since the birth of her fifth child in 1990.

Partially as a result of these success stories, a most interesting and sad revelation took place on German television in 1994. Olga Kovalenko, a gold medal gymnast, revealed that she was asked by the Russian government to become pregnant as part of her preparation for the 1968 Olympics and then undergo an abortion a short time later. The powers that ruled Russian sport at that time apparently believed that pregnancy was actually a boon to training and athletic performance. (Women's Sports and Fitness, 1998).

With regard to exercising during pregnancy, recent research by Sternfeld, Quesenberry, Eskenazi, and Newman (1995) demonstrates that there are many similarities with the findings related to elite athletes. Sternfeld et al. studied 388 pregnant women, mean age 31.7, and found that participation in a regular program of aerobics did not adversely affect birth weight or other maternal or infant outcomes and was associated with fewer perceived pregnancy-related discomforts. A later review of the literature on the topic (Sternfeld, 1997), supported the findings of Sternfeld et al. The position statement of the American College of Obstetricians and Gynecologists (ACOG) as presented by Pivarnik (1994) lends additional support. Based on the results of 85 published studies since 1985 and input based on clinical experience, the ACOG recommendation encourages a proactive consultative partnership between a woman and her obstetrician concerning an individualized program of exercise during pregnancy. Pivarnik (1998) conducted a later review of the literature on this issue and has concluded that a sensible regimen of physical activity during pregnancy offers no great health risks to the fetus. Both Pivarnik and the Sternfeld group do issue a caveat that heavy regimens of exercise may be problematic.

All things considered, fears of menstrual problems and pregnancy complications as a function of sport participation and/or exercise may be largely unfounded. Perhaps Gerber et al. (1974, pp. 514–515) summarize the research best: "On the whole, female athletes can look forward to a normal, vigorous and robust life, for the most part free of menstrual disorders and complications with marriage, pregnancy, and childbirth."

Other Problems

Coakley (1982) discusses at length a number of myths that serve as means for excluding women from total participation in sport. Three myths that Coakley cites have already been discussed; others include damage to the breasts and reproductive organs, a more fragile bone structure in females, and the notion that sport participation creates bulging muscles in females. All of these concerns, according to Coakley, are myths. No convincing evidence exists that either the breasts or the reproductive organs are at risk. The breasts are spared risk for the early years because of lack of maturation and can readily be protected when potential harm is a factor. In a study of 361 colleges and universities, Gillette (1975) indicated that breast injuries associated with sport were the least common among nine areas of injury. Similarly, Hunter and Torgan (1982) found no instance of injury to any University of Washington female athlete during the period 1976 through 1981. As for the uterus, Dunkle (1974) and Eitzen and Sage (1982) both indicate that it is a most shock-resistant organ. In terms of actual risk, males are much more susceptible because their sexual organs are external and thus vulnerable to trauma.

The bone structure of women is indeed smaller than that of men, but it's not more fragile. According to Gerber et al. (1974), the average male is 20% stronger than the average female, has a 25% faster reaction time, and has a cardiovascular capacity advantage of 25% to 50%. These gender differences translate into more power, speed, quickness, and strength for males. The same factors also contribute to what appears to be high injury rates among males. Coakley indicates that the injury rates are actually about as high for females as for males, but these equal rates are more attributable to poor coaching, training, and general carelessness in the case of female competitors than to any inherent "fragile" structures.

Bulging muscles simply do not occur to any great extent in the absence of male sex hormones. Normal exercise has a facilitative effect on muscle tone, and females should not shy away from exertion out of fear of becoming mannish. In a study of 116 American elite female athletes from seven different sports, May, Veach, Daily-McKee, and Furman (1985) indicated that the majority did not feel that vigorous training resulted in a masculine appearance. Moreover, even among those who believed that their training was conducive to muscle development, the consensus was that the effects were positive.

Count all-time tennis great Martina Navratilova among the enthusiasts of muscle development, though such was not always the case. When she defected to the United States from Czechoslovakia in 1975, Martina was embarrassed by her powerful build and did her best to hide her muscular physique. As time passed, it became apparent to her that muscles were acceptable, thanks in part to the growing fitness movement among women. When she realized that, Navratilova felt free to dress as she pleased (Donnelly, 1990).

In summary, it does not appear that there are any severe physical or physiological repercussions for females who seek to play sports or engage in fitness activities. However, some lingering concern exists with regard to rigorous training that interferes with menstrual functioning. Additional research is necessary to bring this issue closer to resolution.

SUMMARY

1. Because of past biases and the current developmental status of women's sport, a separate chapter has been devoted to the female athlete.

2. Though women in ancient Greece were generally oppressed athletically, they did have their own analogue to the Olympics, the Heraean Games, named after Hera, the wife of Zeus.

3. Not until 1896, with the founding of the modern Olympic Games, were women accorded much of a place in sport. With each successive Olympics since then, the athletic menu for women has gradually expanded. Over 3,500 women took part in the 1996 Games.

4. Title IX of the Higher Education Act of 1972 has served as another landmark in women's sports. Its main effect has been to set the stage for equal opportunity in sport. Some unintended consequences of Title IX have had an impact on job opportunities and salaries for female coaches and men's and women's athletic programs at the collegiate level.

5. Contemporary factors such as increased opportunity, fallout produced by the women's movement, the recent fitness boom, and the presence of female role models have all served as additional forces in enhancing women's sport involvement.

6. Relevant physiological issues include menstrual functioning, pregnancy, and childbirth, and myths related to female participation in sport.

7. Menstrual functioning has attracted much interest among sport scientists. Early speculation was that menstruation and physical exertion did not mix,

thereby creating a host of problems for the involved females.

8. Early 1960s research by Erdelyi with Hungarian female athletes and by Zaharieva with Olympic athletes from 10 countries did much to dispel the earlier skepticism about the effect of athletic participation on menstrual function.

9. Recent studies have complicated our understanding of the relationship between menstruation and sport. Though not as negative as the earliest speculations, they are not quite as positive as the findings of Erdelyi and Zaharieva.

10. Causes of menstrual difficulties in athletes are numerous. Frisch has advanced a theory suggesting that these problems are reactions to a disturbed body mass to percentage of body fat ratio. Other authorities point to an endocrinological explanation, excessively strenuous training, and heavy training prior to menarche as possible etiological agents.

11. The consequences of these menstrual cycle disruptions appear to be minimal or nonexistent in terms of pregnancy or childbirth. Female athletes compete well in the early stages of pregnancy, appear to have easy, uncomplicated deliveries, and in some cases compete even more effectively after childbirth.

12. The myth that sport participation by women endangers their breasts and internal sexual structures has not been supported. Further myths lacking support include the notion that women are structurally less able than men to compete and that sport produces bulging, unattractive muscles.

KEY TERMS

Frisch's hypothesis (316)
Heraean Games (310)
Title IX Compliance Test (312)
Title IX Provision (311)
Unintended consequences of Title IX (312)

SUGGESTED READINGS

Important dates, significant suits in law's history. (1997). *USA Today,* June 20, 11C.

This brief article discusses the history of the Title IX legislation from its enactment in 1972 to the filing of a lawsuit on behalf of 25 colleges and universities for sex discrimination against female athletes by the National Women's Law Center. This chronology hits the legal high points, with emphasis on the *Grove City College v. Bell* and the *Cohen v. Brown University* cases, which have been pivotal in focusing attention on abuses of Title IX legislation.

International encyclopedia of women and sports. (2001). New York: Macmillan.

This book provides scholars, students, and sports enthusiasts with a comprehensive coverage of the history and culture of women in sport throughout the world. Sections include Culture of Sports, Contemporary Issues, Health and Fitness, and Biographies. Entries range from 250-word biographies to 4,000-word survey articles addressing a multitude of topics relevant to women in sport.

Nelson, M. B. (1994). *The stronger women get, the more men love football: Sexism and the American culture of sports.* New York: Harcourt and Brace.

Mariah Burton Nelson's second book after *Are we winning yet: How women are changing sports and sports are changing women* (1991) provides an in-depth look at how sports have influenced attitudes about gender in American culture.

Ryan, J. (1995). *Little girls in pretty boxes: The making and breaking of elite gymnasts and figure skaters.* New York: Doubleday.

This grim account of the underbelly of competing in gymnastics and figure skating at the elite level details eating disorders, out-of-control parents, and abusive coaches. The book offers a rare glimpse into the world of sports in which dreams of glory go awry in the face of pressure, eating disorders, and career and/or life-threatening injuries.

INFOTRAC COLLEGE EDITION

For additional readings, explore Infotrac College Edition, your online library. Go to: http://www.infotrac-college.com/wadsworth *Hint:* Enter these search terms: neural transmission, sympathetic nervous system, cerebral cortex, brain imaging, behavioral genetics, Educational Amendments Act of 1972, women's sports, Women's Sport Foundation, amenorrhea.

The Female Sport Experience: Sport Socialization, Psychological Variables, and Other Issues

CHAPTER 20

Socialization Into Sport
Psychological Variables
Other Issues Involving Women in Sport
Summary
Key Terms
Suggested Readings

The graceful and talented professional tennis star, Anna Kournakova, has helped promote women's athletics throughout the world.

© AP/Wide World Photos

Babe Didrikson Zaharias

In 1950, the Associated Press (AP) named Mildred Ella Didrikson Zaharias, or "the Babe," the top female athlete of the first half of the twentieth century. There have been, and continue to be, many outstanding female athletes in the world, but most were exceptional within a narrow range of activity. Not so the Babe; her awe-inspiring list of accomplishments crosses a variety of athletic endeavors.

Golf

Amateur

First to win U.S. Women's Amateur title
First to win British Women's Amateur title
Won 17 Amateur Tournaments in succession in 1946–1947

Professional

Leading money winner on Ladies Professional Golf Association (LPGA) tour in 1948, 1949, 1950, 1951
Won world championship in 1948, 1949, 1950, 1951
Won U. S. Women's Open championship in 1948, 1950, 1954, the last by 12 strokes

Track and Field

Amateur Athletic Union (AAU) National Championships

First Place, Javelin (1930)
First Place, 80-Meter Hurdles (1931)
First Place, Long Jump (1931)

First Place, Eight-Pound Shot Put (1932)
First Place, Baseball Throw (1930, 1931, 1932)

The Olympic Games (1932)

Gold Medal, Javelin
Gold Medal, 80-Meter Hurdles
Silver Medal, High Jump

Miscellaneous Sports

Baseball

Pitched and played infield for touring House of David men's team
Pitched spring training for major league men's teams (it was reported that she once struck out Joe DiMaggio)

Basketball

Three-time All-American (1930, 1931, 1932)

Softball

Played on two city championship teams in Dallas

Honors

Woman Athlete of the Half Century by Associated Press
AP Female Athlete of the Year (1932, 1945, 1946, 1947, 1950, 1954)
Elected to LPGA Hall of Fame (1951)
Elected to National Track and Field Hall of Fame (1974)

The emergence of women in sport and fitness, as we saw in Chapter 19, is a relatively new occurrence. Getting society to accept the idea that women can compete in sport and fitness activities has been a tough sell. Nevertheless, a number of agents of socialization have been at work over the years, and we will look at some of them. The psychological makeup of women taking part in sports has also been of interest over the past several decades, and sport attribu-

tions, psychological androgyny, and fear of success have been dominant research themes in the psychological literature.

The gradual socialization of women into the world of sport and fitness has had its downside. Media coverage of females is often sparse or negative. Homophobic discrimination also continues to be problematic for women in sports. Finally, eating disorders are a major societal problem, and sport and exercise have seen

Elected to the International Women's Sports Hall of Fame (1980)

Elected to the U.S. Olympic Hall of Fame (1983)

In addition to the preceding accomplishments, Babe Didrikson Zaharias was an accomplished seamstress, gourmet cook, interior decorator, harmonica player, and pool player. Throughout all of her competitions, Babe enjoyed the support of her 300-pound husband, ex-professional wrestler George ("the Crying Greek from Cripple Creek") Zaharias (Whatta Woman, 1947).

The Babe died of cancer at the age of 45 in 1956, leaving behind a sport legacy that may never be matched. In a touching memorial to Babe Didrikson Zaharias, the legendary sportswriter Grantland Rice summarized much of her athletic career with this bit of what Johnson and Williamson (1975, p. 48) have called "tin-ear doggerel":

> From the high jump of Olympic fame,
> The hurdles and the rest
> The javelin that flashed its flame
> On by the record test—
> The Texas Babe now shifts the scene
> Where slashing drives are far

In the Olympic Games, August 3, 1932, Mildred Didrikson (*second from left*) winner of the javelin throw, came back with her second world record performance, winning the first heat of the 80-meter hurdles. © Copyright 2001 PhotoDisc, Inc.

> Where spoon shots find the distant green
> To break the back of par.

more than their share of this enigmatic behavior, particularly among women. In this chapter we will explore each of these issues in detail.

SOCIALIZATION INTO SPORT

Sport socialization is the process whereby young females are socialized into taking part in sports. This process is often facilitated by family members, but faces obstacles in the form of role conflict with traditional expectancies for females as well as the notion that some sports are more gender-appropriate than others.

Csikszentmihalyi and Bennett (1971) have suggested that game complexity and skill levels demanded

---

Sport socialization the process whereby females are socialized into taking part in sports; often facilitated by family role models but complicated by conflict with traditional female roles and the acceptability of various sports.

for various activities favor young males. These writers suggest that the "ceiling" on boys' games is higher than that on girls' games. For example, tee ball baseball may be most captivating for 6- or 7-year-olds. Those who stick with the sport for the next several years and who acquire the necessary skills will continue to find the game of baseball intriguing. In contrast, games that first-grade girls enjoy, such as jumping rope or playing tag, they will still play four or five years later, but with little enjoyment; in effect, the girls reached their ceiling of skill long before. These sorts of differences lie at the heart of the issue of sex role socialization and sport. Though this situation has changed greatly of late, males are rewarded for competing, whereas females are seen as sacrificing femininity if they throw themselves into competitive situations, such as athletics. In an effort to explain women's sports participation, we shall look, in turn, at role conflict, agents of socialization, acceptability of various sports, and reasons that females compete.

Role Conflict

Oglesby (1984) cites evidence indicating that parents consistently perceive sex differences between their male and female children even though no objective differences exist. For example, Rees and Andres (1980) found no significant grip strength differences in 4- to 6-year-old boys and girls, though 72% of their respondents reported that boys are stronger. Oglesby further indicates that bipolar trait definitions of the two genders imply that males are active, aggressive, public, cultural, rule governed, instrumental, goal oriented, organized, dominating, competitive, and controlled (i.e., possessing instrumentality). In contrast, females are viewed as passive, submissive, private, natural, idiosyncratic, expressive, chaotic, disorganized, subordinate, cooperative, and uncontrolled (i.e., possessing expressiveness). When a female chooses to be active, aggressive, and goal oriented and to engage in instrumental behaviors, she is at risk for experiencing **role conflict.**

Role conflict in the sports context, when a female chooses to be active, aggressive and goal oriented and to engage in instrumental behaviors, she may experience inner conflict about appropriating a "male" role.

An early investigation of role conflict in sport was carried out by Brown (1965). Using the semantic differential technique (Osgood, Suci, & Tannenbaum, 1957) in which concepts are evaluated through responses to words arranged in a bipolar fashion (e.g., weak–strong, hot–cold, beautiful–ugly), Brown investigated attitudes toward such female roles as cheerleader, sexy girl, twirler, tennis player, feminine girl, swimmer, and basketball player. In general, the athletic roles were deemed less desirable than the other female activities by both college males and females. In another early investigation, Griffin (1973) reported that semantic differential responses to the concepts of ideal woman, girlfriend, mother, housewife, woman professor, and woman athlete indicated that the latter two concepts were least favorably viewed by a large sample of undergraduate students. A model representing the semantic distance between these six roles is reported in Figure 20.1. Griffin viewed these results as indicative of no shift in attitudes toward nontraditional roles for women.

Snyder, Kivlin, and Spreitzer (1975) found that 65% of college women respondents reported feeling that a stigma is attached to female participation in sport. Sage and Loudermilk (1979), in a study of college female athletes, reported that 26% of these women reported great or very great role conflict.

Subsequent reports have been more encouraging. For instance, Snyder and Spreitzer (1978), in a comparison of the attitudes of high school girls participating in sports or music, found no real stigma attached to female participation in sports. Female athletes were as adjusted as the female nonathletes in this study. Kingsley, Brown, and Seibert (1977) compared college students' attitudes toward the concepts of dancer with high and low success aspirations and softball player with high and low success aspirations. Results indicated that athletes, regardless of sport, rated the softball player as more acceptable than the dancer; nonathletes did not rate the dancer significantly higher than the softball player; and the softball player was rated significantly higher than the dancer by all subjects. Vickers, Lashuk, and Taerum (1980) used a semantic differential technique to evaluate four concepts: male, male athlete, female, and female athlete. Subjects were students from seventh-grade, tenth-grade, and college classes, and all subjects were positive toward both male

FIGURE 20.1

A Model Representing the Semantic Distance Among Six Women's Roles

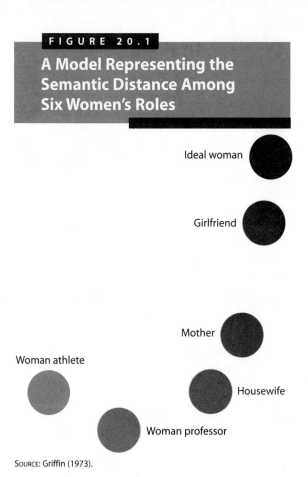

Ideal woman

Girlfriend

Mother

Woman athlete

Housewife

Woman professor

SOURCE: Griffin (1973).

A father teaching his daughter to play golf. The role of parents in fostering an interest in sports among females has been well-documented.
© AP/Wide World Photos

and female athletes. In fact, female athlete was the highest rated of the four concepts. Michael, Gilroy, and Sherman (1984) asked equal numbers of male and female athletes and nonathletes to evaluate hypothetical female athletes and nonathletes. Athletes and nonathletes of both sexes found the athlete to be more attractive than the nonathlete.

Brown (1988), in summarizing a survey conducted under the auspices of the Women's Sport Foundation and Wilson Sporting Goods, found that as females get older, they view females who play sports as either very popular (55%) or a little popular (41%). Seventy-eight percent of the respondents did not think that boys made fun of girls who play sports. Apparently, female involvement in sports is gaining acceptance with both genders and may actually be positively related to popularity in high-school-age girls. Overall there have been positive changes toward female involvement in athletics. How-

ever, much remains to be done to ensure that women are accorded proper respect for sport participation.

Twenge (1997) conducted a meta-analysis of data from studies looking at changes in attitudes toward women for the years 1970–1995 and found a substantial liberalization and feminization of attitudes among males and females alike, particularly for the time period 1986–1995. Though not based on sport literature per se, these findings suggest that role conflict associated with sport participation is less a problem in recent years than in the past.

The Family

The family is the primary socialization force for children in the early formative years; in women's athletics, this appears to be equally true. Malumphy (1970) has indicated that the family is the primary source of socialization into sport, not only for females but also for males. Greendorfer (1977) states that the family is most influential in childhood, but this influence becomes weaker in adolescence and adulthood. Snyder and Spreitzer (1978) support this notion, indicating that parental interest is a big factor in sport involvement by females. Weiss and Knoppers (1982), in a study of collegiate volleyball players, found that parents, peers, and teachers/coaches were most influential in childhood, but the influence of brothers was most salient in college. Finally, Higginson (1985), in a study of 587 participants in the Empire State Games in Syracuse, New York, found that parents were the most influential socialization forces prior to age 13, being replaced in adolescence by coaches and physical education teachers.

Weiss and Barber (1995) have taken this line of inquiry to a new level in their study of socialization of female athletes over the ten-year period 1979–1989. They found that there were essentially three sources of encouragement in 1979: coaches, father, and mother. In 1989, this base of support and encouragement had broadened to include six sources: coaches, mother, father, older brother, female friend, and older sister. Paternal support was rated significantly higher than the other sources by female athletes taking part in collegiate athletics.

An interview with Tammy Pearman, a defender on the U.S. National soccer team in 1995, gets to the heart of this family support issue. Asked about the role played by her family in her choice of sport and subsequent success, Pearman said: "They [her brothers] were a big influence. To this day, my soccer-playing brothers tease me and say I 'stole' all of their moves. To that, I just tell them, I didn't steal them, I just improved on them" (On the Spot, 1996, p. 1). She points out that her father was a soccer player and her mother ran track, and their influence was considerable (p. 1): "Although I played soccer, I was really daddy's little girl in his eyes; it was my mom who took me to practices and motivated me a lot. She [the mother] said, 'You can do anything you want. If you think you can fly, you show me you can sprout wings and you can take off.' "

Acceptability of Various Sports

Early studies indicated individual sports for women were more acceptable than team sports (Harres, 1968; Layman, 1968). Support for this notion was suggested by Snyder and Kivlin (1975), who asked a large sample of college female athletes: "Do you feel that there is a stigma attached to women who participate in the sport you specialize in?" Fifty-eight percent of basketball players said yes, followed by 47% of track and field athletes, 38% of swimmers, and 27% of gymnasts.

Following up on the idea that some sports are more acceptable for females than others, Snyder and Spreitzer (1973) asked a random sample of the citizens of Toledo, Ohio, the question, "In your opinion, would participation in any of the following sports enhance a girl's/woman's feminine qualities?" Two-thirds approved of swimming, followed by slightly over half for gymnastics. Only one in seven was positive about basketball, softball, and track and field. Sage and Loudermilk (1979) reported that female athletes in what they called the less approved sports (softball, basketball, volleyball, field hockey, and track and field) experienced significantly more role conflict than those in more accepted sports (tennis, golf, swimming, gymnastics). Ostrow, Jones, and Spiker (1981), in a study of undergraduate nursing majors, isolated a number of sex-appropriate sports. For example, figure skating and ballet were rated as significantly feminine; no significant differences were noted for swimming, bicycling, and bowling. Marathon running, the shot put, basketball, archery, tennis, racquetball, and jogging were seen as masculine activities.

Hoferek and Hanick (1985) asked people in a small town in Iowa to respond to a questionnaire related to women and sports and concluded that sport participation by females neither enhanced nor detracted from their image. Another interesting finding was that basketball was not seen in the Iowa study as enhancing or detracting but nevertheless was the sport of choice. In response to the question, "If you had a daughter, what sports would you prefer that she participate in?" 53% of the respondents cited basketball; no other sport was cited in more than 9% of the cases. The authors concluded that the comparison of the Ohio and Iowa results suggests that traditional, rigid sex role stereotypes were transcended and the opportunity set was dominant.

Comparing responses from people in Toledo, Ohio, in 1973 with those from citizens of a small Iowa town in the early 1980s may be a bit like the proverbial comparison of oranges and apples. The finding that basketball was so popular may also easily be attributed to the long-term popularity of the sport in Iowa.

For most of its interscholastic sport history, Iowa played a brand of six-on-six basketball in which each team had three players on offense and three on defense, none of whom was allowed to cross the mid-court line. The typical offense in this format was built around a tall, high-scoring center and two quick ball handlers. Iowa abandoned this format in 1994, leaving Oklahoma as the last state to play six-on-six basketball. Toward the end of the six-on-six era, the superintendents of all schools, in consultation with their coaches, actually voted whether to play full-court five-on-five or half-court six-on-six basketball by individual districts. Oklahoma finally did away with the six-on-six format in 1995 (The End, 1995). Undoubtedly, six-on-six basketball serves as a reminder of the time when endurance sports were viewed as excessively demanding for females, physically and psychologically.

Why Women Compete

Kidd and Woodman (1975) created a tripartite notion of reasons that females compete in sports, with "have fun," "play well," and "to win" serving as the respective parts. Nicholson (1979) used the same conditions in a study of athletes and nonathletes in the eighth and ninth grades in Michigan. Generally speaking, Nicholson found few differences between the two groups on "having fun" and "winning." However, sport participants placed much more emphasis on "playing well." Nicholson's results were corroborated by Siegel and Newhof (1984) in their study of basketball players in Divisions I, II, and III of the Association for Intercollegiate Athletics for Women (AIAW). They found no statistically significant differences across divisions in participation satisfaction.

An interesting development related to female competitiveness concerns the ability of women to respond to what is considered to be a standard "gut-check" in sport, namely, coming from behind to win. Weinberg and various associates (Weinberg, Richardson, & Jackson, 1981; Weinberg, Richardson, Jackson, & Yukelson, 1983; Ransom & Weinberg, 1985) have been at the forefront in studying this dimension. In the 1983 study, 2,400 collegiate and professional men's and women's basketball games and 1,900 collegiate and open men's and women's volleyball matches for 1980–1981 were dissected for sex differences in the ability to come from

behind. Being behind in basketball was determined by halftime scores, and the loss of the first set in volleyball. In professional basketball, men's teams came from behind to win 30% of the time; only 7% of the women's teams did. At the collegiate level, these figures were 37% and 24%, respectively. No significant gender differences in volleyball were noted.

In the 1981 and 1985 studies, coming from behind was studied in male and female tennis players. The 1981 study found that male tennis players at both the amateur and professional levels came from behind (i.e., after losing the first set) more often than did female players. The more recent of the two studies was conducted along the same lines. The top 20 male and female players in the 1980 U.S. Tennis Association yearbook were studied, and particularly the 242 matches in which they dropped the first set. No gender differences in ability to come back were noted, thereby indicating that elite players of both genders appear to possess equal ability in overcoming adversity. This equality notion is further substantiated when these top 20 athletes are compared with the ability to come from behind of the top 500 players. In this situation, 39% of males and 37% of females in the top 20 came from behind to win; in the case of the top 500, the figures drop rather precipitously to 15% for males and 9% for females.

The come-from-behind phenomenon represents an interesting aspect of competitiveness in females. Preliminary evidence from Weinberg and associates indicates that elite females are as capable as men of responding positively to potential defeat, at least in tennis. Males at a lower level of competitiveness show a slight superiority to equal-ability females, but both groups are inferior to the top-flight females in coming from behind to win.

PSYCHOLOGICAL VARIABLES

Though an unlimited number of psychological variables deserve mention here, only a few have a sufficient literature to justify elaboration; foremost among them are attribution theory, fear of success, and psychological androgyny.

Attribution Theory

Some overlap between the discussions here and in Chapter 9 will permit us to fully develop issues related to attribution theory and female participation in sport. One significant area of research has been **gender differences.** Deaux and Emswiller (1974) have suggested that sex role stereotypes are conducive to the distortion of one's cognitive processes, particularly in the area of attributions. Deaux and Farris (1977) indicated that adult males are likely to make internal attributions (e.g., ability) for success, whereas females are likely to view their successes as less attributable to ability and more a function of situational factors such as luck. For example, Iso-Ahola (1979) studied the motor performance of male and female fourth graders from physical education classes and found that boys are less likely to admit to ability deficiencies when they fail in competitive situations involving girls than in situations where they are surpassed by other boys. Also, girls tended to see the ability of boys as a more significant factor in losses to boys than in defeats by other girls. Applying generalizations from the preceding studies to sport led McHugh, Duquin, and Frieze (1978, pp. 182–183) to make the following conclusions:

1. Based on women's internalization of beliefs in their own physical inferiority, female athletes attribute success to external factors such as luck and failure to low ability. This pattern may be found in young girl athletes or women in general, but the female that makes this type of attribution is probably not found in advanced athletic programs.

2. Alternatively, the societal attitudes that allude to females' natural inability in sports may produce a pattern of external attributions. Thus, the female athlete who reports playing just for fun and winning by luck or task ease conforms more to society's view than the female who admittedly tries hard.

3. A third prediction of female athletes' attributional patterns could be based on the fact that female athletes have been found to be generally self-confident, autonomous, persevering, and achievement oriented. Preliminary studies have suggested that highly motivated women imply more effort

attributions for both success and failure than low achievement oriented women.

As a result of observations such as these, a fair amount of related research has been generated, though it is not universally supportive of the McHugh et al. position. Bird and Williams (1980) studied 192 males and an equal number of females divided into four age groups (7 to 9, 10 to 12, 13 to 15, 16 to 18). Subjects were asked to respond to stories about various athletic events in which failure or success themes were programmed. Based on in-depth analysis of the results, Bird and Williams concluded that by late adolescence sex role stereotypes in sport do exist and that the directional bias is positive for males and negative for females. They further concluded that by age 13 male successes were explained by effort, whereas by age 16 female successes were viewed as a function of luck.

Two additional studies with adults lend further credence to sex differences in attribution. One, by Reiss and Taylor (1984), involved an analysis of male and female alpine ski racers of various skill levels. A second, by Riordan, Thomas, and James (1985), included female racquetball players. Both studies concluded that females were more likely to make external attributions than were males.

A second area of interest in attribution theory research with females is the *self-serving attributional bias.* Research on the self-serving bias has been equivocal, as was pointed out in Chapter 9. Studies related to female athletes do little to clarify the picture. Riordan et al. (1985) found partial support for the notion in their study of racquetball players, whereas Reiss and Taylor (1984), in a study of alpine skiers, interpreted their findings as not supportive of the self-serving bias. In general, so many inconsistencies occur along methodological and sampling lines that, as stated earlier, it would seem premature to stop researching the topic.

A third thrust in attributions has to do with self versus team responses. Bird and Brame (1978), Bird, Foster, and Maruyama (1980), and Scanlan and Passer (1980a) have all looked at self-versus-team attributions. In the first of these three studies, Bird and Brame selected subjects from several collegiate basketball conferences and found that winners perceived themselves as having less ability than they were perceived to have by their teammates. Winners viewed their teams as having

---

Gender differences an important area of sport psychology research, based on attribution theory, that studies distortion of cognitive processes in relation to sex role stereotypes.

more ability and saw effort as playing a greater role than losers did. Winners also saw their own individual task assignments as more difficult than that of the team. Finally, losers viewed luck as playing a greater role in team success than did winners. Overall, their most salient finding was that the team-ability attribution most powerfully separated winners from losers.

Bird and her associates also looked at female basketball players but added the dimension of team cohesion into the formula. In general, cohesive teams made more convergent attributions for both self and team at the end of the season. Players from less cohesive teams saw luck as more significant than did their winning counterparts. Players from cohesive teams, in the face of occasional adversity, behaved in ways that preserved the team's integrity. In general, the Bird et al. study also supported the team-self distinction as an important one in sport.

Scanlan and Passer studied young female soccer players, and their overall conclusions were generally in agreement with those of Bird and her various associates. Based on the findings of the preceding study and those of four others (Scanlan & Passer, 1978, 1979a, 1979b, 1980b), these researchers point out that sex differences in attributional styles are more similar than dissimilar. This position, of course, runs counter to much of our earlier discussion but does point to the need for continuing research on athletes of both genders and their attributional efforts.

Fear of Success

One aspect of the literature on women's issues that has drawn considerable attention has been the concept of **Fear of Success (FOS),** as formulated by Matina Horner (1968, 1972). Blucker and Hershberger (1983), summarize Horner's 1968 basic premises as follows:

1. The motive to avoid success is a stable characteristic of the personality acquired early in life in conjunction with sex-role standards. It is conceived as a disposition: (a) to feel uncomfortable when successful in competitive achievement situations because such behavior is inconsistent with one's femininity (an internal standard), and (b) to expect to become concerned about social rejection following success in such situations.

2. It is probably not equally important for all women.

3. Fear of success should be more strongly aroused in women who are highly motivated to achieve and/or who are highly able (e.g., who aspire to and/or are readily capable of achieving success).

4. It is more strongly aroused in competitive achievement situations than where competition is directed against an impersonal standard. (pp. 353–354)

Horner apparently viewed FOS as a highly feminine characteristic that would be manifested most noticeably in competitive situations.

In her original work, Horner asked women to respond to the following verbal lead: "After first-term finals, Anne finds herself at the top of her medical school class." For men, "John" was substituted for "Anne." In their responses, the females wrote many more negative responses to their cues than did the males; 65% of the women wrote fear of success themes, whereas only 9% of the men did. For a variety of reasons, subsequent research on FOS has not yielded such clearcut results, but the construct has caught the attention of sport researchers.

One of the first research efforts in this area was that of McElroy and Willis (1979). Female varsity athletes in five different sports attending three large East Coast universities responded to a series of yes–no statements related to sport-specific situations, and no evidence of FOS was noted in these participants. McElroy and Willis concluded that FOS did not generalize to athletic situations, that changing women's roles were at work, or that women had legitimized their athletic participation and felt no need for rationalizing or justifying it. The authors summarize their results as follows: "The absence of fear of success suggested that the female athlete does not seem to be bothered by role conflicts surrounding achievement activities" (p. 246).

Silva (1982b), using the Objective Fear of Success Scale (FOSS) created by Zuckerman and Allison (1976), studied undergraduate athletes and nonathletes of both genders. As with the Zuckerman and Allison study, Silva's females (when grouped together)

Fear of Success (FOS) concept developed by Matina Horner to explain female fear of succeeding.

scored higher on the FOSS than did the males. However, because the mean scores of the female athletes were lower than those of both the male and female nonathletes as well as those reported by Zuckerman and Allison, it appears that women in sport are not particularly fearful of succeeding.

In view of the consistent results of research on FOS, it seems safe to conclude that female athletes do not appear to have fear of success problems. Perhaps the following anecdote from a 24-year-old woman cited by Loverock (1991, p. 85) summarizes the FOS transition from the days of the original work by Horner to the more common view of achievement in competitive situations today:

> As a kid I played a lot of tennis. I signed up for lessons when I was ten and I became pretty good at the game. When I met my first "serious" boyfriend, around age sixteen, he saw the tennis racquets in our garage and suggested we go out to the courts at a nearby school and play a game. After a few serves it was obvious to me I was better at tennis than he was. He was really frustrated because I was winning the game. I hate to say this, but I was afraid he wouldn't like me as much if I beat him, so I played a lousy game and let him win. Of course, young love didn't last and we broke up anyway! Now I'm married to a man who plays tennis badly, but he doesn't mind when I beat him.

At this juncture, the FOS research is probably important mostly in terms of its historical contribution to how women's sport has evolved and serves as a reminder of just how far women and women in sport have come in the past several decades.

Psychological androgyny the state of encompassing, in one's personality, the best of both gender roles and expectations, including both expressive and instrumental behaviors.
Bem Sex-Role Inventory (BSRI) standardized measure of psychological androgyny developed by Sandra Bem to test her theory that traits of masculinity and femininity are a continuum, not a dichotomy.
Personal Attributes Questionnaire (PAQ) standardized measure of psychological androgyny yielding male-valued and female-valued scores; less used in sport research than the BSRI.

Psychological Androgyny

Measurement of gender differences in personality is not new. A number of instruments of the 1940s and 1950s (i.e., the Minnesota Multiphasic Personality Inventory, the Guilford–Zimmerman Temperament Survey, and the California Psychological Inventory) included subscales concerned with gender differences. More recent efforts from the 1970s have been oriented toward the measurement of psychological androgyny (Bem, 1974; Spence, Helmreich, & Stapp, 1974).

Psychological androgyny is generally viewed as a mixture of the best of both gender roles and expectations; that is, "combining assertiveness and competence with compassion, warmth, and emotional expressiveness" (Anastasi, 1982, p. 557). Duquin (1978) differentiates among these various traits by talking of expressive and instrumental behaviors. *Expressive behaviors* are stereotypically associated with women, who may be seen as understanding, sympathetic, affectionate, compassionate, tender, sensitive, warm, and shy. Conversely, males are thought to show more *instrumental behavior* by being independent, ambitious, assertive, aggressive, competitive, and risk taking. Duquin further states that while society generally attributes instrumentality to males and expressiveness to females, the validity of these attributions is questionable. This ambivalence lies at the heart of the role conflict facing female athletes in the traditionally male proving ground of sport.

To Bem (1974), masculinity and femininity have long been viewed as bipolar ends of a single continuum, or as dichotomous variables, but the manifestation of both is entirely possible in males and females. To put it another way, Bem feels that people with healthy self-concepts will be capable of freely engaging in both "masculine" and "feminine" behaviors and will not be restrained by traditional sex role definitions. Bem's positive perception is shared by Spence, Helmreich, and Stapp (1974). As a result of their combined speculations, both Bem and Spence and associates have devised scales aimed at measuring this propensity toward expressing both the masculine and feminine aspects of the self, or what is popularly known as psychological androgyny.

The two most notable of the measures of androgyny are the **Bem Sex-Role Inventory (BSRI)** (Bem, 1974) and the **Personal Attributes Questionnaire (PAQ)** (Spence, Helmreich, & Stapp, 1974). Of the two measures, the BSRI has been used more often in sport. For example, Hilburn and LeUnes (2001) identified 42 studies prior to the year 2000 in which the BSRI was used in sport and exercise research and only 11 in which the PAQ was the instrument of choice.

Spence, Helmreich, and Stapp (1974) developed the PAQ in response to what they perceived to be a need for an instrument that would add to our understanding of masculinity, femininity, and androgyny. The PAQ is a 15-item five-choice response format instrument yielding a male-valued (MV) score and a female-valued (FV) score. In turn, the MV and FV can be subdivided through a four-way median split into the following categories:

1. *Androgynous,* operationally defined as scores above the median on both MV and FV.

2. Stereotypically *masculine,* consisting of a score at or above the median on MV and below the median on FV.

3. Stereotypically *feminine,* defined as a median score or above on FV and below median on MV.

4. *Undifferentiated,* defined as scores below the median on both MV and FV.

In a study using the PAQ, Del Rey and Sheppard (1981) administered the instrument to 119 female athletes from three universities covering 10 sports. Collapsing across the three universities, 33% of the athletes were androgynous, 23% masculine, 22% feminine, and 23% undifferentiated (100% is surpassed here because of rounding errors). Of more importance, a highly significant relationship was seen between the androgynous description and athlete self-esteem as measured by the Texas Social Behavior Instrument (TSBI) (Helmreich, Stapp, & Ervin, 1974).

Another investigation involving the PAQ was conducted by Hochstetler, Rejeski, and Best (1985). Their subjects were 149 undergraduate students, all of whom were moderate to low in cardiovascular fitness and not participating in intercollegiate sport. Thirty-three of the original 149 females were then randomly selected for further testing, 11 in each of the androgynous, masculine, and feminine conditions. The exertion tasks used in the experiment involved a treadmill task and a 30-minute jog, and the subjects were asked to rate their perceptions of the exertion involved therein. Feminine women perceived the rate of physical exertion as higher than did masculine and androgynous subjects, though all subjects worked at the same intensity. Interestingly, the feminine subjects were also the least fit of the three groups. Hochstetler et al. suggest that feminine-type women who enter fitness or rehabilitation programs may be at high risk for noncompliance.

A more recent study using the PAQ has been conducted by Andre and Holland (1995), who studied large numbers of male and female adolescents. Chief among their findings were that the PAQ discriminated between athletes and nonathletes, that female athletes had higher masculine sex role scores than did female nonathletes, and that male athletes expressed more stereotypically masculine attributes than did male nonathletes. Miller and Levy (1996) used the PAQ and found that female collegiate athletes, when compared with nonathletic peers, see themselves as significantly more masculine in sex role orientation. This finding is in line with that of Giuliano, Popp, and Knight (2000), who found that childhood play involving masculine toys and games, playing in mixed or predominantly male groups, and viewing themselves as "tomboys" were predictive of college sports participation. Though they used the BSRI rather than the PAQ, Guiliano et al. also found that female athletes endorsed a more masculine sex role orientation.

In the main, these studies lend validity to the use of the PAQ in sport-related research. They further suggest that androgyny and related issues are important ones within the female sport domain. Bem's work in the area lends even more substantiation to the findings.

The *Bem Sex-Role Inventory (BSRI)* (Bem, 1974) is a 60-item scale made up of 20 masculine, 20 feminine, and 20 neutral statements requiring responses based on a seven-point continuum from "Never or almost never true" to "Always or almost always true." Scoring is essentially similar to that of the PAQ in that an individual's position above or below the median determines classification as masculine, feminine, androgynous, or undifferentiated. Satisfactory factorial validity for the BSRI has been established by Campbell, Gillaspy, and Thompson (1997). An interesting artifact of the Campbell et al. research was that a published short form of the BSRI was actually more reliable than the long form. This finding suggests that further study of the utility of the short form is in order.

Sample items from the BSRI include:

Masculine	Feminine	Neutral
self-reliant	yielding	helpful
defends own beliefs	cheerful	moody
independent	sly	conscientious
athletic	affectionate	theatrical
assertive	flatterable	happy

Research in which the BSRI has been used is considerable, as pointed out earlier, and a number of conclusions can be drawn from this literature. One is that female athletes do not express a feminine sex role orientation. Rates such as 17% of elite racquetball players (Myers & Lips, 1978), 13% of elite field hockey players in New Zealand (Chalip, Villiger, & Duignan, 1980), 22% of gymnasts taking part in the NCAA championships (Edwards, Gordin, & Henschen, 1984), and 17% of individual sport participants (Colley, Roberts, & Chipps, 1985) lend credence to this finding. Myers and Lips did find a 43% femininity rate in a group of Canadian badminton, handball, and squash players, thereby suggesting that the issue is not totally conclusive. Nevertheless, a strong trend exists toward a less feminine sex role orientation among widely diverse female athletes.

A second conclusion is that a masculine sex role orientation is indeed an integral part of female participation in sport. Gackenbach (1982) reported that collegiate swimmers viewed themselves as significantly more masculine in sex role orientation than did nonathletes. Kane (1982) reported 39% of junior college athletes in three sports scored masculine on the BSRI. Twenty-five percent of 84 gymnasts reported a masculine orientation in the study of Edwards, Gordin, and Henschen (1984). Again, these rates of masculine sex role endorsement were not universal. For example, Colley et al. report only a 17% rate among individual sport participants in their study. Henschen, Edwards, and Mathinos (1982) found no differences between rates of femininity and masculinity in their study of high school track athletes and nonathletes, though masculinity was significantly related to the need to achieve.

A third conclusion is that the measurement of androgyny among female athletes yields mixed results. The range of androgynous responses in female athletes is from 65% reported by Chalip and associates (1980), to 17% of the individual sport subjects studied by Colley et al. (1985). In between are percentages of 25% (Edwards et al.), 42% (team sport participants, Chalip et al.), 43% (Henschen et al.), and 44% (Myers and Lips). Given the substantial heterogeneity of these various samples, these discrepancies are possibly to be expected.

The sex role orientation of female athletes is substantially more masculine or androgynous than feminine or undifferentiated. Holding athletic ability constant, this conclusion suggests that the androgynous or masculine female should succeed in sport without experiencing nearly the sex role conflict that the feminine female would. Duquin (1978) sums up the issue: "Sport, when perceived as an instrumental, cross sex-typed activity has little overall appeal to women and has a low appeal to the feminine female who, in fact, has the greatest need for experiencing such instrumental activities" (p. 271). Duquin further suggests that in the best of all possible worlds sport would be regarded not as masculine or feminine, but as androgynous. In this ideal setting, androgynous and masculine females would find sport to be a great outlet for their expressive and instrumental energies. Best of all, perhaps, is the fact that in Duquin's view feminine females would also find reinforcement in physical activity and competition. Sport perceived as an androgynous activity is portrayed in Table 20.1.

A lively debate, meanwhile, has sprung up over whether or not the PAQ and the BSRI are interchangeable in assessing sex role orientation (Spence & Buckner, 2000; Spence & Hall, 1996). While there are clear differences in the theories that drove the creation of each of these measures, it is likely that they are measuring essentially the same constructs. To be sure, the androgyny construct has been an intriguing one for researchers in sport and exercise, regardless of the measurement device used.

OTHER ISSUES INVOLVING WOMEN IN SPORT

Currently research focuses on other issues related to women's sports. One issue is the way in which female

TABLE 20.1

Sport Perceived as an Androgynous Activity

Females Classified on the BSR1	Expected Performance	Expected Attraction
Masculine	moderate–high	moderate–high
Androgynous	high	high
Feminine	moderate	moderate

SOURCE: Duquin (1978).

athletes are portrayed in the media. Another is the emerging literature on homophobia, particularly aimed at females in sport; it appears that there is a widespread perception of rampant lesbianism among women athletes. Finally, eating disorders will be discussed, as there appears to be a problem in this area among athletes, particularly females. Let us begin with media portrayals of female athletes.

The Media

According to McGregor (1989), the term *hegemony* is synonymous with authority, leadership and systems that go unquestioned. One such system is the "good old boy" network in sports. **Male hegemony** is particularly noticeable in media coverage of sports and fitness. Three relevant studies exemplify this point, one dealing with sports publications, another with sports photography, and the final one with the naming of athletic teams. In the first instance, Lumpkin and Williams (1991) conducted a content analysis of nearly 4,000 feature articles in *Sports Illustrated* from 1954 through 1987. Chief among the findings were the following: males were featured in nearly 91% of these articles, nearly 92% were written by male authors, most dealt with exclusively male sports, more white males were featured than were blacks or females, the articles on the white males were longer, and the descriptors in articles on females were blatantly sexist in content.

In a similar vein, Shifflett and Revelle (1994) analyzed articles and pictures chosen from the *NCAA News* for the years 1988–1991 and found that twice the number of paragraphs and pictures were allocated to male sports, players, and coaches than to females.

These findings support earlier work conducted by Gilbert and Williamson (1973b) and Rintala and Burrell (1984). Interestingly, this general picture has also been reported from Australia (McKay & Rowe, 1987), Canada (Theberge, 1991), and China (Chow & Hon, 1998). In the case of Australia, McKay and Rowe report an overwhelming male bias in their media. When Theberge analyzed print media accounts of sports in four major Canadian newspapers over a six-month period, she found little emphasis on female sports and physical activity and equally little effort devoted to changing stereotypes of females who engage in these activities. In China, Chow looked at four Hong Kong newspapers for the years 1984 and 1994. Substantial increases were seen in the space allocated to male athletes and sports, with the coverage of females dropping from 10–12% in 1984 to 4–7% in 1994.

Wann, Schrader, Allison, and McGeorge (1998) have looked at coverage in university sports pages from a small, medium, and large university for a six-month period. Wann et al. found that male athletes and male athletics received far more coverage in university newspapers than did female athletics and female athletics, with the largest inequity in coverage occurring in the newspaper from the large university.

A study by Duncan (1990) on sports photography is instructive. Duncan looked at the portrayal of women in the 1984 and 1988 Olympic Games by analyzing photographs from such popular magazines as *Life, Sports Illustrated, Newsweek, Time, Maclean's* and *Ms.* Chief among Duncan's findings were that the more

---

Male hegemony implicit powers of social authority and leadership granted to men only; the "good old boy" network.

attractive females, such as Katarina Witt and Florence Griffith Joyner, received a disproportionate amount of photographic attention. Many references to their sexiness accompanied the photos. Another point made was that the poses and camera angles employed in the photographs often bordered on the soft pornography variety. Yet another conclusion was that women are often photographed crying, thereby promoting an image of female athletes, and females in general, as incapable of controlling their emotions. The net effect of these kinds of photographic nuances, contends Duncan, is that women are placed in a position of weakness through a deliberate political strategy that has such subjugation as its objective.

Speaking of photography and prominent sports publications, it would be difficult to discuss the area without at least a cursory reference to the controversial but immensely financially profitable swimsuit editions published annually by *Sports Illustrated* and *Inside Sports.* Norman Jacobs, the publisher of *Inside Sports,* refers to the annual exercise as a "little fun," while Twiss Butler (1991, p. 10C), in a letter to *USA Today,* calls it "an annual exercise for hit and run sexual harassment." Undoubtedly, swimsuit editions will be around for the foreseeable future and much indignation will accompany their publication. It is not likely, however, that they do much for the women's movement in sport or society in general.

A third discriminatory mechanism, according to Eitzen and Zinn (1989), exists in the form of the naming and gender marking of sports teams. Eitzen and his colleague looked at data from nearly 1,200 four-year colleges or universities and found that over half have team names, mascots, or logos that are demeaning to women. Examples cited by Eitzen and Zinn (p. 367) which, in their words, "de-athleticize" women's teams include physical markers (Belles, Rambelles), *girl* or *gal* (Green Gals), feminine suffix (Tigerettes, Duchesses), *lady* (Lady Aggies, Lady Eagles), *male* as a false generic (Cowboys, Hokies, Tomcats), male name with a female modifier (Lady Rams, Lady Dons), double gender marking (Choctaws/Lady Chocs, Jaguars/Lady Jags) and male/female paired polarity (Panthers/Pink Panthers, Bears/Teddy Bears). This tendency was

strongest in the South, thought by some to be the last bastion of male domination in the United States. Based on these data and other sources of information not reported here, Eitzen and Zinn conclude that "institutional sexism is deeply entrenched in college sports" (p. 369).

Homophobia

Yet another concern for the female athletes is the common perception that women's sport is filled with lesbians. The term **homophobia** connotes a fear and/or hatred of individuals who engage in homosexual behavior or behavior deemed outside the boundaries of traditional gender role expectations (Griffin, 1989).

Cahn (1993) traces the societal and sport roots of homophobia in a most informative historical article. It is Cahn's contention that the emergence in the early to middle part of this century of women's athletics, sport heroines like Babe Didrikson Zaharias, and professional physical education departments ignited a veritable firestorm in the way society viewed females. Much talk was made of "mannish" females who participated in sport, and athletic teams and physical education departments were eternally vigilant in promoting the most effeminate image possible. Sports, most particularly softball, offered an opportunity for lesbians to gather in socially acceptable surroundings. At the same time, the prevailing negative societal attitudes about lesbianism and homosexuality were such that it was best to keep one's sexual preference a secret. Out of this suspicion and secrecy, homophobia was born.

Homophobia has taken on considerable political baggage as a result of the continuing furor within our society surrounding gay and lesbian issues. Undoubtedly, there are individuals inside and outside of sport who are homosexual, others who are supportive of the behavior, yet others who are tolerant, some who are opposed, and a segment who are actively homophobic. The degree to which each of these groups might zero in on homosexuality in the world of sport and fitness is conjectural, with the exception of homophobes, who are probably predisposed to seeing it everywhere. This last group is probably the same 15% Baumann (1991) found in his *USA Today* survey of sports fans who would ban homosexuals from all competition.

Homophobia fear or hatred of persons engaging in homosexual behavior or behavior deemed outside the boundaries of traditional role expectations.

Incidentally, in the same survey, 59% of all respondents considered homosexual behavior to be morally wrong.

Gays are not unknown in the sports world. Professional football player Dave Kopay, major league baseball umpire Dave Pallone, Olympic champion diver Greg Louganis (an AIDS victim), Olympic decathlete Tom Waddell, and major league baseball player Glenn Burke are just a few of the male athletes who have come out of the closet in the past several years. Burke died of AIDS in 1995, as did Waddell in 1996. Before his death, Waddell teamed with sports personality Dick Schaap to write a book entitled *Gay Olympian: The Life and Death of Dr. Tom Waddell.*

Among females, the numbers of high-profile athletes who have come out of the closet is smaller. Professional tennis stars Billie Jean King and Martina Navratilova are two such luminaries who have admitted to being lesbians. It is interesting that so few prominent examples of lesbianism have been uncovered, given the widely held assumption that lesbianism in sport is so common. For example, Carson (1987) conducted a survey of 250 introductory psychology students in which they were asked to estimate the percentage of female athletes who are lesbians; the mean response was 47%.

"Sweaty lesbians," "dyke," "butch," "lezzies," and "jock" are just a few of the pejorative epithets female athletes hear bandied about as a function of homophobia. To combat this image problem, some coaches have instituted a "no lesbian" policy insofar as such a stricture can be enforced. Other coaches remove players from the team if lesbianism is discovered. Still others have started hairstyle and makeup seminars to give their female players a more acceptable image. Some coaches have even engaged in quasi-ethical behavior by telling the parents of prospective athletes undergoing the recruitment process not to send their daughter to School X because lesbianism is widespread there (Griffin, 1993; Thorngren, 1990).

Several authorities have recently suggested ways to combat homophobia in women's sports (Griffin, 1993; Lenskyj, 1991). Chief among their suggestions include attacking homophobia through education, continuing to seriously address the problem within the organizational structure of the various sports sciences professional societies, and being aware of our own homophobic tendencies and those of others.

Eating Disorders

The American Psychiatric Association has published their *Diagnostic and Statistical Manual* (4th ed.) in an effort to enhance the reliability of psychiatric diagnoses. The DSM–IV is the bible for most practicing psychologists and psychiatrists; it represents the collective wisdom of both groups of practitioners with regard to the diagnostic process. One inclusion in the DSM–IV involves two interrelated eating disorders known as *anorexia* and *bulimia*. The distinction between these two disorders essentially has to do with restricted food intake (anorexia) or excessive food intake (bulimia). Of primary concern in our discussion is anorexia.

According to Comer (2001), anorexia occurs almost exclusively in adolescence or young adulthood, 90–95% of the victims are females, and it has a mortality rate of 2–10%.

Experts in the field of eating disorders constantly refer to the **female athletic triad,** composed of disordered eating, amenorrhea, and osteoporosis. *Amenorrhea* or a disrupted menstrual period is considered to be the red flag for the triad, but the presence of any of the three puts the athlete in the triad and screening should be done to look for the presence of the other two ailments (Dobie, 2000a). Diagnostic high points include the aforementioned amenorrhea; distorted body image; brief binges of overeating (a link with bulimia) followed by self-induced vomiting or excessive use of laxatives; compulsive or excessive exercising; lanugo (soft downy hair on the body); and eroded dental enamel from frequent vomiting. In many instances, the excessive exercising is calculated to the nth degree as a means of keeping weight to a minimum and as a method of exerting control over what may seem to the victim to be an uncontrollable world.

Anorexia is quite well known among female athletes, particularly in those sports requiring what Yates, Leehey, and Shisslak (1983) refer to as **grim asceticism.**

Female athletic triad a food-related psychological complex composed of three factors: disordered eating, amenorrhea, and osteoporosis. Disordered eating includes bulimia (excessive food intake) and, especially for female athletes, anorexia (restricted food intake).

Grim asceticism a term describing those sports that require extreme training and pain endurance, such as gymnastics and distance running.

Here, Yates et al. are referring to sports such as gymnastics and distance running that require a lot of endurance and pain tolerance. In documenting the problem, Halliburton and Sanford (1989) indicate that 10% of all female athletes at the University of Texas were diagnosed as having an eating disorder within an 18-month period. Overall statistics indicate an incidence of 4% to 5% among female nonathletes at the same university. Walberg and Johnston (1991) report that 42% of a sample of competitive female body builders they studied had been anorexic at some point in their lives; 67% reported being terrified of becoming fat, and an additional 58% were obsessed with food. Perhaps most inclusive in terms of statistics, Dick (1991) asked senior female administrators at 803 NCAA institutions to respond to a question about the prevalence of anorexia or bulimia in their respective programs during the period 1988-1990. Nearly 500 administrators responded; 40% of them reported at least one case during the specified time frame. Wrestling for males and gymnastics, cross country, swimming, and the running events in track (in that order) for females had the highest prevalence of eating disorders by sport. As might be predicted, 93% of the cases involved females. Dick's survey certainly substantiates the fact that eating disorders are a serious problem in big-time intercollegiate sports, and particularly in those where women are involved. Other data suggest that the problem is not restricted to collegiate competitors. Results of a recent survey found that 5.4% of high school athletes (and 6.6% of college female athletes) met the criteria for an eating disorder (Dobie, 2000b).

A poignant reminder of the effects of an eating disorder, anorexia, was the premature and tragic death of gymnast Christy Henrich, a member of the United States national team in the early 1990s. At her competitive peak, Christy was 4 feet, 10 inches tall and weighed 95 pounds. When she died in July 1994, her weight had dropped below 50 pounds. Christy was a perfectionist with an incredible work ethic. However, like many anorexics, she had a poor self-image and low self-esteem; she fought these problems along with obsessions about eating and exercise. At one point during her most competitive phase, she had reduced her dietary intake to an apple a day. The crash diet ended her career as a gymnast and ultimately took her life (IG Staff, 1994).

Thus far, the discussion has centered on females and eating disorders, but certainly these are concerns for male athletes as well. Particularly at risk among male athletes are competitive wrestlers, who are often asked to drop or gain weight in a short period of time to make a particular weight class. It is not unheard of for these athletes to lose enough weight to drop down two competitive weight classes in a matter of days. Laxatives and induced vomiting are two ways to accomplish this weight loss goal in a very short time. This sort of situational weight loss raises questions about whether or not athletes such as wrestlers who periodically go on weight-loss (and occasionally, weight-gaining) regimens really meet the DSM–IV standards for inclusion as an eating disorder. Possibly what we have here is a matter of disordered eating. At any rate, one study of low-weight wrestlers and rowers supports the ongoing discussion; Thiel, Gottfried, and Hesse (1993) found the incidence of subclinical eating disorders to be sufficiently high that they recommended that both groups of athletes be considered high-risk populations.

Other groups of males at risk are chronic exercisers, obligatory runners, and other endurance athletes. It is socially acceptable to work out and become fit. Indeed, a great deal of time and money is devoted to promoting fitness through exercise adherence, as we will see in Chapter 25.

To date, the sport psychology and sport medicine literature has had little to say about what might be done to combat the eating disorders problem in athletes. Martin and Hausenblas (1998) have studied commitment to exercise among aerobics instructors and related eating-disorder symptomatology. In general, they found that their sample of aerobics teachers had health eating habits and wholesome attitudes about exercise. Perhaps most important were their recommendations of things aerobics instructors can do to combat the eating disorders problem: First, these instructors need to be constantly aware of how their behavior influences other people. Exercising when ill or overdoing exercise only reinforces undesirable health practices among their clientele. Second, instructors should use their influence to promote healthy exercise and weight management; they should discard the "buns of steel" and "washboard abs" mentality and talk about realistic fitness and weight loss goals. Third, instructors should make themselves aware of the danger signs of eating

Are Cheerleaders Athletes?

West Virginia and Michigan answered this question in the affirmative years ago by designating cheerleading as an official high school sport (Dorsey & Coomes, 1991).

Cheerleading is big business, with hundreds of thousands of participants spending tens of millions of dollars annually on equipment, apparel, and camps. According to Gems (1997), the original cheerleaders were all males, with the first female cheerleader emerging at Tulane University in 1914. Gems does admit that the 1914/Tulane date and place is highly debatable, but the fact that some universities had female cheerleaders by the 1920s seems indisputable.

Webb (1992) cites demographics about cheerleaders that suggest that they are indeed athletes; 70% of them are involved in other athletic activities in addition to cheerleading. In his study of high school cheerleaders, Freischlag (1989) found that cheerleaders endorsed the term *athletic* to a significantly higher degree than did noncheerleading controls. He also noted that 41% of his sample had training in gymnastics. It is this gymnastic and tumbling ability that is often invoked in discussions of whether cheerleaders are athletes or not. Certainly, in organized cheerleading competitions, gymnastics ability appears to be at a premium.

Psychologically, there are some data worth discussing on cheerleaders. One psychological variable that has received some attention is stress. Anecdotal reports suggest high levels of stress associated with cheerleading. Three quotes from Snowden (1992) serve to underscore this point:

> Was it a disappointment not to make the squad? Was it upsetting? Gee, well, it's hard to describe using only those words. It's probably the single most character-molding moment of female adolescence, way beyond getting your period in math class, buying your first bra or being the wallflower at the school dance. Not making the cheerleading squad is when you transcend "disappointed" and suddenly understand when you say you're "bitter."

> What girls need to be told when they don't make cheerleader is that the worst is over. While business has its corollaries, no company policy, no matter how heartless and inhumane, will ever match the level of public humiliation and institutionalized cruelty of cheerleader tryouts.

> Generally speaking, cheerleaders go through life with a quiet confidence, as if they never have to prove anything again, and failed cheerleaders tend to have a weird intensity, as if they have to prove everything a million times.

To underscore the intensity of these stress conditions, Reel and Gill (1996) have looked at eating disorders among cheerleaders. They found that cheerleaders express considerable body dissatisfaction that may predispose them to eating disorders. Certainly, there are pressures to be slim and attractive in the cheerleading uniforms. For example, Reel and Gill found that 84% of their sample of 155 high school and college female cheerleaders responded "yes" to the question, "Do you think there are pressures associated with cheerleading to lose weight or maintain a below average weight?" There were no differences between high school and college cheerleaders on this question. The sometimes revealing uniform and pressure from sponsors/coaches were also seen as problematic in terms of weight and appearance. Forty percent also agreed with the notion that they would be better cheerleaders if they could lose 5 pounds.

On a related note, Finkenberg, DiNucci, McCune, and McCune (1992) looked at anxiety in a sample of cheerleaders at a national collegiate competition. There were males and females in the Finkenberg et al. sample, and both cheerleader groups differed from normative scores on somatic anxiety as measured by the Competitive State Anxiety Inventory, again pointing to stress in cheerleading.

One shift in the way cheerleaders are perceived has been provided by Suitor and Reavis (1995). They gathered attitudinal data from almost 500 college students from the years 1979–1982 and 1988–1989 and found an increase in acquisition of prestige through female sport participation and a concomitant decline in prestige gained through taking part in cheerleading. Perhaps this finding is not so much a criticism of cheerleading but rather a reflection of the increasing acceptance of female sport participation.

SOURCES: Dorsey & Coomes (1991); Finkenberg, DiNucci, McCune, & McCune (1992); Freischlag (1989); Gems (1997); Reel & Gill (1996); Snowden (1992); Suitor & Reavis (1995); Webb (1992).

disorders so that they may encourage potential victims to seek help. Martin and Hausenblas stress, however, that instructors should not get in the business of diagnosing or treating eating disorders. Finally, instructors should be aware of their attire and its effect on participants. Overdoing the "body beautiful" image through careful selection of attire that overly enhances the instructor's physical attributes may subtly alienate participants, who might somehow feel that they could never measure up to that image no matter how hard they tried. One does not have to have a perfect body to derive the benefits of aerobic exercise.

Another area in which the battle against eating disorders might be launched is at the coaching level. Who interacts more with athletes on a continuing basis, and often has more sway with them, than the coach? Turk, Prentice, Chappell, and Shields (1999) surveyed 138 college coaches about their knowledge of eating disorders and concluded that coaches could benefit from comprehensive education in all facets of the eating disorders. If coaches were to become more knowledgeable in this area through training provided by professionals in medicine, nutrition, and psychology, they could in turn pass on their knowledge, insights, and wisdom to their athletes.

Clearly, informed and concerned aerobics instructors and coaches are not enough to stem the tide. Athletes need to be reminded and remind themselves of problems associated with the eating disorders. There will always be cases from time to time, such as Christy Henrich, that transcend the treatment capabilities of coaches or aerobics instructors, and this is the point where protracted medical and psychological intervention must take place. Fortunately, the cases among athletes where this intervention is necessary constitute the exception rather than the rule.

SUMMARY

1. Socialization into sport is a complex issue. Some of the more relevant subaspects of socialization into sport include role conflict, socialization agents, sport acceptance, and the reasons that females compete.

2. Traditional definitions of the concepts of male and female have generated much research interest within psychology. Research from the mid-1960s showed a preference for traditional female roles and a rejection of the female athlete. Even as late as 1975, 65% of college women saw a stigma attached to women's participation in sport. Recent research indicates healthy changes in perceptions of the female athlete.

3. Parents and coaches were the prime inspirations for female sport participation in the late 1970s. The base of support has broadened over the years to include parents, coaches, older siblings, and peers.

4. The acceptability of the broad array of sport for females varies. In general, the more feminine sports carry slightly more acceptance; sports such as basketball, volleyball, and softball appear to be regarded more unfavorably. Research in Iowa suggests positive changes concerning the acceptance of a greater number of sport activities.

5. Though the evidence is sparse, female athletes appear to place more importance on having fun and playing well than on winning. In another facet of competition, women participating in some sports seem to be less likely than men to come from behind to win. Males at lower levels of skill in tennis appear to be better than females of similar skill level at coming from behind, but this finding diminishes somewhat at the elite level. In professional basketball, substantial differences favor the male players; male collegiate players also come from behind to win more often. Volleyball studies show no sex differences in the ability to come from behind to win.

6. Three psychological variables of considerable interest to sport psychologists include attribution theory, fear of success, and psychological androgyny.

7. Research in the late 1970s showed that young females attributed success to external factors such as luck. Like males, they also attributed male success to ability, an internal attribute. Further research indicates that by age 13, sex role stereotypes are in effect. These stereotypes attribute male success to effort, female success to luck. A more recent area of interest, self versus team attribution, has emerged and bears more investigation.

8. Horner suggested in 1972 that females manifested a fear of success (FOS) in a variety of competitive

situations. Subsequent research has not supported her original position.

9. The concept of psychological androgyny was introduced to the literature in 1974. Androgyny is viewed as an optimal amalgamation of the best of what have been viewed as bipolar traits, masculinity and femininity. Research using both the Personal Attributes Questionnaire (PAQ) and the Bem Sex-Role Inventory (BSRI) have been widespread. In general, successful female athletes are either androgynous or masculine on these measures. Feminine females do not find sports and fitness particularly rewarding, though they may need their benefits most. Overall, it appears that females feel little sex role conflict in their sport involvement.

10. Over the past two decades, new issues of concern to women athletes have emerged. Among these are portrayal of women in the media, homophobia, and eating disorders.

11. It is clear that women receive a less than optimal coverage in the major sports periodicals, sports photography, and the naming and marketing of athletic teams.

12. There is a widespread perception that women in sports violate traditional gender role expectations, one manifestation of which is lesbianism. The admission of lesbianism by athletes such as Martina Navratilova and Billie Jean King has reinforced the notion in the minds of many that female athletes are gay.

13. Eating disorders, such as anorexia, are particularly prominent in sports where thinness is rewarded, such as gymnastics, running, and swimming. The incidence of anorexia appears to be higher among women athletes than among females in general. Specific guidelines for dealing with anorexic athletes should involve aerobics instructors, coaches, sport psychologists, and clinical or counseling psychologists in cases where the disorder has become pathological.

KEY TERMS

Bem Sex-Role Inventory (BSRI) (330)
Fear of Success (FOS) (329)
female athletic triad (335)
gender differences (328)
grim asceticism (335)
homophobia (334)
male hegemony (333)
Personal Attributes Questionnaire (PAQ) (330)
psychological androgyny (330)
role conflict (324)
sport socialization (323)

SUGGESTED READINGS

Birrell, S., & Cole, C. L. (Eds). (1994). *Women, sport, and culture.* Champaign, IL: Human Kinetics.
A reader with 24 entries dealing broadly with such topics as women, sport, and ideology; gender and the organization of sport; women in the male preserve of sport; media, sport, and gender; and sport and the politics of sexuality. Subtopics include the African-American athlete, Title IX, coaching, cheerleaders, the male hegemony in sport, gender stereotyping in the media, homophobia, and feminist bodybuilding.

Cahn, S. K. (1994) *Coming on strong: Gender and sexuality in twentieth-century women's sport.* New York: Free Press.
Cahn approaches gender and sexuality from both a historical and contemporary viewpoint, taking on such issues as sexual sensation in the Flapper Era, African-American women in track and field, the All-American Girls Baseball League, the lesbian threat, and homophobia.

Cayleff, S. E. (1995). *Babe: The life and legend of Babe Didrikson Zaharias.* Urbana, IL: University of Illinois Press.
An engaging biography of arguably the greatest female athlete ever. Thorough in its scholarship, this book also reveals quite a bit about the societal context in which her many accomplishments took place.

Leon, G. R. (1990) Bulimia and athletics: The need to maintain a low body weight. In G. R. Leon (Ed.), *Case histories of psychopathology* (4th ed.). Needham Heights, MA: Allyn & Bacon.

Leon describes a case history of a 21-year-old collegiate gymnast, Ginny N., who had an eating disorder in which she was binging and purging. Her MMPI and other psychological test results indicated anxiety, depression, and feelings of alienation. The therapy provided was a ten-week cognitive-behavioral program with specific emphasis on the irrational beliefs she held about her eating behavior. Progress was made over the ten weeks of counseling, though Ginny's case required periodic monitoring beyond that point. The author concludes with a description of bulimia as described in DSM-III–R and its causes from the standpoint of available research on the topic.

Spence, J. T. (1991). Do the BSRI and PAQ measure the same or different concepts? *Psychology of Women Quarterly, 15,* 141–165.
Janet Spence, a past president of the American Psychological Association and an author of the PAQ, deliberates at length about the merits of the BSRI and her own instrument, discussing issues such as reliability, validity, and comparability of the masculinity and femininity scales. Spence concludes that both measures are valid in terms of the potential for assessing instrumental and expressive traits so pivotal to an understanding of gender issues and the concept of psychological androgyny.

INFOTRAC COLLEGE EDITION

For additional readings, explore Infotrac College Edition, your online library. Go to:
http://www.infotrac-college.com/wadsworth.
Hint: Enter these search terms: androgyny, Bem Sex-Role Inventory, cheerleading, exercise for women, fear of success, homophobia, physical fitness for women, sexual harassment.

Youth Sport: Motives for Participating and Withdrawing

CHAPTER 21

A Brief History

Motives for Participating in Sport

Motives for Withdrawing From Participation

AFA Recommendations for Making Youth Sport More Enjoyable

Summary

Key Terms

Suggested Readings

Teammates. One of the joys of youth sports is the sense of belonging to a team and the resultant sense of well-being.

© Copyright 1999 PhotoDisc, Inc.

When I was a small boy in Kansas a friend of mine and I went fishing and as we sat there in the warmth of a summer afternoon on a river bank we talked about what we wanted to do when we grew up. I told him that I wanted to be a real major league baseball player, a genuine professional like Honus Wagner. My friend said that he'd like to be president of the United States. Neither of us got our wish.

DWIGHT D. EISENHOWER,
THIRTY-FOURTH PRESIDENT OF THE UNITED STATES

Whatever happened to the good old days when if you felt like playing baseball you would round up your buddies, get a bat and a ball and would go out and play? What do we do now? We dress up our kids in uniforms, give them professional equipment, tell them where to play, when to play, organize their games for them, give them officials, and put them in the hands of a coach who doesn't know the first thing about the sport or what's good for an eight year old.

JOE PATERNO, FOOTBALL COACH, PENN STATE, CITED IN HARRIS (1973)

Man is most nearly himself when he achieves the seriousness of a child at play.

HERACLITUS, GREEK PHILOSOPHER (500 B.C.)

Youth sport is a popular topic of conversation for professionals and laypersons alike. At the same time, it is a controversial topic. On one hand, early participation in sport is widely believed to be a mechanism for building character, encouraging sportsmanship, and promoting healthy physical, psychological, and social development. On the other, sport participation may also be viewed as an emotional pressure cooker in which children are subjected to a host of undesirable stresses. Where the truth actually lies, of course, is a matter of conjecture.

Most agree that youth sport is high drama. The cast is varied and includes the following actors: (1) *The athletes.* Some are very young participants who are merely striving to acquire the most rudimentary skills. Others, perhaps at a level somewhat beyond entry status, are trying to have fun and meet a variety of social and physical needs. At a more advanced level, others are working on perfecting skills that will allow them to continue participation at points well beyond their cur-

rent states of sophistication. (2) *The coaches.* These individuals, very often volunteers, come in all sizes, shapes, and descriptions and are vital to the immediate enjoyment and later involvement of youth athletes. Undoubtedly, most mean well, but many are ill prepared to provide for meaningful sport experiences for young athletes, both psychologically and in terms of possessing the requisite sport skills (the proverbial x's and o's). Much remains to be done in training these vital cast members, and some of the more innovative approaches in this connection are discussed in Chapter 13. (3) *The extras.* Foremost among these players are parents, siblings, and peers, though program administrators are also vital cogs in the youth sport network. Mix this varied cast of characters together and what unfolds is the intense drama known as youth sport.

A BRIEF HISTORY

Several factors have contributed to the development of youth sport in the United States. First was an increasing societal awareness of the rights of children; before the twentieth century, children were exploited in the workplace and accorded little status. Another impetus to the development of youth involvement was the fact that sport had secured a firm foothold in the fabric of American everyday life. A third positive agent of change in creating the youth sport movement was the emergence of social agencies such as the Boy Scouts, the Boys' Club, and the YMCA. These youth-oriented organizations took it upon themselves to provide a broad array of programming aimed at constructive use of leisure time. Prominently displayed were organized athletic activities that were believed to be useful in keeping young people off the streets and out of trouble. These social agencies also saw character building as a significant duty, and sports were thought to facilitate this process. Their impact was further enhanced by the fact that public schools generally took the view that sports prior to age 12 were too physically and mentally strenuous. As a consequence, little programming was offered by the public schools to meet the sporting needs of the preadolescent. This philosophy gradually changed in the 1940s and 1950s, and a significant force in altering attitudes was Little League baseball, which began in Williamsport, Pennsylvania, in 1939.

Little League Baseball

A Pennsylvania businessman, Carl Stotz, was the architect of **Little League baseball.** So popular was his product that by 1954 there were 4,000 leagues nationwide (Hale, 1956) involving some 70,000 young men (Skubic, 1995). Today, Little League has grown to what Franklin (1989, p. 64) has called an "amiable monster" of some 2.5 million youngsters playing baseball in more than 7,500 leagues in the United States, Africa, Asia, Australia, Canada, and South America. There are 37 countries represented in the European region alone. An additional 400,000 young women play in the Little League softball program.

The first Little League championship was played in 1947 and was won by a team from Williamsport, Pennsylvania. In 1957, an international element was added when a team from Monterrey, Mexico won the Little League championship. In 1960, Berlin became the first European entry in the championship playoffs. Venezuela and Spain followed suit in 1965, and a team from West Tokyo, Japan won the World Series in 1967. The presence of an international team or two in the series is commonplace today, and press and television coverage of the games is considerable.

However, this meteoric growth in the popularity of youth baseball has not always been smooth. Critics in the early years were vociferous in their opposition to the Little League program, and their views reflected the concern of educators, physical educators, and laypersons over possible mental and physical harm that might result from early, intense athletic competition. Slowly but surely, many of the critics of youth baseball were quieted by research extolling the benefits of organized competition.

The first of these research efforts was reported by Scott (1953) in *Research Quarterly,* which was to publish a series of articles over the next decade that generally were supportive of Little League baseball. Based on results of a questionnaire, Scott indicated that parents of Little League players approved of their sons' participation. Skubic (1955), in an attempt to debunk the claim that intense competition was too physically

Little League coach talking to his team in the dugout prior to a game. Coaches serve as important role models for youth athletes.
© Copyright 1999 PhotoDisc, Inc.

strenuous for young athletes, carried out an interesting study of players and nonplayers. Skubic observed 206 boys, ages 9 through 15 (75 Little Leaguers, 51 Middle Leaguers, and 80 nonparticipants) in several stress conditions and measured their responses through Galvanic Skin Response (GSR). Based on her observations, Skubic concluded that GSR variations were not significant regardless of whether boys were competing in league games, championship contests, or games generated in physical education classes. Skubic concluded: "Insofar as the GSR can be taken to be a valid measure of the emotional excitation of boys of this age level, the results of the present study suggest that youngsters were no more stimulated by competition in league games than they were by competition in physical education games" (pp. 350–351).

In 1956, Skubic reported results of four questionnaires aimed at ascertaining parental attitudes toward Little League play. In general, parental attitudes were quite positive toward the activity, though some concern was expressed that not all boys got to play in league games. Other results from her study showed that

---

Little League baseball network of children's baseball teams started by Carl Stotz and now an international organization numbering more than 2.5 million boys; a corresponding softball program for girls numbers 400,000 members.

Little League participants were higher achievers in school and showed better overall personal adjustment than did nonparticipants. These positive findings were substantiated by Seymour (1956) in a study of five leagues in Atlanta, Georgia.

All of the early reports centered around the benefits of sport participation for young boys. However, Little League baseball was not exempt from the effects of the growing women's movement of the 1970s. In 1973, a young girl named Maria Pepe from Hoboken, New Jersey, attempted to become the first girl to compete in Little League baseball. Though Maria Pepe's efforts were rebuffed, she paved the way for Amy Dickinson to become the first female Little Leaguer. According to Jennings (1981, p. 81), Amy Dickinson was "First player selected in town draft in 1974; All Star for three years; 1976 starting pitcher (4–2 record including a 1-hitter and another game with 13 strikeouts) and shortstop; excellent at completing the double play; .382 batting average."

Concerns About Youth Fitness

A second historical force that served to promote youth sport and fitness resulted from research conducted in the early 1950s in which American children were shown to be generally unfit when compared with matched samples of European youth. Kraus and Hirschland (1954) were the prime architects of this legendary research, and their findings were ultimately brought to the attention of President Dwight Eisenhower. Alarmed at the fitness gap presented to him, Eisenhower convened a 1955 meeting of leading educators and fitness experts aimed at responding to this crisis. One noteworthy outgrowth of these deliberations, which were chaired by Vice President Richard Nixon, was the President's Council on Youth Fitness (now known as the President's Council on Physical Fitness and Sports), which has served since that time as a major force behind national youth fitness.

Youth fitness measures initiated out of national concerns about low youth fitness during the 1950s, these tests have evolved from motoric measures to tests of flexibility, body composition, and cardiorespiratory fitness.

In addition to generating national-level concern with youth fitness, Eisenhower's actions led the American Alliance for Health, Physical Education and Recreation (AAHPER) to develop its Youth Fitness Test. As the components of the AAHPER test make clear, physical educators at that time viewed fitness in a motoric sense, and this philosophy was to dominate thinking for the next 20 years. In the mid-1970s, it became clear that fitness involved more than speed, strength, or endurance. Flexibility, body composition, and cardiorespiratory fitness came to be a part of the fitness formula (Blair, Falls, & Pate, 1983). This transition from the Kraus–Weber approach of the 1950s to the more modern **youth fitness measures** can be seen in Table 21.1.

Despite the debate surrounding youth fitness, the impetus given the youth sport movement by the 1950s data clearly has been considerable. Most significantly, it sent out an alert that emphasized the need for constructive exercise and physical activity, thereby serving as a significant force in shaping our views of the interaction between sport and fitness in children.

MOTIVES FOR PARTICIPATING IN SPORT

Estimates are that 23 million young people between the ages of 5 and 16 are involved in nonschool-sponsored sports programs (Brady, 1989) and yet another 6.5 million take part in activities that are school sponsored (Participation Survey, 1999–2000). In school-sponsored activities, it is interesting to note in light of discussion in the previous chapter that participation by females has risen from 17.8% of the total in 1972–1973 (Girls in Varsity Sports, 1997) to 40% for the year 1999–2000 (Participation Survey, 1999–2000).

What, then, prompts this fascination with youth sport? To arrive at an authoritative answer to this question, an examination of several studies conducted with diverse youth groups is instructive. Among the various studies surveyed are those of the Athletic Footwear Association (American Youth, 1990), Gill, Gross, and Huddleston (1981), Gould, Feltz, Weiss, and Petlichkoff (1982), Griffin (1978), Sapp and Haubenstricker (1978), and the University of California at Los Angeles (UCLA) Sport Psychology Laboratory (Sewell, 1992).

TABLE 21.1

Comparison of 1958 and 1976 Youth Fitness Tests With AAHPERD

Physical Best Test (1988) and the President's Challenge (1991)

Test Item	Fitness Components
AAHPERD youth fitness test (1958)	
Pull-ups (boys) or modified pull-ups (girls)	Muscular strength/endurance
Sit-ups	Muscular strength/endurance
Shuttle run	Agility/speed
Standing broad jump	Power
50-yard dash	Speed
Softball throw	Skill/muscular strength
600-yard run-walk	Cardiorespiratory endurance/speed
AAHPERD youth fitness test (1976)	
Flexed-arm hang	Arm and shoulder girdle strength/endurance
1-minute bent-knee sit-ups	Abdominal strength/endurance
AAHPERD shuttle run	Agility in running/changing directions
Standing long jump	Leg power
50-yard dash	Speed
600-yard run	Cardiorespiratory function
AAHPERD Physical Best (1988)	
1-mile walk/run	Aerobic endurance
Triceps and calf skinfold measurement	Body composition
Sit-and-reach	Lower back/hamstring flexibility
1-minute bent-knee sit-ups	Abdominal strength/endurance
Palm forward pull-ups	Upper body strength/endurance
The President's Challenge (1991)	
Curl-ups	Abdominal strength/endurance
AAHPERD shuttle run	Speed and agility
1-mile run/walk	Heart/lung endurance
Pull-ups or flexed-arm hang	Upper body strength/endurance
V-sit reach or sit-and-reach test	Lower back/hamstring flexibility

Sources: AAHPERD Youth Fitness Test Manual (1980); AAHPERD Physical Best (1988); Pate (1983); The President's Challenge Physical Fitness Program (1991).

Of these various efforts, the **Athletic Footwear Association (AFA) research** merits special consideration, particularly in view of its scope. Martha Ewing and Vern Seefeldt of the Youth Sport Institute at Michigan State University were commissioned by the AFA to look at variables contributing to staying with or dropping our of sport. These investigators asked 10,000 young people between the ages of 10 and 18 to complete questionnaires they had devised. This sample of young people was made up of respondents from 11

Athletic Footwear Association (AFA) research comprehensive study commissioned in 1990 to examine variables contributing to youth participation and withdrawal from sport.

cities representing diverse geographical locations and demographic factors. The cities involved were: Hartford, Connecticut; Atlanta, Georgia; Lawrence, Kansas; Baltimore, Maryland; Lansing, Michigan; Cortland, New York; Akron/Kent, Ohio; Arlington, Texas; Brownsville, Texas; and Yakima, Washington. Factors of significance that were predictive of **motives for participation** in sport experience among youth in the AFA study, as well as others to varying degrees, were having fun, skill improvement, fitness benefits, socialization, and a host of miscellaneous and less salient positive variables.

Having Fun

In the middle 1950s, Skubic (1956) found that a high priority for youth participating in sport was to have fun. Little has transpired in the interim to alter this perception. For example, the 1990 AFA report indicated that the highest rated reason among 11 possible participation motives was to have fun; on a five-point scale, having fun received a 4.5 from the respondents. These results are very similar to those of Sapp and Haubenstricker in their 1978 research with youngsters in the state of Michigan. Sapp and Haubenstricker looked at the participation objectives of 579 boys and 471 girls ages 11 to 18 participating in 11 nonschool related sports, and found that the most common reason for participation in their sample was to have fun. Gould, Feltz, Weiss, and Petlichkoff (1982) studied 365 swimmers from ages 8 to 19. Fun was first in importance out of 30 variables studied. Gender differences were noted; girls rated having fun as significantly more important. Scanlan and Lewthwaite (1986), in a study of youth wrestlers ages 9 to 14, found sport enjoyment to be closely linked to parental and coach satisfaction, with a lack of maternal pressure and negative reactions to performance, and positive adult involvement in their sport. Perhaps Kleiber (1981, p. 83) said it best: "Winning is important, but fun is more important, at least for children."

Motives for participation in youth sport, having fun, skill improvement, fitness benefits, team atmosphere, and socialization, among others.

Skill Improvement

Another reason that young people choose sport participation is to improve their skills. The AFA study indicated that skill improvement ran a close second to having fun with their sample. In the Sapp and Haubenstricker report, skill improvement was second only to "having fun" and was mentioned by 80% of the respondents. Other studies have not accorded skill development quite as lofty a state, but nevertheless are supportive. Wankel and Kreisel (1985), in a study of 310 soccer, 338 hockey, and 174 baseball participants, found that youth in all three groups rated improving game skills as fourth in importance. On a related note, however, comparing their skills with those of others was rated highest of 10 enjoyment factors by soccer and baseball players and second by the hockey contingent. Gould et al (1985), in their study of youth swimmers, also found the skill development factor to be ranked fourth of 14 factors studied. No appreciable differences were noted by either sex or age considerations in the Gould et al (1985) sample.

One study in which personal performance was considered to be of paramount importance was that of McElroy and Kirkendall (1980). More than 2,000 participants in the summer portion of the 1979 National Youth Sports Program (average age 11.9 years) responded to a questionnaire about their reasons for taking part in sport. A particularly pertinent question asked of the subjects was:

In playing a sports game, which of the following is most important?

(a) to defeat your opponent, or the other team (winning orientation)

(b) to play as well as you can (personal performance)

(c) to play fairly, by the rules at all times (fair play)

(d) everyone on the team should get to play (total participation)

The results of the responses to this question are summarized in Table 21.2. Clearly, to play as well as one can was overwhelmingly most important in this investigation. Other points of interest include the fact that a winning orientation was endorsed by less than 10% of the total sample.

In summary, its relative rank can be argued, but skill development obviously is an important aspect of

TABLE 21.2

Competitive Orientation Among Youth Sport Participants

	Males (n = 1236)	Females (n = 1096)
Winning orientation	13.5%	4.6%
Personal performance	51.0	48.3
Fair play	24.4	37.6
Total participation	11.0	9.4
	100.0%	100.0%

Source: McElroy & Kirkendall (1980).

youth sports, and coaches and others should be alert to its significance with children.

Fitness Benefits

The AFA study indicated that staying in shape was fourth of 11 variables in terms of importance to their sample. The UCLA sample ranked feeling fit fourth of seven variables but still gave it a higher priority than winning. Fifty-six percent of the Sapp and Haubenstricker respondents saw fitness benefits as an important aspect of sport participation, thereby ranking it third behind having fun and skill development. Gould, Feltz, Weiss, and Petlichkoff (1982), in their study of competitive youth swimmers, reported that their subjects actually saw fitness benefits as a close second to having fun. Others who have stressed the fitness aspect in their research include Gill et al. (1981), Gould et al. (1985), and Griffin (1978).

Team Atmosphere

Team membership and interaction was particularly significant in the UCLA sample, ranking second in importance. The AFA report was less enthusiastic on this point but still accorded team involvement some status. Sapp and Haubenstricker (1978) found team atmosphere to be fourth in importance with their respondents. Wankel and Kreisel (1985) found that being on a team was fifth in importance for each of the sport groups in their study. Closely allied with this aspect is the social dimension of making friends, and this is a consistent finding across vir-

tually all of the studies. Clearly, the social dimension of youth sport participation cannot be overlooked by those who are in the business of providing sport experience for young people.

Other Reasons

In addition to the reasons for participating already cited, others are perhaps less salient but nevertheless worth mentioning. Among them are sportsmanship, excitement or challenge, travel, and such extrinsic rewards as trophies, citations in the newspapers, and feeling important.

A Final Note

Having fun in sports has generally been accorded a lofty position in the hierarchy of reasons that young people play sports. At the same time, fun has an elusive quality to it; for a minority of youth, winning is the only way to have fun. For others, playing well, achieving fitness, or being part of a team is paramount. In an attempt to arrive at what constitutes fun, a study by Wankel and Sefton (1989) is instructive. They had 55 females and 67 males ages 7 to 15 fill out questionnaires before and after ringette and hockey games at various points in their respective seasons. Fun was parsimoniously assessed on a five-point Likert scale from 1 (no fun at all) to 5 (a lot of fun). Other variables studied included age, sex, pre- and postgame affect, motivation mood states, how well one expected to play, confidence in team outcome, and how well one played. Positive postgame affect was the most powerful predictor of fun, followed by how well one played and degree of challenge of the competition. This research strongly suggests that having fun is not a unidimensional concept but is rather a complex phenomenon. Nevertheless, having fun remains a major reason that youth take part in athletic events.

MOTIVES FOR WITHDRAWING FROM PARTICIPATION

Clearly, youth sport is immensely popular and participation is multidimensionally determined. However,

Motives for Youth Sport Participation

An interesting sidelight of the study conducted by the Athletic Footwear Association (AFA) is a categorization scheme for analyzing youth sport participation motives. Accordingly, youth may be viewed as Reluctant Participants, Image-Conscious Socializers, or Competence-Oriented Participants.

Of the respondents, the image-conscious socializers make up the majority, accounting for 40% of all participants; of the remainder, those youth who are competence oriented make up 35%, and those who take part reluctantly account for the remaining 25%. The three groups can be described as follows:

Image-Conscious Socializers

Sports are important to this group, but their behavior is maintained greatly by what others think of them, being made to feel important, and winning trophies and other tangible rewards.

Image-conscious socializers AFA study category of youth sport participants who are motivated by having friends, winning peer approval, and staying fit but are likely to withdraw if peer approval lessens.
Competence-oriented participants AFA study category of youth sport participants who are motivated by skill improvement and intrinsic rather than extrinsic reward; likely to continue in sport in adulthood.
Reluctant participants AFA study category of youth sport participants who are motivated by what others think of them, being made to feel important, and winning awards; comprises the smallest group.

Competence-Oriented Participants

This group is motivated by skill improvement, and their behavior is maintained by intrinsic rather than extrinsic reward. As a consequence, this group is more likely to stay with sport and physical fitness after the adolescent years are over.

Reluctant Participants

Being with or making new friends, winning peer approval, and staying fit are strong motivational keys for this group. However, if their chosen sport becomes quite demanding and/or peer approval lessens, the physical fitness benefits are not likely to be a strong enough incentive for them to continue sport participation.

Interestingly, the focus on winning is about the same for all three groups: of 25 possible responses as to why they might participate in sport, the Reluctant Participants ranked winning as thirteenth, the Image-Conscious Socializers as tenth, and the Competence-Oriented Participants as seventh. While there are some differences placed on winning by these three groups, it clearly does not carry a high priority with youth athletes.

Other key findings from the AFA report indicated the Competence-Oriented Participants and the Image-Conscious Socializers are quite similar in perceived athletic ability, importance placed on team membership, and perceived sport enjoyment. However, the Reluctant Participants rate themselves as far below their teammates (and, hence, the other two groups discussed herein) in athletic ability, place a lower value on team membership, and report much less participation satisfaction.

---

participation in sports is not rewarding to equal degrees for all participants. As a consequence, a formidable dropout problem is associated with the various youth sports.

Motives for withdrawal in youth sport, primary reasons are not having fun, concerns about coaching, and conflict of interest with other life activities; secondary reasons are too much pressure from parents and peers, overemphasis on winning, and not getting to play enough.

Primary Concerns

Among youngsters' primary **motives for withdrawal** from sport include not having fun, concerns about coaching, and conflict of interest with other life activities. Each of these concerns will be addressed in turn.

NOT HAVING FUN. Up to adolescence, fun is the main reason that young people participate in sport. This fact, in turn, should dictate that all involved in setting up youth programs must do their best to guarantee that fun is awarded the highest priority when planning takes place. Although this is easy to say, the doing is more complicated. The "win-at-all-cost" mentality is an unfortunate reality.

CONCERNS ABOUT COACHING. The potential for misperception of what the coach may be trying to accomplish is considerable. The potential for poor coaching procedures is equally possible. Not enough has been done in terms of training coaches to work with youth; coaches are often very interested in young people and have the best of intentions but simply lack the interpersonal and sport-related skills to be successful. Also, some probably think they are latter-day Vince Lombardis living out some sort of fantasy through the use of strong-arm methods, badgering officials, and other tactics used or perceived to have been used by their coaching idols. Young people deserve coaches who have the best training available, who have an appreciation of the principles of child development, and who use a soft touch in dealing with people. Many of the other reasons for dropping out could be avoided or greatly buffered by informed and sensitive coaches.

One of the more consistent findings about why young people drop out of sports is conflict with other life demands. It is unreasonable to think that sports is the be-all and end-all for everyone, and it would be naive to assume that other priorities do not exist. In the earliest years of athletic performance, little else is available and parents tend to dictate the course of organized activities, sporting or otherwise. However, with increasing maturation comes a natural progression toward independence. This greater independence is manifested in a number of ways, not the least of which is dropping out of sport. The skill selection process is partly responsible, but equally powerful are the pulls of growing social needs, academic pursuits, part-time employment, debating, drama, music, and an endless array of other worthwhile and rewarding activities.

A number of studies have substantiated the significance of this conflict-of-interest finding. For instance, Fry, McClements, and Sefton (1981), in a study of

hockey dropouts in Canada, found that 31% reported conflicts as the main reason for dropping out of their sport. Similarly, Orlick (1974), in his study of five sports reported earlier, found that 31% cited general life conflict as the reason for dropping out of their respective sports. In a study by Gould et al. (1985), even stronger results were found with swimmers in the age range of 10 to 18. "Other things to do" was cited by 84% of their subjects.

Burton and Martens (1986) address this issue in a study of youth wrestlers, ages 7 to 17, and their parents and coaches. The dropouts in their study reported conflict-of-interest problems as paramount in importance. However, Burton and Martens suspect that threats to perceived ability were the actual culprits in the dropouts in their study. Despite the caveat provided by Burton and Martens, a major factor in dropping out of sport is simple conflict of interest with other activities, a not altogether unhealthy reason. However, the fact that dropping out is so tied in with increasing age does little to ameliorate the aggravations associated with dropping out in the earlier age groups, such as 8 through 12. The younger the participants, the more vulnerable they appear to be to the kinds of things over which the adult leadership has some degree of control, namely, getting to play, having fun, and developing skills with the help of an informed and sensitive coach.

Secondary Concerns

Secondary motives for discontinuing sports involvement include stress generated by parents and peers, an overemphasis on winning, and not getting to play enough.

TOO MUCH PRESSURE FROM PARENTS AND PEERS. Youth participants are greatly swayed by parents and peers in both initiating and discontinuing sport involvement. Probably everyone is familiar with the parent who reacts to every sport event in which his or her child plays as if it were the Super Bowl and the World Series wrapped into one. Undoubtedly, the chemistry at work here is part ego and part genuine concern for the happiness and well-being of the child. Irrespective of where the true motivation lies, this parental reaction serves as a potential source of stress for the child involved (and for those around the child, too). The issue of the role of the spectators has been the subject of more than one heated debate in both lay and professional groups.

Martens and Seefeldt (1979), reacting to the problems caused by overzealous parent/spectators, have suggested a number of steps that can be taken to curb potentially stress-inducing and embarrassing displays. Among the suggested steps are (1) requiring parents to remain seated in the specified spectator viewing area during all contests; (2) restricting the yelling of instructions, and more particularly criticisms, during the events; (3) not allowing parents to make any derogatory comments to opposing players, officials, and league administrators; and (4) brooking no parental interference with the coach(es) of their children. Parents should have the character to temporarily relinquish their child to the coach for the duration of the event at hand. Though the measures suggested by Martens and Seefeldt may seem unduly harsh, experience has shown that they are often justified. Games should always be oriented philosophically toward making sport physically healthy and psychosocially rewarding for the participants rather than as a means for parents to live vicariously through their children.

Too Much Emphasis on Winning or on Competition.

As can be seen, the emphasis on winning pervades virtually all of the reasons that sport is not always fun for a sizable number of children. Orlick (1974), in a study of dropouts from five sports, noted that 67% cited competitive emphasis as the major reason for their discontinuation of competition. Pooley (1981), in a study of youth soccer players, found that 33% of his respondents dropped out because of too much emphasis on competition. Gould, Feltz, Horn, and Weiss (1982) found his figure to be 16% in a group of dropouts from competitive swimming. Results from these three studies should serve as fair warning that too much emphasis can indeed be placed on the competitive aspects of youth sports.

Not Getting to Play Enough.

Because of the emphasis placed on winning by coaches, parents, and society as a whole, a strong tendency exists to always play the best athletes in order to satisfy the hunger, however misguided, for victory. Lost in the shuffle are the less talented performers. Some of them will never become

athletes of any consequence; however, the distressing fact is that a fair number will be turned off long before they ever find out the ultimate verdict on their sports skills. Knowing what we do about the tremendous variability in physical maturation rates, it seems ludicrous to make premature assessments of talent, judgments with far-reaching implications for future sport participation. One can only wonder how many potentially fine athletes have been turned off at an early age because some coach or administrator decided that winning was more important than total participation of all involved.

AFA RECOMMENDATIONS FOR MAKING YOUTH SPORT MORE ENJOYABLE

The answer to making youth sport more enjoyable is most likely embedded in the results published by the AFA in their survey of 10,000 youth (American Youth, 1990). Asked the most important prompt, "Changes you would make for more enjoyment or to stay involved in a sport you dropped," the top 11 responses of the youth surveyed were nested under two major areas, conflict with other activities (4) and coaching (7). Concerns and the ranking of each response were expressed as follows (T = tie in the rankings):

Conflict with other activities

Schedule didn't conflict with studies (2)
Schedule didn't conflict with social life (3T)
Games/practice schedule were changed (7T)
It didn't take so much time (10T)

Coaching

Practices were more fun (1)
Coaches understood players better (3T)
I could play more (3T)
Coaches were better teachers (6)
Coach understood the sport better (7T)
There was less emphasis on winning (9)
Coach didn't yell so much (10T)

The preceding points appear to possess considerable validity and should be taken as legitimate expressions of the concerns young people have about sport participation. Obviously, administrators, coaches, sport scientists, and parents would do well to take these suggestions to heart in future planning of youth sport activities.

It is once again interesting to note the importance of fun imbedded in the preceding responses, with "making practices more fun" the primary suggestion that young people would make in terms of improving their own sport experience. At all levels of inquiry, the theme of fun pervades virtually every study of youth sport.

SUMMARY

1. Youth sport is a multifaceted enterprise, one fraught with controversy on its positive and negative consequences.

2. Formal sport involvement is a relatively new phenomenon. The growth of organized sport in general in this country and a concomitant increasing awareness of the rights of children gave considerable impetus to the youth sport movement. Also, the emergence of agencies such as the Boy Scouts, Boys' Club, and YMCA pushed youth sport to the forefront of American life. The reluctance of the public schools to provide physical education and sport experiences for youngsters under the age of 12 made the activities provided by these various agencies even more significant.

3. Little League baseball began in 1939 in Pennsylvania and has experienced a meteoric rise, currently serving 2.5 million participants. In its earliest days, Little League baseball met with substantial resistance from a variety of critics who saw the sport as too physically dangerous and psychologically demanding. Research published in the 1950s and 1960s countered many of these claims, and Little League baseball continues to prosper. The equal rights movement led to Amy Dickinson's becoming the first female Little Leaguer.

4. A second force that propelled youth sport was an increasing concern about physical fitness. A landmark study conducted in the early 1950s indicated that American youngsters were inferior to their European peers in overall fitness. President Dwight Eisenhower was appalled by the results of the fitness study. This information led him to convene a panel of education and fitness leaders in an effort to respond to what many regarded as a true national crisis. The President's Council on Youth Fitness and the AAHPER Youth Fitness Test, with later alterations, were two significant products of this presidential response.

5. Approximately 29 million children under age 18 participate in nonschool and school-sponsored athletic activities.

6. Having fun consistently appears to be the primary reason why children take part in sport, followed in no particular order by improving athletic skills, achieving a higher level of fitness, and experiencing the social rewards offered by team sports. Extrinsic rewards, such as trophies or media coverage, appear to be of secondary importance.

7. Just what fun is remains elusive, but postgame positive affect, how well one played, and the level of challenge of the competition have emerged as predictors of fun. Research suggests that fun is a multidimensional rather than a unidimensional concept in the view of youth athletes.

8. The dropout rate in youth sport is, in the view of some, alarmingly high and constitutes a problem for which too few answers have been found. Significant reasons that youngsters discontinue sport participation include not having fun, conflict of interest with other life activities, concerns about coaching, too much parental and peer pressure, too much emphasis on winning, and not getting to play enough.

9. Sport participation could be made more enjoyable, according to youth respondents in the Athletic Footwear Association (AFA) study, through improvement in two primary areas: minimization of conflicts with other life activities and improvements in the quality of coaching. Of the top 11 suggestions for improving youth sport, all could be subsumed under one of these two areas.

KEY TERMS

Athletic Footwear Association (AFA) research (345)
competence-oriented participants (348)

image-conscious socializers (348)
Little League baseball (343)
motives for participation (346)
motives for withdrawal (348)
reluctant participants (348)
youth fitness measures (344)

SUGGESTED READINGS

Kuchenbecker, S. Y. (2000). *Raising winners.* New York: Times Books.

This book combines the author's interest in self-efficacy with her work, known as the Sports Proactive Information Formative Feedback Inventory (SPIFFI). Chapters deal with topics such as self-efficacy, motivation, balance in one's life, correct eating and sleeping habits, growth and development, injuries, the mental game, academic success, and other topics of interest to people involved with youth sport. A hearty endorsement of her work is provided by college basketball coaching legend John Wooden.

Miller, D. K. (1994). *Measurement by the physical educator. Why and how.* (2nd ed.) Dubuque, IA: Brown and Benchmark.

Chapter 16 of this text addresses the assessment of physical fitness among youth in considerable detail. Programs such as the Prudential FITNESSGRAM (1992), the Manitoba Schools Fitness Test (1989), the South Carolina Physical Fitness Test (1983), Fit Youth Today (1986), the YMCA Physical Fitness Test (1989), AAHPERD Physical Best (1988), the Chrysler Fund AAU Physical Fitness Program (1991), the President's Challenge (1991), and the AAHPERD Youth Fitness Test (1976) are compared and contrasted in a most readable fashion. Miller also points out that an "agreement to agree" was generated in 1992 by the leadership of the President's Council on Youth Fitness and Sports (PCYFS) and the American Alliance for Health, Physical Education, Recreation and Dance (AAHPERD) on creating one test for the assessment of fitness in young people.

Orlick, T., & Botterill, C. (1975). *Every kid can win.* Chicago, IL: Nelson-Hall.

A classic that remains useful to an understanding of youth sport. The authors have attempted to bridge the communications gap that exists between people who generate ideas and those who apply them, in this case, coaches, parents, and others who interact with young people in the athletic arena. Practical suggestions are made about how to keep children in sport and how to make the experience as rewarding as possible in the process. A chapter on the female athlete is particularly interesting given the date of the publication of this work.

RQES forum. (1992). *Research Quarterly for Exercise and Sport, 63,* 95–36.

Eight articles address various aspects of youth fitness, focusing primarily on such topics as the fitness level of American youth from several perspectives and measurement problems in assessing youth fitness. This collection serves to reinforce and expand upon many of the points made in our discussion of youth fitness and related concerns.

INFOTRAC COLLEGE EDITION

For additional readings, explore Infotrac College Edition, your online library. Go to:
http://www.infotrac-college.com/wadsworth
Hint: Enter the search terms: Little League baseball, school sports, sports for children (health aspects), sports for children (psychological aspects), sports for children (social aspects), youth fitness.

Youth Sport: Stress and Other Issues

CHAPTER 22

Stress and Youth Sport

Measures of Stress

Cognitive Aspects of
Competitive Stress

Antecedents of Competitive Stress

Elite Performance in Youth Athletes

Violence in Youth Sports

Health Risks Associated With
Youth Sport

Recommendations for Improving
Youth Sport

Summary

Key Terms

Suggested Readings

Coach and umpire arguing over a call made at a baseball game. It is important that youth coaches limit this sort of interaction to minimum, as it can send the wrong message to young baseball players.

Unquestionably, a certain amount of stress is associated with participating in youth sports. The pressures from parents, peers, friends, and coaches as well as individual expectancies all coalesce to produce stress. Clearly, some children are more vulnerable to stress than others, and we shall explore some antecedents and outcomes of the sport experience. Also, elite performance, violence in youth sport, health risks associated with participation, and some recommendations for improving the youth sport experience will be discussed.

STRESS AND YOUTH SPORT

Simon and Martens (1979) conducted research involving 749 boys ranging in age from 9 to 14 years to look at pre-event state anxiety responses in a variety of sport and nonsport situations. Required school activities such as classroom examinations, nonrequired nonsport activities such as band solos, and several nonschool team versus individual and contact versus noncontact sports were studied. One of the more revealing findings of the Simon and Martens effort was that, of 11 activities, band solos evoked more pre-event state anxiety than did any of the sports. Results of their thought-provoking analyses can be seen in Figure 22.1.

Results of the Simon and Martens study notwithstanding, youth sports can be stressful for some youngsters, and a number of factors contribute to this situation. Among the stress factors are the general emphasis on winning as the measure of success and the constant pressure of social evaluation provided by coaches, parents, and peers. One's perceived ability, success expectancy, the expectation of negative evaluation, and the expectancy to feel bad in the face of poor performance are additional anxiety producers.

Product orientation to competition an attitude toward sport that emphasizes "product" over process: winning above all else, tangible rewards, seeking of adulation, and dehumanization of the opponent.

Process orientation to competition an attitude toward sport that emphasizes participation as an end in itself, striving for personal or team excellence, aesthetic activity, and rapport with competitors.

Competition: Product or Process?

The word *competition* comes to us from the Latin *com* and *petere,* which collectively mean "to seek together." Clearly, much of sport at all age levels has drifted away from the "seeking together" idea, and youth sport is no exception. Part of the problem in youth sport and sport in general, according to DuBois (1980), is an emphasis on sport as product rather than process. Characteristics of a **product orientation to competition** are: (1) *Winning above all else.* Events in any contest become meaningful in this context so long as they contribute to winning and the concomitant feeling of domination that goes with beating an opponent. (2) *Tangible rewards.* Competition is magnified if a prize of some kind is more important than the competition itself. (3) *Seeking of adulation.* The product-oriented competitor plays more for the admiration of others than for the intrinsic enjoyment that competition can provide. DuBois suggests that this adulation issue may, in part, explain the difficulties faced by women in their efforts to join the sport subculture. Women have long been viewed as providers as opposed to recipients of adulation. (4) *Dehumanization of the opponent.* The feeling of dominating an opponent is of primary importance here. Feelings of worth are enhanced not from competing but from dominating. At best, this can be viewed as a neurotic motivation for play.

On the other side of the coin, and much more optimistically, the **process orientation to competition** has much to recommend it. Key to this process point of view are: (1) *Participation as an end in itself.* Winning is secondary to taking part. Sport takes on the trappings of an intrinsically rewarding activity because the players participate for the sake of participation; winning is left to take care of itself. (2) *Striving for personal or team excellence.* Playing as best one can is paramount here. The old cliché, "It's not whether you won or lost, but how you played the game," exemplifies this approach to participation. (3) *Aesthetic sensitivity.* There is absolutely no reason that sport, with all its rough-and-tumble activities, cannot be viewed as an aesthetic experience. Harmony, "oneness," and rhythm then become integral parts of a sport process experience. (4) *Rapport with competitors.* Competitors are viewed as catalytic agents in the pursuit of mutual goals, namely,

FIGURE 22.1

Children's Precompetitive State Anxiety in 11 Sport and Nonsport Evaluative Activities

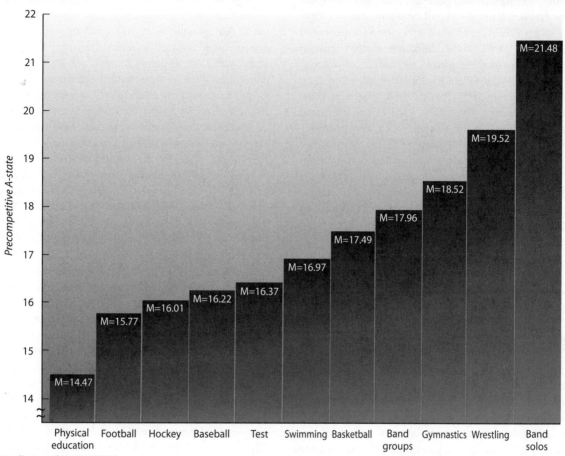

SOURCE: Simon and Martens (1979).

excellence in personal and team performance. Without the opponent, no standard exists against which to measure one's own performance. Therefore, the opponent becomes not an enemy but a valued ally.

The competition as process approach is the one we choose to support. Competition as process is not a sentimental notion of what ought to be; rather, it represents an attainable goal toward which all involved with youth sport should be oriented. Not only does youth sport take on new meaning in this framework, but the lifetime carryover can be significant. We might actually end up with adults with a lifelong interest in sports and physical fitness, adults who also appreciate good ability and effort, sportsmanship, and aesthetic properties inherent in physical activity.

Competitive Stress

The scientific study of the interaction of youth sport and stress owes a debt of gratitude to the research efforts of Rainer Martens and various associates and the separate and collaborative efforts of Michael Passer and Tara Scanlan. Accordingly, the following discussion reflects their substantial efforts in this important aspect of youth sport. Researchers generally agree that **competitive stress** is a negative emotional state that is generated when a child feels unable to respond adequately to competitive performance demands, thereby risking failure. Subsequent negative evaluation of athletic competence and resultant loss of self-esteem may then occur (Martens, 1977; Passer, 1984; Scanlan, 1984; Scanlan & Passer, 1978, 1981). Vital to understanding competitive stress is the awareness that the entire sequence of events is highly personal and subjective. It is not real or objective failure that matters, but how the child perceives competitive adequacy. Also, great individual differences exist in response to competition; not all situations evoke a stress response, and the overall reaction is greatly mediated by a psychologically systemic stress tolerance. Suffice it to say, competitive stress is an incredibly complex phenomenon.

Competitive stress may occur at any time. It may take place at home the day of an important contest or shortly before competition, especially when precompetition inadequacies are experienced. A second forum for competitive stress is during actual competition. If an awareness of inability surfaces, competitive stress becomes a reality. Finally, stress may rise after the fact in situations where game performance may be viewed as inadequate. Giving up a game-winning home run or striking out with the bases loaded in the bottom of the last inning are familiar events for many who have participated in baseball, and postgame competitive stress reactions to such events are common.

MEASURES OF STRESS

Scanlan (1984) suggests that stress may be measured through behavioral, physiological, and psychological

---

Competitive stress a negative emotional state generated when a child feels unable to respond adequately to competitive performance demands.

Competitive trait anxiety (CTA) a condition identified by Martens, who posits a significant correlation between high trait anxiety and subsequent state-related anxiety responses to competition.

means. Behaviorally, sleep difficulties, appetite loss, digestive disturbances, or self-reports of "nerves" might be used as indices of stress. Physiologically, increases in heart rate, respiration, or alterations brought about through activation of the autonomic nervous system could be monitored and used to indicate the presence of stress. An example of physiological monitoring mentioned earlier involved a Galvanic skin response (GSR) study with Little Leaguers (Skubic, 1955). Yet another effort in physiological monitoring of stress by Hanson (1967) is noteworthy. Also using Little Leaguers, Hanson reported that players' heart rates rose to an average of 166 beats per minute while they were batting. No other game situation evoked anywhere near this much stress. Psychologically, the standard stress assessment procedures have been various paper-and-pencil measures, particularly those capable of highlighting state and/or trait anxiety. A general example of the former is Spielberger's State Anxiety Inventory for Children (SAIC) (Spielberger, 1973). A sport specific measure of significance is the children's version of the Competitive State Anxiety Inventory (CSAIQ; Martens, Burton, Rivkin, & Simon, 1980). Both of these tests have been used extensively within the youth sport context. A third important test, discussed earlier, is the Sport Competition Anxiety Test (SCAT) (Martens, 1977), purportedly a measure of **competitive trait anxiety (CTA).**

CTA has been of considerable interest to researchers in sport-related anxiety. Martens' contention is that there will be a significant correlation between high trait anxiety and subsequent state-related anxiety responses to competition. Research by Gill and Martens (1977) and Weinberg and Genuchi (1980) as well as that reported in the various reports by Passer and Scanlan have been most supportive of this line of investigation.

In the various studies conducted on competitive trait anxiety, at least two preliminary but significant findings emerge. One is that CTA appears to increase with age, particularly in precollege samples. This increase in anxiety is, no doubt, linked with the increased importance placed on winning as the athlete grows older and more experienced. A second finding is that CTA is higher in females than in males. Passer (1984) issues several caveats related to these age and gender generalizations, however. One reservation has to do with the cross-sectional rather than longitudinal nature of the differences; it has not been demonstrated over time with groups of athletes that these results would be replicated. Also, laboratory and field studies of state anxiety reactions prior to competition reveal few gender differences (Passer, 1984). Clearly, additional research in the area of age and gender differences in CTA is needed.

COGNITIVE ASPECTS OF COMPETITIVE STRESS

Passer (1984) suggests that the extent to which an athlete experiences competitive stress will largely be dictated by at least four cognitive mediators: perceived ability, success expectancy, expectancy of negative evaluation, and expectancy of experiencing negative affect or emotion.

Perceived Ability

Perceived ability is a function of a continuing comparison process that begins in the preschool years and continues throughout life. In their earliest years, children have an undifferentiated sense of self that is gradually altered by a myriad of environmental events. However, this sense of self eventually must be measured against a multidimensional rather than a unidimensional set of standards. At age 4 or 5 years, the evaluative process begins in earnest and thereafter intensifies, perhaps reaching a peak in the adolescent years, that period in which the search for personal identity is so important. One forum that provides much feedback concerning this self-perception of ability is that of sport. To be selected first (or last) in a pickup baseball game or to be the star (or goat) of an important soccer match has far-reaching consequences for the self-perception of the young athlete. Through a long series of informal and formal events within sports comes a cognitive state that is labeled perceived ability. And with varying perceptions of this ability to compete comes the potential for competitive stress in its various manifestations.

Success Expectancy

Success in youth sport means different things to different people; success may mean winning or losing to some and playing well and having fun to others. Nevertheless, **success expectancy** (as well as failure expectancy) is an important mediator of competitive stress. Passer (1984) reports that high-CTA youth athletes often feel that they are as physically talented as their low-CTA peers but consistently report lower expectancy of success. Obviously, CTA is an important part of success expectancy.

Expectancy of Negative Evaluation

Sport offers numerous opportunities for appraisal of self and others. Home runs and errors, touchdowns and fumbles, and hustling or failing to hustle all are occasions for assessing ability and effort on the part of coaches, parents, and peers. Interestingly, adult significant others appear to be more of a source of competitive stress in the form of **expectancy of negative evaluation** than are peers (Passer, 1983, 1984). Also, competitive trait anxiety is an integral part of this dimension of competitive stress; high-CTA youngsters do not necessarily expect more disapproval when they perform poorly, but they may be more susceptible to negative feedback from significant other adults than low-CTA youngsters.

Expectancy of Negative Affect

High-CTA youth appear to expect the results of their poor performance to be more emotionally painful than do low-CTA children. Passer (1983), in a study of youth soccer players, found that shame and being generally upset were more common among high-CTA players who performed poorly than among those who performed well. Passer explained these observed feelings of guilt, shame, and dejection in terms of a number of

---

Perceived ability a continuing comparison process that begins in the preschool years and continues throughout life; one of Passer's four cognitive mediators of competitive stress.
Success expectancy though success is measured in different terms by individuals, expectancy of success in whatever form creates stress; Passer's second cognitive mediator of competitive stress.
Expectancy of negative evaluation as powerful as success expectancy and more influential from adults than peers; Passer's third cognitive mediator of competitive stress.

factors. Among the factors producing **expectancy of negative affect** were greater expectancy of criticism for poor performance, an overblown emphasis on success, or a simple classically conditioned response in which past failures have been paired with negative emotional feelings, thereby eliciting a conditioned negative emotional state related to competing.

ANTECEDENTS OF COMPETITIVE STRESS

Obviously there must be antecedent events that create a favorable climate for the development of competitive trait anxiety or competitive stress. While it is likely, as suggested by Martens (1977), that individual variations in experiencing competitive stress have strong roots in recurring competitive sport situations, there must be other predispositional factors to consider. Passer (1984) suggests that parent–child interactions, interactions with other adults and peers, and history of success and failure are three such antecedents.

Parent–Child Interactions

There is sufficient research to suggest that parent–child relationships are a salient factor in the development of personality. Parental use of positive and negative feedback for various behaviors is a most crucial part of this childrearing process. Children raised with substantial inconsistencies in the use of reinforcement and punishment tend to behave accordingly; they behave erratically because they are not sure just what the exact rules governing the game of life are. This inability, of course, generalizes to the games we play daily. Children who are raised on a steady diet of punitive measures represent a different issue. They tend to become immune to the effects of punishment and represent discipline problems in school, on the playground, and in the various sport settings.

Expectancy of negative affect an individual's anticipation that poor performance will be emotionally painful, more common among high-CTA children than among low-CTA children; Passer's fourth cognitive mediator of competitive stress.

Interactions With Other Adults and Peers

The role of coaches and parents in the creation of competitive stress was discussed earlier, but little has been said about peer pressure. The fact that children spend the majority of their time playing in situations not supervised by adults tells us something about the potential for peer evaluation opportunities. Sports, unlike the academic world, also creates such an environment of interdependence that performance failures affecting others must necessarily be viewed with a jaundiced eye by those significant other peers.

History of Success and Failure

Passer (1984) indicates that failure can contribute to competitive trait anxiety in at least two ways. One is that frequent failures enhance the chances for negative adult and peer evaluations. Second, repeated failure may lead to the perception of all competition as unduly threatening.

ELITE PERFORMANCE IN YOUTH ATHLETES

Much of the research on youth sport has focused on two areas, participation motives and psychological stress. A healthy literature is now developing on the psychology of the elite youth performer (Feltz & Ewing, 1987). There is a constant bombardment of media accounts concerning precocious athletes. Examples include Jennifer Capriati in tennis, Tiger Woods in golf (he first broke 50 for nine holes just short of his third birthday), and a whole host of diminutive gymnasts who, as a group, probably reach the world stage earlier than any other athletes.

An interesting study of what makes youth athletes tick from the perspective of coaches was reported in 1999 by Kuchenbecker and a host of co-authors (23, to be exact). These researchers asked 658 youth sport coaches from 43 sports to evaluate the characteristics that contribute to exceptional performance in youth athletes. The coaches, who averaged eight years of experience, were given 64 physical and 64 psychological traits that the research team felt had a potential bearing on perfor-

A Parent Talks to a Child Before the First Game

This is your first game, my child, I hope you win.
I hope you win for your sake, not mine.
Because winning's nice.
It's a good feeling.
Like the whole world is yours.
But it passes, this feeling.
And what lasts is what you've learned.

And what you learn about is life.
That's what sports is all about. Life.
The whole thing is played out in an afternoon.
The miseries.
The joys.
The heartbreaks.
There's no telling what'll turn up.
There's no telling whether they'll toss you out in the first five
minutes or whether you'll stay for the long haul.

There's no telling how you'll do.
You might be a hero or you might do absolutely nothing.
There's just no telling.
Too much depends on chance.
On how the ball bounces.

I'm not talking about the game, my child.
I'm talking about life.
But it's life that the game is all about.
Just as I said.

Because every game is life.
And life is a game.
A serious game.
Dead serious.

But that's what you do with serious things.
You do your best
You take what comes.
You take what comes.
And you run with it.
Winning is fun.
Sure.
But winning is not the point.

Wanting to win is the point.
Not giving up is the point.
Never being satisfied with what you've done is the point.
Never letting up is the point.
Never letting anyone down is the point.

Play to win.
Sure.
But lose like a champion.
Because it's not winning that counts.
What counts is trying.

Unknown source, quoted in Wooden & Jamison (1997).

mance. Psychological traits received far more overall endorsement than did physical traits. A runaway number one, in the estimation of the coaches, was love of the game, that is, athletes who play for the sheer joy it brings them; 43% of the coaches endorsed this trait. A positive attitude (33%), being coachable (30%), being self-motivated (27%), and being a team player (26%) were also heavily endorsed. Two items, criticism (17%) and pressure (12%), were the most commonly nominated damaging performance inhibitors. Physical traits received far less endorsement, with being a natural athlete (10%), having good hand–eye coordination (9%), and being coordinated for one's age (4%) mentioned most often.

On a related note, Watkins and Montgomery (1989) asked 232 young people in grades 3, 6, 9, and 12 to rate what they thought contributed to excellence in sports as well as the source of these attributes. For example, on the item, "How excellent athletes are different from other people," third and sixth graders did not feel that there were differences other than ability, whereas the older two groups invoked such social psychological traits as attitude and motivation. On the next item, "How excellent athletes are different from other athletes," scoring and winning were most important to the third graders. The older groups thought concentration and use of strategy were more important contributors to excellence. Incidentally, the finding about scoring and winning among third graders runs counter to our discussion of what youth value in sport.

Interesting gender differences emerged in the items dealing with ability versus other contributors: Males were more likely to endorse natural ability, whereas females made external attributions to sources such as parents, siblings, and peers. Luck as a contributor to excellence received very little endorsement across the board.

The work of Ericsson has demonstrated in earlier treatments of athletic excellence that hard work and focus are instrumental in forging excellence in a spectrum of human endeavors including athletics. Rowley (1987) indicates that an 8-year-old elite gymnast will probably devote 10–15 hours a week to the sport. In contrast, elite tennis players or swimmers might not work up to this level until age 10–12. By early adolescence, all of these athletes will devote nearly 30 hours a week to their sport. These hours of devotion represent the price of excellence, in the view of many.

One among many who has taken issue with this conclusion is Rowland (2000) in an editorial in *Pediatric Exercise Science.* Rowland contends that this seemingly ascetic approach to achieving elite performance is driven primarily by parents, coaches, and the general public rather than by the athletes themselves. After observing the 1996 Olympics, Tofler, Stryer, and Micheli (1996) concluded that elite performance is really a forum for parents and coaches to live vicariously through their children, a phenomenon Tofler et al. label **achievement by proxy.** They also believe that this pressure may also constitute a form of child abuse. Joan Ryan (1995), in her book *Little Girls in Pretty Boxes,* points out that child labor laws were passed in the United States during the Industrial Revolution to protect children. She maintains that we would never let a 13-year-old work 40 hours a week behind a cash register, yet we

think nothing of having a gymnast or ice skater put in that many hours in the gym or on the rink.

Rowland also cites interesting data from 45 retired Canadian elite athletes reported by Donnelly (1993, 1997). Getting to travel and prestige were commonly cited extrinsic benefits of participating at the elite level, and enjoyment of the sport, friendships, good health and fitness, and the pleasure of skill development were all seen as pluses. On the negative side, family conflicts were mentioned by two-thirds of the athletes, and 40% reported eating-related problems. When asked if they would do their sport again, 10% said yes, 30% said no, and 60% said yes with modifications. Would they want their own children to follow in their elite footsteps? Sixty percent said yes, 40% said no.

Rowland brings the philosophy of Immanual Kant to bear on the ethics issue by suggesting that persons should always be treated as an end rather than a means. Implicit in this ethic is not bringing harm to another, respecting that person's rights, enhancing his or her well-being, and generally trying to further his or her welfare. Exploiting elite youth athletes for the benefit of others is not in the best interest of the child and constitutes a violation of Kantian ethics. Rowland says flatly: "Behavior becomes unethical in this view when the child's best interests are subjugated by the interests of others" (p. 2).

In the final analysis, early talent identification and preparation for participation at the elite levels will undoubtedly continue at a pell-mell pace throughout most of the sporting world. The process can continue, however, in the spirit of the ethical issues raised by Rowland. Ultimately, protecting the well-being of youth should be of paramount importance to us all, and no one should be more forceful in this pursuit than the sport psychologist.

VIOLENCE IN YOUTH SPORTS

A relatively recent problem, and one that seems to be increasingly of concern to all involved in youth sports, is violence. Certainly, there are cases where youth athletes engage in aggressive acts against each other during practice or play, but a greater concern centers around parental violence toward children (usually their own), coaches, and officials.

Achievement by proxy tendency of coaches and parents to live vicariously through elite child athletes.

The headlines read:

"Hockey dad indicted in assault on kid's coach"
"Umpires say sports for kids becoming brawl games"
"Losing season prompts dad to sue son's coach"

Among the many players in this drama are:

Ray Knight, a former Cincinnati Reds third baseman and father of a 12-year-old female softball player, who punched the father of a player on the opposing team. He is charged with simple assault.

Fifty parents who physically fought each other at the end of a youth football game in Pennsylvania.

A father in New York who struck a youth hockey coach in the face with two hockey sticks.

A Little League coach who assaulted the manager of an opposing team and was sentenced to 180 days of work furlough.

A Pennsylvania policeman who gave a 10-year-old Little League pitcher $2 to intentionally hit another boy. He was convicted of corruption of a minor and solicitation to commit simple assault.

A Nebraska corrections officer who was sentenced to thirty days in jail for hitting a 16-year-old referee in a flag football game for 6–7 year olds.

A father dressed in a nice shirt and slacks who waded off into waist deep water to berate his son for failing to win a 25-meter swimming race.

A youth baseball coach in Florida who broke the jaw of an umpire during an argument.

A hockey father who beat another man to death in front of the children at a hockey game because he felt that the victim's son was unnecessarily roughing up his own son.

These incidents, reported in an article in *Sports Illustrated* (Nack & Munson, 2000), are among the more sensational examples of violence against coaches, children, and referees but seem to occur with increasing frequency and fury. They certainly run counter to the generally favorable view of fan behavior reported in Highlight 22.2.

Why do these sorts of things occur? Nack and Munson (2000) call this misbehavior **Parentis vociferous** and maintain that it is a direct result of the usually mistaken belief that their children are all potential "Mozarts in cleats." This mentality is fueled by the burgeoning club sport movement whereby children are subtly (and not so subtly) forced to make a choice of sport they plan to specialize in so that they may get a college scholarship or play professionally at a later point. Also imbedded here is parents' inability to realistically size up the true capabilities of their children, so that hope is allowed to spring eternal. Many a child who matures early and excels because of his or her size and strength has learned that these things have a way of evening out over the years. Competing activities like work, cars, dating, and debate also siphon off many youth athletes who excelled early on but lost interest or were passed up by children who matured later, had more interest and drive, and had what is known in sports as a "better head." How many youth athletes never really excel because they engage in counterproductive behaviors that interfere with performance? One of the greatest challenges for the future in sport psychology is to make inroads through coaching programs and consultation on what is known as the "bad head" in youth sports. Unfortunately, bad heads in sport have a way of being bad heads in life.

The violence problem has reached a state where measures to curb these acts have been implemented. One such example is the sportsmanship classes in Jupiter, Florida, where thousands of parents were asked to sign pledges to behave properly at youth sport events. Cleveland (Ohio) parents were asked to observe Silent Sunday, in which they agreed to remain silent during a youth soccer game. Nack and Munson (2000) report that some parents coped with this pressure by sucking on suckers or duct-taping their mouths shut for the duration of the game.

The Arizona legislature has attempted to enact legislation that would stiffen penalties for assault on sports officials. The Youth Sports Official Protection Act, as it was called, passed the state house of representatives by a large margin but was voted down in the senate. Perhaps we shall see more legislative moves in the future to toughen penalties against those who violate the law and our sense of propriety.

Parentis vociferous nickname for overinvolved parents who engage in verbal and physical abuse against coaches, opposing players, and their own children.

Adult Verbalizations at Youth Sport Events

Most of us are familiar with the obnoxious sports fan, who is nowhere more noticeable than at youth sporting events. Data from a number of studies, however, appear to support the notion that these noisy persons are actually in the minority. They stand out precisely because they are so vociferous in expressing their dislike for players, coaches, officials, and other fans. Youth sport studies by Faucette and Osinski (1987) and Walley, Graham, and Forehand (1982) in baseball, Crossman (1986) in hockey, and Randall and McKenzie (1987) in soccer point to a generally well-behaved spectator. In the Faucette and Osinski study, spectators at a youth baseball Mustang World Series served as subjects. During a four-day period, 64 spectators attending 11 games were observed by two trained researchers. Results showed that spectators spend over 80% of their time silently watching the proceedings or conversing with friends. When verbal comments were made, they were predominantly neutral or positive in tone. Negative comments accounted for slightly over 1% of all verbalizations. Walley et al. found virtually identical behaviors in their observations of youth T-ball spectators. Four male raters who observed four fans at 18 games found that 92% of the fans offered no verbalizations and far less than 1% of these verbalizations were negative. Walley and associates did suggest, however, that negative verbalizations may be a linear function; that is, as the stakes go up, so may negativity.

Crossman (1986) had observers view 272 spectators at 91 minor league hockey games in Canada. Spectator behavior varied according to the age and skill level of the athletes, the importance of the competition, and the sex of the onlooker but did not support the stereotype of the verbally abusive fan. In the Randall and McKenzie (1987) investigation involving youth soccer, nearly 75% of the verbalizations made by fans were rated instructive, while 5.8% were negative.

A more recent update from New Zealand by Kidman, McKenzie, and McKenzie (1999) shows a slightly less optimistic picture. Using a system of recording based on the work of Walley and adapted for their work by the authors, Kidman et al. amassed and analyzed almost 9,000 verbalizations made by 250 parents of children ages 6–12 in seven team sports across 147 games/matches. They found a ratio of positive to negative to neutral verbalization of 4:3:2; that is, four positive responses for every three negative ones and two neutral ones. While there were more positive than other responses in this study, the frequency of negative verbalizations far exceeded that of previous studies cited here. Soccer and rugby parents accounted for 80% of the negative responses; governing bodies in these two sports are justifiably concerned by these kinds of reports.

These studies have served to shed light on a fascinating aspect of youth sport, that of spectator behavior. In general, the picture they have presented dispels the negative stereotype so often held about spectators at youth sporting events, though the New Zealand study does give pause. Nevertheless, most fans appear to be quiet, neutral, or positive, with the negative spectator a statistical rarity.

SOURCES: Crossman (1986); Faucette & Osinski (1987); Kidman, McKenzie, & McKenzie (1999); Randall & McKenzie (1987); Walley, Graham, & Forehand (1982).

HEALTH RISKS ASSOCIATED WITH YOUTH SPORT

As part of the hue and cry associated with youth sport since its inception, critics have pointed the finger at physical risks and psychological trauma. Most certainly there are risks associated with rough-and-tumble physical activity, whether organized or informal. How many youngsters have broken an arm or a collarbone in a fall from a tree? Or dislocated a finger or injured a knee in a hastily thrown-together baseball game in someone's backyard? These kinds of things happen all too frequently, but it is our contention that organizers of formalized youth activities have an opportunity and an obligation to provide proper leadership in reducing the risk of physical injury for participants. With proper care and supervision, much of the injury potential in organized sport can be brought under control, a situation that does not exist in the unorganized sector. Summarizing the results of several epidemiological studies, Maffulli (1990) indicates that 3 to 11% of school-age children are injured each year in sport.

There are a number of potential problem areas that raise concern about youth sport injuries. One is the discrepancies in the maturation rates from child to child, thus creating substantial size and strength discrepancies. These size and strength differences suggest that grouping young people by chronological age for sports participation may not be such a good idea. Gomolak (1975, p. 96) sums this situation up very well: "At thirteen . . . boys can vary physically from 90 pounds of baby fat and peach fuzz to 225 pounds of muscle and mustache." A good example of this discrepancy is found in one Nick Stuart of Chesapeake, Virginia ("Strapping Youth," 1998) who was 5 feet, 3 inches tall and weighed 160 pounds at age 9. As a result, he was banned from a youth football league for fear that he would hurt smaller players. As you might guess, this situation has resulted in litigation by Nick's parents. Similarly, Bobby Carter and Andrew Michel, 9-year-olds from Fairfax, Virginia, who weighed 135 and 130 pounds, respectively, were excluded from playing in a youth football league (New Rules, 1996). Andrew's father responded by placing him on a fruit and vegetable diet in hopes that he would lose 25 pounds by the league registration deadline.

One proposed solution for dealing with these maturation, size, and strength differences is to organize play around biological age (BA) as opposed to chronological age (CA), a notion dating back to 1901 (Crampton, 1908). Roche, Tyleshevski, and Rogers (1983) have proposed an alternative to CA, a maturity index composed of the athlete's current height, body mass, exact age, and height of the two parents. They admit that the latter consideration is problematic because the relevant data are not always readily available and usually are nothing more than a rough estimate of eventual youth size. Nevertheless, such efforts to equalize the playing fields are to be applauded. No child should be put at risk unnecessarily.

A second problem area with young athletes is impatience with restrictions on their activities when they are undergoing the diagnosis or treatment of an injury. Running too soon after a leg injury, removing a cast without medical approval and attention, or failing to stay off an injured knee are only a few of the many impulsive actions young athletes have been known to do.

Yet another troublesome concern is the musculoskeletal immaturity of young athletes, which leaves them susceptible to joint and other injuries. A particularly controversial aspect of this problem area concerns what has come to be known as **Little League elbow.** A brief look at the injury picture in the early days of Little League baseball is instructive.

Hale (1961), reacting to criticisms of Little League baseball, conducted a five-year study of nearly 800,000 players and found a relatively low injury rate. Hale's analysis reported 15,444 injuries requiring medical attention, or an incidence of around 2%. Given the number of exposures to potentially injurious situations inherent in baseball (Hale indicates that there were 148 million pitched balls alone), Little League does not appear to be especially hazardous.

In a study of 328 former Little Leaguers, Francis, Bunch, and Chandler (1978) found that injury to the throwing elbow was less common in these individuals than it was in a matched sample of 70 people who had never played baseball at any level. The injury rate in the form of residual elbow lesions for the ex-Little Leaguers was 1.5%, compared with 2.8% for the control group. Overall, seven of 398 total subjects had residual elbow difficulties. Of the 328 ex-Little Leaguers, 28 had gone on to play at the collegiate level; one of these players, a pitcher, had residual damage to the throwing arm. Francis and his associates concluded that psychological trauma might be more of a problem than physical damage in Little League baseball. In any event, the Francis et al. study indicates that Little League elbow does exist, but not at the alarming rate suggested by critics of the game. Nevertheless, the admonition of Congeni (1994, p. 64) cannot be ignored: "Pitching is *not* a 'no pain, no gain' activity."

Some researchers are convinced that the data on Little League elbow are not as reassuring as has been reported by Hale and Francis et al. Among those with a

---

Little League elbow injury to the throwing arm suffered by youth pitchers in baseball.

Headgear in Soccer: Is It An Innovation Whose Time Has Come?

Recently, much controversy has surrounded the potential dangers of heading the ball in soccer. Heading, simply put, occurs when a player attempts to redirect the flight of the ball with his or her forehead (Christensen, 1999). This practice has come under scrutiny because of the immense and growing popularity of soccer on the world scene. It has been estimated that 120 million people worldwide play the game, 15 million of them in the United States, where the sport is growing by leaps and bounds (Delany & Drummond, 1999).

Many studies and conjectural works have suggested that damage to the brain can occur from two sources in soccer. One of the sources is acute trauma and other repetitive blows to the head. In the worst cases, the athlete may take on the characteristics of the proverbial punch-drunk boxer. Concussions occur often in soccer, usually as a function of collision with another player or hitting the head on the ground as a result of a fall. There is little to suggest that these concussions arise from heading. Repeated heading coupled with concussions from other on or off-the-field acci-

dents make it difficult to conclude that brain damage might result from heading alone.

Soccer athletes at most risk are children, players who have suffered previous concussions, and those playing in risky positions, such as the goalie. Of particular concern is the last group, and this has led to a call for protective headgear from some quarters. One concern about protective headgear is that it may open up a Pandora's box involving even more aggressive and dangerous styles of play.

Though the verdict is still out on the issue of brain injury from heading, it is better to be safe than sorry, and recommendations for safer play have been made from several sources (Christensen, 1999; Timms, 1999). Chief among these recommendations are education of coaches, players, and parents; the promotion of proper heading technique; the avoidance of high-risk plays that place the head in jeopardy; and strict enforcement of the rules of the game.

SOURCES: Christensen (1999); Delaney & Drummond (1999); Timms (1999).

---

dissenting view are Wells and Bell (1995), who believe that elbow problems in youth baseball are common. They suggest some preventive and treatment measures that stress education of athletes, parents, and coaches. Chief among their recommendations are proper pitching mechanics, proper stretching regimens, sound strength programs, and, most important, limiting the number of pitches thrown daily. This latter point is supported by Ciccantelli (1994), Congeni (1994), and Whiteside, Andrews, and Fleisig (1999). In the latter group of authors is Dr. James Andrews, a prominent orthopedic surgeon who has performed surgery on a number of the world's most famous injured athletes.

A fourth problem is the possibility of undiagnosed or unrecognized medical conditions that can actually cause premature death. The concern about death is highlighted periodically by reports in the media of

young, talented, and superbly conditioned high school or college athletes who have died on the basketball court or the football field, deaths often attributed by examining medical authorities to covert, undiagnosed congenital heart conditions.

A report in *USA Today* highlights the extent of this problem, though the study was not restricted completely to youth participants (Study of Sudden Death, 1996). Covering the years 1985–1995, it was the joint effort of the Minneapolis (Minnesota) Heart Institute Foundation and the National Center for Catastrophic Sports Injury Research. Data analysis revealed that there were 158 sudden deaths noted in the 10-year period under scrutiny, 134 from cardiac arrest. Aneurysm, coronary artery disease, and deformed valves accounted for 55 deaths. Hypertrophic cardiomyopathy (thickened heart muscle) accounted for 48 deaths and was found much more commonly in black than white athletes. Of the total number of deaths, 83 occurred in high school athletes and 12 in younger athletes. A solid case for appropriate screening by the health authorities prior to each sport season can be made from these data.

A fifth problem is conditioning. Considerable evidence dating back to the physical fitness studies of the 1950s reported earlier in this chapter suggests that our young people are not in optimal physical condition. The conditioning deficiency has obvious ramifications for sport; too many youngsters are not physically prepared for the demands of their chosen sport and all too often resist becoming properly conditioned. These liabilities in fitness enhance injury risk, of course.

Pappas and Zawacki (1991) have suggested an antidote to this fitness deficiency with their emphasis on musculo-skeletal flexibility, aerobic conditioning, and lower extremity strength and endurance. Though specific to youth baseball, the program suggested by Pappas and Zawacki emphasizes injury prevention through total fitness. It seems reasonable to believe that their approach could easily be adapted and implemented across the majority of the youth sport spectrum.

A sixth area of concern is protective equipment. Young athletes are often uninformed, indifferent, or uninterested in the fitting, adjustment, or maintenance of protective equipment.

Finally, youth participants all too often are not provided with access to the services of qualified athletic trainers. Poorly trained or unqualified parents, coaches, or an on-call physician usually provide the services that should be the province of the qualified trainer, a condition that is less than desirable.

RECOMMENDATIONS FOR IMPROVING YOUTH SPORT

Youth sport is a positive experience for most participants. In the best of all possible worlds, it should be so for all youngsters. Developing an appreciation for the skills required within a particular sport, achieving and maintaining a high level of physical fitness, learning to be a team player, and developing the ability to confront and overcome adversity are all attainable through sport. Opportunities for attaining these benefits should be readily available to every participant.

A number of sport agencies and organizations have published articles and/or position papers on ways of improving youth sport, and the following discussion will summarize their recommendations. Among the agencies and organizations are the American Academy of Pediatrics (AAP), American College of Sports Medicine (ACSM), the Association for the Advancement of Applied Sport Psychology (AAASP), the International Society for Sport Psychology (ISSP), and the European Federation of Sport Psychology (FEPSAC). Their combined reflections cut across several sport science subspecialties including medicine, psychology, and sociology.

First, the medical aspects of improving youth sport must be addressed. All youth players should be monitored with periodic health status checkups. Also, professional care should be readily available in all competitive settings (including practices, where many injuries occur). The provision of proper equipment, geared to minimize chances for injury, is also important. It is also important to provide the best in arenas or playing fields. Monetary constraints often force youth activities to take place in less than optimal physical surroundings. However, given the importance we attach to participation, every effort should be made to obtain the best facilities possible. Another way to reduce injury is to modify the rules to fit the age and skill level manifested. Instead of tackle football, the flag variety is encouraged; baskets should be lowered to age-appropriate heights for peewee basketball players; and extremely young baseball pitchers should not be allowed to throw curve balls. These reasonably simple variants can reduce injury and enhance enjoyment at the same time. Finally, another way to reduce injury and promote enjoyment is to encourage and provide the opportunity for proper sport conditioning.

On the psychological side, reinforcement of effort over that old bugaboo, the win–loss record, is of considerable importance. Coaches who are trained through one of the various youth coaching workshop programs to be discussed in Chapter 23, ones who stress the importance of consistent improvement and skill acquisition, would be a most welcome addition. It is also important for coaches to downplay competitive and social evaluation aspects of sports as much as possible. Setting realistic sport mastery goals is another way of shaping positive attitudes and skills. Liberal use of positive reinforcement is a further essential in dealing with young people; they respond predictably well to positive strokes and generally unpredictably or unsatisfactorily to negativism from coaches, parents, or peers. A clear focus on continual development of positive feelings about oneself is also recommended; youth sport should play a pivotal role in self-concept development. Positive sport experiences should result in enhanced feelings of self-worth.

From the sociological perspective, a number of recommendations have been made. One is to structure youth sport in such a way that it only vaguely resembles big-time amateur or professional sport. This requires that league officials downplay such things as pep squads, elaborate awards ceremonies, and excessive recognition through the various media. League officials could be of further assistance by adopting a zero-tolerance policy on inappropriate spectator behavior. Aggression and violence by players or spectators, temper tantrums, and similar negative emotional displays should not be tolerated. The occasional highly publicized misbehaviors of potential role models at the collegiate or professional level should not be glorified. Finally, positive social behavior by parents might be facilitated by involving them in the conduct of some aspects of the action. Working together in the concession stand or in field maintenance and improvement can serve to promote good relations among parents.

As a final note, parents would do well to reinforce their children's involvement in sports other than the "Big Three" of baseball, basketball, and football. Sports such as golf, racquetball, or tennis involve generally lower stakes and emphasize individual participation over group involvement; parental and peer pressure are typically less influential.

If all of the preceding recommendations were put into effect, the goals of youth sport would surely be better realized, and none is pie in the sky. Each of them, with proper urging and support, could be easily implemented and would ensure that young people have a chance at achieving the best that youth sport has to offer.

SUMMARY

1. Sources of stress in youth sport include too much emphasis on winning and pressures associated with constant social evaluation by significant others. One's perceived ability and its association with expectancy of success are other sources of competitive anxiety.

2. Competition may be viewed as a product or as a process. In the product orientation, the emphasis is on winning above all else, tangible rewards, seeking of adulation, and dehumanization of one's opponent. In the process orientation, participation becomes an end in itself, personal or team excellence is sought, activities are appreciated for their aesthetic properties, and there is respect for the opposition.

3. Competitive stress is a negative emotional state that is generated when a person feels unable to cope with competitive demands. This subjective perception of failure results in negative evaluation of athletic ability and resultant loss of self-esteem.

4. Competitive stress may be measured physiologically, behaviorally, or psychologically. Heart rate changes relate to the physiological dimension, quantified sleep loss relates to the behavioral dimension, and using the Sport Competition Anxiety Test (SCAT) represents a psychological measurement tool.

5. Research has suggested that competitive stress is mediated by at least four cognitive variables: perceived ability, expectancy of success, expectancy of negative evaluation, and expectancy of experiencing negative emotional states.

6. General parent–child interactions, interactions with other adults and peers, and history of success or failure are major antecedents of competitive stress.

7. Elite performance in youth sport is characterized most, according to a survey of coaches, by a love of the game. Other psychological contributors to excellence are seen by coaches as having more relevance than innate ability. There are age and gender differences in how athletic excellence is viewed. Females, for instance, make more external attributions for excellence than do males, who are more prone to talk in terms of innate ability, an obviously internal attribution. The ethics of early training for competition at the elite level must be addressed to protect the rights of developing athletes.

8. Occasionally, athletes inflict physical damage on each other, but in youth sport the problem is more one of verbal and physical aggression directed at children, coaches, or game officials by otherwise normal adult parents. While there are considerable data to suggest that most parents are positive or benign, those who get out of control grab the media headlines, thus creating the image that youth sport is one big "brawl game." Measures are being taken at the local level, as has been done in Jupiter, Florida, to curb out-of-control fan behavior at youth sport events. Though it was voted down, the fact that the Arizona legislature even addressed legislation aimed at curbing parental abuse of officials serves as an index of the escalating problem.

9. A number of health risk factors that contribute to injury rates have been identified by the American Council of Pediatrics and others. Among these are discrepancies in size, strength, and skill at various ages; impatience with restrictions when injured; musculo-skeletal immaturity; possible undetected congenital predisposers to injury; overall physical conditioning deficits; poor utilization of protective equipment; and limited access to services of qualified trainers.

10. Recommendations for improving youth sport involve attacking the problem from medical, psychological, and sociological perspectives. Thorough physical examinations, proper equipment, and adapting the rules to fit various age and/or skill levels are a few of many medical recommendations. Psychologically, reinforcement of effort (process) over the win–loss (product) standard is highly recommended. Sociologically, not tolerating inappropriate behavior and reinforcing prosocial efforts among fans and players will go a long way in making youth sport more rewarding.

KEY TERMS

achievement by proxy (360)
competitive stress (356)
competitive trait anxiety (CTA) (356)
expectancy of negative affect (358)

expectancy of negative evaluation (357)
Little League elbow (363)
Parentis vociferous (361)
perceived ability (357)
process orientation to competition (354)
product orientation to competition (354)
success expectancy (357)

SUGGESTED READINGS

Larson, R. (2000). Toward a psychology of positive youth development. *American Psychologist, 55,* 170–183.

This is an innovative and somewhat complex call to consider the role of initiative in the development of a positive life perspective. Sports, arts, and participation in organizations where intrinsic motivation and deep attention are combined appear to the author to be the most likely vehicles for the development of initiative. Mention is made of the work of Glyn Roberts in motivation and Ron Smith and Frank Smoll in youth coaching.

Martens, R. (1978). *Joy and sadness in children's sports.* Champaign, IL: Human Kinetics.

In this classic in the literature of youth sport, Martens, a strong proponent of youth sports, attempts to portray the joy of sports but acknowledges the difficulty of addressing the issues without confronting the downside. Created for all people who care about youth sport, the book is sufficiently scholarly and readable to be of interest to coaches, parents, and sports professionals alike. Martens chose 36 articles from a broad array of sources to address the many issues in youth sport.

Murphy, S. (1999). *The cheers and tears: A healthy alternative to the dark side of youth sports today.* San Francisco: Jossey-Bass.

Shane Murphy, a sport psychologist with extensive experience at the U.S. Olympic Training Center in Colorado, views youth sport as serving two functions: identifying and training talented performers who will eventually play at the more elite levels and to promote lifetime fitness and sport involvement. At the same time he warns about the negative features of the youth sport scene in the form of stress, eating disorders, premature disaffection from sports and fitness, and injury. Comprehensive in its coverage, this book is a must read for all interested in youth sport.

Rowland, T. W. (2000). The creatine conundrum: Or is there really a free lunch? *Pediatric Exercise Science, 11,* 1–4.

    The journal's editor raises some interesting issues related to a problematic area of youth sport, the use of legal but questionable drugs to enhance performance. Rowland cites figures from *USA Today* indicating that over $100 million a year is spent in the United States annually for creatine, and his handling

of the pros (the just-say-no approach) and cons (the permissive perspective) of creatine use is interesting. This is a highly readable handling of a complex topic relevant to youth (and adult) sport.

 INFOTRAC COLLEGE EDITION

For additional readings, explore Infotrac College Edition, your online library. Go to: http://www.infotrac-college.com/wadsworth *Hint:* Enter these search terms: athletic trainer, sports injuries, sportsmanship, trait anxiety.

The Coach: Roles, Communication, and Psychological Variables

CHAPTER 23

Roles of the Coach

What Makes a Good Coach?

Advantages and Disadvantages of Coaching

Communication and Coaching

The Coach and the Sport Psychologist

The Coach's Personality

Summary

Key Terms

Suggested Readings

The legendary Paul "Bear" Bryant is often equated with excellence in coaching college football. Many of his players have followed in his footsteps and become successful coaches, also.
© Bettman/CORBIS

Dear Coach Rockne:

As you may know, I have been interested for some years in many of the problems of psychology and athletics. I am writing you now because during the past season I heard a few comments about you and your team that were of interest to my work, having always taken the point that men on a team play best when they love the game they are playing. I have said that I did not believe such a team would have to be keyed up to its games. A team that is keyed up is bound to have a slump. Men who are always playing their best because they like the game are far more apt to go through a season without a serious slump. Now the point I am getting at is this: I have heard it said that you do not key your men up to their games: that you select such men as play the game joyously for its own sake and that you try to develop in them as much of this spirit as you can.

I am wondering if you care to tell me directly about these things? I am asking for information only because of my psychological interest in athletic sports.

Cordially yours,

Coleman R. Griffith

Dear Mr. Griffith:

I feel very grateful to you for having written me, although I do not know a great deal about psychology.

I do try to pick men who like the game of football and who get a lot of fun out of playing. I never try to make football hard work. I do think your team plays good football, because they do like to play and I do not make any effort to key them up, except on rare, exceptional occasions. I keyed them up for the Nebraska game this year, which was a mistake, as we had a reaction the following Saturday against Northwestern.

I try to make our boys take the game less seriously than, I

Coleman Griffith a professor at the University of Illinois who started the first sport psychology course; known as the "father of sport psychology."
Knute Rockne legendary football coach at the University of Notre Dame in the 1920s.

presume, some others do, and we try to make the spirit of the game one of exhilaration and we never allow hatred to enter into it, no matter against whom we are playing.

Thanking you for your kindness, I am

Yours cordially,

[Knute Rockne]

My dear Mr. Rockne:

Let me thank you most heartily for your comments about the play spirit in football. If you are so inclined, I would like to hear about the plans you make for playing a postseason game and what efforts you have to make to reawaken the interest of the men. I doubt very much whether teams that have to be keyed up to a game will be able to do so well weeks after the season is closed as a team which plays in the spirit in which yours seems to play. I do not mean, of course, to trouble you about this before your trip to the coast but I will be most grateful for any comments you may have to make after you come back.

Cordially yours,

Coleman R. Griffith

Dear Mr. Griffith:

Regarding our trip to the coast, we took it mostly in the way of a pleasure trip and an educational trip, and we made the workouts short and snappy, so as not to make them hard work in any sense of the word. We had just one real hard workout and that was at Tucson, which served to sort of get the boys in a mood for a game. The climate of California sort of took the resiliency and drive out of their legs before the second half began. However, the spirit of play manifested itself and the boys were so alert that they took advantage of every mistake made by Stanford. I think a keyed-up team would have been too tense and too excited to have profited by these opportunities.

From an educational point of view, we had a very profitable trip and the boys missed but one day of classes.

Yours sincerely,

[Knute Rockne]

My dear Mr. Rockne:

I am doubly indebted to you for your letter of February 10.
I was almost sure that the plan which you say you followed
would bring success. I know that other teams have gone to
the coast so keyed-up and excited that their own mental
states fought against them.

Cordially yours,

Coleman R. Griffith

(LeUnes, 1986)

This exchange of letters took place in 1924–1925 between one of college football's most successful coaches, Knute Rockne of Notre Dame, and the father of sport psychology, Coleman Griffith of the University of Illinois. The letters serve as a poignant reminder that the coaching practices of 75 years ago have much in common with those of today, as well as some differences (LeUnes, 1986). Coaching at any level, but particularly in the collegiate or professional ranks, has become a pressure-laden enterprise, one in which win–loss record is generally viewed as the standard by which success is measured. Our quest here is for a better understanding of the kinds of people who choose this enigmatic profession and what psychology has to offer coaches in their pursuit of excellence for themselves and their players.

ROLES OF THE COACH

Coaches, regardless of whether they are working with individuals or teams, live a pressure-laden, fishbowl kind of existence. Coaches are expected to win, be a positive reflection on the organization for which they toil, build character in young athletes, and make money for the organization. Frank Kush, while head football coach at Arizona State University, said: "My job is to win football games. I've got to put people in the stadium, make money for the university, keep the alumni happy, and give the school a winning reputation. If I don't win, I'm gone" (Michener, 1976, p. 324). The coach, in this context, becomes a slave to many masters.

Figure 23.1 offers some additional insight into the complex role facing the typical coach. There are mul-

tiple pressures impinging on the coach, and success in large part will depend on how well these pressures are handled.

At the administrative level, the coach must get along with owners, general managers, athletic directors, and other administrators, depending on the level at which the coaching is being done. This serving of many masters is no small task; often, much money and even bigger egos are involved, greatly increasing the pressure to win at all costs. Also, the prerogatives of the coach can be severely circumvented by a meddling administrator. For example, chronic failures to win among several organizations in professional baseball, basketball, and football are testimonials to mismanagement.

Players are another demand on the resources of the coach. If the coach is not successful in dealing with the players, the other roles are largely inconsequential. The coach must care about the athletes, must be able to motivate them, and must be concerned with their overall welfare. Equally important, the players must sense this commitment to their athletic and personal well being.

Assistant coaches are also factors to be reckoned with. These aides are invaluable in terms of ultimate success and must be treated accordingly. Assistants should be paid what they are worth in terms of the free market, must be given a free rein to coach their various specialties, and should always be treated as trusted allies. Where feasible, they should be groomed for better jobs. It must be very rewarding to look around and see protégés everywhere. In the case of the late football legend Bear Bryant of the University of Alabama, his former players who are now coaches are too numerous to mention, and undoubtedly were a continuing source of immense satisfaction to him. In basketball, the controversial Bobby Knight of Indiana had 15 protégés coaching in major programs at the end of 1986 (Allen, 1987).

The media demand yet another role of the coach. Media people are paid to promote listeners, viewers, or subscribers for the organizations for which they work and put a lot of pressure on coaches for interesting, salable material. An endless array of interviews before and after each game, on Monday morning, and at midweek to explain wins or losses and exceptional players along with the need to respond to continuous media speculation on team prospects and the ultimate fate of the coaches themselves all require the ability to express

FIGURE 23.1

Roles Coaches Are Expected to Play

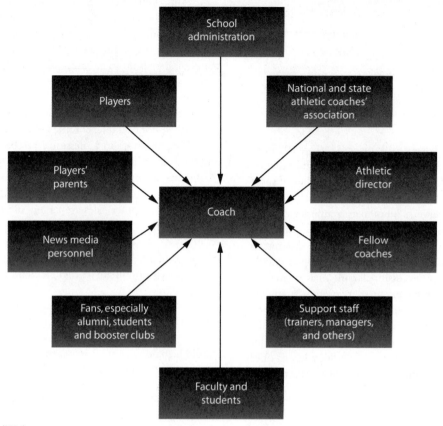

SOURCE: Coakley (1994).

oneself under pressure. The coaches' diplomacy and tact will be taxed at these times. Media exposure is important to the welfare of the teams and athletes, but the inherent pressures create further role demands for coaches.

A recent nuisance and source of stress for some coaches is the Internet chat room, where every Tom, Dick, and Harry in the world is free to make negative comments about coaches and players. The ongoing discussion has a way of fanning the flames of team disloyalty and, at least in a subtle way, exerting pressure on beleaguered coaches.

Dealing with fans represents still another challenge to coaches. Sports require fans to survive, and fans can

greatly determine the fate of a particular program, either through support or lack of it. As a consequence, a good relationship with fans is important. At the professional level, their support is essential to the financial success of the organization. At the intercollegiate level, they provide ticket sales, alumni contributions, and overall program support. At the interscholastic level, fans are often parents with considerable ego involvement with the activities, and they require a delicate, supportive touch.

Of particular interest in the collegiate area of late has been the booster, who is often an overzealous university supporter. Boosters have subverted the very educational goals for which their universities were created through illegal payments to players or prospects, unethical inducements to perform, and, in some cases, blatantly illegal actions, such as plying athletes with cocaine. It is absolutely essential to the academic–athletic balance in universities that these kinds of fans not be allowed to function with university sanction. At the same time, well-meaning alumni have much to offer university athletic programs, and it would not be prudent for the coach to turn them away. Knowing the good guys from the guys in black is unfortunately not an easy distinction for the coach to make, however. Needless to say, alumni should be encouraged to support their teams and universities; they should never be encouraged or allowed to subvert the ultimate reason that universities exist, namely, to provide an education.

Other role demands are made on coaches, depending on the level at which they function, but the roles described here partially explain why coaching is such a demanding profession. In summary, Sabock (1979) says the good coach will be a teacher, disciplinarian, salesperson, public relations specialist, diplomat, organizer, role model, psychologist, leader, judge and jury, mother or father figure, dictator, politician, actor, fundraiser, director, field general, equipment manager, trainer, community citizen, and citizen of the school, university, or organization. With these challenges in mind, it is easy to see why coaches undertake such a career. It is equally easy to see why there are not many old coaches.

WHAT MAKES A GOOD COACH?

Though there may be a few diehards in the group, most coaches are aware that **good coaching** is more than just winning games. This is not to downplay the technical side of sports, but more an attempt to underscore the importance of being able to motivate athletes to do their best. Perhaps a personal experience from the background of your senior author would be instructive. A short time before we were to start fall drills on our junior high school football team, we found ourselves without a coach. For whatever reason, a young (and most capable) science teacher named Carl Davidson was assigned the extra duties as junior high football coach. Despite vehement protests that he had never touched a football or attended a football game,

and thus knew absolutely nothing about the sport, Mr. Davidson took over the coaching reins two or three weeks prior to the first game. The principal referred him to several of the older players as resources, and as a result he read Bud Wilkinson's then very popular book on the split-T formation (Wilkinson, 1952) and installed it as his offense. Despite this inauspicious debut, Mr. Davidson was able to survive and, ultimately, excel. He lost no games that year and only five in the next seven years. He demonstrated that excellence is perhaps achieved more through motivation than sheer knowledge of the game. I (LeUnes) am convinced that I owe my fascination with the psychological side of sport to those serendipitous events of the early 1950s and am deeply indebted to Carl Davidson for providing invaluable insights into the importance of motivation (and of generally being a good human being) in fostering skilled athletic performance.

What is it, then, that makes a good coach? Inasmuch as *coaches are teachers,* and all coaching is ultimately nothing more than teaching, the coach should be knowledgeable about the activity being taught. Athletes need to be taught the basic skills or fundamentals essential to excellent performance. A technology for accomplishing skill acquisition has been provided by behavioral psychologists, as outlined earlier in this book, and all coaches need to become familiar with the behavioral approach to coaching. Coaches who are methodical in teaching skills and who are expert in the proper application of positive reinforcement and punishment (with emphasis on reinforcement) are miles ahead of their lesser-informed contemporaries. At the same time, coaches should have sessions in which the knowledge aspects of the game are stressed. For example, sessions on proper utilization of the rules of a particular activity could be most helpful.

In addition to being a good teacher who knows his or her sport, the coach should also be a *good student* of the game. Studying various sport periodicals on how to improve one's product, attending seminars that have the same goals in mind, and attending university courses in

---

Good coaching even more than technical knowledge of the game, coaches must be able to motivate players, be teachers and students at the same time, be aware of individual differences among athletes, be good listeners, be disciplinarians when necessary, lead by example, and be a goal setter.

John Chaney has had a long and successful career as the basketball coach at Temple University. He is known as a fair but tough task master. Balancing fairness and discipline is a major undertaking for coaches in all sports.
© Reuters NewMedia Inc./CORBIS

sport and sport psychology are readily accessible activities for the coach who wants to grow and improve.

The successful coach is a *motivator.* Successful coaches are successful wherever they go. Programs in the doldrums are often revived by coaches who have been successful elsewhere. The ability to motivate is part and parcel of this success formula. Getting athletes to run through the proverbial brick wall seems to come far easier for some coaches than others. Clearly, the former group are motivators, people who are able to generate the desire to excel in their athletes. Perhaps Mike Vreeswyk, a former basketball player at Temple University, captures the essence of the coach as motivator in the following remark about his mentor, John Chaney: "If Coach says a flea can pull a plough, we say hitch him up" (Kirkpatrick, 1988, p. 30).

Being *aware of individual differences* in athletes is also an important ingredient in coaching excellence. Some athletes are turned on by yelling, screaming, throwing things, and other emotional displays. Others are turned off by these shows of emotion, preferring a more serene, meditative approach to getting ready to participate. Individualizing motivation becomes important here. Knowing which athletes to pat on the back and which ones to cajole and emotionally exhort to perform are vital skills in coaching. Watching for signs of under- or overarousal is also important. As we saw in our earlier discussion of the inverted-U hypothesis, there is an optimum level of arousal that is conducive to good performance. The good coach has a responsibility to acquire some sense of what this optimum level is for the team and for individual players as well. Though numbers cannot be attached to individual levels of arousal in sport, sensitive coaches attempt to make some skillful assessment of the appropriate level for each player.

The good coach is also a *good listener,* keeping eyes open and an ear to the ground to achieve a sense of individual and team subtleties and undercurrents. Consistent with being a good listener, the coach should be a sensitive sounding board for problems, complaints, and wishes of the players. The good coach will also utilize the team leaders as allies in working with other participants. Finally, the good coach will be forceful but democratic, allowing for considerable individual input into the everyday management of the sport at hand, whether team or individual. Players should certainly not run the operation, but they should have input because they are invaluable sources of insights and information.

At times, people step out of line, and athletes are no exceptions to the rule. When misbehavior occurs, the coach must become a *disciplinarian.* Players need to adhere to a reasonable set of rules both on and off the field, and penalties must be meted out for violations of the conduct code. The good coach clearly states the code of player conduct up front and adheres to it with reasonable regularity. When violations occur, punishment should be levied. Consistent with the time-honored rules learned in both the animal laboratory and in human research, if punishment is to be successful in changing behavior, it must be mild, prompt, and consistent. *Mildness* means that counterproductive emotionality will be minimal, thereby allowing the intended message to get through. *Promptness* means that

Football as Fun: Some Coaches Who Dared to Be Different

John Gagliardi of St. John's (Minnesota), a 52-year coaching veteran, has seen his football teams win 377 games and three small-college national championships under his tutelage. All of these achievements have been attained with a unique coaching philosophy that includes such novelties as never using blocking sleds or tackling dummies, no scrimmages, and practices conducted in sweats and/or shorts only. Gagliardi's opposition to the "no pain, no gain" mentality so pervasive among football coaches is legendary; he says he likes to conduct "kinder, more gentle practices," preferring to view football as an exercise in finesse rather than brute strength. Though he has been tendered a number of lucrative offers from big-time football programs, Gagliardi feels that his philosophy is best suited for St. John's.

In a similar vein, the senior author of this text played his final year of high school football many years ago with coaches who instituted a similar philosophy and has seen its merits firsthand. Emphasis in practices was on brevity, speed, timing, conditioning, mental preparation, and *esprit de corps*. There were no scrimmages after two-a-days were over, and pads were almost never worn. The team eventually won 11 of 13 games, was ranked number one or two in its classification for the entire season, and ended up losing in the quarterfinals of the state playoffs 13–12 to the eventual state runnerup after having a 12–0 lead at the end of the third quarter. Many thanks go to coaches Kester "Tractor" Trent and L. E. "Hooter" Brewer, particularly the latter, for their lessons in unorthodox but fun football.

SOURCE: Nance (1990).

---

the punishment and behavior will be tied together temporally in such a way that no mixed messages are sent; to wit, this is the transgression and here is the specified penalty. Finally, punishment that is *consistent* conveys a firm message that there are rules, that no one is above the law, and that all violations will carry a uniform punishment. Athletes, like the rest of us, can live within a punitive policy that is applied only when absolutely necessary and meets the tripartite standards of mildness, promptness, and consistency.

The good coach also *leads by example*. This implies that the coach who demands hard work from others is also a hard worker. It means that the coach who demands fitness is an exemplar of fitness. Obviously, coaches need not need to be in as good a condition as their players, but they should serve as fitness role models for their athletes. It means that the coach who commands respect should show respect for others. It means that the coach who expects unbridled enthusiasm should be an enthusiastic person. It means that the

coach who asks that the players be good listeners also listens when players and assistant coaches are communicating. Finally, though this list is by no means exhaustive, the coach who expects athletics to build character should be a role model and facilitator of the character-building aspects of athletic participation.

Finally, the good coach must be a *goal setter*. Substantial research on goal setting has emerged of late in the sport psychology literature, and the up-to-date coach would do well to incorporate the best of these findings into his or her motivational repertoire.

ADVANTAGES AND DISADVANTAGES OF COACHING

Undoubtedly, there are many rewards associated with coaching. Prevailing in one-to-one competition with your peers has a tremendous amount of appeal. Equally attractive is the pride in molding a group of individuals

TABLE 23.1

Coaching Tenure in Selected Professional Sports, 1980–1989

League	Number of Changes	Percent Change Annually	Average Tenure in Years
NFL	53	21.0	4.75
NBA	76	36.4	2.75
NHL	96	50.7	1.96
MLB	103	44.0	2.27

SOURCE: Pro Coaches (1989).

into a productive and cohesive team. Another source of great satisfaction has to be watching young people master skills and, at the same time, grow up to be useful, contributing citizens. For an increasing number of coaches, substantial monetary rewards and fame accompany such success. Though these various incentives hardly exhaust the myriad possibilities, they serve as reminders that coaching can be a most exhilarating calling.

Fuoss and Troppmann (1981) indicate that coaches will also confront a number of features of their chosen field that fall into the category of hazards of the profession. For one thing, *everyone is an expert on sport.* Few would tell a watchmaker, a welder, or an electronics wizard how to do their respective jobs, yet most of us are more than willing to tell a coach how to run his or her team. Second-guessing by the so-called Monday-morning quarterback is a way of life in the United States and many other countries.

Another pitfall comes in the form of *endless work hours.* Coaches put in many arduous hours in their search for the winning formula. Coaches seem to subscribe wholeheartedly to the prevailing work ethic, as manifested in the various slogans they use to guide their own work and that of their players:

"The will to win is the will to work."
"Success is 99 percent perspiration and 1 percent inspiration."
"By failing to prepare yourself, you are preparing to fail."
"There is no substitute for hard work."

"Alertness plus hard work equals a winner."
"Winners are workers."

Because these ideas are so deeply ingrained in the coaching mentality, they contribute to the idea that the coach who works longest will prevail over the one who is not so diligent. Craig Morton, when coaching the Denver Gold of the now-defunct U.S. Football League, was branded as not very dedicated because he refused to work more than a 40-hour week. His feeling was that coaches spend far more time at the job than is required. Morton may or may not have been correct, but he violated a time-honored coaching norm that the person who works longest and hardest prevails.

A third occupational hazard of coaching is *constant evaluation,* and this appraisal is largely based on the performance of other people (players). The coach's record is a matter of public record and the pressure to notch wins over losses seems endless. Few of us in other professions are so unfailingly scrutinized. The college professor's product is difficult to measure; we often operate in a vacuum as to our proficiency. Not so the coach, whose win–loss record is out there for all to see.

Another negative feature of the coaching business is its *lack of job security.* The coach is only as good as last year's record, as far as management is concerned. To quote Norm Sloan (1977, p. 2), the former head basketball coach at North Carolina State University: "Coaching is the only profession in which you have to prove yourself as much in the thirtieth year as in the first year." Phil Jackson, commenting on the pressures he faced as coach of the 1991 NBA champion Chicago Bulls, puts it succinctly: "I had to win. I knew it was either win or be gone" (Vancil, 1991, p. 19). The prevailing attitude of management and the fans seems to have a "What have you done for me lately?" flavor to it.

Statistics from four of the big-time team sports for the years 1980 through 1989 tell a poignant story about the fragile nature of coaching tenure. Table 23.1 vividly attests to the brief tenure of head coach/managers in big-time sports.

Other noteworthy statistics from the professional and collegiate ranks that underscore the data in Table 23.1 include the following:

- In the NBA in 1990, there were nine first-year coaches, eight second-year coaches, seven third-year coaches, and three coaches with over three years' tenure (New Faces, 1990). At the start of the 1994 season, there were again nine new coaches (NBA Coaching Changes, 1994).

- In men's Division I collegiate basketball, there were 49 coaching changes made following the 1999–2000 season (Coaching Changes, 2000). In Division I women's basketball, the picture is little different. Thirty-three coaches were replaced at the end of 1999–2000 season (NCAA Division I Coaching Changes, 2000).

- In the NFL, there were eight coaching changes made in the first 32 days of the year 2000 (National Football League Head Coaching Changes, 2000). There were 133 head coaches fired in the NFL between 1969 and 1989. As of 1990, only five coaches had more than nine years' tenure with the same team (NFL Veterans, 1990).

- At the collegiate level in football, there were 14 coaching changes made following the 1999–2000 Division I season. At the supposedly lower pressure Division II level, another 19 coaches lost their jobs during that same season (Coaching Changes, 2000). Approximately half of all Division I programs were coached by men with less than four years' tenure. Only 17 have lasted as long as ten years. Joe Paterno at Penn State led the pack with 32 years (Unsteady Ground, 1997).

When one considers the ripple effect created among assistant coaches if the head coach is fired, the unsettled nature of the profession of coaching, at least in the high-profile sports, takes on even more significant proportions. Because of the lack of security, frequent moves are common. Also, getting ahead in coaching calls for additional moves that are not dictated so much by failure to win but rather an opportunity to get a better situation.

The unsettled nature of the business and the frequent moving brings us to a fifth drawback, and that is that coaching takes a *toll on family life.* Hasbrook, Hart, Mathes, and True (1990) surveyed several thousand male and female interscholastic coaches and found that "incompatibility with family life" was ranked high among both genders as a reason for leaving coaching. These researchers also found that 79% of the male coaches in a state survey and 87% in a national survey were married; the figures for female coaches were 53%

and 42%. In this connection, Thorngren (1990) points out that females in coaching may be more susceptible to the effects of job stress by the fact that they are more likely to be single and are thereby deprived of the support system inherent in a good marriage. A final point made by Hasbrook et al. is that parenting, not marital pressure, may be the biggest culprit in job dissatisfaction among coaches; to date, there are no studies of parenting and coaching satisfaction.

A final concern to be addressed here is coaching as a terminal career. Very few coaches actually retire at the usual age of 65 or 70. One must go back to collegiate football legends such as Amos Alonzo Stagg at Pacific (retired from coaching at the age of 84), John Dorman at Upper Iowa (age 81), George Allen at Long Beach State (who died on the job at the age of 72), the legendary Eddie Robinson at Grambling (age 72), and the still-active Joe Paterno at Penn State (age 75) to find examples of older, active coaches. Given the job demands of the profession today, it is unlikely that we will ever see many people coaching into their seventies or eighties again, at least in the high-profile sports. Even the most serious fan among us would be hard-pressed to name five currently employed collegiate head football coaches who are over the age of 55, and the picture is much the same for their assistants.

Fred Jacoby (1978), then Commissioner of the Mid-American Conference, found that only six of 84 assistant coaches in his league were over 50 years of age; only one of the ten head coaches was over 50. Clearly, the coaching of football is a young person's game. Parallels are likely to exist in most other sports. It would appear that coaches, like players, should be aware that they are in a career with a short life expectancy and should prepare for that eventuality, both psychologically and financially.

All things considered, individuals who choose coaching stand to reap many rewards, but they should also be aware of another side of the coin. In order to thrive and survive in coaching, there are many issues to confront. Dealing with the never-ending array of critics, working endless hours, having one's future depend heavily on the behavior of others, having little job security, living a sometimes disjointed family life, and being a member of a career with a short life expectancy are things that have to be dealt with to persist and thrive in the profession of coaching.

Pressures Associated With Coaching at the Collegiate and Professional Level

"Fame breeds exhaustion," says Menninger Clinic staff psychologist Harriet Lerner ("Breaking Point," 1995 p. 58). One arena in which Lerner's sentiment seems to hold true is in big-time collegiate and professional basketball. In 1994 and 1995, a number of college coaches, including Ricky Byrdsong at Northwestern, Tim Grgurich at the University of Nevada at Las Vegas, and Mike Krzyzewski at Duke, were notable casualties of job-related coaching stress. At the professional level, the difficulties in dealing with problem athletes, such as Vernon Maxwell of the Houston Rockets and Dennis Rodman of the San Antonio Spurs, during the 1995 NBA playoffs illustrate just one of the many stresses facing those coaches and their peers.

The stresses and strains of coaching in college and professional sports increasingly grace the headlines of our sports pages. Some of the causes of this phenomenon can be ascertained from quotes from prominent basketball coaches who are currently trying to survive the "win-at-all-costs" pressures from administrators, alumni, fans, the media, and owners (quotes from other observers of the basketball scene are also illustrative and have been added for emphasis).

> Why the recent wave of burned-out basketball coaches? Sports gives them tremendous responsibilities but ultimately, little control. Coaches can only coach; they can't actually run the plays. But if the team loses, they still get fired. (Bureau report, *Time*)

> I don't want this to sound like I'm comparing what we do to war, because I'm not. But this job is a lot like it was for those guys over in Vietnam. If you're not careful, it can really turn you into somebody else, somebody you don't want to be. (Rudy Tomjanovich, NBA coach)

> And I think in a lot of ways, sometimes you have to compromise—compromise your coaching values and your coaching philosophy—just to accommodate people and make things work. And that's the toughest thing about it, the tendency of this job to change you and your losing control of it. (Pat Riley, NBA coach)

> The problem starts because you've got a lot of young people with huge egos. They are corporations in short pants. And they have been pampered all their lives. (Chuck Daly, ex-NBA coach)

> There's a certain aspect of coaching a professional team that leads one to paranoia, because there are a lot of times when you feel like there is just you and your dog. (Del Harris, NBA coach)

> Always there has been pressure on college coaches to win. But never, it seems, have there been so many complications: Pampered and hard-to-handle players, a pile-up of non-coaching responsibilities and unprecedented scrutiny from twenty-four-hour all-sports radio and other media. The toll they're taking is noticeable. (Steve Wieberg, *USA Today* writer)

> It's always been a hard job, but it's more difficult now because of the cost of a franchise and the pressure to win. And the players are different—more demanding, more money. It takes a special guy to do a good job. (Don Nelson, NBA coach)

> When you're a surrogate father for 14, 15 kids, you're shackled with this mind-boggling responsibility. (Terry Holland, University of Virginia basketball coach)

> You spend a great part of your time in activities that have nothing to do with coaching, and many times coaches aren't qualified to deal with those areas. You're dealing with drugs, agents, gambling, academics, all the spillovers from everyday society. (George Raveling, ex-college coach)

SOURCES: Boeck (1995); Breaking Point (1995); Coaching Exodus (1994); Seiko (1995); Weiberg (1995); What They Say (1994); Working Your Nerves (1995).

COMMUNICATION
AND COACHING

In all likelihood, the coach who communicates best is most often the winner in athletic contests. Traditional theory in the psychology of communication indicates that there are four elements in the **communication process:** the source, the message, the channel, and the receiver. The *source* is the person originating the communication, the coach in this case. The effectiveness of the coach will depend on such factors as credibility with his or her players, perceived competence, personal and psychological attractiveness, status, and power. The *message* is the meaning conveyed and may involve shrugs, facial expressions, vocal influences, and the use of sarcasm or sincerity. The *channel* refers to the method used, either verbal or nonverbal. The *receiver* obviously is the target of the message, and such variables as intelligence, motivation, and personality will dictate how much and what is perceived.

Mehrabian (1971) has indicated that message transmission is only slightly weighted by what is actually said; he says that any message is 7% verbal, 38% vocal emphasis, and 55% facial expression. Coaches should be aware that much of what they transmit to their players is nonverbal. Such things as **kinesics** (body language), **proxemics** (social distance or territoriality), and **paralanguage** (inflection or tone) become significant determinants of what is communicated. In kinesics, visual gaze posture, facial gestures, and hand movements are involved; in proxemics, personal space issues are paramount; in paralanguage, slow speech, fast speech, high pitch, sarcasm, and variable use of phrases are manipulated for desired effect. The effective coach motivates and educates through verbalizations, but is also aware of the strategic use of the various elements of kinesics, proxemics, and paralanguage.

Despite the richness of possibilities mentioned by Mehrabian, the preponderance of communication engaged in by coaches is undoubtedly transacted through the verbal modality of speaking, though much information is probably conveyed concomitantly through kinesics and proxemics as well as the skillful use of paralanguage. In their study of teaching behaviors of coaches, Bloom, Crumpton, and Anderson (1999) identified an even dozen verbal mechanisms that coaches use in the day to day teaching of their sport. They applied these mechanisms to an analysis of the coaching behaviors of Jerry Tarkanian (aka Tark the Shark), the highly successful basketball coach at the University of Nevada–Las Vegas (UNLV) and Fresno State University. Tactical instructions, hustles, technical instructions, praise and encouragement, general instructions, and scolding were, in order, the most commonly used verbal strategies. Interestingly, only 6% of Tarkanian's comments were negative (i.e., scolding). Equally engaging in the context of the present discussion is the fact that less than 1% of Tarkanian's coaching behaviors involved nonverbal reward or punishment. Overall, these results are similar in a number of ways to those found by Tharp and Gallimore (1976) in their study of the coaching methods of the legendary UCLA basketball coach John Wooden, widely regarded as a master teacher and coach.

THE COACH AND THE
SPORT PSYCHOLOGIST

The role of the sport psychologist in assisting coaches is a highly ambiguous one. Traditionally, coaches have been skeptical of psychology in general. Other coaches who have had contact with well-intentioned sport psychologists who were not able to produce or with outright charlatans using the title have added fuel to the anti-psychologist fire. However, coaches are becoming increasingly aware of the role of psychological factors in physical performance and are also admitting that they do not have all the answers in this area. At the same time, sport psychologists have increasingly become attuned to their own assets and liabilities and are

---

Communication process a four-element process in which the source, the person originating the communication, is the coach; the message is the meaning he or she is trying to convey; the channel is the method used, verbal or nonverbal; and the receiver is the target of the message, who perceives it according to variables of intelligence, motivation, personality, and the like.
Kinesics body language used to convey a message in the communication process.
Proxemics social distance or territoriality, part of the message conveyed in the communication process.
Paralanguage inflection or tone of voice used to convey a message in the communication process.

Slogans: An Alternate Way of Communicating With Athletes?

Coaches are legendary for dispensing slogans or aphorisms designed to inspire greater performance from their athletes. It is a rare coach who does not employ them around the locker room or in pre-game speeches. We have attempted, however arbitrarily, to categorize some of these slogans gleaned from personal experience, talking with athletes and coaches, or reading the related literature. We think these bits of sports folklore are important because of their relationship to the communication process in coaching.

Emphasis on Winning

Triumph is when *try* meets *umph*.

To explain a triumph, start with the first syllable.

Winning isn't everything, it's the only thing.

Winning beats anything that comes in second.

Playing a tie ball game is like kissing your sister.

Attitude/Belief in What You Are Doing

You must believe to achieve.

It's the attitude, not the aptitude, that carries you to the altitude.

By failing to prepare yourself, you are prepared to fail.

Don't make excuses ... make good.

Mental Preparation

Keep on your toes and you won't get caught flatfooted.

Good luck is what happens when preparation meets opportunity.

Landing on your feet sometimes requires that you use your head.

It takes a cool head to win a hot game.

Tough times never last, but tough people do.

Work Ethic

The harder I work, the luckier I get.

If you can't put out, get out.

More sweat in training, less blood in combat.

It's easy to be ordinary, but it takes guts to excel.

Good, better, best; never rest until your good is better and your better best.

Team Orientation

There is no *I* in team.

There is no *U* in team.

Remember the banana ... every time it leaves the bunch, it gets skinned.

A player doesn't make the team, the team makes the player.

United we stand, divided we fall.

The main ingredient of stardom is the rest of the team.

Animal Exhortations/Comparisons

Any nag can start, but it takes a thoroughbred to finish.

It's not the size of the dog in the fight, but the size of the fight in the dog.

A hungry dog hunts best.

You can't run a zoo without the animals.

He who flies with the owls at night cannot keep up with the eagles during the day.

offering their services to coaches and athletic teams in areas in which they can truly be productive. Further, sport psychologists are increasingly cognizant of the need for tact and diplomacy in dealing with coaches and athletes. All of these attitudinal improvements should result in much more cooperation in the future between coaches and sport psychologists.

A necessary first step in the process of providing sport psychology services is *establishing credibility* with coaches. Lanning (1980) and Suinn (1986) offer a number of suggestions for effectiveness in the sport environment. The guidelines that follow are a synthesis of their various suggestions:

1. The sport psychologist's interest in the problems of sport should be clearly evident.

2. The ability to objectively evaluate sport situations is critical to success.

3. There should be an awareness that, as the level of performance escalates, the problems of the coach and the sport psychologist concurrently increase.

4. The sport psychologist, as an outsider to athletes and coaches, must prove his or her skills to them.

5. The sport psychologist can have a substantial impact on assistant coaches, athletes, and others related to a team; diplomacy in dealing with these various persons is a necessity.

6. A realization that each player and team is unique should guide the efforts of the sport psychologist.

7. Maximization of strengths and recognition of limitations is essential to effective functioning.

8. The role of the sport psychologist is always as psychologist and not as coach.

9. The sport psychologist serves as consultant, not as expert; he or she is a collaborator with others involved with the team and the individual athletes.

10. The ability to listen is one of the sport psychologist's most valuable tools.

If these guidelines are followed in a consistent fashion, the sport psychologist should increasingly become a contributing member in the attainment of athletic excellence. The future can be bright for sport psychologists working hand in hand with coaches to make sport even more fun through increased standards of performance.

THE COACH'S PERSONALITY

In all frankness, there have been few systematic studies of the personality makeup of coaches. Early studies took two major directions, one having to do with authoritarianism and the other with Machiavellianism.

The Authoritarian Personality

Ogilvie and Tutko (1966) studied coaches from the four major American sports: football, basketball, baseball, and track. Based on this early work, Tutko and Richards (1971) identified five types of coaches, one being the hard-nosed or authoritarian coach. Gallon (1980, p. 19) summarizes the **authoritarian personality** of Tutko and Richards as follows:

> These coaches leave no doubt about who is boss. They possess well-formulated goals, know exactly what they are trying to achieve, and expect and demand certain responses from those under them. They take the credit or blame for both achievement and mistakes. The advantages and disadvantages of authoritarianism are the same as those for any dictatorship. Most coaches fall into this category.

The veracity of Gallon's assertions is subject to question, but his last statement, that most coaches are authoritarians, has been popularly accepted for many years.

Research by LeUnes and Nation (1982) may have relevance to the issue of authoritarianism among coaches. Undoubtedly most coaches are ex-players who choose to enter the profession upon graduation. Our 1982 study of collegiate football players shows that, when compared with a sample of college peers who played high school football and a sample of nonathletes from the same university, football players were significantly more authoritarian on virtually every subscale and the total score than the other two groups. The assessment device used in this study was the **California F-Scale,** a traditional measure of authoritarianism (Adorno, Frenkel-Brunswik, Lewinson, & Sanford, 1950).

Authoritarian personality in coaching, one who asserts absolute leadership, has well-formulated goals, demands certain responses from athletes, takes credit or blame for wins and losses alike.
California F-Scale a traditional measure of authoritarianism or psychological rigidity.

If one assumes that this is a representative sample of football players and that some of them will become coaches, it should not be a shock that coaches appear to be authoritarian personalities. On the other hand, there were a number of low authoritarian players in the sample, and these players may go into coaching rather than the authoritarian players. For the time being, it seems sufficient to say that the stereotype of a coach as an authoritarian personality is not strongly supported, but the issue warrants further investigation.

The Machiavellian Personality

Christie and Geis (1970) are responsible for furthering scientific interest in the **Machiavellian personality.** Drawing from the writings of Machiavelli (*The Prince* and *The Discourses*), Christie and Geis devised a scale purporting to measure Machiavellianism (i.e., the **Mach Scale**) or "a person's strategy for dealing with people, especially the degree to which he feels other people are manipulable in interpersonal situations" (Robinson and Shaver, 1973, p. 590). Scott (1971) has stated that coaches as a group are rather insensitive in their dealings with others and are prone to manipulate players and others in order to win. Sage has challenged the assertions of Scott in a pair of studies conducted in the mid-1970s. In the first study, Sage (1972a) administered the Machiavellian Scale to 496 college and high school coaches and a sample of male college students from fourteen different universities. No significant differences were found among the various coaching groups and the university students except on age and years of experience. Interestingly, the relationship was negative, with older, more experienced coaches scoring lower than their younger contemporaries. Additionally, there was no indication of even a mild relationship between win–loss record and a coach's Machiavellian personality, a finding also substantiated by Walsh and Carron (1977) in their survey of a Canadian coaching sample.

Sage's second study (1972b) took a slightly different tack, replacing the Machiavellian measure with the Polyphasic Values Inventory (PVI) (Roscoe, 1965), a

---

Machiavellian personality in coaching, one who manipulates others indirectly rather than laying down the law.
Mach Scale a scale designed to measure Machiavellianism, or the tendency to be manipulative in social interactions.

scale designed to assess conservatism on a variety of philosophical, political, economic, educational, social, religious, and personal-moral issues. A group of randomly selected coaches ($n = 246$) were then compared with large numbers of college students ($n = 4,005$) and businessmen ($n = 479$). Coaches were found to be considerably more conservative than the college students and generally more liberal than the businessmen. Sage concluded that coaches are in fact conservative but probably no more so than American males in most other professions.

When all is said and done, coaches may be authoritarian, conservative, and Machiavellian, but probably no more so than members of a number of other professions. Furthermore, being authoritarian may not be totally negative. At times, a firm hand controlling things may be a real asset. The meetings between coaches and players at critical times in athletic contests call for someone to be assertive and exercise control, and that person often is and should be the coach. Finally, coaches may be authoritarian or conservative in the job situation because it serves them well, but they may not be that way at all in dealings with others outside of work.

The preceding discussion summarizes two avenues of personality research related to coaching and are not compelling in terms of conclusiveness. Authoritarianism and Machiavellianism represent only two of many personality dimensions that characterize coaches and point up the need for much more extensive research in the area of personality and coaching.

SUMMARY

1. Roles of the coach include getting along with management, being committed to the athletes, having a good working relationship with assistant coaches and being an advocate on their behalf, establishing contact with the various media, dealing with parents, fans, and boosters; and meeting a broad variety of other demands necessary to success in coaching.

2. The qualities of the good coach include being knowledgeable about the sport, being a student of the game, having the ability to motivate athletes, being aware of individual differences in athletes, being a good listener, exercising discipline when necessary, and leading by example.

3. With such a premium placed at all levels on winning, coaching has become a pressure-laden profession. The many pluses are offset by occupational hazards. Being second-guessed by all the onlookers who believe themselves to be experts on sport, a seemingly endless work schedule, the pressures of constant evaluation, the lack of job security, the strain on family life, and the fact that coaching is a terminal career are all drawbacks to entering and staying in the coaching business.

4. Communication involves four components: the source, the message, the channel, and the receiver. The source originates the communication, the message is the meaning conveyed by a communication, the channel refers to verbal or nonverbal mechanisms in communication, and the receiver is the target of the communication. By becoming more familiar with the nuances of communication theory, coaches could substantially improve their ability to relate to players and others. All things considered, however, coaches still communicate most often through a verbal medium.

5. Sport psychologists can be of considerable service in supplementing the efforts of a coach. A skilled psychologist has areas of expertise related in varying degrees in coaching, and coaches could profit from these capabilities. The insightful sport psychologist should make his or her interest in sport very clear, should be capable of objectively evaluating the problems to be solved, should be aware of psychological demands at all levels of competition, should be aware that he or she is an outsider to coaches and athletes and must exert measures to change this perception, should be aware that his or her impact extends beyond the head coach to the assistants, should appreciate the unique aspects and commonalities among athletes and coaches, should maximize strengths and recognize limitations; should always be aware that his or her role is as psychologist, not as coach; should be a collaborator, not an expert; and should be a constantly tuned-in listener.

6. Coaches have been widely assumed to possess authoritarian, dogmatic, and Machiavellian personalities. Research conducted in the 1970s and 1980s has partially supported this contention. Overall, coaches appear to be generally conservative but probably are no more so than adults of similar age and education in a number of other vocations.

KEY TERMS

authoritarian personality (381)
California F-Scale (381)
Coleman Griffith (370)
communication process (379)
good coaching (373)
kinesics (379)
Knute Rockne (370)
paralanguage (379)
proxemics (379)
Mach Scale (382)
Machiavellian personality (382)

SUGGESTED READINGS

Martens, R. (1997). *Successful coaching.* (2nd ed.). Champaign, IL: Human Kinetics.

This book by Martens, publisher of *Human Kinetics,* is useful for coaches at all levels. It discusses philosophy of coaching, sport psychology (communication, reinforcement, motivation), sport pedagogy, sport physiology, and sport management. Published in conjunction with Martens' American Sport Education Program (ASEP), discussed earlier in this text.

Martin, G. L., & Lumsden, J. A. (1987). *Coaching: An effective behavioral approach.* St. Louis: Times Mirror/Mosby.

This book on coaching incorporates the best of what is known about basic behavioral principles into the process. Such topics as assessing behavioral baselines, rewarding desirable sport behaviors, things to consider in pre- and postseason goal setting, increasing motivation to succeed, and strategies for decreasing problem behaviors are skillfully addressed. "Nuts-and-bolts" issues such as budgets, equipment, facilities, conditioning, nutrition, ethics, and public relations are also discussed. Useful for students hoping to become coaches as well as for those already entrenched in the profession who simply desire to become more effective in dealing with the multiple demands they face.

Wooden, J., & Jamison, S. (1997). *A lifetime of observations and reflections on and off the court*. Chicago, IL: Contemporary Books.

Wooden, the most successful collegiate basketball coach in history, has been described as a "philosopher-coach" by Bill Walsh, an accomplished professional football coach in his own right. Intermixed throughout this short, enjoyable book is Wooden's philosophy of life and sports, observations about famous athletes he coached (i.e., Kareem Abdul-Jabbar and Bill Walton), poetry, and advice on how to be a good athlete and an even better person.

Includes tributes by Abdul-Jabbar, Walsh, Walton, and other sport celebrities.

INFOTRAC COLLEGE EDITION

For additional readings, explore Infotrac College Edition, your online library. Go to: http://www.infotrac-college.com/wadsworth
Hint: Enter these search terms: authoritarian personality, black coaches, coaching (psychological aspects), coaching (teamwork), coaching (technique), Knute Rockne, women coaches.

Youth, Female, and Black Coaches; Coaching Burnout

CHAPTER 24

Coaching and Youth Sport

The Female Coach

The Black Coach

Coaching Burnout

Summary

Key Terms

Suggested Readings

Ranked by many as the finest women's basketball player in history, Cheryl Miller was head coach of the women's basketball team at the University of Southern California. A four-time NCAA All-American as a player on the USC team, she was also an Olympic gold medalist and has been inducted into the Basketball Hall of Fame.

© Sports Illustrated/Peter Read Miller

In this chapter, we will explore dimensions of the coaching experience not discussed in Chapter 23. One is that of coaching youth; there may not be a higher calling in sports than that of sensitively helping to mold young people into good athletes and even better men and women. Another important undertaking with relatively modern roots is that of coaching women. As discussed earlier in the book, the task of coaching females often falls into the hands of other females. Thus, we will take a look at the female coach. Finally, there are issues to be addressed concerning African-American coaches, who are underrepresented in most aspects of sport life despite the fact that many athletes in the high-profile sports are black.

Given the role demands and pressures alluded to in the preceding chapter, it should come as no surprise that coaching burnout is a substantial problem in sports. Definitional issues, possible causative factors, and suggestions for preventing burnout will be discussed.

COACHING AND YOUTH SPORT

One of the more prominent coaching situations is coaching youth. In many cases, such as with children ages 6 to 12, this kind of coaching is low profile and does not involve pay. In other cases, particularly at the interscholastic level, the profile is higher, money is indeed involved, and the stakes are often quite a bit higher. Regardless of age or level of sophistication, youth athletes are significant figures in the sport world and good coaching is vital to their successful participation.

Lombardo (1986) indicates that there are more than 4 million youth coaches in the United States, and many are not qualified to properly coach children regardless of how well intentioned they may be. To quote Lombardo: "Many leagues are totally dependent upon volunteers and, short of being a convicted felon, all are welcomed" (p. 199). The situation is probably not as desperate as Lombardo portrays, but his position has some validity. For that reason, the Institute for the Study of Youth Sport at Michigan State, among others, has suggested some guidelines organizations might employ in screening coaches to work with young people (Seefeldt, 2000). Coaching programs such as the Coaching Behavior Assessment System (CBAS) and related variants also have much to offer in upgrading the coaching of youth.

The Coaching Behavior Assessment System (CBAS)

In an effort to reduce the magnitude of the problem of well-intentioned but poorly prepared coaches in youth sport, a number of coaching programs have been developed. One of the leaders in coaching improvement is the innovative **Coaching Behavior Assessment System (CBAS)** developed by Smith, Smoll, and Hunt (1977) and shown in Table 24.1. The CBAS was developed to allow for direct observation and subsequent coding of coaching behaviors. Its twelve behavioral categories are divided into two larger categories, reactive or elicited and spontaneous or emitted behaviors. The *reactive behaviors* category refers generally to responses to player behaviors, whereas the *spontaneous behaviors category* refers primarily to game-related or game-irrelevant acts.

After preliminary refinement of the CBAS through repeated studies, Smoll and Smith used it in a study of 51 male coaches and 542 players in the Seattle, Washington, area. Trained observers coded an average of 1,122 behaviors per coach over a four-game period. Results indicated, among other things, that two-thirds of the coaches' behaviors fell within the three instructional and support categories, and the rate of punitive behaviors was generally quite low. The correlation between coaches' ratings of the frequency with which they used a particular behavior and their awareness of the fact was low and insignificant except for the category of punishment. Coaches were generally aware of their use of punitive approaches but were less aware of other behaviors in which they engaged.

Other conclusions drawn from the Smoll and Smith study were that players evaluated their teammates and the sport of baseball more positively if they played for coaches who used high levels of reinforcement and support. Self-esteem was enhanced by the positive coaches, and positive coaches were liked much better than the more punitive ones. Interestingly, win–loss record was generally unrelated to the youngsters' feelings about their coaches.

Coaching Behavior Assessment System (CBAS) a standardized measure developed by Smoll and Smith for direct observation and coding of twelve coaching behaviors grouped as reactive or spontaneous.

TABLE 24.1

CBAS Response Categories

Class I. Reactive Behaviors

Responses to desirable performance

| Reinforcement | A positive, rewarding reaction, verbal or nonverbal, to a good play or good effort |
| Nonreinforcement | Failure to respond to a good performance |

Responses to mistakes

Mistake-contingent encouragement	Encouragement given to a player following a mistake
Mistake-contingent technical instruction	Instructing or demonstrating to a player how to correct a mistake
Punishment	A negative reaction, verbal or nonverbal, following a mistake
Punitive technical instruction	Technical instruction that is given in a punitive or hostile manner following a mistake
Ignoring mistakes	Failure to respond to a player mistake

Response to misbehavior

| Keeping control | Reactions intended to restore or maintain order among team members |

Class II. Spontaneous Behaviors

Game-related responses

General technical instruction	Spontaneous instruction in the techniques and strategies of the sport (not following a mistake)
General encouragement	Spontaneous encouragement that does not follow a mistake
Organization	Administrative behavior that sets the stage for play by assigning duties, responsibilities, positions, etc.

Game-irrelevant responses

| General communication | Interactions with players unrelated to the game |

SOURCE: Smoll & Smith (1984).

In another study, Smoll and Smith examined the impact of coaching behaviors on self-esteem in Little League baseball players (Smoll, Smith, Barnett, & Everett, 1993). Smoll et al. compared the results of behavioral training of eight baseball coaches with that of a no-treatment control group of 10 coaches. Consistent with previous findings, the trained coaches were evaluated more positively by their players and the players reported having more fun despite no differences in win–loss records when compared with controls. Also, boys with low self-esteem as determined by a preseason assessment who played for a trained coach demonstrated significant increases in self-esteem over the season. Unfortunately, such boys playing for the untrained

coaches did not show concomitant improvements in self-esteem. The efficacy of the Smoll and Smith approach appears to be incontrovertibly supported. There appears to be no substitute for good training of coaches in terms of enhancing the youth sport experience.

In yet another effort, Smith, Smoll, and Barnett (1995) conducted a field experiment in which they assessed the efficacy of a preseason training package aimed at teaching anxiety-reduction strategies to coaches. As has been the case over and over, the players of the trained coaches evaluated them more favorably and reported having more fun playing the game. There was also a significant reduction in trait anxiety among the players with coaches who had received the anxiety-reduction training.

A major outcome of this research agenda was the creation of a training program for youth coaches. Smoll and Smith have labeled their training program **Coach Effectiveness Training (CET).** To validate the effectiveness of their three-hour training program, 31 Little League baseball coaches were randomly assigned to either an experimental (training) group or to a control group that did not receive the CET instruction. Interviews with 325 players at the end of the season were supportive of CET. The trained coaches used more reinforcement and less punishment, were liked better by the players, and were seen as better teachers. Additionally, self-esteem gains were seen in the players who had CET-trained coaches. Significantly, there were no differences in win–loss records of the two groups, indicating that the gains afforded by CET are primarily expressed in the psychosocial domain.

Coach training programs such as that developed by Smoll and his associates have been shown to be effective in improving coaching success at the youth level. As a result, a number of other systems have been developed to improve youth coaching, which we will discuss now.

Other Approaches to Improving Youth Coaching

One program aimed at improving coaching in youth sport is the **National Youth Sporting Coaches Association (NYSCA) training program,** founded in

---

Coach Effectiveness Training (CET) a training program for youth coaches developed by Smoll and Smith that teaches anxiety-reduction strategies, reinforcement over punishment, and other psychosocial techniques.

National Youth Sporting Coaches Association (NYSCA) training program a clinic featuring a three-hour video session for youth coaches that teaches positive philosophy, psychology of children, and other topics; coaches must sign a pledge to follow the organization's Code of Ethics.

American Sport Education Program (ASEP) a training program founded by Rainer Martens that includes youth coaches, parents, and administrators.

Institute for the Study of Youth Sport (YSI) a training program administered by Michigan State University to research youth sport and provide educational materials and programs for coaches, administrators, officials, and parents.

Canadian National Certification Program (CNCP) a five-level training program for youth coaches that emphasizes theory, technique, and application.

1981 and headquartered in West Palm Beach, Florida. In 1993, the NYSCA was expanded to form the National Alliance for Youth Sports (NAYS) to broaden their focus from coaches to the inclusion of parents, administrators, and officials. The NYSCA/NAYS clinic involves watching a three-hour video training session. A positive coaching philosophy, the psychology of children, and ways to organize effective practices are only a few of the topics covered. At the end of the clinic, each participant coach must pass an exam and sign a pledge to abide by their Code of Ethics. All coaches completing the training are provided with the official continuing education publication, *Youth Sport Journal,* which comes out quarterly. As of 2000, more than 1.3 million youth coaches participated in the training at one of the 2,500 NYSCA/NAYS chapters.

Another well-received training program is the **American Sport Education Program (ASEP),** originally known as the American Coaching Effectiveness Program (ACEP). Founded at the University of Illinois in 1981 by Rainer Martens, ASEP's motto is "Athletes first, winning second." In 1994, the original coaches' training program was broadened to include parents and administrators, and this larger focus resulted in the name change from ACEP to ASEP. Over 1 million coaches, parents, and administrators have received ASEP training.

The **Institute for the Study of Youth Sport (IYSI),** an outgrowth of the 1978 legislature-mandated Michigan study concerning youth sport mentioned in Chapter 21, operates as a special unit within the Department of Kinesiology at Michigan State University. IYSI has been charged by the Michigan legislature to research the benefits and detriments of youth sport participation and to provide educational materials and programs for coaches, administrators, officials, and parents. It also puts out a six-page newsletter three times a year, the *Spotlight on Youth Sport Newsletter;* it is free to people in the state of Michigan and costs $5 per year for out-of-state subscribers.

In Canada, the **Canadian National Certification Program (CNCP)** serves as an invaluable source of guidance for coaches of youth. CNCP is a five-level program ranging from Level 1, the grassroots level, to Level 5, in which youth are being trained to represent their home country in international competition. Emphasis at all levels is placed on theory, technique, and application.

Behavioral Guidelines of Youth Sports Coaches

Ron Smith and Frank Smoll have generated some of the more useful research in the area of coaching youth participants. One important outcome of their work has been the creation of a set of guidelines for working with young athletes that consists of sensible applications of behavioral principles discussed earlier in the book.

I. Reactions to player behaviors and game situations

A. Good plays

Do: Reinforce! Do so immediately. Let the players know that you appreciate and value their efforts. Reinforce effort as much as you do results. Look for positive things, reinforce them, and you'll see them increase. Remember, whether the kids show it or not, the positive things you say and do stick with them.

Don't: Take their efforts for granted.

B. Mistakes, screw-ups, boneheaded plays, and all the things that pros seldom do

Do: Encourage immediately after mistakes. That's when the kid needs encouragement most. Also, give corrective instruction on how to do it right, but always do so in an encouraging manner. Do this by emphasizing not the bad thing that just happened, but the good things that will happen if the kid follows your instruction (the "why" of it). This will motivate the player to correct positively the mistake rather than negatively to avoid failure and your disapproval.

Don't: Punish when things go wrong. Punishment isn't just yelling at kids; it can be any indication of disapproval, tone of voice, or action. Kids respond much better to a positive approach. Fear of failure is reduced if you work to reduce fear of punishment.

C. Misbehaviors, lack of attention

Do: Maintain order by establishing clear expectations. Emphasize that during a game all members of the team are part of the game, even those on the bench. Use reinforcement to strengthen team participation. In other words, try to prevent misbehaviors from occurring by using the positive approach to strengthen their opposites.

Don't: Constantly nag or threaten the kids in order to prevent chaos. Don't be a drill sergeant. If a kid refuses to cooperate, quietly remove him or her from the bench for a while. Don't use physical measures (e.g., running laps). The idea here is that if you establish clear behavioral guidelines early and work to build team spirit in achieving them, you can avoid having to repeatedly keep control. Remember, kids want clear guidelines and expectations, but they don't want to be regimented. Try to achieve a healthy balance.

II. Getting positive things to happen

Do: Give instruction. Establish your role as a teacher. Try to structure participation as a learning experience in which you're going to help the kids develop their abilities. Always give instruction in a positive fashion. Satisfy your players' desire to become the best athletes they can be. Give instructions in a clear, concise manner; if possible, demonstrate how to do it.

Do: Give encouragement. Encourage effort; don't demand results. Use it selectively so that it is meaningful. Be supportive without acting like a cheerleader.

Do: Concentrate on the game. Be "in the game" with the players. Set a good example for team unity.

Don't: Give either instruction or encouragement in a sarcastic or degrading manner. Make a point, then leave it. Don't let "encouragement" become irritating to the players.

SOURCE: Smoll & Smith (1984).

More and more provinces and municipalities in Canada are requiring CNCP training for youth coaches.

A healthy movement is clearly growing in the United States and Canada, among other countries, to ensure that young people are provided with as positive an early sport experience as possible. Training of volunteer coaches through the various available programs is a necessary step in the process of improving youth sport. In the not too distant future, we hope, all youth coaches will be graduates of one of the training programs in operation today.

THE FEMALE COACH

Two events greatly shaped the face of women's sports in the 1970s. One was the implementation of the Title IX legislation in the early 1970s. Though the intent of the legislation was to assist in the achievement of parity between men and women across the spectrum to include sport, a reverse effect has been generated for female coaches, who find themselves on the outside looking in with regard to career options in the coaching field.

A second factor in promoting female sport involvement was an explosion of participation by young females at both the interscholastic and intercollegiate levels. In 1971, 294,000 young women were participating in high school sports; by 1995, this number had jumped to 2.7 million (Participation Survey, 2000). At the collegiate level, these numbers were 32,000 and 123,000 respectively (Wulf, 1997).

The Female Interscholastic/ Intercollegiate Coach

At the interscholastic level, Hart and Mathes (1982) reported that the percentage of women coaching girls' teams in Wisconsin dropped from 92 in 1975 to 46 in 1981. In assessing the situation in Colorado, Schafer (1984) reported that 89% of coaches of women's high school teams in 1973–1974 were themselves women, whereas this figure dropped to 41% by 1983–1984. In a study conducted in Virginia, Heishman, Bunker, and Tutwiler (1990) report a 271% increase from 1972 to 1987 in coaching opportunities for women's sport; at the same time, the number of female coaches declined

from 80% to slightly under 44% during that 15-year period. A research effort by True (1983) isolated similar trends; data from eight states indicated a 40–50% decrease in women coaches, depending on the state considered. Acosta and Carpenter (1985), in reviewing the coaching situation in the states of Illinois, Kansas, Nebraska, and Wisconsin, found nearly identical declines, generally in the 40–50% range.

A comparable trend toward a reduction in the number of female coaches at the intercollegiate level was first noted by Holmen and Parkhouse (1981), who found that the number of female coaching positions in colleges and universities increased by 37% from 1974 to 1979. However, during the same time period the number of female coaches dropped by 20%. Interestingly and perhaps prophetically, the number of male coaches coaching female athletic teams grew by a whopping 137%. Data from Brewington and White (1988) offer little consolation; since the early 1970s, the number of female coaches has dropped from 90% to 50%. Accompanying data indicate that the number of female sports administrators had declined during the same time period from 90% to 15%.

There is no denying that many female coaches have been replaced with males over the past several decades. However, it does appear that currently things may be stabilizing. Herwig (1994) indicates a 1.3% gain for female coaches at the collegiate level from 1992 to 1994; at the same time, there has been a 4.2% gain during the same time period in number of females administering women's sports programs. Also encouraging is the increase in the number of sports offered for women per NCAA school; in 1978, the average number of female sports per school was 5.61%; in 1992, it was 7.02%, and an all-time high of 7.22% was reached in 1994.

Clearly, there have been some unintended shifts in the career patterns for female coaches over the past two to three decades. Their numbers have steadily declined at both the interscholastic and intercollegiate levels, though there is some evidence that the figures may be reversing ever so slightly. There can be no disputing the fact, however, that 79% of all athletic administrators involved in women's athletics are male, as are 50.6% of the coaches (Herwig, 1994). An inspection of some of the variables that may have led to this situation is therefore warranted.

Reasons for the Decline in the Number of Female Coaches

As we have seen, in the early 1970s most coaches of women's teams were female. According to Sisley and Capel (1986), this situation arose as a natural outgrowth of the existing girls' physical education classes and athletic associations. However, as these programs expanded in terms of popularity, salaries, and public visibility, the number of women filling the existing coaching slots decreased and many positions were taken over by males. Why has female involvement in the coaching of other females declined? One of the more credible explanations proposed is that of Hart, Hasbrook, and Mathes (1986), who contend that one or a combination of each of the following factors is at the heart of the issue: (1) role conflict, (2) incomplete occupational socialization, and (3) outright sex discrimination.

Role conflict is an appealing, common-sense explanatory mechanism because we would all agree that balancing the multiple demands of teacher, coach, wife, and mother represents quite a juggling act for any woman. However, research by Locke and Massengale (1978) and Massengale (1980, 1981a, 1981b) suggests that role conflict is not the exclusive domain of female coaches; in fact, male coaches find the varying demands on their time and energy to be highly conflicting and stressful. Results of a survey of over 4,000 high school coaches by Hasbrook, Hart, Mathes, and True (1990) found that males felt more affected by time constraints and resultant conflicts because of family responsibilities than did the females in their sample. "Incompatibility with family life" was the fourth most cited reason for leaving coaching for males in the sample and sixth most frequent for the females. Interestingly, 87% of the male coaches were married and 42% of the females. The latter statistic may account for the role conflict difference noted by Hasbrook et al. In any event, there can be little doubt that role conflict is an important issue for both male and female coaches.

It has been suggested that failure in various work settings may be a function of **incomplete occupational socialization,** a concept proposed by Burlingame (1972). In this case, the individuals involved simply have not acquired the knowledge, skills, and values to be successful at their jobs. The lack of ex-

pectancy of becoming a coach, the dearth of female role models for coaching, and a shortage of top competitive experience all contribute to the failure of female coaches to acquire the fundamental knowledge, skills, and values so critical to success. Though appealing at an intellectual level, there is some evidence to suggest that at least part of this model is not true. For example, studies by Anderson and Gill (1983), Eitzen and Pratt (1989), and Hasbrook et al. (1990) indicate that, at least for the sport of basketball, female coaches at both the interscholastic and collegiate levels had more varsity playing experience than did male coaches. However, Sisley and Capel did not find this difference to be a factor for a variety of other sports they studied in Oregon. These conflicting results may result from a host of extraneous variables, but they do point out the need for research in this aspect of the coaching experience. Also, playing experience is only one relatively small aspect of occupational socialization for coaching, and there is much to ponder about Burlingame's notion as it relates to the profession of coaching.

The third possible explanation, sex discrimination, is also an attractive one. Mathes (1982) reported that female coaches feel restricted to minor sports, believe their mobility to be limited in terms of becoming head coaches or athletic directors, and generally see coaching as a limited source of job opportunity. Mathes also reported other areas in which inequities are seen, particularly in pay, general support, and facilities.

Evidence in several of the areas cited by Mathes indicates that sex discrimination is alive and well in interscholastic and intercollegiate sport, particularly but not exclusively in hiring and retention practices. For example, Heishman, Bunker, and Tutwiler (1990), in their study of coaching changes from 1971–1972 to 1986–1987 in Virginia, found that the sports where males replaced female coaches at the highest rates were track and field, basketball, and softball, in that order. In contrast, female coaches were much less likely to be replaced in sports such as field hockey, gymnastics,

---

Incomplete occupational socialization condition in which a person has not acquired the knowledge, skills, and values to be successful at a given job; in coaching, a common predicament of female coaches.

volleyball, and tennis. Stangl and Kane (1990) found a strong relationship between gender of the athletic director and gender of coaches who were hired, resulting in what they call **homologous reproduction.** Knoppers, Meyer, Ewing, and Forrest (1989) provide support for this relationship; they suggest that since athletic directors hire coaches, they serve as the "gatekeepers to the profession of coaching" (p. 358). Supporting evidence bearing on this point is provided by Herwig (1994), who indicates that 57% of coaches of NCAA programs are females in situations where the athletic director is also a female.

The intimations of Knoppers et al. and Stangl and Kane give rise to the suspicion that a **"good old boy" network** of men with lifetime professional and personal relationships may be operating in the hiring and retention of coaches and could account for some of the decline in numbers of female coaches. Pastore and Meacci (1994) emphasize that the situation is exacerbated by the absence of a corresponding "good old girl" network. The data on other issues related to sex discrimination are less clear, but there is ample evidence that such practices do occur in interscholastic and intercollegiate sports.

A Final Note

A final point concerns the perceptions athletes have of male and female coaches. Parkhouse and Williams (1986), in a study of male and female interscholastic basketball players in California, found a substantial gender bias favoring male coaches. Though this discovery of possible gender bias is somewhat at variance with earlier research (Cottle, 1982; Rikki & Cottle, 1984; Weinberg, Reveles, & Jackson, 1984), it may suggest that the decline in the number of female coaches is partially due to a "male is better" bias in evaluating coaching ability.

Homologous reproduction in sports, tendency of the person with hiring authority (the athletic director) to hire persons of his or her own gender (the coach), resulting in gender clustering.
"Good old boy" network a group of men whose lifetime association, both personal and professional, results in an informal favoritism in hiring and job advancement.

THE AFRICAN-AMERICAN COACH

African-American coaches are a relative rarity at all levels of competition, but their absence is most noticeable in the high profile world of the major collegiate and professional sports. In an early report, Yetman, Berghorn, and Thomas (1980) indicated that slightly over 5% of the head coaches in NCAA Division I college basketball were black. Another early summary (Black Head Coaches, 1982) showed only thirty black head coaches in all major sports at predominantly white universities. Similarly, Latimer and Mathes (1985) studied the racial composition of 47 Division I colleges and found a total of 80 black coaches, only one of whom was a head coach. Interestingly, the social and educational backgrounds of these coaches were similar to those of a comparable sample of white coaches. Further, the African-American coaches were almost always employed as coaches of athletes playing peripheral as opposed to central positions, a finding not inconsistent with results reported in some detail in Chapter 17. More recent statistics (There's No Question, 1990) indicate that there were 32 black head coaches in predominantly white schools and 17 others at predominantly black schools among the 293 Division I men's basketball programs. The basketball data are particularly striking when we consider the fact that less than 17% of the coaches are black in a sport where the ratio of black to white players is approximately 60–40. For the year 1997–1998, 5.8% of Division I coaches across all sports were African American and another 2.1% were other minorities, yielding an overall figure of 7.9%. This figure represents a gain from the 6.8% figure for 1995–1996 (Lapchick & Matthews, 2000).

In women's collegiate basketball, of the 64 teams making the NCAA Division I playoffs in 1994, five were coached by a black male and five by black females (Becker & Herwig, 1994). Interestingly, 38 others were coached by white females; when the five black female coaches and one Asian-American female coach are added to this total, this means that 44 of the final 64 teams were coached by females. Thus, the percentage of female coaches was 69%, a figure quite a bit above what one would predict based on earlier discussion of this issue. In 1997–1998, 7.1% of all Division I athletic teams were coached by minorities, down from 7.6% in 1995–1996 (Lapchick & Matthews, 2000).

At the professional level of play, a similar overall picture emerges. As of 1998, there were only 10 minority head coaches and managers in the NBA, NFL, and MLB combined, the lowest figure since 1993 (Lapchick, 1999). Given the percentage of black athletes in these three sports (79%, 65%, and 15%, respectively), there is clear underrepresentation of black coaches. Interestingly, only four Hispanics were head coaches in major league soccer, a sport with substantial popularity among that diverse ethnic group.

The focus to this point has been entirely on the collegiate and professional levels of the more visible sports. We are not currently aware of any meaningful summary related to African-American coaches operating at the interscholastic level. This group of coaches might well be a research gold mine in terms of expanding the knowledge base on this most important issue.

COACHING BURNOUT

One possible outcome of prolonged stress associated with coaching is emotional and physical exhaustion; this exhausted state has often been referred to as **coaching burnout.** Maslach and Jackson (1984, p. 134), have defined burnout as "a psychological syndrome of emotional exhaustion, depersonalization and reduced personal accomplishment that can occur among individuals who work with people in some capacity." One of the outgrowths of Maslach and Jackson's work is the Maslach Burnout Inventory (MBI) which will be discussed later and can be seen in Highlight 24.1. A well-accepted model of burnout is that of Ronald Smith and it will guide our discussion here.

Smith's Cognitive-Affective Model of Athletic Burnout

In 1986, Ronald Smith introduced the nuances of burnout to sport psychology with an innovative and comprehensive conceptual model. According to Smith, burnout is a reaction to chronic stress and is made up of physical, mental, and behavioral components. The interaction of this assortment of environmental and personal variables causes burnout. **Smith's cognitive-affective model of burnout** shows the parallel relationships among the situational, cognitive, physiological, and behavioral components of stress and burnout. This conceptual model can be seen in Figure 24.1.

Essentially, Smith states that burnout occurs when the available resources are insufficient to meet the demands being placed on the system by the various sources of life stress. Smith further indicates that there is a sequential response to stress that begins with a cognitive appraisal. The resultant emotional responses to this appraisal will be tempered by how the demands are assessed, by an appraisal of what resources are available to deal with the demands, the likely consequences if the demands are not met, and the personal meaning of the demands for the individual. Self-efficacy, expectancy of success, self-concept, and a host of other variables discussed in earlier chapters all come into play at this point in the Smith model. The third sequential response in the model, the physiological component, occurs if danger or harm is feared. Finally, a variety of coping behaviors, some positive and others counterproductive, will be manifested as moderated by other components of the model. One of these counterproductive behaviors is burnout. In offering his model, Smith has raised some interesting questions about the operationalizing of burnout, its measurement, its epidemiological properties, and related causative and moderator variables.

Causes of Burnout

Like most human behaviors, burnout in coaching is determined by a number of interacting factors. Taking the job too seriously, problem parents, problem athletes, disenchantment with life and/or coaching, pressures to win at all costs, feeling unappreciated, and feeling entrapped are just some of the variables that can contribute to coaching burnout.

Coaching burnout a psychological state in which the coach experiences extreme emotional exhaustion, depersonalization, and reduced accomplishment.
Smith's cognitive-affective model of burnout a model that posits that burnout is a reaction to chronic stress and has situational, cognitive, physiological, and behavioral components.

FIGURE 24.1

A Conceptual Model for Burnout

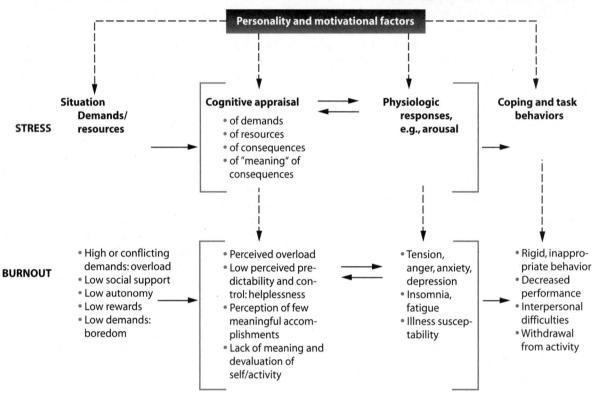

SOURCE: Smith (1986).

Note: This model shows the parallel relationships assumed to exist among situational, cognitive, physiologic, and behavioral components of stress and burnout. Individual differences in motivation and personality are assumed to influence all of the components.

TAKING THE JOB TOO SERIOUSLY. Probably the single biggest cause of coaching burnout is taking oneself and one's job too seriously. Coaching is an important challenge, but there is more to life than work. Maintaining a balanced perspective on work would seem to be a valuable first step in avoiding burnout.

PROBLEM PARENTS. Parents of youthful players constitute a considerable source of stress. When the coach–parent relationship is unhealthy, stress is generated that can ultimately contribute to coaching burnout.

PROBLEM ATHLETES. Darrell Royal, a highly successful football coach at the University of Texas, retired from coaching at a relatively early age, professing symptoms of burnout. One of the major contributing factors, he said, was the loss of interest in coddling 18-year-old prima donnas during the recruiting process. Getting young people to choose one's school, keeping them academically eligible, and getting the most out of their often immense athletic talents is a challenging task that is made considerably more demanding by problem athletes. At another level, the player excesses seen in professional football and basketball have most certainly sent any number of coaches to an early retirement.

DISENCHANTMENT. When the thrill of coaching disappears, burnout cannot be far behind. The notion of a

A Measure of Burnout

Maslach and Jackson have developed the **Maslach Burnout Inventory (MBI)** (Maslach & Jackson, 1981), which has received much attention in assessing the presence of burnout among coaches and athletes. The MBI is composed of 22 items designed to measure both frequency and intensity of feelings and consists of three subscales: Emotional Exhaustion (EE), Depersonalization (D), and Personal Accomplishment (PA). By reversing the direction of the scoring of PA, which is the inverse of EE and D, the result is that the higher the score, the greater the degree of burnout.

Studies of the reliability and validity of the MBI have been conducted by Abu-Hilal and Salameh in Jordan (1992) and Walkey and Green (1992) in New Zealand. In both studies, the factorial validity of the MBI was supported with only minor caveats.

Early studies in the area of burnout and coaching using the MBI were reported by Caccese and Mayerberg (1984), Capel (1986), and Capel, Sisley, and Desertrain (1987). Caccese and Mayerberg indicated that female coaches in their study reported significantly higher levels of emotional exhaustion (EE) and significantly lower levels of personal accomplishment (PA) than did the male coaches they surveyed. The largest gender differences were found on the item, "I feel frustrated by my job," insofar as frequency was concerned. In terms of intensity, "I feel burned out by my job"

showed the largest difference. Overall, however, none of the two groups reported any excessive amount of burnout. Capel studied athletic trainers using the MBI and found little evidence for burnout among these allied professionals. Hendrix, Acevedo, and Hebert (2000) did find excessive burnout in a sample of 118 certified athletic trainers they studied but noted a lower Personal Accomplishment score than was found in coaches, coach/teachers, and mental health professionals from other related studies. Capel, Sisley, and Desertrain, in a study of high school basketball coaches from six western states, found burnout to be at a low to medium level. Nevertheless, there were burned-out coaches in the Capel et al. sample.

Smith (1986), pointing to other successful sport-specific measures that have been outgrowths of assessment devices aimed at nonsport populations, has issued a call for a sport-specific conceptualization and measurement of burnout.

SOURCES: Abu-Hilal & Salameh (1992); Caccese & Mayerberg (1984); Capel (1986); Capel, Sisley, & Desertrain (1987); Hendrix, Acevedo, & Hebert (2000); Maslach & Jackson (1981); Smith (1986); Walkey & Green (1992).

Maslach Burnout Inventory (MBI) a standardized measure of psychological burnout designed to assess frequency and intensity of feelings in the areas of emotional exhaustion, depersonalization, and personal accomplishment.

---

career change may become prominent in the coach's thoughts at this point. An athletic directorship or the broadcasting booth are prominent outlets for burned-out coaches.

PRESSURE TO WIN. Coaches care inordinately about winning, and losing seasons (or strings of them) are frustrating for them. A losing season when preseason expectancies have been extremely high is also disconcerting.

OTHER PRESSURES. Lack of appreciation by administrators, family pressures, too many coaching and teaching duties, and having to share strained resources with

other programs in and out of athletics all take their toll on coaches.

ENTRAPMENT. Schmidt and Stein (1991) have taken a different slant on the burnout issue but confine their elaborations to players as opposed to coaches. However, others have extended their work to the coaching profession. Schmidt and Stein talk of a *commitment perspective* and have suggested three profiles of commitment among athletes. One of these profiles is a commitment based on enjoyment; this athlete wants to compete and derives great returns for their investment. The second profile is that of the entrapped athlete, who participates more out of obligation than joy. The third is the dropout, who gives up participating because of a low sport commitment.

Raedeke (Raedeke, 1997; Raedeke, Granzyk, & Warren, 2000) has adapted Schmidt and Stein's work to analyzing burnout in coaches, suggesting that the problem is one of **entrapment.** According to Raedeke and his colleagues, entrapment occurs when coaches lose some or all of their attraction to coaching but feel they must continue on anyway. Reasons for these feelings of entrapment may arise because the coach feels (a) that there is no attractive alternative available, (b) that they have too much invested to quit, or (c) that they must continue on because of pressure arising from the expectations of others.

To gain insights into the relationship between commitment and burnout, Raedeke et al. mailed a questionnaire to 295 male and female swimming coaches. Chief among their findings was general support for the entrapment hypothesis; that is, coaches who felt trapped reported higher than average exhaustion scores. Overall, however, this sample of coaches had a fairly favorable outlook on coaching and expressed low levels of burnout. It may be that the sample used in this study partially accounts for the low levels of burnout expressed. Sixty-five percent of the sample were part-time coaches, and their coaching may have represented a break from the routine of their everyday job. It is even possible that doing coaching as an avocation could have been a preventive for job burnout in their primary vocation.

PSYCHOLOGICAL FACTORS. In a somewhat different vein, Vealey, Udry, Zimmerman, and Soliday (1992) looked at some of the preceding situational causes of burnout but added state anxiety to the mix. Vealey and her associates administered the State–Trait Anxiety Inventory (STAI), the Maslach Burnout Inventory (MBI), and a Demographic/Cognitive Appraisal Questionnaire to 381 high school and 467 college coaches in 10 different sports. The high school coaches were from Ohio, and the college coaches were drawn from a national coaching registry. Data analysis revealed that there was considerable burnout in this sample, perhaps as high as 29% of the males and 27% of the females. The biggest single predictor of burnout by far was state anxiety. This finding was particularly salient when male and female coaches were categorized as high or low in burnout as defined by the MBI; high burnout coaches of both genders reported significantly more state anxiety. Interestingly, actual time spent in coaching was not predictive of burnout, a finding that ran counter to their research hypothesis as well as to Maslach's earlier work in other applied settings. Finally, Vealey et al. concluded that their findings are partially supportive of the theoretical framework suggested by Smith.

Another attempt to introduce personality variables into the analysis of coaching burnout was made by Kelley (1994). Like Vealey et al., Kelley used the MBI to assess burnout in 131 male and 118 female NCAA Division III and NAIA baseball and softball coaches. The psychological variable studied was hardiness, a construct introduced to the literature by Kobasa (Kobasa, 1988; Kobasa, Maddi, & Courington, 1981). **Hardiness** is characterized by three factors: control, commitment, and challenge. *Control* refers to the tendency of the hardy individual to believe that he or she can influence the course of life events. *Commitment* means approaching life with a sense of purpose, a healthy curiosity, and willingness to invest oneself in relationships. As for *challenge,* the hardy personality believes that change rather than stability is the norm; as such, changes are seen as interesting, positive, and an impetus for additional growth. The Third Generation Hardiness Test (Kobasa, 1988) was used to arrive at a hardiness score for each coach in Kelley's sample. As reported elsewhere, coaches in this sample reported high levels of burnout. Hardiness was predictive of burnout; male and female coaches who were low in psychological hardiness reported high levels of burnout and less job satisfaction in general. It was concluded that this research was supportive of the previous work on hardiness, and its efficacy as a personality construct in burnout research was also demonstrated.

In a related study, Kelley, Eklund, and Ritter-Taylor (1999) looked at hardiness, trait anxiety, and burnout among male and female collegiate tennis coaches. The level of burnout found among these coaches was similar to that found among helping pro-

---

Entrapment a component of burnout that occurs when coaches lose their enthusiasm for the job but feel they must stay on for a variety of reasons.

Hardiness a trait identified by Kobasa that includes three components: control, commitment, and challenge; the hardy personality welcomes change as an impetus to growth.

Does Perfectionism Contribute to Burnout?

Perfectionism has been linked to a number of pathological states to include anorexia and bulimia, depression, obsessive-compulsive disorder, and personality disorders. In sport, there have been studies with ballet dancers (Neumarker, Bettle, Neumarker, & Bettle, 2000), male adult body builders (Blouin and Goldfield, 1995), cross-country runners (Hall, Kerr, & Matthews 1998), competitive rowers (Haase, Prapavessis, & Owen, 1999), and youth tennis athletes (Gould, Udry, Tuffey, & Loehr, 1996; Gould, Tuffey, Udry, & Loehr, 1997). Each of these studies has demonstrated to varying degrees that burnout and perfectionism are related in unhealthy ways within some members of their respective athlete samples. This relationship suggests that similar results might be found among coaches in high pressure situations, though little if anything has been done in sport to look at perfectionism as a cause of coaching burnout.

An important first step for future research in this area is to identify a valid and reliable instrument for measuring perfectionism. Currently, the leading measure of perfectionism is that of Frost, Marten, Lahart, and Rosenblate (1990), known as the Multidimensional Perfectionism Scale (FMPS). The FMPS is a 35-item scale that assesses six subdimensions,

though Stober (1998) has suggested the scale is more robust as a measure of four of the six. At any rate, Frost and his colleagues indicate that the FMPS measures Concern Over Mistakes (CM), Personal Standards (PS), Parental Expectations (PE), Parental Criticism (PC), Doubts About Actions (D), and Organization (O). Of these dimensions, by far the most salient is Concern Over Mistakes followed by Doubting of Actions, both of which correlate highly with measures of depression. It would seem, at least on the surface, that worry about mistakes and self-doubt would be common problems for coaches and thus contribute to burnout. Of course, in the final analysis the question is an empirical one, begging for answers through sound research.

Sources: Blouin & Goldfield (1995); Frost, Marten, Lahart, & Rosenblate (1990); Gould, Tuffey, Udry, & Loehr (1996; 1997); Haase, Prapavessis, & Owen (1999); Hall, Kerr, & Matthews (1998); Neumarker, Bettle, Neumarker, & Bettle (2000); Stober (1998).

Perfectionism a trait that compels a person to seek perfection at all costs; linked with a number of pathological states and a possible contributor to burnout.

fessionals in higher education. The scores on exhaustion, depersonalization, and sense of personal accomplishment among their sample were moderate to high, not a very reassuring picture.

The research efforts of Vealey et al. and Kelley and various associates are important because they represent an attempt to integrate personality variables into the understanding of coaching burnout. Obviously, other work linking personality variables and coaching burnout is needed.

Effects of Burnout

According to Pate, Rotella, and McClenaghan (1984), the effects of burnout will be seen in the two parties

closest to the coach, namely, athletes and family. Pate et al. further state that three attributions for explaining burnout will become dominant. The first response tendency is to *blame the athletes* for the existing problems, looking at them as being low in ability or low in motivation. The second tendency is to look inward (self-blame), thereby attributing the problems to *lack of coaching ability*. The third is to point the accusing finger at *the situation* itself. Administrators, lack of overall support, and emphasis on more preferred sport programs become sources of blame for difficulties. The net result of these three blaming strategies is that the coach will sink into some sort of despondent coaching mediocrity or make a career change aimed at restoring motivation and mental well-being.

Coach Rick Pitino's Ten Steps to Success

Rick Pitino, a well-known college and professional basketball coach, has written *Success Is a Choice: Ten Steps to Overachieving in Business and Life* (1998). In this book, Pitino outlines the ten main ingredients of success in business and life. The ten steps would appear to be useful for coaches and athletes, also. The steps are summarized by Balog (1997) as follows:

1. *Build self-esteem.* "Before we truly can start to achieve, we must believe that our value is worth improving."

2. *Set demanding goals.* Identify your weaknesses and set short-term goals to overcome them.

3. *Always be positive.* Block out negativity, accept and adapt to change, and live in the present.

4. *Establish good habits.* For instance: Get to work early. First thing in the morning, tackle all the things you don't want to do.

5. *Master the art of communication.* Communicate directly, not through someone else. Don't let problems fester. Listen four times as much as you speak.

6. *Learn much from role models.* Role models should be people you look up to daily for specific traits, people who can help you.

7. *Thrive on pressure.* If "no one is demanding a superior performance from you, demand it of yourself."

8. *Be ferociously persistent.* Remember the harder you work, the tougher it is to surrender. The "only time failure is truly bad is if you use it as an excuse to quit."

9. *Learn from adversity.* Adversity requires that you step back, evaluate, and determine the lessons you can take away.

10. *Survive success.* Once you become successful, never forget that failure lurks just around the corner. Create a mental one-year contract with yourself to retain a sense of urgency.

Source: Balog (1997).

Preventing Burnout

A well-rounded life is the key to avoiding burnout. Allowing coaching duties to take over one's life to the exclusion of family, friends, and other aspects of life simply does not work in the long run. Burnout is inevitable or highly likely if one has a unidimensional perspective on life. A number of measures can be taken to help prevent burnout.

MAINTAINING AN AWARENESS THAT NO ONE IS IMMUNE TO BURNOUT. Maintaining the awareness that no coach is immune to burnout is an important preventive measure. Winners and losers alike can burn out, and minor sport coaches are not exempt from the burnout so often associated with coaching in major sports. Nor is burnout the exclusive province of collegiate or professional coaches; it can happen at all levels. Finally,

burnout is not an exclusively male phenomenon; in fact, there is evidence to suggest just the opposite. Caccese and Mayerberg (1984), in a study of 138 male and 93 female coaches from NCAA and AIAW Division I, found that female coaches reported significantly higher levels of emotional exhaustion and lower levels of personal accomplishment than did members of a comparable male sample. Clearly, female coaches are susceptible to coaching burnout, perhaps even more so than their male counterparts.

ADOPTING A HEALTHY LIFESTYLE. Keeping one's physical health at an optimal level is an important inoculation against burnout. Coaches who are healthy and fit are likely to feel good, radiate enthusiasm, and serve as role models for their athletes. This overall sense of well-being is contagious; others sense their enthusiasm, take it in, return it to them, and a cycle of enthusiasm is generated.

MAINTAINING SUPPORT SYSTEMS. Having associations with others who understand the coaching situation is important. Other coaches know only too well what an individual coach is going through, and they can serve as sources of tension release. Pate et al. (1984) calls this "blowing out," a process whereby coaches selectively release tension by expressing their frustrations and stresses in the presence of others who will understand these occasional outbursts.

MAINTAINING A SENSE OF HUMOR. Maintaining a sense of humor is crucial to preventing burnout. Being able to laugh at oneself and the frailties and foibles of others can be a real tension reducer. There is considerable humor in life and athletics, and athletes and coaches are rich sources of such material. Daily quotes and numerous books describing the lighter side of sports are commonplace. The coach who contributes to this literature and who appreciates it from others may well be a step up in burnout avoidance.

Undoubtedly, other ingredients of the mentally healthy person merit discussion. Suffice it to say, however, that the points covered here are basic to keeping one's head when all others around seem to be losing theirs, and the end result will be an enjoyable athletic experience for players, coaches, and fans alike. Kelley et al. (1999, p. 127) nicely summarize the issue by stating that "coaches who have a sense of commitment (rather than alienation) with respect to work, family self, and hobbies; who view challenges as opportunities rather than problems; and who believe they control their destinies are likely to appraise situations as less stressful and are less prone to burnout."

SUMMARY

1. Many of the more than 4 million youth coaches in the United States are poorly qualified for their duties, but several programs have been created to improve the situation.

2. The Coaching Behavior Assessment System (CBAS) has been developed with the ultimate goal of upgrading youth coaching. An outgrowth of the CBAS research with Little League coaches and players in Seattle, Washington, was Coach Ef-

fectiveness Training (CET). CET was tried with a sample of coaches matched with a group of coaches who were not given CET. Results indicated that the trained coaches used more reinforcement and less punishment when coaching, were liked better by their players, and were seen as better teachers. Self-esteem gains were noted in their players, though no win–loss advantage occurred as a result of training.

3. Other approaches to improving youth coaching include the National Association for Youth Sport (NAYS), formerly known as the National Youth Sport Coaches Association (NYSCA); Rainer Martens' American Sport Education Program (ASEP); the Institute for the Study of Youth Sport (YSI) at Michigan State University; and the Canadian National Certification Program (CNCP), a program with five levels ranging from instructing novice athletes to coaching the elite youth of Canada.

4. In 1995, approximately 2.5 million young women participated in interscholastic sports and another 123,000 competed at the intercollegiate level. Although female sport participation is on a substantial upswing, female coaches are not faring nearly as well. Their numbers decreased at a rate as high as 40% to 50% in many states in a recent 15-year period. Role conflict, incomplete occupational socialization, and sex discrimination have all been cited as possible explanations for this decline in the number of women in coaching.

5. African-American coaches at the highest levels of the sport of football are rare, particularly as head coaches. Black coaches, like black athletes, are overrepresented at the peripheral and underrepresented at the central positions.

7. Burnout is a common problem in many vocations, and its insidious effects are felt throughout the coaching profession.

8. Taking the job too seriously, having to deal with problem parents and problem athletes, losing the thrill of coaching, feeling the constant pressure always to win, and being underpaid and underappreciated are some of the more prominent situational causes of coaching burnout. Recently,

psychological factors such as state anxiety and psychological hardiness have also been linked to burnout. High-state-anxious coaches and those low in hardiness appear to be susceptible to burnout. These two efforts represent an attempt to link burnout in coaches to psychological constructs, whereas the preponderance of the existing research has looked largely at situational variables.

9. The cognitive-affective model of athletic burnout proposed by Smith represents an attempt to bring additional sophistication to the definition and assessment of the phenomenon.

10. Athletes and the immediate family will be most seriously affected by a coach's burnout, and they interact to exacerbate the problem.

11. Living a broadly based, rewarding life outside of work is an important preventive measure related to coaching burnout. Being aware that burnout can happen to anyone regardless of level of coaching or gender of the coach, keeping one's physical health at an optimum level, having friends with whom one can release tension, and maintaining a sense of humor are other important preventive measures.

KEY TERMS

American Sport Education Program (ASEP) (388)
Canadian National Certification Program (CNCP) (388)
Coach Effectiveness Training (CET) (388)
Coaching Behavior Assessment System (CBAS) (386)
coaching burnout (393)
entrapment (396)
"good old boy" network (392)
hardiness (396)
homologous reproduction (392)
incomplete occupational socialization (391)
Institute for the Study of Youth Sport (YSI) (388)
Maslach Burnout Inventory (MBI) (395)
National Youth Sporting Coaches Association (NYSCA) (388)
perfectionism (397)
Smith's cognitive-affective model of burnout (393)

SUGGESTED READINGS

Feltz, D. L., Chase, M. A., Moritz, S. E., & Sullivan, P. J. (1999). A conceptual model of coaching efficacy: Preliminary investigation and instrument development. *Journal of Educational Psychology, 91,* 765–776.

Coaching efficacy refers to the extent to which coaches think they can affect the performance and game outcome of their athletes. The authors here have attempted to create a measure of coaching efficacy, and preliminary results appear to be supportive. Game strategy, motivation, team technique, and character building were the factors identified through a confirmatory factor analysis procedure. In a study with basketball coaches, preliminary support was found for the instrument. Further research is indicated to see if indeed this is a valid measure for sport psychology.

Horn, T. S. (1993). The self-fulfilling prophecy theory: When coaches' expectations become reality. In J. M. Williams (Ed.), *Applied sport psychology: Personal growth to peak performance* (pp. 68–81). Palo Alto, CA: Mayfield.

Illustrates how Rosenthal and Jacobson's 1968 research study on self-fulfilling prophecy can be turned to the advantage of the youth coach; emphasis is placed on how the expectations set at the beginning of a sport season can become reality. Behavioral recommendations that will assist coaches in the expectancy-performance process are also delineated.

Smoll, R L., & Smith, R. E. (2001). Conducting sport psychology training programs for coaches: Cognitive-behavioral principles and techniques. In J. M. Williams (Ed.), *Applied sport psychology: Personal growth to peak performance* (4th ed., pp. 379–393). Mountain View, CA: Mayfield.

Outlines the Coaching Effectiveness Training program in detail. The implementation of sport psychology workshops for coaches is extensively discussed. Emphasis is placed on getting coaches to use two proven behavioral change procedures, behavioral feedback and self-monitoring, as well as Smoll and Smith's four-part philosophy of winning: (1) Winning isn't everything, nor is it the only thing; (2) failure is not the same thing as losing; (3) success is not equivalent to winning; and (4) athletes should be taught that success is found in striving for victory (i.e., success is related to effort).

INFOTRAC COLLEGE EDITION

For additional readings, explore Infotrac College Edition, your online library. Go to:
http://www.infotrac-college.com/wadsworth

Hint: Enter these search terms: burnout, burnout (prevention), burnout (research), Maslach Burnout Inventory, perfectionism.

Exercise Psychology: Physical Fitness, Adherence, and the Cognitive and Affective Benefits

CHAPTER 25

Physical Fitness

Exercise Adherence

Cognitive and Affective
Consequences of Exercise

Summary

Key Terms

Suggested Readings

This family is skiing together. Skiing is a very popular sport and serves as a good source of exercise for recreational skiers of all ages.

Thus far, we have focused on the more formalized aspects of sport for men, women, and children. However, a number of sport psychologists have devoted their time and energy to promoting an understanding of fitness apart from the everyday world of sport. The popularity of fitness has been the driving force in the broadening of the field of sport psychology to include sport *and exercise* psychology. This chapter will examine issues of general fitness, exercise adherence, and prevention or alleviation of anxiety and depression through exercise.

This fascination with physical fitness has led to a rush of activity that can be measured, informally at least, by a concurrent explosion of facilities for working out, equipment and paraphernalia, television shows demonstrating or extolling the virtues of looking good and being fit, nutritional aids, and other related enterprises. Despite what appears on the surface to be major interest in fitness, the available statistics on adherence to the various exercise regimens are not particularly reassuring. This issue will be addressed shortly, and some recommendations will be made on ways to improve on adherence. Various models used to explain adherence will also be presented, along with the pros and cons of each.

These young people are taking part in a step aerobics class. The use of weights adds an additional exercise component to their workout.
© Copyright 1999 PhotoDisc, Inc.

PHYSICAL FITNESS

Starting in the 1980s, much excitement was generated about a fitness boom in North America. It appeared that everyone was jogging, working out at a fitness center, swimming, walking, or otherwise "getting in shape." One index of the collective penchant for fitness has been the sales of exercise equipment and paraphernalia. An assortment of statistics from a number of editions of *USA Today* in 1994 and 1995 are revealing; in excess of $10 billion is spent annually on active wear, footwear, and exercise equipment.

Nike, the athletic footwear leader, was founded in 1962 by Bill Bowerman, the University of Oregon track coach and one of his runners, Phil Knight. In its first year of operation (1964), Nike sold 1,300 pairs of shoes. In 1993, the company sold 200 pairs of shoes

every minute, or a total of 100 million pairs. By 1998, Nike had garnered 34% of the athletic footwear market over leading competitors Reebok (13%), Adidas (6%), New Balance (5%), and Easy Spirit (2%). Nike sales for the fiscal year 1999 reached $8.8 billion. Profits are now such that golf star Eldrick (Tiger) Woods recently signed an endorsement deal with the shoe company that will pay him $80 million over the life of the contract. The Swoosh symbol so tied to Nike's identification symbolizes a wing from the Greek goddess by the same name and was drawn by a student for the magnificent sum of $35 (Strategic Analysis, 2000).

In terms of actual exercise accomplished, however, the reports are not especially encouraging. Data from the Centers for Disease Control indicate that fewer than 10% of all Americans exercise enough to attain fitness benefits (Westcott, 1995). Data reported by Caspersen and Merritt (1995) based on responses of almost 35,000 adults in 26 states support Westcott's observation; they report that less than one person in 10 in their study was regularly active in intensive exercise. Perhaps an observation by Brown (1993, p. 2C) summarizes the state of the fitness movement at this time: "The fitness boom hasn't exactly pooped out, but it's definitely taking a rest." It is clear from the preceding data and observations that the fitness movement is in need of new life. The challenge to do so is a big one for health and sport psychologists interested in fitness.

Physical Fitness Defined

The terms *physical activity, exercise,* and *physical fitness* tend to be used interchangeably by professionals and laypersons alike. However, Caspersen (1985) suggests that the three terms actually connote quite different activities and should be treated accordingly. **Physical activity** refers to any bodily movement produced by the skeletal muscles that results in an expenditure of energy. Physical activity may be expended as a function of exercise, but the housewife chasing after three young children, the teenager waxing a new automobile, or the water meter reader attempting to elude a dog are also expending energy. **Exercise** is a subset of physical activity characterized by planned, organized, and repetitive components aimed at improving or maintaining physical fitness. Finally, **physical fitness** refers to a set of attributes that are either health or skill related. The President's Council on Physical Fitness (Guidelines, 2000, p. 1) defines physical fitness as follows: "The ability to perform daily tasks vigorously and alertly, with energy left over for enjoying leisure-time activities and meeting emergency demands. It is the ability to endure, to bear up, to withstand stress, to carry on in circumstances where an unfit person could not continue, and it is a major basis for good health and well-being."

According to guidelines from the President's Council, four basic parts of fitness are essential:

1. *Cardiorespiratory endurance:* level of delivery of oxygen and nutrients to body tissues and of waste removal over sustained periods of time. This component is typically measured through swimming and long runs.

2. *Muscular strength:* the ability of a muscle to exert force for brief periods of time. Various weight-lifting activities are used for measurement here.

3. *Muscular endurance:* the ability of a muscle or group of muscles to sustain repeated contractions and exert force against a fixed object. Push-ups, for example, are an example of an activity used to test the muscles in the arms and shoulders.

4. *Flexibility:* the ability to move joints and use muscles through the full range of motion. The sit-and-reach test brings the lower back and the backs of the upper legs into play for assessment of flexibility.

Other researchers argue that *body composition,* the ratio of fat to lean body mass, should also be a part of assessing physical activity. An optimal balance of fat to lean body mass is often regarded as an index of fitness.

A slightly different way of looking at many of the same issues is found in the position stand of the American College of Sports Medicine (ACSM). It is their belief that the following standards constitute the essence of a comprehensive cardiorespiratory fitness, body composition, and muscular strength and endurance program:

1. Frequency of training: three to five days per week.

2. Intensity of training: 60% to 90% of maximum heart rate, or 50% to 85% of VO2 Max (a measure of maximal aerobic capacity for endurance exercise).

3. Duration of training: 20 to 60 minutes each time, depending on the type of activity.

4. Mode of activity: any activity that uses large muscle groups that can be maintained over time and is rhythmic and aerobic in nature.

5. Resistance training: strength training of a moderate intensity.

Proponents of physical fitness are adamant in their claims about the benefits to be gained from physical activity in the sport and exercise context. Many authorities point to a host of physical and psychological benefits.

Physical Benefits

A 2000 report from the Centers for Disease Control mentions several physical benefits associated with physical fitness. One is a reduction in the likelihood of premature death, either from cardiovascular disease mortality and what Cantwell and Fontanarosa (1996)

Physical activity any bodily movement produced by the skeletal muscles that results in an expenditure of energy.
Exercise a subset of physical activity characterized by planned, organized, and repetitive components aimed at improving or maintaining physical fitness.
Physical fitness a set of attributes that are related either to health or to skills.

call **all-cause mortality.** To this point, Blair, Kampert, Kohl, Barlow, Macera, Paffenbarger, and Gibbons (1996) reported data from a study of fitness levels of 32,000 men and women. Their data indicated that low fitness was a significant risk factor for early mortality, even when other variables such as high blood pressure and smoking were taken into consideration. Another related study by Lee, Hsieh, and Paffenbarger (1995) reported that vigorous but not nonvigorous physical activity is associated with longevity. Their claims were based on the results of a study conducted on over 17,000 Harvard University alumni who entered the university as undergraduates in the years 1916 through 1950. Physical activity was assessed by asking alumni about flights of stairs climbed, city blocks walked, types of sports and recreational activities engaged in, and the amount of time devoted each week to these sports and recreational activities. Mortality statistics were gathered from the Harvard Alumni Office, which keeps weekly rosters of deceased alumni. Statistical analyses indicated a very strong relationship between vigorous physical activity and longevity in this sample. Lee et al. made an additional important point: Nonvigorous exercise is preferable to being sedentary in terms of overall health if not longevity.

Another physical benefit may well be found in *resistance to disease.* One of these diseases discussed by Shephard and Shek (1998) is colon cancer, where fitness is linked to a reduction in risk, though the precise nature of the linkage remains speculative. The explanation may well reside in something as simple as the suggestion by Williams and Long (1983) that digestive and excretory functioning may be enhanced by being physically fit. Obesity has also been linked with colon cancer, and fitness and obesity are largely antithetical states. Other reports point to the efficacy of physical fitness in preventing or ameliorating the effects of HIV/AIDS (Stringer, 1999), menopause (Shangold & Sherman, 1998), and pregnancy complications (Koltyn & Schultes, 1997; Williams, Reilly, Campbell, & Sutherst, 1988). Legwold (1985) has suggested yet another fitness benefit in terms of an improved sex life, a notion also mentioned by Williams and Long (1983).

All-cause mortality death for any reason; reduction in premature all-cause mortality has been associated with physical fitness.

There has also been the suggestion that fitness promotes *healthy sleep habits.* Given that insomnia affects perhaps as many as one-third of all adults (Youngstedt, 1997), it would certainly be nice if the assertion about the fitness–sleep interplay were true. Singh, Clements, and Fiatarone (1997) found that sleep quality improved as a function of an exercise regimen in their subjects. Youngstedt (1997) and Youngstedt, O'Connor, and Dishman (1997), based on their review of the literature in this area, raise some serious methodological questions about sleep and exercise research. One caveat they raise is that most studies have been conducted on people with generally good sleep habits in the first place. Related to this point is the discrepancy often found between what people report about their sleep habits and what more objective measures indicate.

A physical fitness benefit often mentioned that may not be a benefit after all is a *lowered resting heart rate.* Authorities such as LaPorte et al. (1985), Legwold (1985), and Rogers (1985) argue that there is little or no evidence that a low resting heart rate is an indicator of superior cardiac functioning. It may tell us nothing about the person other than the fact that he or she is still alive.

Psychological Benefits

Among the psychological gains associated with physical fitness, some authorities point to *anxiety or stress reduction,* a topic we will discuss in detail later. There may also be benefits in terms of socialization, that is, meeting new people and creating new friendships and acquaintances and maintaining old ones. How many of us who exercise regularly have our exercise behavior maintained by working out with a friend or several friends? And how many of us would continue our exercise regimen if our partner(s) suddenly stopped going?

Another psychological benefit for the more serious fitness buff is the *thrill of competition.* To see this competitive urge in action, just line up some Saturday in the nearest triathlon, 10-kilometer run, or marathon event. One of the virtues of these competitions is that they serve as a showcase for most of the other physical and psychological benefits of fitness.

Steinberg, Sykes, Moss, Lowery, LeBoutillier, and Dewey (1997) suggest yet another psychological benefit of exercise, and that is *enhancement of creativity.* Using an adjective checklist mood measure and the Torrance

Does Riding a Bike Cause Impotence?

Some authorities have suggested that one of the benefits of vigorous exercise is an improved sex life. Certainly, publishers of popular magazines such as *Men's Health* capitalize on this belief in promoting their product. Each edition has an article devoted to the fitness/sexuality theme. But what about riding a bicycle for exercise? It seems to be a tremendously popular forum for exercise and fitness, but a growing literature suggests that riding a bicycle can actually be linked to impotence or erectile dysfunction.

One authority, Dr. Irwin Goldstein, cites a statistic that 100,000 men have suffered permanent impotence from bicycling (New Findings, 1999). Goldstein traces riding-related impotence back several thousand years ago to Hippocrates, who noted that sexual problems were common among horsemen of that era. The physical problem, as Goldstein sees it, has to do with the archaic design and lack of anatomic fit of the typical bicycle seat and the compression damage done to nerves and blood supply in the genital area. Several studies comparing bicyclists with controls show significantly more moderate-to-complete impotency in the cyclists.

Others believe that Goldstein and others have overstated their case concerning the bicycle–impotency relationship, but Goldstein contends that even if the rates of impotency are lower than found in his and other studies, a rate as low as 4% is still significant when one takes into account that probably 50 million people ride bikes. Goldstein is also quick to point out that there are bike riders and there are bike riders. What he means, of course, is that there are degrees of seriousness about cycling. If the activity places the participant at risk for erectile disorder, it is going to be proportional to at least two things, the bicycle seat used and the sheer amount of time spent on the bicycle. The competitive seat, he says, is the most damaging, and those are the same people who log lots of time and miles on a bicycle.

Interestingly, and perhaps predictably, women are not exempt from problems related to riding a bicycle. Traumatic contact with the seat, perineal numbness, urethral stricture, and pelvic fractures (in rare instances) are potential complications women bicyclists must contend with.

SOURCE: New Findings (1999).

---

test of creativity, Steinberg et al. assigned their subjects to a dance aerobics group, an aerobics group, and a neutral group that watched videos. Mood was improved in both aerobics groups by 25%, and there were noticeable but not statistically significant changes in aspects of creativity as measured by the Torrance tests.

EXERCISE ADHERENCE

Perhaps as many as 20–25 million people in the United States exercise on a regular basis, and most extol its many physical, psychological, and social virtues. Substantial numbers of others would like to obtain the benefits of exercise but cannot stay with a program long enough to do so; the virtue of **exercise adher-** ence eludes them. This inability to stick with an exercise regimen is one of the more perplexing problems facing professionals in sport and exercise psychology as well as health psychology.

Godin, Desharnais, Valois, and Bradet (1995) state that it is generally accepted in the exercise adherence literature that 50% of the individuals who start a fitness campaign will drop out in six months or less. These statistics refer to individuals with no known cardiovascular problems. In individuals with a documented history of cardiovascular problems, adherence rates to postmyocardial infarction exercise prescriptions are

---

Exercise adherence ability to follow an exercise regimen on a regular basis over an extended period of time.

equally poor. Sanne (1973) studied 148 post-MI patients in Sweden and found that 29% of the group never began prescribed exercise programming. At the end of two years, 29% of the original 148 patients were working out under a hospital administered exercise program (another 17% said they were working out at home on their own). By the four-year mark, 14% were still working out at the hospital and 18% reported exercising on their own, an overall adherence rate for four years of 32%. In another study, Andrew, Oldridge, Parker, Cunningham, Rechnitzer, Jones, Buck, Kavanagh, Shephard, Sutton, and McDonald (1981) found an exercise noncompliance rate of over 44% in their longitudinal study of 728 postcoronary men in Ontario, Canada. While some of the patients in each of these studies either never started or dropped out of prescribed exercise due to valid medical contraindications, the adherence rate in MI patients appears to be less than satisfactory. Overall, Oldridge (1988) indicates that 40% to 50% of referred patients drop out of cardiac rehabilitation programs in 12 months or less from the time of initial physician referral.

With regard to healthy individuals, the Centers for Disease Control (CDC) has released a series of statistics that are less than reassuring. Among the statistics are: (1) Nearly half of American youths ages 12–21 are not involved in a program of regular exercise; (2) daily enrollment in physical education classes has dropped from 42% to 25% among high school students between 1991 and 1995; (3) approximately 60% of adults do not engage in the recommended amount of physical activity daily, and 25% are not active at all; (4) among older adults, 33% of men and 50% of women ages 75 and older engage in no physical activity whatsoever.

Because adherence rates are low for both healthy individuals and those with a history of heart problems, it seems worthwhile to take a look at predictors of exercise adherence, reasons that people fail to comply with exercise programs, and some ways that exercise adherence might be improved.

Predictors of Exercise Adherence

There are a number of physical, psychological, and social predictors of exercise adherence. Perhaps the most salient of these predictors is *physical proximity* to the exercise area, which, as Roth (1974) points out, under-

scores the importance of practical considerations in exercise adherence. Studies in which geographical proximity to the exercise area has been cited include Teraslinna, Partanen, Koskela, Partanen, and Oja (1969), with Finnish business executives; Andrew et al. (1981), with Canadian heart patients; and Hanson (1977), with American college professors. In each of the studies, proximity was important to the continuance of exercise; in the Teraslinna et al. study, proximity was the single biggest determinant.

Another finding is that *spousal support* is important in exercise adherence. McCready and Long (1985) point to a positive though not overwhelming correlation between spousal support and continuance in exercise programs. Dishman (1984, p. 425) states that "a spouse's attitude toward a participant's involvement is a greater influence in the participant's behavior than is his or her own attitude."

It has been suggested that *exercising in small as opposed to large groups* is conducive to exercise continuance (Dishman, 1984). It seems logical that most of the reinforcement associated with exercise should be realized when groups are small and attention from instructors and peers is maximized. Shephard (1985) indicates that many people are intimidated by mixed classes, so provisions should be made in certain instances to have male and female groupings for exercise.

Another mild indicator of exercise adherence is apparently *socioeconomic status*. That exercise may not be reaching an optimal number of people is a challenge issued by Shephard (1985), who states that greater targeting of blue-collar workers and people at the lower end of the white-collar work strata should be carried out by the exercise leadership.

At a psychological level, preliminary data has implicated an *internal locus of control* as a correlate of exercise adherence. Levenson (1981) has intimated that subjects engaged in health-related activities tend to be more internal on her IPC scale (discussed at several other points in this book), a finding corroborated by McCready and Long (1985) and Noland (1981).

Why People Drop Out of Exercise Programs

A number of negative predictors of exercise adherence have been identified. From the discussion of positive

Models for Analyzing Exercise Behavior

Godin and Shephard (1990) have written an informative review article on six theoretical frameworks borrowed from the broader field of psychology that have been used for analyzing exercise behavior. They are:

1. *Health Belief Model (HBM):* This model, which has its origins in the work of Becker and associates (1977), supposes that the likelihood of adopting a particular behavior appropriate to preventing or controlling a disease is a function of the perceived threat it represents for health and a concomitant belief that the appropriate response will reduce this threat.

2. *Protective Motivation Theory (PMT):* This model is similar to HBM but relies more heavily on fear communication. Rogers (Maddux & Rogers, 1983; Rogers, 1983) has extended HBM by incorporating Bandura's self-efficacy theory into the original model. In HBM, four factors govern the motivation to protect oneself: (1) perceived severity of a threatening event, (2) perceived probability of its occurrence, (3) efficacy of the proposed preventive behavior, and (4) perceived self-efficacy of the individual making the response.

3. *Social Cognitive Theory (SCT):* Essentially, this is a recapitulation or restatement of Bandura's social learning theory, with considerable emphasis on self-efficacy.

4. *Theory of Reasoned Action (TRA):* Fishbein and Ajzen (1975) are the prime proponents of this model, which places much emphasis on individual attitudes toward a particular behavioral response and the social factors that bear on the decision-making process. TRA has been used extensively and is, according to Godin and Shephard, very useful in understanding the decision-making process underlying exercise behavior. These authors present a summary table in their 1990 article of 13 studies involving exercise and TRA.

5. *Theory of Interpersonal Behavior:* Advanced by Triandis (1977), this theory specifies that the likelihood of engaging in a particular behavior is a function of three variables: habit strength, intention, and conditions that encourage or discourage performance of the intended behavior. Much emphasis in this model is placed on the affective dimension of attitude as opposed to the cognitive aspect.

6. *Theory of Planned Behavior:* Ajzen (1985), in a departure from the TRA model of Ajzen and Fishbein (1980), suggests that TRA is useful in explaining voluntary behaviors but is less so with involuntary ones. Perceived behavioral control, an essential component of this theory, represents an extension of facets of TRA and has much in common with Bandura's notion of self-efficacy. Currently, few investigators have employed this model as a vehicle for conducting their research.

A test of three of these exercise behavior models has been made by Yordy and Lent (1993). They compared the reasoned action, planned behavior, and social cognitive models in explaining exercise intentions and behavior by asking 284 introductory psychology students to respond to scenarios related to each of the models. At the same time, previous exercise activity and future exercise intentions and actual behaviors were assessed. Results showed support for the reasoned action and social cognitive models in predicting intentions and behaviors; less support was found for the reasoned action model. Though the Yordy and Lent study acknowledged possible methodological flaws and dealt with only three of the six competing models, we expect this sort of research to accelerate over the next several years, thereby lending insights into exercise behavior.

SOURCES: Ajzen (1985); Becker, Haefner, Kasl, Kirscht, Maiman, & Rosenstock (1977); Fishbein & Ajzen (1975); Godin & Shephard (1990); Maddox & Rogers (1983); Triandis (1977); Yordy & Lent (1993).

predictors, it seems clear that poor accessibility to the exercise area, lack of spousal support, and exercising in large and potentially impersonal groups have considerable impact on whether a person complies with an exercise regimen. Beyond these problems, *time* appears to be a significant determinant of exercise adherence (Dishman, 1986; Shephard, 1985). Time and *accessibility* probably constitute a grouping that accounts for much of the variance in exercise adherence. The extent to which the time–accessibility interaction is true, however, remains to be determined. Sime, Whipple, Stamler, and Berkson (1978) found that dropouts in their study perceived time and accessibility to be problems even though they actually lived closer to their workout environment than did the exercise compliers with whom they were compared.

Another problem associated with exercise adherence is *smoking*. Several authorities have noted the tendency of smokers to drop out of exercise programs (e.g., Massie & Shephard, 1971) and, at the other extreme, the equal tendency on the part of nonsmokers to comply (McCready & Long, 1985).

A third negative predictor is *poor choice of exercise*. Persons beginning an exercise program should weigh the merits of various forms of exercise and choose one that is within their physical capabilities and their general interests. A poorly chosen exercise program is destined to fail. A listing of some of the more popular forms of exercise and their benefits and costs can be seen in Table 25.1.

Related to choice of exercise is the issue of *injury*. All too often, the beginning exerciser is looking for a quick fix, and this misplaced emphasis often results in an injury that in turn dampens enthusiasm for further exercise. Poor choice of type of exercise, too much exercise too soon, and poor equipment selection all interact to produce the injury effect. The beginning exerciser should choose appropriate exercise, opt for a proper workout environment (to include proper instruction), and select suitable equipment.

Type A personality an aggressive, hard-driving, competitive person, at risk for coronary heart disease.
Extraversion a personality trait defined by greater interest in the environment than in oneself; "outgoing" rather than inward looking.

In addition to the locus of control dimension mentioned earlier, two other psychological constructs have been positively linked to the exercise adherence literature, and they are the Type A personality and extraversion. The **Type A personality** is associated with an aggressive, hard-driving, hard-working, time-pressured, and highly competitive individual who is prone, among other things, to being at high risk for coronary heart disease (Friedman & Rosenman, 1974). According to research reported by Oldridge, Wicks, Hanley, Sutton, and Jones (1978), Type A individuals appear to have relatively poor exercise adherence rates. Dishman (1984) interprets the results reported by Oldridge and his colleagues as reflective of either a lack of patience with the seemingly slow pace of the typical fitness program or as a result of setting other competing goals that eventually take priority over exercise. It may be that these competing activities provide the more immediate feedback necessary to the psychological sustenance of the Type A personality.

As for **extraversion,** several studies have mentioned higher compliance rates for extraverted as opposed to introverted personalities (Blumenthal, Williams, Wallace, Williams, & Needles, 1982; Courneya & Hellsten, 1998; Massie & Shephard, 1971). Since extraverts assuredly derive more reinforcement from group interactions than introverts, it is not surprising that the extravert/exercise relationship has been noted.

While the concepts of the Type A personality and the extravert are interesting ones, they need further research. Any number of other personality dimensions are surely pertinent to exercise compliance, and studies should be undertaken with the goal of expanding our knowledge base about psychological constructs and fitness.

Improving Exercise Adherence

Dishman (1984, 1991) has reviewed 56 studies that used behavior modification procedures, and much of the ensuing discussion will be based on his synthesis of the research. Dishman suggests that while we may have varying amounts of control over situational variables such as spousal support, socioeconomic class, professional or blue-collar status, and so forth, we must acknowledge these multiple realities and work within the constraints they create.

TABLE 25.1

Benefits and Costs of Some Popular Forms of Physical Activity

Activity	Aerobics	Fat Loss	Strength	Muscle Endurance	Flexi-bility	Total	Injury rate	Workout Time (min.)	Start-Up Costs
Maximum Score	★★★★	★	★★	★★	★	10			
Swimming	★★★★	★	★	★★	★	9	low	30	$20–$975*
Cross-country skiing (outdoors)	★★★★	★	★	★★	↗	8.5	medium	25	$100–$200
Circuit weight training	★★↗	↗	★★	★★	↗	7.5	medium	30	$200–$675*
Running	★★★★	★	↗	★↗		7	high	25	$40–$85
Aerobic dance	★★★	★	★	★↗	↗	7	high	35	$30–$675*
Cycling (outdoors)	★★★↗	★	★	★		6.5	high†	35	$150–$750
Rowing machine	★★★	★	★	★↗		6.5	medium	35	$100–$400
Walking	★★★↗	★	↗	★		6	low	45	$40–$85
Stair climbing (machine)	★★★↗	★	↗	★		6	low	25	$120–$2,000
Golf (carrying clubs)	★★↗	★	↗	★↗	↗	6	low	45	$200–$725
Rope skipping	★★★↗	↗	↗	★		5.5	medium	25	$45–$80
Racquetball/squash	★★★	★	↗	↗	↗	5.5	medium	35	$70–$815*
Basketball/soccer	★★★	↗	↗	★		5	high	40	$30–$125
Weight training	★		★★	★↗	↗	5	medium	60	$130–$675*
Tennis (singles)	★★↗	↗	↗	↗	↗	4.5	medium	45	$80–$315
Calisthenics	★↗		★	★	★	4.5	low	60	$40–$55

Source: Health and Fitness (1990).
*Upper range includes club fees. †Includes collisions without helment.

One of the approaches suggested by Dishman is **behavioral contracting.** In this situation, exercise specifics are spelled out with the cooperation of both the exerciser and the person(s) supervising the workout. Once the details are worked out to the satisfaction of both parties, a behavioral contract is signed that more or less publicly binds the exerciser to the mutually determined agreement.

Lotteries represent a second behavioral technique for maximizing exercise adherence. Exercise is determined on a daily basis through a lottery system, or what might be referred to as "luck of the draw." Various exercise programs are thrown into the lottery formula, and the person using this approach simply works out according to what he or she draws on any particular day. This approach makes an attempt to reward the exerciser on a random basis, which should relieve some of the boredom found in repetitive programs of exercise.

Self-monitoring and stimulus cueing are two goal-setting techniques that have been effective. In **self-monitoring,** objective records are kept and serve as

---

Behavioral contracting exercise adherence strategy in which the exerciser and his or her trainer enter a binding contract about the program to be followed.
Lotteries exercise adherence strategy in which the exerciser draws the day's regimen at random as a way of relieving boredom.
Self-monitoring exercise adherence strategy in which the exerciser monitors his or her weight loss, heart rate, or blood pressure, generating objective records that serve as reinforcers.

highly identifiable reinforcers for exercise. Variables such as weight loss and heart rate or blood pressure can be monitored for feedback purposes. Examples of event-specific items include mileage in jogging and varying degrees of resistance, repetitions, and sets in weight programs. **Stimulus cueing** involves exercising using the same activity at the same time and place every day. There is much to be said for the adherence potential of such regimentation, since exercise thus becomes a part of everyday activities.

Crucial to an understanding of the various behavioral approaches is the concept of **reinforcement** or **reward.** The more reinforcement that can be provided in the exercise environment, the more likely exercisers are to repeat the desired response of adherence. This relationship between reinforcement and response, of course, is at the heart of conditioning and learning, discussed in detail in Chapter 5. Shephard (1985), at a very practical level, suggests that exercise rewards may be symbolic (badge, T-shirt), material (money, time off from work), or psychological (friendship, recognition). Regardless of how the various rewards may be structured and dispensed, they are essential in some form or fashion if the goal of exercise adherence is to be achieved.

Speaking of stamping in behavior through reinforcement, there is considerable evidence that things learned early in the individual's reinforcement history are among the most powerful. It follows that early reinforced experiences with exercise and fitness will have long-term positive consequences. In this context, the work of Shephard and associates is most salient (Shephard, 1995, 1997; Shephard, Laurencelle, Tremblay, Rajic, & Shephard, 1999). In the first two articles, Shephard makes a strong plea for the institution and support of regular physical education classes in public schools. In support of this call, the 1999 Shephard et al. study compared male and female adults who had five physical education classes per week through the first six years of elementary school with a matched sample drawn at random from an existing data bank. Each sub-

ject gave a self-report of current physical activity, attitudes toward physical activity, intentions to exercise, and perception of barriers to exercise. A frequency distribution revealed higher physical activity rates among the female experimental subjects. Similarities were also noted in attitudes, intentions, and perceived barriers to exercise between experimental and control group subjects. The authors concluded that daily physical education at the primary school level set a tone for long-term continuation of exercise, at least with women, despite existing similarities in attitudes, intentions, and perceived barriers.

COGNITIVE AND AFFECTIVE CONSEQUENCES OF EXERCISE

A regular program of exercise is thought to have positive cognitive and affective consequences for both normal and clinical populations. The actual data bearing on this important and complex issue of fitness and its psychological benefits are less compelling. Not all research has found the purported benefits, and many of the existing studies have been plagued with a host of theoretical and methodological ills. The end result is a cloudy picture of the relationship between fitness and psychological well being.

In this section an attempt will be made to shed light on what is known about exercise and its consequences for cognitive and affective functioning. Much of what will follow is an amalgamation of review articles by Folkins and Sime (1981) and Tomporowski and Ellis (1986).

Cognitive Effects

The pioneering work of Jean Piaget (1936) on the relationship between motor development and cognitive development in children has sparked considerable research in various areas of psychology for more than 60 years. Folkins and Sime (1981) reviewed the available literature on the relationship between exercise and cognitive functioning and concluded that while success has been achieved with geriatric mental patients, the picture was much less clear with normal children and adults, where conflicting results dominate. Tomporowski and Ellis (1986) have reviewed several dozen

---

Stimulus cueing exercise adherence strategy in which the exerciser performs the same activity at the same time and place every day.

Reinforcement behavioral control strategy that stimulates response; also known as **reward.**

studies and have generally arrived at the same conclusions as Folkins and Sime. In their review, Tomporowski and Ellis categorized the available studies in one of four ways: (1) very brief, high-intensity anaerobic exercise; (2) short duration, high-intensity anaerobic exercise; (3) short duration, moderate-intensity aerobic exercise; and (4) long duration aerobic exercise.

VERY BRIEF HIGH-INTENSITY ANAEROBIC EXERCISE. By the very nature of the type of exercise used in anaerobic studies, the physical measures involved a variety of strength tests (e.g., hand dynamometers, weights suspended on pulleys). Most of the research was aimed at testing the inverted-U hypothesis. Results generally indicated that moderate levels of anaerobic exercise facilitate cognitive performance, as measured by such things as addition problems, digit-span tests, perception of geometric figures, and paired associate learning. High and low levels of tension, in contrast, did not facilitate cognitive functioning.

SHORT-DURATION HIGH-INTENSITY ANAEROBIC EXERCISE. The results here are most inconclusive. Six of 11 studies surveyed showed no effects; several showed facilitation of cognitive functioning up to 10 or 15 minutes of exercise, at which time impaired performance became dominant. One additional study showed cognitive impairment at all points. Bicycle pedaling, step-up tasks, or treadmill running were paired with discrimination or arithmetic tasks in these various studies.

SHORT-DURATION MODERATE-INTENSITY AEROBIC EXERCISE. Calisthenics, step-up tasks, bicycle pedaling, treadmill running, and run–jog–walk tasks were used as exercises, and a host of cognitive tasks were employed in this group of studies. Studies in which moderate levels of exercise were used tended to report improved cognitive functioning with increases in arousal. Also, highly fit subjects performed better than less physically fit people on cognitive tasks that were administered in the moderate intensity exercise condition.

LONG-DURATION AEROBIC EXERCISE. Tomporowski and Ellis cited only three studies within this category. A marathon race, a 5-mile march carrying a 40-pound pack, and a treadmill task to fatigue were used as long-duration aerobic events, with signal detection, perceptual organization, and a free-recall memory test serving as the cognitive measures. Facilitation was found in two studies (Gliner, Matsen-Twisdale, Horvath, & Maron, 1979; Lybrand, Andrews, & Ross, 1954), and no effect was found in the third (Tomporowski, Ellis, & Stephens, 1985). Clearly, there is a dearth of research related to assessing the effects of long-duration aerobic exercise and cognitive functioning.

The inability of the available research to arrive at a consensus concerning exercise and cognitive functioning has been brought about by a variety of problems. Little of what has been done has been tied to theory, and methodological flaws are numerous. For example, selection bias is found whereby many subjects are volunteers who are often physically fit and highly motivated prior to any interventions. These volunteers are often compared with themselves or with control groups who differ greatly in fitness, motivation, and many other attributes. Folkins and Sime (1981, p. 386) sum up the selection bias problem as follows: "Self-selected, motivated volunteers may demonstrate improvement in psychological functioning simply because they are motivated for overall self-improvement. It is therefore necessary to arrange for control groups that have time exposure equal to that of trainees, as well as equal and justified expectations for benefit."

Both Folkins and Sime and Tomporowski and Ellis have made suggestions for improving future research in fitness and cognitive functioning. One suggestion is to pay more attention to the measurement of the physical effects brought about by exercise. An example would be the measurement of lactic acid produced by exercise (Fox, 1984). Another is employment of the perceived exertion methodology of Borg (1973). Yet a third measure of precision is cardiovascular functioning. A fourth improvement suggestion has to do with assessing pre-intervention levels of fitness. Comparing highly fit, highly motivated subjects with less fit and perhaps unmotivated individuals undoubtedly contributes little to our understanding of the important issues at hand. Fifth, greater attention should be devoted to systematic analysis of the intensity and duration of exercise and the temporal placement of the measures of cognitive functioning (that is, during or after exercise). Finally, the veritable smorgasbord of cognitive tests used across the variable research studies has contributed to the currently inconclusive picture of the exercise–cognition

Rest and Meditation: Good as Exercise?

Many sport and health psychologists maintain that exercise is a tension reducer. Raglin and Morgan (1985) believe that the distraction or diversion associated with exercise may account for the assumed anxiety reduction. In an earlier test of this hypothesis, Bahrke and Morgan (1978) randomly assigned 75 males to three conditions, one involving *aerobic exercise,* another *meditation,* and a third *quiet rest.* Predictions were that the aerobic exercise and meditation conditions would result in reduced state anxiety as measured by the State–Trait Anxiety Inventory (STAI); in fact, both treatments resulted in reduced anxiety. Surprisingly, however, the quiet rest group experienced similar reductions in state anxiety.

Morgan and his associates point out that their findings may suggest a *quantitative* difference in state anxiety that in no way addresses the *qualitative* issues associated with exercise. A number of physiological changes, such as lowered blood pressure, may not occur as a result of quiet rest or meditation. Also, it is possible that the desirable effects associated with exercise may be much more long lasting than those related to meditation or rest.

SOURCES: Bahrke & Morgan (1978); Raglin & Morgan (1985).

---

issue. In all likelihood, many dimensions of cognition have been tapped in the past, and greater selectivity in choosing future cognitive tasks might yield more valid results.

Effects on Mood

Affect and *mood* are terms that have long been used synonymously in the psychological literature; of the various mood states, two that have come under considerable scrutiny in the exercise literature are anxiety and depression, and the discussion will be limited to these two constructs.

EXERCISE AND ANXIETY. One of the generally assumed outcomes of exercise is anxiety reduction, and the literature is supportive of this claim. Folkins and Sime (1981) cite 14 studies dealing with exercise and affect, 13 of which reported improvement in mood. Of the 13 positive reports, seven dealt with anxiety and all pointed to improvement related to that particular affective dimension.

As noted earlier, one of the more popular measures of anxiety has been the State–Trait Anxiety Inventory (STAI) (Spielberger, Gorsuch, & Lushene, 1970), which has been used widely in the exercise and affec-

tive state research. For example, Long (1984) studied 61 volunteers from a selected community using the STAI, among other things. Long's subjects were administered the STAI prior to being assigned to an aerobics conditioning program involving jogging, a waiting list control group, or a stress inoculation training group that was treated for 10 weeks in accordance with the system popularized by Meichenbaum (1977). A posttreatment and a three-month follow-up testing session were also used in Long's research. Results indicated that self-report statements concerning anxiety (the STAI) decreased in both the jogging and the stress inoculation training groups. These changes were still in effect for both groups at the three-month measurement. In a 15-month follow-up study, Long (1985) reported data from 45 of her original 61 subjects, and continued reports of less anxiety were noted. Consistent with data reported earlier in this chapter, only 40% of the jogging treatment group were still working out at the time the 15-month follow-up was conducted. Generally supportive of Long's findings is the work of Berger (1987), who found decreases in state but not trait anxiety in a study of individuals trying to achieve fitness through swimming. Similar decreases in anxiety have been noted by Boutcher and Landers (1988) with regular runners and by Roth (1989) with both active and inactive subjects working on a stationary cycling regimen.

In an effort to bring closure to the anxiety–exercise relationship, Long and van Stavel (1995) conducted a meta-analysis of 40 studies and found that exercise training improved overall anxiety levels .36 standard deviations over alternative or control conditions. Adults living high-stress lifestyles appeared to profit the most from exercise training.

It thus appears that anxiety reduction can be achieved through a regular program of exercise. However, critics point either to negative findings found elsewhere but not reported here or to research flaws in the studies reporting positive effects. Accordingly, Raglin and Morgan (1985, p. 182) assert that it would be best to view the relationship between exercise and anxiety reduction as follows: "physical activity of a vigorous nature is associated with improved mood state but available research does not support the commonly held view that exercise causes their observed alterations in mood." Until such time as causative links are clearly delineated, it seems appropriate to accept the Raglin and Morgan caveat as illustrative of the current state of the art related to exercise and anxiety reduction.

Additional testimony to the fragile nature of the anxiety and exercise relationship is offered by Desharnais, Jobin, Cote, Levesque, and Godin (1993), who indicate that there may be a strong placebo effect associated with exercise. Desharnais et al. placed 48 healthy adults engaged in a 10-week exercise program into two equal groups, experimentals and controls. They led the experimental subjects to believe that their regimen was specifically designed to facilitate psychological well-being. No such intervention was made with the second group. Subsequent measures of fitness indicated improvements for both groups over the 10-week exercise program; however, the experimental subjects improved significantly with regard to scores on a measure of self-esteem when compared with the controls. While these findings need replication, they are further testimony to the tenuous nature of the anxiety and exercise connection.

EXERCISE AND DEPRESSION. Depression is a well-documented source of human suffering. According to Comer (2001), 5% to 10% of Americans suffer from depression in any given year; one of six people world-wide will experience depression in their lifetime. Depression is at the root of most suicides, with perhaps 80% or more being depression related (Monahan, 1986). Depression is characterized by withdrawal, inactivity, a sense of hopelessness, and loss of control. Through its potential for acting on some or all of these symptoms, physical exercise has become popular as a therapeutic intervention in depression.

The use of physical exercise as part of the treatment of depression received much impetus in the late 1970s from a scientific report by Greist, Klein, Eischens, and Faris (1978) as well as from popular books extolling the virtues of running as a means of promoting overall well-being (Fixx, 1977). Considering the pivotal role the work of Greist and his associates has played in the exercise-as-therapy-for-depression movement, a brief elaboration on their work seems warranted. In their study, subjects (men and women) who had been diagnosed as clinically depressed were assigned to one of three groups, a time-limited psychotherapy group ($n = 9$), a time-unlimited psychotherapy group ($n = 7$), and a running treatment group ($n = 8$). The time-limited psychotherapy group received 10 therapy sessions emphasizing immediate change strategies; the time-unlimited group was given a form of psychodynamic therapy; and the eight runners met with a running therapist (not a psychologist or psychiatrist). Stretching, 30 to 45 minutes of walking and running, discussions while exercising with little emphasis on the depression itself, and further stretching characterized the intervention for the running group. According to Greist et al., six of the eight patients were essentially well at the end of three weeks, another at the end of the sixteenth week, and one neither improved nor deteriorated although her overall fitness level improved. The overall conclusion was that running was as successful as traditional psychotherapy and at a considerable saving in terms of money and time for the clients. Though the Greist et al. study is not above criticism, the work has been well received concerning the possible utility of exercise as a means of dealing with depression. Brown, in a burst of enthusiasm, says, "It's almost too good to be true. If you could bottle it and sell it over the counter, you'd make hundreds" (Monahan, 1986, p. 197).

Greist et al. are quick to point out that while other exercise modalities are probably quite useful, they used

Hypotheses Used to Account for Anxiety Reduction Associated With Exercise

Morgan (1985) and Raglin and Morgan (1985) have suggested that the purported anxiolytic (i.e., anxiety reducing) properties of exercise may be associated with at least four assumptions:

1. The **distraction hypothesis:** This hypothesis hinges on the proposition that various exercise strategies serve to divert or distract subjects from anxiety-producing stressors. It thus serves as a psychological explanation for the anxiety-reducing properties of exercise.

2. The **endorphin hypothesis:** Here, the emphasis is on the release of "morphine-like" chemicals within the pituitary gland and the brain that serve to reduce the painful effects while concurrently enhancing the euphoric aspects of exercise. Reports by Droste, Greenlee, Schreck, and Roskamm (1991) in Germany and Kraemer, Dzewaltowski, Blair, Rinehardt, and Castracane (1990) in the United States in which the endorphin hypothesis has not been substantiated cast suspicion on its validity. Nevertheless, the hypothesis remains intriguing and will undoubtedly continue to generate future research.

3. The **thermogenic hypothesis:** In essence, this hypothesis asserts that the tension reduction associated with exercise is produced by the elevation of body temperature.

Among other things, it works in favor of the tension-reducing properties of, for example, sauna baths.

4. The **monoamine hypothesis:** Largely a model based on research with animals, the monoamine hypothesis asserts that anxiety reduction is brought about by exercise through its alteration of various neurotransmitter substances—namely, norepinephrine and serotonin—within the brain.

SOURCES: Morgan (1985); Raglin & Morgan (1985); Droste, Greenlee, Schreck, & Roskamm (1991); Kraemer, Dzewaltowski, Blair, Rinehardt, & Castracane (1990).

Distraction hypothesis the subject's distraction or diversion from stressors produces the anxiety reduction associated with exercise.

Endorphin hypothesis the release of chemicals within the subject's pituitary gland and brain produces the anxiety reduction associated with exercising.

Thermogenic hypothesis the elevation of the subject's body temperature produces the anxiety reduction associated with exercising.

Monoamine hypothesis the alteration of neurotransmitter substances within the subject's brain produces the anxiety reduction associated with exercise.

---

only running in their treatment and research programs. Bearing on this point, Brown, Ramirez, and Taub (1978) found decreases in depression in their study of high school and college students with wrestling, mixed exercise, and jogging. Tennis produced marginal but positive effects, while softball had no effect at all on depression scores. The greater reduction in depression in the Brown et al. study was in the subjects who engaged in a 10-week program of jogging that required the subjects to work out five times per week.

In two studies of clinically depressed women (Doyne, Ossip-Klein, Bowman, Osborn, McDougall-Wilson, & Neimeyer, 1987; Ossip-Klein, Doyne, Bowman, Osborn, McDougall-Wilson, & Neimeyer, 1989), it was found that running and weight lifting were equally effective in both alleviating the depressive symptoms and improving self-concept in their samples. These findings suggest that the alleviation of depression does not depend entirely on an aerobic exercise component, as would be suggested in the running literature.

Despite the strength of the research findings and the exuberance of the various testimonials by practitioners, the depression research suffers from many of the same deficiencies as does anxiety research. Better use of theory and more focused attention to methodological issues are clearly called for. Also, the link between exercise and depression is, as with anxiety, more correlational than causal at this point. More research is needed to establish the supposed causal link between the two.

CONSIDERATIONS IN USING EXERCISE AS THERAPY FOR ANXIETY OR DEPRESSION. A number of issues need to be addressed when prescribing exercise as therapy for either anxiety or depression, and a careful delineation of these concerns has been made by Buffone (1984). One issue brought up is that of proper psychological diagnosis and a corresponding *individually tailored exercise prescription*. Choice of type of exercise enters in here, as does the notion of combining running with other possible therapeutic modalities, such as stress inoculation training mentioned earlier in the Long studies (1984, 1985). A second issue to consider is the *proficiency of the exercise therapist*. This person should have mental health training as well as skill in conducting proper exercise; he or she should also serve as a *model* for the advantages of exercise and ideally should possess expertise in the prevention and treatment of exercise-related injuries. Finally, *reinforcement of exercise behaviors* must be a concern of all involved parties. Care should be taken to ensure that the exercise regimen, once introduced, becomes a positive therapeutic force and not a negative addiction for the client. The consequences of negative addiction to exercise may be such that the client ends up merely trading one problem for another.

Additional caveats related to the exercise-as-therapy movement are offered by Martinsen (1990) and Raglin (1990). Both authorities suggest that exercise may be more useful with certain types of mood disorders and of limited utility with others. If this hypothesis is true, the exercise professional should select clients with the most potential to profit from physical activity. Raglin goes on to indicate that in those cases where exercise exerts a beneficial effect on mood, it may be sufficient merely to exercise; that is, fitness as it is usually defined is not necessary for exercise to generate the desired effects on anxiety or depression. Raglin also indicates that too vigorous an exercise regimen is capable of producing undesirable mood swings in people with previously stable emotional patterns. Thus, care should be taken to avoid creating problems in so-called normal people when there is a crying need for competent and effective treatment of individuals with genuine mood-related problems.

Recent literature has suggested that exercise as therapy may actually extend beyond mood disorders to encompass clinical syndromes such as schizophrenia (Faulkner & Sparkes, 1999) and body image disorders, conversion disorder, and alcohol dependence (Tkachuk & Martin, 1999). Tkachuk and Martin emphatically state that there is clear and abundant evidence that exercise is a viable, cost effective therapeutic medium.

SUMMARY

1. The continuing fascination with fitness has led to much speculation and research aimed at promoting a better understanding of exercise and its relationship to mental and physical fitness. Why people value fitness, why some cannot adhere to fitness regimens, and the consequences of exercise for prevention and alleviation of anxiety and depression are some of the more significant issues confronting health professionals.

2. An apparent fitness boom of major proportions has seen 50 to 60 million Americans involved in some kind of exercise. However, a large number of so-called exercisers may not work out regularly enough to realize the possible gains in level of fitness. The commitment to fitness is often more verbal than behavioral.

3. Caspersen (1985) suggests that there are differences among the categories of physical activity, exercise, and physical fitness, and these distinctions have served as a guide for subsequent discussion.

4. Among the more prominent physical benefits of physical fitness are increased blood flow to the heart, lowered blood pressure, increased lung capacity, lower blood lactate levels, more effective digestive and excretory functioning, improved sex life, and weight control. Whether or not a lowered resting heart rate is actually a benefit or just an artifact of cardiovascular fitness remains unresolved.

5. The psychological benefits of exercise are less well documented but are thought to include reductions in anxiety and depression, increased

socialization, self-confidence, and the thrill of competition against oneself, external standards, or other competitors.

6. Statistics on exercise adherence are generally not good. Exercise dropout rates of up to 50% are seen both in exercisers with no history of coronary problems who want to become more fit and in those who are postmyocardial infarction patients.

7. Predictors of exercise adherence include geographical proximity to the exercise area, spousal support, exercising in small as opposed to large groups, higher socioeconomic status, and, more tentatively, an internal locus of control.

8. Negative predictors of adherence include lack of time, lack of accessibility, being a smoker, poor choice of exercise, early injury, Type A personality, and being introverted.

9. A number of behavioral approaches to increase exercise compliance that have been used with some success are behavioral contracts, lotteries, self-monitoring, stimulus cueing, and reinforcement of exercise behavior.

10. Concerned professionals have shown interest in the contribution of exercise to cognitive and affective functioning.

11. Many studies have been conducted on various kinds of exercise as they relate to cognitive functioning, and the results so far are highly equivocal. This is generally true for both anaerobic and aerobic exercise conducted at varying degrees of intensity and time. Flaws in methodology and a failure to tie the research to any theoretical base have hampered these studies.

12. Exercise is thought to have an impact on both anxiety and depression, two affective states that have been of considerable interest to scientists across many professional fields.

13. In an extensive review of the literature, Folkins and Sime (1981) cite studies pointing to improved affective functioning as a result of exercise. Evidence also suggests that reductions in anxiety can be achieved by pairing exercise with other approaches, such as stress inoculation training.

14. Depression is a major mental health problem in the United States, and a variety of approaches have been used in an attempt to deal with the condition. Greist and his colleagues (1978) brought the use of running as therapy for depression to the forefront from the scientific perspective, whereas Fixx (1977) served the same function for the general public with his popular book on the many virtues of running. Like the link between anxiety and exercise, the one involving depression is best thought of as correlational as opposed to causative at this point. More research is needed to make the desired causal connection between exercise and improved affect.

15. In using exercise as therapy for anxiety or depression, first priority should be given to making an accurate psychological diagnosis of the client(s). Exercises should be carefully tailored to the individual and should be performed under the guidance of a skilled exercise therapist who serves as an adjustment and fitness model. The therapy situation requires liberal use of reinforcement.

KEY TERMS

all-cause mortality (406)
behavioral contracting (411)
cardiorespiratory endurance (405)
distraction hypothesis (416)
endorphin hypothesis (416)
exercise (405)
exercise adherence (407)
extraversion (410)
lotteries (411)
monoamine hypothesis (416)
physical activity (405)
physical fitness (405)
reinforcement (412)
reward (412)
self-monitoring (411)
stimulus cueing (412)
thermogenic hypothesis (416)
type A personality (410)

SUGGESTED READINGS

Brown, D. R., Wang, Y., Ward, A., Ebbeling, C. B., Fortlage, L., Puleo, E., Benson, H., & Rippe, J. M. (1995). Chronic psychological effects of exercise and exercise plus cognitive strategies. *Medicine and Science in Sports and Exercise, 27,* 765–775.
This research paper presents results of a variety of exercise treatment conditions on the psychological well-being of healthy, sedentary adults (69 females, 66 males). Four groups took part in the experiment: a control group (C), a moderate-intensity walk group (MW), a low-intensity walking plus relaxation group (LWR), and a mindful exercise (ME) group engaging in Tai-Chi meditation. Greatest mood changes as measured by the Profile of Mood States (POMS) were for women in the ME group. Women in the MW group reported the greatest changes in attitudes about physical attributes. It is interesting to note that two activities not much discussed in the fitness and exercise literature, Tai-Chi and walking, created positive effects.

Physical activity and psychological benefits: A position statement from the International Society of Sport Psychology. (1992). *International Journal of Sport Psychology, 4,* 94–98.
ISSP has reviewed the research and adopted the following position on the potential psychological benefits of regular physical exercise: (1) exercise can be associated with reduced state anxiety; (2) exercise can be associated with a decreased level of mild to moderate depression; (3) long-term exercise is usually associated with reductions in neuroticism and anxiety; (4) exercise may be an adjunct to the professional treatment of severe depression; (5) exercise can result in the reduction of various stress indices; and (6) exercise can have beneficial emotional effects across all ages and both genders.

Shephard, R. J. (1994). *Aerobic fitness and health.* Champaign, IL: Human Kinetics.
One of the leading authorities on exercise and health behavior has written a book that authoritatively summarizes the existing literature on the interaction among physical activity, aerobic fitness, and health. Topics discussed include physiological determinants of aerobic fitness; fitness issues of youth, adults, and the elderly; and the health outcomes of a regular program of exercise. Citing over 1,300 references, Shephard's book is unique in its comprehensiveness.

Walking—RX for health, happiness. (2000). August 17. http://apma.org/topics/Walking.html.
This information from the website to the American Preventive Medicine Association extols the benefits of a walking exercise regimen, gives some helpful tips on how to do it effectively, makes recommendations for appropriate footwear, and gives a formula for measuring proper walking heart rate. A good brief read for a person preparing to start a walking program.

 INFOTRAC COLLEGE EDITION

For additional readings, explore Infotrac College Edition, your online library. Go to:
http://www.infotrac-college.com/wadsworth
Hint: Enter these search terms: all-cause mortality, athletic shoe industry, endorphins, extraversion, physical fitness, President's Council on Physical Fitness and Sports, type A personality.

Exercise Psychology: Running Addictions and Exercise for Senior Citizens

CHAPTER 26

The Runner's Addictions

Exercise and Competition
for Senior Citizens

Summary

Key Terms

Suggested Readings

Walking as exercise reduces stress on the lower joints, and is increasingly popular among senior citizens.
© Copyright 1999 PhotoDisc, Inc.

This final chapter will address some of the remaining important issues within sport and fitness. Runners, marathoners, and ultramarathoners (ultrarunners) will be discussed within the context of the notions of positive and negative addiction. Recently there has also been an explosion of interest in exercise, fitness, and competitive activities for senior citizens, and we shall attempt to survey the sport scene with this rapidly growing segment of our population.

THE RUNNER'S ADDICTIONS

For whatever reasons, running has become a popular means of achieving fitness. Some people approach running (and other forms of exercise) reasonably, and this approach is referred to as a *positive addiction*. Others seem to lose sight of what exercise is all about, and the rabidity with which they pursue the elusive goal of fitness is so excessive that they may be said to have a *negative addiction*.

Sachs (1982) has addressed the addiction issue by suggesting that if exercise addiction does in fact exist, it might be viewed as a continuum in which exercise for the negatively addicted individual has gone from mere importance to a controlling factor that dominates other life choices. To put it another way, Sachs says that the positively addicted individual controls the activity and the negatively addicted person is controlled by the activity.

Positive Addiction

Perhaps the most comprehensive popular discussion of exercise addiction has been made by the psychiatrist William Glasser. Glasser (1976, p. 104) discusses positive addiction in a book by the same name and suggests that running is most likely of all the exercises to produce the highly prized positive addiction.

I believe that running creates the optimal condition for positive addiction because it is our most ancient and still most effective survival mechanism. We are descended from those who ran to stay alive, and this need to run is programmed genetically into our brains. When we have gained the endurance to run long distances easily, then a good run reactivates the ancient neural program. As this occurs, we reach a state of mental preparedness that leads to a basic feeling of satisfaction that is less-critical than any other activity that we can do alone.

Though one could argue with Glasser as to the origin of our propensity to run, he does make a compelling case for the positive and addictive qualities of running.

Just what is this quality known as positive addiction to running and/or exercise? **Positive addiction** is characterized, first of all, by an element of controllability; that is, the person involved controls the exercise regimen. Beyond the control factor, the positively addicted person carefully programs exercise into his or her daily life. Careful organization of competing activities takes place so as to reduce possible sources of interference with the exercise program. Exercise is blended in with work and family life in such a way as to add to rather than detract from those important life dimensions. As one becomes more positively addicted, feelings of control, competence, and physical and psychological well-being increase. Conversely, if the positively addicted person is forced by scheduling conflicts, illness, or injury to miss working out, there is a sense of loss, guilt, and physical and mental discomfort. One runner who responded to Glasser summed up his feelings about missing his running workouts as follows: "When I miss my workouts I feel as though I have let myself down. My personal integrity suffers a blow. Guilt feelings mount continuously until I run again. . . . I am glad, however, that I feel this way because it is the watchdog that makes sure I do my running." (107) If all who exercise could maintain this attitude, adherence to exercise would become a nonissue.

One of the first studies attempting to substantiate the positive addictive qualities of running was conducted by Carmack and Martens (1979). These researchers administered a Commitment to Running Scale to 250 male and 65 female runners of various competence and experience levels, and support for both the validity of the scale and the positive addiction

---

Positive addiction in running or other exercise, a love of the activity that is tempered by controllability, integration into everyday activities, and ability to forgo exercise when necessary, resulting in increased feelings of control, competence, and physical and psychological well-being.

A Tribute to Positive Addiction and Flow

Why Do They Run

And they asked me, "Why do you run?"

I answered,

"I run to celebrate the joy of my being . . . the ecstasy that I am!

I run that I may be alone with myself and together with the universe.

I run to find the rhythm of the pounding rush of my own heart which sets its beat to the pulsing of time.

I run in time ever present as it passes through my world garbed in the white robes of winter, the patch-work of fall, stripped to the simplicity of summer or gar-landed with the new growing things of spring . . .

I run seeking the feeling of inner harmony that is mine if I will but open to it.

I run to feel the earth chains break and drop along my path.

I run until I am numb to the everyday cares and woes and I flow forward;

A part of the air which I suck into thirsty lungs the earth which softens the placement of my feet.

The sounds of this space through which I pass are music to my soaring spirit

The sights lure me ever onward

The process carries me ever upward—higher

And higher."

I turned and I asked them,

"How can you not run?"

Bonnie Beach

SOURCE: Used by permission of Bonnie Beach.

notion was demonstrated. Chapman and DeCastro (1990) report supportive results; these researchers found that addiction to running was associated with positive personality characteristics.

Negative Addiction

If exercise is viewed as a continuum, as suggested by Sachs (1984), noncompliance would represent one end of the continuum and addiction the other. In turn, addiction would also be viewed as bipolar, with the range running from the positive to the negative dimensions. All who have exercised for any length of time have been exposed to persons for whom exercise has become their master. Their behavior is so out of the ordinary that it is easily detected: They run until they drop. Their life is dominated by running. They fail to

use good judgment about their strengths and weaknesses as runners. They run to the detriment of their health, career, family, and interpersonal relationships.

Pierce (1994) has expanded our insights into the exercise addiction issue by introducing the term *exercise dependence,* which is another way to describe the symptoms previously mentioned. Other terms that have been used to account for the addictive qualities of exercise, and most particularly running, are *obligatory running* (Yates, Leehey, & Shisslak, 1983), *morbid exercising* (Waldstreicher, 1985), and *compulsive jogging* (Veale de Coverley, 1987).

Negative addiction in running or other exercise, a compulsive need to exercise that overrides considerations of health, relationships, and career. Also known as *exercise dependence, obligatory running, morbid exercising,* and *compulsive jogging.*

Research and speculation about negative addiction was initiated by Morgan (1979), who felt that such a state had been reached if the person believed that running was necessary in order to cope with everyday life and if withdrawal symptoms emerged when running was withdrawn.

One index of running gone awry is found in injury statistics. Diekhoff (1984), in a study of highly committed male and female runners, administered a Type A/B Scale, an Addiction to Running Scale, and a Commitment to Running Scale. He found that those individuals who had suffered injuries while running tended to be Type A personalities, were addicted to running, had a strong commitment to running, ran more miles, and were more likely to run in fun runs and races than were the noninjured runners. A significant correlation was found between addiction to running and number of doctor visits and between running and the use of drugs or physical therapy. Layman and Morris (1986) studied more than 1,000 runners of all levels of ability and experience and found a highly significant relationship between addiction to running and injuries. Almost 60% of the runners in their study reported running-related injuries in the preceding 12 months. Sixty percent of the injured runners considered themselves to be addicted to running. Hailey and Bailey (1982), as part of their attempt to validate the Negative Addiction Scale, found a linear relationship between years of running and negative addiction. Addiction scores on their scale were significantly higher for runners who had run from one to four years than for those who had been running for less than a year.

A recent addition to the literature in this area has featured the development of a measure of maladaptive beliefs about the consequences of not exercising called the Exercise Beliefs Questionnaire (EBQ) (Loumidis & Wells, 1998). The EBQ is a 21-item scale measuring social desirability, physical appearance, mental and emotional functioning, and vulnerability to disease and aging. Time will tell, but the EBQ appears to have promise as a means of assessing exercise dependence.

Runner's high a state experienced by distance runners that is characterized by a sudden heightened sense of well-being; also known as *flow, natural laxative, transcendence, euphoric sensation, steady state stimulation, peak experience, centering state, existential drift, runner's calm, general happiness,* and *total euphoria.*

Mood and Running

Perhaps the most consistent line of research related to runners is found in 37 studies cited by LeUnes (LeUnes & Burger, 1998; LeUnes 2000) in which the Profile of Mood States (POMS) was used. Summing across all of these pieces of research, several conclusions may be drawn. One is that running appears to have a facilitative effect on mood. In the majority of studies in which runners were compared with groups of nonrunners, there were clear differences in mood in favor of the runners. Second, the studies in which an attempt was made to tease out the role of endogenous opiates (endorphins) were equivocal, which is representative of the overall literature on the exercise–endorphin relationship. Finally, it appears that runners of all levels of competence share somewhat equally in the mood benefits associated with their selected exercise medium. The research on this latter point, however, is scant, and any conclusions drawn at this time should be considered as tentative.

Runner's High

Much interest has been shown in what has come to be known as the **runner's high,** a state characterized by an unexpected and heightened sense of well-being that may vary from runner to runner in frequency, intensity, and duration. It apparently occurs only in distance runners and probably will not be experienced by runners who log only 6 to 10 miles per week (Weltman & Stamford, 1983). Wagemaker and Goldstein (1980) indicate that runner's high only occurs only in individuals who run for 25 to 30 minutes or more. Sachs (1984) says that at least 30 minutes of running is necessary; in addition, he thinks that distances of 6 miles or more are required. There is a lively debate about whether many distance runners experience the phenomenon at all. James Menegazzi, an exercise researcher and avid runner, believes that the runner's high is a function of endorphin infusion that only takes place at high intensity. As a consequence, Menegazzi altered his own weekly workout schedule from 50 miles at a moderate clip to 25 miles of hard running (Scanning Sports, 1989).

Estimates of the occurrence of the runner's high range from 9% to 10% of all runners (Weinberg, 1980) to 77% or 78% (Lilliefors, 1978; Sachs, 1980). As Sachs

Runner's High: A Case Study

JRN and I visited Bruce Ogilvie for three days in 1981 at his home in Los Gatos, California. On the morning of the second day, we joined Bruce and several of his friends for a 6-mile run at 5:30 A.M. The first two miles of the chosen course involved the ascent of a steep incline, most certainly what would be called a mountain in most of our home state of Texas, but a sore knee left me far behind the pack. Eventually, I lost sight of the other joggers. In the process, I missed a critical turn up the side of a mountain that ultimately led back down to the starting point in Los Gatos. This error added an additional 5 or 6 miles to the overall trip. Somewhere along the way, a mixture of exhaustion, cool early morning air, excitement of the trip to California, beauty of the landscape, smell of anise, and an unscheduled running tour of the wineries along the way produced what had to have been the elusive "runner's high" so often alluded to by runners and researchers. Though the distance covered far exceeded anything I had run before, the feeling at the end was one of light-headed giddiness as well as disappointment and frustration because no one wanted to continue the run. Was this the "runner's high"? I suspect so, and I doubt that it will ever happen again. I'm just glad I was there to be a part of what may be, for most of us, a once-in-a-lifetime experience.

(1984) has pointed out, a range of 9% to 78% indicates that we have much to learn about the mysterious phenomenon of the runner's high.

The diversity of descriptive terms used to describe the runner's high illustrates just how complex and elusive the phenomenon is. Csikszentmihalyi (1975) describes the runner's high as *flow*. To Henderson (1977) it is a *natural laxative* that throws off the waste in the body and mind. *Transcendence* and *euphoric sensation* are descriptive terms used by Sachs (1980, 1984). Peoples (1983) talks in terms of *steady state stimulation*. For Ravizza (1984), the runner's high is merely one example of *peak experience* associated with sport. Johnsgard (1985) draws parallels between the runner's high and the tranquil state often thought to be a part of transcendental meditation, and he uses terms like *centering state* and *existential drift* for purposes of enhancing his explanation. Murray Allen, a physician and kinesiologist, says that *runner's calm* brought about by the quieting as opposed to excitatory effects is the key descriptor (Hopson, 1988). Masters (1992), in a study of 30 male and female marathoners, indicated that 73% of his sample had experienced runner's high at some point, and 66% experienced it during the marathon under scrutiny. The most common term applied to the runner's high for Masters' sample was *general happiness;* in contrast, *total euphoria* was the least descriptive term used in his study.

Agreement exists that the runner's high is a real but esoteric phenomenon that almost defies description. Problems in operationally defining the experience are a result of this verbal richness, and research in the area is problematic as a result. Nevertheless, further investigation into the fascinating phenomenon known as the runner's high is warranted.

Marathon Runners

Tradition has it that the marathon event was named in honor of the city of Marathon, located some 26 miles from Athens and the scene of one of the most significant battles between the Greeks and the invading Persians in the year 490 B.C. The Greeks inflicted a great defeat on the numerically superior Persian forces, and news of the victory was carried from Marathon to Athens by a runner named **Pheidippides.** Pheidippides reportedly died of exhaustion after his victory

---

Pheidippides legendary runner who brought news of the Greek victory over the Persians from the town of Marathon to Athens; origin of the term *marathon* for a cross-country footrace.

announcement (Howell, 1983). Grogan (1981), in a disclaimer, suggests that the legendary runner was probably named Pheidippides, may or may not have run from Marathon to Athens, and most probably did not die after his victory announcement because he was an accomplished ultrarunner. Well-documented accounts indicated that Pheidippides had made the 100-mile run from Athens to Sparta and back in three or four days while searching for support troops for the upcoming battle at Marathon. This run reportedly had taken place only days or weeks before his relatively short run from Marathon to Athens.

Arguments on the origin of the marathon aside, it was a part of the first modern Olympics in 1896, with a field of 25 entrants. Only 19 ran in 1900, and 14 finished the event in 1904. With each successive Olympics, however, the number of runners has increased. Women participated in the marathon for the first time in the 1984 Olympics in Los Angeles.

Several studies related to personality variables have pointed to marathoners being introverted as opposed to extraverted personalities (Silva & Hardy, 1986). Silva and Hardy also point to low anxiety levels in these athletes. Still others have found superior mood profiles, primarily using the POMS (Morgan & Pollock, 1977; Tharion, Strowman, & Rauch, 1988). A slightly different approach to studying these runners is that of Horton and Mack (2000) who looked at the extent to which runners see themselves as athletes. Using the Athletic Identity Measurement Scale (AIMS) (Brewer, Van Raalte, & Linder, 1993), Horton and Mack found that those runners high in athletic identification exhibited better athletic performance, more commitment to running, and had a healthier social network when compared with runners low in athletic identity. Also, they did not neglect other aspects of their lives in the name of competing in distance events.

Although the evidence so far is insufficient to create a marathon runner personality profile, a number of psychological benefits do appear to be associated with such an undertaking, a finding that is consistent with claims made about the positive effects of running and exercise in general.

The most comprehensive summary to date on motives to participate in marathon running is that of Masters, Ogles, and Jolton (1993). Based on a thorough review of the literature and conclusions drawn from their own research, these investigators have identified four major reasons for running marathons: psychological, physical, social, and achievement. Each of these four major variables is then broken into subcomponents, and they can be seen in the general model provided in Figure 26.1.

In addition to presenting a workable model to guide future research on the "mind" of the marathoner, Masters et al. have created an instrument to assess motives for competing in marathons called the **Motivations of Marathoners Scales (MOMS).** A subsequent study of 472 runners of varying degrees of marathon experience in which the MOMS was used has lent further validity to the scale (Masters & Ogles, 1995). In the Masters and Ogles study, the MOMS successfully differentiated among the motivations of experienced, mid-level experienced, and beginning marathoners. In their most recent effort (Ogles & Masters, 2000), 20- and 50-year-old marathoners were compared with regard to their training habits for an upcoming competition. The older runners were more motivated by concerns about health and weight and affiliation with other runners, whereas the younger runners were driven more by personal goal achievement. Interestingly, both groups trained at about the same mileage each week. In view of the success of the MOMS, Masters and his colleagues will undoubtedly play an active role in future research in this intriguing area of inquiry within sport psychology.

Ultramarathoners/Ultrarunners

McCutcheon and Yoakum (1983) define an **ultramarathon** (the competitors are often referred to as **ultrarunners**) as any race that exceeds the official marathon distance of 26 miles, 385 yards. Maron and Horvath (1978) divide ultramarathons into those that require repetitive days of running long distances and those that are continuous for distances up to 100 miles. Maron and Horvath, in a study of runners participating in the first type of ultramarathon, were interested

---

Motivations of Marathoners Scale (MOMS) a standardized measure for assessing motives for competing in marathons.
Ultramarathon any footrace that exceeds the official marathon distance of 26 miles, 385 yards.
Ultrarunners participants in an ultramarathon.

FIGURE 26.1

Model of Motives for Running Marathons

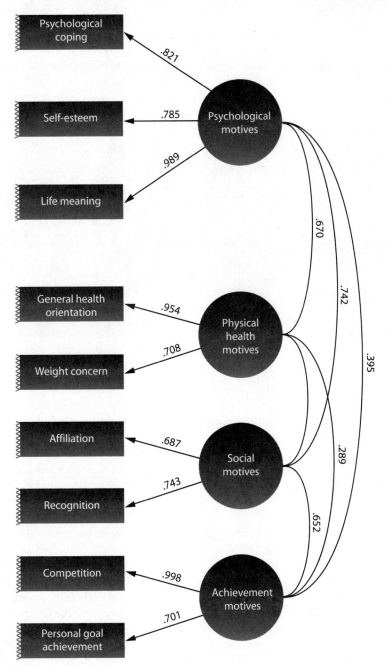

SOURCE: Masters, Ogles, & Jolton (1993).

These senior Olympics competitors are just starting the 10,000 meter run. The Senior Olympics are conducted for participants 55 years of age and older, and involve competition in 18 different sports.
© Bettman/CORBIS

in physiological variables only. The race in question was run in 1928 and involved running the 3,484 miles between Los Angeles and New York City. The 25 entrants who finished the event averaged 41 miles a day for 84 consecutive days; interestingly, few and only minor physiological problems were found at the end of the grueling competition.

In an ultramarathon race similar to the one in 1928 described by Maron and Horvath, Lewis (1992) describes the trials and tribulations of a trek from California to New York, an event won by David Warady of Huntington Beach, California. Warady completed the 3,000 miles in 521 hours and 35 minutes spaced over 64 days. One of the competitors, Al Howie of Scotland, had recently run 4,500 miles across Canada, averaging 62 miles per day in the process. Unlike the results reported by Maron and Horvath in which no physiological consequences were noted, Howie and 15 other ultrarunners eventually dropped out of the competition, most because of injury.

Psychological descriptions of ultrarunners are scant. Folkins and Wieselberg-Bell (1981), in a study of entrants in what they consider to be the toughest endurance run in the United States (a 100-mile trail over the crest of the Sierra Nevada mountains known as the Western States Endurance Run), found deviant MMPI scores on several subscales in comparisons of finishers and nonfinishers. The finishers had higher Psychopathic deviate (Pd), Depression (D), and Schizophrenia (Sc) scores. On the whole, however, Folkins and Wieselberg-Bell concluded that the ultrarunners as a group appeared to be reasonably normal, and they interpreted the deviant MMPI scores as being perhaps necessary for completion of basically what may be a deviant task. Another study of ultrarunners by McCutcheon and Yoakum (1983) revealed no personality differences between their

The Interplay Between Exercise and Aging

Waneen Wyrick Spirduso has carved out a significant research niche in the area of aging and exercise. In a comprehensive survey of the available literature up to 1980, she concluded that methodological shortcomings aside, there is indirect evidence to suggest that the decline in some aspects of brain functioning in the motoric sense may be substantially allayed by chronic exercise. Because it is largely inexpensive, unobtrusive, and self-imposed, exercise may actually offer significant intervention in the aging process, according to Spirduso. The psychological and societal ramifications of this assertion are considerable and merit further attention.

Spirduso's *reaction time studies* maintain that simple reaction time as measured by response to a visual stimulus is affected not so much by age as physical condition. Spirduso and Clifford (1978) looked at young runners, young racket-sports competitors, older racket-sports competitors, older runners, young inactives, and older inactives (young was defined as ages 20–30, while older was ages 50–70). The linear relationship between extent of physical involvement and simple reaction and movement time is graphically displayed in Figure 26.2. The significant differences are most noticeable between inactive young and old people and the other four groups. This suggests that differences in simple reaction and movement time are more a function of fitness level than of age.

In a more recent study, Light, Reilly, Behrman, and Spirduso (1996) looked at simple reaction time (RT) and movement time (MT) using arm-reaching tasks with 40 subjects ages 20–29 and 20 older subjects ages 60–82. After pretesting and considerable practice of the experimental task, a posttest indicated that the practice reduced the simple reaction time of the older subjects to that of the younger subjects. Movement times for both groups improved but the gap between the older and younger subjects remained con-

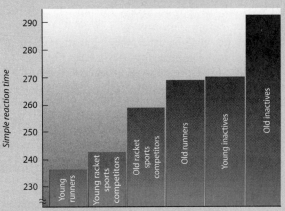

FIGURE 26.2

Age, Physical Fitness, and Reaction Time*

Simple reaction time

290
280
270
260
250
240
230

Young runners | Young racket sports competitors | Old racket sports competitors | Old runners | Young inactives | Old inactives

SOURCE: Spirduso & Clifford (1978).
*Critical values are in milliseconds.

stant. This study does attest to the efficacy of training in improving some aspects of motoric capacity in older persons. It thus suggests that good exercise programs could be beneficial in improving fitness and overall health in geriatrics.

SOURCES: Light, Reilly, Behrman, & Spirduso, 1996; Spirduso (1980, 1983); Spirduso & Clifford (1978).

Spirduso's reaction time studies research by Waneen Wyrick Spirduso that maintains that reaction time (measured by response to a visual stimulus) is affected by physical condition, with older actives having better reaction times than young inactives.

subjects and a matched group of runners who had never competed at distances over 10 miles.

An interesting variant related to the ultrarunner is provided by Bull (1989). In a comprehensive case study of one competitor, Bull administered four psychometric tests and developed a training, evaluation, and crisis intervention program to assist the runner in question through a grinding 20-day run across the 500-mile perimeter of the Mojave Desert in California. Tests administered included the Sixteen Personality Factor Questionnaire (16PF), the Tennessee Self-Concept Scale (TSCS), the State–Trait Anxiety Inventory (STAI), and the Sport Competition Anxiety Test (SCAT). Test results indicated that the ultrarunner in question was generally within the normal range on the traits measured by the 16PF, was high on trait-anxiousness on both the STAI and the SCAT, and was slightly below the population mean on self-concept score. Overall, however, little of the deviance suggested by Folkins and Wieselberg-Bell was found in this runner.

Clearly, not very much is known about the psychological makeup of these interesting athletes. Perhaps future research will be directed toward gaining an understanding of a sport that may, as suggested by Folkins and Wieselberg-Bell, require a little deviance.

EXERCISE AND COMPETITION FOR SENIOR CITIZENS

How old would you be if you didn't know how old you was?

Satchel Paige, legendary baseball pitcher

A 1987 graphic in *USA Today* indicated that the median age of the American population was 31.7 years in 1986 and would rise to 41.6 by the year 2050. One repercussion of this "graying of America" has to do with the role of fitness and competition as a means of adding to the quality of life for senior citizens. Fitness advocates and sport scientists have spent very little time studying the physical fitness and competitive needs, wishes, and talents of people 45 years of age and older. More attention will be paid to these older citizens in the future with the goal of improving the quality, if not the quantity, of life.

Myths permeate the literature concerning the effects of exercise on the aging process. In this section we will look at what we know about exercise and competition for senior citizens.

Fitness Issues for Seniors

Veschi (1963) has quoted Rousseau, the eighteenth-century French philosopher, as follows: "When a body is strong, it obeys; when it is weak, it gives orders." Perhaps this observation is nowhere more applicable than to senior citizens. We have all seen an older person who shuffles, a characteristic related to the inevitable shrinkage of connective tissue that limits length and resiliency of stride. One can go on and on about other examples of the effects of sedentary living among older people. Suffice it to say that many of these results of physical deterioration could have been fended off or ameliorated with a good physical activity program.

We have some measure of control over the biological dimension of the aging process. We can apparently moderate the effects of aging through diet, exercise, and prudence in everyday matters. Smith and Gilliam (1983) and Stamford (1984) all indicate that 50% of the physical decline associated with age is a result of disuse rather than senescence. Substantiation for this point comes from Steinhaus, Dustman, Ruhling, Emmerson, Johnson, Shearer, Latin, Shigeoka, and Bonekat (1990). This research team monitored a four-month fast walking or jogging and stretching exercise regimen for 28 sedentary males and females, ages 55 to 70, and found significantly improved aerobic capacity and other indicators of fitness among their subjects. A four-year follow-up showed a 64% exercise adherence rate for the group. Similarly, Morey, Cowper, Feussner, DiPasquale, Crowley, and Sullivan (1991), using a two-year exercise regimen, found significant gains in cardiovascular fitness and flexibility in a group of elderly subjects residing in a Veteran's Administration Hospital in North Carolina. Looking at gains in muscle strength as an indicator of fitness, Fiatarone, Marks, Ryan, Meredith, Lipsitz, and Evans (1990) studied a most unusual sample of men and women ages 86 to 96. These researchers placed six women and four men with extreme sedentary habits and significant health problems on an eight-week strength program of progressive resistance involving the lower leg only. An average strength gain across all subjects of 174% was noted over the eight-week exercise period. The researchers concluded that much of the strength loss associated with aging is modifiable through exercise. Safety concerns about weight training with senior citizens were also greatly allayed.

In an interesting follow-up to her earlier work, Fiatarone and colleagues (Fiatarone, O'Neill, Ryan, Clements, Solares, Nelson, Roberts, Kehayias, Lipsitz, & Evans, 1994) randomly assigned 100 frail nursing home residents to one of four groups for a ten-week experiment designed to see if weakness and immobility in these individuals could be partially allayed. Group 1 received resistance training three times per week for thigh and hip muscles. Groups 2 and 3 received vitamin-fortified, 360-calorie drinks. Group four received none of these potentially helpful aids. Positive results were found in the muscle resistance training group: gait velocity in exercisers improved nearly 12%, stair-climbing power improved over 28%, and thigh muscle size grew by 2.7%. As an added extra, four members of the weight-training group were able to get out of their walkers and begin using a cane. All gains noted were achieved irrespective of initial frailty, age, gender, or medical condition.

All wishes to the contrary aside, there are legitimate physiological changes associated with age and we would be remiss to ignore them. There are unassailable declines in muscle mass and increases in weight and body fat because of a slowing of basal metabolism. Flexibility is affected by aging, as is bone mineral content. Cardiovascular changes involving the heart, the blood vessels, lung surface area, and elasticity are real (Smith & Zook, 1986). These must all be taken into account when drawing up an exercise prescription for an older client. At the same time, lifelong fitness should be encouraged as a means for altering the course of deterioration of these various bodily systems.

At the psychological level, little is known about people who either have exercised throughout their lives or have only recently begun such a program. Physical benefits have been found in the case of people who have begun an exercise regimen after age 60 (e.g., Lord, Ward, Williams, & Strudwick, 1995; Williams & Lord, 1995). The comparable data on psychological benefits

of such efforts is scant. Supposition of improved well being and higher self-esteem are easily invoked, but actual supportive data are rare. Sidney and Shephard (1976) did find a decrease in anxiety levels in a sample of men and women over 60 years of age undergoing a 14-week conditioning program. Hickey, Wolf, Robins, Wagner, and Harik (1995), in their study of chronically impaired geriatrics, found exercise-related improvements in three measures of psychological well being, including optimism about the future. Much more research needs to be conducted to help substantiate the psychological benefits of exercise for senior citizens.

The Competitive Senior

Beyond accounts found largely in the popular press, not a great deal more is known about competitive seniors, those athletes who choose to enter assorted sporting events for the thrill and challenge provided. Rudman (1986), in an attempt to assess how sports are viewed by three different age groups (18 to 34, 35 to 54, 55 plus), queried 1,319 subjects about their participation in 14 different athletic events. Age, marital status, income, occupational status, and geographic location served as independent variables in the Rudman study. Among the more notable, though not surprising, results was a clear age-related bias in sport involvement. A steady age-related decrease was found; only golf was exempt from differential participation as a function of chronology. The largest drop-off in sport involvement occurred between the 18–34 and the 35–54 age groups, suggesting that discontinuation from competition takes place fairly early in life.

A most fascinating exception is former Olympic sprint star Thane Baker of Dallas, Texas. Baker won a silver medal in the 1952 Olympics and a silver in the 100 meters, a bronze in the 200 meters, and a gold as a member of the winning 400-meter relay team in the 1956 Olympic Games. He continued competing in track over the years and set world records in the 100 meters for men aged 40 to 44 (10.7), 45 to 49 (11.0), and 50 to 54 (11.3) as well as the world mark in the 200 meters for ages 50 to 54 (23.4). As a 52-year-old in 1986, he ran a 10.99 for 100 yards in an all-comers meet at Southern Methodist University (SMU) in Dallas, Texas. Of his time, Baker said: "I hasten to add that I had a

Retirement From Athletics

From the minute practice starts in July until the season ends, you make yourself mean. You get mad and stay mad. Then, boom, the season is over and in 10 minutes you have to change your way of living. For a few weeks, it was hard to calm my nerves. It got easier to be mean every year and harder to get it out of your system. Pretty soon, there's no in-between. You're mean all year around. That's when you know you've been in pro football too long.

Sam Huff, Retired NFL Hall of Fame linebacker

You get tired of hurting. And I'm not even talking about the major injuries. . . . My body can't do it anymore.

Joe Jacoby, Retired Washington Redskins offensive lineman

The trouble with retirement is that you never get a day off.

Abe Lemons, Retired college basketball coach

Athletic retirement can occur at a number of junctures and for several reasons. One popular point of departure for discussing career termination is retirement from intercollegiate athletics and another is termination of a professional career. In turn, these retirements may occur for at least three reasons—the selection process, chronological age, or incapacitating injury (Ogilvie & Howe, 1986).

The selection process is particularly brutal. According to Paul Dietzel (1983), a former head football coach and athletic director, only one out of every 235 high school players will ever "start" for a Division 1 college team. Even more remote is the possibility of a professional football career, in which only one out of each 5,635 (.018%) high school football players will play for a professional team. To compound this problem, only a few of those who make it into the professional ranks will stay long. The average career in the National Football League is 4.2 years; in the National Basketball Association, the statistics are even worse; the career expectancy of an NBA player is 3.4 seasons. Making it to the professional level is a long shot at

best and survival in such a "Darwinian sports world" (Ogilvie & Howe, 1986, p. 366) is a gargantuan undertaking in its own right. Another view of the selection process discussed so far is also provided by Ogilvie and Howe (1986, p. 366):

	Basketball	Football
High school	700,000	1,300,000+
College (NCAA today)	15,000	75,000
Draft	200	320 (NFL)
Final selection	50	150

What becomes of people who retire from sport? The answer to this question is best understood in terms of two perspectives, that of the collegiate athlete terminating an athletic career and that of the professional player leaving what may amount to a lifetime of sports involvement.

The Collegiate Athlete

Two studies (Greendorfer & Blinde, 1985; Kleiber, Greendorfer, Blinde, & Samdahl, 1987) have generated some understanding of the dynamics surrounding the collegiate athlete who "hangs it up" after expiration of eligibility. Reviewing these two research efforts, we can draw several conclusions. One is that termination of athletics at this level is far from traumatic for the majority of athletes involved. In the Greendorfer and Blinde study of 1,123 male and female athletes, 89% of the 697 females and 90% of the 426 males looked forward to life after college. Additionally, 55% of the women and 57% of the men indicated that they were quite or extremely satisfied with themselves upon career termination; also, 75% of the athletes were still participating in their sport at some less formal level. Finally, 81% of the men and 55% of the women continued to follow their respective sports through the media on a "regular" or "religious" basis.

A second conclusion from the two studies is that there were no gender differences in adjustment to termination. Past research has completely neglected the adjustment of female athletes to career termination, so these two studies represented a significant point of departure concerning research about this issue.

Athletic retirement usually a function of the selection process, chronological age, or incapacitating injury.

Third, career termination because of injury resulted in a feeling of reduced life satisfaction for those athletes. Apparently, a sense of unfulfilled promise permeated the attitudes of these injured athletes, resulting in lower life satisfaction scores on the measure used. In one study of retired Notre Dame athletes, Webb, Nasco, Riley, and Headrick (1998) found that those ex-athletes in their sample who had to retire because of injury expressed less overall life satisfaction. Perna, Ahlgren, and Zaichkowsky (1999) also found that there was reduced life satisfaction in their sample of Division 1 athletes among those who were injured. They also found that African-American athletes reported less life satisfaction than Caucasians.

Finally, a shifting of priorities over the collegiate years took place in the majority of the athletes, with sport becoming less significant in their lives and education assuming an increasingly prominent role. These data support the earlier findings of Haerle (1975), who studied professional baseball players and found a strong relationship between amount of education and postretirement occupational achievement. It is also interesting to note that subjects in the Perna et al. study who had formed clear plans for life beyond sports reported more life satisfaction than did athletes with unfocused life after sport goals. This finding may fuel the success of a recent initiative of NFL franchises in Green Bay, Philadelphia, and Seattle whereby money is being pumped into a program to facilitate life adjustment among retiring players called *Invest in Yourself* (Forbes, 2000). The idea behind this program is to assist players in making sound financial and interpersonal decisions after their NFL playing days are over.

The Professional Athlete

Presumably, the adjustment to career termination is more complex at the professional level because the stakes are higher. The money involved is substantially greater, with the average 1995 salary in the NBA at $2.6 million, the NFL $1.1 million, and MLB $2.3 million. Also, the "sports only" identification is probably more operational at this stratified performance level. Partial support for the unidimensionality found in professional athletes is provided by Ogilvie and Howe (1986), who indicate that only 20% of NBA players and 32% of NFL athletes had a college degree.

The popular literature is rife with reports of brain-damaged boxers, football players who cannot get out of bed without assistance, and athletes from all sport persuasions who are wife-battering, drug-addicted, alcoholic deadbeats. It is all too easy to infer from these sensationalized accounts that adjustment problems are rampant among ex-athletes. Little, of course, is made of the ex-athlete who quietly goes to work and becomes an adjusted and contributing citizen. Few statistics are available from which to derive an accurate composite picture of the retired professional athlete.

Mihovilovic (1968) conducted one of the first studies of athletic termination using retired Yugoslavian soccer players. Ninety-five percent of these athletes were forced to retire, and 53% reported missing the camaraderie afforded by team members; 39% took up smoking for the first time and 16 percent increased their alcohol consumption upon retirement.

Adaptation to family life constitutes another challenge to athletic retirement. Ogilvie and Howe (1986) cite statistics from the NFL Players Association in which 50% of all marriages of ex-professional football players end in divorce. Mihoces (1988) sets this divorce figure at 33.5%, still a high number. Bob LaMonte, an educator, agent, and the creator of *Invest in Yourself*, says that 78% of all NFL players are bankrupt, divorced, or unemployed within two years after leaving the game (Forbes, 2000).

Inability to adjust to serious injury associated with sports also affects the overall adjustment to retirement. Taylor and Ogilvie (1994), in summarizing six studies of a variety of athletes, place the career-ending injury rate at a conservative 14% to 32%. In professional football, Mihoces indicates that 66% of all NFL players retire with permanent injury. Underwood (1979, p. 80), in discussing football injuries, poignantly portrays the plight of the seriously injured retiree: "Statistics do not show, however, how many ex-pros can no longer tie their shoe laces, or curl their fingers about a golf club. Statistics do not show many can't sleep without narcotics and have to call their wives for help to get out of bed."

(continued)

Retirement From Athletics—*continued*

Though there is much to be learned about the adjustment of professional athletes to retirement, it seems obvious that all is not a bed of roses for the athletes involved. Inadequate education, a paucity of job skills, physical infirmity, and interpersonal difficulties variously contribute to the problems facing all too many retired athletes. Athletic administrators, counselors, agents, coaches, sport psychologists, and the athletes themselves all have a vested interest in doing what they can to smooth the transition from what clearly is a brief career as an athlete to the more long-term proposition of being a working man. Perhaps Dietzel (1983, p. 162) sums the situa-

tion up best: "The 'average' NFL player will have 42.4 years remaining after his playing career. That means that even if he does 'make it' in the pros, he will have to earn a living for the remaining two-thirds of his life. He has a .018 percent chance of being a pro but he has a solid 100 percent chance of being a 'breadwinner' for the overwhelming majority of his life."

Sources: Dietzel (1983); Forbes (2000); Greendorfer & Blinde (1985); Haerle (1975); Kleiber, Greendorfer, Blinde, & Samdahl (1987); Mihoces (1988); Mihovilovic (1968); Ogilvie & Howe (1986); Perna, Ahlgren, & Zaichkowsky (1999); Taylor & Ogilvie (1994); Underwood (1979); Webb, Nasco, Riley, & Headrick (1998).

---

pretty good tailwind when I did it, but I am fully aware that it might be the last time I break 11 seconds, so I'll take it any way I can get it" (Vernon, 1984, p. 2C).

THE SENIOR GAMES. Competitions at the city and state level have blossomed into the **U.S. National Senior Games,** which have been held every two years since 1987. Several hundred thousand men and women over age 55 compete at these lower levels in hopes that they can qualify for the National Games. Age groups by gender are 55–59, 60–64, 65–69, 70–74, 75–79, 80–84, 85–89, 90–94, 95–99, and 100 plus. Competitions are held in 18 different sports including archery, badminton, basketball, bowling, cycling, golf, horseshoes, race walk, racquetball, road race, shuffleboard, softball, swimming, table tennis, tennis, track and field, triathlon, and volleyball.

Tom Bill, a gymnast in the 1956 Olympic Games, and a competitor at the senior level in badminton where he is a multiple medal winner has perhaps captured the essence of the seniors competition as follows: "In '56, we were competing for fame and glory. Now, whether we win or lose comes second to having fun. There is great camaraderie here" (Sports Camaraderie, 1989, p. 8C).

U.S. National Senior Games 18-sport held every two years for athletes from 55 to 100 years of age.

A Final Note

More research is needed to help gain insight into the requirements of older citizens so that a greater quality of life can be provided through carefully chosen exercise or physical activity. Increasingly, professionals in the health business are reassessing running and superior cardiovascular functioning as the major indicators of fitness. Those who prefer brisk walking, ardent gardening, enthusiastic carpentry, or chopping wood are probably getting the same health benefits and enjoyment as the people who choose jogging, calisthenics, or aerobic dancing as their physical activity of choice. Much remains to be done in tailoring exercise or physical activity to individuals' needs, wishes, and capabilities.

SUMMARY

1. Runners and senior citizens represent two populations of interest to sport, exercise, and health professionals.

2. Much has been made, with some justification, about the merits of running as a means of promoting physical fitness. Some runners (and other exercisers) form a positive addiction and others a negative addiction to their exercise regimen.

3. The notion of positive addiction was popularized in 1976 by psychiatrist William Glasser. To Glasser, the positively addicted person has a healthy attitude toward exercise, has worked it nicely into everyday life, and does not let exercise control his or her life. Evidence from a number of sources supports a generally healthy psychological state among runners, who Glasser would say are most likely to become positively addicted because they are using the exercise of choice.

4. The negatively addicted person has relinquished control of exercise. Work, family life, and health may be sacrificed for the sake of the search for fitness. Injury statistics indicate that negatively addicted runners are at higher risk of injury while working out or competing.

5. The phenomenon of the runner's high is generally agreed to exist, but attempts to operationalize it have not been successful. Estimates indicate that from 9% to 78% of all runners have experienced runner's high.

6. The marathon event was named after a small Greek town in which a prominent battle was fought between the Greeks and the Persians in 490 B.C. The marathon was introduced as an Olympic event in 1896, and its popularity has increased ever since. Women began marathon competition in the 1984 Olympics. Studies of marathoners suggest that they are introverts, have low anxiety levels, and have superior mood profiles in general.

7. Ultramarathoners (or ultrarunners) run distances above the 26 miles, 385 yards found in the marathon event. Ultramarathons may involve long distances over several days or weeks or distances up to 100 miles in a given day. Little is known about the psychology of ultramarathoners. Highly preliminary evidence suggests that they are generally psychologically healthy, with just enough personality deviance to help them participate in what may itself be a deviant event.

8. There will be an increase of 10 years in the median age of the typical American by the year 2050. This "graying of America" is a phenomenon that will place added pressure on a variety of services, not the least of which is exercise and fitness for senior citizens.

9. Chronological age is unalterable; biological age can be modified to an unknown extent, and it remains the task of the exerciser and the exercise and fitness specialists to determine this limit. It is likely that exercise offers one point of intervention in this biological aging issue.

10. Seniors who still have a competitive streak are increasingly being provided with outlets for their energies and talents. One such example is the National Senior Games, an 18-event competition for men and women over age 55.

11. Although exercise may represent one way to achieve fitness, physical activities of any kind that keep people occupied, interested, and moving about may be just as productive in promoting health.

KEY TERMS

athletic retirement (432)
Motivations of Marathoners Scale (MOMS) (426)
negative addiction (423)
Pheidippides (425)
positive addiction (422)
runner's high (424)
Spirduso's reaction time studies (429)
U.S. National Senior Games (434)
ultramarathon (426)
ultrarunners (426)

SUGGESTED READINGS

Adams, J., & Kirkby, R. J. (1998). Exercise dependence: A review of its manifestation, theory and measurement. *Sports Medicine: Training and Rehabilitation, 8,* 265–276.

Discusses research on exercise dependence, also called negative addiction, morbid exercise, athletic neurosis, and obligatory running. Some mention is made of devices used in assessing exercise dependence as well as several theories on how this dependence may be created. Catecholamine theory, elevated blood levels of beta-endorphins, and a "sympathetic hormonal arousal hypothesis" are all discussed, as is an addiction model similar to that used to account for other types of common addictions.

Cheng, J. (1999). Tai chi chuan: A slow dance for health. *Physician and Sportsmedicine, 27*(6), 109–111.

Cheng makes a case for a low-velocity, low-impact exercise with potential broad appeal called tai chi chuan (pronounced *tie jee choo-on*). This variant of the traditional Chinese program combines deep breathing, relaxation, and structured movement. Benefits of such a program, according to Cheng, include balance, lower blood pressure, and healthier heart circulation. It is suggested that tai chi chuan be practiced for 20 to 30 minutes at least two to three times per week. Additional information can be obtained from the American Tai Chi Health Association in Aliso Viejo, California.

Emery, C. F., Schein, R. L., Hauck, E. R., & MacIntyre, N. R. (1998). Psychological and cognitive outcomes of a randomized trial of exercise among patients with chronic obstructive pulmonary disease. *Health Psychology, 17,* 232–240.

Patients with chronic obstructive pulmonary disease (COPD) were randomly assigned to (1) ten weeks of exercise, education, and stress management; (2) education and stress management; and (3) a waiting list. Group 1 received 37 exercise sessions, 16 educational lectures on COPD, and 10 weekly stress management classes. Group 2 received 16 COPD lectures and 10 stress management classes. Pretreatment and posttreatment evaluations were made of pulmonary functioning, exercise endurance, anxiety, depression, and several measures of cognitive functioning. As predicted, there were noticeable improvements in the first group on several indices including improved endurance, lower levels of anxiety, and cognitive functioning. The authors believe that the intensity of the exercise component was a major contributor to the improvements noted.

McNab, T. (1982). *Flanagan's run.* New York: William Morrow and Company.

McNab, an elite triple jumper in track, coach for various British national teams for 11 years, and a consultant for the highly acclaimed movie *Chariots of Fire,* has written a highly sensitive and humorous novel based on the 1928 ultramarathon race from California to New York. Populated with a fascinating collection of personalities, and their trials and tribulations as they run their way across the United States, the book makes for very interesting reading. Peter Gent, ex-Dallas Cowboys wide receiver and author of *North Dallas Forty,* praised it as "a grand epic of America. Wonderful! The celebration of brotherhood, individual strength, and the defeat of fear and greed."

INFOTRAC COLLEGE EDITION

For additional readings, explore Infotrac College Edition, your online library. Go to: http://www.infotrac-college.com/wadsworth
Hint: Enter these search terms: jogging, marathon runners, runners' attitudes, runners' biographies, runners' injuries, runners' training, Senior Olympics, sports for the aged.

References

AAASP online, July 1999, p. 2.

AAHPERD physical best. (1988). Reston, VA: American Alliance for Health, Physical Education, Recreation and Dance.

AAHPERD youth fitness test manual. (1980). Reston, VA: American Alliance for Health, Physical Education, Recreation and Dance.

Abramson, L. Y., Seligman, M. E. P., & Teasdale, I. D. (1978). Learned helplessness in humans: Critique and reformulation. *Journal of Abnormal Psychology, 87,* 49–74.

Abu-Hilal, M. M., & Salarneh, K. M. (1992). Validity and reliability of the Maslach Burnout Inventory for a sample of non-western teachers. *Educational and Psychological Measurement, 52,* 161–169.

Acosta, R., & Carpenter, L. (1985). Women in athletics: A status report. *Journal of Physical Education, Recreation and Dance, 56* (7), 30–34.

Adler, A. (1927). *The theory and practice of individual psychology.* New York: Harcourt Brace.

Adorno, T., Frenkel-Brunswik, E., Levinson, D., & Sanford, N. (1950). *The authoritarian personality.* New York: John Wiley and Sons.

Aiken, L. (1982). *Psychological testing and assessment.* Boston: Allyn & Bacon.

Aiken, L. (1987). *Psychological testing and assessment* (2nd ed.). Boston: Allyn & Bacon.

Ajzen, L. (1985). From intention to actions: A theory of planned behavior. In J. Kuhl & J. Beckman (Eds.), *Action-control: From cognition to behavior.* Heidelberg: Springer.

Ajzen, L., & Fishbein, M. (1980). *Understanding attitudes and predicting social behavior.* Englewood Cliffs, NJ: Prentice-Hall.

Albrecht, R. R., Anderson, W. A., & McKeag, D. B. (1992). Drug testing of college athletes. *Sports Medicine, 14,* 349–352.

Albrecht, R. R., & Feltz, D. L. (1987). Generality and specificity of attention related to competitive anxiety and sport performance. *Journal of Sport Psychology, 9,* 231–248.

Alcohol-free seating not solution to some. (1987, June 29). *USA Today,* p. 7C.

Allen, K. (1987, March 20). Coaches too close to go head-to-head too often. *USA Today,* p. 4C.

Allen, K. (2000, February 24). McSorley is out for the season: Longest suspension in history of NHL is doled out. *USA Today,* pp. C1, C6.

Allison, M. G., & Ayllon, T. (1980). Behavioral coaching in the development of skills in football, gymnastics, and tennis. *Journal of Applied Behavioral Analysis, 13,* 297–314.

Allison, M. G., & Ayllon, T. (1983). Behavioral coaching in the development of skills in football, gymnastics, and tennis. In G. L. Martin & D. Hrycaiko (Eds.), *Behavior modification and coaching: Principles, procedures, and research.* Springfield, IL: Charles C. Thomas.

Allport, G. W. (1937). *Personality: A psychological interpretation.* New York: Holt.

Allport, G. W., & Odbert, H. S. (1936). Trait names: A psycho-lexical study. *Psychological Monographs, 47*(211), 1–171.

Alzado, L. (1991, July 8). I'm sick and I'm scared. *Sports Illustrated,* 20–27.

Ambah, E. (1994, September 4). World population conference. *Houston Chronicle,* p. 24A.

American Psychological Association. (1974). *Standards for educational and psychological tests and manuals.* Washington, DC: Author.

American youth and sports participation. (1990). North Palm Beach, FL: Athletic Footwear Association.

Anastasi, A. (1982). *Psychological testing* (5th ed.). New York: Macmillan.

Anastasi, A. (1988). *Psychological testing* (6th ed.). New York: Macmillan.

Andersen, M. B., & Williams, J. M. (1988). Stress and athletic injury. *Journal of Sport & Exercise Psychology, 10,* 294–306.

Anderson, C. A. (1989). Temperature and aggression: Ubiquitous effects of heat on occurrence of human violence. *Psychological Bulletin, 106,* 74–96.

Anderson, C. A., Anderson, K. B., & Deuser, W. E. (1996). Examining an affective aggression framework weapon and temperature effects on aggressive thoughts, affect, and attitudes. *Personality and Social Psychology Bulletin, 22,* 366–376.

Anderson, C. A., Bushman, B. J., & Groom, R. W. (1997). Hot years and serious and deadly assaults: Empirical tests of the heat hypothesis. *Journal of Personality and Social Psychology, 73,* 1213–1223.

Anderson, C. A., Deuser, W. E., & Deneve, K. M. (1995). Hot temperatures, hostile affect, hostile cognition, and arousal: Tests of general-model of affective aggression. *Personality and Social Psychology Bulletin, 21,* 434–448.

Anderson, D. F., & Gill, K. S. (1983). Occupational socialization patterns of men's and women's interscholastic basketball programs. *Journal of Sport Behavior, 6,* 105–106.

Anderson, K. J. (1990). Arousal and inverted-U hypothesis: A critique of Neiss's "reconceptualizing arousal." *Psychological Bulletin, 107,* 96–100.

Andre, T., & Holland, A. (1995). Orientation and attitude toward women among high school males and females. *Journal of Sport Behavior, 18,* 241–253.

Andrew, G., Oldridge, N., Parker, J., Cunningham, D., Rechnitzer, R., Jones, N., Buck, C., Kavanagh, T., Shephard, R., Sutton, J., & McDonald, W. (1981). Reasons for dropout from exercise programs in post-coronary patients. *Medicine and Science in Sports and Exercise, 13,* 164–168.

Annesi, J. J. (1999). Effects of minimal group promotion on cohesion and exercise adherence. *Small Group Research, 30,* 542–557.

Anshel, M. H. (1979). Effect of age, sex, and type of feedback on performance and locus of control. *Research Quarterly, 50,* 305–317.

Anshel, M. H. (1992). The case against the certification of sport psychologists: In search of the phantom expert. *The Sport Psychologist, 6,* 265–286.

Anshel, M. H. (1993). Against the certification of sport psychology consultants: A response to Zaichkowsky and Perna. *The Sport Psychologist, 7,* 344–353.

Anshel, M. H. (1997). *Sport psychology: From theory to practice* (3rd ed.). Scottsdale, AZ: Gorsuch Scarisbrick.

Anshel, M. H., & Weinberg, R. S. (1995). Sources of stress in American and Australian basketball referees. *Journal of Applied Sport Psychology, 7,* 11–22.

Ardrey, R. (1966). *The territorial imperative: A personal inquiry into the animal origins of property and nations.* New York: Atheneum.

Arnold, E. H. (1924, October). Athletics for women. *American Physical Education Review,* 452–457.

Astrand, R. O., Eriksson, B. O., Nylander, I., Engstrom, I., Karlberg, R., Saltin, B., & Thoren, C. (1963). Girl swimmers with special reference to respiratory and circulatory adaptation and gynaecological and psychiatric aspects. *Acta Paediatrica Scandinavica* (Suppl. 147).

Atkinson, J. W. (1957). Motivational determinants of risk-taking behavior. *Psychological Review, 64,* 359–372.

Atkinson, J. W. (1974). Strength of motivation and efficiency of performance. In J. W. Atkinson & J. O. Raynor (Eds.), *Motivation and achievement* (pp. 193–218). Washington, DC: V. H. Winston.

Bachman, R. (1994). *Violence against women.* Washington, DC: U.S. Department of Justice.

Bachrach, A. (1970). Diver behavior. *Human Performance and SCUBA Diving, 11,* 9–13.

Bahrke, M. S., & Morgan, W. P. (1978). Anxiety reduction following exercise and meditation. *Cognitive Therapy and Research, 2,* 323–333.

Bandura, A. (1969). *Principles of behavior modification.* New York: Holt, Rinehart and Winston.

Bandura, A. (1973). *Aggression: A social learning analysis.* Englewood Cliffs, NJ: Prentice-Hall.

Bandura, A. (1977). Self-efficacy: Toward a unifying theory of behavioral change. *Psychological Review, 84,* 191–215.

Bandura, A. (1990). Perceived self-efficacy in the exercise of personal agency. *Journal of Applied Sport Psychology, 2,* 128–163.

Baron, R. (1977). *Human aggression.* New York: Plenum.

Baron, R., & Ransberger, V. (1978). Ambient temperature and the occurrence of collective violence. The "long hot summer" revisited. *Journal of Personality and Social Psychology, 36,* 351–360.

Baron, R. A., & Richardson, D. R. (1994). *Human aggression* (2nd ed.). New York: Plenum.

Bartholomew, J. B., Brewer, B. W., Van Raalte, J. L., Linder, D. E., Cornelius, A. E., & Bart, S. M. (1998). A psychometric evaluation of the Sports Inventory for Pain. *The Sport Psychologist, 12,* 29–39.

Bartholomew, J. B., Edwards, S. M., Brewer, B. W., Van Raalte, J. L., & Linder, D. E. (1998). The Sports Inventory for Pain: A confirmatory factor analysis. *Research Quarterly for Exercise and Sport, 69,* 24–29.

Basketball coaches shift jobs at a record pace: 123 in top division have moved in 2 years. (1986). *Chronicle of Higher Education, 33*(13), 27.

Bass, B. (1981). *Stogdill's handbook of leadership.* New York: Free Press.

Baumann, M. (1991, September 18). Mixed feelings on gay athletes. *USA Today,* p. 10C.

Baumeister, R. F. (1984). Choking under pressure: Self-consciousness and paradoxical effects of incentives on skillful performance. *Journal of Personality and Social Psychology, 46,* 610–620.

Baumeister, R. F. (1995). Disputing the effects of championship pressures and home audiences. *Journal of Personality and Social Psychology, 68,* 644–648.

Baumeister, R. F., & Steinhilber, A. (1984). Paradoxical effects of supportive audiences on performance under pressure: The home field disadvantage in sports championships. *Journal of Personality and Social Psychology, 47,* 85–93.

Baumeister, R. F., Hamilton, J., & Tice, D. (1985). Public versus private expectancy of success: Confidence booster or performance pressure? *Journal of Personality and Social Psychology, 48,* 1447–1457.

Baumler, G. (1997). Sports psychology. In W. Bringman,

H. E. Luck, R. Miller, & C. E. Early (Eds.), *A pictorial history of psychology*. Carol Stream, IL: Quintessence.

Beaton, R., & Myers, J. (1993, February 25). Stacked deck: Stereotypes and the system keep Mexicans out of the major leagues. *USA Today*, pp. C1–C2.

Beaumaster, E. J., Knowles, J. B., & MacLean, A. W. (1978). The sleep of skydivers: A study of stress. *Psychophysiology, 15,* 209–213.

Becker, D., & Herwig, C. (1994, March 30). Women's hoops scene not all serene. *USA Today*, pp. 1C–2C.

Becker, M. H., Haefner, D. R., Kasl, S. V., Kirscht, J. R., Maiman, L. A., & Rosenstock, I. M. (1977). Selected psychosocial models and correlates of individual health-related behaviors. *Medical Care, 15,* 27–46.

Behling, O., & Schriesheim, C. (1976). *Organizational behavior theory, research, and application*. Boston: Allyn & Bacon.

Bell, J. (1994, July 8). Bears' Anderson decides to retire. *USA Today*, p. 7C.

Bem, S. (1974). The measurement of psychological androgyny. *Journal of Consulting and Clinical Psychology, 42,* 155–162.

Benjamin, L. T., Hopkins, J. R., & Nation, J. R. (1994). *Psychology* (3rd ed.). New York: Macmillan.

Berg, R. (1995). A gain of inches: In women's college sports, good news comes in small packages. *Perspective, 18*(10), 9.

Bergandi, T. A., Shryock, M. G., & Titus, T. G. (1990). The basketball concentration survey: Preliminary development and validation. *The Sport Psychologist, 4,* 119–129.

Berger, B. G. (1987). Swimmers report less stress: A series of investigations. In W. P. Morgan & S. E. Goldston (Eds.), *Exercise and mental health* (pp. 139–143). New York: Hemisphere.

Berger, B. G., & McInman, A. (1993). Exercise and the quality of life. In R. N. Singer, M. Murphey, & L. K. Tennant (Eds.), *Handbook of research in sport psychology* (pp. 729–760). New York: Macmillan.

Berkowitz, L. (1986). *A survey of social psychology*. New York: Holt, Rinehart and Winston.

Bernstein, I. H., & Gesn, P. R. (1997). On the dimensionality of the Buss/Perry Aggression Questionnaire. *Behaviour Therapy and Research, 35,* 563–568.

Berry, L. M., & Houston, J. P. (1993). *Psychology at work: An introduction to industrial and organizational psychology*. Dubuque, IA: Brown & Benchmark.

Best, C. (1987). Experience and career length in professional football: The effect of positional segregation. *Sociology of Sport Journal, 4,* 410–420.

Betts, J. (1953). The technological revolution and the rise of sport, 1850–1900. *Mississippi Valley Historical Review, 40,* 231–256.

Betts, J. (1971). Home front, battlefield, and sport during the Civil War. *Research Quarterly, 42,* 113–132.

Betts, J. R. (1974). *America's sporting heritage, 1850–1950.* Reading, MA: Addison-Wesley.

Bhushan, S., & Agarwal, V. (1978). Personality characteristics of high and low achieving Indian sports persons. *International Journal of Sport Psychology, 9,* 191–198.

Biddle, S. J. H. (1993). Attribution research and sport psychology. In R. N. Singer, M. Murphey, & L. K. Tennant (Eds.), *Handbook of research on sport psychology* (pp. 437–464). New York: Macmillan.

Biddle, S. J. H., & Hill, A. B. (1992). Attributions for objective outcome and subjective appraisal of performance: Their relationship with emotional reactions in sport. *British Journal of Social Psychology, 31,* 215–226.

Bird, A. M. (1977). Development of a model for predicting team performance. *Research Quarterly, 48,* 24–32.

Bird, A. M., & Brame, J. (1978). Self versus team attributions: A test of the "I'm OK, but the team's so-so" phenomenon. *Research Quarterly, 49,* 260–268.

Bird, A. M., & Cripe, B. K. (1986). *Psychology and sport behavior*. St. Louis, MO: Times Mirror/Mosby.

Bird, A. M., Foster, C., & Maruyama, G. (1980). Convergent and incremental effects of cohesion on attributions for self and team. *Journal of Sport Psychology, 2,* 181–194.

Bird, A. M., & Horn, M. E. (1990). Cognitive anxiety and mental errors in sport. *Journal of Sport & Exercise Psychology, 12,* 217–222.

Bird, A. M., & Williams, J. M. (1980). A developmental-attributional analysis of sex role stereotypes for sport performance. *Developmental Psychology, 16,* 319–322.

Birkeland, K. I., & Hemmersbach, P. (1999). The future of doping control in athletes. *Sports Medicine, 28,* 25–33.

Black head coaches: Taking charge on major campuses. (1982, May). *Ebony,* 57–62.

Blair, S., Falls, H., & Pate, R. (1983). A new physical fitness test. *Physician and Sportsmedicine, 1*(4), 87–95.

Blair, S. N., Kampert, J. B., Kohl, H. W., Barlow, C. E., Macera, C. A., Paffenbarger, R. S., & Gibbons, L. W. (1996). Influences of cardiorespiratory fitness and other precursors on cardiovascular disease and all-cause mortality in men and women. *Journal of the American Medical Association, 276,* 205–210.

Blaser, R., & Schilling, G. (1976). Personality tests in sport. *International Journal of Sport Psychology, 7,* 22–35.

Blau, G. (1984). Brief note comparing the Rotter and Levenson measures of locus of control. *Perceptual and Motor Skills, 58,* 173–174.

Bleak, J. L., & Frederick, C. M. (1998). Superstitious behavior in sport: Levels of effectiveness and determinants of use in three collegiate sports. *Journal of Sport Behavior, 21,* 1–15.

Blood, K. J. (1990). Non-medical substance use among athletes at a small liberal arts college. *Athletic Training, 25,* 335–339.

Bloom, G. A., Crumpton, R., & Anderson, J. E. (1999). A systematic observation study of the teaching behaviors of an expert basketball coach. *The Sport Psychologist, 13,* 157–170.

Bloom, M. (1986, December). You've come a long way, baby. *The Runner,* 26–36.

Bloomberg, R. (1977). Coach says running affects menstruation. *Physician and Sportsmedicine, 5*(9), 15.

Blouin, A. G., & Goldfield, G. S. (1995). Body-image and steroid use in male bodybuilders. *International Journal of Eating Disorders, 18,* 159–165.

Blucker, J., & Hershberger, E. (1983). Causal attribution theory and the female athlete: What conclusions can we draw? *Journal of Sport Psychology, 5,* 353–360.

Blumenthal, J., Williams, R., Wallace, A., Williams, R., & Needles, T. (1982). Physiological and psychological variables predict compliance to prescribed exercise therapy in patients recovering from myocardial infarction. *Psychosomatic Medicine, 44,* 519–527.

Boeck, G. (1995, January 31). Hospital stay shows Nelson he must change. *USA Today,* p. 2C.

Bond, C. F. (1982). Social facilitation: A self-presentational view. *Journal of Personality and Social Psychology, 42,* 1042–1050.

Bond, C. F., & Titus, L. J. (1983). Social facilitation: A meta-analysis of 241 studies. *Psychological Bulletin, 94,* 265–292.

Bontemps, A. (1964). *Famous Negro athletes.* New York: Dodd, Mead.

Booth, E. (1958). Personality traits of athletes as measured by the MMPI. *Research Quarterly, 29,* 127–138.

Booth, E. (1961). Personality traits of athletes as measured by the MMPI: A rebuttal. *Research Quarterly, 32,* 421–423.

Bootzin, R. R., Acocella, J. R., & Alloy, L. B. (1993). *Abnormal psychology: Current perspectives* (6th ed.). New York: McGraw-Hill.

Borg, G. (1973). Perceived exertion: A note on history and methods. *Medicine and Science in Sports, 5,* 90–93.

Boutcher, S., & Landers, D. M. (1988). The effects of vigorous exercise on anxiety, heart rate, and alpha activity of runners and nonrunners. *Psychophysiology, 25,* 696–702.

Brady, E. (1989, June 19). Being heard often leads to disruption. *USA Today,* pp. 1C–2C.

Brady, E., & Weiberg, S. (1997, April 22). Ex-Brown player hails Title IX court move. *USA Today,* p. 3C.

Bramwell, S. T., Minoru, M., Wagner, N. N., & Holmes, T. H. (1975). Psychosocial factors in athletic injuries. *Journal of Human Stress, 1,* 6–20.

Brannigan, A., & McDougall, A. A. (1983). Peril and pleasure in the maintenance of a high risk sport: A study of hang-gliding. *Journal of Sport Behavior, 6,* 37–51.

Brant, J. (1988, February). The choke: Lament for a species of overreactors. *Outside,* 23–26.

Brasch, R. (1970). *How did sports begin? A look at the origins of man at play.* New York: David McKay.

Brawley, L. R. (1990). Group cohesion: Status, problems, and future directions. *International Journal of Sport Psychology, 21,* 355–379.

Brawley, L. R., Carron, A. V., & Widmeyer, W. N. (1987). Assessing the cohesion of teams: Validity of the Group Environment Questionnaire. *Journal of Sport Psychology, 9,* 275–294.

Bray, S. R. (1999). The home advantage from an individual team perspective. *Journal of Applied Sport Psychology, 11,* 116–125.

Bray, S. R., & Carron, A. V. (1993). The home advantage in alpine skiing. *The Australian Journal of Science and Medicine in Sport, 25,* 76–81.

Breaking point. (1995, March 6). *Time,* 56–61.

Bredemeier, B. J. L. (1978). Applications and implications of aggression research. In W. F. Straub (Ed.), *Sport psychology: An analysis of athlete behavior.* Ithaca, NY: Mouvement.

Bredemeier, B. J. L. (1994). Children's moral reasoning and their assertive, aggressive, and submissive tendencies in sport and daily life. *Journal of Sport & Exercise Psychology, 16,* 1–14.

Breivik, G. (1996). Personality, sensation seeking and risk taking among Everest climbers. *International Journal of Sport Psychology, 27,* 308–320.

Brewer, B. W. (1994). Review and critique of models of psychological adjustment to athletic injury. *Journal of Applied Sport Psychology, 6,* 87–100.

Brewer, B., Van Raalte, J., & Linder, D. (1993). Athletic identity: Hercules' muscle or Achilles' heel? *International Journal of Sport Psychology, 24,* 237–254.

Brewer, B. W., Van Raalte, J. L., Petitpas, A. J., Bachman, A. D., & Weinhold, R. A. (1998). Newspaper portrayals of sport psychology in the United States, 1985–1993. *The Sport Psychologist, 12,* 89–94.

Brewington, R., & White, C. (1988, February 4). Women fight to keep the door from closing. *USA Today,* p. 1C.

Brichin, M., & Kochian, M. (1970). Comparison of some personality traits of women participating and not participating in sports. *Ceskoslovenska Psychologie, 14,* 309–321.

Brown, B. (1988, June 8). Study: Girls find activities for a lifetime. *USA Today,* p. 9C.

Brown, B. (1993, April 13). Keeping fit on decline. *USA Today,* p. 2C.

Brown, J. A. (1954). *The social psychology of industry.* New York: Penguin Books.

Brown, R. (1965). *A use of the semantic differential to study the image of girls who participate in competitive sports and certain other school related activities.* Unpublished doctoral dissertation, Florida State University.

Brown, R., Ramirez, D., & Taub, J. (1978). The prescription

of exercise for depression. *Physician and Sportsmedicine,* *6*(12), 35–45.

Browne, A., Lachance, V., & Pipe, A. (1999). The ethics of blood testing as an element of doping control in sport. *Medicine and Science in Sports and Exercise, 31,* 497–501.

Brownlee, S. (1988, May). Moms in the fast lane. *Sports Illustrated,* 56–60.

Brunelle, J. P., Janelle, C. M., & Tennant, L. K. (1999). Controlling competitive anger among male soccer players. *Journal of Applied Sport Psychology, 11,* 283–297.

Brustad, R., & Weiss, M. R. (1987). Competence perceptions and sources of worry in high, medium, and low competitive trait-anxious youth athletes. *Journal of Sport Psychology, 9,* 97–105.

Bryant, J., & Zillman, D. (1983). Sports violence and the media. In J. Goldstein (Ed.), *Sports violence* (pp. 195–211). New York: Springer-Verlag.

Bryant, J., Brown, D., Comisky, R. W., & Zillman, D. (1982). Sports and spectators: Commentary and appreciation. *Journal of Communication, 32,* 109–119.

Bryant, J., Comisky, R., & Zillman, D. (1977). Drama in sports commentary. *Journal of Communication, 27,* 140–149.

Bryant, J., Comisky, R., & Zillman, D. (1981). The appeal of rough-and-tumble play in televised football. *Communication Quarterly, 29,* 256–262.

Buchanan, D. (1975). *Roman sport and entertainment.* Essex, England: Longmans.

Buffone, G. W. (1984). Exercise as a therapeutic adjunct. In J. M. Silva & R. S. Weinberg (Eds.), *Psychological foundations of sport* (pp. 445–451). Champaign, IL: Human Kinetics.

Bukowski, W., & Moore, D. (1980). Winners' and losers' attributions for success and failure in a series of athletic events. *Journal of Sport Psychology, 2,* 195–210.

Bull, S. J. (1989). The role of the sport psychology consultant: A case study of ultra-distance running. *The Sport Psychologist, 3,* 254–264.

Bunker, L., & Owen, D. (1985). *Golf: Better practice for better play.* West Point, NY: Leisure Press.

Bunker, L., & Rotella, R. (1980). Achievement and stress in sport: Research findings and practical suggestions. In W. F. Straub (Ed.), *Sport psychology: An analysis of athlete behavior.* Ithaca, NY: Mouvement.

Bunker, L., Williams, J. M., & Zinsser, N. (1993). Cognitive techniques for improving performance and building confidence. In J. M. Williams (Ed.), *Applied sport psychology: Personal growth to peak experience* (pp. 225–242). Mountain View, CA: Mayfield.

Burfoot, A. (1992). White men can't run. *Runner's World, 27*(8), 89–95.

Burke, K. L. (1999). Comments on Balague's 1997 A.A.A.S.P. conference keynote address. *The Sport Psychologist, 13,* 231–234.

Burlingame, M. (1972, Winter). Socialization constructs and the teaching of teachers. *Quest, 18,* 40–56.

Burns, J. M. (1978). *Leadership.* New York: Harper & Row.

Buros, O. K. (1986). *Ninth mental measurements yearbook.* Highland Park, NJ: Gryphon Press.

Burton, D. (1988). Do anxious swimmers swim slower? Re-examining the elusive anxiety-performance relationship. *Journal of Sport & Exercise Psychology, 10,* 45–61.

Burton, D., & Martens, R. (1986). Pinned by their own goals: An exploratory investigation into why kids drop out of wrestling. *Journal of Sport Psychology, 8,* 183–197.

Bushman, B. J., & Wells, G. L. (1998). Trait aggressive and hockey penalties: Predicting hot tempers on the ice. *Journal of Applied Psychology, 83,* 969–974.

Buss, A. H., & Perry, M. (1992). The Aggression Questionnaire. *Journal of Personality and Social Psychology, 63,* 452–459.

Butcher, J. N., Dahlstrom, W. G., Graham, J. R., Tellegen, A., & Kaemmer, B. (1989). *Minnesota Multiphasic Personality Inventory: MMPI–2.* Minneapolis: University of Minnesota Press.

Butler, J. L., & Baumeister, R. F. (1998). The trouble with friendly faces: Skilled performance with a supportive audience. *Journal of Personality and Social Psychology, 75,* 1213–1230.

Butler, R. J. (1989). Psychological preparation of Olympic boxers. In J. Kramer & W. Crawford (Eds.), *The psychology of sport: Theory and practice* (pp. 74–84). Belfast, Northern Ireland: British Psychological Society Northern Ireland Branch: Occasional Paper.

Butler, R. J. (1991). Amateur boxing and sports science II: Psychology. *Coaching Focus, 18,* 14–15.

Butler, R. J., & Hardy, L. (1992). The performance profile: Theory and application. *The Sport Psychologist, 6,* 253–264.

Butler, R. J., Smith, M., & Irwin, I. (1993). The performance profile in practice. *Journal of Applied Sport Psychology, 5,* 48–63.

Butler, T. (1991, February 19). Media unwittingly protecting sexual harassers. *USA Today,* p. 10C.

Buzas, H. P., & Ayllon, T. (1981). Differential reinforcement in coaching tennis skills. *Behavior Modification, 5,* 372–385.

Byrnes, J. P., Miller, D. C., & Schafer, W. D. (1999). Gender differences in risk taking: A meta-analysis. *Psychological Bulletin, 125,* 367–383.

Caccese, T., & Mayerberg, C. (1984). Gender differences in perceived burnout of college coaches. *Journal of Sport Psychology, 6,* 279–288.

Cahn, S. K. (1993). From the "muscle moll" to the "butch" ballplayer: Mannishness, lesbianism, and homophobia in U.S. women's sport. *Feminist Studies, 19,* 343–368.

Calhoun, J., & Acocella, J. (1983). *Psychology of adjustment* and human relationships (2nd ed.). New York: Random House.

Campbell, T., Gillaspy, J. A., & Thompson, B. (1997). The factor structure of the Bem Sex-Role Inventory (BSRI): Confirmatory analysis of long and short forms. *Educational and Psychological Measurement, 57,* 118–124.

Cancio, L. C. (1991). Stress and trance in freefall parachuting: A pilot study. *American Journal of Clinical Hypnosis, 33,* 225–234.

Cantwell, J. D., & Fontanarosa, P. B. (1996). An Olympic medal legacy. *Journal of the American Medical Association, 276,* 248–249.

Capel, S. A. (1986). Psychological and organizational factors related to burnout in athletic trainers. *Athletic Training, 21,* 322–327.

Capel, S. A., Sisley, B. L., & Desertrain, G. S. (1987). The relationship of role conflict and role ambiguity to burnout in high school basketball coaches. *Journal of Sport Psychology, 9,* 106–117.

Carfagno, D. G. (1998). Physically challenged athlete: An update. http://www.hypermedic.com/warthog/rounds/Physical.html

Carmack, M. A., & Martens, R. (1979). Measuring commitment to running: A survey of runners' attitudes and mental states. *Journal of Sport Psychology, 1,* 25–42.

Carron, A. V. (1980). *Social psychology of sport.* Ithaca, NY: Mouvement.

Carron, A. V. (1984). Cohesion in sport teams. In J. M. Silva & R. S. Weinberg (Eds.), *Psychological foundations of sport* (pp. 340–351). Champaign, IL: Human Kinetics.

Carron, A. V., & Chelladurai, P. (1981). The dynamics of group cohesion in sport. *Journal of Sport Psychology, 3,* 123–139.

Carron, A. V., & Spink, K. S. (1992). Internal consistency of the Group Environment Questionnaire modified for an exercise setting. *Perceptual and Motor Skills, 74,* 304–306.

Carron, A. V., & Spink, K. S. (1995). The group-cohesion relationship in minimal groups. *Small Group Research, 26,* 86–105.

Carron, A. V., Widmeyer, W. N., & Brawley, L. R. (1985). The development of an instrument to assess cohesion in sport teams: The Group Environment Questionnaire. *Journal of Sport Psychology, 7,* 244–266.

Carson, K. (1987). *The effects of sex-role orientation and fear of success on attitudes toward women in sport.* Unpublished master's thesis, Texas A&M University.

Carson, R. C., Butcher, J. N., & Mineka, S. (1998). *Abnormal psychology and modern life* (10th ed.). New York: Longman.

Carter, J. E., & Kelley, A. E. (1997). Using traditional and paradoxical imagery interventions with reactant intramural athletes. *The Sport Psychologist, 11,* 175–189.

Casher, B. (1977). Relationship between birth order and participation in dangerous sports. *Research Quarterly, 48,* 33–40.

Caspersen, C. J. (1985). Physical activity, exercise, and physical fitness: Definitions and distinctions for health-related research. *Physician and Sportsmedicine, 13*(5), 162.

Caspersen, C. J., & Merritt, R. K. (1995). Physical activity trends among 26 states, 1986–1990. *Medicine and Science in Sports and Exercise, 27,* 713–720.

Catlin, D. H., & Murray, T. H. (1996). Performance-enhancing drugs, fair competition, and Olympic sports. *Journal of the American Medical Association, 276,* 231–237.

Cattell, R. B. (1949). Manual for the *Sixteen Personality Factor Questionnaire.* Champaign, IL: Institute for Personality and Ability Testing.

Caudill, D., Weinberg, R. S., & Jackson, A. (1983). Psyching-up and track athletes: A preliminary investigation. *Journal of Sport Psychology, 5,* 231–235.

Celestino, R., Tapp, J., & Brumet, M. (1979). Locus of control correlates with marathon performances. *Perceptual and Motor Skills, 48,* 1249–1250.

Chalip, L. (1980). Social learning theory and sport success. *Journal of Sport Behavior, 3,* 76–85.

Chalip, L., Villiger, J., & Duignan, R. (1980). Sex-role identity in a selected sample of women field hockey players. *International Journal of Sport Psychology, 11,* 240–248.

Chapman, C. L., & DeCastro, J. M. (1990). Running addiction: Measurement and associated psychological characteristics. *Journal of Sports Medicine and Physical Fitness, 30,* 283–290.

Chartrand, J. M., Jowdy, D. R., & Danish, S. J. (1992). The Psychological Skills Inventory for Sports: Psychometric characteristics and applied implications. *Journal of Sport & Exercise Psychology, 14,* 405–413.

Chelladurai, P. (1984a). Discrepancy between preferences and perceptions of leadership behavior and satisfaction of athletes in varying sports. *Journal of Sport Psychology, 6,* 27–41.

Chelladurai, P. (1984b). Leadership in sports. In J. M. Silva & R. S. Weinberg (Eds.), *Psychological foundations of sport* (pp. 329–339). Champaign, IL: Human Kinetics.

Chelladurai, P. (1986). Applicability of the Leadership Scale for Sports to the Indian context. In J. Watkins, T. Reilly, & L. Burwitz (Eds.), *Sport science* (pp. 291–296). New York: E. & F. N. Spon Ltd.

Chelladurai, P. (1989). Decision style choices of university basketball coaches and players. *Journal of Sport & Exercise Psychology, 11,* 201–215.

Chelladurai, P. (1990). Leadership in sports: A review. *International Journal of Sport Psychology, 21,* 328–354.

Chelladurai, P., & Carron, A. V. (1978). *Leadership* (Monograph). Ottawa: Canadian Association of Health, Physical Education and Recreation.

Chelladurai, P., & Carron, A. V. (1981). Applicability to

youth sport of the Leadership Scale for Sports. *Perceptual and Motor Skills, 53,* 361–362.

Chelladurai, P., & Carron, A. V. (1983). Athletic maturity and preferred leadership. *Journal of Sport Psychology, 5,* 371–380.

Chelladurai, P., Haggerty, T. R., & Baxter, P. R. (1989). Decision style choices of university basketball coaches and players. *Journal of Sport & Exercise Psychology, 11,* 201–215.

Chelladurai, P., Imamura, H., Yamaguchi, H., Oinuma, Y., & Miyauchi, T. (1988). Sport leadership in a cross-national setting: The case of the Japanese and Canadian university athletes. *Journal of Sport & Exercise Psychology, 10,* 374–389.

Chelladurai, P., & Saleh, S. (1978). Preferred leadership in sports. *Canadian Journal of Applied Sport Sciences, 3,* 85–92.

Chelladurai, P., & Saleh, S. (1980). Dimensions of leader behavior in sports: Development of a leadership scale. *Journal of Sport Psychology, 2,* 24–35.

Chow, B. C., & Hon, S. (1998, Fall). Reporting of female athletes in the newspapers. *Journal of the International Council for Health, Physical Education, Recreation, Sport, and Dance Journal,* 59–63.

Christensen, D. (1999, November 27). Heading for injury: The danger of heading soccer balls up in the air. *Science News,* pp. 348–349.

Christie, R., & Geis, F. (1970). *Studies in Machiavellianism.* New York: Academic Press.

Chu, D. (1982). *Dimensions of sport studies.* New York: Wiley.

Cialdini, R. B., Borden, R. J., Thorne, A., Walker, M. R., Freeman, S., & Sloan, L. R. (1976). Basking in reflected glory: Three (football) field studies. *Journal of Personality and Social Psychology, 34,* 366–375.

Ciccantelli, P. (1994). Avoiding elbow pain: Tips for young pitchers. *Physician and Sportsmedicine, 22*(3), 65–66.

Clark, W. J., Vaz, E., Vetere, V., & Ward, T. A. (1978). Illegal aggression in minor league hockey: A causal model. In F. Landry and W. A. R. Orban (Eds.), *Ice hockey: Research, development and new concepts* (pp. 81–88). Miami, FL: Symposium Specialists.

Clarke, K., & Braslow, A. (1978). Football fatalities in actuarial perspective. *Medicine and Science in Sports, 10*(2), 94–96.

Closed doors to gold glory. (1996, June 10). *Newsweek,* 82.

Cloud, J. (2000, April 24). Never too buff. *Time,* 64–68.

Coaching changes. (2000, August 11). http://www.espn.go.com/ncf/1999/1210/225

Coaching exodus sends Big Eight reeling. (1994, November 24). *Bryan–College Station Eagle [TX],* p. C6.

Coakley, J. (1982). *Sports in society: Issues and controversies* (2nd ed.). St. Louis, MO: Mosby.

Coakley, J. J. (1994). *Sport in society: Issues and controversies* (5th ed.). St. Louis, MO: Mosby.

Coddington, R. D., & Troxell, J. R. (1980). The effect of emotional factors on football injury rates: A pilot study. *Journal of Human Stress, 6,* 3–5.

Cohen, R. J., Swerdlik, M. E., & Smith, D. L. (1992). *Psychological testing and assessment* (2nd ed.). Mountain View, CA: Mayfield.

Cohn, E. G., & Rotton, J. (1997). Assault as a function of time and temperature: A moderator-variable-time series analysis. *Journal of Personality and Social Psychology, 72,* 1322–1334.

Colley, A., Roberts, N., & Chipps, A. (1985). Sex-role identity, personality, and participation in team and individual sports by males and females. *International Journal of Sport Psychology, 16,* 103–112.

Collins, B. (1974). Four components of Rotter internal–external scale. *Journal of Personality and Social Psychology, 29,* 381–391.

Comer, R. J. (1992). *Abnormal psychology.* New York: W. H. Freeman.

Comer, R. J. (2001). *Abnormal psychology* (4th ed.). New York: Worth.

Comisky, P., Bryant, J., & Zillman, D. (1977). Commentary as a substitute for action. *Journal of Communication, 27,* 150–153.

Congeni, J. (1994). Treating—and preventing—Little League elbow. *Physician and Sportsmedicine, 22*(3), 54–64.

Congress considers ban on mail order steroids. (1989). *Physician and Sportsmedicine, 17*(5), 34.

Corby, B. (1993). *Child abuse.* Philadelphia: Open University Press.

Corrington, K. (1994, July). Personal communication. College Station, TX.

Corrington, K. A. (1994, November 15). Personal communication. College Station, TX.

Costa, R. T., & McCrae, R. R. (1985). *The NEO Personality Inventory Manual.* Odessa, FL: Psychological Assessment Resources.

Costa, R. T., & McCrae, R. R. (1992). Normal personality assessment in clinical practice. *Psychological Assessment, 4,* 5–13.

Cotman, C. W., & McGaugh, J. L. (1980). *Behavioral neuroscience.* New York: Academic Press.

Cottle, S. (1982). *Sex bias and professional status level effects in the evaluations of coaching ability.* Unpublished master's thesis, California State University, Fullerton.

Cottrell, N. B. (1972). Social facilitation. In C. G. McClintock (Ed.), *Experimental social psychology* (pp. 185–236). New York: Holt, Rinehart and Winston.

Courneya, K. S., & Carron, A. V. (1990). Batting first versus last: Implications for the home advantage. *Journal of Sport & Exercise Psychology, 12,* 312–316.

Courneya, K. S., & Carron, A. V. (1991). Effects of travel and length of home stand/road trip on the home advantage. *Journal of Sport & Exercise Psychology, 13,* 42–49.

Courneya, K. S., & Carron, A. V. (1992). The home

advantage in sport competitions: A literature review. *Journal of Sport & Exercise Psychology, 14,* 13–27.

Courneya, K. S., & Hellsten, L. A. M. (1998). Personality correlates of exercise behavior, motives, barriers, and preferences: An application of the five-factor model. *Personality and Individual Differences, 24,* 625–633.

Cox, R. H. (1985). *Sport psychology: Concepts and applications.* Dubuque, IA: Wm. C. Brown.

Cox, R. H. (1990). *Sport psychology: Concepts and applications* (2nd ed.). Dubuque, IA: Wm. C. Brown.

Cox, R. H. (1998). *Sport psychology: Concepts and applications* (4th ed.). Dubuque IA: Wm. C. Brown/McGraw-Hill.

Cox, R. H., Qiu, Y., & Liu, Z. (1993). Overview of sport psychology. In R. N. Singer, M. Murphey, & L. K. Tennant (Eds.), *Handbook of research on sport psychology* (pp. 3–31). New York: Macmillan.

Crafts, L. W., Schneirla, T. C., Robinson, E. E., & Gilbert, R. W. (1938). *Recent experiments in psychology.* New York: McGraw-Hill.

Crampton, C. W. (1908). Physiological age: A fundamental principle. *American Physical Education Review, 8,* 141–154.

Cratty, B. J. (1981). *Social psychology in athletics.* Englewood Cliffs, NJ: Prentice-Hall.

Cratty, B. J. (1989). *Psychology in contemporary sport* (3rd ed.). Englewood Cliffs, NJ: Prentice-Hall.

Crockett, D. (1961). Sports and recreational practices of Union and Confederate soldiers. *Research Quarterly, 32,* 335–347.

Cronbach, L. J. (1970). *Essentials of psychological testing* (3rd ed.). New York: Harper & Row.

Crossman, J. E. (1986). Spectator behavior at minor league hockey games. *Perceptual and Motor Skills, 63,* 803–812.

Crowne, D. P., & Marlowe, D. (1964). *The approval motive: Studies in evaluative independence.* New York: Wiley.

Cryan, P. D., & Alles, W. F. (1983). The relationship between stress and college football injuries. *Journal of Sports Medicine and Physical Fitness, 23,* 52–58.

Csikszentmihalyi, M. (1975). *Beyond boredom and anxiety.* San Francisco: Jossey-Bass.

Csikszentmihalyi, M., & Bennett, S. (1971). An exploratory model of play. *American Anthropologist, 73,* 45–58.

Cullen, J., & Cullen, E. (1975). The structural and contextual conditions of group norm violation: Some implications from the game of ice hockey. *International Review of Sport Sociology, 10,* 69–78.

Curry, T. J., & Jiobu, R. (1984). *Sport: A social perspective.* Englewood Cliffs, NJ: Prentice-Hall.

Dabbs, J. M., & Morris, R. (1990). Testosterone, social class, and antisocial behavior in a sample of 4462 men. *Psychological Science, 1,* 209–211.

Daiss, S., LeUnes, A., & Nation, J. R. (1986). Mood and locus of control of a sample of college and professional football players. *Perceptual and Motor Skills, 63,* 731–734.

Dalton, K. (1961). Menstruation and crime. *British Medical Journal, 3,* 1752–1753.

Dalton, K. (1964). *The pre-menstrual syndrome.* Springfield, IL: Charles C. Thomas.

Daniels, F. S., & Landers, D. M. (1981). Biofeedback and shooting performance: A test of disregulation and systems theory. *Journal of Sport Psychology, 3,* 271–282.

Danielson, R. R. (1976). Leadership motivation and coaching classification as related to success in minor league hockey. In R. Christina & D. Landers (Eds.), *Psychology of motor behavior and sport, Vol. 2* (pp. 183–189). Champaign, IL: Human Kinetics.

Danielson, R. R., Zelhart, P. E., & Drake, C. J. (1975). Multidimensional scaling and factor analysis of coaching behavior as perceived by high school hockey players. *Research Quarterly, 46,* 323–334.

Dashiell, J. R. (1935). Experimental studies of the influence of social situations on the behavior of individual human adults. In C. Murchison (Ed.), *A handbook of social psychology* (pp. 1097–1158). Worcester, MA: Clark University Press.

Davis, H. (1991). Criterion validity of the Athletic Motivation Inventory: Issues in professional sport. *Journal of Applied Sport Psychology, 3,* 176–182.

Davis, S. F., Huss, M. T., & Becker, A. H. (1995). Norman Triplett and the dawning of sport psychology. *The Sport Psychologist, 9,* 366–375.

Deaux, K., & Emswiller, T. (1974). Explanations of successful performance on sex-linked tasks: What is skill for the male is luck for the female. *Journal of Personality and Social Psychology, 29,* 80–85.

Deaux, K., & Farris, E. (1977). Attributing causes for one's own performance: The effects of sex, norms, and outcome. *Journal of Research in Personality, 11,* 59–72.

DeCharms, R. (1968). *Personal causation.* New York: Academic Press.

Deci, E. (1975). *Intrinsic motivation.* New York: Plenum.

Dedera, D. (1975). *Hang gliding: The flyingest flying.* Flagstaff, AZ: Northland Press.

Delany, J. S., & Drummond, R. (1999). Has the time come for protective headgear for soccer? *Clinical Journal of Sports Medicine, 9,* 121–123.

Delcomyn, F. *Foundations of neurobiology.* (1998). New York: W. H. Freeman.

Delk, J. (1973). Some personality characteristics of skydivers. *Life Threatening Behavior, 3*(1), 51–57.

Del Rey, R., & Sheppard, S. (1981). Relationship of psychological androgyny in female athletes to self-esteem. *International Journal of Sport Psychology, 12,* 165–175.

Demant, T. W., & Rhodes, E. C. (1999). Effects of creatine

supplementation on exercise performance. *Sports Medicine, 28,* 49–60.

DeMinzi, M. C. R. (1991). A new multidimensional children's locus of control scale. *The Journal of Psychology, 125,* 109–118.

DePalma, D., & Nideffer, R. (1977). Relationships between the Test of Attentional and Interpersonal Style and psychiatric subclassification. *Journal of Personality Assessment, 41,* 622–631.

Desharnais, R., Jobin, J., Cote, C., Levesque, L., & Godin, G. (1993). Aerobic exercise and the placebo effect: A controlled study. *Psychosomatic Medicine, 55,* 149–154.

Dewar, C. (1979). Spectator fights at professional baseball games. *Review of Sport and Leisure, 4,* 14–25.

Dewey, D., Brawley, L. R., & Allard, E. (1989). Do the TAIS attentional-style scales predict how visual information is processed? *Journal of Sport & Exercise Psychology, 11,* 171–186.

DeWitt, D. J. (1979). Biofeedback training with university athletes. In *Proceedings of the Biofeedback Society Annual Meeting,* Denver, CO: The Biofeedback Society.

DeWitt, D. J. (1980). Cognitive and biofeedback training for stress reduction with university athletes. *Journal of Sport Psychology, 2,* 288–294.

Dicara, L. (1970). Learning in the autonomic nervous system. *Scientific American, 22,* 30–39.

Dick, R. W. (1991). Eating disorders in NCAA athletic programs. *Athletic Training, 26,* 136–140.

Dickey, G. (1982). *The history of National League baseball since 1876.* New York: Stein & Day.

Dickinson, J. A. (1977). *A behavioral analysis of sport.* Princeton, NJ: Princeton University Press.

Diekhoff, G. (1984). Running amok: Injuries in compulsive runners. *Journal of Sport Behavior, 7,* 120–129.

Di Giuseppe, R. (1973). Internal–external control of reinforcement and participation in team, individual, and intramural sports. *Perceptual and Motor Skills, 36,* 33–34.

Dietzel, P. (1983). There is life after football. *Physical Educator, 40,* 161–162.

Dishman, R. K. (1983). Identity crisis in North American sport psychology: Academics in professional issues. *Journal of Sport Psychology, 5,* 123–134.

Dishman, R. K. (1984). Motivation and exercise adherence. In J. M. Silva & R. S. Weinberg (Eds.), *Psychological foundations of sport* (pp. 420–434). Champaign, IL: Human Kinetics.

Dishman, R. K. (1986). Exercise compliance: A new view for public health. *Physician and Sportsmedicine, 14*(5), 127–145.

Dishman, R. K. (1991). Increasing and maintaining exercise and physical activity. *Behavior Therapy, 22,* 345–378.

Division I men's college basketball 2000 coaching changes. (2000, July 17). *USA Today,* p. 16C.

Dobie, M. (2000a, July 21). Danger and mystery: Triad ailments can be very serious, but information is scarce. http://www.newsday.com/features/health/triad/tcov0728.html

Dobie, M. (2000b, July 21). On thin ice: Eating disorders are a huge medical concern. http://newsday.com/features/health/triad/tcov0727.html

Dodd, M. (1994, July 9). Baseball gets "C" on "racial report card." *USA Today,* pp. 1C–2C.

Dollard, J., Doob, L., Miller, N., Mowrer, O. H., & Sears, R. (1939). *Frustration and aggression.* New Haven, CT: Yale University Press.

Domjan, M. (1998). *The principles of learning and behavior* (4th ed.). Pacific Grove, CA: Brooks/Cole.

Donahue, J. A., Gillis, J. H., & King, K. (1980). Behavior modification in sport and physical education: A review. *Journal of Sport Psychology, 2,* 311–328.

Donnelly, P. (1993). Problems associated with youth involvement in high-performance sport. In B. R. Cahill & A. J. Pearl (Eds.), *Intensive participation in children's sports* (pp. 95–126). Champaign, IL: Human Kinetics.

Donnelly, P. (1997). Child labour, sport labour. Applying child labour laws to sport. *International Review of the Sociology of Sport, 32,* 389–406.

Donnelly, P., Carron, A. V., & Chelladurai, R. (1978). *Group cohesion and sport* (Sociology of Sport Monograph Series). Ottawa, Ontario: Canadian Association for Health, Physical Education, and Recreation.

Donnelly, R. (1975). *An analysis of the relationship between organizational half-life and organizational effectiveness.* Paper completed for an advanced topics course, Department of Sport Studies, University of Massachusetts, Amherst.

Donnelly, S. B. (1990, Fall). Work that body! *Time* (Special issue), 68.

Donnerstein, E., & Wilson, D. (1976). Effects of noise and perceived control on ongoing and subsequent aggressive behavior. *Journal of Personality and Social Psychology, 34,* 774–781.

Dorsey, V. L., & Coomes, M. (1991, May 30). Michigan athletic association makes cheerleading a competitive sport. *USA Today,* p. 9C.

Doyne, E. J., Ossip-Klein, D. J., Bowman, E. D., Osborn, K. M., McDougall-Wilson, B., & Neimeyer, R. A. (1987). Running versus weight lifting in the treatment of depression. *Journal of Consulting and Clinical Psychology, 55,* 748–754.

Droste, C., Greenlee, M. W., Schreck, M., & Roskamm, H. (1991). Experimental pain thresholds and plasma beta-endorphin levels during exercise. *Medicine and Science in Sports and Exercise, 23,* 334–342.

Druckman, D., & Swets, J. A. (1987). *Enhancing human performance: Issues, theories, and techniques.* Washington, DC: National Academy Press.

Drug testing in sports. (1985). *Physician and Sportsmedicine, 13*(12), 69–82.

Duarte, J. (1998, February 8). First familia. *Houston Chronicle,* pp. 19B–20B.

DuBois, R. (1980). Competition in youth sport: Process or product? *Physical Educator, 37,* 151–154.

Duncan, M. C. (1990). Sports photographs and sexual differ- ence: Images of women and men in the 1984 and 1988 Olympic Games. *Sociology of Sport Journal, 7,* 22–43.

Duncan, T., & McAuley, E. (1987). Efficacy expectations and perceptions of causality in motor performance. *Journal of Sport Psychology, 9,* 385–393.

Dunkle, M. (1974). Equal opportunity for women in sport. In B. Hoepner (Ed.), *Women's athletics: Coping with contro- versy.* Washington, DC: American Association for Health, Physical Education, and Recreation.

Dunn, J., & Lupfer, M. (1974). A comparison of black and white boys' performance in self-paced and reactive sports activities. *Journal of Applied Social Psychology, 4,* 24–35.

Dunning, E. (1983). Social bonding and violence in sport: A theoretical–empirical analysis. In J. H. Goldstein (Ed.), *Sports violence* (pp.129–146). New York: Springer-Verlag.

Dunning, E., Maguire, J., Murphy, P., & Williams, J. (1982). The social roots of football hooligan violence. *Leisure Studies, 1,* 139–146.

Duquin, M. E. (1978). The androgynous advantage. In C. A. Oglesby (Ed.), *Women and sport: From myth to reality* (pp. 89–106). Philadelphia: Lea and Febiger.

Duval, S., & Wicklund, R. (1972). *A theory of objective self- awareness.* New York: Academic Press.

Dweck, C. S. (1980). Learned helplessness in sport. In K. M. Newell & G. C. Roberts (Eds.), *Psychology of motor behav- ior and sport—1979* (pp. 1–11). Champaign, IL: Human Kinetics.

Dweck, C. S. (1986). Motivational processes affecting learn- ing. *American Psychologist, 41,* 1040–1048.

Dworkin, B. R., & Miller, N. E. (1986). Failure to replicate visceral learning in the acute curarized rat preparation. *Behavioral Neuroscience, 100,* 299–314.

Dyer, K. (1982). *Challenging the men: The social biology of fe- male sporting achievement.* St. Lucia, Queensland, Australia: University of Queensland Press.

Edwards, H. (1973). *Sociology of sport.* Homewood, IL: Dorsey.

Edwards, S. W., Gordin, R. D., & Henschen, K. R. (1984). Sex-role orientations of female NCAA championship gymnasts. *Perceptual and Motor Skills, 58,* 625–626.

Egstrom, G., & Bachrach, A. (1971). Diver panic. *Skin Diver, 20*(11), 36–37, 54–55, 57.

Eitzen, D. S. (1989). *Sociology of North American sport.* Dubuque, IA: Wm. C. Brown.

Eitzen, D. S., & Pratt, S. R. (1989). Gender differences in

coaching philosophies: The case of female basketball teams. *Research Quarterly, 60,* 152–158.

Eitzen, D. S., & Sage, G. (1978). *Sociology of American sport.* Dubuque, IA: Wm. C. Brown.

Eitzen, D. S., & Sage, J. (1982). *Sociology of American sport* (2nd ed.). Dubuque, IA: Wm. C. Brown.

Eitzen, D. S., & Zinn, M. B. (1989). The deathleticization of women: The naming and gender marking of collegiate sport teams. *Sociology of Sport Journal, 6,* 362–370.

Ekkekakis, P., Hall, E. E., & Petruzzello, S. J. (1999). Measuring state anxiety in the context of acute exercise using the State Anxiety Inventory: An attempt to resolve the brouhaha. *Journal of Sport & Exercise Psychology, 21,* 205–229.

Eklund, R. C., Gould, D., & Jackson, S. A. (1993). Psycho- logical foundations of Olympic wrestling excellence: Reconciling individual differences and nomothetic char- acterization. *Journal of Applied Sport Psychology, 5,* 35–47.

Ellin, A. (1995, October/November). Out of bounds: Is student–athlete crime out of control? *The College Maga- zine,* 18–22, 24.

Emery, L. (1984). Women's participation in the Olympic Games. *Journal of Physical Education, Recreation and Dance, 55*(5), 62–63, 72.

Emmelkamp, P. M. G., & Wessels, H. (1975). Flooding in imagination vs. flooding in vivo: A comparison with agoraphobics. *Behavior Research and Therapy, 13,* 7–15.

Endler, N. S., & Hunt, J. McV. (1966). Source of behavioral variance as measured by the S–R Inventory of Anxious- ness. *Psychological Bulletin, 65,* 336–346.

Endler, N. S., Hunt, J. McV., & Rosenstein, A. J. (1962). An S–R Inventory of Anxiousness. *Psychological Monographs, 76* (17, Whole No. 536).

Endler, N., & Okada, M. (1975). Multidimensional measure of trait anxiety: The S–R Inventory of General Trait Anxiousness. *Journal of Consulting and Clinical Psychology, 43,* 319–329.

Endler, N. S., Parker, J. D., Bagby, R. M., & Cox, B. J. (1991). Multidimensionality of state and trait anxiety: Factor structure on the Endler Multidimensional Anxiety Scales. *Journal of Personality and Social Psychology, 60,* 919–926.

Englehardt, G. M. (1995). Fighting behavior and winning National Hockey League games: A paradox. *Perceptual and Motor Skills, 80,* 416–418.

Erdelyi, G. (1962). Gynecological survey of female athletes. *Journal of Sports Medicine and Physical Fitness, 2,* 174–179.

Erdelyi, G. (1976). Effects of exercise on the menstrual cycle. *Physician and Sportsmedicine, 4*(3), 79–81.

Ericsson, K. A. (1996). Expert and exceptional performance: Evidence of maximal adaptation to task constraints. *An- nual Review of Psychology, 47,* 273–305.

Eron, L. D. (1987). The development of aggressive behavior

from the perspective of a developing behaviorism. *American Psychologist, 42,* 435–442.

Essing, W. (1970). Team line-up and team achievement in European football. In G. Kenyon (Ed.), *Contemporary psychology of sport* (pp. 349–354). Chicago: Athletic Institute.

Estabrooks, P., & Carron, A. V. (1999). The influence of the group with elderly exercisers. *Small Group Research, 30,* 438–452.

Ethics of blood doping. (1985). *Physician and Sportsmedicine, 13*(8), 151.

Evans, M., Weinberg, R., & Jackson, A. (1992). Psychological factors related to drug use in college athletes. *The Sport Psychologist, 6,* 24–41.

Evans, V., & Quarterman, J. (1983). Personality characteristics of successful and unsuccessful black female basketball players. *International Journal of Sport Psychology, 14,* 105–115.

Eysenck, H. J., & Eysenck, S. B. G. (1963). *The Eysenck Personality Inventory.* San Diego, CA: Educational and Industrial Testing Service.

Eysenck, H. J., Nias, D. K. B., & Cox, D. N. (1982). Sport and personality. *Behavior Research and Therapy, 4*(l), 1–56.

Fans say alcohol sponsorship and sports mix. (1991, February 19). *USA Today,* p. 10C.

Faucette, N., & Osinski, A. (1987). Adult spectator verbal behavior during a Mustang League world series. *Journal of Applied Research in Coaching and Athletics, 2,* 141–152.

Faulkner, G., & Sparkes, A. (1999). Exercise as therapy for schizophrenia. *Journal of Sport & Exercise Psychology, 21,* 52–69.

Federal Bureau of Investigation. (1993). *Uniform Crime Reports.* Washington, DC: Federal Bureau of Investigation.

Feedback. (2000, October 16). *Sports Illustrated, 93*(15), 40.

Feher, P., Meyers, M. C., & Skelly, W. A. (1998). Psychological profiles of rock climbers: State and trait attributes. *Journal of Sport Behavior, 21,* 167–180.

Feicht, C., Johnson, T., Martin, B., Sparkles, K., & Wagner, W. (1978, November 25). Secondary amenorrhea in athletes. *Lancet,* 1145–1146.

Felsten, G., & Hill, V. (1999). Aggression Questionnaire hostility scale predicts anger in response to mistreatment. *Behaviour Research and Therapy, 37,* 87–97.

Feltz, D. L. (1982). Path analysis of the causal elements in Bandura's theory of self-efficacy and an anxiety based model of avoidance behavior. *Journal of Personality and Social Psychology, 42,* 764–781.

Feltz, D. L. (1984). Self-efficacy as a cognitive mediator of athletic performance. In W. F. Straub and J. M. Williams (Eds.), *Cognitive sport psychology. Personal growth to peak experience* (pp. 114–148). Lansing, NY: Sport Science Associates.

Feltz, D. L. (1988). Self-confidence and sports performance.

In K. B. Pandolf (Ed.), *Exercise and sport sciences review, Vol. 16.* New York: Macmillan.

Feltz, D. L., & Ewing, M. E. (1987). Psychological characteristics of elite young athletes. *Medicine and Science in Sports and Exercise, 19,* S98–S105.

Fenz, W. D. (1985). Coping mechanisms and performance under stress. In D. M. Landers & R. W. Christina (Eds.), *Psychology of sport and motor behavior II* (pp. 64–84). University Park, PA: College of HPER, Pennsylvania State University.

Fenz, W. D., & Epstein, S. (1967). Changes in gradients of skin conductance, heart rate and respiration rate as a function of experience. *Psychosomatic Medicine, 29,* 33–51.

Fenz, W. D., & Jones, G. B. (1972). Individual differences in physiological arousal and performance in sport parachutists. *Psychosomatic Medicine, 34,* 1–8.

Festinger, L., Pepitone, A., & Newcomb, T. (1952). Some consequences of de-individuation in a group. *Journal of Abnormal and Social Psychology, 47,* 382–389.

Festinger, L., Schachter, S., & Back, K. (1950). *Social pressures in informal groups.* New York: Harper.

Fiatarone, M. A., Marks, E. C., Ryan, N. D., Meredith, C. N., Lipsitz, L. A., & Evans, W. J. (1990). High intensity strength training in nonagenarians: Effects on skeletal muscle. *Journal of the American Medical Association, 263,* 3029–3034.

Fiatarone, M. A., O'Neill, E. F., Ryan, N. D., Clements, K. M., Solares, G. R., Nelson, M. E., Roberts, S. B., Kehayias, J. J., Lipsitz, L. A., & Evans, W. J. (1994). Exercise training and nutritional supplementation for physical frailty in very elderly people. *The New England Journal of Medicine, 330,* 1769–1775.

Fiedler, F. (1967). *A theory of leadership effectiveness.* New York: McGraw-Hill.

Fiedler, F. (1978). The contingency model and the dynamics of the leadership process. In L. Berkowitz (Ed.), *Advances in experimental social psychology, Vol. 11.* New York: Academic Press.

Fielding, L. (1977). Sport and the terrible swift sword. *Research Quarterly, 48,* 1–11.

Fighters aren't always winners. (1990, March 1). *USA Today,* p. 3C.

Finkenberg, M. E., DiNucci, J. N., McCune, E. D., & McCune, S. L. (1992). Cognitive and somatic state anxiety and self-confidence in cheerleading competition. *Perceptual and Motor Skills, 75,* 835–839.

Finlayson, I. (1984). Obituary. *New Zealand Gliding Kiwi, 16*(1), 21.

Finn, R. (1987, April 16). Players to hit books as well as serves. *USA Today,* p. 12C.

Finn, J., & Straub, W. F. (1977). Locus of control among

Dutch and American women softball players. *Research Quarterly, 48,* 56–60.

Fishbein, M., & Ajzen, L. (1975). *Belief, attitude, intention, and behavior.* Don Mills, NY: Addison-Wesley.

Fisher, A. C. (1977). Sport personality assessment: Fact, fiction, and methodological re-examination. In R. E. Stadulis, C. O. Dotson, V. L. Katch, & J. Schick (Eds.), *Research and practice in physical education* (pp. 188–204). Champaign, IL: Human Kinetics.

Fisher, A. C. (1984). New directions in sport personology research. In J. M. Silva & R. S. Weinberg (Eds.), *Psychological foundations of sport* (pp. 70–80). Champaign, IL: Human Kinetics.

Fisher, A. C., Horsfall, J. S., & Morris, H. H. (1977). Sport personality assessment: A methodological re-examination. *International Journal of Sport Psychology, 8,* 92–102.

Fitts, W. (1965). *Manual: Tennessee Self-Concept Scale.* Nashville, TN: Counselor Recordings and Tests.

Fixx, J. (1977). *The complete book of running.* New York: Random House.

Fleming, S. L., Bourgeois, A. E., LeUnes, A., & Meyers, M. C. (1992). *A psychometric comparison of the full scale Profile of Mood States with other abbreviated POMS scales with selected athletic populations.* Paper presented to the Association for the Advancement of Applied Sport Psychology, Colorado Springs, CO.

Foa, E. B., Grayson, J. B., Steketee, G. S., Doppelt, H. G., Turner, R. M., & Latimer, P. R. (1983). Success and failure in the behavioral treatment of obsessive-compulsives. *Journal of Clinical and Consulting Psychology, 51,* 287–297.

Folkins, C., & Sime, W. (1981). Physical fitness training and mental health. *American Psychologist, 36,* 373–389.

Folkins, C., & Wieselberg-Bell, N. (1981). A personality profile of ultramarathon runners: A little deviance may go a long way. *Journal of Sport Behavior, 4,* 119–127.

Forbes, C. (1973). The Spartan agoge. In E. F. Zeigler (Ed.), *The history of sport and physical education to 1900* (pp. 133–138). Champaign, IL: Stipes.

Forbes, G. (2000, March 31). Buying into life outside the NFL: Owners look at Invest in Yourself program to educate players. *USA Today,* p. 21C.

Ford, S. K., & Summers, J. J. (1992). The factorial validity of the TAIS attentional-style subscales. *Journal of Sport & Exercise Psychology, 14,* 283–297.

Former Husker fesses up. (1987, January 5). *Sports Illustrated,* 24.

Fosdick, D. (1972). *The relationship of the Athletic Motivational Inventory and the 16 Personality Factor Questionnaire as measures of the personality characteristics of college varsity swimmers.* Unpublished master's thesis, San Jose State University.

Foster, W. (1977). A discriminant analysis of selected personality variables among successful and unsuccessful male high school athletes. *International Journal of Sport Psychology, 8,* 119–127.

Fox, E. (1984). *Sports physiology.* Philadelphia: Saunders.

Fox, K. R., & Corbin, C. B. (1989). The Physical Self-Perception Profile: Development and preliminary validation. *Journal of Sport & Exercise Psychology, 11,* 408–430.

Francis, L. J., Jones, S. H., & Kelly, P. (1999). Personality and church attendance among female hockey players. *Social Behavior and Personality, 27,* 519–521.

Francis, L. J., Kelly, P., & Jones, S. H. (1998). The personality profile of female students who play hockey. *Irish Journal of Psychology, 19,* 394–399.

Francis, R., Bunch, T., & Chandler, B. (1978). Little League elbow: A decade later. *Physician and Sportsmedicine, 6*(4), 88–94.

Franken, R. E. (1982). *Human motivation.* Belmont, CA: Wadsworth.

Franklin, K. (1989, September). Field of dreams: Little League's not so little anymore. *Sport,* 64–67.

Fratzke, M. R. (1975). Personality and biographical traits of superior and average college basketball officials. *Research Quarterly, 46,* 484–488.

Freedman, J. (1975). *Crowding and behavior.* San Francisco: W. H. Freeman.

Freischlag, J. (1989). More than a nice smile: A psycho-social analysis of high school cheerleaders. *Journal of Applied Research in Coaching and Athletics, 4,* 63–74.

Freischlag, J., & Freischlag, T. (1993). Selected psychosocial, physical, and technical factors among rock climbers: A test of the flow paradigm. In W. K. Simpson, A. LeUnes, & J. S. Picou (Eds.), *Applied research in coaching and athletics annual 1993.* Boston: American Press.

French, S. N. (1978). Electromyographic biofeedback for tension control during gross motor skill acquisition. *Perceptual and Motor Skills, 47,* 883–889.

Friedman, M., & Rosenman, R. (1974). *Type A behavior and your heart.* New York: Knopf.

Frieze, I. (1976). Causal attributions and information seeking to explain success and failure. *Journal of Research in Personality, 10,* 293–305.

Frisch, R. (1976). Fatness of girls from menarche to age 18 years, with a nomogram. *Human Biology, 48,* 353–359.

Frisch, R., & McArthur, J. (1974). Menstrual cycles: Fatness as a determinant of minimal weight for height necessary for their maintenance or onset. *Science, 185,* 949–951.

Frisch, R., Gotz-Welbergen, A., McArthur, J., Albright, T., Witschi, J., Bullen, B., Birnholz, J., Reed, R., & Hermann, H. (1981). Delayed menarche and amenorrhea of college athletes in relation to age of onset of training. *Journal of American Medical Association, 246,* 1559–1563.

Frost, R. O., Marten, P., Lahart, C., & Rosenblate, R.

(1990). The dimensions of perfectionism. *Cognitive Therapy and Research, 14,* 449–468.

Fry, D., McClements, J., & Sefton, J. (1981). *A report on participation in the Saskatoon Hockey Association.* Saskatoon, Saskatchewan, Canada: SASK Sport.

Fuchs, C., & Zaichkowsky, L. (1983). Psychological characteristics of male and female body-builders. *Journal of Sport Behavior, 6,* 136–145.

Fung, L., & Fu, F. H. (1995). Psychological determinants between wheelchair sport finalists and non-finalists. *International Journal of Sport Psychology, 26,* 568–579.

Fuoss, D., & Troppmann, R. (1981). *Effective coaching: A psychological approach.* New York: Wiley.

Furst, D. M. (1989). Career contingencies: Patterns of initial entry and continuity in collegiate sports officiating. *Journal of Sport Behavior, 14,* 93–102.

Gackenbach, J. (1982). Collegiate swimmers: Sex differences in self-reports and indices of physiological stress. *Perceptual and Motor Skills, 55,* 555–558.

Gallon, A. (1980). *Coaching: Ideas and ideals.* Boston: Houghton Mifflin.

Game winning drives. (1999, April 25). *Austin American Statesman,* p. C6.

Gammon, C. (1985, June 10). A day of horror and shame. *Sports Illustrated,* 20–35.

Garland, D. J., & Barry, J. R. (1988). The effects of personality and perceived leader behaviors on performance in collegiate football. *The Psychological Record, 38,* 237–247.

Gates, D., & Miller, S. (1996, May 27). A case of altitude chicness. *Newsweek,* 58.

Gates, H. L. (1991, August 19). Delusions of grandeur. *Sports Illustrated,* 78.

Gauron, E. F. (1984). *Mental training for peak performance.* Lansing, MI: Sport Science Associates.

Gavzer, B. (1990, October 21). Is it time to investigate boxing? *Parade Magazine,* pp. 3–7.

Gayton, W. F., & Coombs, R. (1995). The home advantage in high school basketball. *Perceptual and Motor Skills, 81,* 1344–1346.

Gayton, W. F., & Langevin, G. (1992). Home advantage: Does it exist in individual sports? *Perceptual and Motor Skills, 74,* 706.

Gayton, W. F., & Nickless, C. J. (1987). An investigation of the validity of the trait and state sport self-confidence inventories in predicting marathon performance. *Perceptual and Motor Skills, 65,* 481–482.

Gayton, W. F., Matthews, G. R., & Nickless, C. J. (1987). The home field advantage in sports championships: Does it exist in hockey? *Journal of Sport Psychology, 9,* 183–185.

Geen, R., & Gange, J. (1977). Drive theory of social facilitation: Twelve years of theory and research. *Psychological Bulletin, 84,* 1267–1288.

Geen, R. G., Beatty, W. W., & Arkin, R. M. (1984). *Human motivation: Physiological, behavioral and social approaches.* Boston: Allyn & Bacon.

Gems, G. (1997). Cheerleading. Grg@noctrl.edu

Gender equity survey numbers. (1992, March 12). *USA Today,* p. 7C.

George, J. (1994). The virtual disappearance of the white male sprinter in the United States: A speculative essay. *Sociology of Sport Journal, 11,* 70–78.

Gerber, E. (1968, Winter). Learning and play: Insights of educational protagonists. *Quest* (Monograph XI), 44–49.

Gerber, E., Felshin, J., Berlin, R., & Wyrick, W. (Eds.). (1974). *The American woman in sport.* Reading, MA: Addison-Wesley.

Geron, E., Furst, D., & Rotstein, P. (1986). Personality of athletes participating in various sports. *International Journal of Sport Psychology, 17,* 120–135.

Gerson, R., & Deshaies, P. (1978). Competitive trait anxiety and performance as predictors of precompetitive state anxiety. *International Journal of Sport Psychology, 9,* 16–26.

Getting tougher on steroid abuse. (1991). *Physician and Sportsmedicine, 19*(2), 46.

Gilbert, B., & Williamson, N. (1973a, June 4). Are you being two-faced? *Sports Illustrated, 38*(22), 45–54.

Gilbert, B., & Williamson, N. (1973b, May 28). Sport is unfair to women. *Sports Illustrated, 38*(21), 88–98.

Gill, D. L. (1986). *Psychological dynamics of sport.* Champaign, IL: Human Kinetics.

Gill, D. L., & Martens, R. (1977). The role of task type and success–failure on selected interpersonal variables. *International Journal of Sport Psychology, 8,* 160–177.

Gill, D. L., Gross, J. B., & Huddleston, S. (1981). Participation motivation in youth sport. *International Journal of Sport Psychology, 14,* 1–14.

Gill, D. L., Ruder, M., & Gross, J. (1982). Open-ended attributions in team competition. *Journal of Sport Psychology, 4,* 159–169.

Gilliland, K. (1974). Internal versus external locus of control and the high-level athletic competitor. *Perceptual and Motor Skills, 39,* 38.

Gillette, J. (1975). When and where women are injured in sport. *Physician and Sportsmedicine, 3*(5), 61–63.

Girls in varsity sports. (1996, June 20). *USA Today,* p. 1C.

Giuliano, T. A., Popp, K. E., & Knight, J. L. (2000). Footballs versus Barbies: Childhood play activities as predictors of sport participation by women. *Sex Roles, 42,* 159–180.

Glamser, E. D. (1990). Contest location, player misconduct, and race: A case from English soccer. *Journal of Sport Behavior, 13,* 41–49.

Glasser, W. (1976). *Positive addiction.* New York: Harper & Row.

Gledhill, N. (1982). Blood doping and related issues: A brief review. *Medicine and Science in Sports and Exercise, 14*(3), 183–189.

Glenn, S. D., & Horn, T. S. (1993). Psychological and personal predictors of leadership behavior in female soccer athletes. *Journal of Applied Sport Psychology, 5,* 17–34.

Gliner, J. A., Matsen-Twisdale, J. A., Horvath, S. M., & Maron, M. B. (1979). Visual evoked potentials and signal detection following a marathon race. *Medicine and Science in Sports, 11,* 155–159.

Godin, G., & Shephard, R. J. (1990). Use of attitude behavior models in exercise promotion. *Sports Medicine, 10,* 103–121.

Godin, G., Desharnais, R., Valois, P., & Bradet, R. (1995). Combining behavioral and motivational dimensions to identify and characterize the stages in the process of adherence to exercise. *Psychology and Health, 10,* 333–344.

Goldman, M., Stockbauer, J., & McAuliffe, T. (1977). Intergroup and intragroup competition and cooperation. *Journal of Experimental Social Psychology, 13,* 81–88.

Goldsmith, P. A., & Williams, J. M. (1992). Perceived stressors for football and volleyball officials from three rating levels. *Journal of Sport Behavior, 15,* 106–118.

Gomolak, C. (1975). Problems in matching young athletes: Body fat, peach fuzz, muscles, and mustache. *Physician and Sportsmedicine, 3*(5), 96–98.

Gorman, C. (1992, December 14). Tackling spinal trauma. *Time,* 57.

Goudas, M., Theodorakis, Y., & Karamousalidis, G. (1998). Psychological skills in basketball: Preliminary study for the development of a Greek from the Athletic Coping Skills Inventory–28. *Perceptual and Motor Skills, 86,* 59–65.

Gough, D. (1989). Improving batting skills with small-college baseball players through guided visual imagery. *Coaching Clinic, 27,* 1–6.

Gould, D. (1990). AAASP: A vision for the 1990's. *Journal of Applied Sport Psychology, 2,* 99–116.

Gould, D., & Krane, V. (1992). The arousal–performance relationship: Current status and future directions. In T. Horn (Ed.), *Advances in sport psychology* (pp. 119–141). Champaign, IL: Human Kinetics.

Gould, D., Eklund, R. C., & Jackson, S. A. (1992a). 1988 U.S. Olympic wrestling excellence: I. Mental preparation, precompetitive cognition, and affect. *The Sport Psychologist, 6,* 358–382.

Gould, D., Eklund, R. C., & Jackson, S. A. (1992b). 1988 U.S. Olympic wrestling excellence: II. Thoughts and affect occurring during competition. *The Sport Psychologist, 6,* 383–402.

Gould, D., Eklund, E. C., & Jackson, S. A. (1993). Coping strategies used by U.S. Olympic wrestlers. *Research Quarterly for Exercise and Sport, 64,* 83–93.

Gould, D., Feltz, D. L., Horn, T., & Weiss, M. (1982). Rea-

sons for discontinuing involvement in competitive youth swimming. *Journal of Sport Behavior, 5,* 155–165.

Gould, D., Feltz, D. L., & Weiss, M. (1985). Motives for participating in competitive youth swimming. *International Journal of Sport Psychology, 16,* 126–140.

Gould, D., Feltz, D. L., Weiss, M., & Petlichkoff, L. M. (1982). Participating motives in competitive youth swimmers. In T. Orlick, J. T. Partington, & J. H. Salmela (Eds.), *Mental training for coaches and athletes* (pp. 57–58). Ottawa: Coaching Association of Canada.

Gould, D., Finch, L. M., & Jackson, S. A. (1993). Coping strategies used by national champion figure skaters. *Research Quarterly for Exercise and Sport, 64,* 453–468.

Gould, D., Horn, T., & Spreeman, J. (1983). Perceived anxiety of elite junior wrestlers. *Journal of Sport Psychology, 5,* 58–71.

Gould, D., Jackson, S. A., & Finch, L. M. (1993a). Life at the top: The experiences of U.S. national champion figure skaters. *The Sport Psychologist, 7,* 354–374.

Gould, D., Jackson, S., & Finch, L. (1993b). Sources of stress in national champion figure skaters. *Journal of Sport & Exercise Psychology, 15,* 134–159.

Gould, D., Petlichkoff, L., Simons, J., & Vevera, M. (1987). Relationships between Competitive State Anxiety Inventory–2 subscale scores and pistol shooting performance. *Journal of Sport Psychology, 9,* 33–42.

Gould, D., Tammen, V., Murphy, S., & May, J. (1989). An examination of U.S. Olympic sport psychology consultants and the services they provide. *The Sport Psychologist, 3,* 300–312.

Gould, D., Tuffey, S., Hardy, L., & Lochbaum, M. (1993). Multidimensional state anxiety and middle distance running performance: An exploratory examination of Hanin's (1980) Zones of Optimal Functioning hypothesis. *Journal of Applied Sport Psychology, 5,* 85–95.

Gould, D., Tuffey, S., Udry, E., & Loehr, J. (1996). Burnout in competitive junior tennis players: 1. A quantitative psychological assessment. *The Sport Psychologist, 10,* 322–340.

Gould, D., Tuffey, S., Udry, E., & Loehr, J. (1997). Burnout in competitive junior tennis players: 2. Individual differences in the burnout experience. *The Sport Psychologist, 11,* 257–276.

Gould, D., Weiss, M., & Weinberg, R. S. (1981). Psychological characteristics of successful and nonsuccessful Big Ten wrestlers. *Journal of Sport Psychology, 3,* 69–81.

Gray, S. W. (1990). Effects of visuomotor rehearsal with videotaped modeling on racquetball performance of beginning players. *Perceptual and Motor Skills, 70,* 379–385.

Greenberg, J. (1991, April 22). Horror show. *Sports Illustrated,* 40–44.

Greendorfer, S. (1977). Role of socializing agents in female sport involvement. *Research Quarterly, 48,* 304–310.

Greendorfer, S., & Blinde, E. (1985). Retirement from inter-collegiate sport: Theoretical and empirical considerations. *Sociology of Sport Journal, 2,* 101–110.

Greist, J., Klein, M., Eischens, R., & Faris, J. (1978). Running out of depression. *Physician and Sportsmedicine, 6*(12), 49–56.

Griffin, L. (1978). *Why children participate in youth sports.* Paper presented at American Alliance for Health, Physical Education and Recreation (AAHPER) Convention, Kansas City, MO.

Griffin, P. (1973). What's a nice girl like you doing in a profession like this? *Quest, 19,* 96–101.

Griffin, R. (1989). Homophobia in physical education. *Canadian Association for Health, Physical Education and Recreation Journal, 55*(2), 27–31.

Griffin, R. (1993). Homophobia in women's sports: The fear that divides us. In G. L. Cohen (Ed.), *Women in sport: Issues and controversies* (pp. 193–203). Newbury Park, CA: Sage.

Griffiths, T. J., Steel, D. H., & Vaccaro, R. (1978). Anxiety levels of beginning SCUBA students. *Perceptual and Motor Skills, 47,* 312–314.

Griffiths, T. J., Steel, D. H., & Vaccaro, R. (1979). Relationship between anxiety and performance in scuba diving. *Perceptual and Motor Skills, 48,* 1009–1010.

Griffiths, T. J., Steel, D. H., & Vaccaro, R. (1982). Anxiety of scuba divers: A multidimensional approach. *Perceptual and Motor Skills, 55,* 611–614.

Griffiths, T. J., Steel, D. H., Vaccaro, R., & Karpman, M. (1981). The effects of relaxation techniques on anxiety and underwater performance. *International Journal of Sport Psychology, 12,* 176–182.

Grogan, R. (1981). Run, Pheidippides, run! The story of the battle of Marathon. *British Journal of Sports Medicine, 15,* 186–189.

Gross, N., & Martin, W. (1952). On group effectiveness. *American Journal of Sociology, 57,* 533–546.

Grossman, S., & Hines, T. (1996). National Hockey League players from North America are more violent than those from Europe. *Perceptual and Motor Skills, 83,* 589–590.

Grove, J. R., & Prapavessis, H. (1992). Reliability and validity data for an abbreviated version of the Profile of Mood States. *International Journal of Sport Psychology, 23,* 93–109.

Gruber, J., & Beauchamp, D. (1979). Relevancy of the Competitive State Anxiety Inventory in a sport environment. *Research Quarterly, 50,* 207–214.

Gruber, J., & Perkins, S. (1978). Personality traits of women physical education majors and nonmajors at various levels of athletic competition. *International Journal of Sport Psychology, 9,* 40–52.

Guarnieri, A., Bourgeois, T., & LeUnes, A. (1998). *A psychometric comparison of inexperienced and minor league umpires.* Paper presented to the Association for the Advancement of Applied Sport Psychology, Hyannis, MA.

Guerin, B., & Innes, J. (1982). Social facilitation and social monitoring: A new look at Zajonc's mere presence hypothesis. *British Journal of Social Psychology, 21,* 7–18.

Guidelines for personal exercise programs. (2000, August 17). http://www.hoptechno.com/book11.html.

Guion, R. M. (1980). On trinitarian doctrines of validity. *Professional Psychology, 11,* 385–398.

Gundersheim, J. (1982). A comparison of male and female athletes and nonathletes on measures of self-actualization. *Journal of Sport Behavior, 5,* 186–201.

Gurin, R., Gurin, G., Lao, R., & Beattie, M. (1969). Internal-external control in the motivational dynamics of Negro youth. *Journal of Social Issues, 25,* 29–53.

Haas, J., & Roberts, G. (1975). Effects of evaluative others upon learning and performance of a complex motor task. *Journal of Motor Behavior, 7,* 81–90.

Haase, A. M., Prapavessis, H., & Owen, R. G. (1999). Perfectionism and eating attitudes in competitive rowers: Moderating effects of body mass, weight classification, and gender. *Psychology and Health, 14,* 643–657.

Hackensmith, C. (1966). *History of physical education.* New York: Harper & Row.

Hackfort, D., & Schwenkmezger, P. (1993). Anxiety. In R. N. Singer, M. Murphey, & L. K. Tennant (Eds.), *Handbook of research on sport psychology* (pp. 328–364). New York: Macmillan.

Haerle, R. K. (1975). Career patterns and career contingencies of professional baseball players: An occupational analysis. In D. W. Ball & J. W. Loy (Eds.), *Sport and social order* (pp. 461–519). Reading, MA: Addison-Wesley.

Hailey, B. J., & Bailey, L. (1982). Negative addiction in runners: A quantitative approach. *Journal of Sport Behavior, 5,* 150–153.

Hale, B. D. (1982). The effects of internal and external imagery on muscular and ocular concomitants. *Journal of Sport Psychology, 4,* 379–387.

Hale, C. J. (1956). Physiological maturity of Little League baseball players. *Research Quarterly, 27,* 276–284.

Hale, C. J. (1961). Injuries among 771,810 Little League baseball players. *Journal of Sports Medicine and Physical Fitness, 1,* 80–83.

Hale, R. (1987, January 5). Don't ban steroids; athletes need them. *USA Today,* p. 10A.

Hall, E. G., Church, G., & Stone, M. (1980). Relationship of birth order to selected personality characteristics of nationally ranked Olympic weight lifters. *Perceptual and Motor Skills, 51,* 971–976.

Hall, E. G., & Erffmeyer, E. S. (1983). The effects of visuo-motor behavioral rehearsal with videotaped modeling on free throw accuracy of intercollegiate female basketball players. *Journal of Sport Psychology, 5,* 343–346.

Hall, E. G., & Hardy, C. J. (1991). Ready, aim, fire . . .

Relaxation strategies for enhancing pistol marksmanship. *Perceptual and Motor Skills, 72,* 775–786.

Hall, H. K., Kerr, A. W., & Matthews, J. (1998). Precompetitive anxiety in sport: The contribution of achievement goals and perfectionism. *Journal of Sport & Exercise Psychology, 20,* 194–217.

Hall, H. K., Weinberg, R. S., & Jackson, A. (1987). Effects of goal specificity, goal difficulty, and information feedback on endurance performance. *Journal of Sport Psychology, 9,* 43–54.

Halliburton, S., & Sanford, S. (1989, July 31). Making weight becomes torture for UT swimmers. *Austin American Statesman,* pp. D1, D7.

Hamachek, D. (1987). *Encounters with the self* (3rd ed.). New York: Holt, Rinehart and Winston.

Hammer, W., & Tutko, T. (1974). Validation of the Athletic Motivation Inventory. *International Journal of Sport Psychology, 5,* 3–12.

Hammermeister, J., & Burton, D. (1995). Anxiety and the Ironman: Investigating the antecedents and consequences of endurance athletes' state anxiety. *The Sport Psychologist, 9,* 29–40.

Hammerton, M., & Tickner, A. (1968). An investigation into the effects of stress upon skilled performance. *Ergonomics, 12,* 851–855.

Handal, P. J. (1973). Development of a social desirability and acquiescence Controlled Repression–Sensitization Scale and some preliminary validity data. *Journal of Clinical Psychology, 39,* 486–487.

Hanin, Y. (1978). A study of anxiety in sports. In W. F. Straub (Ed.), *Sport psychology: An analysis of athlete behavior* (pp. 236–249). Ithaca: NY: Mouvement.

Hanin, Y. (1986). State–trait anxiety research on sports in the USSR. In C. D. Spielberger & R. Diaz-Guerrero (Eds.), *Cross-cultural anxiety* (pp. 45-64). Washington, DC: Hemisphere.

Hanin, Y., & Syrja, P. (1995). Performance affect in soccer players: An application of the IZOF model. *International Journal of Sports Medicine, 16,* 260–265.

Hanson, D. (1967). Cardiac response to participation in Little League baseball competition as determined by telemetry. *Research Quarterly, 38,* 384–388.

Hanson, M. (1977). Coronary heart disease, exercise, and motivation in middle aged males. (Doctoral dissertation, University of Wisconsin, Madison, 1976). *Dissertation Abstracts International, 37,* 2755B.

Harbrecht, T., & Barnett, C. R. (1979). College football during World War II: 1941–1945. *Physical Educator, 36,* 31–34.

Hardman, K. (1973). A dual approach to the study of personality and performance in sport. In H. T. Whiting, K. Hardman, L. B. Hendry, and M. G. Jones (Eds.), *Personality and performance in physical education and sport* (pp. 77–122). London: Henry Kimpton.

Hardy, C. J. (1990). Social loafing: Motivational losses in collective performance. *International Journal of Sport Psychology, 21,* 305–327.

Hardy, L. (1990). A catastrophe model of performance in sport. In J. G. Jones & L. Hardy (Eds.), *Stress and performance in sport* (pp. 81–106). Chichester, England: Wiley.

Hardy, L., & Fazey, J. A. (1987). *The inverted-U hypothesis—a catastrophe for sport psychology and a statement of a new hypothesis.* Paper presented at the annual conference of the North American Society for the Psychology of Sport and Physical Activity, Vancouver, Canada.

Hargreaves, J. (1990). Changing images of the sporting female. *Sport and Leisure, 3*(3), 14–17.

Harkins, S. G., & Syzmanski, K. (1987). Social loafing and social facilitation: New wine in old bottles. In C. Hendrick (Ed.), *Review of personality and social psychology, Vol. 9* (pp. 167–188). Beverly Hills, CA: Sage.

Harres, R. (1968). Attitudes of students toward women's athletic competition. *Research Quarterly, 39,* 278–284.

Harris, D. V. (1973). *Physical activities for children: Effects and affects.* Paper presented at American Alliance for Health, Physical Education and Recreation (AAHPER) Convention, Minneapolis, MN.

Harris, D. V., & Robinson, W. J. (1986). The effects of skill level on EMG activity during internal and external imagery. *Journal of Sport Psychology, 8,* 105–111.

Harris, H. A. (1972). *Sport in Greece and Rome.* Ithaca, NY: Cornell University Press.

Harris, J. A. (1995). Confirmatory factor analysis of the Aggression Questionnaire. *Behaviour Research and Therapy, 33,* 991–993.

Hart, B., Hasbrook, C., & Mathes, S. (1986). An examination of the reduction in the number of female interscholastic coaches. *Research Quarterly for Exercise and Sport, 57,* 68–77.

Hart, B., & Mathes, S. (1982). *Women coaches—Where are they?* Paper presented at 1982 Wisconsin Association for Health, Physical Education and Recreation, Glendale, WI.

Harter, S. (1978). Effectance motivation reconsidered: Toward a developmental model. *Human Development, 21,* 34–64.

Harter, S. (1980). The development of competence motivation in the mastery of cognitive and physical skills: Is there still a place for joy? In G. C. Roberts & D. M. Landers (Eds.), *Psychology of motor behavior and sport* (pp. 3–29). Champaign, IL: Human Kinetics.

Hasbrook, C. A., Hart, B. A., Mathes, S. A., & True, S. (1990). Sex bias and the validity of believed differences between male and female interscholastic athletic coaches. *Research Quarterly for Exercise and Sport, 61,* 259–267.

Hathaway, S., & McKinley, J. (1943). *MMPI Manual.* New York: Psychological Corporation.

Hayes, S. C., Munt, E., Korn, Z., Wulfert, E., Rosenfarb, I.,

& Zettle, R. D. (1986). The effects of feedback and self-reinforcement instructions on studying performance. *Psychological Record, 36,* 27–37.

Hayes, S. C., Rosenfarb, I., Wulfert, E., Munt, E. D., Korn, Z., & Zettle, R. D. (1985). Self-reinforcement effects: An artifact of asocial standard setting? *Journal of Applied Behavioral Analysis, 18,* 201–214.

Health and fitness. (1990, August). *Changing Times,* 64–66.

Hecker, J. E., & Kaczor, L. M. (1988). Application of imagery theory to sport psychology: Some preliminary findings. *Journal of Sport & Exercise Psychology, 10,* 363–373.

Heider, F. (1944). Social perception and phenomenal causality. *Psychological Review, 51,* 358–377.

Heider, F (1958). *The psychology of interpersonal relations.* New York: Wiley.

Heil, J., & Fine, P. (1993). The biopsychology of injury-related pain. In D. Pargman (Ed.), *Psychological bases of sports injuries* (pp. 33–43). Morgantown, WV: Fitness Information Technology.

Heishman, M. F., Bunker, L., & Tutwiler, R. W. (1990). The decline of women leaders (coaches and athletic directors) in girls' interscholastic sport programs in Virginia from 1972 to 1987. *Research Quarterly for Exercise and Sport, 61,* 103–107.

Helmreich, R., Stapp, J., & Ervin, C. (1974). The Texas Social Behavior Inventory (TSBI). *Journal Supplement Abstract Service Catalog of Selected Documents in Psychology, 4,* 79 (Ms. No. 681).

Henderson, J. (1977). Running commentary. *Runner's World, 13*(9), 15.

Hendrix, A. E., Acevedo, E. O., & Hebert, E. (2000). An examination of stress and burnout in certified athletic trainers at Division 1-A universities. *Journal of Athletic Training, 35,* 139–144.

Henry, B. (1976). *History of the Olympic Games.* New York: Putnam's.

Henschen, K., Edwards, S., & Mathinos, L. (1982). Achievement motivation and sex-role orientation of high school female track and field athletes versus nonathletes. *Perceptual and Motor Skills, 55,* 183–187.

Hersey, R., & Blanchard, K. (1977). *Management of organizational behavior: Utilizing human resources.* Englewood Cliffs, NJ: Prentice-Hall.

Hersey, R., Blanchard, K. L., & Hambleton, R. K. (1980). Contracting for leadership style: A process and instrumentation for building effective work relationships. In R. Hersey & J. Stinson (Eds.), *Perspectives in leader effectiveness* (pp. 95–119). Athens, OH: Center for Leadership Studies, Ohio University.

Hershey, S. (1989, May 1). Hoch responds to pressure, wins with 8-foot birdie putt. *USA Today,* p. 10C.

Herwig, C. (1994, June 29). NCAA programs hiring more female coaches and administrators. *USA Today,* p. 12C.

Heusner, W. (1952). *Personality traits of champion and former champion athletes.* Unpublished master's thesis, University of Illinois.

Heyman, S. R., & Rose, K. G. (1979). Psychological variables affecting scuba performance. In C. H. Naudeau, W. R. Halliwell, K. M. Newell, & G. C. Roberts (Eds.), *Psychology of motor behavior and sport—1979* (pp. 180–188). Champaign, IL: Human Kinetics.

Hickey, T., Wolf, F. M., Robins, L. S., Wagner, M. B., & Harik, W. (1995). Physical activity training for functional mobility in older persons. *Journal of Applied Gerontology, 14,* 357–371.

Hicks, B. (1993). The legendary Babe Didrikson Zaharias. In G. L. Cohen (Ed.), *Women in sport* (pp. 38–48). Newbury Park, CA: Sage.

Higgins, N. C., Zumbo, B. D., & Hay, J. L. (1999). Construct validity of attributional style: Modeling context-dependent item sets in the Attributional Style Questionnaire. *Educational and Psychological Measurement, 59,* 804–820.

Higginson, D. (1985). The influence of socializing agents in the female sport-participation process. *Adolescence, 20,* 73–82.

High jump. (1985). *Track and Field News, 37*(12), 38.

Hightower, J. (1973). *A comparison of competitive and recreational baseball players on motivation.* Unpublished master's thesis, Louisiana State University.

Hilburn, K., & LeUnes, A. (2001). A selected bibliography in sex role orientation in sport and exercise: Bem Sex Role Inventory (BSRI), Personal Attributes Questionnaire, and related readings. In W. K. Simpson, A. LeUnes, and J. S. Picou (Eds.), *Applied research in coaching and athletics annual, 2001* (pp. 1–4). Boston: American Press.

Hinshaw, K. E. (1991). The effects of mental practice on motor skill performance: Critical evaluation and meta-analysis. *Imagination, Cognition, and Personality, 11,* 3–35.

Hirst, J. (1972). *Differences in motivation between successful and unsuccessful high school basketball teams.* Unpublished master's thesis, San Jose State University.

Hirt, E. R., Zillman, D., Erickson, G. A., & Kennedy, C. (1992). Costs and benefits of allegiance: Changes in fans' self-ascribed competencies after team victory versus defeat. *Journal of Personality and Social Psychology, 63,* 724–738.

Hochstetler, S., Rejeski, W. J., & Best, D. (1985). The influence of sex-role orientation on ratings of perceived exertion. *Sex Roles, 12,* 825–835.

Hodges, L., & Carron, A. V. (1992). Collective efficacy and group performance. *International Journal of Sport Psychology, 23,* 48–59.

Hoeksema–van Orden, C. Y. D., Gaillard, A. W. K., & Buunk, B. P. (1998). Social loafing under fatigue. *Journal of Personality and Social Psychology, 75,* 1179–1190.

Hoepner, B. (1970). John Swett's experience with physical exercise at the Rincon School: Foundation for the first state physical education law in the U.S. *Research Quarterly, 41,* 365–370.

Hoferek, M., & Hanick, P. (1985). Woman and athlete: Toward role consistency. *Sex Roles, 12,* 687–695.

Hogan, R. (1989). Review of the NEO Personality Inventory. In J. C. Conoley and J. J. Kramer, (Eds.), *The tenth mental measurements yearbook.* Lincoln, NE: Buros Institute of Mental Measurements.

Hogg, M. A. (1992). *The social psychology of group cohesiveness.* New York: New York University Press.

Hollander, E. R. (1967). *Principles and methods of social psychology.* New York: Oxford University Press.

Holmen, M., & Parkhouse, B. (1981). Trends in the selection of coaches for female athletes: A demographic inquiry. *Research Quarterly for Exercise and Sport, 52,* 9–18.

Holmes, I. H., & Rahe, R. (1967). The social readjustment rating scale. *Journal of Psychosomatic Research, 11,* 213–218.

Hopson, J. L. (1988, July–August). A pleasurable chemistry. *Psychology Today,* 28–33.

Horner, M. (1968). *Sex differences in achievement motivation and performance in competitive and noncompetitive situations.* Unpublished doctoral dissertation, University of Michigan.

Horner, M. (1972). Toward an understanding of achievement-related conflicts in women. *Journal of Social Issues, 28,* 157–175.

Horton, R. S., & Mack, D. E. (2000). Athletic identity in marathon runners: Focus or dysfunctional commitment? *Journal of Sport Behavior, 23,* 101–119.

Houlihan, B. (1997). *Sport, policy and politics.* London: Routledge.

House, R. J. (1971). A path-goal theory of leader effectiveness. *Administrative Science Quarterly, 16,* 321–338.

House, R. J., & Dessler, G. (1974). The path–goal theory of leadership: Some post hoc and a priori tests. In J. Hunt & L. Larson (Eds.), *Contingency approaches to leadership* (pp. 29–62). Carbondale, IL: Southern Illinois University Press.

House, R. J., & Mitchell, T. R. (1974, Autumn). Path–goal theory of leadership. *Journal of Contemporary Business,* 81–97.

Howe, B. L. (1991). Imagery and sport performance. *Sports Medicine, 11,* 1–5.

Howell, M. (1969). Seal stones of the Minoan period in the Ashmolean Museum, Oxford, depicting physical activities. *Research Quarterly, 40,* 509–517.

Howell, R. (1983). History of the Olympic marathon. *Physician and Sportsmedicine, 11*(11), 153–158.

Huddleston, S., & Gill, D. L. (1981). State anxiety as a function of skill level and proximity to competition. *Research Quarterly for Exercise and Sport, 52,* 31–34.

Hume, K. M., & Crossman, J. (1992). Musical reinforcement of practice behaviors among competitive swimmers. *Journal of Applied Behavior Analysis, 25,* 665–670.

Hunt, P., & Hillery, J. (1973). Social facilitation in a coaction setting. An examination of the effects over learning trials. *Journal of Experimental Social Psychology, 9,* 563–571.

Hunter, L. Y., & Torgan, C. (1982). The bra controversy: Are sports bras a necessity? *Physician and Sportsmedicine, 10*(11), 75–76.

Hymbaugh, K., & Garrett, J. (1974). Sensation seeking among skydivers. *Perceptual and Motor Skills, 38,* 118.

Ibrahim, H., & Morrison, N. (1976). Self-actualization and self-concept among athletes. *Research Quarterly, 47,* 68–79.

IG Staff. (1994). Christy Henrich: 1972–1994. *International Gymnast, 36*(10), 49.

Inciong, R. (1974). *Leadership style and team success.* Unpublished doctoral dissertation, University of Utah.

Ingham, A., Levinger, G., Graves, J., & Peckham, V. (1974). The Ringelmann effect: Studies of group size and group performances. *Journal of Experimental Social Psychology, 10,* 371–384.

Ingman, O. (1952). *Menstruation in Finnish top class sportswomen.* International symposium on the medicine and physiology of sports and athletes. Finnish Association of Sports Medicine.

Inside the USOC. (1999). www.olympics-usa.org/inside1-14

Irvine, M., & Gendreau, P. (1974). Detection of the fake "good" and "bad" response on the Sixteen Personality Factor Inventory in prisoners and college students. *Journal of Consulting and Clinical Psychology, 42,* 465–466.

Irving, P. G., & Goldstein, S. R. (1990). Effect of home-field advantage on peak performance of baseball pitchers. *Journal of Sport Behavior, 13,* 23–27.

Isberg, L., & Chelladurai, R. (1990). *The Leadership Scale for Sports: Its applicability in the Swedish context.* Unpublished manuscript, University College of Falun/Borlange, Sweden.

Iso-Ahola, S. (1975). A test of attribution theory of success and failure with Little League baseball players. *Mouvement, 7,* 323–327.

Iso-Ahola, S. E. (1977). Effects of team outcome on children's self-perceptions in Little League baseball. *Scandinavian Journal of Psychology, 19,* 38–42.

Iso-Ahola, S. (1979). Sex-role stereotypes and causal attributions for success and failure in motor performance. *Research Quarterly, 50,* 630–640.

Issari, P. (1998). Women, drug use, and drug testing: The case of the intercollegiate athlete. *Journal of Sport and Social Issues, 22,* 153–169.

Jable, J. T. (1976). Sunday sports comes to Pennsylvania: Professional baseball and football triumph over the Commonwealth's archaic blue laws, 1919–1933. *Research Quarterly, 47,* 357–365.

Jackson, J. H. (1932). On the nature of the duality of the brain. In J. Taylor (Ed.), *Selected writings of John Hughlings Jackson: Volume 2. Evolution and dissolution of the nervous system* (pp. 129–145). London, England: Hodder and Stoughton. (Reprinted from *Medical Press and Circular,* 1874, 1, 19)

Jacobson, E. (1938). *Progressive relaxation.* Chicago: University of Chicago Press.

Jacoby, E. (1978). Where is your next job? *Summer Manual* (American Football Coaches Association), 73–75.

Jambor, E. A., & Zhang, J. J. (1997). Investigating leadership, gender, and coaching level using the Revised Leadership Scale for Sport Scale. *Journal of Sport Behavior, 20,* 313–321.

James, W. (1890). *Principles of psychology.* New York: Henry Holt & Company.

Jennings, S. (1981). As American as hot dogs, apple pie, and Chevrolet: The desegregation of Little League baseball. *Journal of American Culture, 4*(4), 81–91.

Jersild, A. (1952). *In search of self.* New York: Teachers College Press, Columbia University.

Johnsgard, K. (1985). The motivation of the long distance runner: 1. *Journal of Sports Medicine, 25,* 135–143.

Johnsgard, K. W., Ogilvie, B. C., & Merritt, K. (1975). The stress seekers: A psychological study of sports parachutists, racing drivers, and football players. *Journal of Sports Medicine, 15,* 158–169.

Johnson, W. O., & Williamson, N. (1975a, October 6). Babe. *Sports Illustrated, 43*(14), 113–127.

Johnson, W. O., & Williamson, N. (1975b, October 20). Babe: Part three. *Sports Illustrated, 43*(16), 48–62.

Johnstone, E. C. (1996). *Biological psychiatry.* New York: Royal Society of Medicine Press Limited.

Jones, J., & Hochner, A. (1973). Racial differences in sports activities: A look at the self-paced versus reactive hypothesis. *Journal of Personality and Social Psychology, 27,* 86–95.

Jones, J. C. H., Ferguson, D. G., & Stewart, K. G. (1993). Blood sports and apple pie: Some economics of violence in the National Hockey League. *American Journal of Economics and Sociology, 52,* 63–77.

Jones, J. G. (1990). A cognitive perspective on the processes underlying the relationship between stress and performance in sport. In J. G. Jones (Ed.), *Stress and performance in sport* (pp. 16–42). New York: Wiley.

Jones, J. G., & Hochner, A. (1973). Racial differences in sports activities: A look at the self-paced versus reactive hypothesis. *Journal of Personality and Social Psychology, 27,* 86–95.

Jones, J. G., Swain, A., & Cale, A. (1990). Antecedents of multidimensional competitive state anxiety and self-confidence in elite intercollegiate middle distance runners. *The Sport Psychologist, 4,* 107–118.

Jones, J. G., Swain, A., & Cale, A. (1991). Gender differences in precompetition temporal patterning and antecedents of anxiety and self-confidence. *Journal of Sport & Exercise Psychology, 13,* 1–15.

Jourard, S. (1974). *Healthy personality: An approach from the viewpoint of humanistic psychology.* New York: Macmillan.

Kane, M. (1971, January 18). On assessment of "black is best." *Sports Illustrated,* 72–83.

Kane, M. (1982). The influence of level of sport participation and sex-role orientation on female professionalization of attitudes toward play. *Journal of Sport Psychology, 4,* 290–294.

Kaplan, J. (1979). *Women and sports.* New York: Viking Press.

Kaplan, R., & Sacuzzo, D. (1989). *Psychological testing: Principles, applications, and issues* (2nd ed.). Monterey, CA: Brooks/Cole.

Kau, M., & Fisher, J. (1974). Self-modification of exercise behavior. *Journal of Behavior Therapy and Experimental Psychiatry, 5,* 213–214.

Kavanaugh, D., & Hausfeld, B. (1986). Physical performance and self-efficacy make happy and sad moods. *Journal of Sport Psychology, 8,* 112–123.

Kearney, A. J. (1996). Some applications of behavioral principles to sport and exercise enhancement. In J. R. Cautela & W. Ishaq (Eds.), *Contemporary issues in behavior therapy: Improving the human condition.* New York: Plenum.

Kelley, B. C. (1994). A model of stress and burnout in collegiate coaches: Effects of gender and time of season. *Research Quarterly for Exercise and Sport, 65,* 48–58.

Kelley, B. C., Eklund, R. C., & Ritter-Taylor, M. (1999). Stress and burnout among collegiate tennis coaches. *Journal of Sport & Exercise Psychology, 21,* 113–130.

Kelley, H. H. (1972). *Causal schemata and the attribution process.* Morristown, NJ: General Learning Press.

Kendall, G., Hrycaiko, D., Martin, G. L., & Kendall, T. (1990). The effects of an imagery rehearsal, relaxation, and self-talk package on basketball game performance. *Journal of Sport & Exercise Psychology, 12,* 157–165.

Kennard, J. (1970). Maryland colonials at play: Their sports and games. *Research Quarterly, 41,* 389–395.

Kenyon, G. (1968). Six scales for assessing attitudes toward physical activity. *Research Quarterly, 39,* 566–574.

Kerr, G. A., & Goss, J. D. (1997). Personal control in elite gymnasts: The relationships of control, self-esteem, and trait anxiety. *Journal of Sport Behavior, 20,* 69–82.

Kerr, J. H. (1985). The experience of arousal: A new basis for studying arousal effects in sport. *Journal of Sports Sciences, 3,* 169–179.

Kerr, J. H. (1990). Stress and sport: Reversal theory. In J. Graham & L. Hardy (Eds.), *Stress and performance in sport* (pp. 107–131). Chichester, England: Wiley.

Kerr, J. H., & Vlaminkx, J. (1997). Gender differences in the experience of risk. *Personality and Individual Differences, 22,* 293–295.

Kerr, N. L., & Bruun, S. E. (1981). Ringelmann revisited: Alternative explanations for the social loafing effect. *Personality and Social Psychology Bulletin, 7,* 224–231.

Kidd, T. R., & Woodman, W. F. (1975). Sex and orientations toward winning in sport. *Research Quarterly, 46,* 476–483.

Kidman, L., McKenzie, A., & McKenzie, B. (1999). The nature and target of parents' comments during youth sport participation. *Journal of Sport Behavior, 22,* 54–68.

...ester, E. (1984). The uses of anger. *Psychology Today, 18*(7), 26.

Killian, K. J. (1988). Teaching swimming using a backward chain sequence. *Journal of Physical Education, Recreation and Dance, 59*(5), 82–86.

Kim, M., & Sugiyama, Y. (1992). The relation of performance norms and cohesiveness for Japanese athletic teams. *Perceptual and Motor Skills, 74,* 1096–1098.

King, J., & Chi, R. (1974). Personality and the athletic social structure: A case study. *Human Relations, 27,* 179–193.

King, M., Stanley, G., & Burrows, G. (1987). *Stress: Theory and practice.* London: Grune and Stratton.

King, R. (1992). The unfortunate 500. *Sports Illustrated, 77*(24), 20–29.

Kingsley, J., Brown, F., & Seibert, M. (1977). Social acceptance of female athletes by college women. *Research Quarterly, 48,* 727–733.

Kirkcaldy, B. (1980). An analysis of the relationship between psychophysiological variables connected to human performance and the personality variables extraversion and neuroticism. *International Journal of Sport Psychology, 11,* 276–289.

Kirkpatrick, C. (1988, February 1). Freshman at work. *Sports Illustrated,* 28–31.

Kirschenbaum, D. S., & Bale, R. M. (1980). Cognitive–behavioral skills in golf: Brain power golf. In R. M. Suinn (Ed.), *Psychology in sports: Methods and applications* (pp. 334–343). Minneapolis, MN: Burgess.

Kirschenbaum, J. (1980, July 21). Uppers in baseball. *Sports Illustrated,* 11.

Klavora, P. (1975). *Application of the Spielberger trait–state theory and STAI in pre-competition anxiety research.* Paper presented to the North American Society for the Psychology of Sport and Physical Activity, State College, PA.

Klavora, P. (1977). An attempt to derive inverted-U curves based on the relationship between anxiety and athletic performance. In D. M. Landers & R. W. Christina (Eds.), *Psychology of sport and motor behavior* (pp. 369–377). Champaign, IL: Human Kinetics.

Kleiber, D. (1981, May). Searching for enjoyment in children's sports. *Physical Educator,* 77–84.

Kleiber, D., Greendorfer, S., Blinde, E., & Samdahl, D. (1987). Quality of exit from university sports and life satisfaction in early adulthood. *Sociology of Sport Journal, 4,* 28–36.

Klein, M., & Christiansen, G. (1969). Group composition, group structure and group effectiveness of basketball teams. In J. W. Loy & G. S. Kenyon (Eds.), *Sport, culture, and society* (pp. 397–408). London: Macmillan.

Klonsky, R. (1991). Leaders' characteristics in same-sex sport groups: A study of interscholastic baseball and softball teams. *Perceptual and Motor Skills, 92,* 943–946.

Knoppers, A., Meyer, B. M., Ewing, M., & Forrest, L. (1989). Gender and the salary of coaches. *Sociology of Sport Journal, 6,* 348–361.

Kobasa, S. C. (1988). *The Hardiness Test.* New York: Hardiness Institute.

Kobasa, S. C., Maddi, S. R., & Courington, S. (1981). Personality and constitution as mediators in the stress–illness relationship. *Journal of Health and Social Behavior, 22,* 368–378.

Koltyn, K. F., & Schultes, S. S. (1997). Psychological effects of an aerobic exercise session and a rest session following pregnancy. *Journal of Sports Medicine and Physical Fitness, 37,* 287–291.

Kornspan, A. S., Lerner, B. S., Ronayne, J., Etzel, E. F., & Johnson, S. (1995). The home disadvantage in the National Football League's conference championship games. *Perceptual and Motor Skills, 80,* 800–802.

Kozar, A. (1984, September). R. Tait McKenzie: A man of noble achievement. *Journal of Physical Education, Recreation and Dance,* 27–31.

Kraemer, R. R., Dzewaltowski, D. A., Blair, M. S., Rinehardt, K. F., & Castracane, V. D. (1990). Mood alteration from treadmill running and its relationship to beta-endorphin, corticotropin, and growth hormone. *Journal of Sports Medicine and Physical Fitness, 31,* 241–246.

Kramer, J., & Schaap, D. (1969). *Instant replay.* New York: Signet.

Kraus, H., & Hirschland, P. (1954). Minimum muscular fitness tests in young children. *Research Quarterly, 25,* 178–188.

Kroll, W. (1970). Current strategies and problems in personality assessment of athletes. In L. E. Smith (Ed.), *Psychology of motor learning* (pp. 349–367). Chicago: Athletic Institute.

Kroll, W. (1976). Reaction to Morgan's paper: Psychological consequences of vigorous physical activity and sport. In M. G. Scott (Ed.), *The academy papers* (pp. 30–35). Iowa City, IA: American Academy of Physical Education.

Kuchenbecker, S. (1999). *Who's a winner? Coaches' views of winning young athletes.* Paper presented to the annual convention of the American Psychological Association, Los Angeles.

Lacayo, R. (2000, April 24). Are you man enough? *Time, 155*(16), 58–64.

Lacoste, P. L., & Laurencelle, L. (1989). *The French validation of the Leadership Scale for Sports.* Unpublished abstract, Université de Quebec à Trois Rivières, Canada.

Lambert, S. M., Moore, D. W., & Dixon, R. S. (1999). Gymnastics in training: The differential effects of self- and coach-set goals as a function of locus of control. *Journal of Applied Sport Psychology, 11,* 72–82.

Lamirand, M., & Rainey, D. (1994). Mental imagery, relaxation, and accuracy of basketball foul shooting. *Perceptual and Motor Skills, 78,* 219–227.

Lan, L. Y., & Gill, D. L. (1984). The relationship among self-efficacy, stress responses, and a cognitive feedback manipulation. *Journal of Sport Psychology, 6,* 227–238.

Landers, D. M. (1980). The arousal–performance relationship revisited. *Research Quarterly for Exercise and Sport, 51,* 77–90.

Landers, D. M., & Boutcher, S. H. (1993). Arousal–performance relationships. In J. M. Williams (Ed.), *Applied sport psychology: Personal growth to peak performance* (2nd ed., pp. 170–184). Mountain View, CA: Mayfield.

Landers, D. M., Brawley, L., & Hale, B. (1978). Habit strength differences in motor behavior. The effects of social facilitation paradigms and subject sex. In D. M. Landers & R. W. Christina (Eds.), *Psychology of motor behavior and sport, 1977* (pp. 420–433). Champaign, IL: Human Kinetics.

Landers, D. M., Wilkinson, M., Hatfield, B., & Barber, H. (1982). Causality and the cohesion–performance relationship. *Journal of Sport Psychology, 4,* 170–183.

Lane, A. M., Sewell, D. F., Terry, P. C., Bartram, D., & Nesti, A. S. (1999). Confirmatory factor analysis of the Competitive State Anxiety Inventory-2. *Journal of Sports Sciences, 17,* 505–512.

Langer, E. J. (1983). *The psychology of control.* Newbury Park, CA: Sage.

Lanning, W. (1980). Applied psychology in major college athletics. In R. M. Suinn (Ed.), *Psychology in sports: Methods and applications* (pp. 362–367). Minneapolis, MN: Burgess.

Lanning, W., & Hisanga, B. (1983). A study of the relationship between the reduction of competitive anxiety and an increase in athletic performance. *International Journal of Sport Psychology, 14,* 219–227.

Lapchick, R. E., & Benedict, J. R. (1993). 1993 racial report card. *CSSS Digest 5*(1), 1–13.

Lapchick, R. E., & Brown, J. R. (1992, Summer). 1992 racial report card: Do professional sports provide opportunities for all races? *CSSS Digest, 4*(1), 1–8.

Lapchick, R., & Matthews, K. (2000, August 11). 1998 racial and gender report card. http://www.bca-org.com/journal.html

LaPlace, J. (1954). Personality and its relationship to success in professional baseball. *Research Quarterly, 25,* 313–319.

LaPorte, R., Dearwater, S., Cauley, J., Slemenda, C., & Cook, T. (1985). Physical activity or cardiovascular fitness: Which is more important for health? *Physician and Sportsmedicine, 13*(3), 145–150.

Larsen, J. D., & Rainey, D. W. (1991). Judgment bias in baseball umpires' first base calls: A computer simulation. *Journal of Sport Behavior, 10,* 183–191.

Last word, The. (1989, December 26). *Houston Chronicle,* p. 6C.

Latane, B. (1973). *A theory of social impact.* St. Louis, MO: Psychonomic Society.

Latane, B., Harkins, S., & Williams, K. (1980). *Many hands make light the work: Social loafing as a social disease.* Unpublished manuscript, Ohio State University.

Latane B., Williams, K., & Harkins, S. (1979). Many hands make light the work: The causes and consequences of social loafing. *Journal of Personality and Social Psychology, 37,* 823–832.

Latimer, S., & Mathes, S. (1985). Black college football coaches' social, educational, athletic, and career pattern characteristics. *Journal of Sport Behavior, 8,* 149–162.

Layman, D., & Morris, A. (1986). *Addiction and injury in runners: Is there a mind–body connection?* Paper presented at the annual convention of the North American Society for the Psychology of Sport and Physical Activity, Scottsdale, AZ.

Layman, E. (1968). *Attitudes towards sports for girls and women in relation to masculinity–femininity stereotypes of women athletes.* Paper presented at symposium of American Association for the Advancement of Science, Dallas, TX.

Lazarus, R. S., & Monat, A. (1979). *Personality* (3rd ed.). Englewood Cliffs, NJ: Prentice-Hall.

Leclerc, G., Lefrancois, R., Dube, M., Hebert, R., & Gaulin, P. (1998). The self-actualization concept: A content validation. *Journal of Social Behavior and Personality, 13,* 69–84.

Leclerc, G., Lefrancois, R., Dube, M., Hebert, R., & Gaulin, P. (1999). Criterion validity of a new measure of self-concept. *Psychological Reports, 85,* 1167–1176.

Ledbetter, B. (1979). Sports and games of the American Revolution. *Journal of Sport History, 6,* 29–40.

Lee, C. (1982). Self-efficacy as a predictor of performance in competitive gymnastics. *Journal of Sport Psychology, 4,* 405–409.

Lee, C. (1990). Psyching up for a muscular endurance task: Effects of image content on performance and mood state. *Journal of Sport & Exercise Psychology, 12,* 66–73.

Lee, I., Hsieh, C., & Paffenbarger, R. S. (1995). Exercise intensity and longevity in men: The Harvard Alumni Health Study. *Journal of the American Medical Association, 273,* 1179–1184.

Lee, M. (1924). The case for and against intercollegiate athletics for women and the situation as it stands today. *American Physical Education Review, 29,* 13–19.

Lee, M. (1931). The case for and against intercollegiate athletics for women and the situation since 1923. *Research Quarterly, 2,* 93–127.

Lee, M. (1983). *A history of physical education and sports in the U.S.A.* New York: Wiley.

Lefcourt, H. M. (1992). Durability and impact of the locus of control construct. *Psychological Bulletin, 112,* 411–414.

Lefrancois, R., Leclerc, G., Dube, M., Hebert, R., & Gaulin,

P. (1997). The development and validation of a self-report measure of self-actualization. *Social Behavior and Personality, 25,* 353–365.

Lefrancois, R., Leclerc, G., Dube, M., Hebert, R., & Gaulin, P. (1998). Reliability of a new measure of self-actualization. *Psychological Reports, 82,* 875–878.

Legwold, G. (1985). Are we running from the truth about the risks and benefits of exercise? *Physician and Sportsmedicine, 13*(5), 136–148.

Lehrer, P. M., Carr, R., Sargunaraj, D., & Woolfolk, R. L. (1993). Differential effects of stress management therapies on emotional and behavioral disorders. In P. M. Lehrer & R. L. Woolfolk (Eds.), *Principles and practice of stress management* (2nd ed., pp. 481–520). New York: Guilford Press.

Leitenberg, H. (1976). Behavioral approaches to treatment of neuroses. In H. Leitenberg (Ed.), *Handbook of behavior modification and behavior therapy* (pp. 41–64). Englewood Cliffs, NJ: Prentice-Hall.

Leith, L. M., & Taylor, A. H. (1992). Behavior modification and exercise adherence: A literature review. *Journal of Sport Behavior, 15,* 60–74.

Lemonick, M. D. (1998, August 10). Le tour de drugs. *Time,* 76.

Lenk, H. (1977). *Team dynamics.* Champaign, IL: Stipes.

Lenskyj, H. (1991). Combating homophobia in sport and physical education. *Sociology of Sport Journal, 8,* 61–69.

Leonard, W. M. (1984). *A sociological perspective of sport* (2nd ed). Minneapolis, MN: Burgess.

Leonard, W. M. (1989). The "home advantage": The case of the modern Olympiads. *Journal of Sport Behavior, 12,* 227–241.

Leonard, W. M. (1996). The odds of transition from one level of sports participation to another. *Sociology of Sport Journal, 13,* 288–299.

Leonard, W. M. (1998). Specification of the home advantage: The case of the World Series. *Journal of Sport Behavior, 21,* 41–52.

Leonard, W. M., & Reyman, J. E. (1988). The odds of attaining professional athlete status: Refining the computation. *Sociology of Sport Journal, 5,* 162–169.

Lepper, M. R., & Greene, D. (1978). *The hidden cost of reward: New perspectives on the psychology of human motivation.* New York: Halstead.

Lepper, M. R., Greene, D., & Nisbett, R. E. (1973). Undermining children's intrinsic interests with intrinsic rewards: A test of the "overjustification" hypothesis. *Journal of Personality and Social Psychology, 28,* 129–137.

LeUnes, A. (1986). A sport psychologist and a football legend discuss the psychology of coaching: Coleman Griffith and Knute Rockne. *Journal of Applied Research in Coaching and Athletics, 1,* 127–134.

LeUnes, A. (2000). Updated bibliography on the Profile of Mood States in sport and exercise psychology research. *Journal of Applied Sport Psychology, 12,* 110–113.

LeUnes, A. (2002, in press). Bibliography of psychological tests used in sport and exercise psychology research. Lewiston, ME: Mellen Press.

LeUnes, A., & Berger, J. (1998). Bibliography on the Profile of Mood States in sport and exercise psychology research, 1971–1998. *Journal of Sport Behavior, 21,* 53–70.

LeUnes, A., Daiss, S., & Nation, J. R. (1986). Some psychological predictors of continuation in a collegiate football program. *Journal of Applied Research in Coaching and Athletics, 1,* 1–8.

LeUnes, A., & Hayward, S. A. (1990). Sport psychology as viewed by chairpersons of APA-approved clinical psychology programs. *The Sport Psychologist, 4,* 18–24.

LeUnes, A., & Nation, J. R. (1982). Saturday's heroes: A psychological portrait of college football players. *Journal of Sport Behavior, 5,* 139–149.

Levenson, H. (1973). *Reliability and validity of the I, P, and C Scales: A multidimensional view of locus of control.* Paper presented at annual convention of the American Psychological Association, Montreal.

Levenson, H. (1974). Activism and powerful others: Distinctions within the concept of internal–external control. *Journal of Personality Assessment, 38,* 377–383.

Levenson, H. (1981). Differentiating among internality, powerful others, and chance. In H. Lefcourt (Ed.), *Research with the locus of control construct: Assessment methods* (Vol. 1, pp. 1–39). New York: Academic Press.

Levenson, M. R. (1990). Risk taking and personality. *Journal of Personality and Social Psychology, 58,* 1073–1080.

Lewin, K. (1935). *A dynamic theory of personality.* New York: McGraw-Hill.

Lewis, B. (1992). The long and winding road. *Runner's World, 27*(2), 82–89.

Lewis, G. (1967). America's first intercollegiate sport: The regattas from 1852–1875. *Research Quarterly, 38,* 637–648.

Lewis, G. (1969). Theodore Roosevelt's role in the 1905 controversy. *Research Quarterly, 40,* 717–724.

Light, K. E., Reilly, M. A., Behrman, A. L., & Spirduso, W. W. (1996). Reaction times and movement times: Benefits of practice to younger and older adults. *Journal of Aging and Physical Activity, 4,* 27–41.

Likert, R. A. (1932). A technique for the measurement of attitudes. *Archives of Psychology, 140,* 1–55.

Lilliefors, F. (1978). *The running mind.* Mountain View, CA: World Publications.

Linder, D. E., Brewer, B. W., Van Raalte, J. L., & DeLange, N. (1991). A negative halo for athletes who consult sport psychologists: Replication and extension. *Journal of Sport & Exercise Psychology, 13,* 133–148.

Linder, D. E., Pillow, D. R., & Reno, R. R. (1989). Shrinking jocks: Derogation of athletes who consult sport psychologists. *Journal of Sport & Exercise Psychology, 11,* 270–280.

Lipsyte, R. (1975). *Sports world: An American dreamland.* New York: Quadrangle Books.

Liukkonen, J., Salminen, S., & Telama, R. (1989, August 7–12). *The psychological climate of training sessions in Finnish youth sports.* Paper presented at the Seventh World Congress in Sport Psychology, Singapore.

Li-Wei, Z., Qi-Wei, M., Orlick, T., & Zitzelsberger, L. (1992). The effect of mental imagery training on performance enhancement with 7–10-year-old children. *The Sport Psychologist, 6,* 230–241.

Locke, E. A. (1968). Toward a theory of task motivation and incentives. *Organizational Behavior and Human Performance, 3,* 157–189.

Locke, E. A., & Latham, G. P. (1985). The application of goal setting to sports. *Journal of Sport Psychology, 7,* 205–222.

Locke, E. A., Shaw, K. N., Saari, L. M., & Latham, G. P. (1981). Goal setting and task performance: 1969–1980. *Psychological Bulletin, 90,* 125–152.

Loggia, M. (1973, July). On the playing fields of history. *Ms.,* 62–65.

Lohr, B. A., & Scogin, F. (1998). Effects of self-administered visuo-motor behavioral rehearsal on sport performance of collegiate athletes. *Journal of Sport Behavior, 21,* 206–221.

Lombardo, B. F. (1986). The behavior of youth sport coaches: Crisis on the bench. In R. E. Lapchick (Ed.), *Fractured focus: Sport as a reflection of society* (pp. 199–205). Lexington, MA: Heath.

Lombardo, J. A., Longcope, C., & Voy, R. O. (1985). Recognizing anabolic steroid abuse. *Patient Care, 19,* 28–47.

Long, B. C. (1980). Stress management for the athlete: A cognitive behavioral model. In C. H. Nadeau (Ed.), *Psychology of motor behavior and sport* (pp. 111–119). Champaign, IL: Human Kinetics.

Long, B. C. (1984). Aerobic conditioning and stress inoculation: A comparison of stress-management interventions. *Cognitive Therapy and Research, 8,* 517–542.

Long, B. C. (1985). Stress-management interventions: A 15-month follow-up of aerobic and stress inoculation training. *Cognitive Therapy and Research, 9,* 471–478.

Long, B. C., & van Stavel, R. (1995). Effects of exercise training on anxiety: A meta-analysis. *Journal of Applied Sport Psychology, 7,* 167–189.

Longstreth, L. (1970). Birth order and avoidance of dangerous activities. *Developmental Psychology, 2,* 154.

Lopez, J. (1998, June 16). Hooligans renew shenanigans. *Houston Chronicle,* p. 9B.

Lord, S. R., Ward, J. A., Williams, P., & Strudwick, M. (1995). The effect of a 12-month exercise trial on balance, strength, and falls in older women: A randomized controlled trial. *Journal of American Gerontology Association, 43,* 1198–1206.

Lorenz, K. (1966). *On aggression.* New York: Harcourt, Brace & World.

Loucks, A. B. (1990). Effects of exercise training on the menstrual cycle: Existence and mechanisms. *Medicine and Science in Sports and Exercise, 22,* 275–280.

Loumidis, K. S., & Wells, A. (1998). Assessment of beliefs in exercise dependence: The development and preliminary validation of the exercise beliefs questionnaire. *Personality and Individual Differences, 25,* 553–567.

Loverock, R. (1991, May). On your mark, get set, go. *Shape,* 83–87.

Loy, J., & McElvogue, J. (1970). Racial segregation in American sport. *International Review of Sport Sociology, 5,* 5–24.

Lufi, D., Porat, J., & Tenenbaum, G. (1986). Psychological predictors of competitive performance in young gymnasts. *Perceptual and Motor Skills, 63,* 59–64.

Lumpkin, A., & Williams, L. D. (1991). An analysis of *Sports Illustrated* feature articles, 1954–1987. *Sociology of Sport Journal, 8,* 16–32.

Lutter, J., & Cushman, S. (1982). Menstrual patterns in female runners. *Physician and Sportsmedicine, 10*(9), 60–72.

Lybrand, W. A., Andrews, T. G., & Ross, S. (1954). Systematic fatigue and perceptual organization. *American Journal of Psychology, 67,* 704–707.

Lynn, R., Phelan, J., & Kiker, V. (1969). Beliefs in internal–external control of reinforcement and participation in group and individual sports. *Perceptual and Motor Skills, 29,* 551–553.

Lyon, L. (1972). *A method for assessing personality characteristics in athletes: The Athletic Motivational Inventory.* Unpublished master's thesis, San Jose State University.

Mace, R. D., & Carroll, D. (1986). Stress inoculation training to control anxiety in sport: Two case studies in squash. *British Journal of Sports Medicine, 20,* 115–117.

Mace, R. D., Eastman, C., & Carroll, D. (1987). The effects of stress inoculation training on gymnastics performance on the pommeled horse: A case study. *Behavioural Psychotherapy, 15,* 272–279.

Machlus, S. D., & O'Brien, R. M. (1988). *Visuo-motor skills and athletic performance.* Paper presented to the Association for the Advancement of Behavior Therapy, Atlanta, GA.

Maddux, J. E., & Rogers, R. W. (1983). Protection motivation and self-efficacy: A revised theory of fear appeals and attitude change. *Journal of Experimental and Social Psychology, 19,* 469–479.

Maehr, M., & Nicholls, J. (1980). Culture and achievement motivation: A second look. In N. Warren (Ed.), *Studies in cross-cultural psychology.* Vol 2. (pp. 53–75). New York: Academic Press.

Maffulli, N. (1990). Intensive training in young athletes: The orthopaedic surgeon's viewpoint. *Sports Medicine, 9,* 229–243.

Mahoney, M. J. (1977). Cognitive skills and athletics performance. Paper presented to the Association for the Advancement of Behavior Therapy, Atlanta, GA.

Mahoney, M. J. (1989). Psychological predictors of elite and non-elite performance in Olympic weightlifting. *International Journal of Sport Psychology, 20,* 1–12.

Mahoney, M. J., & Avener, M. (1977). Psychology of the elite athlete: An exploratory study. *Cognitive Therapy and Research, 7,* 135–141.

Mahoney, M. J., Gabriel, T. J., & Perkins, T. S. (1987). Psychological skills and exceptional athletic performance. *The Sport Psychologist, 1,* 181–199.

Maier, S. F., & Seligman, M. E. P. (1976). Learned helplessness: Theory and evidence. *Journal of Experimental Psychology: General, 105,* 3–46.

Malumphy, T. (1970). The college woman athlete—questions and tentative answers. *Quest, 14,* 18–27.

Mandell, A. (1975, June). Pro football fumbles the drug scandal. *Psychology Today,* 39–47.

Mann, L. (1974). On being a sore loser: How fans react to their team's failure. *Australian Journal of Psychology, 26,* 37–47.

Marcus, B., Selby, V. C., Niaura, R. S., & Rossi, J. S. (1992). Self-efficacy and the stages of exercise behavior change. *Research Quarterly for Exercise and Sport, 63,* 60–66.

Mark, M. M., Bryant, F. B., & Lehman, D. R. (1983). Perceived injustice and sports violence. In J. Goldstein (Ed.), *Sports violence.* New York: Springer-Verlag.

Mark, M. M., Mutrie, N., Brooks, A. R., & Harris, D. V. (1984). Causal attributions of winners and losers in individual competitive sports: Toward a reformulation of the self-serving bias. *Journal of Sport Psychology, 6,* 184–196.

Marks, I., Boulougouris, J., & Marset, P. Flooding versus desensitization in the treatment of phobic patients: A cross over study. *British Journal of Psychiatry, 119,* 353–375.

Maron, M., & Horvath, S. (1978). The marathon: A history and review of the literature. *Medicine and Science in Sports, 10,* 137–150.

Marsh, H. W. (1987). The factorial invariance of responses by males and females to a multidimensional self-concept instrument: Substantive and methodological issues. *Multivariate Behavioral Research, 22,* 457–480.

Marsh, H. W. (1990a). *The Self-Description Questionnaire (SDQ): A theoretical and empirical basis for the measurement of multiple dimensions of late adolescent self-concept—An interim test manual and a research monograph.* San Antonio, TX: The Psychological Corporation.

Marsh, H. W. (1990b). *The Self-Description Questionnaire (SDQ): A theoretical and empirical basis for the measurement of multiple dimensions of late adolescent self-concept—An interim test manual and a research monograph.* San Antonio, TX: The Psychological Corporation.

Marsh, H. W. (1990c). *The Self-Description Questionnaire (SDQ): A theoretical and empirical basis for the measurement of multiple dimensions of late adolescent self-concept: An interim test manual and a research monograph.* San Antonio, TX: The Psychological Corporation.

Marsh, P., Rosser, E., & Harre, R. (1978). *The rules of disorder.* London: Routledge and Kegan Paul.

Martens, R. (1969). Effects of an audience on learning and performance of a complex motor skill. *Journal of Personality and Social Psychology, 12,* 252–260.

Martens, R. (1974). Arousal and motor performance. *Exercise and Sport Science Reviews, 2,* 155–188.

Martens, R. (1975a). The paradigmatic crisis in American sport personology. *Sportswissenschaft, 5,* 9–24.

Martens, R. (1975b). *Social psychology and physical activity.* New York: Harper & Row.

Martens, R. (1977). *Sport Competition Anxiety Test.* Champaign, IL: Human Kinetics.

Martens, R. (1980). From smocks to jocks: A new adventure for sport psychologists. In P. Klavora & K. Wipper (Eds.). *Psychological and sociological factors in sport* (pp. 20–26). Toronto: University of Toronto Press.

Martens, R. (1981). Sport personology. In G. R. E. Luschen & G. E. Sage (Eds.), *Handbook of social science of sport* (pp. 492–508). Champaign, IL: Stipes.

Martens, R., Burton, D., Rivkin, F., & Simon, J. (1980). Reliability and validity of the Competitive State Anxiety Inventory (CSAI): A modification of Spielberger's state anxiety inventory. In C. H. Nadeau, W. R. Halliwell, K. M. Newell, & G. C. Roberts (Eds.), *Psychology of motor behavior and sport—1979* (pp. 91–99). Champaign, IL: Human Kinetics.

Martens, R., Burton, D., Vealey, R. S., Bump, L. A., & Smith, D. (1982). *Cognitive and somatic dimensions of competitive anxiety.* Paper presented to the North American Society for the Psychology of Sport and Physical Activity, University of Maryland, College Park.

Martens, R., Burton, D., Vealey, R. S., Bump, L. A., & Smith, D. E. (1990). Development and validation of the Competitive State Anxiety Inventory–2 (CSAI–2). In R. Martens, R. S. Vealey, & D. Burton (Eds.), *Competitive anxiety in sport* (pp. 117–123). Champaign, IL: Human Kinetics.

Martens, R., Gill, D., Simon, J., & Scanlan, T. (1975). *Competitive anxiety: Theory and research.* Proceedings of the Seventh Canadian Society for Psychomotor Learning and Sport Psychology Symposium, Quebec City, Canada.

Martens, R., & Landers, D. M. (1970). Motor performance

makes stress: A test of the inverted-U hypothesis. *Journal of Personality and Social Psychology, 16,* 29–37.

Martens, R., & Landers, D. M. (1972). Evaluation potential as a determinant of coaction effects. *Journal of Experimental Social Psychology, 8,* 347–359.

Martens, R., & Peterson, J. (1971). Group cohesiveness as a determinant of success and member satisfaction in team performance. *International Review of Sport Sociology, 6,* 49–61.

Martens, R., & Seefeldt, V. (1979). *Guidelines for children's sports.* Washington, DC: Alliance for Health, Physical Education, Recreation and Dance.

Martens, R., Vealey, R. S., & Burton, D. (1990). *Competitive anxiety in sport.* Champaign, IL: Human Kinetics.

Martin, G. L., & Hrycaiko, D. (1983). Effective behavioral coaching: What's it all about? *Journal of Sport Psychology, 5,* 8–20.

Martin, G. L., & Pear, J. (1992). *Behavior modification: What it is and how to do it* (4th ed.). Englewood Cliffs, NJ: Prentice-Hall.

Martin, J. J., & Gill, D. L. (1991). The relationship among competitive orientation, sport-confidence, self-efficacy, anxiety, and performance. *Journal of Sport & Exercise Psychology, 13,* 149–159.

Martin, K. A., & Hall, C. R. (1995). Using mental imagery to enhance intrinsic motivation. *Journal of Sport & Exercise Psychology, 17,* 54–69.

Martin, K. A., & Hausenblas, H. A. (1998). Psychological commitment to exercise and eating disorder symptomatology among female aerobics instructors. *The Sport Psychologist, 12,* 180–190.

Martinsen, E. W. (1990). Benefits of exercise for the treatment of depression. *Sports Medicine, 9,* 380–389.

Maslach, C. (1976). Burned-out. *Human Behavior, 5,* 16–22.

Maslach, C., & Jackson, S. E. (1981). The measurement of experienced burnout. *Journal of Occupational Behavior, 2,* 99–113.

Maslach, C., & Jackson, S. E. (1986). *Maslach Burnout Inventory: Manual* (6th ed.). Palo Alto, CA: Consulting Psychologists Press.

Maslow, A. (1970). *Motivation and behavior* (2nd ed.). New York: Harper & Row.

Massengale, J. (1980). Role conflict and the occupational milieu of the teacher/coach: Some real working world perspectives. In *National Association for Physical Education in Higher Education Proceedings, 11,* 47–52.

Massengale, J. (1981a). Researching role conflict. *Journal of Physical Education, Recreation and Dance, 52*(9), 23.

Massengale, J. (1981b). Role conflict and the teacher/ coach: Some occupational causes and considerations for the sport sociologist. In S. Greendorfer and A. Yiannakis (Eds.), *Sociology of sport: Diverse perspectives* (pp. 149–157). West Point, NY: Leisure Press.

Massie, J., & Shephard, R. (1971). Physiological and psychological effects of training: A comparison of individual and gymnasium programs, with a characterization of the exercise "drop-out." *Medicine and Science in Sports, 3,* 110–117.

Masters, K. S. (1992). Hypnotic susceptibility, cognitive dissociation, and runner's high in a sample of marathon runners. *American Journal of Clinical Hypnosis, 34,* 193–201.

Masters, K. S., & Ogles, B. M. (1995). An investigation of the different motivations of marathon runners with varying degrees of experience. *Journal of Sport Behavior, 18,* 69–79.

Masters, K. S., Ogles, B. M., & Jolton, J. A. (1993). The development of an instrument of measure motivation for marathon running: The Motivations of Marathoners Scales (MOMS). *Research Quarterly for Exercise and Sport, 64,* 134–143.

Mathes, S. (1982). *Women coaches: Endangered species?* Paper presented at the American Alliance for Health, Physical Education, Recreation and Dance National Convention, Houston, TX.

May, J. R., Veach, T. L., Daily-McKee, D., & Furman, G. (1985). A preliminary study of elite adolescent women athletes and their attitudes toward training and femininity. In N. K. Butts, T. T. Gushiken, & B. Zarins (Eds.), *The elite athlete* (pp. 163–169). New York: Spectrum.

Maynard, I. W., Hemmings, B., & Warwick-Evans, L. (1995). The effects of a somatic intervention strategy on competitive state anxiety and performance in semiprofessional soccer players. *The Sport Psychologist, 9,* 51–64.

McAndrew, F. T. (1992). The home advantage in individual sports. *The Journal of Social Psychology, 133,* 401–403.

McAuley, E. (1985). Success and causality in sport: The influence of perception. *Journal of Sport Psychology, 7,* 13–22.

McAuley, E. (1992). Understanding exercise and achievement behavior: A self-efficacy perspective. In G. C. Roberts (Ed.), *Motivation in sport and exercise* (pp. 107–127). Champaign, IL: Human Kinetics.

McAuley, E., & Duncan, T. E. (1989). Causal attributions and affective reactions to disconfirming outcomes in motor performance. *Journal of Sport & Exercise Psychology 11,* 187–200.

McAuley, E., Duncan, T. E., & Russell, D. W. (1992). Measuring causal attributions: The revised Causal Dimension Scale (CDSII). *Personality and Social Psychology Bulletin, 18,* 566–573.

McAuley, E., & Gross, J. (1983). Perception of causality in sport: An application of the Causal Dimension Scale. *Journal of Sport Psychology, 5,* 72–76.

McClelland, D., Atkinson, J., Clark, R., & Lowell, E. (1953).

The achievement motive. New York: Appleton-Century-Crofts.

McCready, M., & Long, B. C. (1985). Locus of control, attitudes toward physical activity, and exercise adherence. *Journal of Sport Psychology, 7,* 346–359.

McCutcheon, L., & Yoakum, M. (1983). Personality attributes of ultramarathoners. *Journal of Personality Assessment, 47,* 178–180.

McElroy, M. A., & Kirkendall, D. R. (1980). Significant others and professionalized sport attitudes. *Research Quarterly for Exercise and Sport, 51,* 645–653.

McElroy, M. A., & Willis, J. (1979). Women and the achievement conflict in sport: A preliminary study. *Journal of Sport Psychology, 1,* 241–247.

McGregor, E. (1989). Mass media and sport: Influences on the public. *The Physical Educator 46*(1), 52–55.

McHugh, M. C., Duquin, M. E., & Frieze, I. H. (1978). Beliefs about success and failure: Attribution and the female athlete. In C. A. Oglesby (Ed.), *Women and sport: From myth to reality* (pp. 173–191). Philadelphia: Lea and Febiger.

McInman, A. D. (1992). *The effects of weight-training on self-concept.* Unpublished master's thesis, University of Western Australia, Nedlands, Australia.

McKay, J., & Rowe, D. (1987). Ideology, the media and Australian sport. *Sociology of Sport Journal, 4,* 258–273.

McKelvie, S., & Huband, D. (1980). Locus of control and anxiety in college athletes and non-athletes. *Perceptual and Motor Skills, 50,* 819–822.

McKenzie, T. L., & Rushall, B. S. (1974). Effects of self-recording on attendance and performance in a competitive swimming training environment. *Journal of Applied Behavioral Analysis, 7,* 199–206.

McNair, D., Lorr, M., & Droppleman, L. (1971). *Profile of Mood States Manual.* San Diego, CA: Educational and Industrial Testing Service.

Mehrabian, A. (1969). Measures of achieving tendency. *Educational and Psychological Measurement, 29,* 445–451.

Mehrabian, A. (1971). *Silent messages.* Belmont, CA: Wadsworth.

Meichenbaum, D. (1977). *Cognitive-behavior modification: An integrated approach.* New York: Plenum.

Meichenbaum, D. (1993). Stress inoculation training: A 20-year update. In P. M. Lehrer & R. L. Woolfolk (Eds.), *Principles and practice of stress management* (2nd ed., pp. 373–406). New York: Guilford Press.

Melzack, R. (1975). The McGill Pain Questionnaire: Major properties and scoring methods. *Pain, 1,* 277–299.

Melzack, R. (1987). The short-form McGill Pain Questionnaire. *Pain, 30,* 191–197.

Menard, V. (1996). Historically underrepresented on the U.S. Olympic team, Hispanics see progress. http://www.hisp.com/jul96/olympics/html

Mento, A. J., Steel, R. R, & Karren, R. J. (1987). A meta-analytic study of the effects of goal setting on task performance: 1966–1984. *Organizational Behavior and Human Decision Processes, 39,* 52–83.

Meyers, A. W., & Schleser, R. (1980). A cognitive behavioral intervention for improving basketball performance. *Journal of Sport Psychology, 2,* 69–73.

Meyers, A. W., Schleser, R., Cooke, C., & Cuvillier, C. (1979). Cognitive contributions to the development of gymnastic skills. *Cognitive Therapy and Research, 3,* 75–85.

Meyers, M. C., Bourgeois, A. E., Stewart, S., & LeUnes, A. (1992). Predicting pain response in athletes: Development and assessment of the Sports Inventory for Pain. *Journal of Sport & Exercise Psychology, 14,* 249–261.

Michael, M., Gilroy, E., & Sherman, M. (1984). Athletic similarity and attitudes towards women as factors in the perceived physical attractiveness and liking of a female varsity athlete. *Perceptual and Motor Skills, 59,* 511–518.

Michener, J. A. (1976). *Sports in America.* New York: Fawcett Crest.

Miedzian, M. (1991). *Boys will be boys: Breaking the link between masculinity and violence.* New York: Doubleday.

Mihoces, G. (1988, May 10). Less-visible players find little glory after football. *USA Today,* p. 12C.

Mihovilovic, M. A. (1968). The status of former sportsmen. *International Review of Sport Sociology, 3,* 73–93.

Miller, J. L., & Levy, G. D. (1996). Gender role conflict, gender-typed characteristics, self-concepts, and sport socialization in female athletes and nonathletes. *Sex Roles, 35,* 111–122.

Miller, L. K. (1997). *Sport business management.* Gaithersburg, MD: Aspen Publishers.

Miller, N. E. (1978). Biofeedback and visual learning. *Annual Review of Psychology, 29,* 373–404.

Mirels, H. (1970). Dimensions of internal vs. external control. *Journal of Consulting and Clinical Psychology, 34,* 226–228.

Mitchell, J. S., Leonard, W. M., & Schmitt, R. L. (1982). Sport officials' perceptions of fans, players, and their occupations: A comparative study of baseball and hockey. *Journal of Sport Behavior, 5,* 83–95.

Molander, B., & Backman, L. (1994). Attention and performance in miniature golf across life-span. *Journal of Gerontology, 49,* 35–41.

Monahan, T. (1986). Exercise and depression: Swapping sweat for serenity? *Physician and Sportsmedicine, 14*(9), 192–197.

Montagu, A. (1975). Is man innately aggressive? In W. Fields and W. Sweet (Eds.), *Neurological symposium on neural bases of violence and aggression* (pp. 431–451). St. Louis, MO: Warren H. Green.

Moolenijzer, N. (1968, Winter). Our legacy from the Middle Ages. *Quest* (Monograph XI), 32–43.

Moran, A. (1993). Conceptual and methodological issues in the measurement of imagery skills in athletes. *Journal of Sport Behavior, 16,* 156–170.

Morey, M. C., Cowper, R. A., Feussner, J. R., DiPasquale, R. C., Crowley, G. M., & Sullivan, R. J. (1991). Two-year trends in physical performance following supervised exercise among community dwelling older veterans. *Journal of the American Geriatric Society, 39,* 549–554.

Morgan, W. P. (1968). Personality characteristics of wrestlers participating in the world championships. *Journal of Sports Medicine, 8,* 212–216.

Morgan, W. P. (1972). Sport psychology. In R. N. Singer (Ed.), *The psychomotor domain* (pp. 193–228). Philadelphia: Lea and Febiger.

Morgan, W. P. (1978, April). The mind of the marathoner. *Psychology Today,* 38–49.

Morgan, W. P. (1979). Negative addiction in runners. *Physician and Sportsmedicine, 7*(2), 56–70.

Morgan, W. P. (1980, July). Test of champions. *Psychology Today,* 92–108.

Morgan, W. P., & Costill, D. (1972). Psychological characteristics of the marathon runner. *Journal of Sports Medicine and Physical Fitness, 12,* 42–46.

Morgan, W. P., Ellickson, K. A., O'Connor, P. J., & Bradley, P. W. (1992). Elite male distance runners: Personality structure, mood states and performance. *Track and Field Quarterly, 92,* 59–62.

Morgan, W. P., O'Connor, P. J., Sparling, P. B., & Pate, R. R. (1992). The elite female distance runner: Psychological characterization. *Track and Field Quarterly, 92,* 63–67.

Morgan, W. P., & Johnson, R. (1978). Personality characteristics of successful and unsuccessful oarsmen. *International Journal of Sport Psychology, 9,* 119–133.

Morgan, W. P., & Pollock, M. (1977). Psychologic characterization of the elite distance runner. In R. Milvey (Ed.), The marathon: Physiological, medical, epidemiological, and psychological studies. *Annals of the New York Academy of Sciences, 301,* 382–403.

Morris, A., Vaccaro, R., & Clarke, D. (1979). Psychological characteristics of age-group competitive swimmers. *Perceptual and Motor Skills, 48,* 1265–1266.

Morris, L. D. (1975). A socio-psychological study of highly skilled women field hockey players. *International Journal of Sport Psychology, 6,* 134–147.

Mottram, D. R. (1999). Banned drugs in sport: Does the International Olympic Committee (IOC) list need updating? *Sports Medicine, 27,* 1–10.

Mottram, D. R., Reilly, T., & Chester, N. (1997). Doping in sport: The extent of the problem. In T. Reilly & M. Orne (Eds.), *The clinical pharmacology of sport and exercise* (pp. 3–12). Amsterdam: Excerpta Medica.

Mount, M. K., Barrick, M. R., & Strauss, J. P. (1994). Validity of the big five personality factors. *Journal of Applied Psychology, 79,* 272–280.

Mouratidis, J. (1984). Heracles at Olympia and the exclusion of women from the ancient Olympic games. *Journal of Sport History, 11,* 41–55.

Mouratidis, J. (1985). Nero: The artist, the athlete, and his downfall. *Journal of Sport History, 12,* 5–20.

Mowrer, O. H. (1960). *Learning theory and behavior.* New York: Wiley.

Muchinsky, R. M. (1987) *Psychology applied to work: An introduction to industrial and organizational psychology* (2nd ed.). Chicago: Dorsey Press.

Mueller, F. O., Blyth, C. S., & Cantu, R. C. (1989). Catastrophic spine injuries in football. *Physician and Sportsmedicine, 17*(10), 51–53.

Mueller, F. O., & Schindler, R. (1984). Annual survey of football injury research, 1931–1983. *Athletic Training, 19,* 189–192, 208.

Murray, H. A. (1938). *Explorations in personality.* New York: Oxford University Press.

Murray, H. A. (1943). *Thematic Apperception Test.* Cambridge: Harvard University Press.

Murrell, A. J., & Dietz, B. (1992). Fan support of sport teams: The effect of common group identity. *Journal of Sport & Exercise Psychology, 14,* 28–39.

Myers, A., & Lips, H. (1978). Participation in competitive amateur sports as a function of psychological androgyny. *Sex Roles, 4,* 571–578.

Myung Woo, H. (1996). Psychological profiles of Korean elite judoists. *American Journal of Sports Medicine, 24,* S67–S71.

Nack, W., & Munson, L. (2000, July 24). Out of control. *Sports Illustrated,* 86–95.

Nance, R. (1990). St. John's (Minn.): Peculiar practices. (1990). *USA Today,* August 22, p. 10C.

Nation J. R., & LeUnes, A. (1983a). Personality characteristics of intercollegiate football players as determined by position, classification, and redshirt status. *Journal of Sport Behavior, 6,* 92–102.

Nation, J. R., & LeUnes, A. (1983b). A personality profile of the black athlete in college football. *Psychology, 20,* 1–3.

Nation, J. R., & Massad, P. (1978). Persistence training: A partial reinforcement procedure for reversing learned helplessness and depression. *Journal of Experimental Psychology: General, 107,* 436–451.

Nation, J. R., & Woods, D. J. (1980). Persistence: The role of partial reinforcement in psychotherapy. *Journal of Experimental Psychology, 109,* 175–207.

NBA coaching changes. (1994, August 30). *Bryan–College Station Eagle [TX],* p. B1.

NCAA Division I coaching changes. (2000, August 11). http://espn.go.com/ncw/s/coaches/new.html

Neil, G., & Kirby, S. (1985). Coaching styles and preferred leadership among rowers and paddlers. *Journal of Sport Behavior, 8,* 3–17.

Neiss, R. (1988). Reconceptualizing arousal: Psychobiological states in motor performance. *Psychological Bulletin, 103,* 345–366.

Nelson, B., & Carron, M. (1991). Home court advantage as perceived by coaches and players in selected division I college sports. In W. K. Simpson, A. LeUnes, & J. S. Picou (Eds.), *Applied Research in Coaching and Athletics Annual.* Boston: American Press.

Neumann, H. (Ed.). (1936). *Der Ritterspiegel.* Halle, Germany: Max Niemeyer.

Neumarker, K. J., Bettle, N., Neumarker, U., & Bettle, O. (2000). Age- and gender-related psychological characteristics of adolescent ballet dancers. *Psychopathology, 33,* 137–142.

New faces on the bench. (1990, November 30). *USA Today,* p. 2C.

New findings reported on biking and impotence. *Physician and Sportsmedicine, 27*(5), 21–22.

New rules a problem (1996, August 16). *USA Today,* p. 3C.

New techniques may catch blood dopers. (1986). *Physician and Sportsmedicine, 14*(2), 36.

NFL veterans. (1990, October 26). *USA Today,* p. IC.

Nicholson, C. (1979). Some attitudes associated with sport participation among junior high school females. *Research Quarterly, 50,* 661–667.

Nicklaus, J. (1974). *Golf my way.* New York: Simon & Schuster.

Nideffer, R. M. (1976a). *The inner athlete.* New York: Crowell.

Nideffer, R. M. (1976b). Test of Attentional and Interpersonal Style. *Journal of Personality and Social Psychology, 34,* 394–404.

Nideffer, R. M. (1981). *The ethics and practice of applied sport psychology.* Ithaca, NY: Mouvement.

Nideffer, R. M. (1986). Concentration and attention control training. In J. M. Williams (Ed.), *Applied sport psychology: Personal growth to peak experience* (pp. 257–269). Palo Alto, CA: Mayfield.

Nideffer, R. M. (1990). Use of the Test of Attentional and Interpersonal Style (TAIS) in sport. *The Sport Psychologist, 4,* 285–300.

Nideffer, R. M., & Bond, J. (1989). *Test of Attentional and Interpersonal Style: Cultural and sexual differences.* Banff, Canada: Proceedings of the Banff International Conference on Psychology, Sport and Health Promotion.

Nisbett, R. E. (1968). Birth order and participation in dangerous sports. *Journal of Personality and Social Psychology, 8,* 351–353.

Nixon, H. L. (1981). Birth order and preference for risky sports among college students. *Journal of Sport Behavior, 4,* 12–23.

Nixon, H. L. (1984). *Sport and the American dream.* New York: Leisure Press.

Noland, M. (1981). *The efficacy of a new model to explain leisure exercise behavior.* Unpublished doctoral dissertation, University of Maryland.

Nolen-Hoeksema, S. (1998). *Abnormal psychology.* New York: McGraw-Hill.

Nowell, P. (2001, January 23). Carruth sentenced to nearly 19 years in jail. *Austin American Statesman,* p. C1.

Nowicki, S., & Strickland, B. (1973). A locus of control scale for children. *Journal of Consulting and Clinical Psychology, 40,* 148–154.

O'Brien, R. M., & Simek, T. C. (1983). A comparison of behavioral and traditional methods for teaching golf. In G. L. Martin and D. Hrycaiko (Eds.), *Behavioral modification and coaching: Principles, procedures, and research.* Springfield, IL: Charles C. Thomas.

O'Dell, J. (1971). Method for detecting random answers on personality questionnaires. *Journal of Applied Psychology, 55,* 380–383.

Ogilvie, B. C. (1974a). *Relationship of AMI traits to three levels of baseball competitors.* Unpublished research paper, San Jose State University.

Ogilvie, B. C. (1974b, October). The sweet psychic jolt of danger. *Psychology Today,* 8–91.

Ogilvie, B., & Howe, M. (1986). The trauma of termination from athletics. In J. M. Williams (Ed.), *Applied sport psychology: Personal growth to peak experience* (pp. 365–382). Mountain View, CA: Mayfield.

Ogilvie, B. C., & Tutko, T. A. (1966). *Problem athletes and how to handle them.* London: Pelham Books.

Ogilvie, B. C., Tutko, T. A., & Lyon, L. (1973). *The Motivational Inventory.* Scholastic Coach, 43, 130–134.

Ogles, B. M., & Masters, K. S. (2000). Older vs. younger adult male marathon runners: Participative motives and training habits. *Journal of Sport Behavior, 23,* 130–143.

Oglesby, C. A. (1984). Interactions between gender identity and sport. In J. M. Silva and R. S. Weinberg (Eds.), *Psychological foundations of sport* (pp. 387–399). Champaign, IL: Human Kinetics.

Oldridge, N. (1988). Cardiac rehabilitation exercise programme. Compliance and compliance enhancing strategies. *Sports Medicine, 6,* 42–55.

Oldridge, N., Wicks, J., Hanley, R., Sutton, J., & Jones, N. (1978). Noncompliance in an exercise rehabilitation program for men who have suffered a myocardial infarction. *Canadian Medical Association Journal, 118,* 361–375.

Oliver, C. (1971). *High for the game.* New York: Morrow.

O'Malley, M. (1977). Some day they'll retire Gordie Howe's sweater—If, of course, he takes it off. *Macleans, 90*(26), 40.

On the spot (1996). November 17. http://www.soccer.org/snnow/spot.html

Orlick, T. (1974, November/December). The athletic dropout: A high price of inefficiency. *CAHPER Journal,* 21–27.

Orlick, T. (1998). *Embracing your potential.* Champaign, IL: Human Kinetics.

Orlick, T., & Partington, J. (1987). The sport psychology consultant: Analysis of critical components as viewed by Canadian Olympic athletes. *The Sport Psychologist, 1,* 4–17.

Orwell, G. (1946). *Animal farm.* New York: Harcourt, Brace.

Osgood, C. D., Suci, G. J., & Tannenbaum, R. H. (1957). *The measurement of meaning.* Urbana, IL: University of Illinois Press.

Ossip-Klein, D. J., Doyne, E. J., Bowman, E. D., Osborn, K. M., McDougall-Wilson, B., & Neimeyer, R. A. (1989). Effects of running or weight lifting on self-concept in clinically depressed women. *Journal of Consulting and Clinical Psychology, 57,* 158–161.

Ostrow, A. G., Jones, D. C., & Spiker, D. D. (1981). Age role expectations and sex role expectations for selected sport activities. *Research Quarterly for Exercise and Sport, 52,* 216–227.

Ottley, W. (1983). USPA secretary killed while making stunt jump. *Parachutist, 24*(3), 35.

Page three. (1985, July 12). *Houston Chronicle,* p. 3.

Palmer, D., & Howell, M. L. (1973). Sports and games in early civilization. In E. F. Zeigler (Ed.), *A history of sport and physical education to 1900* (pp. 21–34). Champaign, IL: Stipes.

Pappas, A. M., & Zawacki, R. M. (1991). Baseball: Too much on a young pitcher's shoulders? *Physician and Sportsmedicine, 19*(3), 107–117.

Parkhouse, B. L., & Williams, J. M. (1986). Differential effects of sex and status on evaluation of coaching ability. *Research Quarterly for Exercise and Sport, 57,* 53–59.

Participation survey 1999–2000. (1999–2000). National Federation of State High School Associations. www.nfhs.org/part_survey99-00.html

Partington, J. (1990). *Personal knowledge in imagery: Implications for novice gymnasts, figure skaters, and their coaches.* Paper presented to the Canadian Society for Psychomotor Learning and Sport Psychology, Windsor, Ontario.

Passer, M. W. (1983). Fear of failure, fear of evaluation, perceived competence, and self-esteem in competitive anxious children. *Journal of Sport Psychology, 5,* 172–188.

Passer, M. W. (1984). Competitive trait anxiety in children and adolescents. In J. M. Silva & R. S. Weinberg (Eds.), *Psychological foundations of sport* (pp. 130–144). Champaign, IL: Human Kinetics.

Pastore, D. L., & Meacci, W. G. (1994). Employment process for NCAA female coaches. *Journal of Sport Management, 8,* 115–128.

Pate, R. (1983). A new definition of youth fitness. *Physician and Sportsmedicine, 11*(4), 87–95.

Pate, R., Rotella, R., & McClenaghan, B. (1984). *Scientific foundations of coaching.* Philadelphia: Saunders.

Patrick, D. (1994, August 15). Torrid Torrence warms up quickly for important week. *USA Today,* p. 12C.

Patrick, D. (1996, July 17). Kenyans remain in lead for the long run. *USA Today,* p. 14C.

Paulus, P. B., & Cornelius, W. L. (1974). An analysis of gymnastic performance under conditions of practice and spectator observation. *Research Quarterly, 45,* 56–63.

Paulus, P. B., Shannon, I. C., Wilson, D. L., & Boone, T. D. (1972). The effects of spectator presence on gymnastic performance in a field situation. *Psychonomic Science, 29,* 88–90.

Pavlov, I. P. (1927). *Conditioned reflex.* London: Oxford University Press.

Pedersen, D. M. (1997). Perceptions of high risk sports. *Perceptual and Motor Skills, 85,* 756–758.

Peoples, C. (1983). A psychological analysis of the "runner's high." *Physical Educator, 40,* 38–41.

Perna, F. M., Ahlgre, R. L., & Zaichkowsky, L. (1999). The influence of career planning, race, and athletic injury on life satisfaction among recently retired collegiate male athletes. *The Sport Psychologist, 13,* 144–156.

Perrotto, R. S., & Culkin, J. (1993). *Abnormal psychology.* New York: HarperCollins.

Pessin, J. (1933). The comparative effects of social and mechanical simulation on memorizing. *American Journal of Psychology, 45,* 263–281.

Pestonjee, D., Singh, R., Singh, A., & Singh, U. (1981). Personality and physical abilities: An empirical investigation. *International Journal of Sport Psychology, 12,* 39–51.

Peterson, C., Semmel, A., von Baeyer, C., Abramson, L. Y., Metalsky, G. I., & Seligman, M. E. P. (1982). The Attributional Style Questionnaire. *Cognitive Therapy and Research, 6,* 287–299.

Peterson, R. (1970). *Only the ball was white.* Englewood Cliffs, NJ: Prentice-Hall.

Petitpas, A. J., Brewer, B. W., Rivera, P. M., & Van Raalte, J. L. (1994). Ethical beliefs and behaviors in applied sport psychology. *Journal of Applied Sport Psychology, 6,* 135–151.

Petrie, T. A. (1993). Coping skills, competitive trait anxiety, and playing status: Moderating effects of the life stress-injury relationship. *Journal of Sport & Exercise Psychology, 15,* 261–274.

Petrie, T. A., & Watkins, C. E. (1994). A survey of counseling psychology programs and exercise/sport science departments: Sport psychology issues and training. *The Sport Psychologist, 8,* 28–36.

Phillips, J. C. (1976). Toward an explanation of racial variations in top-level sports participation. *International Review of Sociology, 11,* 39–55.

Piaget, J. (1936). *The origins of intelligence in children.* New York: New York University Press.

Pierce, E. F. (1994). Exercise dependence syndrome in runners. *Sports Medicine, 18,* 149–155.

Pivarnik, J. M. (1994). Maternal exercise during pregnancy. *Sports Medicine, 18,* 215–217.

Pivarnik, J. M. (1998). Potential effects of maternal physical activity on birth weight: Brief review. *Medicine and Science in Sports and Exercise, 30,* 400–406.

Plowman, S. A. (1989). Exercise and puberty: Is there a relationship for the female athlete? In D. Nudel (Ed.), *Pediatric sports medicine.* New York: PMA Publishing.

Poff, J. (1995) Donnie Moore: A racial memoir. *Elysian Fields Quarterly, 14,* 11–20.

Pooley, J. (1981). *Dropouts from sport. A case study of boys' age group soccer.* Paper presented at American Alliance for Health, Physical Education, Recreation and Dance (AAHPERD) Convention, Boston.

Porretta, D. L., & Moore, W. (1996/1997). A review of sport psychology research for individuals with disabilities: Implications for future inquiry. *Clinical Kinesiology, 50,* 83–93.

Porter, K., & Foster, J. (1988, January). In your mind's eye. *World Tennis,* 22–23.

Position statement: The use of anabolic-androgenic steroids (AAS) in sport and physical activity. (1993). *International Journal of Sport Psychology, 24,* 74–78.

Postmes, T., & Spears, R. (1998). Deindividuation and antinormative behavior: A meta-analysis. *Psychological Bulletin, 123,* 238–259.

Powell, F. M., & Verner, J. P. (1982). Anxiety and performance relationships in first time parachutists. *Journal of Sport Psychology, 4,* 184–188.

Powell, J. W., & Barber-Foss, K. D. (1999). Injury pattern in selected high school sports: A review of the 1995–1997 seasons. *Journal of Athletic Training, 34,* 277–284.

Predebon, J., & Docker, S. B. (1992). Free-throw shooting performance as a function of preshot routines. *Perceptual and Motor Skills, 75,* 161–171.

Premack, D. (1962). Reversability of the reinforcement relation. *Science, 136,* 235–237.

The president's challenge physical fitness program. (1991). Washington, DC: President's Council on Youth Fitness and Sports.

Pro coaches won't find security. (1989). *Inside Sports, 11,* 11–12.

Pufahl, A. (1987). Title IX: Boon or bust to intramural programs. *NIRSA Journal, 11*(2), 48–51.

Quain, R. J., & Purdy, D. A. (1988). Sports officials: Who are these people? *Journal of Applied Research in Coaching and Athletics, 3,* 60–74.

Rader, B. (1983). *American sports from the age of folk games to the age of spectators.* Englewood Cliffs, NJ: Prentice-Hall.

Raedeke, T. D. (1997). Is athlete burnout more than just stress? A sport commitment perspective. *Journal of Sport & Exercise Psychology, 19,* 396–417.

Raedeke, T. D., Granzyk, T. L., & Warren, A. (2000). Why coaches experience burnout: A commitment perspective. *Journal of Sport & Exercise Psychology, 22,* 85–105.

Raglin, J. (1990). Exercise and mental health. *Sports Medicine, 6,* 323–329.

Raglin, J., & Morgan, W. R. (1985). Influence of vigorous exercise on mood state. *Behavior Therapist, 8,* 179–183.

Raglin, J. S., & Morris, M. J. (1994). Precompetition anxiety in women volleyball players: A test of ZOF theory in a team sport. *British Journal of Sports Medicine, 28,* 47–51.

Rainey, D. W. (1995). Sources of stress among baseball and softball umpires. *Journal of Applied Sport Psychology, 7,* 1–10.

Rainey, D. W., & Duggan, P. (1998). Assaults on basketball referees: A statewide survey. *Journal of Sport Behavior, 22,* 113–121.

Rainey, D. W. & Hardy, L. (1999). Assaults on Rugby Union referees: A three union survey. *Journal of Sport Behavior, 23,* 105–113.

Rainey, D. W., & Larsen, J. D. (1988). Balls, strikes, and norms: Rule violations and normative rules among baseball umpires. *Journal of Sport & Exercise Psychology, 10,* 75–80.

Rainey, D. W., Larsen, J. D., & Stephenson, A. (1989). The effects of a pitcher's reputation on umpires' calls of balls and strikes. *Journal of Sport Behavior 12,* 139–150.

Rainey, D. W., Larsen, J. D., Stephenson, A., & Olson, T. (1991). Normative rules among umpires: The "phantom tag" at second base. *Journal of Sport Behavior, 14,* 147–155.

Rainey, D. W., Larsen, J. D., & Williard, M. J. (1987). A computer simulation of sport officiating behavior. *Journal of Sport Behavior, 10,* 183–191.

Rainey, D. W., & Schweickert, G. J. (1988). An exploratory study of team cohesion before and after a spring trip. *The Sport Psychologist, 2,* 314–317.

Rainey, D. W., & Schweickert, G. (1991). Evaluations of umpire performance and perceptions of appropriate behavior toward umpires. *International Journal of Sport Psychology, 22,* 66–77.

Rainey, D. W., Schweickert, G., Granito, V., & Pullella, J. (1990). Fans' evaluations of major league baseball umpires' performances and perceptions of appropriate behavior toward umpires. *Journal of Sport Behavior, 13,* 122–129.

Rajagopalan, K. (1973). Early Indian physical education. In E. F. Zeigler (Ed.), *A history of sport and physical education to 1900* (pp. 45–55). Champaign, IL: Stipes.

Randall, L. E., & McKenzie, T. L. (1987). Spectator verbal behavior in organized youth soccer: A descriptive analysis. *Journal of Sport Behavior, 10,* 200–211.

Ransom, K. & Weinberg, R. S. (1985). Effect of situation criticality on performance of elite male and female tennis players. *Journal of Sport Behavior, 8,* 144–148.

Rasch, R. J., Hunt, M. B., & Robertson, R. G. (1960). The Booth Scale as a predictor of competitive behavior of college wrestlers. *Research Quarterly, 31,* 117.

Rathus, S. A., & Nevid, J. S. (1991). *Abnormal psychology.* Englewood Cliffs, NJ: Prentice-Hall.

Ravizza, K. (1984). Qualities of the peak experience in sport. In J. M. Silva & R. S. Weinberg (Eds.), *Psychological foundations of sport* (pp. 452–461). Champaign, IL: Human Kinetics.

Reel, J. J., & Gill, D. L. (1996). Psychosocial factors related to eating disorders among high school and college cheerleaders. *The Sport Psychologist, 10,* 195–206.

Rees, C. R. (1983). Instrumental and expressive leadership in team sports: A test of leadership role differentiation theory. *Journal of Sport Behavior, 6,* 17–27.

Rees, C. R., & Andres, F. (1980). Strength differences: Real and imagined. *Journal of Physical Education and Research, 2,* 61.

Rees, C. R., & Segal, M. (1984). Role differentiation in groups: The relationship between instrumental and expressive leadership. *Small Group Behavior, 15,* 109–123.

Reid, R., & Hay, D. (1979). Some behavioral characteristics of rugby and association footballers. *International Journal of Sport Psychology, 10,* 239–251.

Reifman, A. S., Larrick, R. P., & Fein, S. (1991). Temper and temperature on the diamond: Heat-aggression relationships in major league baseball. *Personality and Social Psychology Bulletin, 17,* 580–585.

Reilly, R. (2000, February 28.), Bringing parents up to code. *Sports Illustrated,* 88.

Reiss, M., & Taylor, J. (1984). Ego-involvement and attribution for success and failure in a field setting. *Personality and Social Psychology Bulletin, 10,* 536–543.

Rejeski, W. J., & Brawley, L. R. (1983). Attribution theory in sport: Current status and new perspectives. *Journal of Sport Psychology, 5,* 77–99.

Renfrow, N., & Bolton, B. (1979a). Personality characteristics associated with aerobic exercise in adult males. *Journal of Personality Assessment, 43,* 261–266.

Renfrow, N., & Bolton, B. (1979b). Personality characteristics associated with aerobic exercise in adult females. *Journal of Personality Assessment, 43,* 504–508.

Revised edition of the manual for the POMS. (1990). *EDITS Research and Developments.* San Diego, CA: Educational and Industrial Testing Service.

Rice, E., Hutchinson, J., & Lee, M. (1969). *A brief history of physical education* (5th ed.). New York: Ronald.

Richards, D., & Landers, D. M. (1980). Test of Attentional and Interpersonal Style scores of shooters. In G. C. Roberts & D. M. Landers (Eds.), *Psychology of motor behavior and sport—1980* (p. 94). Champaign, IL: Human Kinetics.

Riem, K., & Hursey, K. (1993). Effects of anabolic-androgenic steroid use in athletes: A coach's guide. In W. K. Simpson, A. LeUnes, & J. S. Picou (Eds.), *Applied research in coaching and athletics annual 1993.* Boston: American Press.

Rikki, R., & Cottle, S. (1984). Sex bias in evaluation of coaching ability and physical performance research. *Perspectives, 6,* 32–41.

Riley, J. F., Ahern, D. K., & Follick, M. J. (1988). Chronic pain and functional impairment: Assessing beliefs about their relationships. *Archives of Physical Medicine and Rehabilitation, 69,* 579–582.

Rintala, J., & Burrell, S. (1984). Fair treatment for the active female: A content analysis of *Young Athlete* magazine. *Sociology of Sport Journal, 1,* 231–250.

Riordan, C., Thomas, J., & James, M. (1985). Attributions in a one-on-one sports competition: Evidence for self-serving biases and gender differences. *Journal of Sport Behavior, 8,* 42–53.

Roberts, G. C. (1975). Win–loss causal attributions of Little League players. *Mouvement, 7,* 315–322.

Roberts, G. C. (1992). Motivation in sport and exercise: Conceptual restraints and convergence. In G. C. Roberts (Ed.), *Motivation in sport and exercise.* Champaign, IL: Human Kinetics.

Roberts, G. C. (1993). Motivation in sport: Understanding and enhancing the motivation and achievement of children. In R. N. Singer, M. Murphey, & L. K. Tennant (Eds.), *Handbook of research on sport psychology.* New York: Macmillan.

Roberts, G. C., & Pascuzzi, D. (1979). Causal attributions in sport: Some theoretical implications. *Journal of Sport Psychology, 1,* 203–211.

Robertson, I. (1981). *Sociology* (2nd ed.). New York: Worth.

Robinson, D. W. (1985). Stress seeking: Selected behavioral characteristics of elite rock climbers. *Journal of Sport Psychology, 7,* 400–404.

Robinson, J., & Shaver, R. (1973). *Measures of social psychological attitudes.* Ann Arbor, MI: Institute for Social Research.

Robinson, J., Shaver, R., & Wrightsman, L. S. (1991). *Measures of personality and social psychological attitudes.* San Diego, CA: Academic Press.

Robinson, R. S. (1955). *Sources for the history of Greek athletics.* Cincinnati: Published by author.

Roche, A. F., Tyleshevski, F., & Rogers, E. (1983). Noninvasive measurement of physical activity in children. *Research Quarterly for Exercise and Sport, 54,* 364–371.

Rodgers, W., Hall, C., & Buckholz, E. (1991). The effect of an imagery training program on imagery ability, imagery use, and figure skating performance. *Journal of Applied Sport Psychology, 3,* 109–125.

Rodrigo, G., Lusiardo, M., & Pereira, G. (1990). Relationship between anxiety and performance in soccer players. *International Journal of Sport Psychology, 21,* 112–120.

Rogers, C. (1985). Of magic, miracles, and exercise myths. *Physician and Sportsmedicine, 13*(5), 156–166.

Rogers, R. W. (1983). Cognitive and physiological processes in fear appeals and attitude change: A revised theory of protection change. In J. T. Cacciopo and R. E. Petty (Eds.), *Social psychology: A sourcebook.* New York: Guilford Press.

Roizen, R. (1996, December 19). Zebra abuse: Some theoretical possibilities. Rroizen@ix.net.com

Rorhlich, J. B. (1998). The meaning of aggression. *Psychiatric Annals, 28,* 246–249.

Roscoe, J. (1965). *The construction and applications of the Polyphasic Values Inventory.* Unpublished doctoral dissertation, Colorado State College.

Rosenstiel, A. K., & Keefe, F. J. (1983). The use of coping strategies in lower back pain patients: Relationship to patient characteristics and current adjustment. *Pain, 32,* 105–109.

Rossi, B., & Cereatti, L. (1993). The sensation seeking in mountain athletes as assessed by Zuckerman's Sensation Seeking Scale. *International Journal of Sport Psychology, 24,* 417–431.

Rostaing, B., & Sullivan, R. (1985, January 21). Triumphs tainted with blood. *Sports Illustrated,* 12–17.

Rotella, R. J. (1985). Strategies in controlling anxiety and arousal. In L. Bunker & R. J. Rotella (Eds.), *Sport psychology* (pp. 185–195). Ann Arbor, MI: McNaughton and Gunn.

Roth, W. (1974). Some motivational aspects of exercise. *Journal of Sports Medicine, 14,* 40–47.

Roth, W. (1989). Acute emotional and psychophysiological effects on aerobic exercise. *Psychophysiology, 26,* 593–602.

Rotter, J. B. (1966). Generalized expectancies for internal versus external control of reinforcement. *Psychological Monographs, 80* (1; Whole No. 609).

Rotter, J. B. (1971). External control and internal control. *Psychology Today, 5*(1), 37–42, 58–59.

Rotter, J. B. (1975). Some problems and misconceptions related to the construct of internal versus external control of reinforcement. *Journal of Consulting and Clinical Psychology, 43,* 56–67.

Rotton, J., & Cohn, E. G. (2000). Violence is a curvilinear function of temperature in Dallas: A replication. *Journal of Personality and Social Psychology, 78,* 1074–1081.

Rowell, G. (1983, November). Mount Everest: Pure and simple. *Sports Illustrated,* 88–102.

Rowland, T. W. (2000). On the ethics of elite-level sports participation by children. *Pediatric Exercise Science, 12,* 1–5.

Rowley, S. (1987). Psychological effects of intensive training in young athletes. *Journal of Child Psychology and Psychiatry, 28,* 171–177.

Ruder, M. K., & Gill, D. L. (1982). Immediate effects of win–loss on perceptions of cohesion in intramural and intercollegiate volleyball teams. *Journal of Sport Psychology, 4,* 227–234.

Rudman, W. (1986). Sport as a part of successful aging. *American Behavioral Scientist, 29,* 453–470.

Ruffer, W. A. (1975). Personality traits in athletes. *Physical Educator, 32,* 105–109.

Ruffer, W. A. (1976a). Personality traits in athletes. *Physical Educator, 33,* 50–55.

Ruffer, W. A. (1976b). Personality traits in athletes. *Physical Educator 33,* 211–214.

Runfola, R. (1974, October 17). He is a hockey player, 17, black and convicted of manslaughter. *New York Times,* p. 2–3.

Rupnow, A., & Ludwig, D. (1981). Psychometric note on the reliability of the Sport Competition Anxiety Test: Form C. *Research Quarterly for Exercise and Sport, 52,* 35–37.

Rushall, B. S. (1972). Three studies relating personality variables to football performance. *International Journal of Sport Psychology, 3,* 12–24.

Rushall, B. S. (1975). Alternative dependent variables for the study of behavior in sport. In D. M. Landers (Ed.), *Psychology of sport and motor behavior–II* (pp. 49–59). College Park, PA: Pennsylvania State University.

Rushall, B. S., & Siedentop, D. (1972). *The development and control of behavior in sports and physical education.* Philadelphia: Lea and Febiger.

Rushall, B. S., & Smith, K. C. (1979). The modification of the quality and quantity of behavioral categories in a swimming coach. *Journal of Sport Psychology, 1,* 138–150.

Russell, D. (1982). The Causal Dimension Scale: A measure of how individuals perceive causes. *Journal of Personality and Social Psychology, 42,* 1137–1145.

Russell, G. W. (1974). Machiavellianism, locus of control, aggression, performance, and precautionary behaviour in ice hockey. *Human Relations, 27,* 825–837.

Russell, G. W. (1986). Does sports violence increase box office receipts? *International Journal of Sport Psychology, 17,* 173–183.

Russell, G. W. (1993). Violent sports entertainment and the promise of catharsis. *Medienpsychologie: Zeitschrift fur Individual- & Massenkommunikation, 5,* 101–105.

Russell, G. W. (1997). *The social psychology of sport.* New York: Springer-Verlag.

Russell, G. W., & Drewry, B. R. (1976). Crowd size and competitive aspects of aggression in ice hockey: An archival study. *Human Relations, 29,* 723–735.

Ryan, E. D. (1968). Reaction to "sport and personality dynamics." In *Proceedings* (pp. 70–75). Minneapolis, MN: National College Physical Education Association for Men.

Ryan, J. (1995). *Little girls in pretty boxes.* New York: Warner Books.

Sabo, D. (1998). Women's athletics and the elimination of men's sports programs. *Journal of Sport and Social Issues, 22,* 27–31.

Sabo, D., Jansen, S. C., Tate, D., Duncan, M. C., & Leggett, S. (2000). The portrayal of race, ethnicity, and nationality in televised international athletic events. http://www.aafla.org/Publications/ResearchReports/Research Report.htm

Sabock, R. (1979). *The coach.* Philadelphia: Saunders.

Sachs, M. (1980). *On the trail of the runner's high: A descriptive and experimental investigation of characteristics of an elusive phenomenon.* Unpublished doctoral dissertation, Florida State University.

Sachs, M. (1982). Compliance and addiction to exercise. In R. C. Cantu (Ed.), *The exercising adult.* Boston: Collamore Press.

Sachs, M. (1984). Psychological well-being and vigorous physical activity. In J. M. Silva & R. S. Weinberg (Eds.), *Psychological foundations of sport* (pp. 435–444). Champaign, IL: Human Kinetics.

Sage, G. H. (1972a). Machiavellianism among college and high school coaches. *Seventy-fifth Proceedings of the National College Physical Education Association for Men,* pp. 45–60.

Sage, G. H. (1972b). Value orientations of American college coaches compared to male college students and businessmen. *Seventy-fifth Proceedings of the National College Physical Education Association for Men,* pp. 174–186.

Sage, G. H., & Loudermilk, S. (1979). The female athlete and role conflict. *Research Quarterly, 50,* 88–96.

Sailes, G. A. (1993). An investigation of campus stereotypes: The myth of black athletic superiority and the dumb jock stereotype. *Sociology of Sport Journal, 10,* 88–97.

Sampson answers a prayer. (1986, May 23). *Bryan–College Station Eagle [TX],* p. 3B.

Sanborn, C. R. (1986). Etiology of athletic amenorrhea. In J. L. Puhl & C. H. Brown (Eds.), *The menstrual cycle and physical activity.* Champaign, IL: Human Kinetics.

Sanday, P. R. (1981). *Female power and male domination: On the origins of sexual inequality.* New York: Cambridge University Press.

Sanders, G. (1981). Driven by distraction: An integrative review of social facilitation theory and research. *Journal of Experimental Social Psychology, 17,* 227–251.

Sanders, G., Baron, R., & Moore, D. (1978). Distraction and social comparison as mediators of social facilitation effects. *Journal of Experimental Social Psychology, 14,* 291–303.

Sanderson, F. H. (1983). Length and spacing of practice sessions in sport skills. *International Journal of Sport Psychology, 14,* 116–122.

Sanderson, F. H., & Ashton, M. (1981). Analysis of anxiety levels before and after badminton competition. *International Journal of Sport Psychology, 12,* 23–28.

Sandweiss, J. H. (1985). Biofeedback and sports science. In J. H. Sandweiss & S. L. Wolf (Eds.), *Biofeedback and sports science* (pp. 1–31). New York: Plenum.

Sandweiss, J. H., & Wolf, S. L. (Eds.). (1985). *Biofeedback and sports science.* New York: Plenum.

Sanne, H. (1973). Exercise tolerance and physical training of non-selected patients after myocardial infarction. *Acta Medica Scandinavica, 551,* 1–124.

Sapp, M., & Haubenstricker, J. (1978). *Motivation for joining and reasons for not continuing in youth sports programs in Michigan.* Paper presented at American Alliance for Health, Physical Education, and Recreation (AAHPER) Convention, Kansas City.

Sarason, I., Davidson, K., Lighthall, F., Waite, R., & Ruebush, B. (1960). *Anxiety in elementary school children.* New York: Wiley.

Sasiene, G. (1983). Secondary amenorrhea among female athletes: Current understandings. *Journal of Physical Education, Recreation and Dance, 54*(6), 61–63.

Sasijima, K. (1973). Early Chinese physical education and sport. In E. F. Zeigler (Ed.), *A history of sport and physical education to 1900* (pp. 35–44). Champaign, IL: Stipes.

Scanlan, T. K. (1984). Competitive stress and the child athlete. In J. M. Silva & R. S. Weinberg (Eds.), *Psychological foundations of sport* (pp. 118–129). Champaign, IL: Human Kinetics.

Scanlan, T. K., & Lewthwaite, R. (1986). Social psychological aspects of competition for male youth participants: IV. Predictors of enjoyment. *Journal of Sport Psychology, 8,* 25–35.

Scanlan, T. K., & Passer, M. W. (1978). Factors related to competitive stress among male youth sport participants. *Medicine and Science in Sports, 10,* 103–108.

Scanlan, T. K., & Passer, M. W. (1979a). Factors influencing the competitive performance expectancies of young female athletes. *Journal of Sport Psychology, 1,* 151–159.

Scanlan, T. K., & Passer, M. W. (1979b). Sources of competitive stress in young female athletes. *Journal of Sport Psychology, 1,* 212–220.

Scanlan, T. K., & Passer, M. W. (1980a). The attributional responses of young female athletes after winning, trying, and losing. *Research Quarterly for Exercise and Sport, 51,* 675–684.

Scanlan, T. K., & Passer, M. W. (1980b). Self-serving biases in the competitive sport setting: An attributional dilemma. *Journal of Sport Psychology, 2,* 124–136.

Scanlan, T. K., & Passer, M. W. (1981). Competitive stress and the youth sport experience. *Physical Educator, 38,* 144–151.

Scanlan, T. K., Stein, G. L., & Ravizza, K. (1989). An in-depth study of former elite figure skaters: II. Sources of enjoyment. *Journal of Sport & Exercise Psychology, 11,* 65–83.

Scanlan, T. K., Stein, G. L., & Ravizza, K. (1991). An in-depth study of former elite figure skaters: III. Sources of stress. *Journal of Sport & Exercise Psychology, 13,* 103–120.

Scanning sports. (1989). *Physician and Sportsmedicine, 17*(2), 21.

Schafer, S. (1984). *Sports needs you. A working model for the equity professional.* Denver, CO: Colorado Department of Education.

Schick, J. (1970). Effects of mental practice in selected volleyball skills for college women. *Research Quarterly, 51,* 88–94.

Schlenker, B. R., Phillips, S. T., Boniecki, K. A., & Schlenker, D. R. (1995a). Championship pressures: Choking or triumphing in one's own territory? *Journal of Personality and Social Psychology, 68,* 632–643.

Schlenker, B. R., Phillips, S. T., Boniecki, K. A., & Schlenker, D. R. (1995b). Where is the home choke? *Journal of Personality and Social Psychology, 68,* 649–652.

Schleser, R., Meyers, A. W., & Montgomery, T. (1980). *A cognitive behavioral intervention for improving basketball performance.* Paper presented to the Association for the Advancement of Behavior Therapy, New York.

Schmidt, G. W., & Stein, G. L. (1991). A model integrating enjoyment, dropout, and burnout. *Journal of Sport & Exercise Psychology, 13,* 254–265.

Schrader. M. P., & Wann, D. L. (1999). High-risk recreation: The relationship between participant characteristics and degree of involvement. *Journal of Sport Behavior, 22,* 426–441.

Schrodt, B. (1981). Sports of the Byzantine Empire. *Journal of Sport History, 8,* 40–59.

Schutz, R. W., Eom, H. J., Smoll, E L., & Smith, R. E. (1994). Examination of the factorial validity of the Group Environment Questionnaire. *Research Quarterly for Exercise and Sport, 65,* 226–236.

Schwartz, B., & Barsky, S. R. (1977). The home advantage. *Social Forces, 55,* 641–661.

Schwartz, G. E. (1993). Foreword: Biofeedback is not relaxation is not hypnosis. In P. M. Lehrer & R. L. Woolfolk (Eds.), *Principles and practice of stress management* (2nd ed., pp. ix–x). New York: Guilford Press.

Schwartz, G. E., Davidson, R. J., & Goleman, D. J. (1978). Patterning of cognitive and somatic processes in the self-regulation of anxiety: Effects of meditation versus exercise. *Psychosomatic Medicine, 40,* 321–328.

Scott, J. (1971). *The athletic revolution.* New York: Macmillan.

Scott, R. (1953). Attitudes toward athletic competition in elementary schools. *Research Quarterly, 24,* 352–361.

Seefeldt, V. (2000). *Selecting and "screening" youth volunteer coaches for youth sports programs.* East Lansing, MI: Michigan State University Youth Sport Institute.

Seff, M. A., Gecas, V., & Frey, J. H. (1992). Birth order, self-concept, and participation in dangerous sports. *The Journal of Personality, 127,* 221–232.

Seligman, M. E. P. (1975). *Helplessness: On depression, development, and death.* San Francisco: W. H. Freeman.

Seligman, M. E. P. (1991). *Learned optimism.* New York: Knopf.

Seligman, M. E. P., Abramson, L., Semmel, A., & von Baeyer, C. (1979). Depressive attributional style. *Journal of Abnormal Psychology, 88,* 242–247.

Seligman, M. E. P., & Beagley, G. (1975). Learned helplessness in the rat. *Journal of Comparative and Physiological Psychology, 88,* 534–541.

Seligman, M. E. P., Nolen-Hoeksema, S., Thornton, N., & Thornton, K. M. (1990). Explanatory style as a mechanism of disappointing athletic performance. *Psychological Science, 1,* 143–146.

Serling, R. J. (1986). Curing a fear of flying. *USAir,* 12–19.

Serpa, S., Pataco, V., & Santos, E. (1991). Leadership patterns in handball international competition. *International Journal of Sport Psychology, 22,* 78–89.

Sewell, D. (1992, Fall). Are parents ruining the games? *Youth Sport Coach, 1,* 16.

Seymour, E. (1956). Comparative study of certain behavior characteristics of participant and nonparticipant boys in Little League baseball. *Research Quarterly, 27,* 338–346.

Shacham, S. (1983). A shortened version of the Profile of Mood States. *Journal of Personality Assessment, 47,* 305–306.

Shangold, M. M., & Sherman, C. (1998). Exercise and menopause: A time for positive changes. *Physician and Sportsmedicine, 26*(12), 45+.

Shapiro, E. S., & Shapiro, S. (1984). Behavioral coaching in the development of skills in track. In J. Silva & R. S. Weinberg (Eds.), *Psychological foundations of sport* (pp. 81–98). Champaign, IL: Human Kinetics.

Shaw, M. (1976). *Group dynamics: The psychology of small group behavior* (2nd ed.). New York: McGraw-Hill.

Sheldon, W. H. (1940). *The varieties of human physique.* New York: Harper.

Sheldon, W. H. (1942). *The varieties of human temperament.* New York: Harper.

Shelton, T. O., & Mahoney, M. J. (1978). The content and effect of "psyching-up" strategies in weight lifters. *Cognitive Therapy and Research, 2,* 275–284.

Shephard, R. J. (1985). Motivation: The key to exercise compliance. *Physician and Sportsmedicine, 13*(7), 88–101.

Shephard, R. J. (1995). Physical activity, health, and well-being at different life stages. *Research Quarterly for Exercise and Sport, 66,* 298–302.

Shephard, R. J. (1997). Curricular physical activity and academic performance. *Pediatric Exercise Science, 9,* 113–126.

Shephard, R. J., Laurencelle, L., Tremblay, J., Rajic, M., & Shephard, R. J. (1999). Daily primary school physical education: Effects on physical activity during adult life. *Medicine and Science in Sports and Exercise, 31,* 111–117.

Shephard, R. J., & Shek, P. N. (1998). Associations between physical activity and susceptibility to cancer: Possible mechanisms. *Sports Medicine, 26,* 293–315.

Shepperd, J. A. (1993). Productivity loss in performance groups: A motivation analysis. *Psychological Bulletin, 113,* 67–81.

Sherrill, C., Gench, B., Hinson, M., Gilstrap, T., Richir, K., & Mastro, J. (1990). Self-actualization of elite blind athletes: An exploratory study. *Journal of Vision Impairment and Blindness, 84,* 55–60.

Sherrill, C., Gilstrap, T., Richir, K., Gench, B., & Hinson, M. (1988). Use of the Personal Orientation Inventory with disabled athletes. *Perceptual and Motor Skills, 67,* 263–266.

Sherrill, C., & Rainbolt, W. (1988). Self-actualization profiles of male able-bodied and elite cerebral palsied athletes. *Adapted Physical Education Quarterly, 5,* 108–119.

Sherrill, C., Silliman, L., Gench, B., & Hinson, M. (1990). Self-actualization of elite wheelchair athletes. *Paraplegia, 28,* 252–260.

Shifflett, B., & Revelle, R. (1994). Gender equity in sports media coverage: A review of the *NCAA News*. *Journal of Sport and Social Issues, 18,* 144–150.

Shostrom, E. (1963). *Personal Orientation Inventory.* San Diego, CA: Educational and Industrial Testing Service.

Sidney, K., & Shephard, R. J. (1976). Attitudes toward health and physical activity in the elderly: Effects of a physical training program. *Medicine and Science in Sports, 4,* 246–252.

Siegel, D., & Newhof, C. (1984). The sports orientation of female collegiate basketball players participating at different competitive levels. *Perceptual and Motor Skills, 59,* 79–87.

Silliman, L. M., & Sherrill, C. (1989). Self-actualization of wheelchair athletes. *Clinical Kinesiology, 43,* 77–82.

Silva, J. M. (1979). Assertive and aggressive behavior in sport: A definitional clarification. In C. H. Nadeau, W. R. Halliwell, K. M. Newell, and G. C. Roberts (Eds.), *Psychology of motor behavior and sport—1979* (pp. 199–208). Champaign, IL: Human Kinetics.

Silva, J. M. (1981). Normative compliance and rule violating behavior in sport. *International Journal of Sport Psychology, 12,* 10–18.

Silva, J. M. (1982a). *The current status of applied sport psychology. A national survey.* Paper presented to the American Alliance for Health, Physical Education, Recreation, and Dance Convention, Houston.

Silva, J. M. (1982b). An evaluation of fear of success in male and female athletes and nonathletes. *Journal of Sport Psychology, 4,* 92–96.

Silva, J. M. (1984a). Factors related to the acquisition and expression of aggressive sport behavior. In J. M. Silva and R. S. Weinberg (Eds.), *Psychological foundations of sport* (pp. 261–273). Champaign, IL: Human Kinetics.

Silva, J. M. (1984b). Personality and sport performance: Controversy and challenge. In J. M. Silva & R. S. Weinberg (Eds.), *Psychological foundations of sport* (pp. 59–69). Champaign, IL: Human Kinetics.

Silva, J. M. (1989). Toward the professionalization of sport psychology. *The Sport Psychologist, 3,* 265–273.

Silva, J., & Hardy, C. (1986). Discriminating contestants at the United States Olympic marathon trials as a function of precompetitive anxiety. *International Journal of Sport Psychology, 17,* 100–109.

Silva, J. M., Shultz, B., Haslam, R., & Murray, D. (1981). A psychophysiological assessment of elite wrestlers. *Research Quarterly for Exercise and Sport, 52,* 348–358.

Sime, W. E., Whipple, I. T., Stamler, J., & Berkson, D. M. (1978). Effects of long-term (38 months) training on middle-aged sedentary males: Adherence and specificity of training. In R. Landry & W. A. R. Orban (Eds.), *Exercise and well-being: Exercise physiology* (pp. 456–464). Miami, FL: Symposium Specialists.

Simek, T. C., & O'Brien, R. M. (1981). *Total golf: A behavioral approach to lowering your score and getting more out of your game.* Bethpage, NY: B-Mod Associates.

Simek, T. C., O'Brien, R. M., & Figlerski, L. B. (1994). Contracting and chaining to improve the performance of a college golf team: Improvement and deterioration. *Perceptual and Motor Skills, 78,* 1099–1105.

Simon, J., & Martens, R. (1979). Children's anxiety in sport and nonsport evaluative activities. *Journal of Sport Psychology, 1,* 160–169.

Simri, U. (1973). The ball games of antiquity. In E. F. Zeigler (Ed.), *A history of sport and physical education to 1900* (pp. 93–99). Champaign, IL: Stipes.

Singer, R. N., Harris, D., Kroll, W., & Sechrest, L. J. (1977). Psychological testing of athletes. *Journal of Physical Education, 48,* 30–32.

Singh, N. A., Clements, K. M., & Fiatarone, M. A. (1997). Sleep, sleep deprivation, and daytime activities: A randomized controlled trial of effect of exercise on sleep. *Sleep, 20,* 95–101.

Sisley, B., & Capel, S. (1986). High school coaching: Filled with gender differences. *Journal of Physical Education, Recreation and Dance, 57*(3), 39–43.

Sitter, R. (1991). 1991 fatalities: General observations. *Parachutist, 32*(7), 39–45.

Skinner, B. F. (1971). *Beyond freedom and dignity.* New York: Knopf.

Skubic, E. (1955). Emotional responses of boys to Little League and Middle League competitive baseball. *Research Quarterly, 26,* 342–352.

Skubic, E. (1956). Studies of Little League and Middle League baseball. *Research Quarterly, 27,* 97–110.

Skydiving fatalities. (2000). http://www.skydivenet.com/fatalities/default.html

Skydiving statistics. (2000). http://www.afn.org/skydive/sta/stats.html

Sloan, N. (1977). Opinions out loud. *NCAA News, 14*(7), 2.

Slusher, H. (1964). Personality and intelligence characteristics of selected high school athletes and nonathletes. *Research Quarterly, 35,* 539–545.

Smelser, N. J. (1962). *Theory of collective behavior.* New York: Free Press.

Smith, E. L., & Gilliam, C. (1983). Physical activity prescription for the older adult. *Physician and Sportsmedicine, 11*(8), 91–101.

Smith, E. L., & Zook, S. K. (1986, January). The aging

process: Benefits of physical activity. *Journal of Physical Education, Recreation and Dance,* 32–34.

Smith, H. W. (1994). *The 10 natural laws of successful time and life management: Proven strategies for increased productivity and inner peace.* New York: Warner.

Smith, M. (1979). Towards an explanation of hockey violence: A reference-other approach. *Canadian Journal of Sociology, 4*(2), 105–124.

Smith, M. (1982). Social determinants of violence in hockey: A review. In R. Magill, M. Ash, & F. Smoll (Eds.), *Children in sport* (pp. 294–309). Champaign, IL: Human Kinetics.

Smith, M. (1986). Sports violence: A definition. In R. Lapchick (Ed.), *Fractured focus: Sport as a reflection of society* (pp. 221–227). Lexington, MA: Heath.

Smith, R. E. (1984). A cognitive-affective approach to stress management training for athletes. In C. H. Nadeau (Ed.), *Psychology of motor behavior and sport, 1979.* Champaign, IL: Human Kinetics.

Smith, R. E. (1986a). Consultation in sport psychology. *Consulting Psychology Bulletin, 38*(1), 17–20.

Smith, R. E. (1986b). Toward a cognitive-affective model of athletic burnout. *Journal of Sport Psychology, 8,* 36–50.

Smith, R. E., & Christensen, D. S. (1995). Psychological skills as predictors of performance and survival in professional baseball. *Journal of Sport & Exercise Psychology, 17,* 399–415.

Smith, R. E., Schutz, R. W., Smoll, F. L., & Ptacek, J. T. (1995). Development and validation of a multidimensional measure of sport-specific coping skills: The Athletic Coping Skills Inventory–28. *Journal of Sport & Exercise Psychology, 17,* 379–398.

Smith, R. E., Smoll, F. L., & Barnett, N. P. (1995). Reduction of children's sport performance anxiety through social support and stress-reduction training for coaches. *Journal of Applied Developmental Psychology, 16,* 125–142.

Smith, R. E., Smoll, F. L., & Hunt, E. (1977). A system for the behavioral assessment of athletic coaches. *Research Quarterly, 48,* 401–407.

Smith, R. E., Smoll, F. L., & Schutz, R. W. (1988). *The Athletic Coping Skills Inventory: Psychometric properties, correlates, and confirmatory factor analysis.* Unpublished manuscript, University of Washington.

Smith, R. E., Smoll, F. L., & Schutz, R. W. (1990). Measurement and correlates of sport-specific cognitive and somatic trait anxiety: The Sport Anxiety Scale. *Anxiety Research, 2,* 263–280.

Smith, S. M. (1979). Remembering in and out of context. *Journal of Experimental Psychology: Human Learning and Memory, 5,* 460–471.

Smith, S. M. (1984). A comparison of two techniques for reducing context-dependent forgetting. *Memory and Cognition, 12,* 447–482.

Smoll, F. L., & Smith, R. E. (1984). Leadership research in youth sport. In J. M. Silva & R. S. Weinberg (Eds.), *Psychological foundations of sport* (p. 375). Champaign, IL: Human Kinetics.

Smoll, F. L., Smith, R. E., Barnett, N. P., & Everett, J. J. (1993). Enhancement of children's self-esteem through social support training for youth sport coaches. *Journal of Applied Psychology, 78,* 602–610.

Snowden, L. (1992). The roots of rejection. *Working Woman,* September, 98–100.

Snyder, C. J. (1990). The effects of leader behavior and organizational climate on intercollegiate coaches' job satisfaction. *Journal of Sport Management, 4,* 59–70.

Snyder, C. R., Higgins, R. L., & Stucky, R. J. (1983). *Excuses: Masquerades in search of grace.* New York: Wiley-Interscience.

Snyder, E. E., & Kivlin, J. (1975). Woman athletes and aspects of psychological well-being and body image. *Research Quarterly, 46,* 191–199.

Snyder, E. E., Kivlin, J., & Spreitzer, E. A. (1975). The female athlete: An analysis of objective and subjective role conflict. In D. Harris and R. Christina (Eds.), *Psychology of sport and motor behavior* (pp. 165–180). University Park, PA: Pennsylvania State University.

Snyder, E. E., & Spreitzer, E. A. (1973). Family influence and involvement in sports. *Research Quarterly, 44,* 249–255.

Snyder, E. E., & Spreitzer, E. A. (1978). Socialization comparisons of adolescent female athletes and musicians. *Research Quarterly, 49,* 342–350.

Snyder, E. E., & Spreitzer, E. A. (1983). *Social aspects of sport* (2nd ed.). Englewood Cliffs, NJ: Prentice-Hall.

Snyder, E. E., & Spreitzer, E. A. (1989). *Social aspects of sport* (3rd ed.). Englewood Cliffs, NJ: Prentice-Hall.

Soccer. (1988). *Bryan–College Station Eagle [TX],* January 9, 2B.

Solso, R. L. (1991). *Cognitive psychology* (3rd ed.). Boston: Allyn & Bacon.

Sonstroem, R. J. (1978). Physical estimation and attraction scales: Rationale and research. *Medicine and Science in Sports, 10,* 97–102.

Sonstroem, R. J. (1984). An overview of anxiety in sport. In J. M. Silva & R. S. Weinberg (Eds.), *Psychological foundations of sport* (pp. 104–117). Champaign, IL: Human Kinetics.

Sonstroem, R. J., & Bernardo, P. (1982). Intraindividual pregame state anxiety and basketball performance: A re-examination of the inverted-U curve. *Journal of Sport Psychology, 4,* 235–245.

Sounding board: Anabolic-androgenic steroid use by athletes (1989, October 12). *New England Journal of Medicine,* 1042–1045.

Speak out on sports. (1990, February 5). *VSA Today,* IC.

Spears, B. (1978). Prologue: The myth. In C. A. Oglesby

(Ed.), *Women and sport: From myth to reality* (pp. 3–15). Philadelphia: Lea and Febiger.

Spears, B. (1984). A perspective of the history of women's sport in ancient Greece. *Journal of Sport History, 11*(2), 32–45.

Spears, R., & Swanson, R. A. (1983). *History of sport and physical activity in the United States.* Dubuque, IA: Wm. C. Brown.

Speigler, M. D., & Guevremont, D. C. (1993). *Contemporary behavior theory.* Belmont, CA: Wadsworth.

Spence, J. T., & Buckner, C. E. (2000). Instrumental and expressive traits, stereotypes, and sexist attitudes. *Psychology of Women Quarterly, 24,* 44–62.

Spence, J. T., & Hall, S. K. (1996). Children's gender-related self-perceptions, activity preferences, and occupational stereotypes: A test of three models of gender constructs. *Sex Roles, 35,* 659–683.

Spence, J., Helmreich, R., & Stapp, J. (1974). The Personal Attributes Questionnaire: A measure of sex role stereotypes and masculinity–femininity. *Journal Supplement Abstract Service Catalog of Selected Documents in Psychology, 4,* 43. (Ms. No. 617)

Spielberger, C. D. (1972). *Anxiety: Current trends in theory and research* (Vol. 1). New York: Academic Press.

Spielberger, C. D. (1973a). *State–Trait Anxiety Inventory for Children: Preliminary manual.* Palo Alto, CA: Consulting Psychologists Press.

Spielberger, C. D. (1973b). *Preliminary test manual for the State–Trait Anxiety Inventory for Children.* Palo Alto, CA: Consulting Psychologists Press.

Spielberger, C. (1983) *State–Trait Anxiety Inventory: A comprehensive bibliography.* Palo Alto, CA: Consulting Psychologists Press.

Spielberger, C. D., Gorsuch, R. L., & Lushene, R. F. (1970). *Manual for the State–Trait Anxiety Inventory.* Palo Alto, CA: Consulting Psychologists Press.

Spielberger, C., Gorsuch, R., Lushene, R., Vagg, P., & Jacobs, G. (1983). *Manual for the State–Trait Anxiety Inventory (Form Y).* Palo Alto, CA: Consulting Psychologists Press.

Spink, K. S. (1990). Group cohesion and collective efficacy of volleyball teams. *Journal of Sport & Exercise Psychology, 12,* 301–311.

Spink, K. S., & Carron, A. V. (1992). Group cohesion and adherence to exercise classes. *Journal of Sport & Exercise Psychology, 14,* 78–86.

Spink, K. S., & Carron, A. V. (1994). Group cohesion effects in exercise classes. *Small Group Research, 25,* 26–42.

Spirduso, W. W. (1980). Physical fitness, aging, and psychomotor speed: A review. *Journal of Gerontology, 35,* 850–865.

Spirduso, W. W. (1983). Exercise and the aging brain. *Research Quarterly for Exercise and Sport, 54,* 208–218.

Spirduso, W. W., & Clifford, P. (1978). Neuromuscular speed and consistency of performance as a function of age,

physical activity level and type of physical activity. *Journal of Gerontology, 33,* 26–30.

Sports camaraderie: The fit will frolic. (1989, June 19). *USA Today,* p. 8C.

Spurgeon, J. H., Blair, S. V., Keith, J. A., & McGinn, C. J. (1978). Characteristics of successful and probationary football officials. *Physician and Sportsmedicine, 6*(5), 106–112.

Stamford, B. (1984). Exercise and longevity. *Physician and Sportsmedicine, 12*(6), 209.

Stampfl, T. G., & Levis, D. J. (1967). Essentials of implosive therapy: A learning theory based psychodynamic behavioral therapy. *Journal of Abnormal Psychology, 72,* 496–503.

Stangl, J. M., & Kane, M. J. (1991). Structural variables that offer explanatory power for the underrepresentation of women coaches since Title IX: The case of homologous reproduction. *Sociology of Sport Journal, 8,* 47–60.

Starek, J., & McCullagh, P. (1999). The effect of self-modeling on the performance of beginning swimmers. *The Sport Psychologist, 13,* 269–287.

Steinberg, H., Sykes, E. A., Moss, T., Lowery, S., LeBoutillier, N., & Dewey, A. (1997). Exercise enhances creativity independently of mood. *British Journal of Sports Medicine, 31,* 240–245.

Steinhaus, L. A., Dustman, R. E., Ruhling, R. O., Emmerson, R. Y., Johnson, S. C., Shearer, D. E., Latin, R. W., Shigeoka, J. W., & Bonekat, W. H. (1990). Aerobic capacity of older adults: A training study. *Journal of Sports Medicine and Physical Fitness, 30,* 163–172.

Sternfeld, B. (1997). Physical activity and pregnancy outcome. *Sports Medicine, 23,* 33–47.

Sternfeld, B., Quesenberry, C. R., Eskenazi, B., & Newman, L. A. (1995). Exercise during pregnancy and pregnancy outcome. *Medicine and Science in Sports and Exercise, 27,* 634–640.

Stewart, L. (1970). *A comparative study measuring the psychological makeup among groups of basketball players and coaches.* Unpublished master's thesis, Western Washington State College.

St. John's (Minn.): Peculiar practices. (1990, August 22). *USA Today,* p. 10C.

Stober, J. (1998). The Frost Multidimensional Perfectionism Scale revisited: More perfect with four (instead of six) dimensions. *Personality and Individual Differences, 24,* 481–491.

Stockbauer, J., & McAuliffe, T. (1977). Intergroup and intragroup competition and cooperation. *Journal of Experimental Social Psychology, 13,* 81–88.

Stone, J., Lynch, C. I., Sjomeling, M., & Darley, J. M. (1999). Stereotype threat effects on black and white athletic performance. *Journal of Personality and Social Psychology, 77,* 1213–1227.

Stone, J., Perry, Z. W., & Darley, J. M. (1997). "White men can't jump": Evidence for the perceptual confirmation of racial stereotypes following a basketball game. *Basic and Applied Social Psychology, 19,* 291–306.

Stowers, C. (1985, October). Danny White: Back in the saddle again. *Inside Sports,* p. 18–23.

Strapping youth. (1998, August 11). *USA Today,* p. 3C.

Strategic analysis of Nike, Inc. (2000, August 17). http://www.depaul.edu/aalmaney/StrategicAnalysisofNike.html

Straub, W. F. (1982). Sensation seeking among high and low-risk athletes. *Journal of Sport Psychology, 4,* 246–253.

Straub, W. F. (1986). Conversation with Bruce Ogilvie. *AAASP Newsletter 1*(2), 4–5.

Straub, W. F., & Davis, S. (1971). Personality traits of college football players who participated at different levels of competition. *Medicine and Science in Sports, 3,* 39–43.

Straub, W. F., & Hinman, D. A. (1992). Profiles and professional perspectives of 10 leading sport psychologists. *The Sport Psychologist, 6,* 297–312.

Strauss, R. H., & Yesalis, C. E. (1991). Anabolic steroids in the athlete. *Annual Review of Medicine, 42,* 449–457.

Stringer, W. W. (1999). HIV and aerobic exercise. *Sports Medicine, 28,* 389–395.

Struna, N. (1981). Sport and colonial education: A cultural perspective. *Research Quarterly for Exercise and Sport, 52,* 117–135.

Study of sudden death in young athletes. (1996, April 22). *USA Today,* p. 12C.

Stull, G. A. (1973). The athletic events of *The Odyssey.* In E. F. Zeigler (Ed.), *A history of sport and physical education to 1900* (pp. 121–131). Champaign, IL: Stipes.

Stull, G. A., & Lewis, G. (1968, Winter). The funeral games of the Homeric Greeks. *Quest* (Monograph XI), 1–13.

STYSA discipline and suspension report. (1998). *STYSA Shootout, 8*(3), 35.

Suinn, R. M. (1972). Behavioral research for ski racers. *Behavioral Therapy, 3,* 519–520.

Suinn, R. M. (1984). *Fundamentals of abnormal psychology.* Chicago: Nelson-Hall.

Suinn, R. M. (1985). The 1984 Olympics and sport psychology. *Journal of Sport Psychology, 7,* 321–329.

Suinn, R. M. (1986). Consultation in sport psychology. *Consulting Psychology Bulletin, 38*(1), 17–20.

Suinn, R. M. (1993). Imagery. In R. N. Singer, M. Murphey, & L. K. Tennant (Eds.), *Handbook on research in sport psychology* (pp. 492–510). New York: Macmillan.

Suinn, R. M. (1996). Imagery rehearsal: A tool for clinical practice. *Psychotherapy in Private Practice, 15,* 27–31.

Suinn, R. M. (1997). Mental practice in sport psychology: Where have we been, where do we go? *Clinical Psychology: Science and Practice, 4,* 189–207.

Suitor, J. J., & Reavis, R. (1995). Football, fast cars, and cheerleading: Adolescent gender norms. *Adolescence, 30,* 265–272.

Summers, J. J., & Ford, S. K. (1990). The Test of Attentional and Interpersonal Style: An evaluation. *International Journal of Sport Psychology, 21,* 102–111.

Swaddling, J. (1980). *The ancient Olympic Games.* Austin, TX: The University of Texas Press.

Swain, A., & Jones, G. (1992). Relationships between sport achievement orientation and competitive state anxiety. *The Sport Psychologist, 6,* 42–54.

Tallant, M. (1997). Women's athletics: The top 25 people and events since 1972. *Athletics Administration,* October, 15–20.

Tammen, V. V., Murphy, S. M., & Jowdy, D. (1990). *Reevaluating the Psychological Skills Inventory for Sports: Factor analysis and implications.* Paper presented to North American Society for the Psychology of Sport and Physical Activity, Asilomar, CA.

Tangen-Foster, J. W., & Lathen, C. W. (1983). Risk sports in basic instruction programs: A status assessment. *Research Quarterly for Exercise and Sport, 54,* 305–308.

Taylor, A. H., & Daniel, J. V. (1987). Sources of stress in soccer officiating: An empirical study. *First world congress on science and football* (pp. 538–544). Liverpool, England: E. & F. N. Spon.

Taylor, J. (1953). A personality scale of manifest anxiety. *Journal of Abnormal and Social Psychology, 48,* 285–290.

Taylor, J., & Ogilvie, B. C. (1994). A conceptual model of adaptation to retirement among athletes. *Journal of Applied Sport Psychology, 6,* 1–20.

Teenagers' motivations for sports participation help predict lifelong habits. (1990). North Palm Beach, FL: Athletic Footwear Association.

Telander, R. (1989, April 3). In the aftermath of steroids. *Sports Illustrated,* 34.

Tenenbaum, G., Pinchas, S., Elbaz, G., Bar-Eli, M., & Weinberg, R. (1991). Effect of goal proximity and goal specificity on muscular endurance performance: A replication and extension. *Journal of Sport & Exercise Psychology, 13,* 174–187.

Teraslinna, R, Partanen, T., Koskela, A., Partanen, K., & Oja, R. (1969). Characteristics affecting willingness of executives to participate in an activity program aimed at coronary heart disease prevention. *Journal of Sports Medicine and Physical Fitness, 9,* 224–229.

Terry, R. C., & Jackson, J. J. (1985). The determinants and control of violence in sport. *Quest, 37,* 27–37.

Thakur, G., & Ojha, M. (1981). Personality differences of Indian table-tennis, badminton, and football players on primary source traits of the 16PF. *International Journal of Sport Psychology, 12,* 196–203.

Tharion, W. J., Strowman, S. R., & Rauch, T. M. (1988). Profile and changes in moods of marathoners. *Journal of Sport & Exercise Psychology, 10,* 229–235.

Tharp, L. R. (1994). The effect Title IX has had on intramural sports. *NIRSA Journal, 18*(1), 29–31.

Tharp, R. G., & Gallimore, R. (1976). What a coach can teach a teacher. *Psychology Today, 9*, 75–78.

Thayer, R. E. (1967). Measurement of activation through self report. *Psychological Reports, 20*, 663–678.

The Babe: A record of achievement. (1993). Beaumont, TX: Babe Didrikson Zaharias Foundation, Inc.

Theberge, N. (1991). A content analysis of print media coverage of gender, women, and physical activity. *Journal of Applied Sport Psychology, 3*, 36–48.

The end. (1995, March 10). *USA Today*, p. 7C.

Thelwell, R. C., & Maynard, I. W. (1998). Anxiety–performance relationships in cricketers: Testing the Zone of Optimal Functioning hypothesis. *Perceptual and Motor Skills, 87*, 675–689.

Theobald, G. (1936, September). Emancipation of women. *American Journal of Public Health*, 871.

The recommended quantity and quality of exercise for developing and maintaining cardiorespiratory and muscular fitness in healthy adults. (1990). *Medicine and Science in Sports and Exercise, 22*, 265–274.

There's no question we can do the job. (1990, March 7). *USA Today*, pp. 1C–2C.

Thiel, A., Gottfried, H., & Hesse, F. W. (1993). Subclinical eating disorders in male athletes: A study of the low-weight category in rowers and wrestlers. *Acta Psychiatrica, 88*, 259–265.

Thompson, C., & Wankel, L. (1980). The effects of perceived activity choice upon frequency of exercise behavior. *Journal of Applied Social Psychology, 10*, 436–444.

Thorngren, C. M. (1990, March). A time to reach out— keeping the female coach in coaching. *Journal of Physical Education, Recreation and Dance*, 57–60.

Throop, W., & MacDonald, A. (1971). Internal–external locus of control. A bibliography. *Psychological Reports, 28*, 175–190.

Thurstone, L. L. (1928). Attitudes can be measured. *American Journal of Sociology, 33*, 529–554.

Timms, K. E. (1999). Is it safe to head the ball? Yes! http://www.stxsoccer.org/from_the_touchline.html

Tippett, L. J. (1992). The generation of visual images: A review of neuropsychological research and theory. *Psychological Bulletin, 112*, 415–432.

Titley, R. W. (1976, September). The loneliness of the long distance kicker. *Athletic Journal*, 74–80.

Tjaden, P., & Thoennes, N. (2000). Extent, nature, and consequences of intimate partner violence. Washington, DC: U.S. Department of Justice.

Tkachuk, G. A., & Martin, G. L. (1999). Exercise therapy for patients with psychiatric disorders: Research and clinical implications. *Professional Psychology: Research and Practice, 30*, 275–282.

Toch, H. (1984). *Violent men*. Cambridge: Schenkman.

Tofler, I. R. K., Stryer, B. K., & Micheli, L. J. (1996). Physical and emotional problems of elite female gymnasts. *New England Journal of Medicine, 335*, 281–283.

Tombor, E. (1970). *Personality correlates of football and basketball performances*. Unpublished master's thesis, San Jose University.

Tomporowski, R. D., & Ellis, N. R. (1986). Effects of exercise on cognitive processes: A review. *Psychological Bulletin, 99*, 338–346.

Tomporowski, R. D., Ellis, N. R., & Stephens, R. (1985). The immediate effects of strenuous exercise on free-recall memory. *Ergonomics, 30*, 121–129.

Toufexis, A. (1989, January). Shortcut to the Rambo look. *Time*, p. 78.

Triandis, H. C. (1971). *Attitude and attitude change*. New York: Wiley.

Triandis, H. C. (1977). *Interpersonal behavior*. Monterey, CA: Brooks/Cole.

Triplett, N. (1898). The dynamogenic factors in pacemaking and competition. *American Journal of Psychology, 9*, 507–533.

True, S. (1983). *Data on the percentage of girls' high school athletic teams coached by women*. Kansas City, MO: National Federation of State High School Associations.

Tubbs, M. E. (1986). Goal setting: A meta-analytic examination of the empirical evidence. *Journal of Applied Psychology, 71*, 474–483.

Tuckman, B. (1965). Developmental sequence in small groups. *Psychological Bulletin, 63*, 384–399.

Turk, J. C., Prentice, W. E., Chappell, S., & Shields, E. W. (1999). Collegiate coaches' knowledge of eating disorders. *Journal of Athletic Training, 34*, 19–24.

Tutko, T. A., Lyon, L., & Ogilvie, B. C. (1969). *Athletic Motivation Inventory*. San Jose, CA: Institute for the Study of Athletic Motivation.

Tutko, T. A., & Richards, J. W. (1971). *Psychology of coaching*. Boston: Allyn & Bacon.

Twenge, J. M. (1997). Attitudes toward women, 1970–1995. *Psychology of Women Quarterly, 21*, 35–51.

Twombly, W. (1976). *200 years of sport in America*. New York: McGraw-Hill.

2000 National Football League head coaching changes. (2000, August 11). wysiwyg://83/http://latimes...ts/fbo/nfl/nfl/nfl.newcoaches.html

Updated POMS bibliography now available. (1995, Spring/Summer). *EDITS Research and Developments*, 4. San Diego, CA: Educational and Industrial Testing Service.

Underwood, J. (1979). *The death of an American game.* Boston: Little, Brown.

Unsteady ground at the top. (1997, September 23). *USA Today,* p. 9C.

US skydiving incident reports-2000. (2000) http://www.skydivenet/fatalities/fatalities_us_00.html

Vallerand, R. (1983). Attention and decision-making: A test of the predictive validity of the Test of Attentional and Interpersonal Style in a sport setting. *Journal of Sport Psychology, 5,* 449–459.

Vancil, M. (1991). Phil Jackson. *Inside Sports, 13,* 19–23.

Van Dalen, D., Mitchell, E., & Bennett, B. (1953). *World history of physical education.* Englewood Cliffs, NJ: Prentice-Hall.

Van Raalte, J. L., Brewer, B. W., Nemeroff, C. J., & Linder, D. E. (1991). Chance orientation and superstitious behavior on the putting green. *Journal of Sport Behavior, 14,* 41–50.

Van Schoyck, R., & Grasha, A. (1981). Attentional style variations and athletic ability: The advantage of a sports-specific test. *Journal of Sport Psychology, 3,* 9–18.

Varca, P. (1980). An analysis of home and away performance of male college basketball teams. *Journal of Sport Psychology, 2,* 245–257.

Vare, R. (1974). *Buckeye: A study of coach Woody Hayes and the Ohio State football machine.* New York: Harper.

Vaughan, G., & Guerin, B. (1997). A neglected innovator in sport psychology: Norman Triplett and the early history of competitive performance. *Journal of the History of Sport, 14,* 82–99.

Vaz, E., & Thomas, D. (1974). What price victory? An analysis of minor hockey league players' attitudes toward winning. *International Review of Sport Sociology, 2*(9), 33–53.

Veale de Coverley, D. M. W. (1987). Exercise dependence. *British Journal of Addictions, 82,* 735–740.

Vealey, R. S. (1986). Conceptualization of sport-confidence and competitive orientation: Preliminary investigation and instrument development. *Journal of Sport Psychology, 8,* 221–246.

Vealey, R. S. (1988). Sport-confidence and competitive orientation: An addendum on scoring procedures and gender differences. *Journal of Sport & Exercise Psychology, 10,* 471–478.

Vealey, R. S., Udry, E. M., Zimmerman, V., & Soliday, J. (1992). Intrapersonal and situational predictors of coaching burnout. *Journal of Sport & Exercise Psychology, 14,* 40–58.

Vernacchia, R., McGuire, R. T., Reardon, J. P., & Templin, D. P. (2000). Psychosocial characteristics of Olympic track and field athletes. *International Journal of Sport Psychology, 31,* 5–23.

Vernon, R. (1984, June 22). Baker says trials changed for better. *Dallas Morning Times,* p. 2C.

Veschi, R. (1963). Longevity and sport. *Journal of Sports Medicine and Physical Fitness, 3,* 44–49.

Vickers, J., Lashuk, M., & Taerum, T. (1980). Differences in attitude toward the concepts "male," "female," "male athlete," and "female athlete." *Research Quarterly for Exercise and Sport, 51,* 407–416.

Volkamer, N. (1971). Investigations into the aggressiveness in competitive social system. *Sportswissenschaft, 1,* 33–64.

Vos Strache, C. (1979). Players' perceptions of leadership qualities for coaches. *Research Quarterly, 50,* 679–686.

Wagemaker, H., & Goldstein, L. (1980). The runner's high. *Journal of Sports Medicine, 20,* 227–228.

Waite, B. T. & Pettit, M. E. (1993). Work experiences of graduates from doctoral programs in sport psychology. *Journal of Applied Sport Psychology, 5,* 234–250.

Walberg, J. L., & Johnston, C. S. (1991). Menstrual function and eating behavior in female recreational weight lifters and competitive body builders. *Medicine and Science in Sports and Exercise, 23,* 30–36.

Waldstreicher, J. (1985). Anorexia nervosa presented as morbid exercising. *Lancet, 1,* 987.

Walkey, F. H., & Green, D. E. (1992). An exhaustive examination of the replicable factor structure of the Maslach Burnout Inventory. *Educational and Psychological Measurement, 52,* 309–323.

Walley, R. B., Graham, G. M., & Forehand, R. (1982). Assessment and treatment of adult observer verbalizations at youth league baseball games. *Journal of Sport Psychology, 4,* 254–266.

Walsh, J., & Carron, A. V. (1977). *Attributes of volunteer coaches.* Paper presented at the annual meeting of the Canadian Association of Sport Sciences, Winnipeg, Canada.

Wankel, L. M. (1980). Social facilitation of motor performance: Perspective and prospective. In C. H. Nadeau, W. R. Halliwell, K. M. Newell, & G. C. Roberts (Eds.), *Psychology of motor behavior and sport—1979* (pp. 41–53). Champaign, IL: Human Kinetics.

Wankel, L. M. (1984). Audience effects in sport. In J. M. Silva & R. S. Weinberg (Eds.), *Psychological foundations of sport* (pp. 293–314). Champaign, IL: Human Kinetics.

Wankel, L. M., & Kreisel, P. (1985). Factors underlying enjoyment of youth sports: Sport and age group comparisons. *Journal of Sport Psychology, 7,* 51–64.

Wankel, L. M., & Sefton, J. M. (1989). A season long investigation of fun in youth sports. *Journal of Sport & Exercise Psychology, 11,* 355–366.

Wann, D. L. (1993). Aggression among highly identified spectators as a function of their need to maintain positive social identity. *Journal of Sport and Social Issues, 17,* 134–143.

Wann, D. L. (1997). *Sport psychology.* Upper Saddle River, NJ: Prentice Hall.

Wann, D. L., & Branscombe, N. R. (1990). Die-hard and fair-weather fans: Effects of identification on BIRGing and CORFing tendencies. *Journal of Sport and Social Issues, 14,* 103–118.

Wann, D. L., Schrader, M. P., Allison, J. A., & McGeorge, K. K. (1998). The inequitable newspaper coverage of men's and women's athletics at small, medium, and large universities. *Journal of Sport and Social Issues, 22,* 79–87.

Ward, E. A. (1994). Construct validity and the need for achievement and locus of control scales. *Educational and Psychological Measurement, 54,* 983–992.

Watkins, B., & Montgomery, A. B. (1989). Conceptions of athletic excellence among children and adolescents. *Child Development, 60,* 1362–1372.

Webb, G. (1992). Cheerleaders: A unique combination of leadership and athleticism. In W. K. Simpson, A. LeUnes & J. S. Picou (Eds.), *Applied research in coaching and athletics annual* (pp. 224–225). Boston: American Press.

Webb, J., Millan, D., & Stolz, C. (1979). Gynecological survey of American female athletes competing at the Montreal Olympic Games. *Journal of Sports Medicine, 19,* 405–412.

Webb, W. M., Nasco, S. A., Riley, S., & Headrick, B. (1998). Athlete identity and reactions to retirement from sports. *Journal of Sport Behavior, 21,* 338–362.

Webster, E. (1989, January 16). Cold courage. *Sports Illustrated,* 62–74.

Weinberg, R. S. (1980). Relationship of commitment to running scale to runners' performances and attitudes. In *Abstracts: Research papers 1980 AAHPERD Convention.* Washington, DC: AAHPERD.

Weinberg, R. S. (1982). The relationship between mental strategies and motor performance: A review and critique. *Quest, 32,* 195–213.

Weinberg, R. S. (1984). The relationship between extrinsic rewards and intrinsic motivation in sport. In J. M. Silva & R. S. Weinberg (Eds.), *Psychological foundations of sport* (pp. 177–187). Champaign, IL: Human Kinetics.

Weinberg, R. S. (1990). Anxiety and motor performance: Where to from here? *Anxiety Research, 2,* 227–242.

Weinberg, R. S., Fowler, C., Jackson, A., Bagnall, J., & Bruya, L. (1991). Effect of goal difficulty on motor performance: A replication across tasks and subjects. *Journal of Sport & Exercise Psychology, 13,* 160–173.

Weinberg, R. S., & Genuchi, M. (1980). Relationship between competitive trait anxiety, state anxiety, and golf performance: A field study. *Journal of Sport Psychology, 2,* 148–154.

Weinberg, R. S., & Gould, D. (1999). *Foundations of sport and exercise psychology* (2nd ed.). Champaign, IL: Human Kinetics.

Weinberg, R. S., Gould, D., & Jackson, A. (1979). Expecta-

tions and performance: An empirical test of Bandura's self-efficacy theory. *Journal of Sport Psychology, 1,* 320–331.

Weinberg, R. S., Hankes, D., & Jackson, A. (1991). Effect of the length and temporal location of the mental preparation interval on basketball shooting performance. *International Journal of Sport Psychology, 22,* 3–14.

Weinberg, R. S., Reveles, M., & Jackson, A. (1984). Attitudes of male and female athletes toward male and female coaches. *Journal of Sport Psychology, 6,* 448–453.

Weinberg, R. S., Richardson, R., & Jackson, A. V. (1981). Effect of situation criticality on tennis performances of males and females. *International Journal of Sport Psychology, 12,* 253–259.

Weinberg, R. S., Richardson, R., Jackson, A. V., & Yukelson, D. (1983). Coming from behind to win: Sex differences in interacting sport teams. *International Journal of Sport Psychology, 14,* 79–84.

Weiner, B. (1972). *Theories of motivation: From mechanism to cognition.* Chicago: Rand-McNally.

Weiner, B. (Ed.) (1974). *Achievement motivation and attribution theory.* Morristown, NJ: General Learning Press.

Weiner, B. (1979). A theory of motivation for some classroom experiences. *Journal of Educational Psychology, 71,* 3–25.

Weiner, B. (1980). *Human motivation.* New York: Holt, Rinehart and Winston.

Weiner, R. (1999, January 22). A great divide. *USA Today,* pp. C1, C2.

Weir, T. (1997, September 29). Hispanics' big league breakthrough. *USA Today,* pp. 1A–2A.

Weiss, M. R., & Barber, H. (1995). Socialization influences of collegiate female athletes: A tale of two decades. *Sex Roles, 33,* 129–140.

Weiss, M. R., & Knoppers, A. (1982). The influence of socializing agents on female collegiate volleyball players. *Journal of Sport Psychology, 4,* 267–279.

Welch, M. (1997). Violence against women by professional football players: A gender analysis of hypermasculinity, positional status, narcissism, and entitlement. *Journal of Sport and Social Issues, 21,* 392–411.

Wells, M. J., & Bell, G. W. (1995). Concerns on Little League elbow. *Journal of Athletic Training, 30,* 249–253.

Weltman, G., & Egstrom, G. H. (1969). Personal autonomy of scuba diver trainees. *Research Quarterly, 40,* 613–618.

Weltman, A., & Stamford, B. (1983). Psychological effects of exercise. *Physician and Sportsmedicine, 11*(1), 175.

Westcott, W. (1995). Converting couch potatoes to fitness fans. *Perspective, 21*(4), 22–25.

What they say about coaching. (1994, December 21). *USA Today,* p. 5C.

Whatta woman. (1947, March 10), *Time*, 69–70.

Whelan, J. P., Mahoney, M. J., & Meyers, A. W. (1991). Performance enhancement in sport: A cognitive behavioral domain. *Behavior Therapy, 22,* 307–327.

Whitcomb, D. (1992). *When the victim is a child* (2nd ed.). Washington, DC: U.S. Department of Justice.

Whiteside, J. A., Andrews, J. R., & Fleisig, G. S. (1999). Elbow injuries in young baseball players. *Physician and Sportsmedicine, 27*(6), 87+.

Whitney, K. (1994). Improving group–task performance: The role of group goals and group efficacy. *Human Performance, 7,* 55–78.

Whorton, J. C. (1981). Muscular vegetarianism: The debate over diet and athletic performance in the progressive era. *Journal of Sport History, 8,* 58–75.

Widmeyer, W. N., & Birch, J. S. (1984). Aggression in professional ice hockey: A strategy for success or a reaction to failure? *Journal of Psychology, 117,* 77–84.

Widmeyer, W. N., Brawley, L. R., & Carron, A. V. (1985). *The measurement of cohesion in sports teams: The Group Environment Questionnaire.* London, Ontario: Sports Dynamics.

Widmeyer, W. N., Brawley, L. R., & Carron, A. V. (1992). *Group dynamics in sport.* In T. S. Horn (Ed.), *Advances in sport psychology* (pp. 124–139). Champaign, IL: Human Kinetics.

Wieberg, S. (1992, June 8). Universities discover good intentions not enough. *USA Today,* p. 10C.

Wieberg, S. (1997, June 20). Grading the progress of Title IX. *USA Today,* p. 11C.

Wieberg, S. (1999, October 26). Women making slow gains. *USA Today,* p. 11C.

Wiggins, D. (1977). Good times on the old plantation: Popular recreations of the black slave in Antebellum South, 1810–1860. *Journal of Sport History, 4,* 260–281.

Wilberger, J. E. (1993). Minor head injuries in American football. *Sports Medicine, 15,* 338–343.

Wilkinson, C. (1952). *Oklahoma split-t football.* New York: Prentice-Hall.

Willard, N. (1978, November). Testing the limits. *World Health,* 22–26.

Williams, A., Reilly, T., Campbell, I., & Sutherst, J. (1988). Investigation of changes in responses to exercise and in mood during pregnancy. *Ergonomics, 31,* 1539–1549.

Williams, J. M., & Hacker, C. (1982). Causal relationships among cohesion, satisfaction, and performance in women's intercollegiate field hockey teams. *Journal of Sport Psychology, 4,* 324–337.

Williams, J., Hoepner, B., Moody, D., & Ogilvie, B. C. (1970). Personality traits of champion level female fencers. *Research Quarterly, 41,* 446–453.

Williams, J. M., & Widmeyer, W. N. (1991). The cohesion–performance outcome relationship in a coaching sport. *Journal of Sport & Exercise Psychology, 13,* 364–371.

Williams, K. D. Harkins, S., & Latane, B. (1981). Identifiability and social loafing: Two cheering experiments. *Journal of Personality and Social Psychology, 40,* 303–311.

Williams, K. D., & Karau, S. J. (1991). Social loafing and social compensation: The effects of expectations and co-worker performance. *Journal of Personality and Social Psychology, 61,* 570–581.

Williams, L. R. T., & Parkin, W. A. (1980). Personality factor profiles of three hockey groups. *International Journal of Sport Psychology, 11,* 113–120.

Williams, P., & Lord, S. R. (1995). Predictors of adherence to a structured exercise program for older women. *Psychology of Aging, 10,* 617–624.

Williams, R., & Youssef, Z. (1972). Consistency of football coaches in stereotyping the personality of each position's player. *International Journal of Sport Psychology, 3,* 3–11.

Williams, R., & Youssef, Z. (1975). Division of labor in college football along racial lines. *International Journal of Sport Psychology, 6,* 1–13.

Willis, J. D. (1982). Three scales to measure competition-related motives in sport. *Journal of Sport Psychology, 4,* 338–353.

Willis, J. D., & Layne, B. H. (1988). A validation study of sport-related motive scales. *Journal of Applied Research in Coaching and Athletics, 3,* 299–307.

Winder, P., O'Dell, J., & Karson, S. (1975). New motivational distortion scales for the 16PF. *Journal of Personality Assessment, 39,* 532–537.

Winning Associates. (1978). *Athlete's homework manual.* Morgantown, WV: Winning Associates.

Wirth, V. J., & Gieck, J. (1996). Growth hormone: Myths and misperceptions. *Journal of Sport Rehabilitation, 5,* 244–250.

Wolko, K. L., Hrycaiko, D., & Martin, G. L. (1993). A comparison of two self-management packages to standard coaching for improving performance of gymnasts. *Behavior Modification, 17,* 209–233.

Wolpe, J. (1982). *The practice of behavior therapy.* New York: Pergamon.

Women's Sports and Fitness (1998, April), 50–51.

Wong, G. M. (1998, March). Payday! Payday! The EEOC's new guidelines augur a windfall for coaches of women's sports. *Athletic Business,* 20–22.

Wooden, J., & Jamison, S. (1997). *Wooden: A lifetime of observations and reflections on and off the court.* Chicago, IL: Contemporary Books.

Woodman, T., & Hardy, L. (2001). Stress and anxiety. In R. N. Singer, H. A. Hausenblas & C. M. Janelle (Eds.), *Handbook of sport psychology* (pp. 290–318). New York: Wiley.

Woolfolk, R. L., Parrish, M. W., & Murphy, S. (1985). The effects of positive and negative imagery on motor skill performance. *Cognitive Therapy and Research, 9,* 335–341.

Woolum, J. (1992). *Outstanding women athletes: Who they are and how they influenced sports in America.* Phoenix, AZ: Oryx Press.

Worchel, S., Hart, D., & Butemeyer, J. (1991). *Is social loafing a group phenomenon? The effect of membership and interdependence on work output.* Unpublished manuscript, Texas A&M University.

Working your nerves: The toughest jobs. (1995, March 6). *Time,* 60.

Worthy, M., & Markle, A. (1970). Racial differences in reactive versus self-paced sports activities. *Journal of Personality and Social Psychology, 16,* 439–443.

WPS 1995–1996 Catalog. (1995). Los Angeles: Western Psychological Services.

Wrisberg, C. A., & Anshel, M. H. (1989). The effect of cognitive strategies on the free throw performance of young athletes. *The Sport Psychologist, 3,* 95–104.

Wulf, S. (1997, May 5). A level playing field for women. *Time,* 79–80.

Wysocki, T., Hall, G., Iata, B., & Riordan, M. (1979). Behavioral management of exercise: Contracting for aerobic point. *Journal of Applied Behavioral Analysis, 12,* 55–64.

Yalouris, N. (Ed.). (1979). *The eternal Olympics: The art and history of sport.* New Rochelle, NY: Caratzas Brothers.

Yates, A., Leehey, K., & Shisslak, C. M. (1983). Running: An analogue for anorexia? *New England Journal of Medicine, 308,* 251–255.

Yeager, R. (1979). *Seasons of shame: The new violence in sports.* New York: McGraw-Hill.

Yerkes, R. M., & Dodson, J. D. (1908). The relation of strength of stimulus to rapidity of habit formation. *Journal of Comparative and Neurological Psychology, 18,* 459–482.

Yes beer or no beer? (1987, October 1). *USA Today,* p. 9C.

Yesalis, C. E. (1990). Winning and performance enhancing drugs—our dual addiction. *Physician and Sportsmedicine, 18*(3), 161–163, 167.

Yetman, N. R., & Berghorn, F. J. (1993). Racial participation and integration in intercollegiate basketball: A longitudinal perspective. *Sociology of Sport Journal, 10,* 310–314.

Yetman, N., Berghorn, F., & Thomas, F. (1980). *Racial participation and integration in intercollegiate basketball, 1958–1960.* Paper presented at the annual program of the North American Society for the Sociology of Sport, Denver, CO.

Yiannakis, A. (1976). Birth order and preference for dangerous sports among males. *Research Quarterly, 47,* 62–67.

Yordy, G. A., & Lent, R. W. (1993). Predicting aerobic exercise participation: Social cognitive, reasoned action, and planned behavior models. *Journal of Sport & Exercise Psychology, 15,* 363–374.

Young, N. (1944). Did the Greeks and Romans play football? *Research Quarterly, 15,* 310–316.

Youngstedt, S. D. (1997). Does exercise truly enhance sleep? *Physician and Sportsmedicine, 25*(10), 72.

Youngstedt, S. D., O'Connor, P. J., & Dishman, R. K. (1997). The effects of acute exercise on sleep. *Sleep, 20,* 203–214.

Yukelson, D., Weinberg, R. S., & Jackson, A. V. (1984). A multidimensional group cohesion instrument for intercollegiate basketball teams. *Journal of Sport Psychology, 6,* 103–117.

Yukelson, D., Weinberg, R. S., Richardson, R., & Jackson, A. V. (1983). Interpersonal attraction and leadership within collegiate sport teams. *Journal of Sport Behavior, 6,* 28–36.

Zaccaro, S. J. (1984). "Social loafing: The role of task attractiveness." *Personality and Social Psychology Bulletin, 10,* 99–106.

Zaharieva, E. (1965). Survey of sportswomen at the Tokyo Olympics. *Journal of Sports Medicine and Physical Fitness, 5,* 215–219.

Zaharieva, E., & Sigler, J. (1963). Maternidad y deporte. *Tokogenic Pract., 144–149.*

Zaichkowsky, L. D., & Fuchs, C. Z. (1989). Biofeedback-assisted self-regulation for stress management in sports. In D. Hackfort & C. D. Spielberger (Eds.), *Anxiety in sports: An international perspective* (pp. 235–245). New York: Hemisphere.

Zaichkowsky, L. D., & Perna, F. M. (1992). Certification of consultants in sport psychology: A rebuttal to Anshel. *The Sport Psychologist, 6,* 287–296.

Zaichkowsky, L. D., & Takenaka, K. (1993). Optimizing arousal level. In R. N. Singer, M. Murphey, & L. K. Tennant (Eds.), *Handbook of research on sport psychology* (pp. 511–527). New York: Macmillan.

Zajonc, R. R. (1965). Social facilitation. *Science, 149,* 269–274.

Zander, A. (1976). The psychology of removing group members and recruiting new ones. *Human Relations, 10,* 969–987.

Zarevski, P., Marusic, I., Zolotic, S., Bunjevac, T., & Vukosav, Z. (1998). Contribution of Arnett's inventory of sensation seeking and Zuckerman's sensation seeking scale to the differentiation of athletes engaged in high and low risk sports. *Personality and Individual Differences, 25,* 763–768.

Zawitz, M. W. (1994). *Violence between intimates.* Washington, DC: U.S. Department of Justice.

Zeigler, E. F. (1973a) Historical foundations: Social and educational. In E. F. Zeigler (Ed.), *A history of sport and physical education to 1900* (pp. 11–19). Champaign, IL: Stipes.

Zeigler, E. F. (Ed.). (1973b). *A history of sport and physical education to 1900.* Champaign, IL: Stipes.

Zeigler, R. G., & Michael, R. H. (1985). The Maryland Senior Olympic Games: Challenging older athletes. *Physician and Sportsmedicine, 13*(8), 159–163.

Zhang, J. J., Jensen, B. E., & Mann, B. L. (1997). Modification and revision of the Leadership Scale for Sport. *Journal of Sport Behavior, 20,* 105–122.

Ziegler, S. G. (1994). The effects of attentional shift training on the execution of soccer skills: A preliminary investigation. *Journal of Applied Behavioral Analysis, 27,* 545–552.

Zimbardo, P. (1969). The human choice: Individuation, reason, and order versus deindividuation, impulse, and chaos. In W. Arnold & D. Levin (Eds.), *Nebraska Symposium on Motivation,* Vol. 17 (pp. 237–307). Lincoln: University of Nebraska Press.

Zuckerman, M. (1971). Dimensions of sensation-seeking. *Journal of Consulting and Clinical Psychology, 36,* 45–52.

Zuckerman, M. (1984). Experience and desire: A new format for Sensation Seeking Scales. *Journal of Behavioral Assessment, 6,* 101–114.

Zuckerman, M., & Allison, S. (1976). An objective measure of fear of success: Construction and validation. *Journal of Personality Assessment, 40,* 422–430.

Zuckerman, M., Kolin, E. A., Price, L., & Zoob, I. (1964). Development of a Sensation-seeking Scale. *Journal of Consulting Psychology, 28,* 477–482.

Author Index

AAHPERD Physical Best, 345
AAHPERD Youth Fitness Test Manual, 345
Abramson, L. Y., 66, 67, 146
Abu–Hilal, M. M., 395
Acevedo, E. O., 395
Acocella, J., 138
Acosta, R., 390
Acosta, R. V., 313
Adams, J., 435
Adler, A., 201
Agarwal, V., 244
Ahern, D. K., 298
Ahlgren, R. L., 433, 434
Aiken, L., 233, 234
Ajzen, L., 409
Albrecht, R. R., 254, 302
Albright, T., 317
Allard, E., 255
Allen, K., 211, 371
Allen, M., 425
Alles, W. F., 297
Alge, B. J., 148
Allison, J. A., 333
Allison, M. G., 57, 58, 60, 61
Allison, S., 329–330
Allport, G. W., 224, 244
Alzado, L., 302
Ambah, E., 197
American Youth, 344, 350
Anastasi, A., 232, 330
Andersen, M. B., 296
Anderson, C. A., 195, 205
Anderson, D. F., 391
Anderson, J. E., 379
Anderson, K. B., 195
Anderson, K. J., 79
Anderson, W. A., 302
Andre, T., 331
Andres, F., 324
Andrew, B., 408
Andrews, J. R., 364
Andrews, T. G., 413
Annesi, J. J., 166
Anshel, M. H., 17, 47, 99, 136, 219
Arai, Y., 246
Ardrey, R., 192
Arkin, R. M., 114, 115, 62, 188
Arnold, E. H., 315
Astrand, R. O., 316, 317
Athletic Footwear Association, 347
Atkinson, J., 127
Atkinson, J. W., 128
Avener, M., 76, 293
Ayllon, T., 57, 58, 60, 61

Bachman, A. D., 19
Bachman, R., 186
Bachrach, A., 284, 285
Back, K., 158

Backman, L., 254
Bagby, R. M., 84
Bagnall, J., 143
Bahrke, M. S., 414
Bailey, L., 424
Bale, R. M., 102
Bandura, A., 61, 65, 120, 123, 137, 192, 198–199, 227
Baradaxoglu, N., 12
Barber, H., 167, 326
Barber–Foss, K. D., 296
Bar–Eli, M., 143
Barlow, C. E., 406
Barnett, N. P., 387
Baron, R., 174
Baron, R. A., 91, 192, 196
Barrick, M. R., 227
Barry, J. R., 158
Barsky, S. R., 175
Bart, S. M., 298
Bartholomew, J. B., 298
Bartram, D., 83, 254
Bass, B., 150, 151
Baumann, M., 334
Baumeister, R. F., 172, 176–182
Baumler, G., 47
Baxter, P. R., 157
Beagley, G., 66
Beaton, R., 275
Beattie, M., 135
Beatty, W. W., 62, 114, 115, 188
Beauchamp, D., 83, 253
Beaumaster, E. J., 279
Becker, A. H., 47
Becker, B., 12
Becker, D., 392
Becker, M. H., 409
Behling, O., 154
Behrman, A. L., 429
Bell, G. W., 364
Bell, J., 209
Bem, S., 330
Benedict, J., 222
Benedict, J. R., 268, 270
Benjamin, L. T., 46, 73, 91
Bennet, S., 323
Bennett, B., 27, 32
Benson, H., 419
Berg, R., 313, 315
Bergandi, T. A., 254
Berger, B. G., 141, 414
Berghorn, F., 392
Berghorn, F. J., 270
Berkowitz, L., 197
Berkson, D. M., 410
Berlin, R., 310, 317, 318
Bernardo, P., 78, 79
Bernstein, I. H., 195
Berry, L. M., 153
Bertilson, H., 205

Best, C., 268, 269
Best, D., 331
Bettle, N., 397
Bettle, O., 397
Betts, J., 42, 43
Betts, J. R., 208
Bhushan, S., 244
Biddle, S. J. H., 115, 117, 118, 119, 125
Birch, J. S., 213
Bird, A. M., 94, 125, 153, 203, 217, 253, 328
Birkeland, K. I., 303
Birnholz, J., 317
Blair, M. S., 416
Blair, S., 344
Blair, S. N., 406
Blair, S. V., 218, 219
Blanchard, K. L., 153–154
Blaser, R., 242
Blau, G., 136
Bleak, J. L., 134
Blinde, E., 432, 434
Blood, K. J., 305
Bloom, G. A., 379
Bloom, M., 317
Bloomberg, R., 316
Blouin, A. G., 397
Blucker, J., 329
Blumenthal, J., 410
Blyth, C. S., 209
Boeck, G., 378
Bolton, B., 244
Bond, C. F., 174
Bond, J., 255
Bonekat, W. H., 430
Boniecki, K. A., 177–178, 181
Boone, T. D., 173
Booth, E., 243
Borden, R. J., 179–180
Borg, G., 413
Botterill, C., 352
Boulougouris, J., 89
Bourgeois, A. E., 250, 256, 298
Boutcher, S. H., 79, 414
Bowman, E. D., 416
Bradet, R., 407
Bradley, P. W., 246, 249
Brady, E., 312, 344
Brame, J., 125, 328
Bramwell, S. T., 297
Brannigan, A., 281
Branscombe, N. R., 180
Brant, J., 181
Brasch, R., 2, 30, 34, 39
Braslow, A., 209
Brawley, L. R., 126, 162, 164, 165, 166, 173, 255
Bray, S. R., 176

Breaking Point, 378
Bredemeier, Brenda Jo Light, 195
Breivik, G., 286
Brewer, B. W., 18, 19, 20, 136, 296, 298, 426
Brewington, R., 390
Brichin, M., 245
Brooks, A. R., 125–126
Brown, B., 325, 404
Brown, D., 202
Brown, D. R., 419
Brown, F., 324
Brown, J. A., 151
Brown, J. R., 268
Brown, R., 324, 416
Browne, A., 303
Brownlee, S., 317
Brumet, M., 134
Brunelle, J. P., 250
Brustad, R., 76
Bruun, S. E., 162
Bruya, L., 143
Bryant, F. B., 217, 220
Bryant, J., 201–203, 202
Brylinsky, J. A., 183
Buchanan, D., 33
Buck, C., 408
Buckholz, E., 98
Buckner, C. E., 332
Buffone, G. W., 417
Bukowski, W., 125–126
Bull, S. J., 430
Bullen, B., 317
Bump, L. A., 83, 84, 253
Bunch, T., 363
Bunjevac, T., 285
Bunker, L., 77, 105, 106, 111, 390, 391
Burfoot, A., 274
Burger, J., 248, 424
Burke, K. L., 14, 23
Burlingame, M., 391
Burns, J. M., 150
Burrell, S., 333
Burton, D., 74, 82, 83, 252, 253, 254, 349, 356
Bushman, B. J., 195, 205
Buss, A. H., 195
Butcher, J. N., 89
Butemeyer, J., 161
Butler, J. L., 172, 182
Butler, R. J., 208, 334
Buunk, B. P., 160–161
Buzas, H. P., 57
Byrnes, J. P., 287

Cable, N. T. 110
Caccese, T., 395, 398
Cahn, S. K., 334, 339
Cale, A., 253

Calhoun, J., 138
Campbell, I., 406
Campbell, T., 331
Cancio, L. C., 279
Cantu, R. C., 209
Cantwell, J. D., 405
Capel, S., 391
Capel, S. A., 395
Carfagno, D. G., 294
Carmack, M. A., 422
Carpenter, L., 390
Carpenter, l. J., 313
Carr, R., 94
Carroll, D., 104
Carron, A. V., 123, 153, 155–158, 160, 164, 162, 165, 166, 176, 382
Carson, K., 335
Carson, R. C., 89
Carter, J. E., 250
Casher, B., 286
Caspersen, C. J., 404, 405
Castracane, V. D., 416
Catlin, D. H., 300
Cattell, R. B., 242, 244
Caudill, D., 109
Cauley, J., 406
Cayleff, S. E., 339
Celestino, R., 134
Cereatti, L., 286
Chalip, L., 137, 332
Chalk, O., 288
Chandler, B., 363
Chapman, C. L., 423
Chappell, S., 337
Chartrand, J. M., 256
Chase, M. A., 400
Chelladurai, P., 153, 155–157, 158, 164
Cheng, J., 436
Chester, N., 298
Chi, R., 244
Chipps, A., 332
Chow, B. C., 333
Christensen, D., 364
Christensen, D. S., 256
Christiansen, G., 167
Christie, R., 382
Chu, D., 264, 266, 269
Church, G., 134, 294
Cialdini, R. B., 179–180
Ciccantelli, P., 364
Clark, R., 127
Clark, W. J., 212
Clarke, D., 136
Clarke, K., 209
Clarkson, P. M., 304
Clements, K. M., 406, 431
Clifford, P., 429
Closed Doors, 311
Cloud, J., 300
Coaching Exodus, 378
Coakley, J. J., 217, 265, 266, 267, 315, 318
Coddington, R. D., 297
Cohn, E. G., 196
Cole, C. L., 339
Coleman, J. K., 22
Colley, A., 332
Collins, B., 135
Comer, R. J., 335, 415
Comisky, P., 201, 202

Comisky, R. W., 202
Congeni, J., 363, 364
Cook, D. L., 95
Cook, T., 406
Cooke, C., 99
Coombs, R., 176
Coomes, M., 337
Corbin, C. B., 141
Corby, B., 186
Cornelius, A. E., 298
Cornelius, W. L., 173
Corrington, K. A., 150–151, 210
Costa, R. T., 227
Cota, A. A., 169
Cote, C., 415
Cotman, C. W., 73
Cottle, S., 392
Cottrell, N. B., 173
Courington, S., 396
Courneya, K. S., 176, 410
Cowper, R. A., 430
Cox, B. J., 84
Cox, D. N., 225, 245, 260
Cox, R. H., 55, 106, 162, 164, 174, 188, 190, 203, 217, 220, 230
Crafts, L. W., 89
Crampton, C. W., 363
Cratty, B. J., 162, 172
Cripe, B. K., 94, 203, 217
Crockett, D., 42
Cronbach, L. J., 232
Crossman, J. E., 60, 362
Crowley, G. M., 430
Crowne, D. P., 298
Crumpton, R., 379
Cryan, P. D., 297
Csikszentmihalyi, M. 148, 323, 425
Cullen, E., 203
Cullen, J., 203
Cunningham, D., 408
Curry, L. A., 95
Curry, T. J., 200, 265
Cushman, S., 316
Cuvillier, C., 99

Dabbs, J. M., 191
Daily-McKee, D., 318
Daiss, S., 135, 247
Dalton, K., 191
Daniel, J. V., 218, 219
Daniels, D. D., 239
Daniels, F. S., 93
Danielson, R. R., 150, 152, 153
Danish, S. J., 256
Darley, J. M., 272
Dashiell, J. R., 172
Davenport, J., 306
Davidson, K., 82
Davidson, R. J., 83–84
Davis, H., 251–252
Davis, S., 244
Davis, S. F., 47
Dearwater, S., 406
Deaux, K., 328
DeCastro, J. M., 423
DeCharms, R., 137
Deci, E., 128, 129
Dedera, D., 282, 288
DeLange, N., 20
Delcomyn, F., 73
Delk, J., 245

Del Rey, R., 331
Demant, T. W., 304
DeMinzi, M. C. R., 137
Deneve, K. M., 195
De Palma, D., 254
Desertrain, G. S., 395
Deshaies, P., 75
Desharnais, R., 407, 415
Dessler, G., 153
Deuser, W. E., 195
Dewar, C., 217
Dewey, A., 406–407
Dewey, D., 255
DeWitt, D. J., 93
Dicara, L., 93
Dick, R. W., 336
Dickey, G., 159
Dickinson, J. A., 62
Diekhoff, G., 424
Dietz, B., 180
Dietzel, P., 432, 434
Di Giueseppe, R., 135
DiNucci, J. N., 337
Dion, K. L., 169
DiPasquale, R. C., 430
Dishman, R. K., 4, 225, 406, 408, 410
Dixon, R. S., 137
Dobie, M., 335, 336
Docker, S. B., 98, 99
Dollard, J., 192
Domjan, M., 54, 55
Donahue, J. A., 55, 59, 61, 63, 66
Donnelly, P., 162, 360
Donnelly, R., 162
Donnelly, S. B., 318
Donnerstein, E., 197
Doob, L., 192
Doppelt, H. G., 90
Dorsey, V. L., 337
Doyne, E. J., 416
Drake, C. J., 150, 152
Drewry, B. R., 203, 204
Droppleman, L., 246
Droste, C., 416
Drug Testing in Sports, 301
Druckman, D., 94
Duarte, J., 275
Dube, M., 139
DuBois, R., 354
Duda, J., 222
Duggan, P., 216
Duignan, R., 332
Duncan, M. C., 273, 275, 276, 333
Duncan, T. E., 119, 122
Dunkle, M., 318
Dunn, J., 272
Dunning, E., 199
Duquin, M. E., 328, 330, 332, 333
Dustman, R. E., 430
Duval, S., 174
Dweck, C. S., 67, 123, 148
Dworkin, B. R., 94
Dyer, K., 317
Dzewaltowski, D. A., 416

Eagly, A. H., 169
Eastman, C., 104
Ebbeling, C. B., 419
Edwards, H., 269
Edwards, S. M., 298

Edwards, S. W., 332
Egstrom, G. H., 284, 285
Eischens, R., 415
Eitzen, D. S., 264, 268, 311, 318, 334, 391
Ekkekakis, P., 250
Eklund, R. C., 294, 396, 399
Elbaz, G., 143
Ellickson, K. A., 246, 249
Ellin, A., 216
Ellis, N. R., 412, 413
Emery, C. F., 436
Emery, L., 311
Emmelkamp, P. M. G., 89
Emmerson, R. Y., 430
Emswiller, T., 328
Endler, N. S., 84, 228–229, 284
Engelhardt, G. M., 203
Engstrom, I., 316, 317
Entine, J., 288
Epstein, S., 279
Erdelyi, G., 316, 317
Erffmeyer, E. S., 102, 103
Erickson, G. A., 180
Ericsson, K. A., 295, 306
Eriksson, B. O., 316, 317
Eron, L. D., 189, 231
Ervin, C., 331
Eskenazi, B., 317
Essing, W., 163
Estabrooks, P., 166
Ethics of Blood Doping, 303
Etzel, E. F., 179
Evans, C. R., 169
Evans, M., 305
Evans, V., 245
Evans, W. J., 430, 431
Everett, J. J., 387
Ewing, M. E., 358, 392
Eysenck, H. J., 225, 231, 242, 245, 260
Eysenck, S. B. G., 231, 242, 245

Falls, H., 344
Faris, J., 415
Farris, E., 328
Faucette, N., 362
Faulkner, G., 417
Feher, P., 283
Feicht, C., 317
Fein, S., 197
Felshin, J., 310, 317, 318
Felsten, G., 195
Feltz, D. L., 121, 122, 142, 254, 344, 346, 347, 349, 350, 358, 400
Fenz, W. D., 76, 279, 280
Ferguson, D. G., 213
Festinger, L., 158, 199
Feussner, J. R., 430
Fiatarone, M. A., 406, 430, 431
Fiedler, F., 152–153, 167
Field, T. M., 95
Fielding, L., 42
Figlerski, L. B., 64
Finch, L. M., 293
Fine, P., 296
Finkenberg, M. E., 337
Finlayson, I., 280
Finn, J., 134, 137
Fishbein, M., 409
Fisher, A. C., 224, 228

Fisher, J., 65
Fitts, W., 139
Fixx, J., 415
Fleisig, G. S., 364
Fleming, S. L., 250
Foa, E. B., 90
Folkins, C., 412, 413, 414, 428
Follick, M. J., 298
Fontanarosa, P. B., 405
Forbes, C., 29
Ford, S. K., 255
Forehand, R., 362
Forrest, L., 392
Fortlage, L., 419
Fosdick, D., 251
Foster, C., 125, 328
Foster, J., 98
Foster, W., 244
Fowler, C., 143
Fox, E., 413
Fox, K. R., 141
Francis, L. J., 246
Francis, R., 363
Frank, M. G., 222
Franken, R. E., 197
Franklin, K., 343
Fratzke, M. R., 218, 219
Frederick, C. M., 134
Freedman, J., 198
Freeman, S., 179–180
Freischlag, J., 283
Freischlag, T., 283
French, S. N., 94
Frey, J. H., 286
Friedman, M., 410
Frieze, I. H., 117, 328
Frisch, R., 316, 317
Frost, R. O., 397
Fry, D., 347
Fu, F. H., 250
Fuchs, C. Z., 94, 245
Fung, L., 250
Fuoss, D., 376
Furman, G., 318
Furst, D. M., 218, 219, 243

Gabriel, T. J., 256
Gackenbach, J., 332
Gaillard, A. W. K., 8, 160–161
Gallimore, R., 379
Gallon, A., 381
Game Winning Drives, 150
Gammon, C., 217
Gange, J., 174
Garland, D. J., 158
Garrett, J., 279, 285
Gates, D., 282
Gates 1991, 269
Gaulin, P., 139
Gauron, E. F., 106
Gavzer, B., 208
Gayton, W. F., 141–142, 176, 179
Gecas, V., 286
Geen, R. G., 62, 114, 115, 174, 188
Geis, F., 382
Gench, B., 139
Gender Equity Survey, 313
Gendreau, P., 245
Genuchi, M., 75
George 1994, 274
Gerber, E., 36, 310, 317, 318
Geron, E., 243

Gerson, R., 75
Gesn, P. R., 195
Gibbons, L. W., 406
Gieck, J., 304
Gilbert, B., 333
Gilbert, N., 333
Gilbert, R. W., 89
Gill, D. L., 75, 76, 118, 122, 141, 167, 230, 258, 337, 344, 347
Gill, K. S., 391
Gillaspy, J. A., 331
Gillette, J., 318
Gilliam, C., 430
Gilliland, K., 135
Gillis, J. H., 55, 59, 61, 63, 66
Gilovich, T., 222
Gilroy, E., 325
Gilstrap, T., 139
Giuliano, T. A., 331
Glamser, E. D., 176
Glasser, W., 422
Gledhill, N., 303
Glenn, S. T., 158
Gliner, J. A., 413
Godin, G., 407, 409, 415
Goldfield, G. S., 397
Goldman, M., 162
Goldsmith, P. A., 218, 219
Goldstein, J. H., 222
Goldstein, L., 424
Goldstein, S. R., 176
Goleman, D. J., 83–84
Gomolak, C., 363
Gordin, R. D., 332
Gorman, C., 209
Gorsuch, R. L., 80, 81, 246, 249, 414
Goss, J. D., 137
Gottfried, H., 336
Gotz-Welbergen, A., 317
Goudas, M., 257
Gough, D., 98, 102
Gould, D., 17, 72, 74, 75, 80, 81, 107, 121, 293, 294, 344, 346, 347, 349, 350, 397
Graham, G. M., 362
Granito, V., 219
Granzyk, T. L., 396
Grasha, A., 254
Graves, J., 161
Gray, S. W., 98
Grayson, J. B., 90
Green, D. E., 395
Greenberg, J., 210
Greendorfer, S., 326, 432, 434
Greene, D., 63, 128
Greenleaf, C. A. 110
Greenlee, M. W., 416
Griest, J., 415
Griffin, L., 344, 347
Griffin, P., 324
Griffin, R., 335
Griffiths, T. J., 284
Grogan, R., 426
Groom, R. W., 195
Gross, J. B., 118, 119, 344, 347
Gross, N., 158
Grossman, S., 213
Grove, J. R., 110
Gruber, J., 83, 244, 253
Guarnieri, A., 256
Guerin, B. J., 47, 174

Guevremont, D. C., 55
Gundersheim, J., 139
Gurin, G., 135
Gurin, R., 135

Haas, J., 174
Haase, A. M., 397
Hackensmith, C., 27, 29, 45
Hacker, C., 163–164, 167
Hackfort, D., 80, 81
Haefner, D. R., 409
Haerle, R. K., 433, 434
Haggerty, T. R., 157
Hailey, B. J., 424
Hale, B. D., 99, 173
Hale, C. J., 343, 363
Hall, C., 98
Hall, C. R., 98
Hall, E. E., 250
Hall, E. G., 102, 103, 134, 294
Hall, G., 65
Hall, H. K., 397
Hall, S. K., 332
Hamachek, D., 138, 140
Hambleton, R. K., 153–154
Hammer, W., 251
Hammermeister, J., 254
Hammerton, M., 279
Handal, P. J., 298
Hanick, P., 326
Hanin, Y., 80, 81
Hankes, D., 99, 100
Hanley, R., 410
Hanson, D., 356
Hanson, M., 408
Hardman, K., 244
Hardy, C. J., 102, 161, 162, 426
Hardy, L., 79, 80, 81, 208, 216
Harkins, S. G., 161
Harre, R., 199, 200
Harres, R., 326
Harris, D. V., 101, 125–126
Harris, H. A., 27, 30, 31
Harris, J. A., 195
Hart, B. A., 377, 390, 391
Hart, D., 161
Harter, S., 122, 124
Hasbrook, C. A., 377, 391
Haslam, R., 294
Hatfield, B., 167
Hathaway, S., 231, 242
Haubenstricker, J., 344, 346, 347
Hauck, E. R., 436
Hausenblas, H. A., 86, 336
Hausfeld, B., 122
Hawkins, R. M. F., 131
Hay, D., 245
Hay, J. L., 147
Hayes, S. C., 61
Hayward, S. A., 20
Headrick, B., 433, 434
Health and Fitness, 411
Hebert, E., 395
Hebert, R., 139
Hecker, J. E., 98, 101
Heider, F., 115
Heil, J., 296
Heishman, M. F., 390, 391
Hellsten, L. A. M., 410
Helmreich, R., 330–331, 331
Hemmersbach, P., 303

Hemmings, B., 254
Henderson, J., 425
Hendrix, A. E., 395
Henry, B., 27
Henschen, K. P., 22, 332
Hermann, H., 317
Hersey, R., 153–154
Hershberger, E., 329
Hershey, S., 180
Herwig, C., 390, 392
Hesse, F. W., 336
Heusner, W., 244
Heyman, S. R., 285
Hickey, T., 431
Hicks, B., 323
Higgs, R., 51
Higgins, N. C., 147
Higgins, R. L., 180
Higginson, D., 326
Hightower, J., 251
Hill, A. B., 119
Hill, V., 195
Hillery, J., 173
Hines, T., 213
Hinman, D. A., 14
Hinshaw, K. E., 101
Hinson, M., 139
Hirschland, P., 344
Hirst, J., 251
Hirt, E. R., 180
Hisamichi, S., 246
Hisanga, B., 101
Hochner, A., 272
Hochstetler, S., 331
Hodges, L., 123
Hoeksema-van Orden, C. Y. D., 160–161
Hoepner, B., 45, 244
Hoferek, M., 326
Hoffman, L. A., 239
Hogan, R., 227
Hogg, M. A., 165
Holder, R. L., 183
Holland, A., 331
Holmen, M., 390
Holmes, T. H., 297
Hon, S., 333
Hopkins, J. R., 46, 73, 91
Hopson, J. L., 425
Horn, M. E., 253
Horn, T. S., 158, 350, 400
Horner, M., 329
Horsfall, J. S., 228
Horton, R. S., 426
Horvath, S. M., 413, 426
Houlihan, B., 302
House, R. J., 153
Houston, J. P., 153
Howe, B. L., 101
Howe, M., 432, 433, 434
Howell, M. L., 26, 27
Howell, R., 426
Hrycaiko, D., 56, 61, 100
Hsieh, C., 406
Huband, D., 135
Huddleston, S., 76, 344, 347
Hume, K. M., 60
Hunt, E., 386
Hunt, J. McV., 228–229
Hunt, P., 173

Hunter, L. Y., 318
Hursey, K. G., 300, 301, 302
Huss, M. T., 47
Hutchinson, J., 29, 32, 34, 41
Hymbaugh, K., 279, 285

Iata, B., 65
Ibrahim, H., 139
IG Staff, 336
Imamura, H., 157
Ingham, A., 161
Ingman, O., 316
Innes, J., 174
Irvine, M., 245
Irving, P. G., 176
Irwin, I., 208
Isberg, L., 157
Iso-Ahola, S. E., 125, 328
Issari, P., 305

Jable, J. T., 44
Jackson, A., 99, 100, 109, 121, 143, 392
Jackson, A. V., 158, 327
Jackson, J. J., 191, 212
Jackson, S. A., 293, 294
Jackson, S. E., 393, 395
Jacobs, G., 249
Jacobson, E., 91
Jacoby, F., 377
Jambor, E. A., 157
James, M., 328
Jamison, S., 359, 384
Janelle, C. M., 86, 250
Jansen, S. C., 273, 275, 276
Janssen, J., 169
Jennings, S., 344
Jensen, B. E., 157
Jersild, A., 138
Jiobu, R., 200, 265
Jobin, J., 415
Johnsgard, K. W., 243, 279
Johnson, R., 243
Johnson, S., 179
Johnson, S. C., 430
Johnson, T., 317
Johnson, W. O., 323
Johnstone, C. S., 336
Johnstone, E. C., 72
Jolton, J. A., 426, 427
Jones, D. C., 326
Jones, G. B., 253, 254, 279
Jones, J., 272
Jones, J. C. H., 213
Jones, J. G., 253
Jones, N., 408, 410
Jones, S. H., 246
Jourard, S., 139
Jowdy, D. R., 256

Kaczor, L. M., 98, 101
Kampert, J. B., 406
Kane, M. J., 267, 332, 392
Kaplan, J., 317
Kaplan, R., 231–232, 242, 243
Karamousalidis, G., 257
Karau, S. J., 161
Karch, S. B., 306
Karlberg, R., 316, 317
Karpman, M., 284
Karren, R. J., 142
Karson, S., 245

Kasl, S. V., 409
Kau, M., 65
Kavanagh, T., 408
Kavanaugh, D., 122
Kearney, A. J., 65
Keefe, F. J., 298
Kehayias, J. J., 431
Keith, J. A., 218, 219
Kelley, A. E., 250
Kelley, B. C., 396, 399
Kelley, S. C., 396
Kelly, P., 246
Kendall, G., 100
Kendall, T., 100
Kennard, J., 41
Kennedy, C., 180
Kenyon, G., 257
Kerr, A. W., 397
Kerr, G. A., 137
Kerr, J. H., 81, 287
Kerr, N. L., 162
Kidd, T. R., 327
Kidman, L., 362
Kiester, E., 190
Kiker, V., 134
Kilik, L., 169
Killian, K. J., 64
Kim, M., 167
King, J., 244
King, K., 55, 59, 61, 63, 66
King, R., 209
Kingsley, J., 324
Kirby, S., 152, 154
Kirby, R. J., 435
Kirkendall, D. R., 346
Kirker, B., 222
Kirkpatrick, C., 374
Kirschenbaum, D. S., 102
Kirschenbaum, J., 299
Kirscht, J. R., 409
Kivlin, J., 324, 326
Klavora, P., 78, 249, 250
Kleiber, D., 346, 432, 434
Klein, H. J., 148
Klein, M., 167, 415
Kleine, D., 86
Klonsky, B. G., 169
Klonsky, R., 252
Knight, J. L., 331
Knoppers, A., 392
Knowles, J. B., 279
Kobasa, S. C., 396
Kocian, M., 245
Kohl, H. W., 406
Kolin, E. A., 279, 285
Koltyn, K. E., 406
Korn, Z., 61
Kornspan, A. S., 179
Koskela, A., 408
Kozar, A., 46
Kozlowski, N. F., 239
Kraemer, R. R., 416
Kraus, H., 344
Kreisel, P., 346, 347
Kroll, W., 292
Kuchenbecker, S. Y., 352

Lacayo, R., 301
Lachance, V., 303
Lacoste, P. L., 157
Lahart, C., 397
Lambert, S. M., 137

Lamirand, M., 99
Lan, L. Y., 122
Landers, D. M., 78, 79, 86, 93, 167, 173, 174, 254, 414
Lane, A. M., 83, 254
Langer, E. J., 137
Langevin, G., 176
Lanning, W., 101, 381
Lao, R., 135
Lapchick, R. E., 239, 268, 270, 392, 393
LaPlace, J., 243
Laporte, R., 406
Larrick, R. R., 197
Larsen, J. D., 218, 219
Larson, R., 367
Lashuk, M., 324
Latané, B., 161
Latham, G. P., 142–145
Lathen, C. W., 277
Latimer, P. R., 90
Latimer, S., 392
Latin, R. W., 430
Laurencelle, L., 157, 412
Layman, D., 424
Layman, E., 326
Layne, B. H., 142
Lazarus, R. S., 224
LeBoutillier, N., 406–407
Leclerc, G., 139
Ledbetter, B., 41
Lee, C., 101, 121
Lee, I., 406
Lee, M., 29, 32, 34, 41, 315
Leehey, K., 335, 423
Lefcourt, H. M., 137, 148
Lefrancois, R., 139
Leggett, S., 273, 275, 276
Legwold, G., 406
Lehman, D. R., 217, 220
Lehrer, P. M., 94, 110
Leitenberg, H., 92
Leith, L. M., 55
Lemonick, M. D., 303
Lenk, H., 159
Lenskyj, H., 335
Lent, R. W., 409
Leon, G. R., 339
Leonard, W. M., 41, 176, 218, 219, 266, 269, 272, 273, 299
Lepper, M. R., 63, 128
Lerner, B. S., 179
Lesyk, J. L., 22
LeUnes, A., 20, 83, 135, 156, 247, 248, 250, 253, 254, 256, 257, 260, 272, 298, 381, 424
Levenson, H., 135, 136, 247, 408
Levenson, M. R., 283, 286
Levesque, L., 415
Levinger, G., 161
Levis, D. J., 89
Levy, G. D., 331
Le-Wei, Z., 101
Lewin, K., 228
Lewis, B., 429
Lewis, B. P., 182
Lewis, G., 27, 41, 43
Lewthwaite, R., 346
Lidor, R., 12
Light, K. E., 429
Lighthall, F., 82

Likert, R. A., 257
Lilliefors, F., 424
Linder, D. E., 19, 20, 136, 182, 298, 426
Lips, H., 332
Lipsitz, L. A., 430, 431
Lipsyte, R., 311
Liu, Z., 106
Liukkonnen, J., 157
Lochbaum, M., 80, 81
Locke, E. A., 142–145, 391
Locke, K. N., 142–143
Loehr, J., 397
Loggia, M., 311
Lohr, B. A., 103
Lombardo, J. A., 301
Long, B. C., 104, 408, 410, 414, 415, 417
Long, J., 406
Longcope, C., 301
Longman, R. S., 169
Longstreth, L., 286
Lopez, J., 200
Lord, S. R., 431
Lorenz, K., 192
Lorr, M., 246
Loucks, A. B., 317
Loudermilk, S., 324, 326
Loumidis, K. S., 424
Loverock, R., 330
Lowell, E., 127
Lowery, S., 406–407
Loy, J., 268
Ludwig, D., 252
Lufi, D., 136, 137
Lumpkin, A., 333
Lumsden, J. A., 383
Lupfer, M., 272
Lushene, R. F., 80, 81, 246, 249, 414
Lusiardo, M., 254
Luthans, F., 131
Lutter, J., 316
Lybrand, W. A., 413
Lynch, C. I., 272
Lynn, R., 134
Lyon, L., 251

MacDonald, A., 134
MacIntyre, N. R., 436
MacLean , A. W., 279
McAndrew, F. T., 176
McArthur, J., 316, 317
McAuley, E., 119, 122
McAuliffe, T., 162
McClelland, D., 127
McClements, J., 347
McClenaghan, B., 299, 397, 399
McCrae, R. R., 227
McCready, M., 408, 410
McCullagh, P., 250
McCune, E. D., 337
McCune, S. L., 337
McCutcheon, L., 426, 428
McDonald, W., 408
McDougall, A. A., 281
McDougall-Wilson, B., 416
McElroy, M. A., 329, 346
McElvogue, J., 268
McGaugh, J. L., 73
McGeorge, K. K., 333
McGinn, C. J., 218, 219

McGregor, E., 333
McGuire, R. T., 293
McHugh, M. C., 328
McInman, A. D., 141
McKay, J., 333
McKeag, D. B., 302
McKelvie, S., 135
McKenzie, A., 362
McKenzie, B., 362
McKenzie, T. L., 61, 62, 362
McKinley, J., 231, 242
McNab, T. 436
McNair, D., 246
McNair, P. J. 110
McNamee, M. J., 23
Mace, R. D., 104
Macera, C. H., 406
Machlus, S. D., 99
Mack, D. E., 426
Maddi, S. R., 396
Maddux, J. E., 409
Maehr, M., 123
Maffulli, N., 363
Maguire, J., 199
Mahoney, M. J., 76, 98, 101, 256,
        293, 294
Maier, N. F., 69
Maier, S. F., 66
Maiman, L. A., 409
Makhijani, M. G., 169
Malumphy, T., 325
Mandell, A., 299
Mann, B. L., 157
Mann, L., 116
Marcus, B., 122
Mark, M. M., 125–126, 217, 220
Markle, A., 272
Marks, E.C., 430
Marks, I., 89
Marlowe, D., 298
Maron, M. B., 413, 426
Marset, P., 89
Marsh, H. W., 141
Marsh, P., 199, 200
Marten, P., 397
Martens, R., 4, 75, 76, 77, 78, 82,
        83, 139, 163, 164, 173, 174,
        252, 253, 256, 349, 350,
        354, 355, 356, 358, 367,
        383, 422
Martin, B., 317
Martin, G. L., 56, 61, 63, 64, 69,
        89, 100, 383, 417
Martin, J. J., 141
Martin, K. A., 98, 336
Martin, W., 158
Martinsen, E. W., 417
Marusic, I., 285
Maruyama, G., 125, 328
Maslach, C., 393, 395
Maslow, A., 139
Massad, P., 67
Massengale, J. D., 51, 391
Massie, J., 410
Masters, K. S., 425, 426, 427
Mathes, S. A., 377, 390, 391, 392
Mathinos, L., 332
Matsen-Twisdale, J. A., 413
Matthews, G. R., 179
Matthews, J., 397
Matthews, K., 392, 393
Mattson, J., 222

May, J., 107
May, J. R., 318
Mayerberg, C., 395, 398
Maynard, I. W., 80, 81, 254
Meacci, W. G., 392
Mehlenback, R. S., 22
Mehrabian, A., 294, 379
Meichenbaum, D., 103, 104, 414
Melzack, R., 298
Menard 1996, 275
Menegazzi, J., 424
Mento, A. J., 142
Meredith, C. N., 430
Merritt, K., 243, 279
Merritt, R. K., 404
Metalsky, G. I., 146
Meyer, B. M., 392
Meyers, A. W., 22, 99, 100, 101,
        102
Meyers, C., 250
Meyers, M. C., 283, 298
Michael, M., 325
Micheli, L. J., 360
Miedzian, M., 215
Mihoces, G., 433, 434
Mihovilovic, M. A., 433, 434
Milan, D., 316
Miller, D. C., 287
Miller, D. K., 352
Miller, J. L., 331
Miller, L. K., 217
Miller, N., 192
Miller, N. E., 93, 94
Miller, S., 282
Mineka, S., 89
Minoru, M., 297
Mirels, H., 135
Mitchell, E., 27, 32
Mitchell, J. S., 218, 219
Mitchell, T. R., 153
Miyauchi, T., 157
Molander, B., 254
Monahan, T., 415
Monat, A., 224
Montagu, A., 193
Montgomery, A. B., 359
Montgomery, T., 102
Moody, D., 244
Moolenijzer, N., 36
Moore, D., 125–126, 174
Moore, D. W., 137
Moore, J. C., 183
Moore, W., 295
Moran, A., 98, 110
Morey, M. C., 430
Morgan, J. R., 415, 416
Morgan, W. P., 4, 243, 245, 246,
        247, 248, 249, 414, 416,
        424, 426
Moritz, S. E., 400
Morris, A., 136, 424
Morris, H. H., 228
Morris, L. D., 251
Morris, M. J., 80, 81
Morris, R., 191
Morris, T., 12
Morrison, N., 139
Moss, J., 406–407
Mottram, D. R., 298, 304
Mount, M. K., 227
Mouratidis, J., 34, 310
Mowrer, O. H., 88, 192

Muchinsky, R. M., 153, 158
Mueller, F. O., 208, 209
Munson, L., 361
Munt, E. D., 61
Murphy, P., 199
Murphy, S., 98, 107, 367
Murphy, S. M., 256, 257
Murray, D., 294
Murray, H. A., 127
Murray, T. H., 300
Murrell, A. J., 180
Mutrie, N., 125–126
Myers, A., 332
Myers, J., 275
Myung Woo, H., 250

Nack, W., 361
Nance, R., 375
Nasco, S. A., 433, 434
Nation, J. R., 46, 66, 67, 73, 91,
        135, 247, 272, 381
Needles, T., 410
Neil, G., 152, 154
Neimeyer, R. A., 416
Neiss, R., 79
Nelson, B., 176
Nelson, M. B., 320
Nelson, M. E., 431
Nemeroff, C. J., 136
Nesti, A. S., 83, 254
Neumann, H., 35
Neumarker, K. J., 397
Neumarker, U., 397
Nevill, A. M., 183
Newcomb, T., 199
New Findings, 407
Newhof, C., 327
Newman, L. A., 317
New Rules, 363
Nias, D. K. B., 225, 245, 260
Niaura, R. S., 122
Nicholls, J., 123
Nicholson, C., 327
Nicklaus, J., 99
Nickless, C. J., 141–142, 179
Nideffer, R. M., 92, 236, 254, 255
Nisbett, M. E., 63
Nisbett, R. E., 128, 286
Nixon, H. L., 6, 286
Nolen-Hoeksema, S., 89, 143–144,
        146
Nowell, P., 214
Nowicki, S., 136, 137
Nylander, I., 316, 317

O'Brien, R. M., 64, 99
O'Connor, P. J., 246, 247, 249, 406
Odbert, H. S., 244
O'Dell, J., 245
Ogilvie, B. C., 243, 244, 251, 279,
        280, 381, 432, 433, 434
Ogles, B. M., 426, 427
Oglesby, C. A., 324
Oinuma, Y., 157
Oja, R., 408
Ojha, M., 245
Okada, M., 284
Oldridge, N., 408, 410
Olivardia, R., 300
Oliver, C., 300
Olson, T., 218

O'Malley, M., 212
O'Neill, E. E., 431
Orlick, T., 19, 99, 101, 347, 350, 352
Osborn, K. M., 416
Osgood, C. D., 257–258, 324
Osinski, A., 362
Osipow, A. C., 260
Ossip-Klein, D. J., 416
Ostrow, A. G., 326
Ottley, W., 279
Owen, D., 105
Owen, R. G., 397

Paffenbarger, R. S., 406
Palmer, D., 26
Pappas, A. M., 365
Pargman, D., 307
Puleo, E., 419
Parker, J., 408
Parker, J. D., 84
Parkhouse, B. L., 390, 392
Parkin, W. A., 244
Parrish, M. W., 98
Parry, S. J., 23
Partanen, K., 408
Partanen, T., 408
Participation Survey, 344
Partington, J., 19, 101
Pascuzzi, D., 117–118, 126
Passer, M. W., 75, 76, 328, 329,
        356, 357, 358
Pastore, D. L., 392
Pataco, V., 157
Pate, R., 299, 344, 345, 397, 399
Pate, R. R., 247, 249
Patrick, D., 274, 317
Paulus, P. B., 173
Paulus, R. B., 173
Pavlov, I., 54
Pear, J., 63, 64, 69, 89
Peckham, V., 161
Pedersen, D. M., 277–278
Pemberton, C. L.,12
Peoples, C., 425
Pepitone, A., 199
Pereira, G., 254
Perkins, S., 244
Perkins, T. S., 256
Perna, F. M., 15–17, 433, 434
Perry, M., 195
Perry, Z. W., 272
Pessin, J., 172
Pestonjee, D., 245
Peterson, C., 69, 146
Peterson, J., 163
Peterson, R., 264
Petitpas, A. J., 18, 19
Petlichkoff, L. M., 74, 75, 344, 346
Petrie, T. A., 20
Petruzzello, S. J., 86, 250
Pettit, M. E., 21
Phelan, J., 134
Phillips, K., 300
Phillips, S. T., 177–178, 181
Piaget, J., 412
Pierce, E. F., 423
Piette, J. M., 239
Pillow, D. R., 19
Pinchas, S., 143
Pipe, A., 303
Pivarnik, J. M., 318
Plowman, S. A., 316

Poczwardowski, A., 22
Poff, J., 267
Pollack, M., 248, 249
Pollock, M., 246, 426
Pooley, J., 350
Pope, H., 300
Popp, K. E., 331
Porat, J., 136, 137
Porretta, D. L., 295
Porter, K., 98
Postmes, T., 199
Powell, F. M., 279
Powell, J. W., 296
Prapavessis, H. 110, 397
Pratt, M. B., 391
Predebon, J., 98, 99
Premack, D., 65
Prentice, W. E., 337
President's Challenge Physical
    Fitness Program, The, 345
Price, L., 279, 285
Pro Coaches, 376
Ptacek, J. T., 256
Pufahl, A., 313
Puffer, J., 301
Pullella, J., 219
Purdy, D. A., 218, 219

Qiu, Y., 106
Qi-Wei, M., 101
Quain, R. J., 218, 219
Quarterman, J., 245
Quesenberry, C. R., 317

Rader, B., 41
Raedeke, T. D., 396
Raglin, J. S., 80, 81, 414–417
Rahe, R., 297
Rainbolt, W., 139
Rainey, D. W., 99, 167, 205, 216, 218, 219
Rajagopalan, K., 26
Rajic, M., 412
Ramirez, D., 416
Randall, L. E., 362
Ransberger, V., 196
Ransom, K., 327
Raub, J., 416
Rauch, T. M., 426
Ravizza, K., 293, 425
Reardon, J. P., 293
Reavis, R., 337
Rechnitzer, R., 408
Reed, R., 317
Reel, J. J., 337
Rees, C. R., 155, 324
Rehm, M., 95
Reid, R., 245
Reifman, A. S., 197
Reilly, M. A., 429
Reilly, R., 217
Reilly, T., 298, 406
Reiss, M., 328
Rejeski, W. J., 126, 331
Renfrow, N., 244
Reno, R. R., 19
Reveles, M., 392
Revelle, R., 333
Reyman, J. E., 269
Rhodes, E. C., 304
Rice, E., 29, 32, 34, 41
Richards, D., 254
Richards, J. W., 381

Richardson, D. R., 191, 192
Richardson, R., 158, 327
Richir, K., 139
Riem, K. E., 300, 301, 302
Rikki, R., 392
Riley, J. F., 298
Riley, S., 433, 434
Rinehardt, K. F., 416
Rintala, J., 333
Riordan, C., 328
Riordan, M., 65
Rippe, J. M. 419
Ritter-Taylor, M., 396, 399
Rivera, P. M., 18
Rivkin, J., 83, 253, 356
Roberts, G. C., 12, 114, 115, 117–118, 122, 124, 125, 126, 131, 174
Roberts, N., 332
Roberts, S. B., 431
Robertson, I., 267
Robins, L. S., 431
Robinson, D. W., 286
Robinson, E. E., 89
Robinson, J., 259, 382
Robinson, R. S., 312
Robinson, W. J., 101
Roche, A. F., 363
Rodgers, W., 98
Rodrigo, G., 254
Rogers, C., 406
Rogers, E., 363
Rogers, R. W., 409
Roizen, R., 216
Ronayne, J., 179
Rorhlich, J. B., 186
Roscoe, J., 382
Rose, K. G., 285
Rosenblate, R., 397
Rosenfarb, I., 61
Rosenman, R., 410
Rosenstein, A. J., 228
Rosenstiel, A. K., 298
Rosenstock, I. M., 409
Roskamm, H., 416
Ross, S., 413
Rosser, E., 199, 200
Rossi, B., 286
Rossi, J. S., 122
Rostaing, B., 303
Rotella, R. J., 77, 106, 299, 397, 399
Roth, W., 408, 414
Rotstein, P., 243
Rotter, J. B., 134, 135, 137
Rotton, J., 196
Rowe, D., 333
Rowell, G., 283
Rowland, T. W., 360
Rowley, S., 360
Rowland, T. W., 368
Ruby, B. C., 95
Ruder, M., 118
Ruder, K., 167
Rudman, W., 431
Ruebush, B., 82
Ruffer, W. A., 224
Ruhling, R. O., 430
Runfola, R., 212
Rupert, P. A., 239
Rupnow, A., 252
Rushall, B. S., 60, 61, 62, 244
Russell, D. W., 119–120

Russell, G. W., 193, 202, 203, 204, 213, 216
Ryan, J., 320, 360
Ryan, N. D., 430, 431

Saari, L. M., 142–143
Sabo, D., 273, 275, 276, 312
Sabock, R., 373
Sachs, M. L., 23, 422–425
Sacuzzo, D., 231–232, 242, 243
Sage, G. H., 318, 324, 326, 382
Sage, J., 268, 311
Salameh, K. M., 395
Salazar, W., 86
Saleh, S., 153, 156
Salminen, S., 157
Saltin, B., 316, 317
Samdahl, D., 432, 434
Sanborn, C. R., 317
Sanday, P. R., 215
Sanders, G., 174
Sanderson, F. H., 65–66
Sandweiss, J. H., 93
Sanne, H., 408
Santos, E., 157
Sapp, M., 344, 346, 347
Sarason, I., 82
Sargunaraj, D., 94
Sasiene, G., 317
Sasijima, K., 26
Scanlan, T. K., 75, 76, 293, 328, 329, 346, 356
Scanning Sports, 424
Schachter, S., 158
Schafer, S., 390
Schafer, W. D., 287
Schein, R. L., 436
Schick, J., 99
Schilling, G., 242
Schindler, R., 208
Schlenker, B. R., 177–178, 181
Schlenker, D. R., 177–178, 181
Schleser, R., 99, 100, 102
Schmidt, G. W., 395
Schmitt, R. L., 218, 219
Schneirla, T. C., 89
Schrader, D., 23
Schrader, M. P., 134, 333
Schreck, M., 416
Schriesheim. C., 154
Schrodt, B., 34
Schultes, S. S., 406
Schutz, E., 343, 346, 356
Schutz, R. W., 84, 256
Schwartz, B., 175
Schwartz, G. E., 83–84, 107
Schweickert, G. J., 167, 219
Schwenkmezger, P., 80, 81
Scogin, F., 103
Scott, J., 382
Scott, R., 343
Sears, H. D., 52
Sears, R., 192
Seefeldt, V., 350, 386
Seff, M. A., 286
Sefton, J. M., 347
Segal, M., 155
Seibert, M. 324
Selby, V. C., 122
Seligman, M. E. P., 66, 67, 69, 104, 137, 143–144, 146, 148
Semmel, A., 146
Serling, R. J., 89

Serpa, S., 157
Sewell, D., 344
Sewell, D. F., 83, 254
Seymour, E., 344
Shacham, S., 250
Shangold, M. M., 406
Shannon, I. C., 173
Shapiro, E. S., 60
Shapiro, S., 60
Shaver, R., 259, 382
Shaw 1976, 158
Shearer, D. E., 430
Shek, P. N., 406
Sheldon, W. H., 225
Shephard, R. J., 406, 408, 409, 410, 412, 431, 412, 419
Sheppard, S., 331
Shepperd, J. A., 161
Sherman, C., 69, 406
Sherman, C. P., 22
Singer, R. N., 86, 222
Sherman, M., 325
Sherrill, C., 139
Shields, E. W., 337
Shifflett, B., 333
Shigeoka, J. W., 430
Shisslak, C. M., 335, 423
Shostrom, E., 139
Shryock, M. G., 254
Shultz, B., 294
Sidney, K., 431
Siedentop, D., 60
Siegel, D., 327
Sigler, J., 317
Silliman, L. M., 139
Silva, J. M., 14, 17, 159, 190, 198, 230, 292, 294, 329, 426
Sime, W. E., 410, 412, 413, 414
Simek, T. C., 64
Simon, J., 75, 76, 83, 253, 354, 355, 356
Simons, J., 74, 75
Simri, U., 26
Singh, A., 245
Singh, N. A., 406
Singh, R., 245
Singh, U., 245
Sisley, B. L., 391, 395
Sjomeling, M., 272
Skelly, W. A., 283
Skinner, B. F., 69
Skubic, E., 343, 346, 356
Skydiving Statistics, 281
Slemenda, C., 406
Sloan, L. R., 179–180
Sloan, N., 376
Smelser, N. J., 194
Smith, D. E., 83, 84, 253
Smith, E. L., 430, 431
Smith, H. W., 143
Smith, K. C., 62
Smith, M., 208, 210–214
Smith, R. E., 55, 84, 89, 90, 92, 104, 256, 386, 387, 389, 393, 394, 400
Smoll, F. L., 84, 256, 386, 387, 389, 400
Snowden, L., 337
Snyder, C. J., 152
Snyder, C. R., 95, 180
Snyder, E. E., 193, 217, 270, 271, 324, 326

Solares, G. R., 431
Soliday, J., 396, 397
Solso, R. L., 98
Sonstroem, R. J., 78, 79, 257
Sparkes, A., 417
Sparkles, K., 317
Sparling, P. B., 247, 249
Spears, B., 310
Spears, R., 41–43, 199, 312
Spence, J. T., 330–332, 340
Spiegler, M. D., 55
Spielberger, C. D., 74, 75, 80, 81, 82, 246, 248–250, 253, 260, 356, 414
Spiker, D. D., 12, 326
Spink, K. S., 166
Spirduso, W. W., 429
Sports Camaraderie 1989, 434
Spreeman, J., 72
Spreitzer, E. A., 193, 217, 270, 271, 324, 326
Spurgeon, J. H., 218, 219
Stainback, R. D., 307
Stajkovic, A. D., 131
Stamford, B., 424, 430
Stamler, J., 410
Stampfl, T. G., 89
Stangl, J. M., 392
Stapp, J., 330–331, 331
Starek, J., 250
Steel, D. H., 284
Steel, R. R., 142
Stein, G. L., 293, 395
Steinberg, H., 406–407
Steinhaus, L. A., 430
Steinhilber, A., 176–181
Steketee, G. S., 90
Stephens, R., 413
Stephenson, A., 218, 219
Sternfeld, B., 317, 318
Stewart, E., 222
Stewart, K. G., 213
Stewart, L., 251
Stewart, S., 298
Stober, J., 397
Stockbauer, J., 162
Stolz, C., 316
Stone, J., 272
Stone, M., 134, 294
Stowers, C., 159
Strategic Analysis, 404
Straub, W. F., 14, 134, 137, 244, 251, 285
Strauss, J. P., 227
Strauss, R. H., 300
Strickland, B., 136, 137
Stringer, W. W., 406
Strowman, S. R., 426
Strudwick, M., 431
Struna, N., 41
Stryer, B. K., 360
Stucky, R. J., 180
Study of Sudden Death, 364
Stull, G. A., 27
Suci, G. J., 257–258, 324
Sugiyama, Y., 167
Suinn, R. M., 99, 101, 102, 103, 107, 110, 140, 381
Suitor, J. J., 337
Sullivan, P. J. 400
Sullivan, R., 303
Sullivan, R. J., 430
Summers, J. J., 255

Sutherst, J., 406
Sutton, J., 408, 410
Swaddling, J., 28
Swain, A., 253, 254
Swanson, R. A., 41–43, 51, 312
Swets, J. A., 94
Sykes, E. A., 406–407
Syrja, P., 80, 81
Syzmanski, K., 161

Taerun, T., 324
Takenaka, K., 108
Tallant, M., 312
Tammen, V. V., 107, 256
Tangen-Foster, J. W. 1983, 277
Tannenbaum, R. H., 257–258, 324
Tapp, J., 134
Tate, D., 273, 275, 276
Taylor, A. H., 55, 218, 219
Taylor, J., 82, 328, 433, 434
Teasdale, I. D., 66, 67
Telama, R., 157
Telander, R., 302
Templin, D. P., 293
Tenenbaum, G., 136, 137, 143, 222
Tennant, L. K., 250
Teraslinna, R., 408
Terry, P. C., 83, 254
Terry, R. C., 191, 212
Thakur, G., 245
Tharion, W. J., 426
Tharp, L. R., 313
Tharp, R. G., 379
Thayer, R. E., 253
Theberge, N., 333
Thelwell, R. C., 80, 81
Theobald, G., 315
Theodorakis, Y., 257
There's No Question, 392
Thiel, A., 336
Thoennes, N., 214
Thomas, D., 212
Thomas, F., 392
Thomas, J., 328
Thomas, P. R., 257
Thompson, B., 331
Thompson, H. S., 304
Thoren, C., 316, 317
Thorne, A., 179–180
Thorngren, C. M., 335, 377
Thornton, K. M., 143–144, 146
Thornton, N., 143–144, 146
Throop, W., 134
Thurstone, L. L., 257
Tickner, A., 279
Timms, K. E., 364
Tippett, L. J., 98, 110
Titley, R. W., 102
Titus, L. J., 174
Titus, T. G., 254
Tjaden, P., 214
Tkachuk, G. A., 417
Toch, H., 215
Tofler, I. R. K., 360
Tombor, E., 251
Tomporowski, R. D., 412, 413
Torgan, C., 318
Toufexis, A., 300, 302
Tremblay, J., 412
Triandis, H. C., 257, 409
Triplett, N., 172
Troppmann, R., 376

Troxell, J. R., 297
True, S., 377, 390, 391
Tubbs, M. E., 142
Tuckman, B., 160
Tuffey, S., 80, 81, 397
Turk, J. C., 337
Turner, R. M., 90
Tutko, T. A., 251, 381
Tutweiler, R. W., 391
Tutwiler, R. W., 390
Twenge, J. M., 325
Twombly, W., 44
Tyleshevski, F., 363

Udry, E. M., 396, 397
Underwood, J., 433, 434
Unsteady Ground, 377

Vaccaro, R., 136, 284
Vagg, P., 249
Vallerand, R., 254
Valois, P., 407
Vancil, M., 376
Van Dalen, D., 27, 32
Van Raalte, J. L., 18, 19, 20, 136, 298, 426
Van Schoyck, R., 254
van Stavel, R., 415
Varca, P., 175, 203
Vare, R., 311
Vaughan, G., 47
Vaz, E., 212
Veach, T. L., 318
Veale de Coverley, D. M. W., 423
Vealey, R. S., 82, 83, 84, 110, 141, 252, 253, 396, 397
Vernacchia, R., 293
Verner, J. P., 279
Vernon, R., 434
Veschi, R., 430
Vetere, V., 212
Vevera, M., 74, 75
Vickers, J., 324
Villiger, J., 332
Vlaminkx, J., 287
Volkamer, N., 203
von Baeyer, C., 146
Vos Strache, C., 153
Voy, R. O., 301
Vukosav, Z., 285

Wagemaker, H., 424
Wagner, M. B., 431
Wagner, N. N., 297
Wagner, W., 317
Waite, B. T., 21
Waite, R., 82
Walberg, J. L., 336
Waldstreicher, J., 423
Walker, M. R., 179–180
Walkey, F. H., 395
Wallace, A., 410
Walley, R. B., 362
Walsh, J., 382
Wang, Y., 419
Wankel, L. M., 174, 346, 347
Wann, D. L., 18, 81, 134, 180, 333
Ward, E. A., 136
Ward, A., 419
Ward, J. A., 431
Ward, T. A., 212
Warren, A., 396
Warwick-Evans, L., 254

Watkins, B., 359
Watkins, C. E., 20
Webb, G., 337
Webb, J., 316
Webb, W. M., 433, 434
Webster, E., 283
Weese, W. J., 169
Weiberg, S., 378
Weinberg, A., 305
Weinberg, R. S., 72, 75, 80, 81, 99, 100, 101, 109, 121, 128, 129, 143, 158, 219, 294, 305, 327, 392, 424
Weiner, B., 115–117, 119, 131
Weiner, R., 151
Weinhold, R. A., 19
Weir, T., 273
Weiss, M. R., 76, 294, 326, 344, 346, 347, 349, 350
Welch, M., 215
Wells, A., 424
Wells, G. L., 195
Wells, M. J., 364
Weltman, A., 424
Weltman, G., 285
Wessels, H., 89
Wesson, M. J., 148
Westcott, W., 404
Whatta Woman, 323
What They Say, 378
Whelan, J. P., 22, 101
Whipple, I. T., 410
Whitcomb, D., 186
White, C., 390
Whiteside, J. A., 364
Whitney, K., 123
Whorton, J. C., 30
Wickland, R., 174
Wicks, J., 410
Widmeyer, W. M., 167
Widmeyer, W. N., 162, 164, 165, 166, 213
Widom, C. S., 206
Wieberg, S., 312, 313
Wieselberg-Bell, N., 428
Wiggins, D., 264
Wilberger, J. E., 209
Wilkinson, C., 373
Wilkinson, M., 167
Willard, N., 281
Williams, A., 406
Williams, J., 199, 244
Williams, J. M., 105, 106, 111, 163–164, 167, 218, 219, 296, 328, 392
Williams, K. D., 161
Williams, L. D., 333
Williams, L. R. T., 244
Williams, P., 431
Williams, R., 243, 269, 406, 410
Williamson, N., 323
Williard, M. J., 219
Willis, J. D., 142, 329
Wilson, D., 197
Wilson, D. L., 173
Winder, P., 245
Winning Associates 1978, 102
Wirth, V., 304
Witschi, J., 317
Wolf, F. M., 431
Wolf, S. L., 93
Wolko, K. L., 61
Wolpe, J., 92

Women's Sports and Fitness 1998, 317
Wong, G. M., 312
Wooden, J., 359, 384
Woodman, T., 79
Woodman, W. F., 327
Woods, D. J., 66
Woolfolk, R. L., 94, 98, 110
Woolum, J., 323
Worchel, S., 161
Working Your Nerves, 378
Worthy, M., 272
Wrightsman, R. S., 259
Wrisberg, C. A., 99
Wulf, S., 390
Wulfert, E., 61

Wyrick, W., 310, 317, 318
Wysocki, T., 65

Yalouris, N., 28, 30, 31
Yamaguchi, H., 157
Yates, A., 335, 423
Yaeger, D., 222
Yalouris, N., 38
Yeager, R., 208, 215
Yesalis, C. E., 300, 302
Yetman, N. R., 270, 392
Yiannakis, A., 286
Yoakum, M., 426, 428
Yordy, G. A., 409
Young, N., 32
Youngstedt, S. D., 406

Youssef, Z., 243, 269
Yukelson, D., 158, 327

Zaccaro, S. J., 161
Zaharieva, E., 316, 317
Zaichkowsky, L. D., 15–17, 94, 108, 245, 433, 434
Zajonc, R. R., 172–173
Zander, A., 163
Zarevski, P., 285
Zawacki, R. M., 371
Zawitz, M. W., 186, 214
Zeigler 1973a, 26
Zelhart, P. E., 150, 152
Zettle, R. D., 61
Zhang, J. J., 157

Ziegler, S. G., 255
Zillman, D., 180, 201–203, 202
Zimbardo, P., 199
Zimmerman, V., 396, 397
Zinn, M. B., 334
Zinsser, N., 105, 106, 111
Zitzelsberger, L., 101
Zolotic, S., 285
Zoob, I., 279, 285
Zook, S. K., 431
Zuckerman, M., 279, 285, 329–330
Zumbo, B. D., 147

Subject Index

AAASP. *See* Association for the Advancement of Applied Sport Psychology
AAHPERD. *See* American Alliance for Health, Physical Education, Recreation and Dance
AAP. *See* American Academy of Pediatrics
AAS. *See* Anabolic-androgenic steroids
AAU. *See* Amateur Athletic Union
ABA design, 61
Ability antecedents, 115–116
Academic sport psychologist, 7–8
Achievement, need for, 127–130
Achievement by proxy, 360
ACSI. *See* Athletic Coping Skills Inventory
ACSM. *See* American College of Sports Medicine
Activation–Deactivation Adjective Checklist (AD–ACL), 83, 253
Actual leader, 155
Adams, Cindy (Dr.), 19
Addiction to Running Scale, 424
Adonis complex, 300
Adrenaline, 73. *See also* Epinephrine
Aerobic exercise, 413
Affective cycle theory, 296
African-American athletes
  male sprinters, 274
  success of, 266–273
African-American coaches, 392–393
Age, exercise and, 429
Age of Chivalry, 35–36
Aggression
  adaptive and maladaptive, 188
  biological theories of, 191
  in boxing, 208
  defined, 186–188
  direct external rewards for, 198–199
  direct and indirect, 188
  displaced, 188
  factors promoting, 195–203
  in football, 208–210
  hockey and, 210
  hostile, 189
  instrumental, 189
  measurement of, 194–203
  physical factors and, 195–198
  physical and verbal, 188
  provoked and unprovoked, 188
  psychological factors and, 198–199
  psychosocial theories of, 191–193
  sociological consideration, 199–203
  sociological explanations, 193–194
  sport-related variables affecting, 203–204
  steroid use and, 302–303
  violence and, 190–191
Agoraphobia, 89
Agreeableness, 227
AIAW. *See* Association for Intercollegiate Athletics for Women

AIMS. *See* Athletic Identity Measurement Scale
AIS. *See* Australian Institute of Sport
Alcohol abuse, 303, 305
Alcoholic beverages at sporting events, 217
Alexander the Great, 31
All-cause mortality, 406
Allen, George, 377
Alomar, Roberto, 273, 275
Alomar, Santos (Sandy), 275
Alou, Felipe, 275
Alou, Jesus, 275
Alou, Matty, 275
Alou, Moises, 273
Alvarez, Wilson, 273
Alzado, Lyle, 302
Amateur Athletic Union (AAU), 42
Amenorrhea, 335
American Academy of Pediatrics (AAP), 365
American Alliance for Health, Physical Education, Recreation and Dance (AAHPERD), 9, 45, 315, 344–345
American Athletic Association of the Deaf, 295
American College of Obstetricians and Gynecologists (ACOG), 318
American College of Sports Medicine (ACSM), 9, 302, 365
American Journal of Psychology, 46, 47
American Medical Association, on boxing, 208
American Psychological Association (APA), 9, 15, 50
  Standards for Educational and Psychological Tests and Manuals, 82, 252
American Sport Education Program (ASEP), 388
AMI. *See* Athletic Motivation Inventory
Amphetamines, 299–300
Anabolic-androgenic steroids (AAS), 300–302
Anabolic effects of AAS, 301
Anabolic Steroids Control Act (ASCA), 302
Anaerobic exercise, 413
Andersen and Williams theory, 296–297
Androgenic effects of AAS, 301
Androgyny, psychological, 330–332
Ankle sprains, 296
Anorexia, 335
ANS. *See* Autonomic nervous system
Anti-asthma drugs, 304
Antonelli, Feruccio, 8
Anxiety
  competitive performance and, 75–77
  competitive trait, 356
  defined, 72
  determinants of, 72–74
  exercise and, 414–416
  psychological measures of, 82–84
  state, 74
  trait, 75

See also Anxiety and arousal
Anxiety and arousal
  neurophysiological mechanisms, 72–75
  psychological mechanisms, 74–75
Aoki, Isao, 276
APA. *See* American Psychological Association
Aparicio, Luis, 275
Application function, 7
Applied sport psychologist, 8
APS. *See* Australian Psychological Society
Aristotle, 29
Armstrong, George, 277
Arousal
  defined, 72
  determinants of, 72–74
  effects on competitive performance, 77–79
  optimal levels, 78
  physiological measures of, 80–82
Arousal. *See also* Anxiety and arousal
ASCA. *See* Anabolic Steroids Control Act
ASEP. *See* American Sport Education Program
Ashford, Emmit, 266
ASQ. *See* Attributional Style Questionnaire
Assessment, psychological. *See* Psychological assessment
Association for the Advancement of Applied Sport Psychology (AAASP), 4, 8–9, 15–18, 50, 365
Association for Intercollegiate Athletics for Women (AIAW), 327
Athens, early, 27–28, 30–31
Athletes
  audience effects on, 173
  cheerleaders as, 337
  collegiate, 432–433
  desirable practice behavior, 56
  with disabilities, 294–296
  drug abusing, 298–305
  female. *See* Female sport experience
  impaired student, 294–296
  injured, 296–298
  minority. *See* Minority athletes
  pursuit of excellence, 7
  youth. *See* Youth sport
  See also Players
Athletic Coping Skills Inventory (ACSI), 256–257
Athletic Footwear Association (AFA) research, 344–345, 348, 350–351
Athletic Identity Measurement Scale (AIMS), 426
Athletic Motivation Inventory (AMI), 251–252
Athletic performance, state anxiety and, 74
Athletic retirement, 432–434
Atlanta Braves, 3
ATPA. *See* Attitudes Toward Physical Activity Scale
A-trait conditions, 75

Attentional conflict, 174
Attentional control, training procedures for, 255
Attitude measurement, 257–259
    Likert scales, 257–258
    Semantic Differential Scales, 258
    Thurstone scales, 258–259
Attributional Style Questionnaire (ASQ), 146–147
Attribution theory, 115–127
    cognitive model, 115–120
    female athletes and, 327–330
    functional model, 125–126
    future directions, 126–127
    social cognitive models, 120–125
Audience effects, 172–181
    home advantage, 175–179
    interactive, 174
Australian Institute of Sport (AIS), 9
Australian Psychological Society (APS), 9
Authoritarian personality, 381–382
Autonomic nervous system (ANS), 73
Aversive stimulus, 188

BAAGI. See Bredemeier Athletic Aggression Inventory
Backward chain, 64
Bagley, Larry, 279
Baker, Thane, 274, 431
Ball Four (Bouton), 299
Baltimore Orioles, 3
Barkley, Charles, 159
Barnes, Randy, 299
Baron de Coubertin, Pierre de Fredy, 43, 310
Baseball
    Civil War and, 42
    drug abuse in professional, 299
    goals for tasks in, 144
    Little League, 342–344. See also Little League baseball
    salaries in major league, 3
    Test of Attentional and Interpersonal Style for, 254
    trait anxiety and, 76
Baseline, 59
Basketball
    assessing performance in, 145
    goals for tasks in, 144
    locus-of-control study for, 134
    salaries in professional, 3
    use of imagery in, 99–100
    use of visuomotor behavioral rehearsal in, 102–103
Basking in reflected glory (BIRG), 175, 179–180
BASES. See British Association for Sport and Exercise Sciences
Becerra, Cheri, 277
Beecher, Catharine, 45
Begay, Notah, 277
Behavior
    aggressive. See Aggression
    exercise, 409
    expressive, 330
    guidelines for youth sport coaching, 389
    instrumental, 330
    interactional model of, 229
    leadership, 154
    reactive coaching, 386
    role-related, 225
    spontaneous coaching, 386
Behavioral coaching techniques, 56–61

football blocks and, 58
    gymnastics and, 60–61
    track and, 60
Behavioral contracting, 411
Behavioral principles
    classical conditioning, 54–55
    cognitive learning, 67
    operant learning, 55–67
Behaviorism, 46, 226–228
Behavior theory, 152
Behavior therapy, counterconditioning model in, 91
Bellan, Esteban, 273
Bem Sex-Role Inventory (BSRI), 285, 330–332
Benard, Marvin, 273
Berra, Yogi, 105
Beta-blockers, 304
Bias, attributions subject to, 115
Bicycle–impotency relationship, 407
Big five personality traits, 227
Binet, Alfred, 46, 232
Biofeedback training, 93–94
Bird, Larry, 3
BIRG. See Basking in reflected glory
Birth order effects, 286
Blankers-Koen, Fannie, 314
Blood doping, 302–303
Blood pressure, 80
Blue laws, 44
Bobick, Dwayne, 67
Body composition, 405
Body contact, 211
Book of Sports, 41
Boosters, collegiate, 372–373
Boosting, 302–303
Borderline violence, 211
Boredom susceptibility (BS), 286
Borzov, Valery, 274
Boucha, Henry, 211
Bouton, Jim, 299
Bowerman, Bill, 404
Bowling, skittles, 41
Boxing
    African Americans in early, 265
    aggression in, 208
    Hamed vs. Sanchez, 207
Boys' Club, 342
Boy Scouts, 342
BPS. See British Psychological Society
Brain, structures for arousal and anxiety, 73
Brashears, Donald, 211
Breathing, as psych-up strategy, 108
Bredemeier Athletic Aggression Inventory (BAAGI), 195
Brisco, Valerie, 317
British Association for Sport and Exercise Sciences (BASES), 9
British Psychological Society (BPS), 9
Brown, Larry, 3
Bryant, Paul "Bear," 369, 371
BS. See Boredom susceptibility
BSRI. See Bem Sex-Role Inventory
Bulimia, 335
Bulletin boards, as psych-up strategy, 109
Bull grappling, 26
Burke, Glenn, 335
Burnout
    causes of, 393–397
    coaching, 393–399
    cognitive-affective model of, 393
    effects of, 397–398

measure of, 395
    perfectionism and, 397
    preventing, 398–399
Burns, Tom, 265
Byrd, William, III, 41
Byrdsong, Ricky, 378
Byzantine Empire, 34–35

Caffeine, 304
California F-Scale, 381–382
California Psychological Inventory, 330–332
Cambria, Joe, 275
Campfire Girls, 45
"Camptown Races," 41
Canadian Association for Health, Physical Education, Recreation and Dance (CAHPERD), 9
Canadian National Certification Program (CNCP), 388
Canadian Society for Psychomotor Learning and Sport Psychology (CSPLSP), 9
Capriati, Jennifer, 358
Cardiorespiratory endurance, 405
Carrasquel, Chico, 275
Carroll, Pete, 53
Carruth, Rae, 214
Castro, Fidel, 275
Catastrophe theory, 81
Catharsis hypothesis, 191–193
Causal antecedents for behavior, 115–116
Causal attributions, 115
Causal Dimension Scale (CDS), 119, 126
Causal Dimension Scale II (CDSII), 120, 126
CDS. See Causal Dimension Scale
Centering state, 425
Centers for Disease Control
    on healthy individuals, 408
    on physical fitness, 404–405
Center for the Study of Sport in Society, 9
Cepeda, Orlando, 275
Cerebral cortex, 72
Certification, 15–16, 21
Certified consultant–AAASP, 16
CET. See Coach Effectiveness Training
Chaining, 64
Challenge, 396
Chamberlain, Darren A., 302
Chaney, John, 374
Chang, Michael, 276
Chariot drivers, 32–33
Chariot racing, 34
Cheerleaders, 337
Children
    trait anxiety in, 75–76
    violence in media and, 200–201
    See also Youth sport
Chin, Tiffany, 276
Chinese civilization, ancient, sports in, 26
Chivalry, Age of, 35–36
Choking under pressure, 175–177, 180–181
Chow, Amy, 276
Christianity, early, sports and, 35
Christie, Linford, 299
Civil Rights Act of 1964, 44
Civil War, 42, 264
Classical conditioning, 46, 54–55
    counterconditioning, 90–92
    extinction, 89–90
    techniques, 88–92
Clemento, Roberto, 275
Cleveland Indians, 3

CNCP. *See* Canadian National Certification Program
Coach Effectiveness Training (CET), 388
Coaches
  African-American, 392–393
  changing behavior of, 62–65
  eating disorders and, 338
  female, 390–393
  good, 373–375
  leadership behavior by, 157
  personality of, 381–382
  slogans of, 380
  roles of, 371–373
  sport psychologist and, 379–381
  sports violence and, 217–218, 220–221
  team cohesion and, 159–160
  youth sport, 349
  See also Coaching
Coaching
  advantages and disadvantages of, 375–378
  communication and, 379–380
  good, 373–375
  pressures of, 378
  tenure in, 376
  youth sport and, 386–390
  See also Coaches
Coaching Behavior Assessment System (CBAS), 386–387
Coaching burnout, 393–399
Coaching techniques, behavioral, 56–61
Coactive sports, 162
Cocaine, 303, 305
Cockfights, Civil War and, 42
Coefficient alpha, 235
Cognitive–affective model of burnout, 393
Cognitive appraisal theory, 296
Cognitive attributional model, 115–120
Cognitive effects of exercise, 412–414
Cognitive learning
  cognitive control, 104–106
  defined, 67
  hypnosis, 106–107
  imagery, 98–102
  Nesmeth example, 67
  psych-up strategies, 108–109
  stress inoculation training (SIT), 103–104
  visuomotor behavioral rehearsal (VBMR), 102–104
  yoga, zen, and transcendental meditation, 107–108
Cognitive evaluation theory, 128
Cognitive–Somatic Anxiety Questionnaire (CSAQ), 83
Cognitive state anxiety, 74–75
Cohesion, 158
  life cycle model of, 160
  See also Team cohesion
COI. *See* Competitive Orientation Inventory
Collective efficacy, 123
College Physical Education Association (CPEA), 45
Collegiate athletes, eligibility and, 432–433
Colonial America, sports in, 40–41
Commitment, 396
Commitment perspective, 395
Commitment to Running Scale, 422
Communication process, 379
Competence, 17
Competence-oriented participants, 348
Competition
  defined, 354
  product or process?, 354–355

senior citizens and, 431–434
stress and, 355–356
women and, 327
Competitive Orientation Inventory (COI), 141
Competitive performance
  anxiety and, 75–77
  arousal and, 77–79
Competitive State Anxiety Inventory (CSAI), 83, 253, 337
Competitive State Anxiety Inventory (CSAIQ), 356
Competitive State Anxiety Inventory-2 (CSAI-2), 83–84, 253–254, 257
Competitive stress, 355–356
  antecedents of, 358
  cognitive aspects of, 357–358
Competitive trait anxiety (CTA), 356
Compulsive jogging, 423
Concern for the welfare of others, 18
Conditioned response (CR), 54
Conditioned stimulus (CS), 54, 88
Confidence, 105
Connolly, Olga, 314
Conscientiousness, 227
Conservative response style, 236
Constitutional theory, 225
Construct validity, 234
Contagion theory, 193
Content validity, 234
Continuous reinforcement, 66
Control, 396
Controlled Repression–Sensitization Scale (CRS), 298
Convergence theory, 193–194
Coop, Richard (Dr.), 18
Cooper, Keith, 200
Coping Strategies Questionnaire (CSQ), 298
Cordero, Will, 214
CORF. *See* Cutting off reflected failure
Cortisol, 81
Costin, Michael, 187
Counterconditioning, 90–92
Countering, 105–106
Courier, Jim, 19
Course of Calisthenics for Young Ladies (Stowe), 45
Courson, Steve, 302
CPEA. *See* College Physical Education Association
CR. *See* Conditioned response
Creatine, 304
Credentialing, 15–17
Crime statistics, 186
Criminal violence, 212
Criterion validity, 234
Crowding, sports violence and, 197–198
CRS. *See* Controlled Repression–Sensitization Scale
Cruz, Cirilo (Tommy), 275
Cruz, Enrique, 275
Cruz, Hector, 275
Cruz, Jose, 275
Cruz, Jose, Jr., 275
CS. *See* Conditioned stimulus
CSAI. *See* Competitive State Anxiety Inventory
CSAI-2. *See* Competitive State Anxiety Inventory-2
CSAIQ. *See* Competitive State Anxiety Inventory
CSAQ. *See* Cognitive–Somatic Anxiety Questionnaire

CSPLSP. *See* Canadian Society for Psychomotor Learning and Sport Psychology
CTA. *See* Competitive trait anxiety
Cutting off reflected failure (CORF), 180
Czyz, Bobby, 186

Dallas Cowboys, 3, 150
Daly, Chuck, 378
Daly, John, 18, 214, 299
Dangerfield, Rodney, 210–211
Davis, Glenn, 274
Davis, Hal, 274
Deindividuation, 199
Deliberate practice, 295
Deluca, Rande, 278
Demographic/Cognitive Appraisal Questionnaire, 396
Denial, 296
Denver Broncos, 150
Depression
  exercise and, 415–417
  MMPI scale, 242
Descartes René, 138
Determined coping, 296
Dewey, John, 46
Diaulos, 28
Dickey, Curtis, 266
Dickinson, Amy, 344
Differential reinforcement, 59
Dihigo, Martin, 275
Diocles, 32–33
Dis. *See* Disinhibition
Disabilities, athletes with, 294–296
Disabled Sports Organizations (DSOs), 295
Disabled Sports USA, 295
Discounting principle, 129
Discourses, The (Machiavelli), 382
Displaced aggression, 188
Dispositional attributions, 115
Dissociative running strategies, 247–248
Distance running, dissociative strategies in, 247–248
Distraction hypothesis, 416
Distress, 296
Distributed practice, 65–66
Diuretics, 304
Dobler, Conrad, 190
Dolichos, 28, 29
Drive theories, 172–174
Drug abuse, 298–305
  blood doping, 302–303
  boosting, 302–303
  prohibited substances, 300–302
  restricted drugs, 303–305
Drugs, classes subject to restriction, 303–305
Drug testing, 302
DSOs. *See* National Disabled Sports Organizations
Dual relationships, 17
Duval, David, 2, 19
Dwarf Athletic Association of America, 295
Dysfunctionally aggressive play, 175

EA. *See* Efficiency average
Eating disorders, 335–338
  cheerleaders and, 337
EBC. *See* Effective behavioral coaching
Ectomorph, 225
Educational Amendments Act of 1972, Title IX, 44
Educational and Industrial Testing Service (EDITS), 250

Education function, 6–7
Edwards, Jonathan, 3
Edwards Personal Preference schedule (EPPS), 279
EEG. *See* Electroencephalography
Effective behavioral coaching (EBC), 56
Efficacy expectancy, 121
Efficiency average (EA), 63
Effort antecedents, 116
Egyptian civilization, ancient, sports in, 26
Eisenhower, Dwight D. (President), 44, 342, 344
Ekblom, Bjorn (Dr.), 302–303
Electroencephalography (EEG), 80
Electromyography (EMG), 80, 93–94
    feedback, hypnotism vs., 107
Eligibility
collegiate, 432–433
    NCAA, 247
Elite athletes, 292–294
Elite Distance Runner Project, 247
Elite performance, in youth athletes, 358–360
Elway, John, 150–151, 158
EMAS. *See* Endler Multidimensional Anxiety Scales (EMAS)
Emergent norm theory, 194
EMG. *See* Electromyography
Empirical validity, 233
Endler Multidimensional Anxiety Scales (EMAS), 84
Endocrine system, 73
Endomorph, 225
Endorphin hypothesis, 416
Enduring personality traits, 242–246
Energizing imagery, 108
Enlightenment, 36–37
Entrapment, 396–396
EPI. *See* Eysenck Personality Inventory (EPPS)
Epinephrine, 73, 81. *See* also Adrenalin
EPQ. *See* Eysenck Personality Questionnaire
ES. *See* Experience *Seeking*
Escobar, Andres, 187
Ethical principals, 17–18
Ethics of testing, 236–237
Etruscans, 33
Euphoric sensation, 425
Euripides, 29
European Federation of Sport Psychology (FEPSAC), 365
Evaluative apprehension, 173–174
Ewing, Martha, 345
Exceptional performance, research on, 292–295
Exercise, 405
    aerobic, 413
    age and, 429
    anaerobic, 413
    anxiety and, 414–416
    cognitive effects of, 412–414
    depression and, 415–417
    Group Environment Questionnaire and, 166–167
    mood and, 414–417
    as psych-up strategy, 108
    senior citizens and, 430–434
Exercise adherence, 407–412
    exercise adherence, 408
        improving, 410–412
        negative predictors of, 408–410
Exercise behavior, models for analyzing, 409
Exercise Beliefs Questionnaire (EBQ), 424
Exercise dependence, 423
Existential drift, 425

Expectancy of negative affect, 357–358
Expectancy of negative evaluation, 357
Experience *Seeking* (ES), 286
Explanatory style, 143–147
Expressive behavior, 330
External locus of control, 134
Extinction, 89–90
Extraversion, 227, 410
Extrinsic motivation, 128
Eysenck Personality Inventory (EPI), 231, 245–246, 279
Eysenck Personality Questionnaire (EPQ), 245–246

Face validity, 234
Fading, 62
Failure
    attributions for, 126
    cutting off, 180
    formula for assessing, 115–120
    history of, 358
    mastery-oriented attitude toward, 67
    to operationalize, 230
Faking bad, 230, 236
Faking good, 230, 236
Faldo, Nick, 18
Fans, coaches' dealings with, 372
Faulty generalizations, 231
Faustian philosophy, 301
Fear of success (FOS), 329–330
Feherty, David, 18
Fehr, Rick, 19
Female athletes, violence among, 214
Female athletic triad, 335
Female coaches, 390–393
Females, aggression in, 191
Female sport experience
    brief history, 310–315
    contemporary forces, 315
    eating disorders and, 335–338
    homophobia and, 334–335
    media and, 333–334
    modern time line, 314
    physiological dimension, 315–319
    psychological variables, 327–332
    sport socialization and, 323–327
    time line of older sentiments, 311
Title IX legislation, 311–315
See also Women
FEPSAC. *See* European Federation of Sport Psychology
Fernandez, Mary Joe, 19
Fiedler's contingency model, 152–153
Figure skaters
    Olympic/USA National Championship, 293
    Henie, Sonja, 309
Fine, Alan, 18
Finley, Charles O., 159
Fischer, Scott, 282
Fitness
    youth sport and, 347
See also Physical fitness
Fitness movement, 7
Fives, 41
Fleisher, Bruce, 2
Flexibility, 405
Flooding, 889
Flow, 425
Fontinato, Lou, 212
Football
    aggression in, 208–210
    assessing performance in, 145

    blocks, behavioral coaching techniques and, 58
    drug abuse in professional, 299
    as fun, 375
    goals for tasks in, 144
    team leaders in, 158
    violence in, 202
    See also National Football League
Football players
    biofeedback training for, 93
    personality of, 243
Forbes, David, 187, 211
Forward chain, 64
Fosbury, Dick, 90
Fosbury Flop, 90
FOSS. *See* Objective Fear of Success Scale
Fowler, John (Bud), 264
Freud, Sigmund, 46, 192, 226
Frisch's hypothesis, 316
Frustration–aggression hypothesis, 192
Fun
    football as, 375
    youth sport and, 346, 349
Functional attributional model, 125–126
Functionalism, 46
Functional leadership model, 154–155
Functionally aggressive play, 175
Funeral games, 27
"Futile caution," 172–173

Gagliardi, John, 375
Galen, 29
Galton, Francis (Sir), 46
Galvanic Skin Response (GSR), 343, 356
Games, 6
Gay Olympian: The Life and Death of Dr. Tom Waddell (Schaap), 335
Gender differences, 328
Gender marking, 334
General Anxiety Scales, 82
GEQ. See Group Environment Questionnaire
Giamatti, A. Bartlett, 150
Gibson, Althea, 266
Gilbert, Brad, 18
Girl Scouts, 45
Gladiatorial combat, 33
Goal achievement model, 123
Goals
    setting performance, 142–143
    SMART, 143
Goal setting, applications of, 146
Goal-setting theory, 143
"Goff," 41
Goldstein, Irwin (Dr.), 407
Golf
    anxiety levels and, 75
    cognitive learning and, 67
    goals for tasks in, 144
    thinking and learning to play, 105
Gonzalez, Mike, 275
Good coaching, 373–375
Gooden, Dwight, 299
"Good old boy" network, 392
Gordon, Jeff, 3
Greece
    ancient, female sport experience in, 310
    sports in ancient, 27–31
Greek Parthenon, 25
Gregg, Forrest, 209
Gretzky, Wayne, 99
Griffith, Coleman R., 50, 370–371
Grim asceticism, 335–336

Group cohesion, 158–167
  conceptual model of, 166
  See also Team cohesion
Group Environment Questionnaire (GEQ),
  164–167
Group integration, 165
Grove City v. Bell, 312
GSR. See Galvanic Skin Response
Guilford–Zimmerman Temperament Survey,
  330–332
Guthrie, Edwin, 46
Guthrie, Janet, 314
Gymnastics
  behavioral coaching techniques and, 60–61
  eating disorders and, 335–336
  stress inoculation training in, 104
Gymnasts, Olympic, 293

Hall, G. Stanley, 46
Hall, Rob, 281
Hamed, Prince NaSeem, 207
Handball, fives, 41
Hang gliding, 280–282
Hansen, Doug, 281
Hardiness, 396
Harpastum, 32
Harris, Andy, 282
Harris, Del, 378
Harris, Dorothy, 314
Haixia, Zheng, 276
Hayes, Woody, 311
Hays, Sue Pirtle, 317
HBM. See Health Belief Model
Health Belief Model (HBM), 409
Heart rate (HR), 80
Hegemony, 333
Henie, Sonja, 309, 314
Henrich, Christy, 336, 338
Heraclitus, 342
Heraean Games, 310, 312
Hereditary Genius (Galton), 46
HGH. *See* Human growth hormone
High jump, 90
High-risk-sport, 277–287
  correlates of participation, 285–287
  hang gliding, 280–281
  rock climbing, 281–284
  scuba diving, 284–285
  sport parachuting/sky diving, 278–280
Hispanic athletes, 273–276
History
  of female sport experience, 310–315
  of physical education, 45–46
  of psychology, 46–47
  of sport psychology, 47–50
  of youth sport, 342–344
History of sports
  ancient Near East and Asia, 26–27
  Greeks, 27–31
  Middle Ages, 34–36
  Renaissance and Enlightenment, 36–37
  Romans, 31–34
  United States, 40–45
HIV/AIDS, physical fitness and, 406
Hoch, Scott, 19, 180
Hockey
  aggression and, 210
  goals for tasks in, 144
  illegal actions, 213
  shinny, 41
  use of imagery in, 99
  violence in, 201

See also National Hockey League
Hogan, Ben, 67
Hogensen v. Williamson, 187
Holland, Terry, 378
Home/away factor, aggression and, 203
Home advantage, 175–179
Home disadvantage, 177
Homer, 27, 150
Homeric Greece, sports in, 27
Homologous reproduction, 392
Homophobia, 334–335
Homosexuality, 334–335
Hooliganism, 199–200
Hostile aggression, 189
Houston Astros, 3
Howard, Jimmy, 266
Howe, Gordie, 212
HR. See Heart rate
Hull, Clark, 46
Hull–Spence drive theory, 172
Human growth hormone (HGH), 304
Humanism, 46, 226
Hypnosis, 106–107
Hypochondriasis, 242, 243
Hypomania, 242
Hypothalamus, 73
Hysteria, 242

Iceberg Profile, 246–247, 283
Iliad, 27, 150
Image-conscious socializers, 348
Imagery, 98–102
  cultivating use of, 101
  defined, 98
  energizing, 108
  internal vs. external, 101
  research not supportive of, 99–100
  stress inoculation training, 98–99
Impaired student athletes, 294–296
Implosive therapy, 89–90
Incomplete occupational socialization, 391
Individual attractions to the group, 165
Individual game performance
  state anxiety and, 79
  trait anxiety and, 79
Individualized zones of optimal functioning
  (IZOF) theory, 80
Industrial/organizational (I/O) psychology, 14
Informational bias, 115
Injured athletes, 296–298
Injuries
  exercise adherence and, 410
  of NFL defensive back, 210
Inside Sports, 334
Instinct theory, 192
Institute for the Study of Youth Sport (YSI),
  386, 388
Instrumental aggression, 189
Instrumental behavior, 330
Integrity, 17
Interactional model of behavior, 228–229
Interactive sports, 162
Intercollegiate Athletic Association, 43
Intermittent reinforcement, 66
Internal consistency, 235
Internal locus of control, 134, 408
International Olympic Committee (IOC)
  drug testing by, 302
  on performance-enhancing substances, 299,
  303
International Society for Sport Psychology
  (ISSP), 8, 302, 365

Intimate violence, 214
Intrapsychic model, 226
Intrinsic motivation, 128
Inverted-U hypothesis, 77–79
  alternatives to, 80–81
  temperature and aggression, 195–196
Invest in Yourself, 433
IOC. *See* International Olympic Committee
IPC scale, Levenson's, 135–136
Irabu, Hideki, 276
Irwin, Hale, 2
Irwin, Juno Stover, 317
ISSP. *See* International Society for Sport
  Psychology
Ivansevic, Goran, 18
IYSI. *See* Institute for the Study of Youth Sport
IZOF theory. See Individualized zones of
  optimal functioning (IZOF) theory

Jackson, John Hughlings, 98
Jacobi, Joe, 209
Jacobs, Andrew (Dr.), 19
Jacobs, Franklin, 266
Jagr, Jaromir, 3
James, William, 46, 138
Jockeys, early African-American, 265
Jogging
  compulsive, 423
  See also Running
Johnson, Ben, 299
Johnson, Doc, 278
Johnson, Jack, 265
Johnson, Lawrence, 269
Johnson, Michael, 2
Jones, Marion, 241
Journals, major sport, 5
Joust, 35–36
Joyner, Florence Griffith, 299, 334

Kania, Karen, 317
Kant, Immanuel, 360
Kazankina, Tatyana, 317
Kennedy, Ted, 212
Kerns, Hubie, 274
Kerrigan, Nancy, 19
Kinesics, 379
King, Billie Jean, 314, 335
King, Martin Luther, Jr., 150
Kiraly, Karch, 3
Klemmer, Grover, 274
Knee injuries, 296
Knight, Bobby, 371
Knight, Phil, 404
Knight, Ray, 361
Knutson, Harold, 283
Kopay, Dave, 335
Koublova, Zdena, 314
Kovalenko, Olga, 317
Kramer, Jerry, 209
Kristiansen, Ingrid, 317
Kroll's personality performance pyramid,
  292–294
Krzyzewski, Mike, 378
Kuder–Richardson reliability, 235
Kupchak, Mitch, 188
Kush, Frank, 371
Kwan, Michelle, 113, 276

Lacrosse, goals for tasks in, 144
LaMonte, Bob, 433
Landry, Tom, 150
Lapchick, Richard, 9

Lawn tennis, 39
Law School Admission Test (LSAT), 231
LBDQ. See Leader Behavior Description
    Questionnaire
Leader Behavior Description Questionnaire
    (LBDQ), 152
Leadership, 150–158
    evaluation of research, 158
    multidimensional model of sport, 155–158
    player, 158
    theories of, 151–155. See also Leadership
        theories
    See also Sport leadership
Leadership Scale for Sports (LSS), 156
Leadership theories
    behavior theory, 151–152
    Fiedler's contingency model, 152–153
    functional model, 154–155
    life cycle theory, 153–154
    path–goal theory, 153
    trait theory, 151
League standing, aggression and, 203
Learned helplessness, 66–67
Learned optimism, 104
Learning, operant, 55–67
Least preferred coworker (LPC) scale, 152–153
Lee, Sammy (Dr.), 276
Leonard, Sugar Ray, 214
Lesbianism, 334–335
Lett, Leon, 299
Levenson's IPC scale, 135–136
Levy, Marv, 19
Licensure, 15
Life cycle model of cohesion, 160
Life cycle theory, 153–154
Likert scales, 257–258
Limon, Tony, 187
Lindros, Eric, 19
Linear–curvilinear debate, 195–196
Linear model of cohesion, 160
Lister, Richard, 19
Little Girls in Pretty Boxes (Ryan), 360
Little League baseball, 2, 342–344, 356, 387
Little League elbow, 363
Llewellyn, Jack (Dr.), 19
Locke, Bernadette, 314
Locus of control
    current status of, 137
    defined, 134
    Levenson's Multidimensional approach,
        135–136
    Nowicki–Strickland Scale, 136–137
    Rotter's I–E scale, 134–135
Loehr, Jim (Dr.), 18–19
Lombardi, Vince, 186
Longboat, Tom, 277
Longitudinal research, 231
Lopez, Nancy, 317
Lotteries, 411
Louganis, Greg, 335
Louis, Joe, 265
Love, Davis, 19
Lowery, Nick, 19
LSS. See Leadership Scale for Sports
Luck antecedents, 116
Lundberg, George (Dr.), 208
Lutter, Judy Mahle, 314

McCann, Sean (Dr.), 19
McClelland–Atkinson model, 127–128
McCormick, Pat, 317
McEnroe, John, 190
McGill Pain Questionnaire (MPQ), 298

McGuire, Mark, 304
McKenzie, R. Tait (Dr.), 45
McKinney, Steve, 283
McSorley, Marty, 211
MAF. See Motive to avoid failure
Machiavellian personality, 382
Male hegemony, 333
Males athletes, violence against females by,
    214–216
Mallor, George, 282
Manual of Physiology and Calisthenics for Schools
    and Families, A (Stowe), 45
MAP. See Motive to achieve power
Marathon runners, 425–426
Marichal, Juan, 275
Marijuana, 303, 305
Marino, Dan, 151
Marlowe Crowne Social Desirability Scale, 298
Maruyama, Shigeki, 276
MAS. See Motive to achieve success
Mashburn, J. W., 274
Maslach Burnout Inventory (MBI), 393, 395,
    396
Maslow, Abraham, 46, 139–140, 226
Maslow's need hierarchy, 140
Massed practice, 66
Maxwell, Vernon, 378
MBI. See Maslach Burnout Inventory
Measures of temporary states, 246
Media
    female sport experience and, 333–334
    glorification of violence by, 200–201
    image of sport psychology in, 18–19
    Olympic Games and, 15
    sport psychology in, 19
    sports violence and, 218–220
    Super Bowl advertising, 3
Meditation, 107–108, 414
Meichenbaum, Donald, 98–99
Melpomene, 314
Mental Measurement Yearbooks
    (MMY), 259
Mere presence hypothesis, 172
Mesomorph, 225
Metcalfe, Ralph, 274
Miami Marlins, 273
Middle Ages
    Age of Chivalry, 35–36
    Byzantine Empire, 34–35
    Christianity, 35
Miller, Cheryl, 385
Milo of Croton, 30
Minnesota Multiphasic Personality Inventory
    (MMPI), 231–232, 235, 242–243, 279
Minoans, 26–27
Minority athletes
    African-American athletes, 264–266
    Asian-American athletes, 276
    Hispanic athletes, 273–276
    Native-American athletes, 276–277
    racial representation in different sports,
        270–271
Minoso, Orestes (Minnie), 275
Mitchell, Dennis, 299
MMPI. See Minnesota Multiphasic Personality
    Inventory
Modification and attrition theory, 292
Molineaux, Tom, 265
Monoamine hypothesis, 416
Mood
    exercise and, 414–417
    running and, 424
Moon, Warren, 214

Morbid exercising, 423
Morgan, William, 234
Morrow, Bobby, 266, 274
Mortality, all–cause, 406
Morton, Craig, 376
Morup, Dorjee, 282
Most Valuable Player (MVP), 128
Motivation
    attribution theory, 115–127
    explanatory style, 143–147
    extrinsic, 128
    intrinsic, 128
    locus of control, 134–137
    for marathon running, 427
    performance goals and, 142–143
    self theory, 137–141
    sport self-confidence and, 141–142
    what is?, 114–115
    Willis's sport motivation scale, 142
    for youth sport participation, 344–348
Motivational bias, 115
Motivations of Marathoners Scales (MOMS),
    426
Motivator, coach as, 374
Motive to achieve power (MAP), 142
Motive to achieve success (MAS), 142
Motive to avoid failure (MAF), 142
Motives for participation, 346
Motives for withdrawal, 348–349
Movement time (MT), 429
MPQ. See McGill Pain Questionnaire
MPS. See Multidimensional Perfectionism
    Scale
MT. See Movement time
Multidimensional model of sport leadership,
    155–158
Multidimensional Perfectionism Scale (MPS),
    397
Mulvey, Paul, 199
Munoz, Anthony, Jr., 275
Murray, Henry, 127
Muscles, strength and endurance, 405
Music, as psych-up strategy, 108
MVP. See Most Valuable Player

Nabozny v. Barnhill, 187
Najera, Eduardo, 275
Namba, Yasuko, 282
NASC. See Native American Sports Council
NASPSPA. See North American Society for
    the Psychology of Sport and Physical
    Activity
NASSH. See North American Society for
    Sport History
NASSM. See North American Society for
    Sport Management
NASSS. See North American Society for the
    Sociology of Sport
National Alliance for Youth Sports (NAYS),
    388
National Association for Physical Education of
    College Women, 45
National Basketball Association (NBA), 176,
    178, 188, 266, 268, 314
National Collegiate Athletic Association
    (NCAA), 44
    African-American coaches in, 392–393
    female coaches in, 390
    on eligibility, 247
    on "impaired student athletes," 294
    NCAA News, 333
    rules, 160
National Crime Victimization Survey, 186

National Disabled Sports Organizations (DSOs), 295
National Football League (NFL), 3, 179, 202, 209
National Hockey League, 175–176, 179, 212–213
National Youth Sporting Coaches Association (NYSCA) training program, 388
National Youth Sports Program, 346
Native American Sports Council (NASC), 277
Navratilova, Martina, 318, 335
NAYS. See National Alliance for Youth Sports
NCAA. See National Collegiate Athletic Association
Need for achievement, 127
Need hierarchy, Maslow's, 140
Negative affect, expectancy of, 357–358
Negative evaluation, expectancy of, 357
Negative reinforcement, 55, 59
Nelson, Don, 378
Nelson, Larry, 2
NEO Five Factor Inventory (NEO-FFI), 227
NEO Personality Inventory (NEO-PI), 227
Nero, 34
Nesmeth, James (Major), 67
Neurophysiological mechanisms, 72–74
Neuroticism, 227
New York Yankees, 3, 159
NFL Players Association, 433
Nguyen, Dat, 276
Nicknames, for aggressive behavior, 198–199
Nideffer, Robert (Dr.), 14
Nixon, Richard, 44, 344–347
Noise, sports violence and, 197
Nomo, Hideo, 276
Nondrive models, 174
Norepinephrine, 81
Norman, Greg, 18
Norms, 235–236
North American Society for the Psychology of Sport and Physical Activity (NASPSPA), 8, 50
North American Society for the Sociology of Sport (NASSS), 11
North American Society for Sport History (NASSH), 11
North American Society for Sport Management (NASSM), 11
Nowicki–Strickland Scale, 136–137
NYSCA. See National Youth Sporting Coaches Association training program, 388

Oakland A's, 159
Oberlin College, 311
Objective Fear of Success Scale (FOSS), 329
Objective tests of personality, 195
Obligatory running, 423
O'Brien, Dan, 13, 19
Odyssey, 27
Officials, violence against, 216–220
Ogilvie, Bruce (Dr.), 19, 425
Ojeda, Augie, 276
Olajuwon, Hakeem, 188
Olympic figure skaters, 293
Olympic Games, 2
    in early Athens, 27–28
    female competitors in, 310–311
    marathon running in, 426
    media attention on, 15
    portrayal of women in, 333
    reinstitution of, 43
    sport psychologists and, 19–20

Olympic gymnasts, 293
Olympic track and field athletes, 293
Olympic weight lifters, 294
Olympic wrestlers, 294
Omission training, 56
One-shot research method, 231
Openness to experience, 227
Operant conditioning
    learned helplessness and, 66–67
    See also Operant learning
Operant learning
    basic principles, 55–56
    behavioral coaching techniques, 56–61
    biofeedback training, 93–94
    changing coaching behaviors and, 62–65
    conditioned reinforcement, 62–63
    defined, 55
    Premack Principle, 65
    public recordings, 61–62
    reinforced practice, 92–93
    response cost, 65
    training variables, 65–66
Orr, Bobby, 99
Osteoporosis, 335
Ottey, Merlene, 299
Outcome, aggression and, 203
Outcome expectancy, 121
Overjustification hypothesis, 129
Owens, Jesse, 274

Paige, Satchel, 430
Pain and Impairment Relationship Scale (PAIRS), 298
Paljor, Tsewang, 282
Pallone, Dave, 335
Palmeiro, Rafael, 273
Pan American Games, 2
Panhellenic Games, 31
Pankration, 27–28, 32
PAQ. See Personal Attributes Questionnaire
Parachuting, 278–280
Parachutists
    personality of, 243
    trait anxiety and, 76
Paralanguage, 379
Parallel forms, 235
Paralympic Games, 291, 295
Paranoia, 242
Parent–child interactions, 358, 359
Parentis vociferous, 361
Parents, youth sport and, 349–350
Park, Chan Ho, 276
Parthenon, 25
Paterno, Joe, 342, 377
Path–goal theory, 153
Patton, Mel, 274
Pavin, Corey, 18
Pavlon, Ivan, 46, 54, 226
Payne, Stewart, 18
Peak experience, 425
Pearman, Tammy, 326
PEAS. See Physical Estimation and Attraction Scales
Pehrson, Eric, 278
Pendular model of cohesion, 160
Pepe, Maria, 344
Pep talks, as psych-up strategy, 108–109
Perceived ability, 357
Perceived competence theory, 122–123
Perceptual bias, 115
Perfectionism, 397
Performance goals, setting, 142–143
Peripheral states, 224

Personal Attributes Questionnaire (PAQ), 330–331
Personality
    authoritarian, 381–382
    defined, 224–225
    Machiavellian, 382
    objective tests of, 195
    projective tests of, 194
    theories of. See Personality theories
    Type A, 410
    See also Sport personality research
Personality performance pyramid, 292–294
Personality structure, Hollander's model of, 225
Personality theories
    behavioral model, 226–228
    biological models, 225
    humanistic model, 226
    interactional model, 228
    psychodynamic model, 226
    trait theory, 228
Personality traits, 227
    enduring, 242–246
Personal Orientation Inventory (POI), 139
Peurifory, Dave, 209
Pheidippides, 425–426
Phi Epsilon Kappa, 45
Phillips, Lawrence, 214
Physical activity, 405
    benefits and costs of specific, 411
Physical education
    history of, 45–46
    use of term, 45
Physical Estimation and Attraction Scales (PEAS), 257
Physical fitness, 404–407
    age, reaction time and, 429
    defined, 405
    physical benefits of, 405–406
    psychological benefits of, 406–407
    senior citizens and, 430–431
    See also Fitness; Fitness movement
Physical Self-Perception Profile (PSPP), 141
Pitino, Rick, 314
    ten steps to success, 398
Pittsburgh Pirates, 159
Plato, 29, 30
Play, defined, 6
Player leadership, 158
Players
    sports violence and, 221
    See also Athletes
Playground Association of America, 45
Plutarch, 29
PMT. See Protective Motivation Theory
POI. See Personal Orientation Inventory
Point spread, aggression and, 203
Political tool, sport as, 7
Polyphasic Values Inventory (PVI), 382
POMS. See Profile of mood states
Positive addiction, 422–423
Positive reinforcement, 55
Precompetitive workout, 108
Preferred leader, 155
Premack Principle, 65
President's Council on Fitness and Sport, 114
President's Council on Physical Fitness and Sports, 344–347
President's Council on Youth fitness, 44
Pride, Dickie, 19
Prince, The (Machiavelli), 382
Process orientation to competition, 354
Product orientation to competition, 354
Professional athletes, retirement and, 433

Professional organizations
  Australian, 9
  British, 9
  Canadian, 9
  emergence of, 45
  international, 8
  related, 9–10
Professional and scientific responsibility, 17
Profile of Mood States (POMS), 246–248
  African-American athletes and, 272
  athletes with disabilities and, 295
  drug users and, 304
  exercise and, 424
  short forms of, 250
  State–Trait Anxiety Inventory (STAI), 248–250
Progressive relaxation, 91–92
Prohibited substances, 299–302
  amphetamines, 299–300
  anabolic–androgenic steroids (AAS), 300–302
Projective tests of personality, 194
Protective Motivation Theory (PMT), 409
Proxemics, 379
Pryde, Ian, 280
PSIS. See Psychological Skills Inventory for Sports (PSIS), 256
PSPP. See Physical Self-Perception Profile
Psychasthenia, 242
Psychoanalytic model, 46
Psychoanalytic theory, 226
Psychobiological theory, 225
Psychological androgyny, 330–332
Psychological assessment, 231–232
  enduring personality traits, 242–246
  sport-specific tests, 251–257
Psychological core, 224
Psychological Skills Inventory for Sports (PSIS), 256
Psychological stress response, 94
Psychological test, 232–233
Psychological variables, female, 327–332
Psychology, history of, 46–47
Psychopathic deviates, 242
Psych-up strategies, 108–109
Public recording, 61–62
Publishers, major sport, 5
Punishment, 56, 59
  vicarious, 198
PVI. See Polyphasic Values Inventory

Quasi-criminal violence, 211
Quiet rest, 414

"Rambo Look," 300
Ramirez, Manny, 273
Raveling, George, 378
Ravizza, Ken, 19
Reaction time studies, 429
Reactive coaching behavior, 386
Reactive tasks, 272
Reardon, Jim, 19
Reciprocal inhibition, 55
Recreation
  Civil War and, 42
  defined, 6
Reeves, Dan, 18
Reframing, 106
Registry, 15–17
Reinforced practice, 92–93
Reinforcement
  conditioned, 62–63

continuous, 66
differential, 59
exercise and, 412
intermittent, 66
negative, 55, 59
positive, 55
vicarious, 198
Relaxation training, 91
Reliability, 234–235
Reluctant participants, 348
Renaissance, 36–37
Renteria, Edgar, 273
Research function, 6
Respect for people's rights and dignity, 17
Response cost, 65
Response distortion, 230
Rest as exercise, 414
Reticular formation, 73
Retirement from athletics, 432–434
Reveal, Jon, 283
Reversal theory, 81
Revolutionary War, 41
Reward, exercise and, 412
Rice, Grantland, 323
Richardson, Rod, 266
Right Stuff, The (Wolfe), 278
Riley, Pat, 378
Ringelmann effect, 161
Rivera, Mariano, 273
Rizzo, Patty, 19
Robinson, Eddie, 377
Robinson, Frank, 266
Robinson, Jackie, 265–266, 268
Robinson, Mack, 274
Rock climbing, 281–284
Rockne, Knute, 158, 370–371
Rodman, Dennis, 274
Rodriguez, Alex, 171
Rodriguez, Chi Chi, 275
Rogers, Carl, 46, 226
"Roid rages," 301
Role conflict, 324–325
Role-related behaviors, 225
Roman civilization, 31–34
Roosevelt, Theodore (President), 43–44
Rorschach Inkblot Test, 194
Rotella, Robert (Dr.), 18–19
Rotter, Julian, 115
Rotter's I–E scale, 134–135, 285
Rousseau, Jean-Jacques, 36, 46
Rowing regatta, 41
Royal, Darrell, 394
Runners
  dissociative strategies in distance, 247–248
  marathon, 425–426
  ultramarathoners/ultrarunners, 426–430
Runner's addictions, 422–430
  mood and running, 424
  negative, 423–424
  positive, 422–423
  runner's high, 424–425
Runner's calm, 425
Runner's high, 424–425
Running, mood and, 424
Russell, Bill, 266

Sabatini, Gabriela, 19
SAIC. See State Anxiety Inventory for Children
Salaries in professional sports, 3, 7
Salas, Jose, 275
Samania, T., 282

Sanchez, Angie, 207
Sargent, Dudley (Dr.), 45
SAS. See Sport Anxiety Scale (SAS), 84
Scale of Children's Action Tendencies in Sport (SCATS), 195
SCAT. See Sport Competition Anxiety Test
SCATS. See Scale of Children's Action Tendencies in Sport
Schaap, Dick, 335
Schizophrenia, 242
Scholastic Aptitude Test (SAT), 231, 234
Schollander, Don, 311
SCQ. See Sports Cohesiveness Questionnaire
Scripture, E. W., 50
SCT. See Social Cognitive Theory
Scuba diving, 284–285
Seattle Mariners, 171
Seefeldt, Vern, 345
Self-actualization, 139–140
Self-concept, 139
Self-Description Questionnaire (SDQ) series, 141
Self-efficacy theory, 120
Self-monitoring, 411
Self-paced activities, 272
Self-serving attributional bias, 115, 328
Self-talk, positive, 105
Self theory, 137–141
  defined, 138
  "self" in, 138–139
  self-actualization, 139–140
  self-concept, 139
  status of research on, 141
Semantic Differential Scales, 258
Senior citizens
  competition for, 431–434
  exercise and, 430–431
Senior Olympics, 428
Sensation Seeking, 285
Sensation Seeking Scale (SSS), 285
Se Ri Pak, 276
Shaping, 57, 60
Shield of Athletes (Tait), 46
Shinny, 41
Shriver, Pam, 72
Siddhartha (Buddha), 26
Silva, John, 9
Sime, Dave, 274
Simms, Phil, 186
Simon, Theodore, 46, 232
Simpson, O. J., 214
Singh, Vijay, 2
SIP. See Sports Inventory for Pain
SIT. See Stress inoculation training
Sixteen Personality Factor Questionnaire (16PF), 244–245, 279, 430
Skaters, figure, 293
Skewed groups, 270
Skiing, 267, 403
Skin, electrical properties of, 80
Skinner, B. F., 46, 59
Skittles, 41
Sky diving, 278–280
Slaney, Mary Decker, 299, 317
Sleep habits, 406
Slogans, coaches', 380
SMART goals, 143
Smithers, Paul, 187
Smith's cognitive-affective model of burnout, 393
Smith's violence typology, 210–214
Smoking, exercise adherence and, 410

Smoltz, John, 19
Soccer
  goals for tasks in, 144
  headgear for children, 364
  hooliganism, 200
  violence, 187
Social and Athletic Readjustment Rating Scale
    (SARRS), 297
Social cognitive models, 120–125
  goal achievement model, 123
  perceived competence theory, 122–123
  self-efficacy theory, 120–122
Social Cognitive Theory (SCT), 409
Social Darwinian hypothesis, 267
Social Desirability Scale, 298
Social facilitation, 172–173
Socialization
  incomplete occupational, 391
  into sport, 323–327. See also Sport
    socialization
Social learning theory, 192–193
Social loafing, 161
Social monitoring theory, 174
Social responsibility, 18
Social striving, 162
Socrates, 29
Softball
  female players, 76, 134
  Test of Attentional and Interpersonal Style
    for, 254
Somatic state anxiety, 74–75
Somatotypes, 225
Sotomayor, Javier, 298–299
Southern, Eddie, 274
Spartan civilization, 28–30
Special Olympics International, 295
Spirduso's reaction time studies, 429
Split-half method, 235
Spontaneous coaching behavior, 386
Sport, defined, 6
Sport Anxiety Scale (SAS), 84
Sport assertiveness, 189–190
Sport Competition Anxiety Test (SCAT),
    82–83, 103, 252–253, 257, 356, 430
Sport leadership, multidimensional model of,
    155–158
Sport Mental Attitude Survey (SMAS), 272
Sport opportunity structure, 268
Sport parachuting, 278–280
Sport personality research
  conceptual problems in, 228–230
  interpretive problems, 231
  methodological problems, 230–231
  theoretical vs. atheoretical, 229–230
Sport psychologists
  academic, 7–8
  application function of, 7
  applied, 7–8
  coaches and, 379–381
  credentialing of, 15–17
  education function of, 6–7
  employment opportunities for, 20–21
  ethical principals of, 17–18
  image of, 18–20
  research function of, 6
  tasks of, 5–8
  training for, 14–15
  websites for, 10
Sport psychology
  certification in, 21
  defined, 4
  history of, 47–50

professional issues in, 14–21
  professional organizations, 8–11
  reasons for, 7
  test ethics and, 236–237
Sports
  fascination with, 2
  history of. See History of sports
Sports Cohesiveness Questionnaire (SCQ), 164
Sport self-confidence, 141–142
Sports Illustrated
  feature articles in, 333
  swimsuit edition, 334
Sports Inventory for Pain (SIP), 298
Sport socialization, 323–327
  acceptability of various sports, 326–327
  family and, 325–326
  reasons women compete, 327
  role conflict, 324–325
Sports officials, violence against, 216–220
Sport-specific tests, 251–257
Sports time line, 48–50
Sport violence
  defined, 191
  glossary of, 215
  See also Violence
"Sport Warrior Golf Program," 277
SR Inventory of Anxiousness, 228
S–R Inventory of General Trait Anxiousness,
    284
SSCI. See State Sport-Confidence Inventory
Stacking, 268
Stadion, 28, 29
Stagg, Amos Alonzo, 377
STAI. See State–trait anxiety inventory
Stanley Cup, 99, 179
Stargell, Willie, 159
State–Trait Anxiety Inventory (STAI),
    248–250, 279, 284, 396, 414, 430
State–Trait Anxiety Inventory for Children, 82
State anxiety, 74, 248
  children's precompetitive, 355
  individual game performance and, 79
  inverted-U hypothesis and, 78
State Anxiety Inventory for Children (SAIC),
    356
State Sport-Confidence Inventory (SSCI), 141
Staubach, Roger, 150, 158
Steady state stimulation, 425
Steinkuhler, Dean, 301
Steroids, anabolic-androgenic, 300–302
Stimulus cueing, 412
Stingley, Daryl, 187
Stotz, Carl, 343
Stowe, Harriett Beecher, 45
Strawberry, Darryl, 214, 299
Street, Picabo, 19
Stress
  competitive, 355–356
  measures of, 356–357
  youth sport and, 354–358
Stress inoculation training (SIT), 98–99,
    103–104
Stretching, as psych-up strategy, 108
Structuralism, 46
Success
  attributions for, 126
  fear of, in women, 329
  formula for assessing, 115–120
  history of, 358
  Pitino's steps to, 398
Success expectancy, 357
Suinn, Richard (Dr.), 19

Sumerian civilization, sports in, 26
Super Bowl, 3
Svec, Joe, 278
Sweet, Judy, 314
Swett, John, 45
Swimming
  public recording and, 61–62
  shaping and, 57, 60
Swoopes, Cheryl, 317
Systematic desensitization, 92

TAIS. See Test of Attentional and
    Interpersonal Style
Tarkanian, Jerry, 379
TAS. See Thrill and Adventure Seeking
Task antecedents, 116
TAT. See Thematic Apperception Test
Taureador sports, 26
Taylor, Terry, 314
Team cohesion
  coaches and, 159–160
  factors affecting, 160–164
  group size and, 160–162
  measures of, 164–167
  models of, 160
  satisfaction and, 163–164
  task and, 162
  team tenure and, 162–163
Team half-life, 162
Teams, gender marking of, 334
Team stability, 163
Technology and sports, 42, 43
Temperature–aggression relationship,
    195–197
Tennes. See Self-Concept Scale (TSCS), 139,
    141
Tennis
  coaching, 57, 59
  fans and enmity among players, 202
  goals for tasks in, 144
Terman, Lewis, 232
Test of Attentional and Interpersonal Style
    (TAIS), 254
Testing
  ethics of, 236–237
  information sources, 259
  psychological, 232–233
  sources of error in, 236
  See also Psychological assessment
Test of Performance Strategies (TOPS), 257
Texas Rangers, 171
Texas Social Behavior Instrument (TSBI), 331
Thematic Apperception Test (TAT), 127,
    194–195
Theodosius I, 34
Theoretical vs. atheoretical research, 229
Theory of Interpersonal Behavior, 409
Theory of Planned Behavior, 409
Theory of Reasoned Action (TRA), 409
Thermogenic hypothesis, 416
Third Generation Hardiness Test, 396
Thorndike, E. L., 46
Thorpe, Jim, 276
Thought stoppage, 105
Thrill and Adventure Seeking (TAS), 286
Thurstone scales, 258–259
Tilted groups, 270
Time line
  sports, 48–50
  women's sports, 314
Tissie, Philippe, 47
Titchener, E. B., 46

Title IX
  Compliance Test, 312–313
  legislation, 44, 311–313, 315, 390
Token system, 63
Tolan, Eddie, 274
Tolman, Edward, 46
Tomjanovich, Rudy, 186, 187, 378
TOPS. *See* Test of Performance Strategies
  (TOPS), 257
Torrance, Gwen, 317
Total chain, 64
Total Golf, 64
TRA. *See* Theory of Reasoned Action
Track and field athletes
  behavioral coaching techniques, 60
  eating disorders and, 335–336
  Olympic, 293
  "Who's Who" of, 274
Training for sport psychologists, 14–15
Training variables
  reinforcement schedules, 66
  session length, 65–66
Trait anxiety, 75, 248
  competitive, 356
  individual game performance and, 79
Trait Sport-Confidence Inventory (TSCI), 141
Trait theory, 151, 228
Transcendence, 425
Transcendental meditation, 107–108
Trevino, Lee, 275
Triplett, Norman, 47
TSBI. *See* Texas Social Behavior Instrument
TSCI. *See* Trait Sport–Confidence Inventory
TSCS. See TennesSee Self–Concept Scale
Tutko, Thomas, 19
Type A personality, 410
Typical responses, 225
Typology of violent men, 215–216
Tyson, Mike, 214

U.S. Cerebral Palsy Athletic Association, 295
U.S. Football League, 376
U.S. National Senior Games, 434
U.S. Olympic Committee (USOC), 14
  on blood boosting, 302, 303
  drug testing by, 302
  Native American Sports Council (NASC)
    and, 277
  Sport Psychology Registry, 15
  on women in sports, 311
U.S. Olympic Training Center, Elite Distance
  Runner Project, 247
UCR. *See* Unconditioned response
UCS. *See* Unconditioned stimulus
Ultramarathoners, 426–430
Ultrarunners, 426–430
Unconditioned response (UCR), 54
Unconditioned stimulus (UCS), 54, 88
Unintended consequences of Title IX, 312
United Association for Blind Athletes, 295
United States, history of sports in, 40–45
  Civil War, 42
  Colonial America, 40–41

milestones in recent, 42–45
  Revolutionary War, 41
  technological revolution, 42
USA National Championship figure skaters, 293
USOC. *See* U.S. Olympic Committee

Validity, 233–234
Value-added theory, 194
VBR. *See* Visuomotor behavioral rehearsal
Venationes, 33
Vicarious punishment, 198
Vicarious reinforcement, 198
Violence
  against females by male athletes, 214–216
  against sports officials, 216–220
  aggression and, 190–191
  among female athletes, 214
  between intimates, 186
  body contact, 211
  chronology of sports, 187
  criminal, 212
  intimate, 214
  inurement to, 199
  quasi-criminal, 211
  recommendations for curbing, 217–221
  Smith's typology, 210–214
  in youth sport, 360–362
  See also Sport violence
Visuomotor behavioral rehearsal (VMBR), 98,
  102–104
VMBR. See Visuomotor behavioral rehearsal
Volleyball, injury rates for, 296
Vreeswyk, Mike, 374

Wagner, Honus, 342
Walker, Moses Fleetwood, 264, 268
Walker, Weldy Wilberforce, 264
Walter, Steffi Martin, 317
Warady, David, 428
Washington, Kermit, 186
Watson, John B., 46, 226
Wayman, Agnes, 311
Weathers, Seaborn Beck, 282
Websites, 10
Wecker, Kendra, 314
Weight lifters, Olympic, 294
Weight lifting, drug abuse in, 299
Weiner's three-dimensional taxonomy, 117
Weiner's two-dimensional taxonomy, 117
Wells, Alan, 274
Western States Endurance Run, 428
Wheelchair Sports USA, 295
White, Danny, 159
Whitman, Charles, 191
Who can be called a psychologist, 17
"Who can do what debate," 14, 16
Wieberg, Steve, 378
Williams, Bernie, 273
Williams, Jason, 19
Williams, Ricky, 3
Williams, Venus, 3
Willis's sport motivation scale, 142
Wimbledon, women participation at, 314

Witt, Katarina, 334
WNBA. See Women's National Basketball
  Association
Wolhuter, Rick, 274
Women
  bone structure of, 318
  menstrual functioning in, 315–318
  muscles development in, 318
  risk experience for, 287
  semantic distance among roles of, 325
  See also Female sport experience
*Women in Intercollegiate sport: A Seventeen-Year
  Update,* 313
Women's National Basketball Association
  (WNBA), 314, 317
Woodhouse, Bill, 266
Woods, Tiger, 1–2, 276, 358
Workout, precompetitive, 108
World Games, 2
World Series, 159, 176, 178
Woronin, Marion, 274
Wrestling
  eating disorders and, 335–336
  goals for tasks in, 144
  Olympic, 294

Yale University, rowing regatta, 41
Yamaguchi, Kristi, 276
Yeager, Chuck, 278
YMCA, 342
Yoga, 107–108
Youth fitness measures, 344–345
Youth sport
  actors in, 342
  adult verbalizations at events, 362
  AFA recommendations for more enjoyable,
    350–351
  biological vs. chronological age, 363
  competition in, 354–356
  competitive orientation, 347
  elite performance, 358–360
  fitness benefits, 347
  fitness concerns, 344
  fun and, 346
  health risks with, 362–365
  history of, 342–344
  motives for participation, 344–348
  motives for withdrawing from
    participation, 347–350
  recommendations for improving, 365–366
  skill improvement and, 346–347
  stress and, 354–358
  team atmosphere, 347
  violence in , 360–362
Youth Sport Institute, 345
Youth Sports Official Protection Act, 361
Yuill, D. G. M., 281

Zaharias, Babe Didrikson, 322–323, 334–335
Zen, 107–108
Zuckerman Sensation Seeking Scale (SSS), 279